SALES MANAGEMENT

ANALYSIS AND DECISION MAKING

THOMAS N. INGRAM
Memphis State University

RAYMOND W. LaFORGE
Oklahoma State University

The Dryden Press
Chicago New York San Francisco Philadelphia
Montreal Toronto London Sydney Tokyo

Acquisitions Editor: Robin Zwettler
Developmental Editor: Rebecca Ryan
Project Editor: Cathy Crow
Design Director: Alan Wendt
Production Manager: Barb Bahnsen
Permissions Editor: Doris Milligan/Mary Ann Lanstrum
Director of Editing, Design, and Production: Jane Perkins

Text and Cover Designer: C. J. Petlick, Hunter Graphics
Copy Editor and Indexer: Maggie Jarpey
Compositor: The Clarinda Company
Text Type: 10/12 Berkeley Oldstyle Book

Library of Congress Cataloging-in-Publication Data

Ingram, Thomas N.
Sales management: analysis and decision making/Thomas N. Ingram, Raymond LaForge.
p. cm.
Includes bibliographies and index.
ISBN 0-03-013457-9
1. Sales management. I. LaForge, Raymond. II. Title.
HF5438.4.I54 1989
658.8′1—dc 19 88-18985
CIP

Printed in the United States of America
890-039-987654321

Address orders:
The Dryden Press
Orlando, Florida 32887

Address editorial correspondence:
The Dryden Press
908 N. Elm St.
Hinsdale, IL 60521

The Dryden Press
Holt, Rinehart and Winston
Saunders College Publishing

To our parents and to Jacque, Susan, and Alexandra.

THE DRYDEN PRESS SERIES IN MARKETING

Balsley and Birsner
Selling: Marketing Personified

Blackwell, Engel, and Talarzyk
Contemporary Cases in Consumer Behavior, *Revised Edition*

Blackwell, Johnston, and Talarzyk
Cases in Marketing Management and Strategy

Block and Roering
Essentials of Consumer Behavior, *Second Edition*

Boone and Kurtz
Contemporary Marketing, *Sixth Edition*

Churchill
Basic Marketing Research

Churchill
Marketing Research: Methodological Foundations, *Fourth Edition*

Czinkota and Ronkainen
International Marketing

Dunn and Barban
Advertising: Its Role in Modern Marketing, *Sixth Edition*

Engel, Blackwell, and Miniard
Consumer Behavior, *Fifth Edition*

Futrell
Sales Management, *Second Editon*

Hutt and Speh
Business Marketing Management: A Strategic View of Industrial and Organizational Markets, *Third Edition*

Ingram and LaForge
Sales Management: Analysis and Decision Making

Kurtz and Boone
Marketing, *Third Edition*

Park and Zaltman
Marketing Management

Patti and Frazer
Advertising: A Decision-Making Approach

Rachman
Marketing Today, *Second Edition*

Rogers and Grassi
Retailing: New Perspectives

Rosenbloom
Marketing Channels: A Management View, *Third Edition*

Schellinck and Maddox
Marketing Research: A Computer-Assisted Approach

Schnaars
MICROSIM
A marketing simulation available for IBM PC® and Apple®

Sellars
Role Playing the Principles of Selling

Shimp and DeLozier
Promotion Management and Marketing Communications

Talarzyk
Cases and Exercises in Marketing

Terpstra
International Marketing, *Fourth Edition*

Weitz and Wensley
Readings in Strategic Marketing: Analysis, Planning, and Implementation

Zikmund
Exploring Marketing Research, *Third Edition*

PREFACE

Our objective in writing *Sales Management: Analysis and Decision Making* is to provide comprehensive and rigorous coverage of contemporary sales management in a readable, interesting, and challenging manner. Findings from recent sales management research are blended with examples of current sales management practice into an effective pedagogical format. Topics are covered from the perspective of a sales management decision maker. This decision-making perspective is accomplished through a chapter format that typically consists of discussing basic concepts, identifying critical decision areas, and presenting analytical approaches for improved sales management decision making. Company examples from the contemporary business world are used throughout the text to supplement chapter discussion.

LEVEL AND ORGANIZATION

This text was written for the undergraduate student enrolled in a one-semester or one-quarter sales management class. However, it is sufficiently rigorous to be used at the MBA level, if supplemented with additional readings.

A sales management model is used to present coverage in a logical sequence. The text is organized into six parts to correspond with the six stages in the sales management model.

Part One: Describing the Personal Selling Function is designed to provide students with an understanding of personal selling prior to addressing specific sales management areas. Colleagues across the country have suggested that available sales management texts do not provide enough coverage of personal selling. We decided to devote three chapters at the beginning of the text to this topic.

Part Two: Defining the Strategic Role of Personal Selling consists of two chapters that discuss important relationships between personal selling and organizational strategies at the corporate, business, marketing, and account levels. Each chapter in this part focuses on how strategic decisions at different organizational levels affect sales management decisions and personal selling practices.

Part Three: Designing the Sales Organization addresses the key decisions required to establish an effective sales organization. The two chapters in this part investigate alternative sales organization structures and examine analytical methods for determining salesforce size, territory design, and the allocation of selling effort.

Part Four: Developing the Salesforce changes the focus from organizational topics to people topics. The two chapters in this part cover the critical decision areas in the recruitment and selection of salespeople, and in training salespeople once they have been hired.

Part Five: Directing the Salesforce continues the people orientation by examining important areas of salesforce motivation and reward systems. The last of three chapters in this part discusses the general supervisory and leadership roles necessary for successful sales management.

Part Six: Determining Salesforce Performance concludes the sales management process by addressing evaluation and control procedures. Differences in evaluating the effectiveness of the sales organization and the performance of salespeople are highlighted and covered in separate chapters. The three chapters in this part focus on evaluation approaches and how they can be used to diagnose problems and develop effective sales management solutions.

PEDAGOGY

The following pedagogical format is used for each chapter to facilitate the learning process.

Learning Objectives. Specific learning objectives for the chapter are stated in behavioral terms so that students will know what they should be able to do after the chapter has been covered.

Opening Vignettes. All chapters are introduced by an opening vignette that typically consists of a recent, real-world company example addressing many of the key points to be discussed in the chapter. These opening vignettes are intended to generate student interest in the topics to be covered and to illustrate the practicality of the chapter coverage.

Key Words. Key words are highlighted in bold type throughout each chapter and summarized in list form at the end of the chapter to alert students to their importance.

Boxed Inserts. Each chapter contains three boxed inserts titled "Sales Trend," "Sales Technology," and "International Sales." These items provide specific company examples illustrating important topics covered in the chapter and related to general sales management trends, the use of new technologies, or international sales management issues.

Figure Captions. Every figure in the text includes a summarizing caption designed to make the figure understandable without reference to the chapter discussion.

Chapter Summaries. A chapter summary recaps the key points covered in the chapter by restating and answering questions presented in the learning objectives at the beginning of the chapter.

Discussion Questions. Ten discussion questions are presented at the end of each chapter to review key concepts covered in the chapter. Some of the questions require students to summarize what has been covered, while others are designed to be more thought-provoking and extend beyond chapter coverage.

Application Exercises. Five application exercises conclude each chapter, requiring students to apply what has been learned in the chapter to a specific sales management situation. Many of the application exercises require data analysis.

CASES

The book contains a mixture of short, medium, and long cases—28 in all. The shorter cases can be used as a basis for class discussion or short written assignments. The longer cases are more appropriate for detailed analysis and class discussions or presentations by individuals or student groups. Most of the cases are located at the end of the six parts of the book. We have tried to match the major focus of each case with the appropriate chapter coverage in the book. In addition, four comprehensive cases that integrate multiple sales management decision areas are presented at the end of the book.

ANCILLARIES

Instructor's Manual, Test Bank, and Transparency Masters. A comprehensive package of ancillary materials is available to make it as easy as possible for professors to teach a rigorous and interesting sales management course. The *Instructor's Manual, Test Bank, and Transparency Masters,* prepared by the authors, contains a separate section for each chapter as well as teaching notes for all of the cases. Each section includes a summary; examples, exercises, and materials not covered in the book that could be incorporated into class discussion; and answers to review questions and application exercises. The manual also contains sample course outlines. The *Test Bank* contains multiple-choice and true-false questions and is available in a computerized version for IBM microcomputers.

A large number of *transparency masters* are in the manual, more than half of which represent figures and tables that do not appear in the book. Finally, the manual concludes with a user-friendly discussion of the microcomputer software available with the book and how this software could be used in a sales management class.

Microcomputer Software. Two microcomputer disks have been developed for use with the book. The first disk contains spreadsheet templates that can be used in solving several of the application exercises and five of the cases. The second disk contains a stand-alone computer exercise, SPREE, for evaluating salesperson performance. The software is designed to be very easy for students to use, and everything necessary to incorporate the microcomputer analysis into a sales management class is provided in the *Instructor's Manual.*

Sales Management Update. We have tried to make the book as current as possible by incorporating recent sales management examples and research results. However, sales management is a dynamic field with new examples and research findings continuously emerging. Therefore, we have decided to prepare a "Sales Management Update" that will be available each year in early January and early August. The update will be organized according to the chapters in the book and will include the latest company examples, new research findings, and other teaching aids geared to each chapter, making it easy for professors to incorporate this current information into their class sessions.

ACKNOWLEDGMENTS

The writing of a book is a long and arduous task that requires the dedicated efforts of many individuals. The contributions of these individuals are greatly appreciated and deserve specific recognition.

First, many colleagues across the country reviewed the book in various stages of development and provided many useful suggestions that improved the final product substantially. We are especially grateful for the efforts of the following colleagues:

Ramon Avila, *Ball State University*

Steve Castleberry, *University of Georgia*

Steve Clopton, *Appalachian State University*

Cathy Cole, *University of Iowa*

Bob Collins, *University of Nevada, Las Vegas*

Bill Cron, *Southern Methodist University*

Ken Evans, *Arizona State University*

Sarah Gardial, *University of Tennessee, Knoxville*

Harrison Grathwol, *California State University, Chico*

David Good, *Central Missouri State University*

Jon Hawes, *University of Akron*

Vince Howe, *University of North Carolina, Wilmington*

Bill Moncrief, *Texas Christian University*

Walter Pachuk, *University of Scranton*

Hal Teer, *James Madison University*

Dan Weilbaker, *Bowling Green State University*

We also sincerely appreciate the willingness of many individuals to allow us to include their cases in the book. These cases have substantially enhanced the effectiveness and interest of the text.

Interaction with sales and marketing executives has produced interesting examples and useful insights that have been incorporated in various ways throughout the book. Special thanks go to Andrew Altendorf, *LORI;* Bob Barrett, *Mobil Chemical;* Clint Butler, *NCR Corporation;* Jerry Colletti, *The Alexander Group;* Charlie Eitel, *Collins and Aikman;* Jim Houts, *Xerox Corporation;* Rick Kasick, *Combustion Engineering;* Dave Moore, *Roserich Designs;* Elliot Prieur, *Lincoln Property Company;* and Kevin Turner, *Jim Walter Papers.* Valuable input was also provided by two long-time friends, Don Becker and Wesley Singleton, entrepreneurs whose extraordinary success is largely attributable to highly developed sales management skills. Sales and Marketing Executives International (SMEI) has also been of great assistance, particularly through support of the authors' research that is reflected in this book.

We would also like to thank Cliff Young (*Oklahoma State University*) for doing a terrific job in developing and refining all of the microcomputer software accompanying the book. Cliff also translated the bits and bytes into an excellent, user-friendly discussion of how to use the software in a sales management class.

A great deal of the credit for this book should go to all of the wonderful people at The Dryden Press. Their expertise, support, and constant encouragement turned an extremely difficult task into a very enjoyable one. We would like to recognize specifically the tremendous efforts of the following professionals and friends: Rob Zwettler, Becky Ryan, Karen Vertovec, Cathy Crow, Maggie Jarpey, and Doris Milligan. However, we also want to thank the many individuals with whom we did not have direct contact, but who assisted in the development and production of this book. We have been treated superbly by everyone at The Dryden Press during this project.

We are also very appreciative of the support provided by our colleagues at the University of Kentucky, Memphis State University, and Oklahoma State University.

Finally, we have been most fortunate to have been supported throughout our academic careers by two of the finest gentlemen and scholars in our field: Danny Bellenger (*Texas Tech University*) and Dave Cravens (*Texas Christian University*). Their influence is exhibited in this book and in all of our work.

Thomas N. Ingram
Raymond W. LaForge

October 1988

ABOUT THE AUTHORS

Thomas N. Ingram (PhD, Georgia State University) is Professor of Marketing and holder of the Sales and Marketing Executives Chair in Sales Excellence at Memphis State University. Dr. Ingram spent eight years at the University of Kentucky, where he received the National Alumni Association Great Teacher Award. He has been active as a researcher, trainer, and consultant in the sales management area. His articles have appeared in the *Journal of Marketing Research, Journal of Marketing, Journal of Personal Selling and Sales Management,* and many other journals and proceedings. Professor Ingram is a member of the Editorial Review Board for the *Journal of Personal Selling and Sales Management* and has previously coauthored *Professional Selling.*

Raymond W. LaForge (DBA, University of Tennessee) is Associate Professor of Marketing at Oklahoma State University. Dr. LaForge has been active in research, consulting, and seminar programs that focus on increasing sales productivity. His articles have appeared in a number of journals and proceedings, including *Decision Sciences, Journal of Business Research, Journal of Personal Selling and Sales Management,* and *Business Horizons.* He is a member of the Editorial Review Board for the *Journal of Personal Selling and Sales Management.*

C O N T E N T S

CHAPTER 1

AN OVERVIEW OF CONTEMPORARY SALES MANAGEMENT

Consider the following job announcement that might appear in the 1990s:

> WANTED: Need an individual that can plan, direct, and control the personal selling activities of a rapidly growing firm. Qualified applicant must be a sales forecaster, market analyst, strategic planner, student of buyer behavior, opportunity manager, intelligence gatherer, scarce-product allocator, accounts receivable collector, cost and profit analyst, budget manager, leader, and master communicator (both verbal and nonverbal). Duties will be performed in an environment characterized by high buyer expertise, high customer expectations, intense foreign competition, revolutionary changes in communications technology, and an influx of women and minorities into personal selling jobs.[1]

This job announcement provides an accurate description of a typical sales management position in the 1990s. The days when a sales manager merely supervised the day-to-day activities of a few salepeople are long gone. Sales management today is a complex and demanding professional occupation, and it will become more so in the future.

This exciting world of sales management is explored in the following manner in this text. First, the present chapter provides an overview of contemporary sales management, with a brief presentation of each stage in the sales management process, a discussion of different types of sales management positions and emerging sales management issues, and a description of the format used in the remaining chapters of the text. Then each area of sales management is covered in a separate chapter with the goal of providing thorough, current, and interesting in-depth information and discussion.

SALES MANAGEMENT PROCESS

The promotional tools available to any firm are typically classified as personal selling, advertising, sales promotion, and publicity. *Personal selling* has been defined as direct communication with an audience through paid personnel of an organization or its agents in such a way that the audience perceives the communicator's organization as being the source of the messages.[2] This definition differentiates personal selling from other promotional tools in two ways. First, personal selling is personal communication, whereas advertising and sales promotion are nonpersonal. Second, in personal selling the audience perceives the message as being delivered by the organization, whereas in publicity, even when it is in the form of personal communication, the audience typically perceives the media, not the organization, as being the source of the message.

Sales management is simply management of an organization's personal selling function. As the job announcement at the beginning of this chapter suggests, managing the personal selling function requires a large number of diverse activities. These activities can be classified into three major categories: planning, implementation, and control. Sales managers are involved in both the strategy (planning) and people (implementation) aspects of personal selling as well as in evaluating and controlling all personal selling activities. They must be able to deal effectively with people in the personal selling function, people in other functional areas in the organization, and with people outside the organization, especially customers. The sales management model presented in Figure 1.1 illustrates the major stages in the sales management process.

Describing the Personal Selling Function

Since sales managers are responsible for managing the personal selling function, they must thoroughly understand it. This text therefore devotes three chapters to that subject before discussing sales management activities. Chapter 2 ("Personal Selling: Evolution, Contributions, and Classifications") presents an overview of personal selling, tracing its evolution from ancient times to the current era of the professional salesperson. The importance of personal selling to society, business firms, and customers is explained, and the diverse forms it can take are examined (that is, alternative approaches to selling and different types of sales jobs).

Chapter 3 ("Personal Selling: Job Activities and the Sales Process") investigates the various activities involved in personal selling in great detail. Although the basic

Figure 1.1 **Sales Management Model**

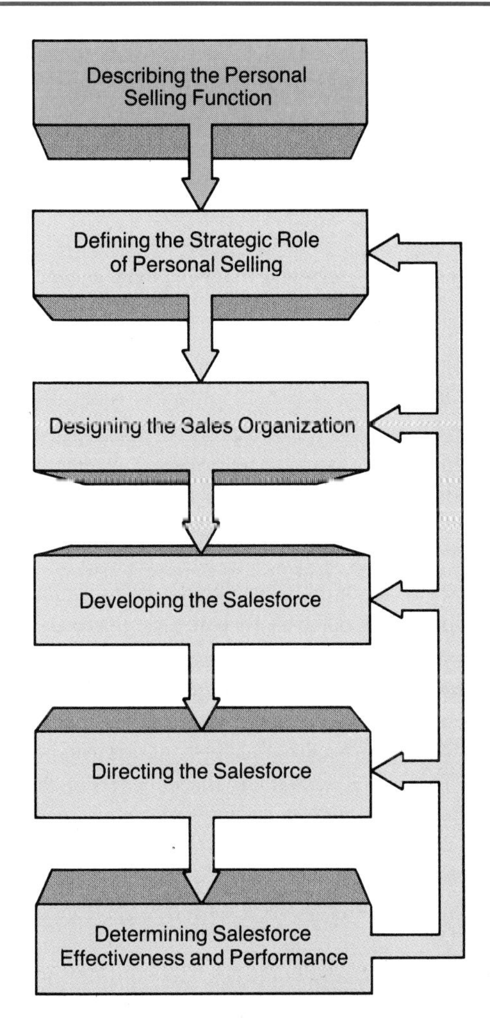

The six major stages of sales management as presented in this model correspond to the six major parts of this textbook.

job of salespeople is to sell, many of them also perform management activities in their relationships with individual accounts and in managing their time and assigned territory. Salespeople are also normally engaged in various support activities for their firm, such as collecting market information, assisting in the recruitment and selection of salespeople, collecting past due accounts, and so on. But, the basic job of salespeople is to sell. The sales process is presented as a series of interrelated steps used to generate initial sales from prospects.

The coverage of personal selling concludes with Chapter 4 ("Sales Careers: Characteristics, Qualifications, and Stages"), in which the basic characteristics of sales careers and the general qualifications for most sales positions are discussed. The progression of salespeople through different stages in a sales career is also examined. Then the factors associated with promotion into sales management are investigated, along with an examination of typical career paths in personal selling and sales management.

Defining the Strategic Role of Personal Selling

Many firms in the contemporary business world consist of collections of relatively autonomous business units that market multiple products to diverse customer groups. These multiple-business, multiple-product firms must develop and integrate strategic decisions at different organizational levels. Chapter 5 ("Personal Selling and Corporate, Business, and Marketing Strategies") discusses the key strategic decisions at the corporate, business, and marketing levels and the basic relationships between these decisions and the personal selling and sales management functions. Corporate and business level strategic decisions typically provide guidelines within which sales managers and salespeople must operate. In contrast, personal selling is an important component of marketing strategies in specific product market situations. The role of personal selling in a given marketing strategy has direct and important implications for sales managers.

Strategic decisions at the corporate, business, and marketing levels must be translated into strategies for individual accounts. Chapter 6 ("Personal Selling and Account Management and Account Coverage Strategies") discusses two types of account strategies: account management strategy and account coverage strategy. Since personal selling is typically important in organizational marketing situations, an explanation of organizational buyer behavior is provided as a foundation for the development of account strategies.

An *account management strategy* entails decisions on developing, maintaining, and expanding relationships with accounts. Relationship marketing and transaction marketing represent the two extremes of account management strategy. An *account coverage strategy* entails decisions on the best methods for providing selling effort coverage to accounts. In addition to regular field selling effort, firms might employ industrial distributors, independent representatives, selling centers, telemarketing, and/or trade shows to provide selling effort coverage to different accounts.

Designing the Sales Organization

The development and integration of corporate, business, marketing, and account strategies establishes the basic strategic direction for personal selling and sales management activites. However, an effective sales organization is necessary to implement these strategies successfully. Chapter 7 ("Organizing the Activities of Sales Managers and Salespeople") presents the basic concepts in designing an effective sales organization structure: specialization, centralization, span of control versus management levels, and line versus staff positions. Different decisions in any of these areas produce different sales organization structures. The appropriate structure for a firm depends upon the specific characteristics of a given selling situation. If major account selling programs are used, specific attention must be directed toward determining the best organizational structure for serving these major accounts.

Closely related to sales organization decisions are decisions on the amount and allocation of selling effort. Chapter 8 ("Allocating Selling Effort, Determining Salesforce Size, and Designing Territories") presents specific methods for making salesforce deployment decisions. Since the decisions on selling effort allocation, salesforce size, and territory design are interrelated, they should be addressed in an integrative manner. A number of different analytical approaches can assist in this endeavor, but "people" issues must also be considered.

Developing the Salesforce

The account strategy, sales organization, and salesforce deployment decisions produce the basic structure for personal selling efforts and can be considered similar to the "machine" decisions in a production operation. Sales managers must also make a number of "people" decisions to ensure that the right types of salespeople are available and have the skills to operate the "machine" structure effectively and efficiently.

Chapter 9 ("Staffing the Salesforce: Recruitment and Selection") discusses the key activities involved in planning and executing salesforce recruitment and selection programs. These activities include determining the type of salespeople desired, identifying prospective salesperson candidates, and evaluating candidates to ensure that the best are hired. Legal and ethical issues are important considerations in the recruiting and selection process. Also, the ramifications of this process for salespeople's subsequent adjustment to a new job (socialization) are also examined.

Chapter 10 ("Continual Development of the Salesforce: Sales Training") emphasizes the need for continuous training of salespeople and the important role that sales managers play in this activity. The sales training process consists of assessing training needs, developing objectives, evaluating alternatives, designing the training program, carrying it out, and evaluating it. Sales managers face difficult decisions at each stage of the sales training process, since it is not only extremely important but also expensive, and there are many sales training alternatives available.

Directing the Salesforce

Hiring the best salespeople and providing them with the skills required for success is one thing; directing their efforts to meet sales organization goals and objectives is another. Sales managers spend a great deal of their time in motivating, supervising, and leading members of the salesforce.

Chapter 11 ("Salesforce Motivation: Theories and Current Issues") presents several content and process theories of motivation that attempt to explain how individuals decide to spend effort on specific activities over extended periods of time. Sales managers can use these theories as a foundation for determining the best ways to get salespeople to spend the appropriate amount of time on the right activities over a period of time. Key issues in and general guidelines for salesforce motivation are also discussed.

Chapter 12 ("Managing Salesforce Reward Systems") builds on the previous discussion of motivation by focusing on the specific salesforce reward systems. Both the compensation type of rewards and the noncompensation types are examined. The advantages and disadvantages of different compensation programs are investigated as well as different methods for sales expense reimbursement. Specific guidelines for developing and managing a salesforce reward system are suggested.

Chapter 13 ("Sales Management Leadership and Supervision") distinguishes between the leadership and supervisory activities of a sales manager. *Leadership activities* focus on influencing salespeople through communication processes to attain specific goals and objectives. In contrast, *supervisory activities* are concerned with day-to-day control of the salesforce under routine operating conditions. The use of power and influence strategies is discussed in the context of an overall sales leadership model. Different styles of sales management are illustrated and key issues and problems in sales management leadership and supervision discussed.

Determining Salesforce Effectiveness and Performance

Sales managers must continually monitor the progress of the salesforce to determine current effectiveness and performance. This is a difficult task, since these evaluations should address both the effectiveness of different units within the sales organization as well as the performance of individual salespeople. Chapter 14 ("Developing Forecasts and Establishing Sales Quotas and Selling Budgets") provides the necessary background for effectiveness and performance evaluations. The different types of forecasts and the methods of bottom-up and top-down forecasting are presented.

It is critically important that forecasts for developing sales quotas and selling budgets be accurate. *Sales quotas* represent specific sales goals that should be achieved by salespeople or sales organization units during a prescribed time period. *Selling budgets* consist of the financial resources that have been allocated to salespeople and sales organization units to achieve sales quotas and other objectives. Both sales quotas and selling budgets are often derived directly or indirectly from sales forecasts.

Chapter 15 ("Evaluating Sales Organization Effectiveness: Sales, Cost, Profitability, and Productivity Analysis") focuses on evaluating the effectiveness of sales organization units, such as territories, districts, regions, and zones. The *sales organization audit* is the most comprehensive approach for evaluating the effectiveness of the sales organization as a whole. Specific methods for assessing the effectiveness of different sales organization units with regard to sales, costs, profitability, and productivity are presented. Skill in using these different analyses helps a sales manager to diagnose specific problems and develop solutions to them.

Chapter 16 ("Evaluating Salesperson Performance and Job Satisfaction") changes the focus to evaluating the performance of people, both as individuals and in groups. These performance evaluations are used for a variety of purposes by sales managers. Specific criteria to be evaluated and different methods for providing the evaluative information are examined, and the use of this information in a diagnostic and problem-solving manner is described. A method for measuring salesperson job satisfaction, which is closely related to salesperson performance, is presented as well.

SALES MANAGEMENT POSITIONS

The complexity of multibusiness, multiproducts firms and the diversity of strategies used by these firms result in many different types of sales management positions. Although these positions might be discussed in several ways, our discussion will be in terms of their level in the sales organization and the type of selling method.

Level in Sales Organization

Most sales organizations have hierarchical structures with different types of sales managers at different levels. One reasonably simple sales organization structure is illustrated in Figure 1.2. This structure has three levels of sales management and thus three different types of sales management positions. A firm with this structure would have to perform all of the sales management activities shown in Figure 1.1; sales managers at different levels would have different responsibilities and would focus on different activities.

Consider the example of David C. Moore, who has been a district sales manager, regional sales manager, and national sales manager for Drawing Board Greeting Cards. His experiences at each sales management level follow:[3]

> The district sales manager is the first level of true sales management. As a *district sales manager,* I had no direct account responsibility (or, if you will, I had responsibility for *every* account in the district). The majority of my time was spent in building business by working with salespeople at different accounts. I had hiring and firing responsibilities, subject to the approval of my regional sales manager. As a district manager, I faced for the first time the harsh reality that my success and continued career growth depended upon my ability to motivate and manage salespeople rather than on my own efforts to develop business.
>
> As a *regional sales manager,* I was unquestionably the chief decision maker in the region. I had *ultimate* hiring and firing responsibilities. Direct contact with salespeople was less frequent, and most of my account contact occurred at the upper management echelons in the major accounts. I was really at the interface

Figure 1.2 **Example of Sales Organization Structure**

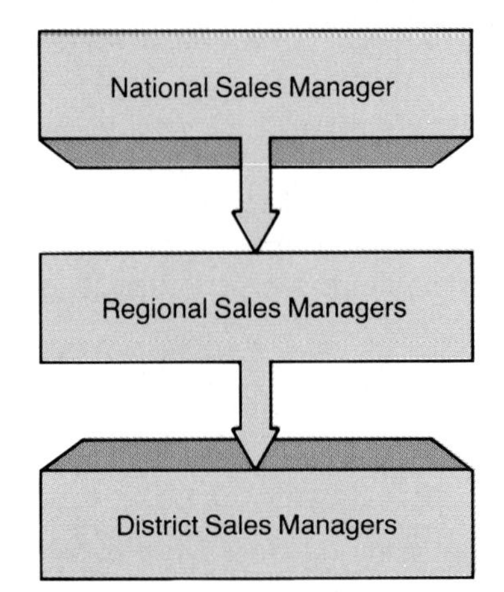

In this example of a sales organization structure, there are three levels of sales management and thus three different types of sales management positions.

between the district managers in the field and the national sales manager at the corporate office. My most difficult task was in getting things done through the district managers under my supervision in a positive manner. At least one day a week was spent in strategic planning activities designed to improve the productivity of the territories and districts within my region.

The national sales manager is the chief headknocker. The buck stops here! As the *national sales manager,* I spent about 75 percent of my time managing the salesforce and 25 percent on internal administration ranging from product line reviews to developing effective performance appraisals. I had little direct contact with salespeople, but provided specific direction to the regional sales managers and would typically accompany them on key account calls when top management from the key account was attending the presentation. One of my difficult tasks was learning to delegate responsibility and authority effectively, since there was a tremendous demand for my time from both the field sales organization and other departments in the company.

In sum, as David C. Moore's experience attests, management skills increase in direct proportion to responsibilities within a sales organization. These skills are refined at lower sales management levels in preparation for promotions to senior level assignments with increased responsibilities. At the same time, the significance and importance of each decision is magnified the higher a person progresses up the corporate ladder. Our focus in this text is typically on the position of *district sales man-*

ager as a field sales manager working directly with salespeople in the field. However, discussion of the other sales management levels is interwoven throughout.

Type of Selling Method

Our description of sales management positions at different sales organization levels assumes that the personal selling effort is provided by a field salesforce that makes personal sales calls to accounts. This assumption is reasonable for most firms today, but some are beginning to employ selling methods other than the typical field personal selling. As these new selling methods replace field selling or are integrated with field selling, sales management responsibilities and activities will change. Oftentimes, new sales management positions must be created.

Recent research investigates the increasing use of major account and telemarketing selling methods by many firms.[4] These new selling methods are being employed as a means of controlling the rapidly rising costs of field selling, as a way to respond to the changing buying habits and service requirements of accounts, and as a potential avenue for securing competitive advantages. An example of using different selling methods for accounts of different sizes and at different stages of the selling process is illustrated in Figure 1.3.

As indicated in the figure, major account management programs might be used for large accounts at all stages of the selling process, while telemarketing might be appropriate for small accounts at all stages of the selling process. Medium accounts might warrant a mixture of selling methods. Telemarketing could be used for prospecting and qualifying accounts and field selling employed to make the sales presentation and close the sale. Servicing the account and obtaining reorders might be accomplished by integrating field selling and telemarketing efforts. Although other types and mixes of selling methods are possible, the use of field selling, major account programs, and telemarketing methods produces some new and interesting sales management positions.

One result of using major account programs for large accounts and telemarketing for small accounts is that the traditional field sales manager and field salesforce are restricted to generating business and servicing medium accounts. Coverage of large and small accounts becomes the responsibility of major account managers and telemarketing managers.

Major account managers operate like product managers. They are typically responsible for mobilizing all required resources of the firm to develop and maintain long-term relationships with the largest and most important accounts. They plan strategies for each major account and coordinate the firm's efforts to implement each strategy successfully.

Telemarketing managers are responsible for developing and managing salespeople to contact accounts by telephone. This telemarketing salesforce might have complete responsibility for generating sales and establishing relationships with all small accounts and/or might be required to perform prospecting and servicing activities for

Figure 1.3 **Examples of Different Selling Methods**

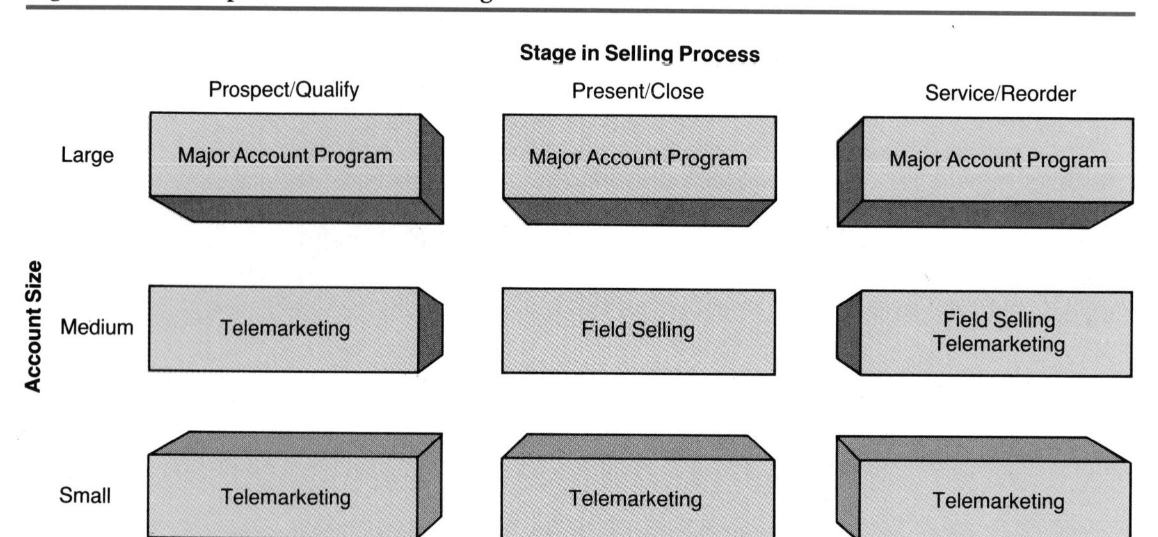

Different selling methods might be employed for accounts of different sizes and at different stages in the selling process.

Source: Adapted from Richard Cardozo and Shannon Shipp, "New Selling Methods Are Changing Industrial Sales Management," *Business Horizons*, September–October 1987, 26.

medium accounts. The telemarketing manager job is similar in many respects to the field sales manager job, but it concerns more tightly specified tasks and is normally performed in a single location.

As firms employ mixtures of field selling, major account programs, and telemarketing, the responsibilities of regional and national sales managers also change. These sales managers must now supervise and coordinate the efforts of field sales managers, major account managers, and telemarketing managers. Some firms are establishing the position of general sales manager to manage the different selling methods. As one CEO commented,[5]

> The general sales manager is like a general officer or a theatre commander, planning ground strategy and moving ground, sea, and air resources against multiple objectives.

The discussion of different types of sales management positions highlights the dynamic nature of sales management. Changes in sales management are occurring at a rapid rate as firms try to adapt to the volatile business environment. Several emerging issues in sales management deserve discussion.

EMERGING ISSUES IN SALES MANAGEMENT

Due to their diversity, changes in sales management are sometimes difficult to classify. Thus, each of the remaining chapters in this book presents a "Sales Trends" box with a trend related to the specific topic of the chapter. These boxes address important, emerging issues in sales management that cannot be classified into the "Sales Technology," "International Sales," and "Sales Ethics" categories of other sales management issues.

Sales Technology

Computer and communication technological development has been exploding in recent years with no end to new development in sight. Many of these new technologies are applicable to the sales management area, although some firms are slow to employ them. For example, as indicated in Exhibit 1.1, actual usage of computers in sales management is much lower than might be expected, with many firms either in the planning mode or having no plans for computer usage in 1986. Specific uses of computer and communication technologies (e.g., teleconferencing, facsimile machines, and cellular telephones) in personal selling and sales management are presented in the "Sales Technology" boxes in each of the remaining chapters of this book.

International Sales

One of the facts of life in the contemporary business world is that most firms operate in a global marketplace. Suppliers, competitors, and customers are located throughout the world and not just in a particular state, region, or country. Many firms are focusing their efforts toward marketing their products in different countries, which often requires the development and management of some type of overseas selling operation. Differences in culture, politics, and other areas make international sales management a challenging task. Some of the nuances of that task are presented in the "International Sales" boxes in each of the remaining chapters of this book.

Sales Ethics

Ethics in business has become an increasingly important issue in contemporary firms. Since salespeople and sales managers operate in the field, situations requiring ethical consideration are commonplace. This text addresses that issue in appropriate places throughout the book rather than confining the discussion to one section. This approach is a realistic one, since ethical considerations are an integral part of many different types of sales management decisions.

Exhibit 1.1 **Use of Computers in Sales Management**

Application	Operational System	Pilot Mode	Planning Phase	No Plans
Order entry	29%	22%	29%	20%
Check order status	27	22	35	16
Check inventory	23	17	32	28
Prepare forecasts	21	18	37	24
Planning and scheduling	20	10	34	36
Territory management	18	6	50	26
Account management	18	6	41	35
Reporting expenses	15	9	30	46
Reporting sales calls	11	8	35	46
Analyze customer requirements	11	6	36	47
Prepare bids or proposals	10	9	27	54
Managing sales leads	10	2	36	52
Computer-based training	8	6	26	60
Personal Applications				
Word processing	23%	25%	25%	27%
Spread sheet	18	16	20	46
Database management	18	15	26	41
Electronic mail	16	12	43	29

Source: Thayer C. Taylor, "Marketers and the PC: Steady as She Goes," *Sales and Marketing Management,* August 1986, 53.

CHAPTER FORMAT

Sales Management: Analysis and Decision Making was written for students. Therefore, its aim is to provide a comprehensive coverage of sales management in a manner that students will find interesting and readable. Each chapter blends recent research results with current sales management practice in a format designed to facilitate the learning process.

At the beginning of each chapter, "Learning Objectives" highlight the basic material that the student should expect to learn. These learning objectives are helpful in reviewing chapters for future study. An opening vignette then illustrates many of the important ideas to be covered in the chapter, using examples of companies in various industries to illustrate the diversity and complexity of sales management. Most of the companies described in the vignettes are well-known, and most of the situations represent recent actions by these firms.

Key words in the body of each chapter are printed in bold letters, and figures and exhibits are used liberally to illustrate and amplify the discussion in the text.

Every figure contains an explanation so that it can be understood without reference to the text.

A chapter summary is geared to the learning objectives presented at the beginning of the chapter, and a listing of key words recaps the bold-type words that appeared throughout the chapter. Finally, each chapter concludes with ten discussion questions and five application exercises. The discussion questions focus on summarizing and/or extending some of the discussion covered in the chapter. The application exercises represent different situations where students must apply basic concepts and/or analytical approaches to realistic sales management situations. Students who can answer the discussion questions and work the application exercises can feel confident that they have mastered the material covered in a chapter.

A CONCLUDING COMMENT

This brief overview of contemporary sales management and summary of the contents and format of *Sales Management: Analysis and Decision Making* sets the stage for your journey into the dynamic and exciting world of sales management. This should be a valuable learning experience as well as an interesting journey. All of the information contained herein should prove extremely relevant to those who begin their careers in personal selling and progress through the ranks of sales management.

References

[1]The job characteristics and environmental situations are adapted from Rolph E. Anderson and Bert Rosenbloom, "Eclectic Sales Management: Strategic Response to Trends in the Eighties," *Journal of Personal Selling and Sales Management,* November 1982, 41–46; and Bert Rosenbloom and Rolph E. Anderson, "The Sales Manager: Tomorrow's Super Marketer," *Business Horizons,* March–April 1984, 50–56.

[2]This definition is taken from David W. Cravens, Gerald E. Hills, and Robert B. Woodruff, *Marketing Management* (Homewood, Ill.: Irwin, 1987), 487.

[3]This description is taken from materials provided by David C. Moore on January 4, 1988. Mr. Moore is no longer with Drawing Board Greeting Cards, and the company is now Carlton Cards, which is a wholly owned subsidiary of American Greetings Corporation.

[4]This discussion is taken from Richard N. Cardozo, Shannon H. Shipp, and Kenneth J. Roering, "Implementing New Business-to-Business Selling Methods," *Journal of Personal Selling and Sales Management,* August 1987, 17–26; and Richard Cardozo and Shannon Shipp, "New Selling Methods Are Changing Industrial Sales Management," *Business Horizons,* September–October 1987, 23–28.

[5]Reported in Richard Cardozo and Shannon Shipp, "New Selling Methods Are Changing Industrial Sales Management, *Business Horizons,* September–October 1987, 27.

PART ONE

DESCRIBING THE PERSONAL SELLING FUNCTION

THE three chapters in Part 1 describe the personal selling function. A clear understanding of personal selling is essential to gain a proper perspective of the issues facing sales managers. In Chapter 2, the historical evolution of selling is presented, along with a contemporary look at the contributions of personal selling to our economic and social system. In addition, classifications of the various approaches to personal selling and types of personal selling jobs are discussed.

Chapter 3 reviews the key job activities of salespeople. In addition to selling, salespeople are involved in time and territory management, assisting sales managers, and providing support for other organizational activities. This chapter also reviews the seven steps in the sales process.

In Chapter 4, sales careers are discussed, including the characteristics of sales jobs, the skills and human characteristics necessary for success in sales and sales management, and the career paths typical in sales.

CHAPTER 2

AN OVERVIEW OF PERSONAL SELLING

Learning Objectives

After completing this chapter, you should be able to

1. Describe the evolution of personal selling from ancient times to the modern era.
2. Explain the contributions of personal selling to society, business firms, and customers.
3. Discuss five alternative approaches to personal selling.
4. Describe different types of personal selling jobs.

COMPUTER SALES: JOE PRIVITERA ON THE JOB

Joe Privitera, 28-year-old computer salesperson, is a busy account executive with Unisys who carefully plans his work days to maximize sales productivity. He cites a well-known key to sales success when he says, "if you want to make it in sales, you must learn to make time work for you." To make time work for him, Privitera starts each work day early and leaves nothing to chance. A business administration graduate of the University of Kansas, Joe Privitera exemplifies the modern version of a professional salesperson.

Each morning, Joe is out of bed by 5:30 a.m. and arrives at work at 7:30 a.m., well ahead of the crowd. He uses the first two hours of the work day to scan his mail and process some paperwork. He then spends the rest of the day calling on both established accounts and new prospects. To conclude the day's work, he plans the next day's activities, makes advance appointments, and returns customer phone calls. By the time he leaves his office at 6:00 p.m., he has set the stage for future sales presentations and prioritized his activities for the immediate future.

Although Unisys put Privitera through an extensive sales training program before he began working on his own accounts, at first he found the task of calling on new accounts to be tedious and difficult, though he realized, of course, that such calls are the foundation of future sales.

"It can be very frustrating, calling on different people and not getting anywhere," he explains. "But as frustrating as it can be, it's also challenging. To make headway, you quickly realize that you have to be very flexible in order to reach people who are potential customers. You have to adapt yourself to any situation you're dealing with and present yourself, company, and product in such a way that somebody is going to part with money in order to buy what you're offering. You also learn to take rejection. The problem with most of us is that we take rejection personally, not realizing that if you present yourself in a professional manner, the person on the other end is not rejecting you, only your product."

During the first few months on the job, Privitera gained the confidence he needed to feel comfortable calling on potential new clients. He also learned a key sales skill:

Source: Excerpted from Bob Weinstein, "Computer Sales: What I Do on the Job," *Business Week's Guide to Careers*, March/April 1985, 30–34.

how to listen to what a prospective client is saying. " A good salesperson cannot be a passive listener," he says. "You must listen aggressively, to uncover specific needs . . . once you uncover a need, you can package your sales solutions accordingly."

Privitera notes that a successful salesperson must have thorough product knowledge, especially in a field like his where the product represents a major purchasing decision. Privitera must be prepared to answer many elaborate questions and speak to specific customer concerns. Furthermore, he must be able to help potential customers find the most cost-effective solution to their needs.

Another important skill required in his job is the ability to manage politics and group dynamics in the organizational buying processes of his customers. Since the purchase of a computer is often a group decision, he must satisfy several different people simultaneously. This can be a complex undertaking, requiring months or even years in some cases.

The most challenging part of Joe Privitera's job, in his opinion, is understanding and meeting customer needs. "A good salesperson has to be concerned with making sure customers are satisfied on a long-term basis," he says. "The relationship between salesperson and customer must be perfect, because the relationship continues long after the sale. The salesperson is, in effect, in business with the customer."

EVOLUTION OF PERSONAL SELLING

Personal selling, as represented by professionals like Joe Privitera, has evolved into a quite different activity than it was merely a few decades ago. Throughout this course you will learn about new technologies and techniques that have contributed to this evolution. This chapter provides an overview of personal selling, affording insight into the operating rationale of today's salespeople and sales managers. In the highly competitive, complex environment of the world business community, personal selling and sales management has never played a more critical role.

Early Origins of Personal Selling

Ancient Greek history documents selling as an exchange activity, and the term *salesman* appears in the writings of Plato.[1] However, true salespeople, those who earned a living only by selling, did not exist in any sizable number until the Industrial Revolution in England, from the mid-eighteenth century to the mid-nineteenth century. Prior to this time, traders, merchants, and artisans filled the selling function. These predecessors of contemporary marketers were generally viewed with contempt since deception was often employed in the sale of goods.[2]

In the latter phase of the Middle Ages, the first door-to-door salesperson appeared in the form of the peddler. Peddlers collected produce from local farmers, sold it to townspeople, and, in turn, bought manufactured goods in town for subsequent sale in rural areas.[3] Like many other early salespeople, they performed other important marketing functions — in this case, purchase, assembly, sorting, and redistribution of goods.

The emergence of the *guild system* represented an important development in the evolution of personal selling. Made up of associations of merchants and artisans, the guild system had the effect of uniting competition and discouraging sales expeditions into new geographic areas. However, it also made a positive contribution to personal selling because the high ethical standards espoused by the guilds elevated the social status of all business people.

Industrial Revolution Era

As the Industrial Revolution began to blossom in the middle of the eighteenth century, the economic justification for salespeople gained momentum. Local economies were no longer self-sufficient, and as inter-city and international trade began to flourish, economics of scale in production spurred the growth of mass markets in geographically dispersed areas. The continual need to reach new customers in these dispersed markets called for an increasing number of salespeople.

It is interesting to note the job activities of the first wave of salespeople in the era of the Industrial Revolution. The following quotation describes a salesperson who served the customer in conjunction with a producer:

> Thus, a salesman representing the producing firm, armed with samples of the firm's products, could bring the latter to the attention of a large number of potential customers — whether buying for sale to others or for their own production requirements — who might not, without the salesman's visit, have learnt of the product's existence, and give them the opportunity of examining and discussing it without having to go out of their way to do so . . . Even if the salesman did not succeed in obtaining an order, he frequently picked up valuable information on the state of the market, sometimes the very reasons for refusal . . . This information could be very useful to the producer.[4]

Post-Industrial Revolution Era

By the early 1800s, personal selling was well-established in England but just beginning to develop in the United States.[5] This situation changed noticeably after 1850, and by the latter part of the century, salespeople were a well-established part of business practice in the United States. As an example, one wholesaler in the Detroit area reported sending out 400 traveling salespeople in the 1880s.[6]

At the dawning of the twentieth century, an exciting time in the economic history of the United States, it became apparent that marketing, especially advertising and personal selling, would play a crucial role in the rapid transition of the economy from an agrarian base to one of mass production and efficient transportation.

Glimpses of the lives of salespeople in the early 1900s gained from literature of that period reveal an adventuresome, aggressive, and valuable group of employees often working on the frontier of new markets. Already, however, the independent maverick salespeople who had blazed the early trails to new markets were beginning to disappear. One clear indication that selling was becoming a more structured activity was the development of a **canned sales presentation** by John H. Patterson of the National Cash Register Company. This presentation, a virtual script to guide NCR salespeople on how to sell cash registers, was based on the premise that salespeople are not "born, but rather they are made."[7]

Sales historians noted the changes occurring in personal selling in the early twentieth century. Charles W. Hoyt, author of one of the first textbooks on sales management, chronicled this transition in 1912, noting two types of salespeople:

> The old kind of salesman is the "big me" species . . . He works for himself and, so far as possible, according to his own ideas . . . There is another type of salesman. He is the new kind. At present he is in the minority, but he works for the fastest growing and most successful houses of the day. He works for the house and the house works for him. He welcomes and uses every bit of help the house sends to him.[8]

Hoyt's observations about the "old" and the "new" salesman summed up the changing role of personal selling. The management of firms in the United States were beginning to understand the tremendous potential of personal selling, and simultaneously, the need to shape the growth of the sales function. In particular, there was a widespread interest in how to reduce the cost of sales. According to Hoyt, this did not mean hiring lower-cost salespeople, but instead called for "distributing much larger quantities of goods with less motion."[9]

The War and Depression Era

The 30–year span from 1915 to 1945 was marked by three overwhelming events — two World Wars and the Great Depression in the United States. Because economic activity concentrated on the war efforts, new sales methods did not develop quickly during those periods. During the Great Depression, however, business firms, starved for sales volume, often employed aggressive salespeople to produce badly needed revenue. Then, with renewed prosperity in the post-World War II era, salespeople emerged as important employees for an increasing number of firms that were beginning to realize the benefits of research-based integrated marketing programs.

Professionalism: The Modern Era

In the middle 1940s personal selling became more professional. Buyers not only began to demand more from salespeople but they also grew intolerant of high pressure, fast-talking salespeople, preferring instead a well-informed, customer-oriented salesperson. In 1946, the *Harvard Business Review* published "Low-Pressure Selling,"[10] a classic article followed by many others that called for salespeople to increase the effectiveness of their sales efforts by improving their professional demeanor.

An emphasis on **sales professionalism** seems to be a keynote of the current era. The term has varied meanings, but in this context we use it to mean a customer-oriented approach that employs truthful, nonmanipulative tactics to satisfy the long-term needs of both the customer and the selling firm. The effective salesperson of today is no longer a mere presenter of information, but now must stand equipped to respond to a variety of customer needs before, during, and after the sale.

The evolution of the sales professional is aptly illustrated by sports management executive Mark McCormack:

> The old foot-in-the-door school of high-pressure, super-assertive techniques has gone the way of the dinosaur. These were never very effective techniques to begin with, but perhaps they were necessary fifty years ago, when a salesman was not likely to see or speak to a customer for another six months. Today in the age of modern communication and transportation, if you are being intrusive and have enough people awareness to sense this, there is no excuse for not picking a better time and coming back. You do, of course, have to be willing to come back.[11]

The importance of a customer-oriented professional approach to selling in today's environment was demonstrated by the "Best Sales Force Survey," in which sales executives were asked, "What factors are the most important in running a quality sales operation?" The factors most frequently cited as being important were (1) reputation among customers and (2) holding old accounts (customer retention).[12] Sales professionalism is a prerequisite for any sales manager interested in success in these competitive times. For more on the subject, see "Sales Trend: Increasing Professionalism around the World."

Evolution: Concluding Thoughts

Salespeople have continually struggled to overcome negative images that were formed in ancient times and have carried forward in some form to the present day. As salespeople become more professional and as the beneficial role of salespeople becomes more evident, the negative image burden grows lighter.

Another factor in the evolution of personal selling is the growing awareness that it is a unique occupation because of its economic contribution. Salespeople are an important resource for businesses, providing strong returns on the investment their employers place in them. Salespeople also make a number of contributions to society outside the strictly defined realm of short-term economics. We will consider some of these contributions in the following section.

SALES TREND

INCREASING PROFESSIONALISM AROUND THE WORLD

Is professionalism in selling really increasing, or is this merely a fantasy of buyers and sellers alike? Michael P. Wynne, president of International Management Consulting Services, believes that, indeed, there is an increase in sales professionalism around the world. He observes that more people read books and magazine articles about selling; companies concentrate more on sales training; and that enrollment in sales courses and seminars is high. Moreover, Wynne cites Latin America as evidence that concern for professionalism is not restricted to the United States. He reports that much is being done in those countries to improve the skills of salespeople. Universities, associations, and private training companies are offering courses and seminars featuring customer-oriented topics such as listening and problem solving.

Another factor cited by Wynne as contributing to sales professionalism is the rapid spread of personal selling to professional fields such as banking, where salespeople are expected to meet existing standards for professional conduct. Further, Wynne thinks that women are taking sales professionalism more seriously than some of their male counterparts, and that the increasing influx of women into sales will hasten the movement toward professionalism in sales.

Source: Michael P. Wynne, "The Time Has Come For Professionalism," *Sales and Marketing Management,* September 10, 1984, 18.

Future evolution is inevitable as tomorrow's salesperson responds to a more complex, dynamic environment. Also, increased sophistication of buyers and of new technologies will demand more from the next generation of salespeople. Exhibit 2.1 summarizes some of the likely events of the future.

Exhibit 2.1 **Continued Evolution of Personal Selling**

Change		Salesforce Response
Increased cost of sales calls	⟶	New sales approaches (less traveling)
Raw material shortages	⟶	Allocation orientation
Improved computer technology	⟶	Computerized selling
Increasing complexity of the marketplace	⟶	Market/sales intelligence system
Upgrading of purchasing function	⟶	Upgrading of sales function
More emphasis on managing customer relationships	⟶	Concentration on long-term benefits, developing trust and credibility

Source: Adapted from Wesley J. Johnston, "The Industrial Salesforce's Response to a Changing Environment," in *Issues in Industrial Marketing: A View to the Future,* edited by Robert Speckman and David Wilson (Chicago: American Marketing Association, 1982), 57–68.

CONTRIBUTIONS OF PERSONAL SELLING

Although advertising has traditionally captured most of the attention of students and researchers, personal selling is actually the most important part of marketing communications for most business firms.[13] Proof of its importance is furnished by surveys and estimates revealing that more money is spent on personal selling than on any other form of marketing communications, whether it be advertising, sales promotion, publicity, or public relations. As the shift to a national economic base more dominated by the service sector continues, all indications point to an even more important role for personal selling in the future.[14]

The sizable investment in personal selling is reflected in the estimated costs of employing a salesperson. First, a firm can expect to spend from $10 thousand to $50 thousand to recruit, hire, and train the salesperson to productive status. Next, the average compensation for an experienced salesperson usually exceeds $40 thousand a year. Sales expenses, fringe benefits, and continual training costs add to the investment.

A common denominator of this investment is the cost per sales call index as calculated by various organizations. For example, *Sales and Marketing Management* magazine, a well-known source, estimates an approximate cost range of $151–$207 for a single sales call.[15] Multiply this estimate by multiple sales calls per day for each salesperson, and extend the mathematics for an entire year, and the conclusion is clear — personal selling is expensive. A sales manager's response is to ask, how can we make such an investment pay off? Indeed, this may be the most crucial question a sales manager deals with, at both strategic and tactical levels. We will now take a look at how this investment is justified by reviewing the contributions of personal selling to society in general, to the employing firm, and to customers.

Salespeople and Society

Since the founding of this nation, our society has consistently supported a goal of economic growth. Salespeople contribute to this process in two basic ways. They act as stimuli for economic transactions, and they further the diffusion of innovation.

Salespeople as Economic Stimuli. Several years ago, baseball star Reggie Jackson described himself as "the straw that stirs the drink" of the championship New York Yankees team. Much like Jackson, salespeople are expected to stimulate action in the business world — hence the term, **economic stimuli**. In a fluctuating economy, salespeople make invaluable contributions by assisting in recovery cycles and by helping to sustain periods of relative prosperity. In fact, the demand for salespeople increases following a decline in profits.[16] As John P. Steinbrink, president of the Dartnell Corporation, a Chicago research and publishing company, observed, "a business always needs a sales staff, especially when the economy is wavering."[17] This is true because salespeople are capable of, and expected to, get results in the short term as well as the long term.

Salespeople and Diffusion of Innovation. Salespeople play a critical role in the **diffusion of innovation**, the process whereby new products, services, and ideas are distributed to the members of society. Consumers who are likely to be early adopters of an innovation often rely on salespeople as a primary source of information. Quite frequently, well-informed, specialized salespeople provide useful information to potential consumers who then purchase from a lower-cost outlet. The role of salespeople in the diffusion of industrial products and services is particularly crucial. Imagine trying to purchase a company-wide computer system without the assistance of a competent salesperson or sales team!

While acting as an agent of innovation, the salesperson invariably encounters a strong resistance to change in the latter stages of the diffusion process. The status quo seems to be extremely satisfactory to many parties, even though, in the long run, change is necessary for continued progress or survival. By encouraging the adoption of innovative products and services, salespeople may indeed be making a positive contribution to society. For example, our educational system has been improved by the addition of computers to the classroom, a development that would have been delayed indefinitely without the efforts of salespeople.

Salespeople and the Employing Firm

A chapter in this book details the job activities of salespeople, but at this point, we will discuss the more general contributions of salespeople to their firms — as revenue producers, sources of market research and feedback, and as candidates for management positions.

Salespeople as Revenue Producers. Sales managers and salespeople rally around the common slogan of "we bring in the money . . . everybody else is just overhead." In fact, they occupy the somewhat unique role as the **revenue producers** in their firms. Consequently, they usually feel the brunt of that pressure along with the management of the firm. While accountants and financial staff are concerned with profitability in bottom-line terms, salespeople are constantly reminded of their responsibility to achieve a healthy "top line" on the profit and loss statement. Their goals are thus distinguished by their narrower focus on revenue production.

Market Research and Feedback. Since salespeople spend so much time in direct contact with their customers, it is only logical that they would play an important role in market research and in providing feedback to their firms. For example, sales representatives at Pfizer Agriculture track competitive pricing, changes in competitive sales coverage, and customers' reactions to other companies' products. This information is transmitted electronically to Pfizer's management, which has used the information for actions as diverse as planning advertising campaigns and acquiring another company.[18]

Another company that relies heavily on the salesforce for market research and feedback is Warner Electric Brake and Clutch, a supplier of clutches for Xerox machines. Each salesperson is required to submit three possible additions to the product line as suggested by customers. Such requirements are fairly routine in sales organizations, but the unusual aspect of this case is that the chairman of Warner Electric reads all 90 reports and regularly requests concrete follow-up action on 30 to 40 of the ideas.[19]

Some would argue that salespeople are not trained as market researchers, or that salespeoples' time could be better utilized than in research and feedback activities. Many firms, however, refute this argument by finding numerous ways to capitalize upon the salesforce as a reservoir of ideas. It is not an exaggeration to say that many firms have concluded that they cannot afford to operate in the absence of salesforce feedback and research.

Salespeople as Future Managers. In recent years, marketing and sales personnel have been in strong demand for upper management positions. Recognizing the need for a top management trained in sales, many firms use the sales job as an entry-level position that provides a foundation for future assignments.[20] The dominance of former salespeople in top management has been cited as the key reason for the success of IBM, Frito-Lay, Procter and Gamble, and Domino's Pizza, among other top firms.[21] As progressive firms continue to emphasize customer orientation as a basic operating concept, it is only natural that salespeople who have learned how to meet customer needs will be good candidates for management jobs.

As competition intensifies, salespeople will continue to be valuable human resources. While they make important contributions as salespeople, many will make even more significant contributions as top managers in customer-oriented firms.

Salespeople and the Customer

A recent survey of purchasing agents emphasizes the expectations that buyers have of salespeople. According to respondents in the survey, professional buyers expect salespeople to exhibit:

- Reliability and credibility
- Professionalism and integrity
- Product knowledge
- Innovativeness in problem solving
- Preparation for the sales presentation[22]

These expectations are consistent with other surveys of buyer expectations of salespeople that span several years.[23] The overall conclusion is that buyers expect salespeople to contribute to the success of the buyer's firm. Buyers value the information furnished by salespeople, and, more than ever before, they value the problem-solving skills of salespeople.

The importance of providing solutions to customer problems is clearly illustrated by IBM. In reviewing the computer industry, one observer said, "More than anything else, it was IBM's awesome sales skills that enabled the company to capture the computer market."[24] Other observers of IBM's sales strategy attributed the company's success to its commitment to solving customer problems, even if company rules of operation had to be temporarily set aside.[25]

As salespeople serve their customers, they simultaneously serve their employers and society. When the interests of these parties conflict, the salesperson can be caught in the midst. By learning to resolve these conflicts as a routine part of their jobs, salespeople further contribute to developing a business system based on progress through problem solving.

CLASSIFICATION OF PERSONAL SELLING APPROACHES

Over 20 years ago, four basic approaches to personal selling were identified: stimulus-response, mental-states, need-satisfaction, and problem-solution.[26] Since that time, another approach to personal selling, termed contingency selling, has gained popularity. All five approaches to selling are practiced today. Furthermore, many salespeople use elements of more than one approach in their own hybrids of personal selling.

Some salespeople use no conscious approach to their sales efforts. But most successful salespeople do benefit from at least a rudimentary working knowledge of the different views of selling.

Stimulus-Response Selling

Of the five views of personal selling, **stimulus-response selling** is the simplest. The theoretical background for this approach originated in early experiments with animal behavior. The key idea is that various stimuli can elicit predictable responses. Salespeople furnish the stimuli from a repertoire of words and actions designed to produce the desired response. This approach to selling is illustrated in Figure 2.1.

An example of the stimulus-response view of selling would be **continued affirmation**, a method in which a series of questions or statements furnished by the salesperson is designed to condition the prospective buyer to answering "yes" time after time, until, it is hoped, he or she will be inclined to say "yes" to the entire sales proposition. This method is often employed by telemarketing personnel, who rely on comprehensive sales scripts read or delivered from memory.

Stimulus-response sales strategies, particularly when implemented with a canned sales presentation, have some advantages for the seller. The sales message can be structured in a logical order. Questions and objections from the buyer can usually be

Figure 2.1 **Stimulus-Response Approach to Selling**

The salesperson attempts to gain favorable responses from the customer by providing stimuli, or *cues,* to influence the buyer. After the customer has been properly conditioned, the salesperson tires to secure a positive purchase decision.

anticipated and addressed before they are magnified during buyer-seller interaction. Inexperienced salespeople can rely on stimulus-response sales methods in some settings, and this may eventually contribute to sales expertise.

The limitations of stimulus-response methods, however, can be severe, especially if the salesperson is dealing with a professional buyer. Most buyers like to take an active role in sales dialogue, and the stimulus-response approach calls for the salesperson to dominate the flow of conversation. The lack of flexibility in this approach is also a disadvantage, as buyer responses and unforseen interruptions may neutralize or damage the effectiveness of the stimuli.

Considering the net effects of this method's advantages and disadvantages, it appears most suitable for relatively unimportant purchase decisions, when time is severely constrained, and when professional buyers are not the prospects. As consumers in general become more sophisticated, this approach will become more problematic.

Mental-States Selling

Mental-states selling, or the *formula approach* to personal selling, assumes that the buying process for most buyers is essentially identical and that buyers can be led through certain mental states, or steps, in the buying process. These mental states are typically referred to as **AIDA** (attention, interest, desire, and action).[27] Appropriate sales messages provide a transition from one mental state to the next.

Like stimulus-response selling, the mental-states approach relies on a highly structured sales presentation. The salesperson does most of the talking, as feedback from the prospect could be disruptive to the flow of the presentation.

A positive feature of this method is that it forces the salesperson to plan the sales presentation prior to calling on the customer. It also helps the salesperson recognize

Exhibit 2.2 **Mental States View of Selling**

Mental State	Sales Step	Critical Sales Task
Curiosity	Attention	Get prospects excited, then get them to like you.
Interest	Interest	Interview: needs and wants
Conviction	Conviction	"What's in it for me?" Product — "Will it do what I want it to do?" Price — "Is it worth it?" "The hassle of change?" "Cheaper elsewhere?" Peers — "What will others think of it?" Priority — "Do I need it now?" (sense of urgency)
Desire	Desire	Overcome their stall
Action	Close	Alternate choice close: which, not if!

Source: Adapted from D. Forbes Ley, *The Best Seller* (Newport Beach, CA: Sales Success Press, 1986).

that timing is an important element in the purchase-decision process, and that careful listening is necessary to determine which stage the buyer is in at a given point in time. The mental-states approach to personal selling has been popular with sales trainers, perhaps because it is easy to formulate major selling points around the attention, interest, desire, and action states.

A problem with the mental-states method is that it is very difficult to determine which state a prospect is in. Sometimes a prospect is spanning two mental states, or moving back and forth between two states, during the sales presentation. Consequently, the heavy guidance structure the salesperson implements may be inappropriate, confusing, and even counterproductive to sales effectiveness. We should also note that this method is not customer-oriented. Although the salesperson tailors the presentation to each customer somewhat, this is done by noting customer mental states rather than needs.

The mental-states, or formula, approach to personal selling is very popular in consumer and industrial sales. One interesting account of this approach is furnished by the Glass Container Group of the Ball Corporation. This firm's sales strategy is based on moving through several stages over a time period that can extend into years. It is founded on the premise that the most important goal in communicating is getting the prospect to listen. This corresponds to the attention stage of AIDA. From the attention-gaining platform, Ball attempts to interest the potential customer in its company as a potential supplier, then it "moves the script along" to an ultimate "lift-off," where the buyer makes a positive decision regarding Ball.[28]

The mental-states method is illustrated in Exhibit 2.2. Note that this version includes "conviction" as an intermediate stage between interest and desire. Such minor variations are commonplace in different renditions of this approach to selling.

Figure 2.2 **Need-Satisfaction Approach to Selling**

The salesperson attempts to uncover customer needs that are related to the salesperson's product or service offering. This may require extensive questioning in the early stages of the sales process. After confirming the buyer's needs, the salesperson proceeds with a presentation based on how the offering can meet those needs.

Need-Satisfaction Selling

Need-satisfaction selling is based on the notion that the customer is buying to satisfy a particular need or set of needs. This approach is shown in Figure 2.2. It is the salesperson's task to identify the need to be met, then to help the buyer meet the need. Unlike the mental-states and stimulus-response methods, this method focuses on the customer, rather than on the salesperson. The salesperson utilizes a questioning, probing tactic to uncover important buyer needs. Customer responses dominate the early portion of the sales interaction, and only after relevant needs have been established does the salesperson begin to relate how his or her offering can satisfy these needs.

Customers seem to appreciate this selling method and are often willing to spend considerable time in preliminary meetings to define needs prior to a sales presentation or written sales proposal. Also, this method avoids the defensiveness that arises in some prospects when a salesperson rushes to the persuasive part of the sales message without adequate attention to the buyer's needs.

As originally conceived, need-satisfaction selling was meant to create a friendly, low-pressure environment for communication between the buyer and seller in which the salesperson would be perceived as a trusted source of information and advice. In recent years, a version of need-satisfaction selling called *nonmanipulative selling* has gained favor with sales trainers. The conversational framework of this method directs salespeople to spend more time on determining prospect needs and wants than on any other part of the sales process.[29]

Although critics charge that the time expenditure in needs-satisfaction selling is too great in both training and time away from actual "selling," the method is nevertheless well entrenched in business practice today. One study attesting to its potency was conducted by Xerox Learning Systems and found that the more successful salespeople were able to[30]

- Ask questions to uncover needs
- Recognize when customers have real needs and show how their products or services could satisfy the needs
- Establish a balanced dialogue with customers

Different approaches, of course, work best in different situations. For most professional salespeople, however, the need-satisfaction approach seems to have the widest applicability.

Problem-Solving Selling

Problem-solving selling is an extension of need-satisfaction selling. It goes beyond identifying needs to developing alternative solutions for satisfying these needs. The problem-solving approach to selling is depicted in Figure 2.3. Sometimes even competitor's offerings are included as alternatives in the purchase decision. For example, a technique called Product Profile Analysis allows the buyer and seller to concentrate on the most relevant criteria in a given purchase situation.[31] Scores are computed for each alternative, including competitors' offerings, in an attempt to make a rational purchase decision.

The Plastics Division of the Mobil Corporation has used the problem-solving approach in selling disposable food service items to hospitals as an alternative to glass and stainless steel utensils. To present the alternatives, Mobil undertakes a complete audit of the hospital's foodservice operation. All cost figures are furnished by the hospital rather than being estimated by the salesperson. Before final computations are made, hospital personnel are asked to verify the accuracy of the information. Then the figures are inputted to an accounting model that assesses the operating costs of the various alternatives and the associated breakeven points. This detailed process, which may take a month or longer to complete, allows the decision maker to make the best possible choice for the hospital.

As the Mobil example points out, the problem-solving approach to selling can take a lot of time. In some cases, the selling company cannot afford this much time with each prospective customer. In other cases, the customers may be unwilling to spend the time. Insurance salespeople, for example, report this to be so in their field. The problem-solving approach appears to be most successful in technical industrial sales situations, where the parties involved are usually oriented toward scientific reasoning and processes and thus find this approach to sales quite amenable.

Contingency Approach

During the last decade, there has been considerable interest in another view of personal selling—one that favors the use of several different sales approaches, depending on what is best in a given situation, rather than a single approach. This **contin-**

Figure 2.3 **Problem-Solving Approach to Selling**

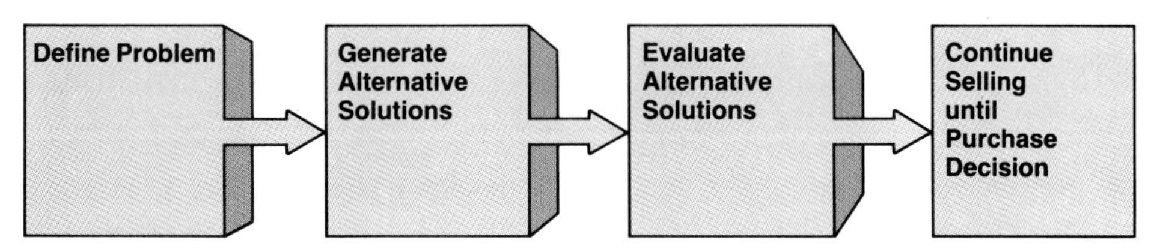

The salesperson defines a customer problem that may be solved by various alternatives. Then an offering is made that represents at least one of these alternatives. All alternatives are carefully evaluated before a purchase decision is made.

gency approach calls for an adaptive salesperson who is capable of reading the situation properly, then reacting to feedback from the prospect with the proper sales tactic. Thus, the stimulus-response, mental-states, need-satisfaction, and problem-solving approaches might all be used at different points in the sales dialogue.

Both common sense and empirical studies tell us that salespeople in different selling environments use varying approaches to selling.[32] As illustrated in Figure 2.4, the contingency approach recognizes four key sets of variables that define a selling situation:

- Characteristics of the salesperson-customer relationship
- Selling behaviors
- Resources of the salesperson
- Characteristics of the customer's buying task

The first variable — the relationship between the salesperson and the customer — depends on more than just how well the two parties get along together. For example, does one party have an extraordinary amount of power over the other party, or is there a relative balance of power? Is there some anticipation of future interaction that could be beneficial to both parties, or is this a one-shot deal? Certainly the answers to these questions help determine which selling approach should be employed.

Salespeople have a multitude of choices in terms of the second variable, which selling behaviors to use when operating on a contingency basis. They may attempt to exercise tight control in the sales interaction or, alternatively, encourage the prospect to dictate the flow and content of the sales interview. They can focus on a product appeal or select from a number of other influence techniques. For an application of the contingency approach to selling, see "International Sales: Selling to the Japanese."

Figure 2.4 Contingency Model of Salesperson Effectiveness

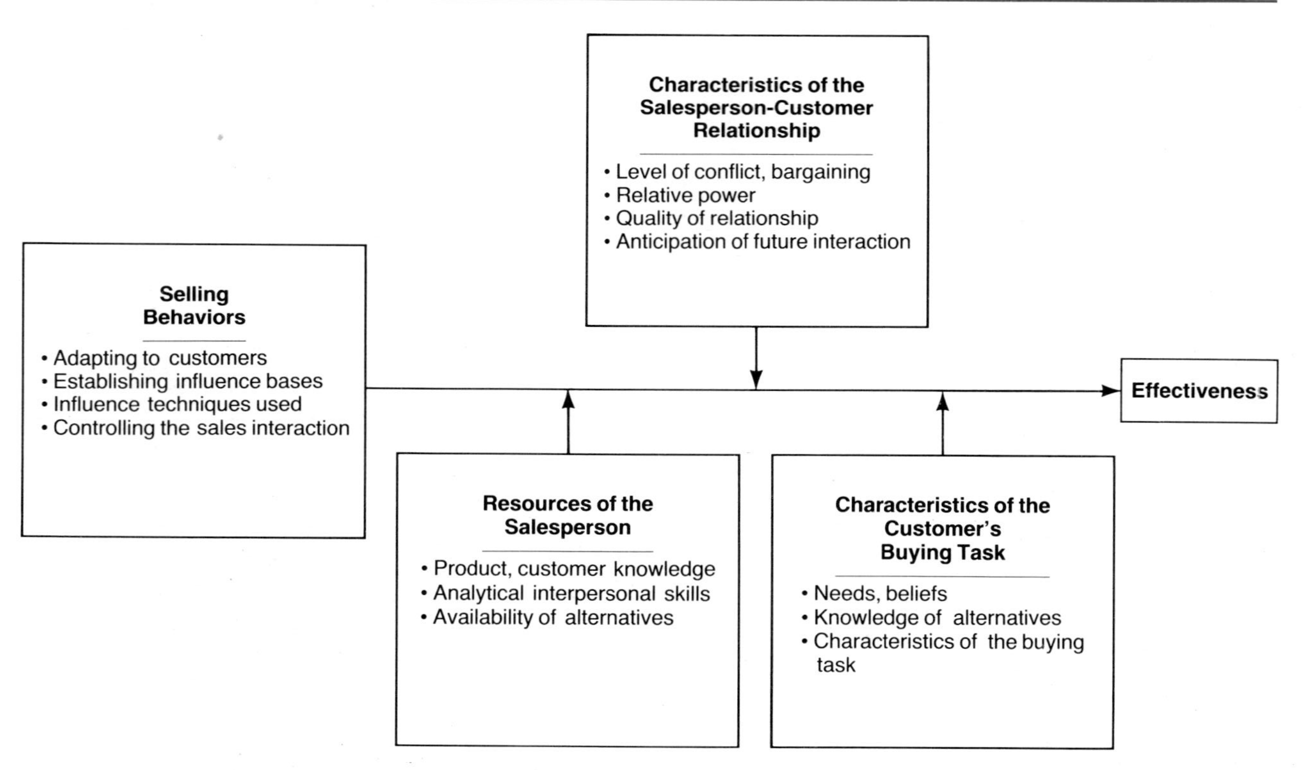

The most effective selling behaviors depend on (1) the resources of the salesperson, (2) the customer's buying task, and (3) the nature of the salesperson-customer relationship.

Source: Barton A. Weitz, "Effectiveness In Sales Interactions: A Contingency Framework," reprinted from *Journal of Marketing* 45 (Winter 1981): 86, published by the American Marketing Association. Used with permission.

INTERNATIONAL SALES

SELLING TO THE JAPANESE

A manager with Borg-Warner in Hong Kong who is experienced in dealing with the Japanese points out that in America, business relationships center on money. In Japan, personal relationships mean a lot more to buyer-seller relationships. He suggests that sellers must first establish trust with potential customers before attempting to make sales presentations. Among his other recommendations are the following:

- Recognize that timing differences exist in Japan. A time limit on an offer to transact business is not acceptable.
- Americans should view themselves as "guests," not "hosts."
- Be patient. Try to be more passive than usual.
- Do not expect Japanese customers to provide all the information requested in a given situation. Americans are often seen as being too straightforward in their requests for information.

Source: Mark F. MacPherson, "When In Toyko," *Business Marketing*, September 1987, 88.

The contingency approach recognizes that the resources of individual salespeople differ. Some are sales "powerhouses," exhibiting formidable product knowledge, an arsenal of well-developed interpersonal skills, and a knowledge of how to use these attributes in an effective manner. Other salespeople must compensate for certain weaknesses. For instance, a salesperson could compensate for a lack of product knowledge in a given situation by utilizing another resource such as willingness to provide follow-up service.

An effective salesperson must be able to assess the buyer's special situation. One buyer might feel reluctant to do business with a new supplier because he is comfortable with his current vendor. Conversely, another might be dissatisfied with her current vendor, which would make her an excellent prospect for the selling company. Some buyers are highly experienced and well aware of various alternatives. Others are heavily dependent on salespeople's assistance.

A good example of the contingency approach to selling is reported by Lowry, Raclin, Harrell, and Howerdd, a Chicago financial consulting firm. Executive Director Mark Raclin spent over $200,000 to produce a computerized video projection system to be used in presentations to Fortune 1000 companies who were seeking financial advice on investment decisions. Mr. Raclin found that his executive audiences were intolerant of delays in answering questions and that the new system allowed him to respond quickly to complex unexpected questions. The contingency approach is evident in Raclin's comments: "The pictures help us communicate large amounts of information in a short period of time, as well as examine various opportunities and options."[33]

SALES TECHNOLOGY

PLANNING THE SALES CALL WITH THE SALES EDGE

The Sales Edge, an off-the-shelf software package, allows salespeople to plan specific strategies for each customer or prospect. The Sales Edge contains three basic steps. First, the salesperson does a self-assessment of his or her own personality. This is done by responding to 86 "agree or disagree" statements such as, "I like to take charge of situations."

Next, the customer's personality is assessed. The salesperson agrees or disagrees with 50 adjectives to describe the customer. For example, the customer is rated on whether or not he is talkative, social, independent, and apprehensive.

The third step in the program is a five- to seven-page sales strategy report that tells the salesperson what to expect from the prospect and how to make the sale. For example, one prospect was profiled as being cynical and somewhat suspicious. The sales strategy report advised the salesperson to appeal to the prospect's intellect and curiosity, rather than trying to charm the prospect with socializing.

As is true with all "self-help" sales software, The Sales Edge is not represented as the definitive word on how to sell a customer. It does, however, encourage development of a specific strategy for each customer, an important element in contingency selling.

Source: Diane Lynn Kastiel, "Computerized Consultants," *Business Marketing*, March 1987, 72–74; and Robert H. Collins, "Artificial Intelligence in Personal Selling," *Journal of Personal Selling and Sales Management* 4 (May 1984): 58–66.

Personal computers are aiding salespeople who prefer the contingency approach. Questions that explore topics ranging from inventory on hand to predicted interest rates are routinely explored via computer as the sales representative makes the sales call. An example of contingency selling with the assistance of sales-planning software is presented in "Sales Technology: Planning the Sales Call with the Sales Edge."

CLASSIFICATION OF PERSONAL SELLING JOBS

Since there are so many unique sales jobs, the term *salesperson* is not by itself very descriptive. A salesperson could be a flower vendor at a busy downtown intersection or the sales executive negotiating the sale of Boeing aircraft to the People's Republic of China.

We have already mentioned that selling services and selling tangible products require distinctly different approaches. Moreover, retail selling differs from selling to institutions. Telemarketing sales attempts are quite different from field selling. The list is probably endless.

We will briefly discuss six types of personal selling jobs:

- Sales support
- New business
- Existing business
- Inside sales (non-retail)
- Direct-to-consumer sales
- Combination sales jobs

Sales Support

Sales support personnel are not usually involved in the direct solicitation of purchase orders. Rather, their primary responsibility is dissemination of information and performance of other activities designed to stimulate sales. They might concentrate at the end-user level or another level in the channel of distribution to support the overall sales effort. They may report to another salesperson, who is responsible for direct handling of purchase orders, or to the sales manager. There are two well-known categories of support salespeople: missionary or detail salespeople and technical support salespeople.

Missionary salespeople usually work for a manufacturer but may also be found working for brokers and manufacturing representatives, especially in the grocery industry. There are strong similarities between sales missionaries and religious missionaries. Like their counterparts, sales missionaries are expected to "spread the word" with the purpose of conversion — to customer status. Once converted, the customer receives reinforcing messages, new information, and the benefit of the missionary's activities to strengthen the relationship between buyer and seller.

In the pharmaceutical industry, the **detailer** is a fixture. Major corporations utilize the detailer to support the sales effort at crucial junctures in the channel of distribution. Detailers working at the physician level furnish valuable information regarding the capabilities and limitations of medications in an attempt to get the physician to prescribe their product. Another sales representative from the same pharmaceutical company will sell the medication to the wholesaler or pharmacist, but it is the detailer's job to support the direct sales effort by calling on physicians.

Technical specialists are sometimes considered to be sales support personnel. These **technical support salespeople** may assist in design and specification processes, installation of equipment, training of the customer's employees, and follow-up service of a technical nature. They are sometimes part of a sales team that includes another salesperson who specializes in identifying and satisfying customer needs by recommending the appropriate product or service.

New Business

New business is generated for the selling firm by adding new customers or introducing new products to the marketplace. Two types of new-business salespeople are pioneers and order-getters.

Pioneers, as the term suggests, are constantly involved with either new products, new customers, or both. Their task requires creative selling and the ability to counter the resistance to change that will likely be present in prospective customers. Pioneers are well-represented in the sale of business franchises, where the sales representatives travel from city to city seeking new franchisees. They are also found in consumer and industrial firms, where new accounts are turned over to another salesperson once the pioneer has established the buyer-seller relationship.

Order-getters are salespeople who actively seek orders, usually in a highly competitive environment. While all pioneers are also order-getters, the reverse is not true. An order-getter may serve existing customers on an ongoing basis, whereas the pioneer moves on to new customers as soon as possible. Order-getters may seek new business by selling an existing customer additional items from the product line. A well-known tactic is to establish a relationship with a customer by selling a single product from the line, then to follow up with subsequent sales calls for other items from the product line.

Most corporations emphasize sales growth, and salespeople operating as pioneers and order-getters are at the heart of sales-growth objectives. The pressure to perform in these roles is fairly intense; the results are highly visible. For these reasons, the new-business salesperson is often among the elite in any company's salesforce.

Existing Business

In direct contrast to new-business salespeople, other salespeople's primary responsibility is to maintain relationships with existing customers. These salespeople are no less valuable to their firms than the new-business salespeople, but creative selling skills are less important to this category of sales personnel. Their strengths tend to be reliability and competence in assuring customer convenience. Customers grow to depend on the services provided by this type of salesperson. As most markets are becoming more competitive, the role of existing business salespeople is sometimes critical to prevent erosion of the customer base.

Many firms, believing that it is easier to protect and maintain profitable customers than it is to find replacement customers, are reinforcing sales efforts to existing customers. A classic example of thwarting competitive efforts through stressing the importance of existing customers occurred when American Hospital Supply Corporation introduced its ASAP (analytical systems automated purchasing) systems. In a nutshell, these systems made it hard for hospitals to switch to another purchasing system after they had become accustomed to the superior features of the ASAP system.[34] In a slow market for hospital admissions, placing priority on serving existing business proved to be an astute move for American Hospital.

Salespeople who specialize in maintaining existing business include **order-takers**. These salespeople frequently work for wholesalers, and as the term order-taker implies, they are not too involved in creative selling. Route salespeople who work an established customer base, taking routine reorders of stock items, are order-takers. They sometimes follow a pioneer salesperson and take over the account after the pioneer has made the initial sale.

Inside Sales

In this text, **inside sales** refers to non-retail salespeople who remain in their employer's place of business while dealing with customers. The inside-sales operation has received considerable attention in recent years, not only as supplementary sales tactic, but also as an alternative to field selling.

Inside sales can be conducted on an active or passive sales basis. Active inside sales include the solicitation of entire orders, either as part of a telemarketing operation or when customers walk into the seller's facilities. Passive inside sales imply the acceptance, rather than solicitation of, customer orders, although it is common practice for these transactions to include add-on sales attempts. We should note that customer service personnel sometimes function as inside-sales personnel as an ongoing part of their jobs.

Direct-to-Consumer Sales

Direct-to-consumer salespeople are the most numerous type. There are over 4 million retail salespeople in this country and perhaps another million selling real estate, insurance, and securities. Add to this figure another several million selling direct to the consumer for companies such as Tupperware, Mary Kay, and Avon.

This diverse category of salespeople ranges from the part-time, often temporary salesperson in a retail store to the highly educated, professionally trained stockbroker on Wall Street. As a general statement, the more challenging direct-to-consumer sales positions are those involving the sale of intangible services such as insurance and financial services.

Combination Sales Jobs

Now that we have reviewed some of the basic types of sales job, let us consider the salesperson who performs multiple types of sales jobs within the framework of a single position. We will use the case of the territory manager's position with Beecham Products, U.S.A, to illustrate the combination sales job concept. Beecham, whose products include Aqua-Fresh toothpaste, markets a wide range of consumer goods to food, drug, variety, and mass merchandisers. The territory manager's job blends responsibilities for developing new business, maintaining and stimulating existing business, and performing sales support activities.

During a typical day in the field, the Beecham territory manager is involved in sales support activities such as merchandising and in-store promotion at the individual retail store level. Maintaining contact and goodwill with store personnel is another routine sales support activity. The territory manager also makes sales calls on chain headquarters personnel to handle existing business and to seek new business. And it is the territory manager who introduces new Beecham products in the marketplace.

SUMMARY

1. **Describe the evolution of personal selling from ancient times to the modern era.** The history of personal selling can be traced as far back as ancient Greece. The Industrial Revolution enhanced the importance of salespeople, and personal selling as we know it today had its roots in the early twentieth century. The current era of sales professionalism represents a further evolution.
2. **Explain the contributions of personal selling to society, business firms, and customers.** Salespeople contribute to society by acting as stimuli in the economic process and by assisting in the diffusion of innovation. They contribute to their employers by producing revenue, performing research and feedback activities, and by comprising a pool of future managers. They contribute to customers by providing timely knowledge to assist in solving problems.
3. **Discuss five alternative approaches to personal selling.** Alternative approaches to personal selling include stimulus-response, mental-states, need-satisfaction, problem-solving, and the contingency approach. Stimulus-response selling often utilizes the same sales presentation for all customers. The mental-states approach prescribes that the salesperson lead the buyer through stages in the buying process. Need-satisfaction selling focuses on relating benefits of the seller's products or services to the buyer's particular situation. Problem-solving selling extends need-satisfaction by concentrating on various alternatives available to the buyer. In the contingency approach, the salesperson adapts to the situation, utilizing whichever sales methods are most appropriate.
4. **Describe different types of personal selling jobs.** Among the countless number of different personal selling jobs are the following six types: sales support, new business, existing business, inside sales (non-retail), direct-to-consumers sales, and combination jobs. Sales support positions include missionary or detail salespeople and technical support salespeople. Two types of new-business salespeople are pioneers and order-getters. The primary responsibility of existing-business salespeople is to maintain relationships with present customers through routine sales calls and follow up. Inside sales in non-retail settings is typified in telemarketing operations and is also used to handle walk-in sales transactions. Direct-to-consumer sales include retail selling, as well as the sale of insurance, securities, and real estate. Combination sales jobs are commonplace, and may combine

new-business selling with sales support and existing-business responsibilities as shown in the Beecham Products example. Other combinations are also frequently encountered.

Key Terms

- canned sales presentation
- sales professionalism
- cost per sales call index
- economic stimuli
- diffusion of innovation
- revenue producers
- stimulus-response selling
- continued affirmation
- mental-states selling
- AIDA
- need-satisfaction selling
- problem-solving selling
- contingency approach
- sales support personnel
- missionary salespeople
- detail salespeople
- technical support salespeople
- pioneers
- order-getters
- order-takers
- inside sales
- combination sales jobs

Review Questions

1. What factors will influence the continued evolution of personal selling?
2. How do salespeople contribute to our society? Are there negative aspects of personal selling from a societal perspective?
3. What are the primary contributions made by salespeople to their employers?
4. Most businesses would have a difficult time surviving without the benefits of the salespeople who call on them. Do you agree?
5. Distinguish between stimulus-response selling and mental-states selling.
6. How are need-satisfaction and problem-solving selling related? How do they differ?
7. The contingency approach to personal selling can incorporate the other approaches to selling within its framework. Give an example of how one of the other views of personal selling might be utilized within the contingency framework.
8. When do you think stimulus-response selling would be most effective?
9. What are the differences in key responsibilities of missionary salespeople amd pioneer salespeople? What recurring problems would you expect each type to encounter as they call on their customers?
10. Sales jobs are essentially the same — they involve satisfying the customer. Do you agree?

Application Exercises

1. Assume you are a telemarketing sales representative for a residential lawncare company. Using the stimulus-response approach, plan a sales presentation designed to persuade a homeowner to utilize your service, which involves four equally priced applications of

fertilizer and weed killer on an annual basis. The presentation, to be conducted by telephone, should not last over two minutes.

2. Imagine that you are a sales manager in the year 2010. You have agreed to address the marketing club at a local university on "the future of personal selling." Outline the key factors that you see affecting personal selling in the post-2010 era. Also comment on the viability of personal selling in this future period.
3. The contingency sales approach requires adapting to differing situations, including the buyer's personality. For each of the following personality traits, discuss how a salesperson might react to facilitate the sale.
   - Argumentative
   - Hesitant
   - Impulsive
   - Decisive
   - Procrastinator
4. Visit your library and locate five articles that portray negative aspects of salespeople and five that portray positive aspects. What factors seem to contribute to the image of salespeople in general? How does the image of salespeople affect sales management? (Note: to complete this assignment, consult popular magazines and newspapers rather than trade periodicals or academic journals.)
5. The need-satisfaction, problem-solving, and contingency approaches to selling recognize that customer motives may differ. For each of the following buyers of liquid carpet cleaner, list the most likely concerns or motives that must be addressed by the salesperson.
   - Hardware store owner
   - Purchasing agent for a janitorial-supplies wholesaler
   - Manager of a municipal airport

Notes

[1]Marjorie J. Caballero, Roger A. Dickinson, and Dabney Townsend, "Aristotle and Personal Selling," *Journal of Personal Selling and Sales Management* 4 (May 1984): 13–18.

[2]William T. Kelley, "The Development of Early Thought in Marketing," in *Salesmanship: Selected Readings,* edited by John M. Rathmell (Homewood, Ill.: Irwin, 1969), 3.

[3]Thomas L. Powers, Warren S. Martin, Hugh Rushing, and Scott Daniels, "Selling before 1900: A Historical Perspective," *Journal of Personal Selling and Sales Management* 7 (November 1987): 5.

[4]Michael Bell, *The Salesman in the Field* (Geneva: International Labour Office, 1980), 1.

[5]Stanley C. Hollander, "Anti-Salesman Ordinances of the Mid-19th Century," in Rathmell, *Salesmanship,* 9.

[6]Ibid., 10.

[7]Jon M. Hawes, "Leaders in Selling and Sales Management," *Journal of Personal Selling and Sales Management* 5 (November 1985): 60.

[8]Charles W. Hoyt, *Scientific Sales Management* (New Haven, Conn.: George W. Woolson and Co., 1913), 3–4.

[9]Ibid., 4.

[10]Edward C. Bursk, "Low-Pressure Selling," *Harvard Business Review* 25 (Winter 1947): 227–242

[11]Mark H. McCormack, *What They Don't Teach You at the Harvard Business School* (New York: Bantam Books, 1984), 92.

[12]"The Qualities of Quality," *Sales and Marketing Management,* June 6, 1986, 55.

[13]Barton A. Weitz, "Relationship between Salesperson Performance and Understanding of Customer Decision Making," *Journal of Marketing Research* 15 (November 1978): 501–516.

[14]William R. George, J. Patrick Kelley, and Claudia E. Marshall, "The Selling of Services: A Comprehensive Model," *Journal of Personal Selling and Sales Management* 6 (August 1986): 29–37.

[15]"1987 Survey of Selling Costs," *Sales and Marketing Management,* February 22, 1988, 12.

[16]Joseph A. Bellizzi, A. Frank Thompson, and Lynn J. Loudenback, "Cyclical Variations of Advertising and Personal Selling," *Journal of the Academy of Marketing Science* 11 (Spring 1983): 142–155.

[17]"Selling More Vital Today Than Ever," *Marketing Times,* January/February 1983, 42.

[18]"Ideas You Can Use: Bird-Dogging the Competition," *Sales and Marketing Management,* December 9, 1985, 52.

[19]Thomas J. Peters and Nancy K. Austin, *A Passion for Excellence* (New York: Random House, 1985), 26.

[20]Alan J. Dubinsky and Thomas N. Ingram, "Important First-Line Qualifications: What Sales Executives Think," *Journal of Personal Selling and Sales Management* 3 (May 1983): 18–26.

[21]Peters and Austin, *A Passion for Excellence,* 107.

[22]"PAs Examine the People Who Sell to Them," *Sales and Marketing Management,* November 11, 1985, 39.

[23]Alvin J. Williams and John Seminerio, "What Buyers Like from Salesmen," *Industrial Marketing Management* 14 (May 1985): 75–78.

[24]"The Colossus That Works," *Time,* July 11, 1983, 46.

[25]Peters and Austin, *A Passion for Excellence,* 92.

[26]Robert F. Gwinner, "Base Theory in the Formulation of Sales Strategy," *MSU Business Topics,* Autumn 1968, 37–44.

[27]Ronald D. Balsey and E. Patricia Birsner, *Selling: Marketing Personified* (Hinsdale, Ill.: The Dryden Press, 1987), 31.

[28]Clayton J. Reichard, "Industrial Selling: Beyond Price and Persistence," *Harvard Business Review* 63 (March-April 1985): 127–133.

[29]Tony Alessandra and Jim Cathcart, "Non-Manipulative Selling," *Industrial Distribution,* June 1985, 49.

[30]Mike Radick, "Training Salespeople to Get Success on Their Side," *Sales and Marketing Management,* August 15, 1983, 63–65.

[31]John I. Coppett and William A. Staples, "Product Profile Analysis: A Tool for Industrial Selling," *Industrial Marketing Management* 9 (July 1980): 207–211.

[32]Robert E. Hite and Joseph A. Belizzi, "Differences in the Importance of Selling Techniques between Consumer and Industrial Salespeople," *Journal of Personal Selling and Sales Management* 5 (November 1985): 19–30.

[33]"Standing Tall on the Sales Call," *Sales and Marketing Management,* January 1987, 76.

[34]Collin Canright, "Seizing the Electronic Information Advantage," *Business Marketing,* January 1988, 81–86.

CHAPTER 3

PERSONAL SELLING: JOB ACTIVITIES AND THE SALES PROCESS

Learning Objectives

After completing this chapter, you should be able to

1. Describe the key job activities of salespeople.
2. Explain how salespeople act as managers in certain situations.
3. Delineate the role salespeople play in supporting their organizations.
4. Discuss the sales process as a series of interrelated steps.

WHERE THREE SALES A YEAR MAKE YOU A SUPERSTAR

Based on the number of deals closed, Zellars C. West hardly sounds like a sales superstar. He made only three sales in 1985, yet he was honored as the top salesperson of the year by his employer, Cray Research, Inc. Cray sells the Porsches of the computer industry — fast, powerful supercomputers that are priced up to $20 million each. Mr. West, whose territory covers New Jersey, Pennsylvania, and Ohio, may work years to close a multimillion-dollar sale. He is firmly established among the world's sales elite.

Like most sellers of big-ticket items, West receives a base salary — about $60,000. He also gets a commission on total sales of 4 percent. It has been estimated that West, along with the other top Cray salespeople, earn in excess of $250,000 per year. Considering the pressure to land huge contracts and his success at doing just that, it would appear that Mr. West definitely earns his pay.

Mr. West is a 30-year veteran of the computer industry. He worked with Univac, Honeywell, and Control Data before joining Cray in 1977. When he came to work for Cray, he took a 50 percent cut in pay and ran his territory with little marketing support. He had no office and no secretary. He was an almost instant success with Cray, landing a $8.5 million contract with AT&T after only three months on the job.

Despite his spectacular sales accomplishments, West does not think of himself as a sales superstar. He lives in the same split-level, three-bedroom home he bought 19 years ago, dresses conservatively, and avoids lavish entertainment of customers.

West prefers a subdued approach with his customers, rather than a hard sell. He says his clients are mostly engineers and scientists who are "ten times smarter than me." One of his customers, James R. Kasdorf, manager of engineering computer services at Westinghouse, confirms West's low-pressure methods by stating, "He doesn't bother us a whole lot when we don't want to be bothered." This tactic fits the overall strategy at Cray, where the emphasis is not on selling a product, but rather on establishing marriage-like relationships.

Source: Patrick Houston and Gordon Bock, "Where Three Sales a Year Make You a Superstar," *Business Week,* February 17, 1986, 76–77.

The biggest challenge facing Mr. West is finding qualified buyers for his products. While many scientists and engineers want supercomputers, a sizable number do not have the money or management support necessary to make a purchase. Once a likely buyer is located, West seeks an insider to help him sell his products to other key personnel. This process took five years in a deal involving General Electric. The result was a $9.5 million contract. A year-by-year review of the General Electric sale follows.

In 1981 West first visited General Electric's research development center in New York. GE's computer programs were tested on Cray hardware. In the fall, Cray made an informal presentation to GE scientists and engineers. In 1982 Cray analyzed the GE divisions to see which ones could benefit the most from its machines.

Late in 1983 Cray made a two-hour presentation to the most likely prospect, GE's Ohio aircraft engine manufacturing facility. A year later, West briefed 50 employees at the Ohio facility on Cray applications.

The year 1985 was a busy one for West. In January GE approached him with inquiries into a specific Cray model. West arranged a two-day seminar on Cray's potential uses. The seminar was conducted in August. In September GE signed a letter of intent to buy a $9.5 million Cray X-MP 28. In early 1986 Cray was anticipating the signing of the purchase agreement.

This story of the General Electric deal illustrates not only the varied activities of salesperson West, but also the interaction of sales with other Cray divisions, the multiple influences on the purchase decision, and the prolonged, sequential order of the sales process.

It has been estimated that salespeople spend only 25 to 40 percent of their time engaged in actual selling. The remainder is spent on various other activities required to execute their sales duties or to support other organizational activities. In this chapter, we will discuss the common job activities that most salespeople perform to some degree. As you read this chapter, use the combination sales job as a frame of reference. More specifically, picture an outside salesperson who is responsible for nurturing old business, developing new business, and performing sales support activities.

The management activities of salespeople will be discussed first. While salespeople do not usually supervise other employees of their firms, they are involved in time and territory management, managing company assets, and assisting sales management. Next, we will review the organization support activities of salespeople. Finally, the majority of the chapter will be devoted to the sales process, beginning with the search for prospective customers and ending with post-sale follow-up activities.

KEY JOB ACTIVITIES OF SALESPEOPLE

A study of 1,393 salespeople in 15 manufacturing industries shows that the job activities of salespeople can be broken into the 10 activity groups shown in Exhibit 3.1. Many of the specific activities comprising these groups will be discussed in this chapter.

THE SALESPERSON AS MANAGER

Salespeople sometimes function in management roles — namely, time and territory management and sales management support as part of their regular sales jobs.

Time and Territory Management

Time and territory management (TTM) involves the planning, organizing, and implementing of sales activities to optimize sales performance. The essential task of TTM is to determine which activities are most conducive to sales success and to perform

Exhibit 3.1 **Activities of Salespeople**

Activity Name	Selected Activities
Selling function	Search out leads; prepare sales presentations; make sales calls; overcome objections.
Working with orders	Correct orders; expedite orders; handle shipping problems.
Servicing the product	Test equipment; teach safety instructions; supervise installation.
Information management	Provide feedback to superiors; receive feedback from clients.
Servicing the account	Inventory; set up point-of-purchase displays; stock shelves.
Conferences/meetings	Attend sales conferences; set up exhibitions, trade shows.
Training/recruiting	Recruit new sales representatives; train new sales representatives.
Entertaining	Take clients to lunch, golfing, fishing, tennis, etc.
Out-of-town traveling	Spend night on road; travel out of town.
Working with distributors	Establish relations with distributors; extend credit; collect past-due accounts.

Source: Adapted from William C. Moncrief, "Selling Activity and Sales Position Taxonomies for Industrial Salesforces," *Journal of Marketing Research* 23 (August 1986): 261–270, published by the American Marketing Association. Used with permission.

these activities on a priority basis. The importance of effective TTM is well articulated by Martin D. Shafiroff, a managing director of Shearson Lehman/American Express:

> Every salesperson worth his or her salt is a good time manager. There are only so many minutes in each day, and how well you make use of them is often what separates star sales performers from mediocre performers. Common sense dictates that if two salespersons have equal ability, and one gives twice as many presentations, he will produce at least twice as many sales. And when you consider the principle of synergy, his productivity may be far greater — resulting in three or four times as many sales. For this reason, every salesperson must carefully prepare his day in advance, making sure his prime selling time is used in front of the customer.[1]

Coming from Mr. Shafiroff, this advice should be easy to accept. He is a leading investment broker whose commissions have sometimes exceeded $10 million a year. Salespeople who wish to improve their TTM skills might start with a self-audit as suggested in Exhibit 3.2. To be effective at TTM, salespeople must complete three major activities: prioritize and plan their work, execute their work in an efficient manner, and analyze their efforts and results to seek continual improvement.

Setting Priorities. In many organizations, salespeoples' priorities are set by annual objectives, which are then decomposed into quarterly, monthly, weekly, daily, and

Exhibit 3.2 **Self-Audit Time Analysis**

This method considers five major categories where salespeople spend their time — travel, office, service, personal, and face-to-face customer contact. Activities should be noted on a worksheet in 30-minute intervals over a period of several weeks.

1. *Travel:* Time spent traveling to and from work, time between calls, and time spent waiting to see customers.
2. *Office time and paperwork:* Time spent in the office reading, writing, listening or talking on the phone, planning calls, preparing proposals, attending meetings, or any other inside activities required to move correspondence in the office.
3. *Service:* Time spent servicing customers, including handling complaints, expediting orders, and resolving design problems.
4. *Personal:* Time spent on meals, coffee breaks, servicing the car, and other personal activities.
5. *Customers:* Time spent in the presence of one or more buyers in an organization where you are seeking an order.

For illustration purposes, say a salesperson spends two and one-half hours per day spending time in the fifth category, seeing customers. If the salesperson can allocate an additional 30 minutes of time to this category, a 20 percent increase in sales calls could be realized. Assuming a constant ratio between sales calls and orders written, this could result in a sales increase of 20 percent.

Source: Vince Pesce, *A Complete Manual of Professional Selling* (Englewood Cliffs, N.J.: Prentice-Hall, 1983), 116–117.

even individual sales-call objectives. Without clear-cut direction provided at least in part by measurable objectives, salespeople (like most people) tend to concentrate on the most pleasant job tasks, which may or may not be the most important tasks. As a result, sales managers have been heard to complain that they are supervising paid tourists rather than salespeople. Actually, the fault probably lies with sales management in such cases for neglecting to establish meaningful objectives for the salesforce.

Another part of setting priorities involves determining how to allocate the salesperson's time among his or her accounts. The **80/20 rule**, which states that 80 percent of a company's volume will come from 20 percent of the customers, is so well-known that it is almost a cliche. Nevertheless, it is surprisingly accurate and emphasizes the need to plan the time spent with various customers on a prioritized basis, recognizing that all customers are not equally important to the firm and that some warrant more sales attention than others.

Efficient Work Execution. In addition to prioritizing their work, salespeople must execute it efficiently. When travel is involved, this requires careful planning and scheduling to avoid inefficiencies such as retracing a route, or unnecessary zig-zagging. Plans can be devised with sophisticated computer algorithms, or they can be as simple as a city map indicating customer locations and the sales-call sequence to be followed. Three simple yet efficient travel plans are shown in Figure 3.1.

Travel plans include more than determining the route to be followed. It may be necessary to make motel or airline reservations, select a site for a business lunch, and handle other logistical details. Another factor in planning is the sales-call schedule, which must allow adequate coverage for all customers.

Salespeople should plan to see each customer on a regular basis, but **call frequency** will vary according to the priority assigned to each account. For example, key accounts might be called on monthly and secondary accounts only quarterly.

The average length of sales calls may vary according to the importance of the account and other situational factors. In planning the average length, salespeople should also consider their customers' preferences in scheduling sales calls. As an example, some organizations will see salespeople only on certain days of the week or only during specified hours.

Increasingly, the questions of sales-call frequency and average duration of sales calls are being addressed with the assistance of the computer. For example, the SalesPro software program allows salespeople to utilize customer ratings and targeted sales volume to compute how much time should be spent with each account.[2] Procedures for deciding how much sales effort should be allocated to various activities are presented in Chapter Eight.

Analysis of Efforts and Results. Salespeople and sales managers should constantly analyze their efforts and results to try to improve the productivity of time spent on various activities. One standard tool for analyzing individual sales calls and, ultimately, sales calls taken collectively, is the **call report.**[3] The report may be completed

Figure 3.1 **Travel Alternatives**

Travel plans such as these are designed to allow adequate account coverage on a regular basis without unnecessary zig-zagging or retracing of steps.

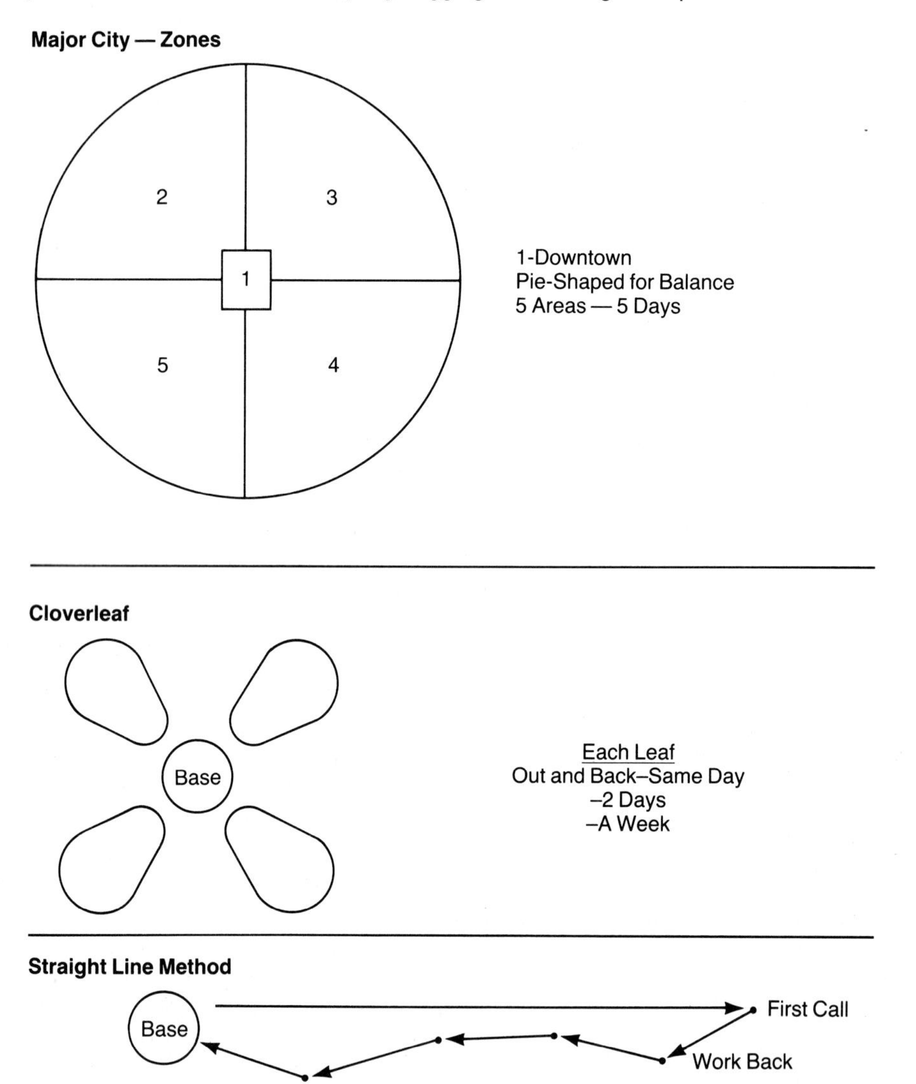

Source: Jim Rapp, *Time and Territory Management* (Orlando, Florida: The National Society of Sales Training Executives, 1982), 17. Used with permission.

SALES TECHNOLOGY

TIME AND TERRITORY MANAGEMENT AT HEWLETT-PACKARD

When Hewlett-Packard surveyed its personal-computer salesforce of 200, company management faced the hard fact that only 31 percent of the reps' time was spent on customer contact activities, which included telephone, face-to-face, and trade-show contact. Other activities such as travel, administrative duties, training, and organization support activities were taking significant amounts of time for the HP salespeople to complete.

The survey also found that salespeople and managers agreed that they would like to increase customer contact and training time while decreasing administrative and non-customer phone time. For HP management, the solution to the problem came naturally from one of their products, the personal computer. By using electronic mail instead of the telephone, they have cut the number and duration of phone calls. HP estimates that the average six-minute phone call can be handled in only one minute via electronic mail, and that salespeople can save several hours per month. The computer is also used to assist in proposal writing, checking on the status of customers, and monitoring competitive activity. HP management also figures that improved productivity will decrease salesforce turnover.

Source: Thayer C. Taylor, "Reduction in Selling Time Underscores Computer Need," *Sales and Marketing Management,* October 7, 1985, 59–60.

in handwritten form, dictated to a portable tape recorder, or entered into a portable computer. Regardless of the means employed, the report should be recorded immediately after the call, since information from a sales call has proved highly perishable.

The contents of call reports vary considerably from one company to the next. Some types of information, however, are routinely found in all:[4]

- Name, address, and key contact at customer or prospect contacted
- Outcome of call — that is,
  - More information needed, if any
  - Business lost (why?)
  - Business won (details)
  - Business "on hold"
  - Date of next scheduled call
  - Competitive information obtained.

The analysis of sales calls on a regular basis by salespeople and sales managers can lead to improved time and territory management, which in turn leads to improved sales performance. For an example, read "Sales Technology: Time and Territory Management at Hewlett-Packard."

In summarizing the TTM responsibilities of salespeople, it is helpful to view salespeople as managers of valuable assets, the most valuable of which is the customer base, which could represent millions of dollars in actual and potential sales. Salespeople are expected to provide a return on the investment their companies have made in salaries, commissions, fringe benefits, and other selling costs. Efficient time and territory management can maximize this return by maximizing productive selling time.

Assisting in Sales Management

As Exhibit 3.1 indicated, salespeople spend some of their time assisting sales managers. Typical sales management support activities carried out by salespeople are recruiting, training, managing warehouses, and supervising manufacturer's representatives.

In the recruiting and selection process, salespeople may be asked to conduct screening interviews or spend a day in the field with the recruit to provide a job preview for the prospective candidate. This may even become a major job activity for some salespeople, as in the case of Exxon salespeople in the retail division, who are responsible for recruiting independent service station operators for the company's leased outlets.

Training new salespeople is a common responsibility of salespeople in most industries. It has become a time-honored tradition for the rookie salesperson to spend some time with the seasoned veteran.

In some companies that use independent warehouses as part of the channel of distribution for their products, salespeople may monitor the operation of the warehouse to ensure prompt handling of orders and conscientious management of the inventory. Since independent warehouses are usually performing for more than one supplier, the salesperson is sometimes expected to encourage the warehouse operator to treat the salesperson's company as a priority supplier whose orders will be filled on a preferred basis.

Salespeople may also be responsible for supervising sales assistants and independent representatives who supplement the company's own salesforce. (Independent representatives are discussed in Chapter Six.)

All these activities contribute directly to the sales management function within a firm. Salespeople also are involved in activities that support other areas within the organization. We will now consider some of those activities.

ORGANIZATION SUPPORT ACTIVITIES

From the same survey that was featured in the "Sales Technology" feature in this chapter, it was determined that Hewlett-Packard salespeople spent 8 percent of their time on "organization support" activities. The HP experience is fairly typical. Three primary types of organization support activities are (1) administrative, (2) market information, and (3) meeting participation.

Administrative Duties

In addition to completing the aforementioned call reports, salespeople may be required to perform other administrative duties, such as tracking account receivables and being responsible for collecting past-due accounts. Also, they may be expected to file expense accounts on a regular basis to receive reimbursement for their sales expenses.

Market Information Activities

In Chapter Two we discussed the role of salespeople in providing market research and feedback to their employers. Some of these activities not only assist sales management, but other areas in the firm such as production, finance, or general management as well. Input from the salesforce may be utilized to formulate marketing strategy and support other marketing tools. For example, when Anheuser-Busch introduced Bud Light to the market, the salesforce was asked to contribute opinions on the product's taste and packaging, the pricing strategy, and ways to identify logical test and rollout markets.[5]

Some firms have put their salespeople in the key role in an interactive communications network that relies on constant input from the salesforce. Westinghouse made a major investment in a system that integrates sales with other parts of the marketing system and with the engineering and production systems to form an integrated system. The system, which is shown in Figure 3.2, relies on the input of the Westinghouse sales representatives.

Examples of firms that have successfully integrated the salesperson into the market research system are plentiful. Even so, the authors would agree with the findings from a survey of 156 firms that concluded, "Without question, there is considerable opportunity for a more effective integration of the salesforce into the marketing information system."[6]

Meeting Participation

As indicated in Exhibit 3.1, salespeople are routinely involved in attending meetings and conferences held for a variety of purposes, such as training, planning, reviewing performance, motivating the salesforce, or rewarding a job well done. Other activities in this area include teleconferences and one-on-one conferences with the sales manager.

Figure 3.2 **Westinghouse Interactive Communications Network**

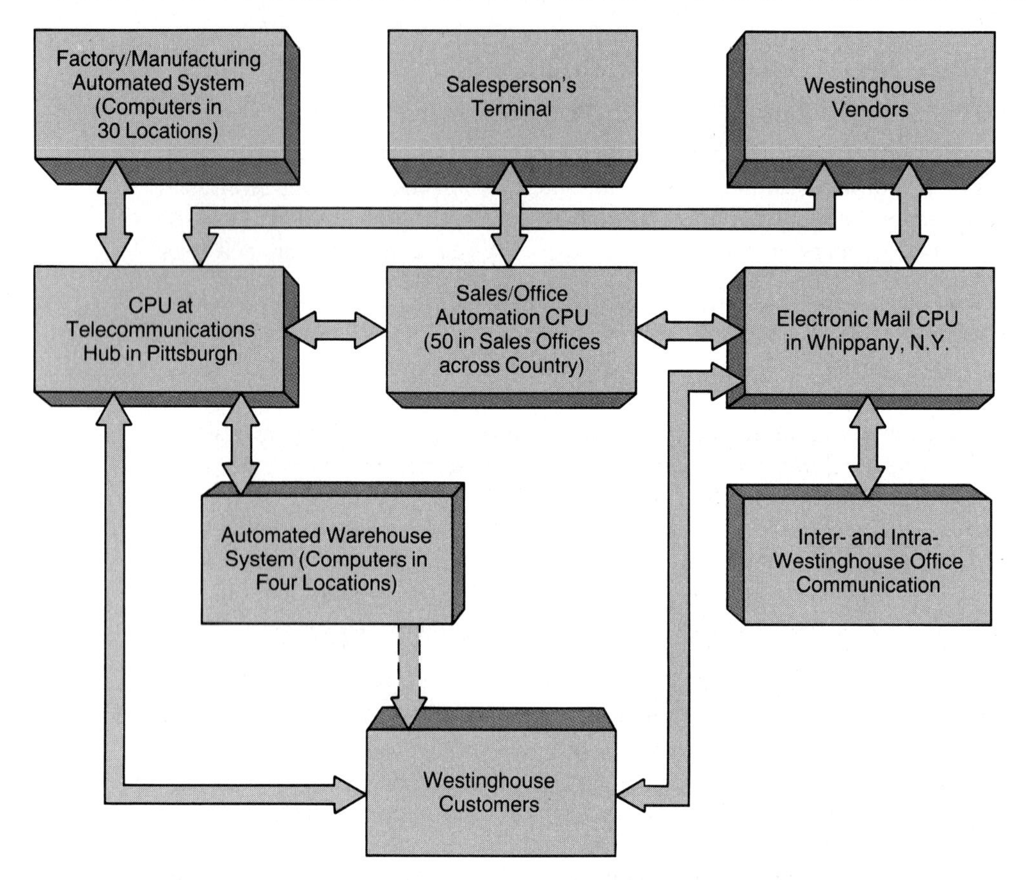

Salespeople provide key inputs into this interactive communications Network. The network links sales, marketing, manufacturing, and other areas into one integrated communication system.

Source: Diane Lynnkastiel, "New Tools for Enhanced Sales Force Productivity," *Business Marketing,* March 1986, 89.

THE SALES PROCESS

The nonselling activities on which most salespeople spend a majority of their time are essential for the successful execution of the most important part of the salesperson's job, the **sales process**. The sales process is usually described as a series of interrelated steps beginning with locating qualified prospective customers. From there, the salesperson plans the sales presentation, makes an appointment to see the customer, completes the sale, and performs post-sale activities. This process is shown in seven steps in Figure 3.3. Before we explore each step in the sales process, a few preliminary comments are in order.

When studying the sales process, we should note that there are countless versions of the process in terms of number of steps and the names of the steps. As an example, one conceptualization of the sales process is only four steps: information gathering, proposal, confirming the sale, and assuring customer satisfaction.[7] Despite language and sequencing differences, however, the various depictions of the sales process are actually quite comparable. Empirical studies of salespeople confirm the rather universal view of the sales process shown in Figure 3.3.[8]

Another point that should be stressed is that the sales process is broken into steps in order to facilitate discussion and sales training, not to suggest discrete lines between the steps. The steps are actually highly interrelated, and in some instances may overlap. Further, the step-wise flow of Figure 3.3 does not imply a strict sequence of events. Salespeople may move back and forth in the process with a given customer, sometimes shifting from step to step several times in the same sales encounter. Finally, completion of the sales process typically will require multiple sales calls.

As we proceed to discuss the steps in the sales process, we will present an overview of each step. The overviews will describe the objectives of each step and identify key issues to be dealt with in each step. Selected techniques and activities that are usually associated with each step will be presented as well.

Prospecting

The term **prospecting** as used in the sales context is analogous to the prospecting process for gold as practiced in the 1800s. The prospector for gold would work a stream, separating the sludge and mud in a search for strains of the precious metal. The contemporary salesperson locates a pool of potential customers and then screens them to determine which ones are qualified prospects.

In some situations, such as in most retail operations, salespeople are only slightly involved in prospecting; usually, however, they play an important role. A survey of 2,500 manufacturers found that salespeople locate more prospects than any other prospecting means, including advertising and direct mail.[9] The importance of the salesperson's role in prospecting was further documented in a study of 170 consumer and industrial goods salespeople in which the prospecting method rated as "most important" was personal observation, where the salesperson looks and listens for evidence of good prospects.[10]

Locating Prospects

The initial part of the prospecting process is the generation of a pool, or list, of potential customers. At this point, these potential customers are sometimes referred to as "suspects" rather than prospects to stress that a screening process must follow

Figure 3.3 **Sales Process Model**

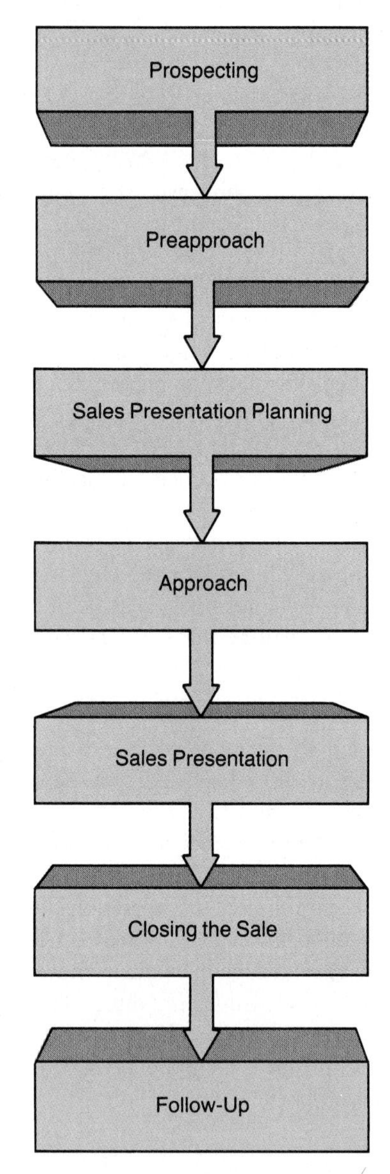

This commonly accepted version of the sales process shows seven highly interrelated steps. It usually takes several sales calls to close a sale with a new customer.

Exhibit 3.3 **Prospecting Methods**

Category	Prospecting Techniques
1. External Sources	Referral approach: Ask each prospect for the name of another potential prospect. Community contact: Ask friends and acquaintances for the names of potential prospects. Introduction approach: Obtain introduction by one prospect to others via phone, letter, or in person. Contact organizations: Seek sales leads from service clubs and chambers of commerce. Noncompeting salespeople: Seek leads from noncompeting salespeople. Cultivate visible accounts: Cultivate visible and influential accounts that will influence other buyers.
2. Internal Sources	Examine Records: Examine company records, directories, telephone books, membership lists, and other written documents. Inquiries to advertising: Respond to customer inquiries generated from company advertising. Phone/mail inquiries: Respond to phone or mail inquiries from potential prospects.
3. Personal Contact	Personal observation: Look and listen for evidence of good prospects. Cold canvassing: Make cold calls on potential prospects (phone or in person.)
4. Miscellaneous	Hold/attend trade shows: Organize or participate in a trade show directed toward potential prospects. Bird dogs: Have junior salespeople locate prospects that senior salespersons will contact. Sales seminar: Prospects attend as group to learn about a topic in which the salesperson's product is involved.

Source: Adapted from A. J. Dubinsky, "A Factor Analytic Study of the Personal Selling Process," *Journal of Personal Selling and Sales Management,* 1, No. 1 (Fall-Winter, 1980–81), 28. Used with permission.

to determine who the real prospects are. Various methods are used to locate potential prospects. As Exhibit 3.3 indicates, a salesperson may utilize sources outside the organization along with internal company sources. Exhibit 3.3 includes some methods in which the salesperson plays a fairly passive role in this part of prospecting and others where the salesperson is directly responsible for locating the potential customer.

Screening Prospects. After potential prospects are located, they must be evaluated in terms of **screening criteria** to see whether they merit further sales attention. These criteria vary from one sales organization to the next, but some that are commonly used follow:

- Compatibility — between the seller's product and the needs or wants of the prospect
- Accessibility — to the prospect

- Eligibility — in terms of geographic location and type of business the prospect is engaged in
- Authority — to make the purchase decision
- Profitability — as estimated based on the prospect's willingness and ability to pay and on predicted sales expenses.

Questions involving these criteria may be hard to answer fully in the prospecting stage. As a case in point, consider the profitability element. A salesperson may not be able to estimate whether a prospect will prove profitable at some future point in time. It is certainly possible for a prospect to become an unprofitable customer in the future and subsequently lose customer and prospect status with the selling firm. However, the prospecting stage does not require irrevocable decisions regarding the suitability of a prospect, only sufficient indications that the prospect is worthy of sales pursuit.

Prospecting Issues. There are three managerial issues of extreme interest in the prospecting stage. One is the persistent question of which method or methods work best for locating qualified prospects. The second is the problem of **cold-call reluctance** in many salespeople. The third is the issue of using technology to complete the basic tasks of prospecting.

Which method or methods work best? There is no answer to this question without some experimentation by the selling firm. For one firm, a trade show may be a bonanza, while another will find it more profitable to rely exclusively on cold canvassing. The question continues to inspire sales researchers, who are seeking insight into how best to utilize the estimated $19 billion per year spent on telephone prospecting.[11] One thought-provoking study examined a prospecting approach featuring prenotification of the prospect that literature would be sent before calling for an appointment. The prenotification produced an extraordinary number of qualified prospects.[12]

The subject of cold-call reluctance is especially important, since this method of locating prospects is crucial in many sales situations. Call reluctance experienced later in the sales process is generally not as acute as in the prospecting stage, where the salespeople are encountering strangers on their (the strangers') turf and may feel as if they are intruding. Many have a hard time dealing with the face-to-face rejection that often accompanies this prospecting method.

Noting that the origins of call reluctance are multiple and complex, experts in this phenomenon have reported that "the lore of fearlessness among salespeople is more fiction than fact. Many, it turns out, are struggling with a bone-shaking fear of prospecting, a fear that persists regardless of what they have to sell, how well they have been trained to sell it, or how much they believe in their product's worth."[13] This problem is of sufficient magnitude that sales managers and sales trainers frequently address it in training and development programs.

Another prospecting topic that is generating considerable discussion among sales managers is the use of technology to perform some or all prospecting. In recent years,

INTERNATIONAL SALES

SCITEX MEETS ITS MATCHMAKER

Scitex America, a marketer of high-tech imaging printing systems, used a computerized Sales & Marketing Information System (SAMIS) to build international sales. Scitex had introduced 12 new products at an exposition in Dusseldorf in May 1986. Results were disappointing. As president George Carlisle recalls, "due to the Chernobyl nuclear disaster and fears of terrorist activity, only one-fifth of the expected American attendees showed up. We had to recoup fast."

Returning to the United States, Scitex (a division of an Israeli corporation) moved swiftly to recreate the Dusseldorf exposition for American customers. Utilizing the sophisticated targeting capabilities of the SAMIS, Scitex invited the best prospects to the expo. The results were phenomenal — more than $7 million in new business versus expenses of $40,000 to $60,000.

Scitex believes they have achieved market leadership at least in part because of the precision with which they can locate and qualify top prospects. Their largest competitors, Siemens of West Germany and De La Rue of the United Kingdom, have 25 salespeople apiece, almost twice the number of Scitex salespeople. In addition to assisting in prospecting, Scitex's SAMIS generates a number of time and territory management reports, including account analysis and sales coverage plans.

Source: "Scitex Meets its Matchmaker," *Sales and Marketing Management*, December 1986, 76–78.

automated systems combining computers with communications equipment have become widely available. Some of systems extend beyond prospecting to include other sales functions such as account tracking and post-sale follow-up. The cost effectiveness of automated prospecting systems has been frequently reported in trade publications. For example, a Baltimore insurance agent invested $5,700 in an Apple ll Plus computer and a software package called Prospector that yielded him $20,000 per month in new business.[14] Research in this area indicates that as the pressure to improve sales productivity continues to mount, the use of technology to perform prospecting tasks will certainly become more commonplace.[15] An innovative prospecting program is presented in "International Sales: Scitex Meets Its Matchmaker."

Preapproach

In the **preapproach**, the salesperson gathers information about the prospect that will be used to formulate the sales presentation. During this step, the salesperson may determine buyer needs, buyer motives, and details of the buyer's situation that are relevant to the upcoming sales presentation.

Various information sources may be consulted in this undertaking. Published materials such as industry newsletters, magazine articles, and newspaper accounts may be useful. Another alternative is to call on the prospect for information-gathering purposes. This tactic is practiced by IBM, as illustrated in the following passage:

> It's a matter of a rep doing enough fact-finding to fully understand what is giving the prospect the greatest challenges. Once this is identified, the rep can begin to take the appropriate IBM equipment and put it in the prospect's office, factory, or perhaps warehouse, and provide a solution to his problem. But the rep can't very well answer any problems unless he's able to draw out the necessary day-to-day bits of information from the prospect. As you can see, a lot of fact-finding is required before an IBM rep can properly do his or her job.[16]

In addition to gathering information to be used in the sales presentation, the preapproach offers other benefits. Because of the information it provides, the salesperson may avoid serious blunders based on false assumptions. Also, the self-confidence of the salesperson is increased by the acquisition of knowledge, and the salesperson's credibility with the prospect is enhanced.

The preapproach raises two issues worthy of management attention. First is the question of how extensive the preapproach should be. Second is the issue of invasion of privacy.

The extensiveness of the preapproach depends on the nature of the sales situation. Specifically, it has been suggested that a more extensive preapproach is appropriate when[17]

- Future interactions (after the initial sale) with the customer are anticipated.
- Customers are making complex, high-involvement decisions.
- The purchase decision will have significant impact on the salesperson.
- The salesperson has a range of alternatives to offer the customer.
- Customers encountered by the salesperson are heterogeneous in terms of their needs.

Sales managers and salespeople should also be sensitive to the issue of invasion of privacy when conducting the preapproach. There have been instances where surreptitious methods were used to learn personal details about prospects. Such tactics are unethical, and they often backfire if the prospect becomes aware of the practice. A related tactic is the use of so-called market research that purports to be "selling nothing" when in reality, selling is precisely the purpose. As was indicated in the previous chapter, straightforward sales techniques have proved more effective over the long run.

Sales-Presentation Planning

During the first two steps of the sales process, the salesperson must locate qualified prospects and gather enough information about the prospect to plan the sales presentation. The third step in the sales process, **sales-presentation planning**, has become more important in recent years, as evidenced by increased coverage on the topic in sales training programs. In contrast, it was not unusual a decade ago to find no coverage of sales-presentation planning in popular sales training materials. Somehow, salespeople were expected to move from the preapproach directly into the sales presentation, without any planned transition. The requirements of professional selling today make such planning imperative, and it is often extensive, since it is increasingly viewed as a critical link in the sales process.

As with other planning processes, the salesperson must begin with a specifically stated objective, or perhaps multiple objectives, for each sales presentation. Typical objectives might be stated as order quantities, dollar values, or even in communications terms, such as reaching an agreement in principle with the prospect. Once a clearly stated objective has been formulated, the salesperson can focus on how the benefits of his or her offering can be related to the prospect in a competitively advantageous manner.

Taken to the ultimate, sales-presentation planning might actually result in a script to guide sales encounters. Not to be confused with a scripted sales message to be delivered over the telephone, this script would be more a guide to expected sales activities given a particular buying situation. Research has been conducted that suggests that scripts could "help the company define the specific information requirements and aids essential for success in the sales encounter itself."[18]

Sales-Presentation Format. To plan the sales presentation, salespeople must decide on a basic presentation format. Alternatives include a canned sales presentation, an organized presentation, and the written sales proposal. A salesperson might utilize one or more of these formats with a particular customer. Each format has unique advantages and disadvantages as follows:

Canned Sales Presentation. The highly structured, inflexible **canned sales presentation** does not vary from customer to customer. When properly formulated, it is logical, complete, and minimizes sales resistance by anticipating the prospect's objections. It can be utilized by relatively inexperienced salespeople and perhaps is a confidence builder for some salespeople.

The major limitation of the canned sales presentation is that it fails to capitalize on the strength of personal selling—the ability to tailor the message to the prospect. Further, it does not handle interruptions well, may be awkward to use with a broad product line, and may alienate buyers who want to participate in the interaction.

In spite of its limitations, the canned sales presentation has been shown to be effective in some situations.[19] If the product line is narrow and the salesforce is relatively inexperienced, the canned presentation may be quite suitable. Also, many salespeople may find it effective to use canned portions in a sales presentation to introduce their company, demonstrate the product, or for some other limited purpose.

Organized Sales Presentations. According to survey data, presentations that are tailored to each prospect are far more popular with salespeople than canned sales presentations.[20] In the **organized sales presentation**, the salesperson organizes the key points into a planned sequence that allows for adaptive behavior by the salesperson as the presentation progresses. Feedback from the prospect is encouraged, and therefore this format is less likely to offend a participation-prone buyer.

One limitation of this presentation format is that it requires a knowledgeable salesperson who can react to questions and objections from the prospect. Further, it could be argued that this format may extend the time horizon before a purchase decision is reached, or that it is vulnerable to diversionary delay tactics by the prospect. Presumably, those who make these arguments feel that a canned presentation forces a purchase decision in a more expedient fashion.

Overall, however, most agree that the organized presentation is ideal for most sales situations. Its flexibility allows a full exploration of customer needs and appropriate adaptive behavior by the salesperson.

Sales Proposal. A written sales presentation, the **sales proposal**, may be developed after careful investigation of the prospect's needs; or, alternatively, a generic proposal may be presented. With the increasing prevalence of word processing, computer graphics, and desktop publishing, the written sales proposal is being used in an increasing number of situations. These technologies have minimized the traditional disadvantage of the written proposal — the time it takes to prepare it. Technological advances are illustrated in "Sales Trend: Using the Computer to Generate Sales Proposals."

The sales proposal has long been associated with important, high-dollar-volume sales transactions. It is frequently used in competitive bidding situations and in situations involving the selection of a new supplier by the prospect. One advantage of the proposal is that the written word is usually viewed as being more credible than the spoken word. Written proposals are subject to careful scrutiny with few time constraints, and specialists in the buying firm often analyze various sections of the proposal.

Sales proposals are often combined with face-to-face presentations and question-and-answer periods. Their content is similar to other sales presentations, focusing on customer needs and related benefits offered by the seller. In addition, technical information, pricing data, and perhaps a timetable are included. Most proposals provide a triggering mechanism such as a proposed contract to confirm the sale, and some specify follow-up action to be taken if the proposal is satisfactory.

Sales Mix Model. To this point, our discussion of the sales presentation planning process should have clearly suggested a need for a specific objective for each presentation and a need to determine the basic format of the presentation. In general terms, we have spoken of blending information into a palatable sales message. This is best done within the context of the sales mix model shown in Figure 3.4. The model

SALES TREND

USING THE COMPUTER TO GENERATE SALES PROPOSALS

Preparing a sales proposal can be a time-consuming process. Dan Dotin of Xerox says, "often, preparing a proposal for a multimillion deal, with all its complex terms and conditions, could mean days spent gathering people and information, talking it through, producing hard copy, and getting approval from the Major Accounts Administration department in Rochester, N.Y. Now, we can do all that just as accurately, and more quickly—in fact it all takes less than half a day."

Xerox cut the time required to complete sales proposals by using their own computers to create workstations for salespeople, who assemble information from various databases, perform necessary calculations, combine text and graphics, and send the finished proposal to Rochester for approval.

In addition to saving a significant amount of time, Xerox salespeople feel they are producing better sales proposals. Dallas-based marketing representative Peg Mayfield says, "I generate better proposals because I can organize the information more effectively using the workstation's windows, and combine text and graphics, such as columns and boxes, to make product and price comparisons, and thus a more persuasive document. I can create a document that will stand on its own so that, even if I can't present it to the final decision maker in person, the document will certainly sell itself.

Source: Thayer C. Taylor, "Xerox: Who Says You Can't Be Big and Fast?" *Sales and Marketing Management,* November 1987, 62–65.

includes five variables that require planning effort: pace of presentation, scope of presentation, depth of inquiry, degree of two-way communication, and variety of sensory appeals.

Pace of presentation refers to the speed with which the salesperson intends to move through the presentation. The appropriate pace will be largely determined by the preference of the prospect and may be affected by variables such as complexity of the product or the number of products to be presented. Another determinant of pace would be past experiences with a particular customer, as a quicker pace may be possible with a familiar customer.

Scope of presentation involves the selection of benefits and terms of sale to be included in the presentation. This narrowing-down process can be a challenge for the knowledge-laden salesperson, who may know more about the product than will be of interest to the prospect. Time and again, we see reports of jargon-spouting salespeople who have talked themselves out of a sale through indiscriminate use of their extensive product knowledge. For example, the stumbling growth of the personal computer market in the formative years was partially attributed to sales presentations that failed to key on the important benefits sought by customers but instead overwhelmed the customer with unimportant technical features of the product.[21]

Depth of inquiry refers to the extent to which the salesperson goes to ascertain the prospect's needs and decision process. Some of this information may have been

Figure 3.4 **Sales Mix Model**

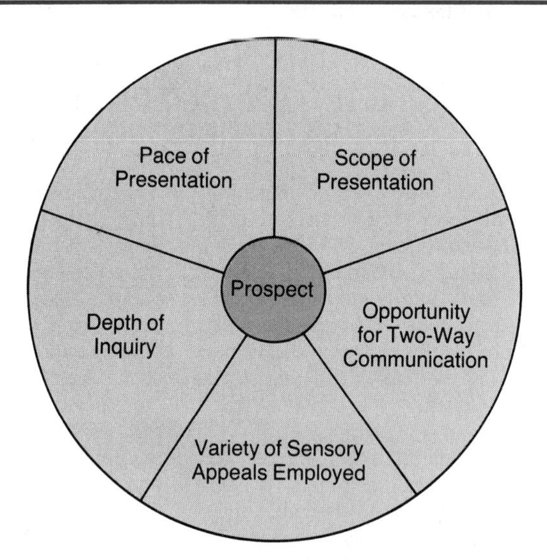

Five variables require planning effort after the salesperson has set objectives for the presentation and selected a basic presentation format.

Source: Reprinted by permission of the publisher from John I. Coppett and William A. Staples, "A Sales Mix Model For Effective Industrial Selling," *Industrial Marketing Management* 9 (1980): 32. Copyright 1980 by Elsevier Science Publishing Co., Inc.

gained in the preapproach, and some probing is usually necessary during the presentation. The planning task is simply to identify gaps in needed information and plan the presentation accordingly.

The issue of **two-way communication** is partially addressed when the salesperson selects a basic format for the presentation. By definition, the canned presentation does not allow for significant two-way communication. The organized presentation allows for, and usually encourages, a two-way flow. The degree of interactive flow is often dictated by buyer expertise, with more allowance for two-way flow planned with expert buyers.

Sensory appeals beyond the spoken word have become an important element in sales presentations, and their use must be carefully planned. Unless sales aids are utilized with caution, they may actually detract from rather than enhance the sales presentation. When properly orchestrated, sensory appeals ranging from flip charts to taste tests can be valuable tools during the sales presentation. The potential for enhancing presentations with relatively inexpensive desktop video productions is becoming an exciting reality. For example, Travelers' Insurance was able to produce a variety of videos for each account representative in each region at a cost of less than

$20,000. The videos are distributed on videocassette, but the master disk is stored on a personal computer, which allows easy modification for different sales situations.[22]

After the sales presentation is planned, the salesperson is ready to shift to an active selling mode. While the customer may have been contacted earlier in the sales process, the emphasis has been on information gathering and planning. Now the actual selling begins as the salesperson seeks an interview with the prospect.

Approach

Approaching the customer involves two phases. The first phase is securing an appointment for the sales interview. The second phase covers the first few minutes of the sales call. Each step in the sales process is critical, and the approach is no exception. In today's competitive environment, a good first impression is essential to lay the groundwork for subsequent steps in the sales process. A bad first impression on the customer can be difficult or impossible to overcome.

Getting an Appointment. Most initial sales calls on new prospects require an appointment. Requesting an appointment accomplishes several desirable outcomes. First, the salesperson is letting the prospect know that the salesperson thinks the prospect's time is important. Second, there is a better chance that the salesperson will receive the undivided attention of the prospect during the sales call. Third, setting appointments is a good tool to assist the salesperson in effective time and territory management. The importance of setting appointments is clearly proclaimed in a survey of purchasing agents, who included "walking in without an appointment" as behavior common to "bad" salespeople.[23] Given this rather strong feeling of buyers, it a good idea to request an appointment if there is any doubt about whether one is required.

Appointments may be requested by phone, mail, or personal contact. By far, setting appointments by telephone is the most popular method. Combining mail and telephone communications to seek appointments is also commonplace. Regardless of the communications vehicle used, the salespeople can improve their chances of getting an appointment by following three simple directives: give the prospect a reason why an appointment should be granted; request a specific amount of time; suggest a specific time for the appointment. These tactics recognize that prospects are busy people who do not spend time idly.

In giving a reason why the appointment should be granted, a well-informed salesperson can appeal to the prospect's primary buying motive as related to one of the benefits of the salesperson's offering. Being specific is recommended. For example, it is better to say "you can realize gross margins averaging 35 percent on our product line" than "our margins are really quite attractive."

Specifying the amount of time needed to make the sales presentation alleviates some of the anxiety felt by a busy prospect at the idea of spending some of his or her already scarce time. It also helps the prospect if the salesperson suggests a time and date for the sales call. It is very difficult for busy people to respond to a question like, "what would be a good time for you next week?" In effect, the prospect is being asked to scan his or her entire calendar for an opening. If a suggested time and date are not convenient, the interested prospect will typically suggest another.

Starting the Sales Call. Having secured an appointment with a qualified, presumably interested prospect, the salesperson should plan to accomplish some important tasks during the first few minutes of the call. First in importance is to establish a harmonious atmosphere for discussion. Common rules of etiquette and courtesy apply here. In addition, recent sales research reveals certain techniques for building rapport with a prospect. One interesting method is **neuro-linguistic programming,** or NLP. Originally developed by psychotherapists to help develop trust, rapport, and understanding with clients, NLP is being used in some sales training programs to teach salespeople how to do the same with customers. Body cues and word selection of the prospect are observed and responded to in specified ways.[24] Some preliminary small talk is usually part of the ritual, then the discussion should turn to business. Adaptive salespeople can learn how to interpret the prospect's signals and move into the sales message on cue.

From a communications standpoint, salespeople are striving for some specific outcomes during these first few minutes of the sales call. They are trying to focus the prospect's attention on the sales offering, build the prospect's interest, and make a transition into the complete sales presentation. In some sales situations, this process of **attention-interest-transition** requires more information gathering and needs definition than can be accomplished in the preapproach, so it must be done in the approach. A **benefit statement** is most helpful for this purpose according to a survey of industrial and consumer salespeople.[25] The salesperson simply states a benefit of the offering and measures the prospect's reaction before proceeding. Another popular method at this point in the approach is to ask a series of questions, thus requiring the prospect to pay attention (in order to answer the questions).

Gimmickry: An Issue in the Approach. An examination of some sales training materials uncovers the disturbing recommendation that to secure attention and interest, salespeople should resort to the *shock approach,* which involves creating fear in the prospect, or the *premium approach,* where the salesperson gives the prospect a token gift to get the interview. It is somewhat comforting to note that these two methods were rated unimportant in a survey of professional salespeople.[26]

Sales Presentation

During the **sales presentation**, the salesperson expands on the basic theme established in the first few minutes of the sales call or during previous sales calls. Specifically, more details are furnished regarding how offered benefits will meet customer needs. If the prior steps in the sales process have been properly implemented, the salesperson is now interacting with a qualified, interested prospect at a convenient time. Given these circumstances, three major goals remain: building credibility, achieving clarity, and coping with questions and objections raised by the prospect.

Building Credibility. With any major purchase, prospects perceive a considerable amount of risk. In order to be able to reduce that perception of risk in the prospect, the salesperson must appear a credible source of information. In a classic study, Harvard professor Theodore Levitt found *source credibility* for salespeople to be a function of three factors: the individual salesperson; the company image, and the product being sold.[27] Additional research has indicated that salespeople's credibility may be affected by their job title. For example, those salespeople holding the designation Chartered Life Underwriter were viewed as being more credible than other insurance salespeople in one study.[28] In our discussion of source credibility, we will concentrate on factors that can, to a significant degree, be controlled by the salesperson. These factors can be divided into two categories — personal behavior and sales techniques.

Personal Behavior. The basics of personal behavior that build credibility are dressing appropriately, showing common courtesy for all personnel in the prospect's organization, and being customer-oriented. More importantly, all words and actions should be consistent with the traits of honesty and integrity. In a survey of purchasing agents, the two most valued traits among salespeople were reliability/credibility and professionalism/integrity.[29] These findings confirm that building credibility is a very worthwhile activity for salespeople.

One approach to building credibility through personal behavior is to become a good listener. As the benefits of listening become more apparent, popular sales training programs have increased their coverage of this subject. Good listening skills enable the salesperson to learn more about the prospect and also keep the prospect interested in the sales proposition, since people are usually more interested in listening to someone else when they, too, are given the chance to talk. Moreover, by listening, the salesperson is, in effect, complimenting the prospect and showing respect for the prospect's point of view. The result is a reciprocation process in which the prospect repays the salesperson by listening to the sales presentation more attentively. The platform for credibility is built by the salesperson's willingness and ability to be an effective listener.

We discussed listening as a personal behavior since most effective listeners practice the art all the time, not just during sales presentations. We would not argue, however, with those who propose that listening is a sales technique rather than a personal behavior.

Sales Techniques. One sales technique used to build credibility with prospects is that of **conservative claims** regarding the benefits of the offering. The idea is that prospects may expect claims to be exaggerated, so upon discovering that the salesperson has conservatively stated the claims, they tend to rate the credibility of the salesperson higher.

Another technique is to use **third-party evidence** to support a contention. **Testimonials** from satisfied customers are sometimes used for this purpose, as are research reports and product reviews from trade magazines. In the early stages of establishing credibility, salespeople often find that third-party information, particularly if it is written, may be more acceptable than the salesperson's spoken word.

Guarantees and warranties are other sales tools that can improve a salesperson's credibility. A strong warranty without a plethora of fine-print exceptions can go a long way toward eliminating the prospect's perceived risk and elevating the salesperson's credibility.

Another method is to let the prospect try the product or service under actual usage conditions. This can be as simple as a test-drive in a new automobile or as extensive as installing a computer system on a trial basis. This method permits the prospect to raise and answer questions without immediate persuasive pressure from the salesperson.

Even salespeople who work for companies with good reputations cannot assume that source credibility is a given. Further, they cannot assume that it will be easy to establish. They must recognize the skepticism and perceived risk in many sales situations and then combine appropriate personal behavior and sales techniques to overcome it.

Achieving Clarity. Salespeople begin the task of **achieving clarity** during sales-presentation planning. Recall the sales mix model, in which the salesperson plans such presentation elements as depth of inquiry, pace, and sensory appeals. The sales mix model also includes the scope of the presentation and the degree of two-way communication to be accomplished. At this point in the sales presentation, we are ready to implement those plans made with the assistance of the sales mix model.

To supplement the forethought given to achieving clarity as implied in the sales mix model, salespeople must adapt to the dynamics of the sales presentation. That is, as changes in the sales situation occur, salespeople must be adept at soliciting, interpreting, and reacting to feedback from the prospect. Again, listening skills emerge as important. Questioning skills are, too. Research has found that sales success can be linked to the number of questions asked during the sales presentation and, in some cases, to the type of questions asked. There is evidence that more successful salespeople ask more questions. Closed questions (those providing a series of potential responses) appear most effective for obtaining relevant information from the prospect.[30]

Sales aids such as charts, graphs, printed literature, photographs, films, slides, and portable computers are excellent tools in a number of sales situations for achieving clarity. Such sales aids should be employed only where they can make the presentation more effective, not merely to "put on a show." After all, the medium should not overpower the message.

Exhibit 3.4 **Selected Methods for Handling Objections**

Method	Action Taken by Salesperson
Forestalling	Mention the anticipated objection before the prospect does, i.e., take the offensive to address the objection. Use early in the presentation to diffuse commonly encountered objections.
Translation	Convert the prospect's reason for not buying into a reason for buying. Use when the the basis for the objection cannot be modified (e.g., "This is the very reason you should buy.")
Denial	In a diplomatic manner, dispute the prospect's objection. Use when the prospect is incorrect on an important point.
Compensation	Recognize the validity of the prospect's objection, then point out other advantages that offset the objection. Use to counteract weaknesses in the salesperson's offering.
Question	Ask the prospect why he or she objects. Use to clarify an objection and to encourage the prospect to reconsider.

Questions and Objections. The solicitation of feedback from the prospect will usually raise concerns the prospect has with the salesperson's offering. Coping with the questions and objections raised by the prospect is a routine part of most sales presentations. In some cases, these questions represent an unwillingness to buy unless the problem is resolved. In other cases, the buyer is asking for clarification of a point, or seeking information, perhaps reassurance on a particular point. In still other cases, prospects raise objections and ask questions as a bargaining tactic in an attempt to negotiate a more favorable deal.

Regardless of the reasons for raising objections and asking questions, the salesperson must be ready to respond effectively. Veteran salespeople generally look forward to dealing with questions and objections, viewing them as indicators of interest and therefore of an imminent purchase decision. Accordingly, they treat objections and questions with respect, even when they must tell the prospect that he or she is in error on a point.

Techniques for uncovering and handling objections and questions abound, varying mostly in terms of salesperson aggression. The idea is to remove or neutralize the prospect's concern in an inoffensive manner. The most popular method for handling questions is the "direct answer" response, where the salesperson provides a straightforward response to the exact question posed by the prospect.[31] Five popular methods for coping with objections — **forestalling**, **translation**, **denial**, **compensation**, and **questioning** — are described in Exhibit 3.4.

Sales Presentation Issue: How Personal? Some industries, such as the grocery industry, are becoming extremely automated in terms of how orders are placed with vendors. In some cases, customer computers are connected to the vendor's computer and orders are placed directly, without the involvement of a salesperson. Such arrangements have caused speculation that salespeoples' roles will become less important or will be redefined to reflect less involvement in the sales-presentation step of the sales process.

The question of just how much salespeople should be involved in the sales presentation has generated a good bit of discussion among sales managers, and, interestingly, among customers. In the grocery industry, buyers are now saying they need more, not less, contact with salespeople. Farm equipment dealers have told Massey-Ferguson that telemarketing is no substitute for personal sales calls. A survey of 1,100 corporate-level buyers of insurance services cited a strong link with the salesperson as their top concern in choosing a vendor.[32] At this time, the prediction that salespeople will become an extinct species seems baseless.

Closing the Sale

During the step of **closing the sale**, the salesperson's goal is to facilitate the prospect's decision-making process toward making the purchase and to furnish a stimulus for the decision at the appropriate time. A great deal of emphasis is put on this step in the sales process. It is unquestionably an important event for both the prospect and the salesperson. Salespeople may feel increased pressure at this step, since their success at closing sales is typically an important performance indicator. Further, their compensation may be directly tied to closing sales.

Closing Techniques. Several techniques have been suggested for closing a sale. The **direct close** (in which the salesperson simply asks for the order in a straightforward manner) has been cited by salespeople as the most important closing method by a narrow margin over the **summary**, **contingency**, **assumptive**, and **choice close**.[33] These methods are described in Exhibit 3.5.

It should be noted that these closing methods, along with other closing methods, may raise new questions and objections from the prospect. This is to be expected, as the deepest concerns a prospect has with an offering may not surface until he or she faces the purchase decision.

Issues in Closing the Sale. Sales managers and sales trainers center a fair amount of attention on the issues of why salespeople fail to close sales and of when the close should be initiated. It is rare to find a salesperson who can implement the previous steps in the sales process adequately yet consistently fail to close sales. Usually, failure to close is due to mistakes in previous steps rather than in the closing method. The prospect may be unqualified, or the sales presentation may be flawed. Perhaps the salesperson has failed to achieve credibility, in which case no closing method can hope to succeed.

Sometimes, of course, the problem does lie in the closing method. Salespeople who fear rejection may avoid providing the stimulus for the purchase decision, fearing that the prospect will reject the attempt. If the salesperson's self-perception is

Exhibit 3.5 **Techniques for Closing the Sale**

Closing Technique	Action Taken by the Salesperson
Direct Close	Simply ask for the order. Appropriate in most situations. Often combined with other closing techniques.
Summary Close	Summarize key points to facilitate a purchase decision. Recommended if sales presentation is complex, or if negotiations have extended over a long time period.
Contingency Close	Isolate the last remaining obstacle to the sale, and make the sale contingent upon removing the obstacle.
Assumptive Close	Assume the sale has been made, and present the order form for the prospect's approval. Use when resistance has been weak or nonexistent.
Choice Close	Ask the prospect which version of the product is preferred. Use when the prospect seems interested but is confused or indecisive about which alternative to choose.

consistent with the negative stereotypical images of unprofessional salespeople, this state of mind may preclude active closing attempts.

The question of when to seek a close remains open. The stock answer in days gone by was "early and often," meaning that salespeople should try to conclude the sale quickly by using repeated closing attempts. This approach is, however, risky; if the closing attempt is inappropriately early, a negative response is more likely; and once a negative response has been voiced by the prospect, principles of *cognitive consistency* dictate that the prospect will tend to reinforce the decision. The question of timing, therefore, is important in the closing step.

Although there are no unimpeachable guidelines to timing, if the presentation has been completed without questions or objections from the prospect, it is logical that a closing attempt should be made without delay. Likewise, if all questions and objections have been satisfactorily handled, closing is in order. In many instances, salespeople can interpret cues, or signals, from the prospect that indicate that closing is the next logical step. For example, the prospect might ask, "Can you deliver by next Tuesday?" Such a question would not be asked by an indifferent or unreceptive prospect. In the final analysis, the question of when to seek the close of a sale is a judgment call to be made by the salesperson, sometimes with the assistance of the prospect.

Follow-Up

There are two basic purposes of the **follow-up** step in the sales process. First, the benefits and satisfaction sought by the customer must be fully delivered. Second, in many cases, follow-up entails the development of a long-term, mutually satisfying relationship with the customer.

Follow-up Activities. Specific follow-up activities vary substantially from company to company, but some of the more common ones are

- Entering orders
- Expediting orders
- Installing the product or service
- Training customer personnel
- Resolving complaints
- Correcting billing errors

In some cases, salespeople may also seek the names of other prospective customers from existing customers as a routine part of follow-up. The follow-up may even provide a recycling of the sales process through subsequent sales calls on existing customers.

Building Relationships with Customers. There has been considerable interest in **relationship marketing** during the past few years. Relationships are developed over time and rely on continual follow-up by the salesperson. Thus, one objective of follow-up is to create a strong bond with the customer that will diminish the probability of the customer terminating the relationship. In effect, the salesperson's firm earns the business through a number of successive trial occurrences and strengthens its position as time passes. Relationship marketing will be discussed further in Chapter Six.

To achieve this bond with the customer, the salesperson must earn his or her trust. **Building trust** begins with pre-call planning prior to the first sales call and generally requires several sales calls. Research has found that trust can be developed if the customer perceives the salesperson to be dependable, honest, competent, customer-oriented, and likable.[34] These customer expectations certainly appear to be reasonable and controllable through recruiting, selection, training, and supervision of sales personnel.

Issue: Is Follow-Up a Cliche? Follow-up has received a flurry of attention in the past few years. Best-sellers have been written on the topic, and even the popular press has given it wide coverage.[35] The question being asked is, how sincere are these customer-oriented programs? Some disciples of service-oriented follow-up are true believers, while others only masquerade as such. Consider this passage:

> All sales experts strongly believe that outstanding service is mandatory in today's selling world. Yet, while the importance of this is so obvious, sadly only a small

percentage of salespeople are ready and willing to provide it. To the mass army of salespeople, "the customer always comes first" is a tired cliche, but to most successful salespeople it represents a code to live by. To them, making a sale and failing to follow up with the best possible service is tantamount to delivering damaged goods. The customer is cheated because he doesn't receive the true value that's due him for his money.[36]

These words provide food for thought for sales managers in an increasingly competitive world. Salespeople who think of the sales process as ending with the prospect's agreement to purchase run the risk of losing that customer in the future to competitors who, in all fields, are ever more numerous. Few companies can afford the high-risk gambling of neglectful follow-up.

SUMMARY

1. **Describe the key job activities of salespeople.** In addition to actual selling, salespeople are involved in service activities, working with their sales managers, relaying information to and from their customers and their employers, travel and entertainment, and attending meetings and conferences. Exhibit 3.1 lists ten key activities. The typical salesperson spends only about 25 to 40 percent of his or her time engaged in actual selling, and constantly tries to increase this percentage.
2. **Explain how salespeople act as managers in certain situations.** Salespeople are, in effect, performing management functions in two areas: They are time and territory managers, which requires setting priorities, efficient execution of work activities, and analysis of efforts and results. They also assist sales managers in recruiting, training, managing warehouses, and supervising manufacturer's representatives.
3. **Delineate the role salespeople play in supporting their organizations.** Salespeople are often relied upon to support the organization in administrative capacities such as collecting past-due accounts. They also are frequently called upon to provide market information used in marketing decisions such as pricing, packaging, and identifying test markets. They spend a fair amount of time participating in meetings and conferences for a variety of purposes.
4. **Discuss the sales process as a series of interrelated steps.** As presented in Figure 3.3, the sales process has seven steps: prospecting; preapproach; sales-presentation planning; approach; sales presentation; closing the sale; and follow-up. It is important to note that one step builds on the previous step, and that it usually takes several sales calls to confirm an initial sale to a prospect.

Key Terms

- time and territory management (TTM)
- 80/20 rule
- call frequency
- call report
- sales process
- prospecting
- screening criteria
- cold call reluctance
- preapproach
- sales presentation planning
- sales presentation format
- canned sales presentation
- organized sales presentation
- sales proposal
- sales mix model
- pace of presentation
- scope of presentation
- depth of inquiry
- two-way communications
- variety of sensory appeals
- approach
- neuro-linguistic programming (NLP)
- attention-interest-transition
- benefit statement
- sales presentation
- building credibility
- conservative claims
- third-party evidence
- testimonials
- guarantees and warranties
- achieving clarity
- objections and questions
- forestalling
- denial
- compensation
- questioning
- closing the sale
- direct close
- summary close
- contingency close
- assumptive close
- choice close
- follow-up
- relationship marketing
- building trust

Review Questions

1. How does a salesperson act as a manager? Do all salespeople act as managers?
2. Describe the critical elements in time and territory management in terms of inputs, outputs, and controls.
3. What are typical organization support activities for salespeople?
4. What is the purpose of each step in the sales process?
5. Describe the key activities and sales techniques associated with each step in the sales process.
6. What are some key sales management issues related to the sales process?
7. Discuss the follow-up step of the sales process as related to the evolution of personal selling, which was covered in Chapter Two.

8. Discuss the elements of the sales mix model shown in Figure 3.4.
9. Describe the three different sales-presentation formats in terms of their advantages and disadvantages.
10. Which do you feel is the most important — planning the sales presentation or delivering it?

Application Exercises

1. Successful salespeople are skilled at gathering information from their prospects during the sales process. Three types of questions that salespeople might use to gather information are verification questions, developmental questions, and evaluative questions.[37] Each is defined below.

    a. *Verification questions* are designed to validate prior knowledge, assumptions, or impressions the salesperson has formed from either the prospect's previous statements or other sources of information.
    b. *Developmental questions* are open-ended. They cannot be answered by "yes" or "no." They are used to encourage discussion by the prospect about ideas, feelings, or events introduced by the prospect or salesperson.
    c. *Evaluative questions* ask the prospect for feedback concerning ideas or information provided by the salesperson.

    Assume you are a salesperson for an automobile leasing firm. Your firm specializes in fleet leasing agreements, and you are planning a sales presentation for a fleet manager for a national firm. The firm currently owns its company cars, but you have heard that the company is considering a switch to leased automobiles. Using examples, illustrate how you might incorporate the three types of questions into your first sales call on the fleet manager.

2. Evaluate these telephone requests for sales appointments:

    a. Good afternoon, Mrs. Baxter. This is Mark Watson with Canon Cameras. We have a new line of fashion cameras that would be ideal for your store, and I would like to stop by this afternoon and show them to you. Would that be possible?
    b. Hello, Mr. Brewer. This William Skinner calling. I am the local representative with 3M. I am calling for two reasons. First, to say welcome to the Chicago area. Second, I would like to introduce you to our full line of industrial adhesives. Your distributor margins could average 30 percent or better, and I was hoping we could get together later today — say around three o'clock. Would that be convenient for you?
    c. Good morning, Mr. Jackson. This is Ron Samuelson with RCA Records. I am only going to be in town a couple of days and I was wondering if we could get together to look over our new compact disc catalog. We have some special pricing you will like, plus an early-order bonus. Could we meet for half an hour around eleven tomorrow?

3. Assume you are a salesperson, and the following information applies to your territory:

Accounts Classified According to Anticipated Sales Volume

A: Large, 15 accounts
B: Medium, 10 accounts
C: Small, 8 accounts

Frequency and Length of Sales Call Per Account Class

A: 60 minutes/call × 48 calls/year
B: 30 minutes/call × 24 calls/year
C: 20 minutes/call × 12 calls/year

Workload in Hours Required for Account Coverage

A: 15 accounts X 48 hours/year = 720 hours
B: 10 accounts X 12 hours/year = 120 hours
C: 8 accounts X 4 hours/year = 32 hours
TOTAL = 872 hours/year

Assume you work 48 weeks per year, and that 40 percent of your time is spent on actual selling. Further assume you work five days per week. How many hours per day must you work to provide the account coverage outlined in the preceding information? How many hours per day must be spent to complete all job activities? What recommendations can you make to salespeople who are trying to maximize selling time?

4. This exercise should be completed in groups of three or more. One person plays the role of the salesperson, one plays the role of the buyer, and the other members of the group will be evaluators. The designated salesperson selects a product with which he or she is familiar, plans a 20-minute presentation, then makes a sales presentation to the designated buyer. The buyer should express sincere questions and realistic objections during the sales presentation. Evaluators should use the rating scale shown here. Constructive criticism should be offered for each sales presentation.

Sales Presentation Evaluation

NAME: ____________________________

1. APPROACH

5	4	3	2	1
Gained attention Built desire to buy Smooth transition to presentation				Failed to gain attention, build desire or make a transition to the presentation.

2. ATTENTIVENESS

5	4	3	2	1
Listened carefully to the buyer's responses and questions				Would rather talk than listen

3. FOCUS ON BENEFITS OF PRODUCT

5	4	3	2	1
Emphasized benefits rather than features				Sold only features; ignored benefits

4. PRODUCT KNOWLEDGE

5	4	3	2	1
Thorough knowledge of the product evidenced				Inadequate level of knowledge

5. SELF-CONFIDENCE

5	4	3	2	1
Extremely relaxed & self-confident				Lacked a confident attitude

6. CLOSING (TIMING)

5	4	3	2	1
Recognized when to close				Missed one or more buying signals

7. CLOSING TECHNIQUE

5	4	3	2	1
Appropriate technique; applied properly				Poor choice of technique; failed to attempt a close; close appeared "forced"

8. ANTICIPATION OF OBJECTIONS/QUESTIONS

5	4	3	2	1
Anticipated and/or uncovered any objections not mentioned by the buyer				Never tried to probe for hidden objections

9. ATTITUDE

5	4	3	2	1
Enthusiastic; acted as if the call were important				Lackadaisical

10. PRESENTATION FORMAT

5	4	3	2	1
Employed a logical, clear format				Formations vague and/or illogical

11. IMPLEMENTATION OF PRESENTATION PLAN

5	4	3	2	1
Plan was closely followed				Plan was of little use during the presentation

continued

12. QUESTIONING

5	4	3	2	1
Questions were pertinent				Questions were poorly directed, irrelevant, inaptly phrased

13. SUPPORT MATERIAL

5	4	3	2	1
Used sales support material to show benefits				Did not use support material during presentation

14. FOLLOW-UP

5	4	3	2	1
Necessary details covered in follow-up				Left out important information

15. NEEDS AND WANTS

5	4	3	2	1
Was the prospect appropriately chosen according to needs and wants?				Prospect not properly qualified

Total Score ______________________

COMMENTS:

Source: Scale developed by Professor John S. Wright, Georgia State University. Reprinted with permission.

5. Assume you are selling PACSEAL, an automatic package-sealing device. One of your current prospects is a manufacturer of windshield wiper blades that ships approximately 5,000 boxes of blades per day to its customers. The cost of PACSEAL is $20,000. The customer can expect to save a penny per box shipped if PACSEAL is installed. The PACSEAL system has a guaranteed life of five years. How could you utilize this information in a sales proposal? How would you illustrate the key selling points derived from this information?

Notes

[1]Robert L. Shook, *The Perfect Sales Presentation* (New York: Bantam Books, 1986), 87–88.

[2]"The Computer in Sales and Marketing," *Sales and Marketing Management,* August 15, 1983, 71.

[3]Arthur Bragg, "Is the Call Report on the Way Out?" *Sales and Marketing Management,* November 1987, 78–83.

[4]*Computers and the Sales Effort* (New York: The Conference Board, 1986), 12.

[5]"Send in the Sales Force," *Sales and Marketing Management,* March 14, 1983, 56–57.

[6]Kenneth R. Evans and John L. Schlacter, "The Role of Sales Managers and Salespeople in a Marketing Information System," *Journal of Personal Selling And Sales Management* 5 (November 1985): 57.

[7]Tony Allesandra and Jim Cathcart, "Non-Manipulative Selling," *Institutional Distribution,* June 1985, 49.

[8]See Alan J. Dubinsky, "A Factor Analytic Study of the Personal Selling Process," *Journal of Personal Selling and Sales Management* 1 (Fall–Winter 1980–81): 26–33; and Robert E. Hite and Joseph A. Belizzi, "Differences in the Importance of Selling Techniques Between Consumer and Industrial Salespeople," *Journal of Personal Selling and Sales Management* 5 (November 1985): 19–30.

[9]"The Computer in Sales and Marketing," *Sales and Marketing Management,* August 15, 1986, 71.

[10]Hite and Belizzi, "Differences In."

[11]Marvin A. Jolson, "Prospecting by Telephone Prenotification: An Application of the Foot-in-the-Door Technique," *Journal of Personal Selling and Sales Management* 6 (August 1986): 39–42.

[12]Ibid.

[13]George W. Dudley and Shannon L. Goodson, "The Fear of Prospecting," *Training* 21 (September 1984): 59.

[14]"The Computer in Sales and Marketing," *Sales and Marketing Management,* August 15, 1983, 71.

[15]Robert H. Collins, "Microcomputer Systems to Handle Sales Leads: A Key to Increased Salesforce Productivity," *Journal of Personal Selling and Sales Management* 5 (May 1985): 77–83.

[16]Shook, *The Perfect Presentation,* 111.

[17]Barton A. Weitz, "A Critical Review of Personal Selling Research: The Need for Contingency Approaches," in *Sales Management: State-of-the-Art and Future Research Needs,* edited by Gerald Albaum and Gilbert A. Churchill, Jr. (Eugene, Oregon: Division of Research, College of Business Administration, University of Oregon, 1979), 110.

[18]Thomas W. Leigh and Arno J. Rethans, "A Script-Theoretic Analysis of Industrial Purchasing Behavior," *Journal of Marketing* (Fall 1984): 30.

[19]Marvin A. Jolson, "The Underestimated Potential of the Canned Sales Presentation," *Journal of Marketing* 39 (January 1975): 75–78

[20]Hite and Belizzi, "Differences In," 25.

[21]"What's Scaring the Customers Away?" *Business Week,* June 24, 1985, 80.

[22]Jeffrey Rothfeder, "Now Playing at an Office Near You," *Business Week,* June 1, 1987, 85–87.

[23]"PAs Examine the People Who Sell to Them," *Sales and Marketing Management,* November 11, 1985, 38–41.

[24]William G. Nickels, Robert F. Everett, and Ronald Klein, "Rapport Building by Salespeople: A Neuro-Linguistic Approach," *Journal of Personal Selling and Sales Management* 3 (November 1983): 1–7.

[25]Hite and Belizzi, "Differences In," 24.

[26]Ibid.

[27]Theodore Levitt, *Industrial Purchasing Behavior: A Study in Communications* (Boston: Division of Research, Harvard School of Business, 1965).

[28]Edwin K. Simpson and Ruel C. Kahler, "A Scale for Source Credibility Validated in the Selling Context," *Journal of Personal Selling and Sales Management* 1 (Fall–Winter 1980–81): 17–25.

[29]"PAs Rate," 39.

[30]Camille P. Schuster and Jeffrey E. Danes, "Asking Questions: Some Characteristics of Successful Sales Encounters," *Journal of Personal Selling and Sales Management* 6 (May 1986): 17–28.

[31]Hite and Belizzi, "Differences In," 26.

[32]"Significant Trends," *Sales and Marketing Management,* March 11, 1985, 162.

[33]Hite and Belizzi, "Differences In," 28.

[34]John E. Swan, I. Frederick Trawick, and David W. Silva, "How Industrial Salespeople Gain Trust," *Industrial Marketing Management* 14 (August 1985): 203–211.

[35]See Karl Albrecht and Ron Zemke, *Service America* (New York: Dow-Jones-Irwin, 1985) and "Pul-eeze! Will Somebody Help Me?" *Time,* February 1987, 48–57.

[36]Shook, *The Perfect Presentation,* 166–167.

[37]Thomas T. Ivy and Louis E. Boone, "A Behavioral Science Approach to Effective Sales Presentations," *Journal of the Academy of Marketing Science* 4 (June 1976): 456–466.

CHAPTER 4

SALES CAREERS: CHARACTERISTICS, QUALIFICATIONS, AND STAGES

Learning Objectives

After completing this chapter, you should be able to

1. Discuss the characteristics of sales careers.
2. List the skills and characteristics required for success in most sales positions.
3. Discuss the concept of career stages as applied to salespeople.
4. Describe the human, technical, and conceptual skills needed in sales management.
5. Name the factors associated with promotion into sales management.
6. Explain the existence of different career paths in sales and sales management.

DON BECKER: PROFILE OF AN ELITE SALES EXECUTIVE

Don Becker is firmly established among the sales elite in the plastics and paper-packaging industry. His Atlanta-based sales and distribution firm, Becker Marketing Services(BMS), is continuing the strong growth pattern that has marked its 10-year history. The company serves as an intermediary in the channel of distribution for a variety of packaging products. In some cases, BMS resells products purchased from manufacturers. The company also represents several vendors as independent manufacturers' agents. Billings and commissions exceed $6 million dollars per year, and gross profits are tracking at approximately three-quarters of a million dollars per year.

The rewards of Becker's hard work are worthy of one of the top sales executives in the country: a beautiful home in a posh Atlanta neighborhood, two vacation homes, and luxury automobiles. Those who know Becker best, however, would say that the other rewards of his work are at least as important to him as the financial ones. They see him as a man who likes a challenge. They would tell you that he has always been a hard worker, and probably always will be, even though his financial security is no longer in question.

Mr. Becker has made a number of critical career decisions in the past 20 years. Perhaps the first major decision was to continue his college education after an interruption for military service. He served in an assault helicopter company in Vietnam, returning to Drury College in Springfield, Missouri, where he graduated in Business Administration in 1969. Becker's first job after graduation was with Procter & Gamble as a sales representative in the Carolinas. In 1972 he joined the packaging division of Mobil Plastics, a Mobil oil subsidiary, as a salesperson in the food packaging division. He and his family moved to Nashville.

Two and a half years later, Becker moved to Atlanta with Mobil to become a product manager. Less than two years later, he was promoted to sales manager for the Southeastern United States. His success led to another opportunity in late 1977, when Mobil asked him to move to New York as a national product manager.

Source: Based on personal interview with Don Becker, President, Becker Marketing Services, Inc., Atlanta, Georgia.

At this point, Becker and his family were enjoying life in Atlanta and simply did not want to move to New York. He changed companies, accepting a job as national sales manager with a division of Clorox. Subsequently, the division was acquired by International Paper. Becker was offered a choice of jobs in New York or California but declined both opportunities. The time had come for Don Becker to establish a new career path — that of the entrepreneur.

The year 1979 was a slow one in the plastics and paper industry. Nonetheless, Becker established a $5,000 credit line with an Atlanta bank and committed his life savings as working capital to found Becker Marketing Services. His wife, Rosie, was his only employee, and she functioned as a partner in the business. The business was run from the basement of their home. Within six months, Becker had exhausted his savings and fully utilized the original credit line extension. In the seventh month, he turned a profit. Since then, results have been truly spectacular. In 1982 Becker leased an office and hired two additional salespeople. Today, he operates from a new office building in which he is half-owner, has an office staff of four people, and has recently computerized his operation.

In reviewing his career, Becker says the hardest decision he ever made was to risk losing the security and comfort of the major corporation career to chart his own course. He says the large company life is a lot like a military career, where frequent relocation is very much a part of the job. He is quick to note that he learned a great deal about business from big companies, but he much prefers the challenges and rewards offered by running his own company. As for the future, he sees the biggest task to be that of assuring future growth and further refining his management skills as his company expands. In particular, he plans to expand direct-marketing operations as a supplement to the personal selling efforts of his firm.

THE career of a successful salesperson, as illustrated in the case of Don Becker, can be extremely rewarding. Although the successful salesperson will often have opportunities in management and in entrepreneurial ventures, many pursue a lifelong career as a salesperson instead. Simply stated, sales offers a variety of career paths, and successful salespeople have the privilege of making a choice based on individual preference.

In this chapter, we will discuss the characteristics of, qualifications for, and stages of sales careers. Their wide diversity forces us to generalize, but a look at several typical career paths should give the reader an idea of whether sales is a suitable place for him or her to start a career in business.

The ideal career has been described by these conditions:[1]

- It should have a future based on economic, political, and technological trends.
- Financial rewards should be adequate.
- It should have the growth potential to support a sizable number of new entrants in the years ahead.

CHARACTERISTICS OF SALES CAREERS

In this discussion, we treat salespeople and sales managers as one occupational group. The characteristics to be discussed are

- Job security
- Advancement opportunities
- Immediate feedback
- Prestige
- Job variety
- Independence
- Compensation
- Boundary-role effects.

Job Security

Salespeople are revenue producers, and thus enjoy relatively good job security when compared to other occupational groups. A recent national survey of hiring practices concluded that "field salespeople seem to be leaders of the pack in job security."[2] Certainly, individual job security depends on the individual performance, but, in general, salespeople are usually the last group to be negatively affected by personnel cutbacks. When AT&T's Information Systems group eliminated 24,000 jobs, none of them were in sales. Although 8,000 management jobs were cut in the company's attempt to eliminate "redundant" jobs, a company spokesperson said that not only would there be no effect on sales, but, in fact, AT&T planned to be even more competitive in future sales activities.[3]

Competent salespeople also have some degree of job security based on the universality of their basic sales skills. In many cases, salespeople are able to successfully move to another employer, maybe even change industries, because sales skills are largely transferrable. For salespeople working in declining or stagnant industries, this is heartening news.

Furthermore, projections by the U.S. Department of Labor indicate strong demand for salespeople in all categories in the future (see Exhibit 4.1). And growth in

Exhibit 4.1 **Occupational Outlook for Salespeople**

Job Type	1984 Employment	1995 Employment	Percent Increase 1984–1995
Insurance	371,000	405,000	9.1
Manufacturer	547,000	598,000	9.3
Real Estate	363,000	415,000	14.4
Retail	4,001,000	4,584,000	14.6
Securities/Financial	81,000	113,000	44.7
Travel Agent	72,000	103,000	43.9
Wholesale	1,248,000	1,617,000	35.3

Source: *Occupational Projections and Training Data,* Bulletin 2251, U.S. Department of Labor, April 1986.

Note: The Department of Labor forecasts are done at three levels: low, moderate, and high. The 1995 figures in this exhibit reflect moderate forecasts.

the number of salespeople should bring a corresponding growth in the numbers of sales management positions.

According to Exhibit 4.1, there are particulary good opportunities in financial services, the travel industry, and in wholesale trades. "Sales Trend: Selling Financial Services" notes the increasing importance of personal selling in the financial services industry.

Advancement Opportunities

The opportunity for salespeople to advance their careers through promotion into management is one of the chief advantages of sales jobs. Evidence of advancement opportunities for salespeople comes from multiple sources:

- 1,100 newly promoted executives polled by the University of Michigan found sales/marketing to be the best preparation for top management positions.[4]
- A worldwide executive-search firm concludes that sales/marketing is the most traveled route to the top and has increased its lead over other functions since 1979.[5]
- A survey of CEOs of the 1,200 largest U.S. firms showed 58 percent want their successors to have a sales/marketing background.[6]
- A best-selling book, profiling "excellent" companies, says such companies promote a disproportionate share of salespeople to general management.[7]

As the business world continues to become more competitive, the advancement opportunities for salespeople will continue to be an attractive dimension of sales careers. The career advancement of a young executive is featured in "International Sales: Ian Fitzwilliam of New World Marketing."

SALES TREND

SELLING FINANCIAL SERVICES

As indicated in Exhibit 4.1, the demand for financial services salespeople is quite strong. An industry source says that since so many bank officers are becoming financial services salespeople, the term banking as we now define it may become obsolete. Bankers are being joined in the sales field by account representatives from large insurance companies, brokerage houses, and accounting firms as this relatively new sales orientation gains momentum in the financial services industry.

Salespeople in this industry work both commercial and personal markets. They offer combinations of savings, risk management, investment, and financing options. These financial services combination packages are tailored to the needs of the client. Since clients are so well-informed, and competition is intense, salespeople in this industry must be extremely knowledgeable and adaptive. There is no question that personal selling is well-established and still gaining momentum in the financial services sector. In such a dynamic environment, the best salespeople will prosper, and the marginal performers will be forced out.

Source: William J. Birnes and Gary Markham, *Selling at the Top,* (Harper & Row, New York, 1985), p. 22

INTERNATIONAL SALES

IAN FITZWILLIAM OF NEW WORLD MARKETING

At age 29, English-born Ian Fitzwilliam is president of New World Marketing Corp., a Canadian book distribution company. Fitzwilliam began his career at the age of 16 as a retail shoe salesperson. Within a year, he moved into direct sales, selling such items as garbage bags, pots and pans, and books door-to-door. In his late teens, Fitzwilliam founded his own direct sales company. The company failed after only three months. Later, Fitzwilliam said, "I was undercapitalized, and I had no good business sense. You learn from your mistakes."

Apparently, he learned well. In 1982, Fitzwilliam founded New World Marketing with twenty-five employees. By the mid-eighties, his firm was selling 50,000 books a week and challenging Canadian direct selling firms such as Mary Kay Cosmetics Ltd. and Avon Canada Inc.

When asked about his successful career, Fitzwilliam claims that his secret is that he uses a "lazy" approach to selling. In reality, his approach could hardly be called lazy. Rather, he uses a soft-sell based on letting the customer examine the product and relies on high-quality products to help make the sale.

By implementing a sales approach consistent with the wants and needs of a mass market, Ian Fitzwilliam has moved from retail salesclerk to the top position in a significant sales and distribution company with offices across North America.

Source: Allan Gould, "Secrets of a Lazy, But Very Rich Salesman," *Canadian Business,* November 1984, 36–50.

Immediate Feedback

Salespeople receive constant, immediate feedback on their job performance. Usually, the results of their efforts can be plainly observed by both salespeople and their sales managers — a source of motivation and job satisfaction.

One interesting study of 500,000 workers found salespeople to have the highest levels of job satisfaction for any occupational group, with immediate feedback being cited as a key reason. The study concluded that job satisfaction is high among salespeople because they "see the results of their efforts almost instantly, instead of having to wait years to obtain some satisfaction for a job well done."[8]

Prestige

Traditionally, sales has not been a prestigious occupation in the eyes of the general public. More recently, the negative stereotypical images of salespeople have begun to slowly disappear. There are some indicators that college students are viewing sales as a more prestigious career than their predecessors. Yet we cannot say that sales is clearly a prestigious career.

Business people generally hold salespeople in higher regard than they are held by members of society who rarely encounter professional salespeople. Even salespeople in oft-maligned fields such as automobile and insurance sales are reporting that their own approach to the job has a major impact on how prestigious it appears to other people. For example, a 26-year old college graduate selling Mercedes-Benzes in New Jersey earns over $140,000 a year utilizing a soft-sell approach. He says, "It's a very prestigious job."[9] His approach is in direct contrast to the fast-talking "tire-kicker," a character clearly lacking in occupational prestige.

Job Variety

Salespeople rarely vegetate due to boredom. Their jobs are multifaceted and dynamic. For a person seeking the comfort of a well-established routine, sales might not be a good career choice. In sales, day-to-day variation on the job is the norm. A recent college graduate working for a New York advertising agency as an assistant account executive describes his activities on the Schlitz Malt Liquor account this way: "The time each day that your mind is engaged, concentrating, is far more than in school."[10]

The opportunity to become immersed in the job and bring creativity to bear is reflected in the thoughts of Jerry Della Femina, one of the most successful advertising executives in the country:

> Selling — both in and out of the advertising industry — has become highly specialized. The science of demographics has been refined to an art. Technology has impacted on advertising as well as on every other industry. If you want to sell — products, services, yourself — you've got to keep current. You've got to know what's happening today . . . It's hard work, and you've got to be creative — and original. Creativity is the key ingredient in all selling — not only in advertising.[11]

Independence

Sales jobs often allow independence of action. This independence of action is frequently a by-product of decentralized sales operations in which salespeople live and work away from headquarters, therefore working from their homes and making their own plans for extensive travel.

Independence of action is usually presented as an advantage that sales positions have over tightly supervised jobs. Despite its appeal, however, independence does present some problems. New recruits working from their homes may find the lack of a company office somewhat disorienting. They may need an office environment to relate to, especially if their past work experience provided regular contact in an office environment.

Work-related travel sounds more exciting than most salespeople find it to be. The realities of extensive travel include boredom, diet modification, adjusting to ever-changing sleep environments, lack of exercise, and loneliness. These negative consequences of travel can be minimized by careful planning, and life on the road need not be drudgery. Nevertheless, a fair summary statement would be that travel more closely approximates demanding work than leisurely recreation. Extensive travel also places some demands on salespeoples' personal lives, whether they are married or not.

The independence of action traditionally enjoyed by salespeople is apparently being scrutinized by sales managers more heavily now than in the past. The emphasis on sales productivity, accomplished in part through cost containment, is encouraging sales managers to take a more active role in dictating travel plans and sales-call schedules.

Compensation

Salesforce compensation will be discussed in detail in a later chapter, but a few generalizations are in order now. Compensation is generally thought to be a strong advantage of sales careers. Pay is closely tied to performance, especially if commissions and bonuses are part of the pay package. To illustrate this point, consider the results of a survey conducted by The Wyatt Company's Executive Compensation Service. In a study of 750 sales organizations, Wyatt found that salespeople who work solely on commission earn an average of $185,600, almost four times what straight salary salespeople earn. The Wyatt study points out that most sales organizations pay some combination of salary and incentives such as bonus and/or commission. Salespeople on such combination pay plans average $85,300 a year.[12]

These figures undoubtedly reflect the pay for highly experienced salespeople. Starting salaries for inexperienced salespeople with a college degree typically range from $25,000 to $30,000. Between the extremes of the highly experienced salesperson and the inexperienced recruit, an average salesperson earns approximately $50,000 per year.[13]

Boundary-Role Effects

Salespeople are **boundary-role performers**. That is, they occupy boundary-spanning positions between their employers and their customers. Their loyalties are sometimes torn between customer demands and the expectations of their company or their sales manager. For example, the company may want to sell at list price, while the customer demands a discount. The salesperson is caught between the two parties, and somehow must resolve the situation. This is but one example of the **role conflict** routinely experienced by salespeople.

Another dimension of boundary-spanning jobs such as sales jobs is **role ambiguity**. It occurs when the salesperson is unsure about what to do in a situation where no policy or procedure applies. This is not an uncommon event, given the variable nature of sales situations which sometimes require innovative problem solving.

The uncertainty arising from a lack of direction can contribute to **role stress**. Role conflict may also contribute to role stress, which salespeople, sales managers, organizational psychologists, and sales researchers all agree is strongly associated with sales careers. There is no escaping the conclusion that sales is a high-visibility, "spotlight" position. The revenue-production responsibilities of salespeople create considerable pressure to perform. When customer expectations are at odds with the employer's expectations, the pressure rises.

Some salespeople thrive in stressful situations. Stockbrokers like Mike Russell of Prudential-Bache flourish in an environment marked by tension, excitement, and uncertainty. A former air traffic controller, Russell enjoys the thrill of trying to second-guess the market and make wise investments.[14] His success in this job setting could not be duplicated by many. For most salespeople, stress is a large part of the job. Some handle it satisfactorily, and some do not.

QUALIFICATIONS AND SKILLS REQUIRED FOR SUCCESS BY SALESPEOPLE

Since there are so many different types of jobs in sales, it is rather difficult to generalize about the qualifications and skills needed for success. This list would have to vary according to the details of a given job. Even then, it is reasonable to believe that for any given job, different people with different skills could be successful. These conclusions have been reached after decades of research that has tried to correlate sales performance with physical traits, mental abilities, personality characteristics, and the experience and background of the salesperson.[15]

It should also be noted that many of the skills and characteristics leading to success in sales would do the same in practically any professional business occupation. For example, the *Occupational Outlook Handbook* published by the U.S. Department of Labor points out the importance of various personal attributes for success in sales, including the following: outgoing, enthusiastic personality; self-confidence; and self-discipline.[16] Who could dispute the value of such traits for any occupation?

Having made these introductory, rather cautionary, remarks, let us consider some of the skills and qualifications that are thought to be especially critical for success in most sales jobs.

Five factors that seem to be particularly important for success in sales are empathy, ego drive, ego strength, verbal communication skills, and enthusiasm. These factors have been selected after reviewing three primary sources of information:

- A study of over half a million salespeople in 11,000 companies (Greenberg and Greenberg)[17]
- A review of 30 years of research on factors related to sales success (Comer and Dubinsky)[18]
- Surveys of sales and marketing executives[19]

Empathy. In a sales context, **empathy** (the ability to see things as others would see them) includes being able to read cues furnished by the customer to better determine the customer's viewpoint. An empathetic salesperson is presumably in a better position to tailor the sales presentation to the customer during the planning stages. More importantly, empathetic salespeople can adjust to feedback during the presentation. Though not verified by research, it is reasonable to link empathy with listening skills. Further, it is more than coincidence that the major sales training programs feature listening as a major topic.[20]

The research of Greenberg and Greenberg found empathy to be a significant predictor of sales success. This finding was partially supported in the review by Comer and Dubinsky, who found empathy to be an important factor in consumer and insurance sales, but not in retail or industrial sales.

Ego Drive. In a sales context, **ego drive** (an indication of the degree of determination a person has to achieve goals and overcome obstacles in striving for success) is manifested as an inner need to persuade others in order to achieve personal gratification. Greenberg and Greenberg point out the complementary relationship between empathy and ego drive that is necessary for sales success. The salesperson who is extremely empathetic but lacks ego drive may have problems in taking active steps to confirm a sale. On the other hand, a salesperson with excessive ego drive relative to empathy may ignore the customer's viewpoint in an ill-advised, overly anxious attempt to confirm the sale.

Ego Strength. The degree to which a person is able to achieve an approximation of inner drives is **ego strength**. Salespeople with high levels of ego strength are likely to be self-assured and self-accepting. Salespeople with healthy egos are better equipped to deal with the possibility of rejection throughout the sales process. They are probably less likely to experience sales call reluctance, and are resilient enough to overcome the disappointment of inevitable lost sales.

Dorothy Cole, a district manager for Compaq Computers, knows the importance of ego strength in selling. Noting that every sales attempt cannot be successful, she points out the importance of being able to handle rejection. One coping tactic she uses is to refuse to take such rejection personally.[21]

Verbal Communication Skills. Executives who recruit salespeople cite **verbal communication skills**, including listening, as being essential for sales success. Mike Russell, the Prudential-Bache stockbroker mentioned earlier, says, "If you don't have good communications skills, I strongly recommend taking a course or two. Some people are naturals when it comes to working with people, others have to work at it to establish a comfortable rapport."[22]

A survey of sales executives from major companies such as Borg-Warner, Phillip Morris, Bassett Furniture Industries, and Litton Industries ranked verbal skills among the most important criteria for sales success.[23] This finding has consistently been corroborated in other surveys. For example, studies by the *Marketing News* and *The Collegiate Forum* found verbal communication skills to be the most important qualification for job candidates in entry-level marketing jobs, many of which are sales positions. The director of placement at the University of North Texas has said that "a good communicator — someone who can go out and sell himself — is the student who will succeed."[24] The director of career development at Temple University adds, "You don't have a prayer . . . if you have not learned to communicate grammatically, with polish and assertiveness."[25]

Research on communication styles in selling indicates that salespeople can be more effective by recognizing different communication styles utilized by their customers and then adapting their own styles of communication. Empirical study has confirmed the role of verbal communication styles in successful sales interactions.[26]

The importance of verbal skills has been recognized by sales managers, recruiters, campus placement directors, and sales researchers. These skills can be continually refined throughout a sales career, a positive factor from both a personal and a career-development perspective.

Enthusiasm. When sales executives and recruiters discuss qualifications for sales positions, they invariably include **enthusiasm**. They are usually referring to dual dimensions of enthusiasm — an enthusiastic attitude in a general sense and a special enthusiasm for selling. On-campus recruiters have told us that they seek students who are well beyond "interested in sales" to the point of truly being enthusiastic about career opportunities in sales. Recruiters are somewhat weary of "selling sales" as a viable career, and they welcome the job applicant who displays genuine enthusiasm for the field.

One survey of sales executives found enthusiasm to be the most important characteristic sought in newly hired salespeople.[27] Further evidence of the importance of enthusiasm in sales comes from Peters and Austin, who observed in top companies: "Early in their career, young men and women on the move clamor for an opportunity to be in sales."[28] Those interested in pursuing a sales career might do so in an innovative manner described in "Sales Technology: On-Line Career Exploration."

SALES TECHNOLOGY

ON-LINE CAREER EXPLORATION

A recent *New York Times* article describes a new college graduate's unique method for seeking a job — he met the rush hour crowd at Grand Central Station, handing out resumes to as many passers-by as possible. Another job hopeful rented a billboard in Pittsburgh in an attempt to land a job. While these methods are unique, they use a scattershot approach. Through on-line technology, a more selective approach to career exploration and job seeking is possible.

A pioneer in the electronic job service industry is Career Placement Registry (CPR). CPR was founded in 1980, specializing in listing entry-level jobs for college graduates. Since then, CPR has expanded to include a variety of job categories, including salespeople.

Another example is the Sales Prospector database, which reports on industrial and commercial expansion in the United States and Canada. This service is usually employed to help sales personnel develop new prospect listings, but it also has been used to locate prospective employers.

On-line job services offer the candidate an opportunity to identify key industry and company characteristics, as well as the appropriate person to contact for employment information. Fees to the user vary with the comprehensiveness of the service.

Source: Kathleen Lane, "The Perfect Match," *On-Line Access Guide*, March-April 1987, 30–41.

Comments on Qualifications and Skills

Our discussion of factors related to sales success is necessarily brief, as a fully descriptive treatment of the topic must be tied to a given sales position. Veteran sales managers and recruiters can often specify with amazing precision what qualifications and skills are needed to succeed in a given sales job. These assessments are usually based on a mixture of objective and subjective judgments that will be discussed in the chapter on recruitment and selection later in the book.

SALESPERSON CAREER STAGES

An interesting way to examine sales careers is to consider the various stages that salespeople pass through over the course of their careers. The **salesperson career cycle** was first discussed by Jolson in 1974.[29] Jolson theorized that salespeople pass through career stages in the same fashion that a product might move through its life cycle. He linked performance to the various stages in the career cycle — improving to a plateau, then declining as the salesperson approached the end of his or her career. The usefulness of the career cycle concept was in its recognition that the

Exhibit 4.2 **Salesperson's Career Stages**

	Career Stage Characteristics			
	Exploration	**Establishment**	**Maintenance**	**Disengagement**
Career Concerns:	Finding an appropriate occupational field.	Successfully establishing a career in a certain occupation.	Holding on to what has been achieved. Reassessing career, with possible redirection.	Completing one's career.
Developmental Tasks:	Learning the skills required to do the job well. Becoming a contributing member of an organization.	Using skills to produce results. Adjusting to working with greater autonomy. Developing creativity and innovativeness.	Developing broader view of work and organization. Maintaining a high performance level.	Establishing a stronger self-identity outside of work. Maintaining an acceptable performance level.
Personal Challenges:	Must establish a good initial professional self-concept.	Producing superior results on the job in order to be promoted. Balancing the conflicting demands of career and family.	Maintaining motivation though possible rewards have changed. Facing concerns about aging and disappointment over what one has accomplished. Maintaining motivation and productivity.	Acceptance of career accomplishments. Adjusting self-image.
Psychosocial Needs:	Support. Peer acceptance. Challenging position.	Achievement. Esteem. Autonomy. Competition.	Reduced competitiveness. Security. Helping younger colleagues.	Detachment from organization and organizational life.

Source: William L. Cron, "Industrial Salesperson Development. A Career Stages Perspective." Reprinted from *Journal of Marketing* 48 (Fall 1984): 45, published by the American Marketing Association. Used with permission.

challenges and desires relevant for a salesperson would change as the salesperson progressed through the stages.

Ten years after Jolson introduced the concept to sales management, other researchers refined the concept and began empirical research on career stages likely to be encountered by salespeople. Cron offered a modified perspective, summarized in Exhibit 4.2. As shown in Exhibit 4.2, salespeoples' careers can be broken down into four distinct stages: exploration, establishment, maintenance, and disengagement. For each of the four stages, there will be different career concerns, developmental tasks, personal challenges, and psychosocial needs.

Exploration

In the **exploration stage**, people are most concerned with finding the right occupational field. They aspire to be accepted as productive members of the organization, and they must learn the basic skills of the job.

Establishment

In the **establishment stage**, salespeople commit to the sales field as an occupation of choice. Their skills are increasing, and they may begin to concentrate on producing better results. They become more autonomous on the job as they no longer rely heavily on direction from supervisors.

Maintenance

The **maintenance stage** is characterized by holding on to achievement levels, and perhaps reassessing future career direction. At this point, performance has reached a satisfactory plateau, and the salesperson strives to maintain the plateau.

Disengagement

The **disengagement stage** is the transition from work to retirement. Salespeoples' perspectives become more oriented toward factors outside the organization such as retirement planning and establishing an identity outside the work environment.

Conclusions on Concept of Salesperson Career Stages

The career stages concept as applied to salespeople has begun to generate considerable research interest. Cron and Slocum studied 446 salespeople in six industrial firms and found that salespeople in the exploration stage often were not convinced they had made the right occupational choice. Salespeople in later stages, however, reported higher levels of job satisfaction. Further, salespeople in the maintenance stage reported quite positive attitudes toward their work and had the highest performance levels of any of the salespeople in the study.[30] In a study of 336 insurance agents, Hafer also reported higher sales levels in the latter stages of the career cycle.[31]

These studies imply that a sales career is not right for everyone, but those who do continue in sales find it rewarding. One reason for this result is that poor performers in the sales field usually exit, leaving those who will prosper, and thus enjoy, their work.

Another important finding from the research on career stages is that salespeople can move into various stages irrespective of their age or job tenure. Cron and Slocum's study found, for example, that salespeople in their forties might be grappling with exploration issues, or alternatively might be concerned with disengagement.[32] Another study found little connection between job tenure and a career-stage indicator, vocational maturity.[33]

A considerable number of salespeople will spend their entire career without advancing into management. Often, these career salespeople form the foundation of a company's salesforce. Other salespeople move into management, with the first assignment quite likely being in sales management. While similarities exist between selling and sales management positions, there are substantial differences in the two types of jobs. A discussion of the skills and characteristics required for success in sales management follows.

QUALIFICATIONS AND SKILLS REQUIRED FOR SUCCESS IN SALES MANAGEMENT

Sales management positions are relatively more complex than personal-selling positions, as suggested by sales executive David Moore in Chapter 1. Sales managers frequently are charged with motivating and supervising salespeople they see on an irregular basis. Moreover, they often retain sales responsibility for designated accounts in addition to their managerial duties such as recruiting, training, and evaluating performance. Sales managers are also involved in planning, forecasting, and budgeting activities to a greater degree than the salespeople they supervise.

The overall perspective of salespeople as compared to sales managers is different. Salespeople have an individual perspective, and they focus on sales development. Salespeople are subordinates within the organization, typically having no supervisory responsibilities. Compared to sales managers, salespeoples' jobs are narrowly defined and in many cases extremely specialized. In contrast, sales managers focus on getting results through the efforts of other people. They have a team perspective in two ways — they see their salesforce as a team of which they are leaders, and they view themselves as being part of a management team. Finally, sales managers' roles as superiors and as subordinates complicates their job.[34]

Figure 4.1 depicts three categories of skills required of sales managers: **technical, human, and conceptual**. The triangular representation in the figure suggests that more candidates for sales management positions acquire the requisite technical skills than acquire the necessary human skills. The narrowing process continues in that fewer still master the conceptual skills needed for sales management.

Technical Skills

The basic foundation of **technical skills** required for sales managers is acquired in the personal selling position. While sales managers generally agree that the best salesperson does not always make the best sales manager, incompetent salespeople are rarely promoted into sales management.

Figure 4.1 **From Selling to Sales Management: A Developmental Model**

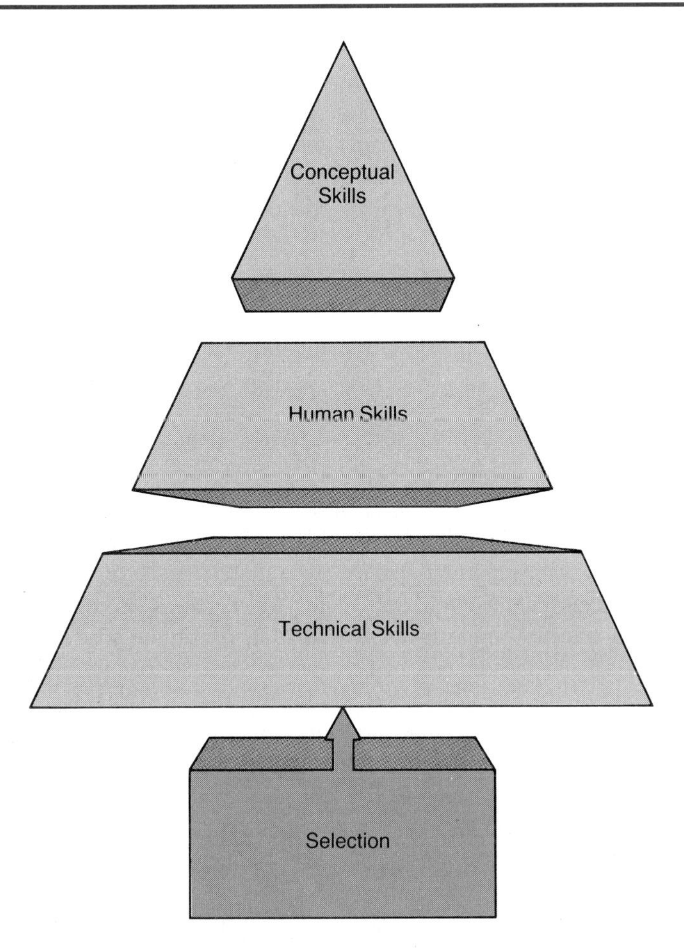

Three categories of skills are necessary in sales management: technical, human, and conceptual. The technical skills required for sales management are acquired primarily as a result of experience gained as a salesperson. Human skills are more difficult to attain than technical skills, and conceptual skills are the most difficult to attain.

Source: Reprinted by permission of the *Harvard Business Review*. An exhibit from "Skills of an Effective Administrator" by Robert L. Katz (September/October 1974). Copyright © 1974 by the President and Fellows of Harvard College; all rights reserved.

It is essential that salespeople learn the basic technical skills of the selling job before moving into sales management because they must prove their competence in that area in order to be able to influence subordinates. Also, they must be able to transfer technical knowledge to their salesforce. Fundamental skills must be acquired in product, market, and company knowledge, sales techniques, and time and territory management before a salesperson is ready for promotion. Further, salespeople are wise to begin developing abilities in managerially oriented technical activities such as sales forecasting while still functioning in a personal selling job.

Human Skills

Human skills, those related to the development and management of effective working relationships, are critical for sales managers. As Figure 4.1 indicates, these skills are more difficult to attain than the technical skills needed for sales management. Three human skills required of sales managers are verbal communication skills, written communication skills, and leadership skills.

We previously noted the importance of verbal communication skills in personal selling positions. These skills become even more important as individuals move into sales management. Group presentations are given more frequently — to customers, to members of the management team, and to the salesforce. Sales managers must become adept at communicating sensitive information relating to matters such as performance appraisals and termination of employment for salespeople.

Written communications are stressed more in sales management than in most sales positions. Producing communications for the entire salesforce as opposed to writing for a single recipient requires a different approach, and planning documents must be precise and clear. Salespeople are being called upon more often to produce credible written communications, but for the most part, the scope of their written communications is much narrower than for sales managers. Salespeople concentrate on sales proposals, sales letters, and reports requested by management. Sales managers must prepare a far wider range of materials and require more versatility in written communication.

Leadership skills are those related to the interpersonal relationships between the sales manager and members of the salesforce. Sales managers act as leaders as they seek to accomplish organizational goals with the support of the salesforce. A later chapter will consider salesforce leadership in detail.

Conceptual Skills

As Figure 4.1 implies, only a relatively small number of salespeople master the final level of skills necessary for successful sales management, **conceptual skills**. Within a sales management context, conceptual skills refer to understanding the operational

Exhibit 4.3 **Factors Associated with Promotion to Sales Management**

Most Important	Least Important
1. Integrity	1. Parent's occupation
2. Dependability	2. Being single
3. Self-motivation	3. Advanced (graduate) degree
4. Positive attitude	4. Upper-management sponsor
5. Good judgment	5. Being married
6. Customer relations	6. Being a workaholic
7. Overall job knowledge	7. Working for successful manager

Note: Results are rank-ordered, with integrity being most important in the survey, and parent's occupation being the least important.

Source: Alan J. Dubinsky and Thomas N. Ingram, "Important First-line Sales Management Qualifications: What Sales Executives Think," *Journal of Personal Selling and Sales Management* 3 (May 1983): 18–25.

rationale of the organization, problem solving, adopting a systems approach, and utilizing a strategic planning perspective.

Understanding the *operational rationale* (why we do what we do) is the foundation for developing other important conceptual skills needed in sales management. This foundation is inextricably linked to the other conceptual skills. Problems cannot be logically solved without understanding the operational rationale of the organization. The *systems approach* dictates that the interactions between various elements in the organization such as marketing, manufacturing, finance, and personnel be taken into account as sales managers perform their jobs. A *strategic planning perspective* begins with an understanding of the organization's mission, which is highly suggestive of the operational rationale of the organization.

Success Factors Ranked By Sales Executives

In summarizing the technical, human, and conceptual skills necessary for sales management, it becomes readily apparent that competence in a selling job is a necessary, but not sufficient, condition for successful sales management. To gain further insight into the skills and characteristics thought to be important in sales management, we will review the findings of a survey that asked sales executives their opinions.

The results of this survey of 176 sales executives disputed the conventional wisdom that sales managers should possess the attributes of "workaholic" tendencies, extrovertedness, and political instinct.[35] Instead, a number of other factors were cited as more important in determining which individuals should be promoted into sales management (see Exhibit 4.3).

Exhibit 4.3 indicates that personality traits are more important than other factors in determining who will be promoted into sales management. Some sales executives noted, however, that factors generally considered less important could, in some cases, become critical for receiving a promotion. For example, having an upper-management sponsor may be the only way to be promoted in some companies. In others, a graduate degree may enhance promotional opportunities.

As you look over the factors thought to be associated with opportunities to enter sales management, it may occur to you that these characteristics would be desirable for managers in any area. This is true, and perhaps this explains, at least in part, why sales and sales management is a solid preparation for upper-management positions.

CAREER PATHS IN SALES AND SALES MANAGEMENT

Generic Career Paths

Individuals who begin their careers as salespeople may pursue any of an almost endless variety of **career paths**. As previously indicated, many salespeople move into management and perhaps entrepreneurial ventures. Two typical generic (that is, not company-specific) career paths, one for career salespeople and one for those who enter management after beginning in sales, are shown in Figure 4.2. Some salespeople become managers, then return to the job of a salesperson. Career paths vary not only from company to company, but also sometimes within the same company. The path followed depends on the individual's strengths, successes, and preferences as well as various circumstantial factors beyond the control of the individual. The career paths shown are for illustrative purposes only. In the career sales path, the individual concentrates directly on actual selling activities throughout the career path. The management path includes jobs where directing the efforts of others in addition to actual selling are key activities.

Company-Specific Examples of Career Paths

Figure 4.3 illustrates the early stages of a potential career path for E. & J. Gallo Winery of Modesto, California. This path would lead an individual through three phases — sales representative, first-level sales manager, and field-marketing manager-in-training. Those who succeed during the first two phases will become field-marketing managers-in-training in approximately two to three years.

Figure 4.2 **Career Paths in Sales and Sales Management**

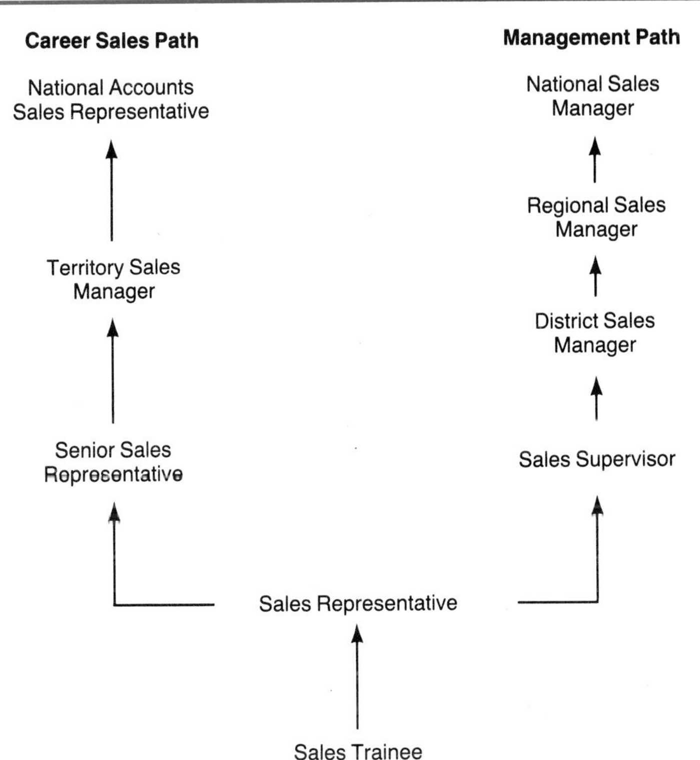

The career paths shown are for illustrative purposes only. In the career sales path, the individual concentrates directly on actual selling activities throughout the career path. The management path includes jobs where directing the efforts of others in addition to actual selling are key activities.

Source: Reprinted with permission of Macmillan Publishing Company from *Professional Selling* by Danny N. Bellenger and Thomas N. Ingram, p. 8. Copyright © 1984 by Macmillan Publishing Company.

In addition to actual selling, a Gallo sales representative would be involved in a variety of other tasks, including territory management, merchandising, servicing, product distribution, and working with distributors. With Gallo, a first-level sales manager begins sales management and executive training with the opportunity to manage other people. In Phase III, Gallo marketing managers are responsible for developing and implementing various marketing programs. Marketing managers are

Figure 4.3 **E. J. Gallo Career Path**

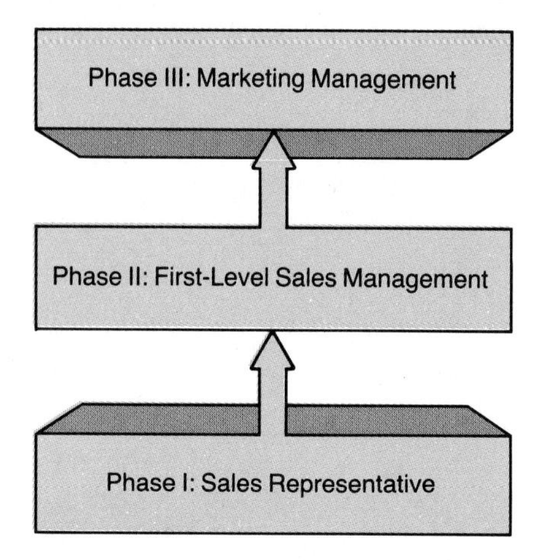

This career path illustrates the first few years in the career of an individual hired as a sales representative for E. J. Gallo Winery. Of course, another individual hired in this capacity might have an entirely different career path.

Source: E. J. Gallo, Modesto, California. Used with permission.

involved in pricing, advertising, new product decisions, and assuring growth in Gallo's markets.

The career path illustrated in Figure 4.3 is relatively simple since it extends only a few years into the future of a newly hired sales representative. A more complex career path is shown in Figure 4.4 for Beecham Products, whose products include Aqua-Fresh toothpaste, Sucrets lozenges, and Cling-Free fabric softener. In the Beecham career path, the territory manager position corresponds closely to Phase I in the Gallo career path. The Beecham district manager holds a first-level sales management position comparable to Phase II in the Gallo career path. While the successful Gallo first-level sales manager would move into marketing management, the Beecham first-level sales manager would continue into other sales management positions, such as sales trainer, regional sales manager, and national account manager.

Figure 4.4 **Beecham Products Company Career Path**

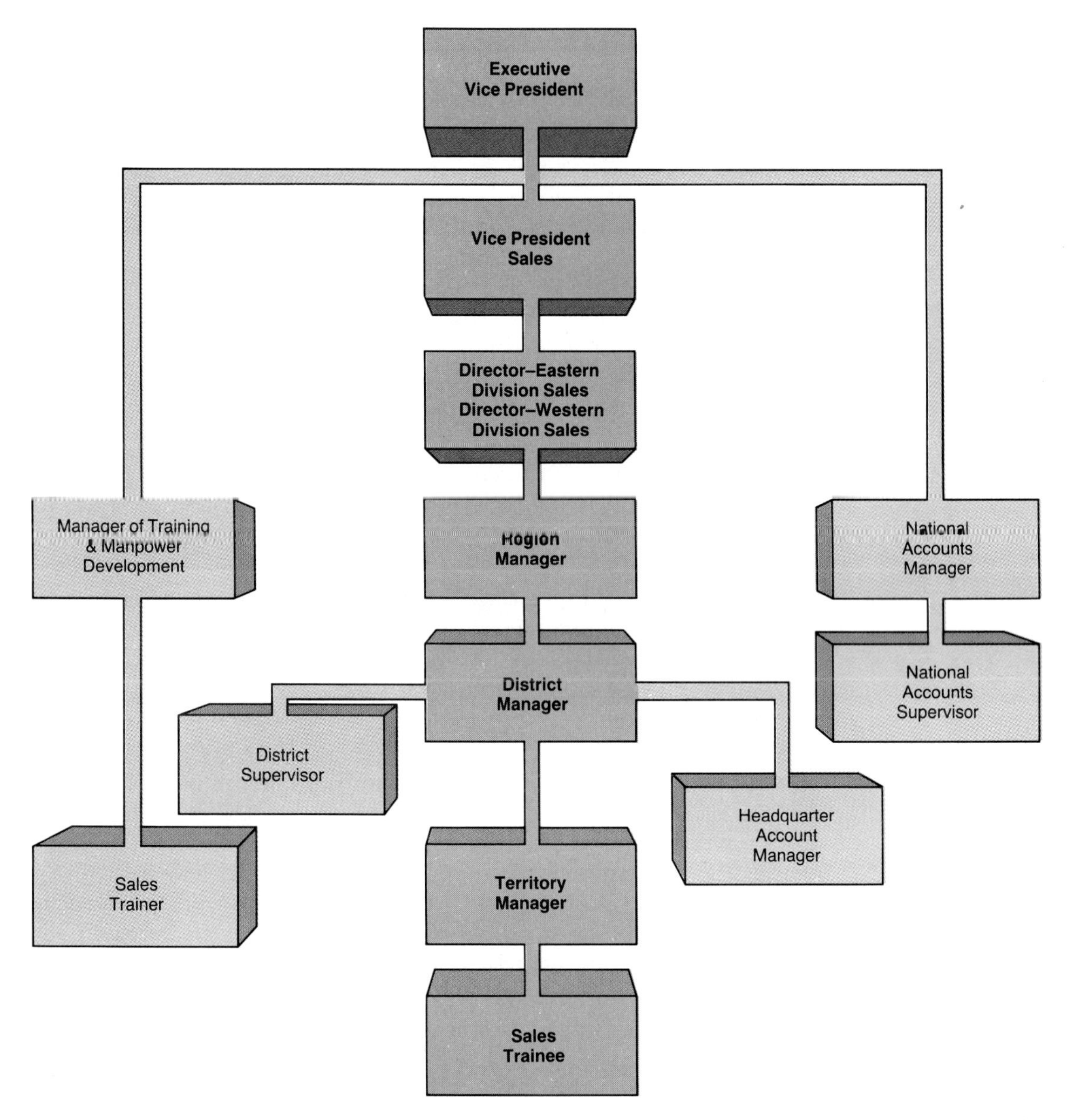

Salespeople might progress in a straight path as indicated by the shaded boxes, or hold other jobs, examples of which are shown in the non-shaded boxes, as their careers advance. This career path at Beecham Products Company, like the one shown in Figure 4.3 for E. J. Gallo Winery, is only one example of several possible paths.

Source: Courtesy of Beecham Products, U.S.A. Training & Manpower Development Department.

SUMMARY

1. **Discuss the characteristics of sales careers.** Sales careers are characterized by relatively good job security and reasonable opportunities for advancement. Salespeople get immediate feedback on the job, and this may explain why job satisfaction for salespeople is higher than in many other occupational groups. The prestige of selling seems to be improving gradually. An advantage of sales careers is that they offer the salesperson the chance to become totally involved in a creative, dynamic occupation where boredom is rare. Sales careers have long been associated with independence of action, although sales managers lately are monitoring sales activities more closely to improve sales productivity. Salespeople are paid fairly well, with those receiving incentive pay such as commissions being paid better than those on a straight salary. Salespeople occupy boundary roles between their customers and their employers. These roles often produce conflict and stress due to pressure to perform well for multiple parties.
2. **List the skills and characteristics required for success in most sales positions.** While there is not a universal profile of the successful salesperson, research indicates certain characteristics may be associated with sales success, namely, empathy, ego drive, ego strength, verbal communication skills, and enthusiasm.
3. **Discuss the concept of career stages as applied to salespeople.** Research indicates that salespeople move through four stages in their careers — exploration, establishment, maintenance, and disengagement. Job performance and attitudes vary as salespeople pass through the career stages. One major study found that salespeople in the maintenance stage generally had the highest levels of job performance.
4. **Describe the technical, human, and conceptual skills needed in sales management.** There are fundamental differences in the job responsibilities of salespeople and sales managers. It is common for salespeople to be promoted into sales management. The technical skills necessary for sales management have been largely acquired in the sales position. Various human skills involving communications and leadership must be developed. Conceptual skills dealing with strategic planning and problem solving must also be developed by sales managers.
5. **Name the factors associated with promotion into sales management.** Limited research into this area suggests that integrity, dependability, and self-motivation are important in determining which individuals will be promoted into sales management. This research also indicates that marital status and having advanced educational degrees are not important in decisions involving promotion into sales management.
6. **Explain the existence of different career paths in sales and sales management.** Many different sales career paths are possible within an industry, and even, sometimes, within a company. Career paths of successful salespeople can include management positions and entrepreneurial ventures.

Key Terms

- boundary-role performers
- role conflict
- role ambiguity
- role stress
- empathy
- ego drive
- ego strength
- salesperson career cycle
- exploration stage
- establishment stage
- maintenance stage
- disengagement stage
- technical skills
- human skills
- conceptual skills
- career path

Review Questions

1. How would you assess sales in terms of the criteria for an ideal career presented in this chapter?
2. From your personal perspective, what are the most positive aspects of a career in sales? What are the most negative aspects?
3. Salespeople enjoy relatively good job security and opportunities for advancement into management. Why is this so, and will these conditions hold true in the foreseeable future?
4. Explain what is meant by the statement that "salespeople are boundary-role performers."
5. What factors contribute to job stress for salespeople?
6. Describe the balance between empathy and ego drive required for sales success.
7. Explain the concept of the salesperson career cycle. Which stages can you identify in the profile of Don Becker at the beginning of the chapter?
8. What are the fundamental differences between sales jobs and sales management jobs?
9. Describe the technical, human, and conceptual skills required for sales management.
10. To become a sales manager, an individual must do more than be a competent salesperson and be in the right place at the right time. What factors are cited by sales executives as being important for promotion into sales management?

Application Exercises

1. Arrange interviews with several sales executives to solicit their opinions about sales careers. Develop a list of questions before you call for an interview appointment. Suggested questions follow:
   - What is the most positive aspect of a career in sales?
   - What is the most negative aspect of a career in sales?
   - What factors are related to sales success in your field?
   - Can a successful salesperson succeed in any selling job?
   - What is the future outlook for women in sales management?
   - Would you recommend selling to a close friend or family member?

Summarize your findings, focusing on differences of opinions among the executives, and be prepared to discuss the results of your interviews in class.

2. An excellent way to learn about career opportunities in sales is to gain experience through an internship in sales. It may be possible for you to earn academic credit through your university for internships. Check with your academic advisor. Even if academic credit is not feasible, you might want to pursue an internship as a sales assistant or as a sales trainee. Contact likely employers (any firm with a salesforce), offering to work as a sales assistant. Stress that you are interested in learning about sales careers. Be flexible on the matter of compensation, as some of the best learning opportunities come in the form of unpaid internships. Clarify job duties and the objectives of the internship with your employer before you start the internship. Keep a daily log of your activities, and write a report at the end of the internship detailing your learning experience.

3. Ethical dilemmas are frequently encountered in all occupational settings, including sales. Some college students encounter their first occupational ethical dilemma during their pursuit of an entry-level job upon graduation. What would you do if you were Rick Gibson in the following scenario?

    Rick Gibson will graduate from a university in the Midwest in two weeks, and he has been seeking an entry-level sales position. His first choice for an employer is Xerox. His interviews with Xerox have gone well, but Xerox has informed Rick that a reorganization of the salesforce is occurring and that hiring has been suspended for 60 days. Xerox management is telling Rick that it is likely that he will receive an offer, but there are no guarantees. Meanwhile, Rick has a firm offer from E. J. Gallo to begin work immediately upon graduation. Gallo has given Rick a week to decide on its offer, which would involve a relocation to its California headquarters. Gallo is an attractive company to Rick, but he has wanted to work for Xerox since he completed a favorable internship with the company last summer. At this point, Rick is considering accepting the Gallo offer, but switching to Xerox if an offer materializes.

4. Changing jobs during a career often mixes risk with opportunity. Consider the case of Bill Hanson, sales representative with a major packaging firm. Bill has been passed over for promotion to sales management and is in the process of switching jobs. He is bitter over his lack of opportunity with his present employer and is planning to go to work for a direct competitor. He has accepted a job with the new company that begins in three weeks. In preliminary discussions with his new employer-to-be, Bill shared some confidential information on his current customers. He also detailed plans for converting these customers to the new employer once the switch had been completed.

    Bill is now planning his resignation, and he plans to unload his frustrations during the regional sales meeting later this week. He is angry, and he wants to be sure that the management of his current company clearly understands his anger. He has been asked to deliver a 10-minute verbal review of his territory for management and the other salespeople. At the conclusion of his review, Bill is planning some derogatory remarks followed by a resignation statement. What do you think will be the consequences of Bill's actions?

5. Personal selling skills and activities are relevant in many different occupations and job positions. Arrange an interview with one individual in a non-sales position (e.g., an accountant, an architect, manager in nonprofit organization or other position). Develop a list of questions concerning the importance of personal selling skills and activities for the individual's job position. Summarize the results of the interview.

Notes

[1]Steven S. Ross, "The Best Job for You," *Business Week Guide to Careers,* December 1984–January 1985, 38.

[2]"The Job Market: Quick, Get Me a Field Sales Manager," *Sales and Marketing Management,* May 1987, 27.

[3]"Cuts Won't Touch AT&T's Sales Force," *Sales and Marketing Management,* October 7, 1985.

[4]"Marketing Newsletter," *Sales and Marketing Management,* December 9, 1985, 29.

[5]"Marketing Newsletter," *Sales and Marketing Management,* February 1987, 27.

[6]"CEO Survey Finds Marketers Sought For Their Successors," *Marketing News,* January 30, 1987, 5.

[7]Thomas J. Peters and Nancy K. Austin, *A Passion for Excellence* (New York: Random House, 1985), 107.

[8]"Industrial Newsletter," *Sales and Marketing Management,* July 1986, 43.

[9]John Huey, "A Mercedes Purveyor Has No Resemblance to a Car Salesman," *The Wall Street Journal,* June 25, 1985, 1.

[10]Randy Ring, "How I Got My Job," *Business Week's Guide To Careers,* Fall Winter 1983, 71.

[11]William J. Birnes and Gary Markham, *Selling At The Top* (New York: Harper and Row, 1985), ix.

[12]"Commissioned Reps Make Out," *Business Marketing,* March 1987, 42.

[13]"Survey of Selling Costs," *Sales and Marketing Management,* February 16, 1987, 57

[14] Bob Weinstein, "Stockbroker: What I Do On the Job," *Business Week's Guide To Careers,* February-March, 1985, 86.

[15]Gilbert A. Churchill, Jr., Neil M. Ford, Steven W. Hartley, and Orville C. Walker, Jr., "The Determinants of Salesperson Performance: A Meta-Analysis," *Journal Of Marketing Research* 22 (May 1985): 103–118.

[16]*Occupational Outlook Handbook, 1986–87 Edition,* (Washington, D.C.: U.S. Department of Labor Statistics, April 1986), 253.

[17]See Herbert M. Greenberg and Jeanne Greenberg, "Job Matching For Better Performance," *Harvard Business Review,* 58 (September–October 1980): 128–133; and Jeanne Greenberg and Herbert Greenberg, "The Personality of a Top Salesperson," *Nation's Business,* December 1983, 30–32.

[18]James M. Comer and Alan J. Dubinsky, *Managing The Successful Sales Force* (Lexington, Mass.: D.C. Heath and Company, 1985), 5–22.

[19]See Ralph M. Gaedeke, Dennis H. Tootelian, and Burton F. Schaffer, "Employers Want Motivated Communicators For Entry-Level Marketing Positions: Survey," *Marketing News,* August 5, 1983; and Stan Moss, "What Sales Executives Look For in New Salespeople," *Sales and Marketing Management,* March 1978, 46–48.

[20]Jeremy Main, "How to Sell By Listening," *Fortune,* February 4, 1985, 52–54.

[21]"Meet The Savvy," *Fortune,* February 4, 1985, 59.

[22]Weinstein, "Stockbroker," 88.

[23]Moss, "What Sales Executives Look For," 46–48.

[24]Gaedeke, Tootelian, and Schaffer, "Employers Want," 1.

[25]Ibid.

[26]Kaylene C. Williams and Rosann L. Spiro, "Communication Style in the Salesperson-Customer Dyad," *Journal of Marketing Research* 22 (November 1985): 434–442.

[27]Moss, "What Sales Executives Look For," 46–48.

[28]Peters and Austin, *A Passion,* 108.

[29]Marvin A. Jolson, "The Salesman's Career Cycle," *Journal of Marketing* 38 (July 1974): 39–46.

[30]William L. Cron and John W. Slocum, Jr., "The Influence of Career Stages on Salespeople's Job Attitudes, Work Perceptions, and Performance," *Journal of Marketing Research* 23 (May 1986): 119–129.

[31]John C. Hafer, "An Empirical Investigation of the Salesperson's Career Stages Perspective," *Journal of Personal Selling and Sales Management* 6 (November 1986): 1–7.

[32]Cron and Slocum, "The Influence of Career Stages," 119–129.

[33]Alan J. Dubinsky, Thomas N. Ingram, and Charles H. Fay, "An Empirical Investigation of the Assumed Job Tenure-Vocational Maturity Linkage in the Industrial Sales Force," *Journal of the Academy of Marketing Science* 12 (Fall 1984): 52–62.

[34]Based on Alan J. Dubinsky and Thomas N. Ingram, "From Selling To Sales Management: A Developmental Model," *Journal of Business and Industrial Marketing* 2 (Spring 1987): 27–36.

[35]Alan J. Dubinsky and Thomas N. Ingram, "Important First-Line Sales Management Qualifications: What Sales Executives Think," *Journal of Personal Selling and Sales Management 3* (May 1983): 18–25.

NATIONAL BUSINESS MACHINES

It was Brad Wilson's first day on the job after completing his product training with National Business Machines Inc. Two months prior to this time, Brad had graduated with a 2.8 G.P.A. with a bachelor of arts degree in business administration from a major university. He had taken a personal selling class as part of his marketing major.

Brad believed strongly that his most positive attribute was his outgoing and enthusiastic personality. It was the reason he had chosen sales as a career. This belief was reinforced by NBM recruiters, who remarked that it was this trait that led them to hire him over other candidates around the nation with more impressive G.P.A.'s.

Brad had been assigned to the typewriter division of NBM, working out of an office located in a medium-sized city, and he was eager to get started. His supervisor had given him a list of customers who might be prospects for the new generation of electronic typewriters NBM had just introduced. Brad scanned the list and noticed Harrison Brothers was located just around the corner from the NBM building. Eager to make his first sale, he picked up his demonstration model and rushed off to Ms. Johnstone, the office manager at Harrison Brothers.

Brad (to receptionist): Good morning, I'm Brad Wilson with NBM. I would like to see Ms. Johnstone, the office manager.

Receptionist: Do you have an appointment?

Brad: Well, er, no, but we have this fantastic new line of typewriters I know she'll want to hear about.

Receptionist: Ms. Johnstone, there's a Mr. Wilson here from NBM who would like to see you about some new typewriters.

Mr. Wilson, Ms. Johnstone says she is busy right now. If you would like to make an appointment she'll be willing to talk to you.

Brad: Tell Ms. Johnstone I will only take 10 minutes of her time and I'm sure increasing office productivity while decreasing costs is something she'll want to hear about!

Receptionist: Ms. Johnstone says O.K. but no more than 10 minutes because she really is busy. Her office door is the last door on the left.

Brad: Hello, Ms. Johnstone, how are you doing? I'm Brad Wilson with NBM. I know you're going to be glad you agreed to see me. (Smiling with hand extended.)

Source: This case was prepared by Stephen E. Calcich, School of Business, Norfolk State University. Copyright 1984 Stephen E. Calcich. Permission granted by the author.

Ms. Johnstone: Well, I don't know about that. Please sit down and say what you have to say. I have some things I have to attend to.

Brad: This is our daisywheel electronic typewriter which has just been introduced. It has automatic one-line correction, automatic underscore, automatic entering, caps lock and keyboard paper movement controls.

Ms. Johnstone: That's all very nice Mr. Wilson, but we bought some of your electronic typewriters just over a year ago for $1,500 each! We can't afford to buy anymore right now.

Brad: It's more a question of can you afford not to invest in this latest model, Ms. Johnstone. What we've been able to do is simplify the design so that manufacturing and servicing costs have been significantly reduced. What this means to you is that with over $420 trade-in on each of your old machines and a total investment of only $1,045 in the new machines, your net investment is only $625. Right now you are paying $291 per year for maintenance. Maintenance on our new model is only $108 per year, a savings of $183 per year. So, in less than four years the savings on maintenance will have covered the cost of the machines. Isn't that impressive, Ms. Johnstone? By the way, when would you like delivery of your new machines, next week or would the end of the month be soon enough?

Ms. Johnstone: Look, Mr. Wilson, I can see where the maintenance savings are substantial, but I'm going to have to think about it.

Brad: That's always a good idea, Ms. Johnstone, but our trade-in allowance on your current machines is only in effect until the end of next month, and you would like to take advantage of that, wouldn't you?

Ms. Johnstone: Why, yes, I would, but I still need to consider the deal.

Brad: Let me leave this demonstrator with you so you can see its advantages over your existing machines, then I'll come back next week to take care of the paperwork. Is that O.K., Ms. Johnstone? I promise to make an appointment with your receptionist on the way out.

Ms. Johnstone: O.K., Mr. Wilson, I'll see you next week, but no promises.

Brad: Thank you for your time, Ms. Johnstone. Good-bye.

Questions

1. How would you evaluate Brad's sales call at Harrison Brothers?
2. Why did Brad leave the demonstrator model? What was he hoping would happen when he returned?
3. What are Brad's chances of succeeding at NBM?
4. How can Brad improve his overall approach and presentation to be successful on future sales calls?

ROYAL CORPORATION

As Mary Jones, a third-year sales representative for the Royal Corporation, reviewed her call plans for tomorrow, she thought about her sales strategy. It was only July, 1983, but Jones was already well on her way toward completing her best year, financially, with the company. In 1982, she had sold the largest dollar volume of copiers of any sales representative in the northeast and was the tenth most successful rep in the country.

But Jones was not looking forward to her scheduled activities for the next day. In spite of her excellent sales ability, she had not been able to sell the Royal Corporate Copy Center (CCC). This innovative program was highly touted by Royal upper management. Jones was one of the few sales reps in her office who had not sold a CCC in 1982. Although Jones had an excellent working relationship with her sales manager, Tom Stein, she was experiencing a lot of pressure from him of late because he could not understand her inability to sell CCCs. Jones had therefore promised herself to concentrate her efforts on selling CCCs even if it meant sacrificing sales of other products.

Jones had five appointments for the day—9:00 a.m., Acme Computers; 9:45, Bickford Publishing; 11:45, ABC Electronics; 12:30, CG Advertising; and 2:00 p.m., General Hospital. At Acme, Bickford, and ABC, Jones would develop CCC prospects. She was in various states of information gathering and proposal preparation for each of the accounts. At CG, Jones planned to present examples of work performed by a model 750 color copier. At General Hospital, she would present her final proposal for CCC adoption. Although the focus of her day would be on CCCs, she still needed to call and visit other accounts that she was developing.

Royal Introduces CCC Concept

In 1980, Royal had introduced its Corporate Copy Center facilities management program (CCC). Under this concept, Royal offered to equip, staff, operate, and manage a reproduction operation for its clients, on the clients' premises (see Exhibit I). After analyzing the needs of the client, Royal selected and installed the appropriate equipment and provided fully trained, Royal employed operators. The CCC equipment also permits microfilming, sorting, collating, binding, covering, and color copying, in addition to high-volume copying.

The major benefits of the program include: reproduction contracted for at a specified price, guaranteed output, tailor-made capabilities, and qualified operators.

As she pulled into the Acme Computers parking lot, she noticed that an unexpected traffic jam had made her ten minutes late for the 9:00 a.m. appointment. This

---

Source: Copyright © 1983. This case was prepared at Babson College by Professor Hubert Hennessey and Barbara Kalunian, graduate student, as the basis for discussion rather than to illustrate either effective or ineffective sales performance. Names and locations have been disguised.

Exhibit I

To see what Royal Corporate Copy Center can do for you—and for your operating budget—take a minute to explore the *true* cost of your *present* system, outlined in the chart below. As you can see, it includes those "hidden" reprographic expenses that *many* organizations fail to consider . . .	**The CCC concept is a familiar one, of course . . . many progressive organizations are now utilizing similar arrangements for their food service and data processing programs.**
Labor Operator (Hrs × 4.3 Wks) Secretary (Hrs × 4.3 Wks) Executive (Hrs × 4.3 Wks) Supervisor (Hrs × 4.3 Wks)	CCC provides expert operators and experienced reprographic managers so all labor costs are included in one convenient monthly invoice.
Paid Benefits Social Security Vacations Sick Leave Pensions Medical Plans	CCC eliminates all "people problems"—your repro staff is on our payroll, and we pay for their benefits.
Recruiting & Training Advertising Costs Personnel Time Interviewer Time Operator Time Supervisor Time	No more recruiting and training . . . we handle that job, and we cover all related expenses!
Administrative Time Purchase Orders Filing Work Calling Service People Talking to Sales People	We handle all repro management—you receive a single monthly invoice for your entire repro system (and supplies)!

made her uncomfortable as she valued her time, and assumed that her clients appreciated promptness. Jones had acquired the Acme Computers account the prior summer and had dealt personally with Betty White, Director of Printing Services, ever since. She had approached White six months earlier with the idea of purchasing a CCC, but had not pursued the matter further until now because Betty had seemed very unreceptive. For today's call, Jones had worked several hours preparing a detailed study of Acme's present reproduction costs. She was determined to make her efforts pay off.

Waste Operator Negligence Unauthorized Copies Equipment Malfunction	You only pay for the copies you use . . .
Downtime Resulting In . . . Vendor Charges Overtime Costs Missed Deadlines	Comprehensive back-up capabilities at your local Royal Reproduction Center—job turnaround times are guaranteed at no extra cost to you!
Price Increases Labor Materials Overhead Interest	The CCC price includes everything and it's guaranteed for the length of our agreement!
Space Requirements Inventory File Cabinets Additional Equipment	Equipment and supplies are our responsibility, eliminating the need for anything extra on your part . . .
Chargeback Control Clients Departments Individuals	At no charge, we maintain a log of all copies made . . . for clients, departments and individuals.

Jones gave her card to the new receptionist, who buzzed White's office and told her that Jones was waiting. A few minutes later, Betty appeared and led Jones to a corner of the lobby. They always met in the lobby, a situation that Jones found frustrating but it was apparently company policy.

"Good morning, Betty, it's good to see you again. Since I saw you last, I've put together the complete analysis on the CCC that I promised. I know you'll be excited by what you see. As you are aware, the concept of a CCC is not that unusual anymore. You may recall from the first presentation that I prepared for you, the CCC can be a tremendous time and money saver. Could you take a few moments to review the calculations that I have prepared exclusively for Acme Computers?" Betty flipped through the various pages of exhibits that Jones had prepared, but it was obvious that she had little interest in the proposal. "As you can see," Jones continued, "the savings are really significant after the first two years."

"Yes, but the program is more expensive the first two years. But what's worse is that there will be an outsider here doing our printing. I can't say that's an idea I could ever be comfortable with."

Jones realized that she had completely lost the possibility of White's support, but she continued.

"Betty, let me highlight some of the other features and benefits that might interest Acme."

"I'm sorry, Mary, but I have a 10:00 meeting that I really must prepare for. I can't discuss this matter further today."

"Betty, will you be able to go over these figures in more depth a little later?"

"Why don't you leave them with me, I'll look at them when I get the chance," White replied.

Jones left the proposal with White hoping that she would give it serious consideration, but as she pulled out of the driveway to Acme Computers, she could not help but feel that the day had gotten off to a poor start.

The Royal corporation established the Royal Reproduction Center (RRC) Division in 1956. With 51 offices located in 24 states in the United States, the RRC specializes in high quality quick-turnaround copying, duplicating, and printing on a service basis. In addition to routine reproduction jobs, the RRC is capable of filling various specialized requests including duplicating engineering documents and computer reports, microfilming, color copying, and producing overhead transparencies. In addition, the RRC sales representatives sell the Royal 750 color copier (the only piece of hardware sold through RRCs) and the Royal Corporate Copy Center program (CCC). Although the RRC accepts orders from "walk ins," the majority of the orders are generated by the field representatives who handle certain named accounts which are broken down by geographic territory.

At 9:45 a.m., Jones stopped at Bickford Publishing for her second sales call of the day. She waited in the lobby while Joe Smith, Director of Corporate Services, was paged. Bickford Publishing was one of Jones's best accounts. Last year her commission from sales to the Bickford totaled 10 percent of her pay. But her relationship with Joe Smith always seemed to be on unstable ground. She was not sure why, but she had always felt that Smith harbored resentment towards her. However, she decided not to dwell on the matter as long as a steady stream of large orders kept coming in. Jones had been calling on Bickford ever since Tim McCarthy, the sales representative before her, had been transferred. Competition among the RRC sales reps for the Bickford account has been keen. But Stein had decided that Jones's performance warranted a crack at the account, and she had proven that she deserved it by increasing sales 40 percent within six months.

"Good morning, Miss Jones, how are you today?" Smith greeted her. He always referred to her formally as Miss jones.

"I'm fine, Mr. Smith," Jones replied. "Thank you for seeing me today. I needed to drop by and give you some additional information on the CCC idea that I reviewed with you earlier."

"Miss Jones, to be perfectly honest with you, I reviewed the information that you left with me, and although I think that your CCC is a very nice idea, I really don't believe it is something that Bickford would be interested in at this particular point in time."

"But Mr. Smith, I didn't even give you any of the particulars. I have a whole set of calculations here indicating that the CCC could save Bickford a considerable amount of time, effort, and money over the next few years."

"I don't mean to be rude, Miss Jones, but I am in a hurry, I really don't care to continue this conversation."

"Before you go, do you think that it might be possible to arrange to present this proposal to Mr. Perry (Tony Perry, V.P. of Corporate Facilities, Joe Smith's immediate supervisor) in the near future? I'm sure that he would be interested in seeing it. We had discussed this idea in passing earlier, and he seemed to feel that it warranted serious consideration."

"Maybe we can talk about that the next time you are here. I'll call you if I need to have something printed. Now I really must go."

As Jones returned to her car, she decided that in spite of what Smith had told her about waiting until next time, she should move ahead to contact Mr. Perry directly. He had seemed genuinely interested in hearing more about the CCC when she had spoken to him earlier, even though she had mentioned it only briefly. She decided that she would return to the office and send Perry a letter requesting an appointment to speak with him.

Although Jones was not yet aware of it, Joe Smith had returned to his desk and immediately began drafting the following memo to be sent to Tony Perry:

To: Tony Perry, V.P. Corporate Facilities
From: Joe Smith, Corporate Services
Re: Royal CCC

Tony:

I spoke at length with Mary Jones of Royal this morning. She presented me with her proposal for the adoption of the CCC program at Bickford Publishing. After reviewing the proposal in detail, I have determined that the program: (a) is not cost effective, (b) has many problem areas that need ironing out, and (c) is inappropriate for our company at this time.

Therefore, in light of the above, my opinion is that this matter does not warrant any serious consideration or further discussion at this point in time.

Royal 750 Color Copier

The Royal 750 color copier made its debut in 1973 and was originally sold by color copier specialists in the equipment division of Royal. But sales representatives did not want to sell the color copier exclusively and sales managers did not want to manage the color copier specialists. Therefore, the 750 was not a particularly successful product. In 1979, the sales responsibility for the color copier was transferred to the RRC division. Since the RRC sales representatives were already taking orders from customers needing the services of a color copier, it was felt that the reps would be in an advantageous position to determine when current customer requirements would justify the purchase of a 750.

Jones arrived back at her office at 10:45. She checked her mailbox for messages, grabbed a cup of coffee, and returned to her desk to draft the letter to Tony Perry. After making several phone calls setting up appointments for the next week and checking on client satisfaction with some jobs that were delivered that day, she gathered up the materials that she needed for her afternoon sales calls. Finishing her coffee, she noticed the poster announcing a trip for members of the "President's Club." To become a member, a sales representative had to meet 100% of his or her sales budget, sell a 750 color copier, sell a CCC program, and sell a short-term rental. Jones believed that making budget would be difficult but attainable, even though her superior performance in 1982 led to a budget increase of 20% for 1983. She had already sold a color copier and a short-term rental. Therefore, the main thing standing in her way of making the President's Club was the sale of a CCC. Not selling a CCC this year would have even more serious ramifications, she thought. Until recently, Jones had considered herself the prime candidate for the expected opening for a senior sales representative in her office. But Michael Gould, a sales rep who also had three years experience, was enjoying an excellent year. He had sold two color copiers and had just closed a deal on a CCC to a large semiconductor manufacturing firm. Normally everyone in the office celebrated the sale of a CCC. As a fellow sales rep was often heard saying, "it takes the heat off all of us for a while." Jones, however, found it difficult to celebrate Michael's sale. For not only was he the office "Golden Boy" but now, in her opinion, he was also the prime candidate for the senior sales rep position as well. Michael's sale also left Jones as one of the few reps in the office without the sale of a CCC to his or her credit. "It is pretty difficult to get a viable CCC lead," Jones thought, "but I've had one or two this year that should have been closed." Neither the long discussions with her sales manager, nor the numerous in-service training sessions and discussions on how to sell the CCC had helped. "I've just got to sell one of these soon," Jones resolved.

On her way out, she glanced at the clock. It was 11:33. She had just enough time to make her 11:45 appointment with Sam Lawless, operations manager, at ABC Electronics. This was Jones's first appointment at ABC and she was excited about getting a foot in the door there. A friend of hers was an assistant accountant at ABC. She had informed Jones that the company spent more than $15,000 a month on printing services and that they might consider a CCC proposal. Jones knew who the competition was, and although their prices were lower on low-volume orders, Royal could meet or beat their prices for the kind of volume of work for which ABC was contracting. But Jones wasn't enthusiastic about garnering the account for reproduction work. She believed she could sell ABC a CCC.

Jones' friend had mentioned management dissatisfaction with the subcontracting of so much printing. Also, there had been complaints regarding the quality of work. Investment in an in-house print shop had been discussed. Jones had assessed ABC's situation and had noticed a strong parallel with the situation at Star Electronics, a multi-division electronics manufacturing firm that had been sold CCCs for each of their four locations in the area. That sale, which occurred over a year ago, was vital in legitimatizing the potential customers in the Northeast. Jones hoped to sell ABC on the same premise that Fred Myers had sold Star Electronics. Myers had been extremely helpful in reviewing his sales plan with Jones and had given her ideas on points he felt had been instrumental in closing the Star deal. She felt well prepared for this call.

Jones had waited four months to get an appointment with Lawless. He had a reputation for disliking to speak with salespeople, but Jones' friend had passed along to him some CCC literature and he had seemed interested. Finally, after months of being unable to reach him by telephone, or get a response by mail, she had phoned two weeks ago and he had consented to see her. Today she planned to concentrate on how adoption of the CCC program might solve ABC's current reproduction problems. She also planned to ask Lawless to provide her with the necessary information to produce a convincing proposal in favor of CCC. Jones pulled into a visitor parking space and grabbed her briefcase. "This could end up being the one," she thought as she headed for the reception area.

Jones removed a business card from her wallet and handed it to the receptionist. "Mary Jones to see Sam Lawless, I have an appointment," Jones announced.

"I'm sorry," the receptionist replied, "Mr. Lawless is no longer with the company."

Jones tried not to lose her composure, "But I had an appointment to see him today. When did he leave?"

"Last Friday was Mr. Lawless's last day. Mr. Bates is now operations manager."

"May I see Mr. Bates, please?" Jones inquired, knowing in advance, the response.

"Mr. Bates does not see salespeople. He sees no one without an appointment."

"Could you tell him that I had an appointment to see Mr. Lawless? Perhaps he would consider seeing me."

"I can't call him. But I'll leave him a note with your card. Perhaps you can contact him later."

"Thank you, I will." Jones turned and left ABC, obviously shaken. "Back to square one," she thought as she headed back to her car. It was 12:05 p.m.

Jones headed for her next stop, CG Advertising, still upset from the episode at ABC. But she had long since discovered that no successful salesperson can dwell on disappointments. "It interferes with your whole attitude," she reminded herself. Jones arrived at the office park where CG was located. She was on time for her 12:30 appointment.

CG was a large, full-service agency. Jones's color copy orders from CG had been increasing at a rapid rate for the past six months, and she had no reason to believe that their needs would decrease in the near future. Therefore she believed the time was ripe to present a case for the purchase of a 750 color copier. Jones had been dealing primarily with Jim Stevens, head of Creative Services. They had a good working relationship, even though on certain occasions Jones had found him to be unusually demanding about quality. But she figured that characteristic seemed to be common in many creative people. She had decided to use his obsession with perfection to work to her advantage.

Jones also knew that money was only a secondary consideration as far as Stevens was concerned. He had seemingly gotten his way on purchases in several other instances, so she planned her approach to him. Jones had outlined a proposal which she was now ready to present to Jim.

"Good morning, Jim, how's the advertising business?"

"It's going pretty well for us here, how's things with you?"

"Great, Jim," Jones lied, "I have an interesting idea to discuss with you. I've been thinking that CG has been ordering large quantities of color copies. I know that you utilize them in the presentations of advertising and marketing plans to clients. I also know that you like to experiment with several different concepts before actually deciding on a final idea. Even though we have exceptionally short turnaround time, it occurred to me that nothing would suit your needs more efficiently and effectively than the presence of one of our Royal 750 color copiers right here in your production room. That way, each time that you consider a revision one of your artists will be able to compose a rough, and you can run a quick copy and decide virtually immediately if that is the direction in which you want to go, with no need to slow down the creative process at all."

"Well, I don't know; our current situation seems to be working out rather well. I really don't see any reason to change it."

"I'm not sure that you're fully aware of all the things that the 750 color copier is capable of doing," Jones pressed on. "One of the technicians and I have been experimenting with the 750. Even I have discovered some new and interesting capabilities to be applied in your field, Jim. Let me show you some of them."

She reached into her art portfolio and produced a wide variety of samples to show Stevens. "You know that the color copier is great for enlarging and reducing as well as straight duplicating. But look at the different effects we got by experimenting with various sizes and colors. Don't you think that this is an interesting effect?"

"Yes, it really is," Stevens said loosening up slightly.

"But wait," Jones added, "I really have the ultimate to show you." Jones produced a sheet upon which she had constructed a collage from various slides that Stevens had given her for enlarging.

"Those are my slides! Hey, that's great."

"Do you think that a potential client might be impressed by something like this? And the best part is you can whip something like this up in a matter of minutes, if the copier is at your disposal."

"Hey, that's a great idea, Mary, I'd love to be able to fool around with one of those machines. I bet I'd be able to do some really inventive proposals with it."

"I'm sure you would, Jim."

"Do you have a few minutes right now, I'd like to bounce this idea off of Bill Jackson, Head of Purchasing, and see how quickly we can get one in here."

Jones and Stevens went down to Jackson's office. Before they ever spoke, Jones felt that this deal was closed. Jim Stevens always got his own way. Besides, she believed she knew what approach to use with Bill Jackson. She had dealt with him on several other occasions. Jackson had failed to approve a purchase for her the prior fall, on the basis that the purchase could not be justified. He was right on that account. Their present 600 model was handling their reproduction needs sufficiently, but you can't blame a person for trying, she thought. Besides, she hadn't had Stevens in her corner for that one. This was going to be different.

"How's it going, Bill. You've met Mary Jones before, haven't you?"

"Yes, I remember Miss Jones. She's been to see me several times, always trying to sell me something we don't need," he said cynically.

"Well, this time I do have something you need and not only will this purchase save time, but it will save money, too. Let me show you some figures I've worked out regarding how much you can save by purchasing the 750 color copier." Jones showed Jackson that, at their current rate of increased orders of color copies, the 750 would pay for itself in three years. She also stressed the efficiency and ease of operation. But she knew that Jackson was really only interested in the bottom line.

"Well, I must admit, Miss Jones, it does appear to be a cost-effective purchase."

Stevens volunteered, "Not only that, but we can now get our artwork immediately, too. This purchase will make everyone happy."

Jones believed she had the order. "I'll begin the paperwork as soon as I return to the office. May I come by next week to complete the deal?"

"Well, let me see what needs to be done on this end, but I don't foresee a problem," Jackson replied.

"There won't be any problem," Stevens assured Jones.

"Fine, then. I'll call Jim, the first of next week to set up an appointment for delivery."

Jones returned to her car at 1:00. She felt much better having closed the sale on the 750. She had planned enough time to stop for lunch.

During lunch, Jones thought about her time at Royal. She enjoyed her job as a whole. If it weren't for the pressure she was feeling to sell the corporate copy center program, everything would be just about perfect. Jones had been a straight "A" student in college where she majored in marketing. As far back as she could remember, she had always wanted to work in sales. Her father had started out in sales, and enjoyed a very successful and profitable career. He had advanced to sales manager and sales director for a highly successful Fortune 500 company and was proud that his daughter had chosen to pursue a career in sales. Often they would get together, and he would offer suggestions that had proven effective for him when he had worked in the field. When Jones's college placement office had announced that a Royal collegiate recruiter was visiting the campus, Jones had immediately signed up for an interview. She knew several recent graduates that had obtained positions with Royal and were very happy there. They were also doing well financially. She was excited at the idea of working for an industry giant. When she was invited for a second interview, she was ecstatic. Several days later, she received a phone call offering her a position at the regional office. She accepted immediately. Jones attended various pre-training workshops for 6 weeks at her regional office preparing her for her 2-week intensive training period at the Royal Training Headquarters. The training consisted of product training and sales training.

She had excelled there, and graduated from that course at the head of her class. From that point on everything continued smoothly . . . until this problem with selling the CCC.

After a quick sandwich and coffee, Jones left the restaurant at 1:30. She allowed extra time before her 2:00 appointment at General Hospital, located just four blocks from the office, to stop into the office first, check for messages, and check in with her sales manager. She informed Tom Stein that she considered the sale of a 750 to CG almost certain.

"That's great, Mary, I never doubted your ability to sell the color copiers, or repro for that matter. But what are we going to do about our other problem?"

"Tom, I've been following CCC leads all morning. To tell you the truth, I don't feel as though I've made any progress at all. As a matter of fact, I've lost some ground." Jones went on to explain the situation that had developed at ABC Electronics and how she felt when she learned that Sam Lawless was no longer with he company. "I was pretty excited about that prospect, Tom. The news was a little tough to take."

"That's okay. We'll just concentrate on his replacement, now. It might be a setback. But the company's still there, and they still have the same printing needs and problems. Besides, you're going to make your final presentation to General Hospital this afternoon, and you really did your homework for that one." Stein had worked extensively with Jones on the proposal from start to finish. They both knew that it was her best opportunity of the year to sell a CCC.

"I'm leaving right now. Wish me luck."

He did. She filled her briefcase with her personals and CCC demonstration kit that she planned to use for the actual presentation and headed toward the parking lot.

Jones's appointment was with Harry Jameson of General Hospital. As she approached his office, his receptionist announced her. Jameson appeared and lead her

Exhibit II **Why Royal Corporate Copy Center?**

- No Hidden Costs
- No Downtime
- No Capital Investment
- No Recruiting or Training
- No People Problems
- No Inventory Problems
- Increased Quality
- Expert Operators — Plus
- Guaranteed Turnaround Time
- Allows You to Devote Full Time to Your Business
- Departmental Budget Control
- RRC Full Center Support
- Tailor Made System
- Full Write Off
- Guaranteed Cost Per Copy
- Short Term Agreement
- Trial Basis

to the board room for their meeting. Jones was surprised to find three other individuals seated around the table. She was introduced to Bob Goldstein, V.P. of operations, Martha Chambers, director of accounting, and Dr. J. P. Dunwitty, chairman of the board. Jameson explained that whenever an expenditure of this magnitude was being considered, the hospital's executive committee had to make a joint recommendation.

Jones set up her demonstration at the head of the table so that it was easily viewed by everyone and began her proposal. She presented charts verifying the merits of the CCC (Exhibit II, III) and also the financial calculations that she had generated based upon the information supplied to her by Jameson.

Forty minutes later, Jones finished her presentation and began fielding questions. The usual concerns were voiced regarding hiring an "outsider" to work within the hospital. But the major concern seemed to revolve around the loss of employment on the part of two present printing press operators. One, John Brown, had been a faithful employee for more than five years. He was married and had a child. There had never

Exhibit III **What is Royal Corporate Copy Center?**

Royal Corporate Copy Center is the means whereby Royal will equip, staff, operate and manage a reproduction operation for you on your own premises. First, we analyze your needs, then we select and install the appropriate equipment. Secondly, we provide two fully trained Royal employed operators and professional reproduction management. Finally, we schedule all work, and protect you with comprehensive back-up capabilities at our Royal Reproduction Center . . . and you receive just one monthly bill for the entire package.

continued

General Hospital Copying Objectives

1. To lower on-hand inventory of forms
2. To be able to upgrade or relocate equipment if needed
3. To have a competent full-time operator as well as back-up operators
4. To increase productivity
5. To be more cost efficient
6. 89-day trial option period
7. To eliminate downtime
8. To eliminate waste
9. To assure fast turnaround
10. To establish an inventory control system for paper and copier supplies
11. To install an accurate departmental charge-back system
12. To improve copy quality
13. To eliminate queuing time
14. To allow administrative support personnel to devote their full time to General Hospital's daily business.
15. To eliminate having to worry about service on machines

General Hospital Offset vs. Printing

1. You won't eliminate all your related printing problems such as:
   A. You will still have to keep Savins for short-run lengths.
   B. You will still have waste problems.
   C. You still need plates and printing supplies.
   D. It is messy and complicated.
   E. You must have a dependable operator every day, and someone for vacations.
   F. You will have to vend some printing.
   G. You won't be able to cut down inventory of form or hand, and you will have to have long-run lengths to be profitable and long turnaround for two-sided copying.
   H. You will be running a copying print shop, but this is still not state of the art.
   I. It is very noisy. You wouldn't be able to put it in this building. You might have to find another location or keep it in the old building.
   J. Only 3 out of about 15 hospitals on the North Shore area have printing presses — those that do have large duplicators that do 100,000 to 200,000 in volume per month besides long-run lengths on presses.
2. You would lose all of the extra benefits the Royal Corporate Copy Center would give you. (See Attached)
3. For the first full year because of expense for press, your cost would be $14,890 higher than Royal Corporate Copy Center, and your estimated price increases over the next two years would not be fixed, thus still costing you more for a less efficient operation.

Royal Corporate Copy Center Will Satisfy These Objectives in the Following Manner:

1. By having a high-speed duplicator and professional operator, you will be able to order forms on an as-needed basis. This will lower your present inventory by at least 80%, thus freeing up valuable space for other use.
2. Because of the flexibility that Royal Corporate Copy Center gives you, you have the opportunity to change or upgrade equipment at any time. If relocation of equipment is necessary because of changes in the hospital's structure, this can be done also.

3. Royal Corporate Copy Center will provide a trained, professional operator whose hours will conform to General Hospital's. Regardless of vacation schedules, sickness, or personal absences, a competent operator will report to General Hospital every day. If these operators do not meet with General Hospital's satisfaction, they can be changed within 24 hours' time. Because Royal will supply the operators, you will be relieved of this person as a staff member. Benefits, sick time, and vacation will be taken care of by Royal. You will receive operators for your facility 52 weeks a year.
4. Our people will report directly to your supervisor for their assignment the same as any other employee under your supervision. These people will be able to sort incoming jobs as we have discussed or may be used for other work in the copy center at non-peak times. These people would also be available to pick up copying work from various central locations throughout General Hospital at specified times, thus eliminating the need for people to come to the copy center. These people may also be used to operate other various types of equipment that General Hospital has.
5. By having a Royal Corporate Copy Center program at General Hospital and letting Royal take care of all your duplicating needs in a professional manner, your copying costs will become much more cost efficient. We believe that the cost savings alone in the first year could be upwards of 10–15% and would increase as your copy volume grows with you. Your present system does not offer several of the important benefits that Royal Corporate Copy Center offers that now will be included in one fixed cost — in dollars and cents, by not having to pay for these services, this is where the additional 10–15% cost savings per year could come in. We also will give you a fixed reproduction cost so that you can budget more accurately. We will also fix all of your cost for the next three years (that includes supplies, machine, support and operators) if you sign a three-year agreement at the end of the trail period. This will enable you to save upwards of another 10% per year.
6. We at Royal feel very confident about this program and its success. We, therefore, wish to minimize our customers' risk for installing a new program. We feel we are able to do this by offering a trial option period of up to 89 days. This program works in the following way:

   General Hospital must sign a trial option pricing addendum and a three-year agreement. This will put into action the following:

   A. $1,050.00 per month credit off the original pricing for the first partial month, the first full month, and the second full month (total of $3,150.00).
   B. At the end of the trial option period General Hospital can elect to:
      a. Remain on the three-year agreement date May 1, 1983.
      b. Execute a 90-day, one-year, or two-year agreement with applicable pricing.
      c. Cancel the agreement date May 1, 1983, without liquidation damages.
7. With Royal Corporate Copy Center you will never experience downtime. Your work will always be done timely. We will back up the machines with a back-up copier running the work there or send it to our closest center to be completed and returned. By being a Royal Corporate Copy Center customer, General Hospital will always receive priority on service. Also, our operators will be able to handle more extensive types of service to the equipment.
8. General Hospital will be charged only for the copies ordered. This will eliminate all of your present waste that is involved with offset.
9. Trained Royal operators should reduce turnaround time on work. These operators will know how to run jobs on the equipment properly and in the fastest way so that productivity will increase and turnaround time will decrease.
10. Royal will order all toner and developer, thus eliminating the need for General Hospital to make large commitments and maintain large inventories. We will order paper also for you on a weekly basis if you so choose.
11. Royal will install an accurate departmental charge-back system, allowing General Hospital to accurately account for all copies. You will receive a copy of this breakdown each month.
12. Royal will provide trained operators, guaranteeing high-quality copies. By using a Xerographic process, you will always have consistently high-quality copies.
13. By providing General Hospital with skilled operators, copying and duplicating requirements will be met in a timely fashion, eliminating the need for General Hospital employees to stand and wait to use other equipment. In essence, General Hospital employees will be free to do General Hospital business; Royal will fulfill the copying and duplicating requirements.
14. Administrative personnel will no longer have to worry about sales people, service problems, obtaining purchase orders, or buying supplies.
15. All machines used will be the responsibility of Royal for service and maintenance.

continued

General Hospital Cash Flow (One-Year Period)
Royal Corporate Copy Center vs. Present System

Corporate Copy Center		Hospital
Royal 900	Equipment	Obsolete presses & mimeo
$ 6,500.00	Supplies and Paper	$ 42,189.00
Included	Toner and Developer	-0-
Included	Labor	$ 22,496.00
Included	Benefits	$ 2,681.00
Included	Administrative Time	-?-
Included	Management Time	-?-
Included	CCC Benefits	None
Eliminated	Savin 680 Rental	$ 4,534.00
Eliminated	Smaller Savin I Rental	$ 1,080.00
Eliminated	Smaller Savin II Rental	$ 1,320.00
Eliminated	Savin Copying Cost	$ 2,400.00
Eliminated	Vending (Forms that could be kept in-house)	$ 7,000.00
Eliminated	Issuing of P.O.s	$ 500.00
Eliminated	Expense for Present Building	$ 2,500.00
$ 80,310.00 ($.029 per copy)	Royal Facilities Management (200,000 copies)	—
$ 86,810.00	TOTAL CASH FLOW	$ 86,700.00

	Fixed	Price Increases	Est.	
$ 86,810.00	0	15 months	5%	$ 91,035.00
$ 89,414.00	3%	2nd year	9%	$ 99,228.00
$ 91,202.00	2%	3rd year	9%	$108,158.00
$267,426.00		PROJECTED 3-YEAR COST		$298,421.00
$ 30,995.00		PROJECTED 3-YEAR SAVINGS		None

Recommendation

Royal feels at this time that it would be very beneficial for General Hospital to change from its present reproduction system of two offset presses, memograph equipment, several smaller copiers, and a collator to a Royal 900 and a professional operator under the Royal Corporate Copy Center program. Royal feels it would be beneficial for General Hospital to effect this change presently for the following reasons:

1. Professional people would replace a part-time operator (20 hours) and an operator that is on leave (20 hours).
2. State-of-the-art equipment would replace the present presses, which are very old and outdated.
3. The large amount of waste presently experienced would be eliminated.
4. The high maintenance cost for the presses would be eliminated.
5. Hand collating and off-line collating would be eliminated.
6. Poor and inconsistent quality in the copies would be eliminated.

7. The back-up problem would be eliminated.
8. You would have better turnaround and accountability.
9. Some of the smaller copiers, and lower copy volumes on the smaller copiers, would be eliminated.
10. You would receive all other Royal Corporate Copy Center benefits unattainable with your present program.

In the following pages I hope to show you how we will accomplish these goals by installing the Royal Corporate Copy Center at General Hospital.

---

been a complaint about John personally, or with regard to the quality or quantity of his work. The second operator was Peter Dunwitty, a recent graduate of a nearby vocational school and nephew of Dr. Dunwitty. Although he had been employed by the hospital for only three months, there was no question about his ability and performance.

In response to this concern, Jones emphasized that the new equipment was more efficient, but different, and did not require the skills of experienced printers like Brown and Dunwitty. She knew, however, that this was always the one point about the adoption of a CCC program that even she had the most difficulty justifying. She suddenly felt rather ill.

"Well, Miss Jones, if you'll excuse us for a few minutes, we'd like to reach a decision on this matter," said Jameson.

"There's no need to decide right at this point. You all have copies of my proposal. If you'd like to take a few days to review the figures, I'd be happy to come by then," said Jones, in a last-ditch attempt to gain some additional time.

"I think that we'd like to meet in private for a few minutes right now, if you don't mind," interjected Dunwitty.

"No, that's fine," Jones said as she left the room for the lobby. She sat in a waiting room and drank a cup of coffee. She lit a cigarette, a habit that she seldom engaged in. Five minutes later, the board members called her back in.

"This CCC idea is really sound, Miss Jones," Jameson began. "However, here at General Hospital, we have a very strong commitment to our employees. There really seems to be no good reason to put two fine young men out of work. Yes, I realize that from the figures that you've presented to us, you've indicated a savings of approximately $30,000 over three years. But I would have to question some of the calculations. Under the circumstances, we feel that maintaining sound employee relations has more merit than switching to an unproven program right now. Therefore, we've decided against purchasing an CCC."

Jones was disappointed. But she had been in this situation often enough not to show it. "I'm sorry to hear that, Mr. Jameson, I thought that I had presented a very good argument for participation in the CCC program. Do you think that if your current operators decided to leave, before you filled their positions, you might consider CCC again?"

"I can't make a commitment to that right now. But feel free to stay in touch," Jameson countered.

"I'll still be coming in on a regular basis to meet all your needs for other work not capable of being performed in your print shop," Jones replied.

"Then you'll be the first to know if that situation arises," said Jameson.

"Thank you all for your time. I hope that I was of assistance even though you decided against the purchase. If I may be of help at any point in time, don't hesitate to call," Jones remarked as she headed for the door.

Now, totally disappointed, Jones regretted having scheduled another appointment for that afternoon. She would have liked to call it a day. But she knew she had an opportunity to pick up some repro work and develop a new account. So she knew she couldn't cancel.

Jones stopped by to see Paul Blake, head of staff training at Pierson's, a large department store with locations throughout the state. Jones had made a cold call one afternoon the prior week and had obtained a sizable printing order. Now she wanted to see whether Blake was satisfied with the job, which had been delivered earlier in the day. She also wanted to speak to him about some of the other services available at the RRC. Jones was about to reach into her briefcase for her card to offer to the receptionist when she was startled by a "Hello, Mary" coming from behind her.

"Hello, Paul," Jones responded, surprised and pleased that he had remembered her name. "How are you today?"

"Great! I have to tell you that report that you printed for us is far superior to the work that we have been receiving from some of our other suppliers. I've got another piece that will be ready to go out in about an hour. Can you have someone come by and pick it up then?"

"I'll do better than that. I'll pick it up myself," Jones replied.

"See you then," he responded as he turned and headed back towards his office.

"I'm glad I decided to stop by after all," Jones thought as she pressed the elevator button. She wondered how she could best use the next hour to help salvage the day. When the elevator door opened, out stepped Kevin Fitzgerald, operations manager for Pierson's. Jones had met him several weeks earlier when she had spoken with Ann Leibman, a sales rep for Royal Equipment Division. Leibman had been very close to closing a deal that would involve selling Pierson several "casual" copying machines that they were planning to locate in various offices to use for quick copying. Leibman informed Jones that Tom Stein had presented a CCC proposal to Pierson's six months earlier but the plan was flatly refused. Fitzgerald, she explained, had been sincerely interested in the idea. But the plan involved a larger initial expenditure than Pierson's was willing to make. Now, Leibman explained, there would be a much larger savings involved, since the "casual" machines would not be needed if a CCC were involved. Jones had suggested to Fitzgerald that the CCC proposal be reworked to include the new machines so that a current assessment could be made. He had once again appeared genuinely interested and suggested that Jones retrieve the necessary figures from Jerry Query, Head of Purchasing. Jones had not yet done so. She had phoned Query several times, but he had never responded to her messages.

"Nice to see you again, Mr. Fitzgerald. Ann Liebman introduced us, I'm Mary Jones from Royal."

"Yes, I remember. Have you spoken with Mr. Query, yet?"?"

"I'm on my way to see him right now," Jones said as she thought that this would be the perfect way to use the hour.

"Fine, get in touch with me when you have the new calculations."

Jones entered the elevator that Fitzgerald had been holding for her as they spoke. She returned to the first floor and consulted the directory. Purchasing was on the third floor. As she walked off the elevator on the third floor, the first thing that she saw was a sign that said, "Salespeople seen by appointment only. Tuesdays and Thursdays, 10 a.m.–12 noon."

"I'm really out of luck," Jones thought, "not only do I not have an appointment, but today's Wednesday. But I'll give it my best shot as long as I'm here."

Jones walked over to the receptionist who was talking to herself as she searched through a large pile of papers on her desk. Although Jones knew she was aware of her presence, the receptionist continued to avoid her.

"This could be a hopeless case," Jones thought. Just then the receptionist looked up and acknowledged her.

"Good afternoon. I'm Mary Jones from Royal. I was just speaking to Mr. Fitzgerald who suggested that I see Mr. Query. I'm not selling anything. I just need to get some figures from him."

"Just a minute," the receptionist replied as she walked towards an office with Query's name on the door.

"Maybe this is not going to be so bad after all," Jones thought.

"Mr. Query will see you for a minute," the receptionist announced as she returned to her desk.

Jones walked into Mr. Query's plushly furnished office. Query was an imposing figure at 6 feet, 4 inches, nearly 300 pounds, and bald. Jones extended her hand, which Query grasped firmly. "What brings you here to see me?" Query inquired.

Jones explained her conversations with Ann Liebman and Kevin Fitzgerald. As she was about to ask her initial series of questions, Query interrupted. "Miss Jones, I frankly don't know what the hell you are doing here!" Query exclaimed. "We settled this issue over six months ago, and now you're bringing it up again. I really don't understand. You people came in with a proposal that was going to cost us more money than we were spending. We know what we're doing. No one is going to come in here and tell us our business."

"Mr. Query," Jones began, trying to remain composed, "the calculations that you were presented with were based upon the equipment that Pierson's was utilizing six months ago. Now that you are contemplating additional purchases, I mentioned to Mr. Fitzgerald that a new comparison should be made. He instructed me to speak with you in order to obtain the information needed to prepare a thorough proposal," Jones tried to explain.

"Fitzgerald! What on earth does Fitzgerald have to do with this? This is none of his damn business. He sat at the same table as I six months ago when we arrived at a decision. Why doesn't he keep his nose out of affairs that don't concern him? We didn't want this program six months ago, we don't want it now!" Query shouted.

"I'm only trying to do my job, Mr. Query. I was not part of the team that presented the proposal six months ago. But from all the information that is available now, I still feel that a CCC would save you money here at Pierson's."

"Don't you understand, Miss Jones? We don't want any outsiders here. You have no control over people that don't work for you. Nothing gets approved around here unless it has my signature on it. That's control. Now I really see no need to waste any more of my time or yours."

"I appreciate your frankness," Jones responded, struggling to find something positive to say.

"Well, that's the kind of man I am, direct and to the point."

"You can say that again," Jones thought. "One other thing before I go, Mr. Query. I was noticing the color copies on your desk."

"Yes, I like to send color copies of jobs when getting production estimates. For example, these are of the bogs that we will be using during our fall promotion. I have received several compliments from suppliers who think that by viewing color copies they get a real feel for what I need."

"Well, it just so happens that my division of Royal sells color copiers. At some time it may be more efficient for you to consider purchase. Let me leave you some literature on the 750 copier which you can review at your leisure." Jones removed a brochure from her briefcase. She attached one of her business cards to it and handed it to Query. As she shook his hand and left the office, Jones noted that she had half an hour before the project of Blake's would be ready for pick-up. She entered the donut shop across the street and as she waited for her coffee, she reviewed her day's activities. She was enthusiastic about the impending color copier sale at CG Advertising, and about the new repro business that she had acquired at Pierson's. But the rest of the day had been discouraging. Not only had she been "shot down" repeatedly, but she'd now have to work extra hard for several days to insure that she would make 100% of budget for the month. "Trying to sell the CCC is even harder than I thought it was," Jones thought.

PART TWO

DEFINING THE STRATEGIC ROLE OF PERSONAL SELLING

THE two chapters in Part 2 discuss personal selling from a strategic perspective. Chapter 5 investigates strategic decisions at different levels in multibusiness, multiproduct firms. The key elements of corporate strategy, business strategy, and marketing strategy are described, and important relationships between each strategy level and the personal selling function are identified. Special attention is directed toward the role of personal selling in a marketing strategy. Chapter 6 changes the strategic focus to the account level. A discussion of organizational buyer behavior is presented to provide a foundation for account strategy development. Account relationship strategy and account coverage strategy are examined as the key types of account strategies. The important roles of personal selling and sales management at the account level are emphasized.

CHAPTER 5

PERSONAL SELLING AND CORPORATE, BUSINESS, AND MARKETING STRATEGIES

Learning Objectives

After completing this chapter, you should be able to

1. Define the different strategy levels for multibusiness, multiproduct firms.
2. Discuss how corporate strategy decisions affect personal selling.
3. Explain the relationships between business strategy and personal selling.
4. List the advantages and disadvantages of personal selling as a promotional tool.
5. Specify the situations when personal selling is typically emphasized in a marketing strategy.
6. Describe ways that personal selling and advertising can be blended into effective promotional strategies.

STRATEGIC CHANGE AND PERSONAL SELLING: CAMPBELL SOUP CO.

What could be a better symbol of American mass marketing than the red and white Campbell Soup can? Since being established in 1869, Campbell Soup Co. has relied on standardization, volume production, and national brand identity to establish strong market positions in several food categories. The most striking measure of this success was the 83 percent share of the soup market achieved in 1954. However, since this 1954 high, Campbell Soup's share has decreased to 62 percent with case soup sales falling from 55.5 million to 49 million during the 1975–1981 period. Total company sales averaged 8 percent growth, while the industry averaged 12 to 13 percent during the past 10 years. What happened?

The food marketing environment changed dramatically throughout the 1980s. The uniform, mass market served so well by Campbell Soup and other companies no longer exists. Increases in the number of working women and minorities, the rise of single-parent households, and the "graying" of America have altered the complexion of American society. In essence, the mass market has fragmented into many different segments. All consumers do not want the same food products. Such criteria as convenience, sophistication, and variety vary in importance depending upon regional location and demographic characteristics.

Before this new environment developed, Campbell Soup's organization consisted of four *strategic business units* (SBUs): canned foods, frozen foods, special products, and fresh foods. Each of these SBUs marketed a large number of products, was administered as a separate profit center, and followed a mass marketing approach. Then, when R. Gordon McGovern took over as president in 1980, a new corporate strategy was designed to address the food market fragmentation. The company divided the four SBUs into fifty SBUs, each with an average annual sales volume of $50 million. A general manager headed each new SBU. This manager had responsibility for the development of new products and the marketing of existing products.

Sources: Adapted from Joel Klotkin, "The Revenge of the Fortune 500," *INC.*, August 1985, 39–44; Rayna Skolnik, "Campbell Stirs Up Its Sales Force," *Sales and Marketing Management*, April 1986, 56–68; "Marketing's New Look," *Business Week*, January 26, 1987, 64–69.

The business strategies of the SBUs were changed from a mass marketing scope to a focus on specific market segments. Instead of developing and marketing the same basic product to everyone, each business unit focuses on achieving competitive advantage by satisfying the specific needs of well-defined market segments. Suddenly, Campbell Soup was developing a Creole soup for Southern markets and a red bean soup for Hispanic markets!

The changes in corporate and business strategies also had a tremendous effect on marketing strategies. The new, focused market orientation pushed much of the strategic planning activities down to the market level. Different geographic and demographic markets required separate marketing strategies. More emphasis was placed on targeted advertising and less on mass advertising vehicles. In sum, Campbell Soup Co. was practicing regional, or localized, marketing.

How did these corporate, business, and marketing strategy changes affect personal selling and sales management? In a word — drastically! The change to fifty SBUs and a regionalized marketing approach necessitated wholesale changes in the personal selling effort. The emphasis is no longer on products, but on markets and customers. Thus, the salesforce was reorganized into 22 geographical regions. Each region has a regional manager and is responsible for all product lines. The only individuals that concentrate on specific product lines are the four brand sales managers assigned to each region. These brand sales managers provide a key link between the SBUs and the salesforce. Both the salespeople and sales managers participate in developing and implementing marketing plans at the regional level. They often work with groups of retailers or even individual retailers in their region to develop tailored promotional programs. This is an enormous change for a company used to mass marketing and central control of promotional expenditures.

Have the new strategies been successful? Although it is too early to make a final judgment, the company is already reporting improved performance. Campbell Soup introduced almost 400 new products between 1980 and 1985. Among them, Prego Spaghetti Sauce and Le Menu Frozen Dinners produced combined sales of $450 million after only two years. Company sales increased 43 percent and profits 57 percent between 1980 and 1984. Changes in the salesforce will take longer to evaluate, but Campbell Soup expects these changes to promote such teamwork at all levels that "there'll be nobody who can beat us."

THE Campbell Soup Co. situation described in the opening vignette illustrates an important reality in the contemporary business world: most firms are really collections of relatively autonomous businesses that market multiple products to diverse customer groups. Strategy development in these multibusiness, multiproduct firms is extremely complex. Different types of strategic decisions must be made at different levels of the organization. However, the different strategies must be consistent with

Exhibit 5.1 **Organizational Strategy Levels**

Strategy Level	Key Decision Areas	Key Decision Makers
Corporate Strategy	Corporate mission Strategic business unit definition Strategic business unit objectives Corporate growth orientation	Corporate management
Business Strategy	Market scope Differentiation emphasis Functional expenditures	Strategic business unit management
Marketing Strategy	Target market selection Marketing mix development Promotional mix development	Marketing management
Account Strategy	Account management strategy Account coverage strategy	Sales management

each other and integrated for the firm to perform successfully. As the Campbell Soup situation suggests, strategic changes at one organizational level can have profound effects on strategies at other organizational levels.

Although our focus is on personal selling and sales management, it is relevant to discuss the different types of organizational strategy and their relationships with the personal selling function. We will discuss corporate strategy, business strategy, and marketing strategy in this chapter.

ORGANIZATIONAL STRATEGY LEVELS

The key strategy levels for multibusiness, multiproduct firms are presented in Exhibit 5.1. **Corporate strategy** consists of decisions that determine the mission, business portfolio, and future growth directions for the entire corporate entity. A separate **business strategy** must be developed for each *strategic business unit* (SBU) (discussed later in this chapter) in the corporate family, defining how that SBU plans to compete effectively within its industry. Since an SBU typically consists of multiple products serving different markets, each product/market combination requires a specific **marketing strategy**. Each marketing strategy includes the selection of target market segments and the development of a marketing mix to serve each target market. A key consideration is the role that personal selling will play in the promotional mix for a particular marketing strategy.

The corporate, business, and marketing strategies represent strategy development from the perspective of different levels within an organization. Although sales management may have some influence on the decisions made at each level, the key decision makers are typically from higher management levels outside the personal selling function. Sales management does, however, play the key role in account strategy development. In discussing account strategy, we must change our perspective from within the organization to the individual customer; therefore, this subject will be discussed in detail in Chapter 6.

CORPORATE STRATEGY AND PERSONAL SELLING

Strategic decisions at the topmost level of multibusiness, multiproduct firms determine the corporate strategy for a given firm, which is what provides direction and guidance for activities at all organizational levels. The process of developing a corporate strategy consists of the following steps:[1]

1. Analyzing corporate performance and identifying future opportunities and threats.
2. Determining corporate mission and objectives.
3. Defining business units and setting objectives for each business unit.
4. Determining directions for future corporate growth.

Once the corporate strategy has been developed, management is concerned with implementation, evaluation, and control of the corporate strategic plan. Although the corporate strategy has the most direct impact on business level operations, each element does affect the personal selling function. Our discussion will focus on the basic relationships between personal selling and corporate mission, business unit definition, business unit objectives, and corporate growth directions.

Corporate Mission

The development of a **corporate mission statement** is an important first step in the strategy formulation process for multibusiness, multiproduct firms. Although corporate mission statements vary considerably across firms, evidence suggests eight key components of an effective statement,[2] shown along with a specific mission statement for Federal Industries in Exhibit 5.2.

The first four components provide a qualitative description of the firm's strategic orientation in relation to customers and markets, products and services, geographic scope, and technology. These statements provide direction for strategy making at all organizational levels. For example, Federal Industries is and intends to remain a diversified company. Its mission statement indicates that the firm might operate in many different markets with many different products. The only strategic limitation in the mission statement is the proviso that the firm not exceed the scope of its ability to provide excellent management.

Exhibit 5.2 Corporate Mission Statements

Key Components of Corporate Mission Statements	Corporate Mission Statement for Federal Industries
1. The specification of target customers and markets 2. The identification of principal products/services 3. The specification of geographic domain 4. The identification of core technologies	To remain diversified, limiting our diversity only by our ability to provide excellent management
5. The expression of commitment to survival, growth, and profitability	To be a growth company, limiting our growth only by fiscal prudence and our ability to provide excellent management To be consistently profitable
6. The specification of key elements in the company philosophy	To contribute positively to every endeavor in which we are involved
7. The identification of the company self-concept	To be a responsible employer
8. The identification of the firm's desired public image	To be a responsible corporate citizen

Source: Adapted from John A. Pearce, II, and Fred David, "Corporate Mission Statements: The Bottom Line," *Academy of Management Executive,* May 1987, 109, and Federal Industries, *The Corporate Long Range Plan 1987/1995,* iv.

The fifth component expresses the firm's basic objectives for growth and profitability. The Federal Industries mission statement indicates a strong commitment to continuous growth. However, this growth must be profitable. Thus, strategy makers are directed to pursue only those growth opportunities that promise desired levels of profitability.

The final three components present the basic philosophy and values of the firm. These statements describe how the firm expects to conduct business and the firm's orientation toward customers, employees, and other publics. Overall, the mission statement for Federal Industries suggests that the firm wants to make positive contributions in all activities and to be responsible in relationships with employees and other publics.

Since sales managers typically play a minor role in the development of corporate, business, and marketing strategies, the first five key components of a mission statement have only limited direct impact on sales management activities. However, the basic philosophies and values expressed in the last three key components have a direct effect on how sales managers manage salespeople and deal with customers and other publics. Of particular importance are the ethical values expressed by the corporate mission statement.

The ethical values of a firm need to be defined and communicated at the highest corporate levels:[3]

> One of the few undisputed findings that emerges from research concerning ethics is that the single most important factor in setting an ethical climate for the organization is the attitude of top management.[4]

Figure 5.1 Ethical Attitude of Federal Industries

KEEP IT SIMPLE REQUIRES

UNQUESTIONABLE ETHICS

THE LAW SAYS WHAT'S LEGAL, BUT
"LAW" HAS BECOME COMPLEX AND UNCLEAR.
GREAT BUSINESSES ARE BUILT ON A
FOUNDATION OF STRICTEST INTEGRITY.
LISTEN TO YOUR HEART TO KNOW
WHAT'S RIGHT, AND ALWAYS DO
THE RIGHT THING.

Federal Industries humorously illustrates its corporate attitude toward ethical behavior in its Corporate Long-Range Plan.

Source: Federal Industries, *Corporate Long Range Plan 1987/1995*, v.

Top management can officially communicate its attitude toward ethics in the corporate mission statement and other corporate policy documents. These official statements concerning ethical behavior need to be reinforced by top management action for maximum effectiveness.[5] For example, the chairman of Rexnord has videotaped a speech on ethics that is shown to all employees. He specifically tells all employees "to walk away from business when it means doing anything unethical or illegal."[6]

Federal Industries communicates the firm's official attitude toward ethics when discussing each element of its mission statement in the Corporate Long Range Plan. Excerpts from this discussion are illustrated in Figure 5.1 and include the following:

> Those who suggest business cannot be conducted profitably on a solid ethical base are wrong. Every decision made in the operation of a Federal business unit must be solidly based in ethics that will stand the test of public scrutiny. When faced with moral and ethical decisions, we ask ourselves this question, "If my decision on this matter was published in the newspaper, would it embarrass Federal's Directors?" If the answer is "yes", or even "maybe," it's time to rethink the decision.[7]

This discussion in the corporate plan provides general direction and a specific criterion to guide the ethical behavior of sales managers, salespeople, and other employees.

Sales managers and salespeople must operate within the ethical guidelines presented in the corporate mission statement and related corporate policies. Furthermore, they can use these corporate guidelines as a basis for establishing specific ethical policies for the entire sales organization. Thus, in this way, the corporate mission statement, especially those portions dealing with ethical values, has a direct effect on sales management activities.

Definition of Strategic Business Units

Defining business units, often called **strategic business units (SBUs)**, is an important and difficult aspect of corporate strategy development. The basic purpose is to divide the corporation into parts in order to facilitate strategic analysis and planning. Cravens defines an SBU as "a single product or brand, a line of products, or a mix of related products that meets a common market need or a group of related needs, and the unit's management is responsible for all (or most) of the basic business functions."[8] The importance of SBU definition is evident in the Campbell Soup example at the beginning of this chapter. Campbell Soup initially followed a centralized, mass marketing approach with only four SBUs. Their new strategy called for a more focused market perspective. This led to a redefinition of the corporation into fifty SBUs. Their new SBU definitions represented a more decentralized orientation that led to a complete reorganization of their personal selling operations.

Firms must continually evaluate their SBU definitions and make changes when warranted. One study of multibusiness corporations found that:[9]

1. When there are too few SBUs, it is difficult to support each product or line of products.
2. When there are too many SBUs, it creates expensive duplication within the corporation.

Major changes in SBU definition often lead to major changes in the personal selling function, as evidenced by the Campbell Soup situation. However, even minor changes in SBU definition can cause sales management problems. For example, AT&T recently moved its computer business unit from the information systems division to the communications division. The purpose of this move was to integrate computer sales in networking arrangements with PBX systems and phone services. The problem facing sales management at AT&T is how to integrate the computer sales organization into the phone service organization. This is a difficult task, since the phone service salespeople concentrate on selling network systems to large national accounts, while the computer salespeople are accustomed to selling individual units to smaller, regular accounts.[10]

The definition of SBUs is an important element of corporate strategy. Changes in SBU definition may increase or decrease the number of SBUs, and these changes typically affect the personal selling function in many ways. Salesforces may have to be merged, new salesforces may have to be established, or existing salesforces may have to perform different activities. These changes may affect all sales management activities from the type of salespeople to be hired to how they should be trained, motivated, compensated, and supervised.

Objectives for Strategic Business Units

Once strategic business units have been defined, corporate management must determine appropriate strategic objectives for each. Many firms view their SBUs collectively as a portfolio of business units. Each business unit faces a different competitive situation and plays a different role in the **business unit portfolio**. Therefore, specific strategic objectives should be determined for each SBU.

Several analytical tools are available to help management evaluate its business unit portfolio and to provide guidelines for determining strategic objectives. The two most popular methods are the growth-share matrix developed by the Boston Consulting Group and the multiple factor screening method developed by General Electric Company.[11] Both of these analytical tools provide a means for classifying SBUs into categories based upon market opportunity and competitive strength considerations. Each category represents a different environmental situation and suggests different strategic objectives. For example, an SBU classified into a category of high market opportunity and high competitive strength signifies a favorable environmental situation. The analytical methods would recommend market share building objectives for all SBUs in this category.

Although the growth-share matrix, multiple factor screening method, and other analytical approaches can provide useful information, they have been overused by many firms.[12] Corporate management has ultimate responsibility for establishing strategic objectives for each SBU whether analytical tools are used or not. As illustrated in Exhibit 5.3, the strategic objective assigned to a business unit has a direct effect on personal selling and sales management activities.

Different market share objectives for an SBU (build, hold, harvest, divest/liquidate) lead to different objectives for the sales organization. Achieving these different sales organization objectives requires that salespeople perform sales tasks appropriate for the objective. Sales management activities must also be consistent with the objec-

Exhibit 5.3 **SBU Objectives and the Sales Organization**

Market Share Objectives	Sales Organization Objectives	Primary Sales Tasks	Recommended Compensation System
Build	Build sales volume Secure distribution outlets	Call on prospective and new accounts Provide high service levels, particularly pre-sale service Product/market feedback	Salary plus incentive
Hold	Maintain sales volume Consolidate market position through concentration on targeted segments Secure additional outlets	Call on targeted current accounts Increase service levels to current accounts Call on new accounts	Salary plus commission or bonus
Harvest	Reduce selling costs Target profitable accounts	Call on and service most profitable accounts only and eliminate unprofitable accounts Reduce service levels Reduce inventories	Salary plus bonus
Divest/ Liquidate	Minimize selling costs and clear out inventory	Inventory dumping Eliminate service	Salary

Source: Adapted from William Strahle and Rosann L. Spiro, "Linking Market Share Strategies to Salesforce Objectives, Activities, and Compensation Policies," *Journal of Personal Selling and Sales Management,* August 1986, 14 and 15. Used with permission.

tives and tasks as indicated by the recommended compensation system for each market share objective.

Determining strategic objectives for each SBU is an important aspect of corporate strategy. These strategic objectives affect the development of the sales organization's objectives, the selling tasks performed by salespeople, and the activities of sales managers.

Corporate Growth Orientation

Another important aspect of corporate strategy is determining how the corporation will grow and develop over the long term. Most firms begin operations in a core business, then as growth opportunities in this core business diminish over time, management must expand the scope of operations to ensure long-term corporate growth. For example, Kodak (Figure 5.2) can no longer achieve corporate growth objectives within its core photographic business. Therefore, it is moving into the pharmaceutical business, data storage business, and other areas.[13] Sometimes firms must change their growth orientation to adapt to rapid changes in the environment. An example of this situation is presented in "International Sales: Responding to Environmental Changes."

Figure 5.2 **Corporate Growth Orientation for Kodak**

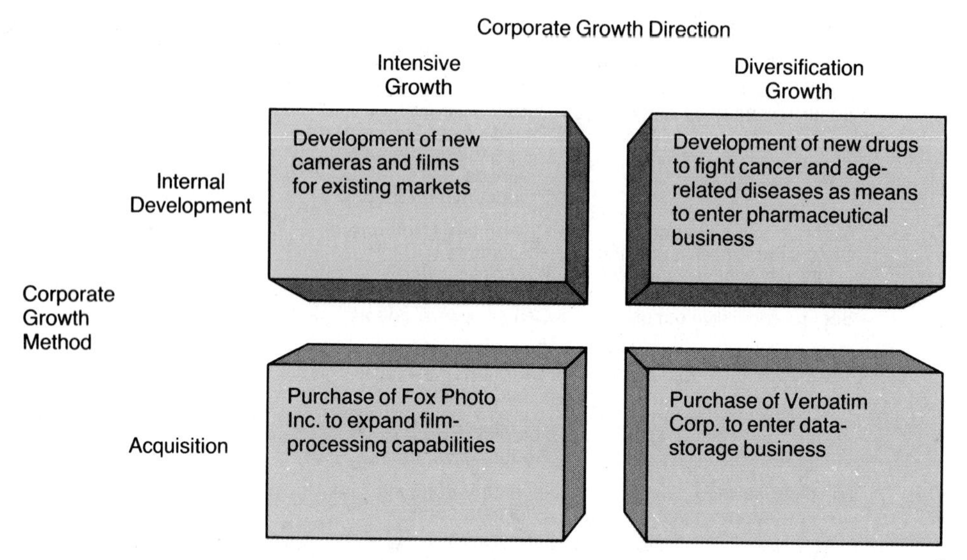

Kodak has chosen to grow in both intensive and diversification directions and by means of both internal development and acquisition.

Source: Leslie Helm, "Why Kodak is Starting to Click Again," *Business Week,* February 23, 1987, 134–138.

The basic corporate growth orientations, presented in Figure 5.3, are **intensive growth** in existing businesses or **diversification growth** by entering new business areas. Corporate strategists can use **internal development** or **acquisition** methods to achieve both intensive growth and diversification growth. Kodak provides a good example of multiple orientations toward corporate growth. The firm is attempting to grow intensively by introducing new products for existing markets and by diversifying into new businesses. These growth directions are being accomplished both through internal development and acquisition.[14]

The corporate growth orientation of a firm has a direct impact on sales management activities. The specific effects depend upon the growth directions and methods employed. Examples of some specific differences in sales management activities for each growth direction and method are presented in Figure 5.3.

Intensive growth through internal development requires sales managers to increase selling effort in existing business areas. This is typically achieved by increasing the size of the salesforce and/or improving the productivity of salespeople. Productivity improvement is normally attempted through training and motivational programs

INTERNATIONAL SALES

RESPONDING TO ENVIRONMENTAL CHANGES

IBM Japan Ltd. had increased its share of installed large computers from 28.1 percent to 32.6 percent in 1985; however, revenues stumbled in 1986 and earnings were down 48 percent in the fourth quarter alone. What caused this poor performance?

IBM Japan Ltd. gets nearly 40 percent of its revenue from computer sales to Japanese manufacturers and about 26 percent from export sales. The strengthening of the yen in world currency markets had a negative impact in both of these areas. The strong yen made Japanese products more expensive in international markets and reduced the export sales of Japanese manufacturers and IBM Japan Ltd. Japanese manufacturers have responded to this situation by scaling back capital expenditures, including those for computer systems.

Takeo Shiina, president of IBM Japan Ltd., is trying to enter new markets to reduce their dependence on manufacturing. Separate marketing and sales teams have been created to focus on financial institutions, retailing, telecommunications, health care, and government markets. Efforts are being made to increase selling effort by hiring more salespeople and increasing the dealer network. More emphasis is also being directed toward improving customer service and toward more aggressive pricing. These strategic changes are expected to return IBM Japan Ltd. to desired growth levels and to provide some protection from volatile changes in world currencies.

Source: *Business Week*, "Just When IBM Was Roaring Back in Japan. . .," February 2, 1987, 70–71.

directed toward increased market penetration and by the use of new technologies in sales operations. For example, firms such as DuPont, Ciba Geigy, John Hancock Mutual Life, GTE, and the Wrangler Division of VF Corp. are equipping salespeople with cellular telephones, laptop computers, and/or hand-held order entry computers to improve their productivity.[15]

Diversification through internal development represents an entirely different sales management challenge. Instead of increasing selling effort in current business areas, sales operations must be developed for new business areas. Since the salesforce must sell different products to different customers, new methods and procedures for recruiting/selecting, training, and motivating salespeople must often be established. The situation faced by Tandy Corp. illustrates some of the difficulties involved. In 1986 Tandy decided to diversify into the business market for personal computers. The Tandy plan was to develop a salesforce of 1,500 to compete against the likes of IBM in the personal computer business market. Tandy expected to be able to apply the retail methods used in its Radio Shack stores to direct sales to business customers. Results for the first year were disappointing. Sales did not meet objectives, turnover was 64 percent for salespeople and 25 percent for store managers, and problems in the sales training and motivational programs were identified. Although Tandy is at-

Figure 5.3 Corporate Growth Orientation and Sales Management Activities

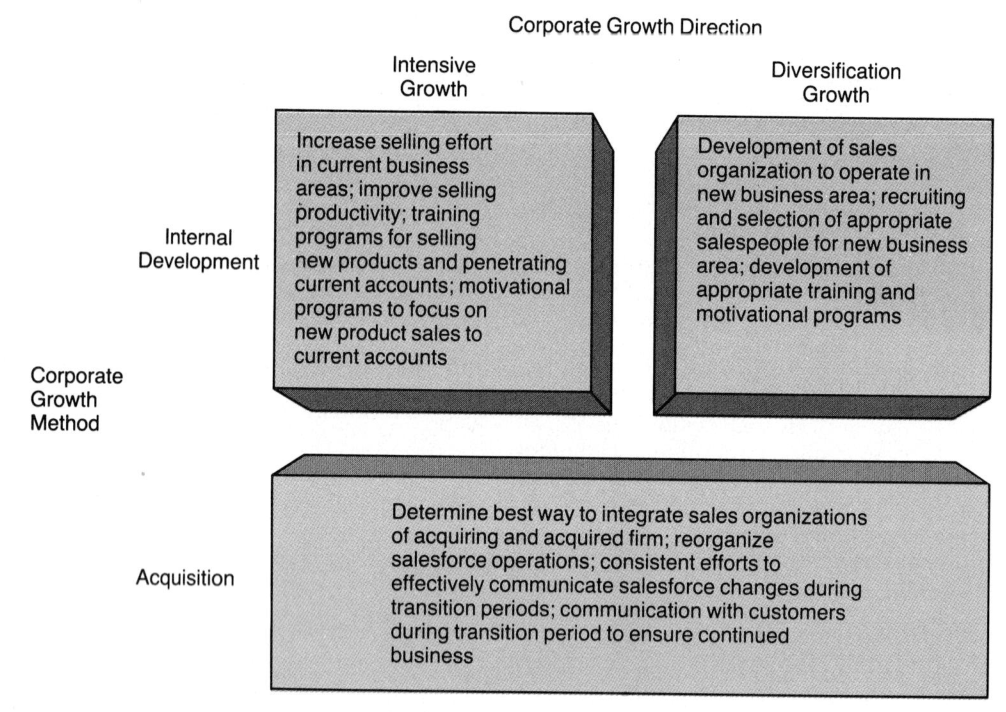

Sales management activities differ considerably depending upon the corporate growth orientation (internal development or acquisitions, intensive growth or diversification growth). Acquisitions present a variety of sales management problems regardless of whether they are used for intensive or diversification growth.

tempting to improve direct sales operations, it serves as an example of diversification bringing difficult and complex sales management problems.[16]

Acquisitions present a different set of problems regardless of whether growth is intensive or by diversification. The key challenge is to determine the best way to integrate the selling operations of the acquiring and acquired firm. Options include a complete merging of the two salesforces, partial merging, or keeping both salesforces separate. Consider the sales management problems associated with the following acquisitions:

- Uniroyal Inc. acquired B. F. Goodrich to form Uniroyal-Goodrich Tire Co. The new company is the nation's second largest tire producer. The firm would like to merge the two salesforces. However, Goodrich has been concentrating on the replacement tire market with selling efforts directed toward tire dealers. In contrast, Uniroyal has been focusing on selling tires to the automobile manufacturers, with General Motors being their largest customer. The critical sales management challenge is to determine how to knit these two different salesforces together.[17]

- Burroughs acquired Sperry to form a new corporation called Unisys. The two companies market incompatible computer lines, so their salesforces remain somewhat separate. Nevertheless, there are areas, such as banking and financial services, where the two lines can supplement each other. Sales management is faced with determining the best way to promote joint selling between the two separate salesforces.[18]

The keys to successful salesforce integration appear to be the development of a specific plan and the effective communication of this plan to salespeople and sales managers from both salesforces and to key customers.[19] One of the major problems during the acquisition and merger process is that rumors abound between the two salesforces and customers, if not addressed effectively by sales managers. Consider the successful approach taken by James River Corp. when acquiring the Northern and Dixie divisions of the then American Can Co. (now Primerica Corp.):

> As soon as the acquisition was announced, key managers were assembled and a personal letter sent to all salespeople to detail what was happening. Every effort was made to communicate with the field salesforce and key customers. Top sales executives met frequently with their sales managers and salespeople to address any and all rumors. Once the integration plan was finalized, sales management began the implementation process. Again, extensive communication between sales management and salespeople and customers was the key to a successful transition.[20]

Although all directions and methods of corporate growth are being employed, there has been an increasing trend toward acquisitions as the preferred route. The number of acquisitions increased from 2,326 in 1982 to approximately 3,600 in 1987.[21] One study found that approximately 70 percent of the 3,788 corporate growth moves by 33 large firms from 1950 to 1986 were acquisitions. Ironically, almost 60 percent of these acquisitions were considered to be failures.[22] Thus, sales managers can expect more opportunities to deal with the problems of acquisition in the future, even though many past acquisitions have failed.

Corporate Strategy Summary

Strategic decisions at the topmost levels of multibusiness corporations provide guidance for strategy development at all lower organizational levels. Even though the personal selling function is often far removed from the corporate level, corporate strategy has both direct and indirect impacts on personal selling and sales management. The corporate mission, definition of strategic business units, determination of strategic business unit objectives, and the establishment of corporate growth orientation all affect sales organization operations. However, corporate strategy decisions have their most immediate impact on business unit strategies.

BUSINESS STRATEGY AND PERSONAL SELLING

Whereas corporate strategy addresses decisions across business units, a separate strategy must be designed for each SBU. The essence of business strategy is competitive advantage: How can each SBU compete successfully against competitive products and services? What differential advantage will each SBU try to exploit in the marketplace? What can each SBU do better than competitors? Answers to these questions provide the basis for business strategies.

Business Unit Strategies

Although developing a business unit strategy is a complex task, several classification schemes have been developed to aid in this endeavor. One of the most popular is Porter's **generic business strategies**,[23] presented in Exhibit 5.4. Each of these generic strategies — **low cost**, **differentiation**, or **niche** — emphasizes a different type of competitive advantage and presents a different challenge for personal selling. For example, Zenith Laboratories follows a low cost strategy by marketing generic drugs in the pharmaceutical industry.[24] Its salesforce concentrates on minimizing costs and emphasizing low price when selling to pharmacy customers. IBM, on the other hand, employs a differentiation strategy that focuses on providing excellent customer service. Its salespeople try to compete not on low price but through high quality products supported by superior customer service. Businesses using niche strategies achieve their competitive advantage by focusing on a specific target market and specializing in meeting the needs of target customers better than competitors. Nichers may also use a low cost or differentiation strategy to appeal to their target segments.

Another useful business strategy typology, suggested by Miles and Snow and presented in Exhibit 5.5,[25] classifies business strategies as prospectors, defenders, or analyzers. Again, the role of personal selling differs depending upon the business strategy category. **Prospectors** are businesses that are continually introducing new products and that use their salesforces to generate more business from existing accounts and to develop new customers. **Defenders** concentrate on maintaining their current market position. The role of their salespeople is to maintain continuing relationships with existing customers. Finally, **analyzers** represent strategies intended to both defend existing business and prospect for new business. The salesforce must, therefore, balance its activities to maintain existing customer relationships and to generate new customers.

Exhibit 5.4 **Generic Business Strategies and Salesforce Activities**

Strategy Type	Role of the Salesforce
Low Cost Supplier	
Aggressive construction of efficient-scale facilities, vigorous pursuit of cost reductions from experience, tight cost and overhead control, usually associated with high relative market share.	Servicing large current customers, pursuing large prospects, minimizing costs, selling on the basis of price, and usually assuming significant order-taking responsibilities.
Differentiation	
Creation of something perceived industrywide as being unique. Provides insulation against competitive rivalry because of brand loyalty and resulting lower sensitivity to price.	Selling nonprice benefits, generating orders, providing high quality of customer service and responsiveness, possibly significant amount of prospecting if high growth industry, selecting customers based on low price sensitivity. Usually requires a high quality salesforce.
Niche	
Service of a particular target market, with each functional policy developed with this target market in mind. Although market share in the industry might be low, the firm dominates a segment within the industry.	To become experts in the operations and opportunities associated with the target market. Focusing customer attention on nonprice benefits and allocating selling time to the target market.

Source: Adapted from William L. Cron and Michael Levy, "Sales Management Performance Evaluation: A Residual Income Perspective," *Journal of Personal Selling and Sales Management*, August 1987, 58. Used with permission.

Both of the business strategy classification schemes are useful, but both oversimplify the situation. Each strategy category actually consists of many different business strategies. For example, firms following a differentiation strategy can attempt to differentiate themselves in any number of ways (customer service, product quality, innovativeness, etc.). The important point is that the role of personal selling must be consistent with the business strategy being employed. For example, an empirical study of the Miles and Snow typology in the financial services industry found that the importance of personal selling and sales management declined when moving from prospector to analyzer to defender strategies.[26]

Salesforce Expenditures

Regardless of the type of strategy employed, a key decision in formulating business strategy is determining the amount to spend on the personal selling function. Business strategists must decide on the relative emphasis warranted for personal selling versus other marketing activities and other business functions as well as the total

Exhibit 5.5 **Miles and Snow Business Strategies and Salesforce Activities**

Strategy Type	Role of the Sales Force
Prospector	
Attempt to pioneer in product/ market development. Offer a frequently changing product line and be willing to sacrifice short-term profits to gain a long-term stronghold in their markets.	Primary focus is on sales volume growth. Territory management emphasizes customer penetration and prospecting.
Defender	
Offer a limited, stable product line to a predictable market. Markets are generally in the late growth or early maturity phase of the product life cycle. Emphasis is on being the low-cost producer through high volume.	Maintain the current customer base. Very little prospecting for new customers is involved. Customer service is emphasized along with greater account penetration.
Analyzer	
Choose high growth markets while holding onto substantial mature markets. Analyzers are an intermediate type of firm. They make fewer and slower product/market changes than prospectors, but are less committed to stability and efficiency than defenders.	Must balance multiple roles: servicing existing customers, prospecting for new customers, uncovering new applications, holding onto distribution of mature products and support campaigns for new products.

Source: Adapted from William L. Cron and Michael Levy, "Sales Management Performance Evaluation: A Residual Income Perspective," *Journal of Personal Selling and Sales Management,* August 1987, 58. Used with permission.

salesforce expenditures. Studies using data from the Profit Impact of Market Strategies (PIMS) provide some general guidelines for these decisions.

One study found that percentage changes in salesforce expenditures had more impact on market share changes than percentage changes in advertising, sales promotion, product quality, customer service, or new products.[27] Although this relationship held across different types of businesses, the study was limited to an investigation of one four-year period. Another study reported that a 5 percent change in salesforce expenditures produced an average 6.5 percent change in market share for both consumer and industrial businesses.[28] Despite the limitations of these studies, the results suggest that management should consider emphasizing personal selling activities and salesforce expenditures when the SBU objective is to increase market share.

Research also suggests complex relationships between salesforce expenditures and different measures of business performance.[29] Relationships between salesforce expenditures and *gross margin* and *return on investment* (ROI) are presented in Figure 5.4. The exhibit indicates a positive relationship between salesforce expenditures and gross margin, confirming the ability of field salesforces to generate sales of high margin products, but a negative relationship with ROI, which emphasizes the high operating costs associated with personal selling. The key implication is that the salesforce expenditure decision is very complex and should be based on analyses that

Figure 5.4 **Salesforce Expense Relationships with Gross Margin and ROI**

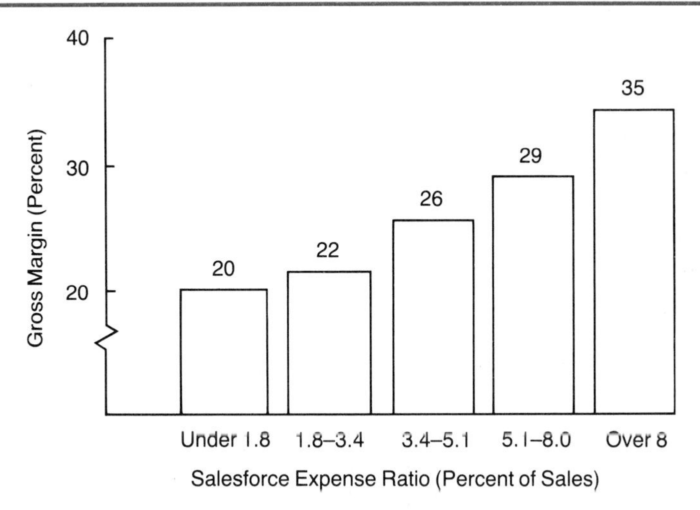

The PIMS (Profit Impact of Market Strategies) results indicate a positive relationship between salesforce expenditures and gross margin. In general, as salesforce expenditures increase, gross margin increases.

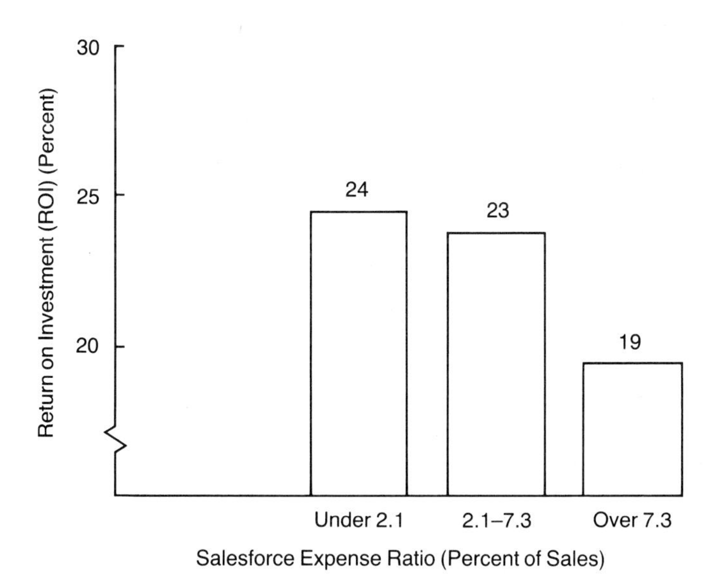

The PIMS (Profit Impact of Market Strategies) results indicate a negative relationship between salesforce expenditures and ROI. In general, as salesforce expenditures increase, ROI decreases.

Source: Dalrymple, Douglas J. and Hans B. Thorelli, "Sales Force Budgeting," *Business Horizons*, July–August 1984, 34.

consider the business unit strategy, market share objectives, and different cost considerations.

Business Strategy Summary

Business strategies determine how each SBU plans to compete in the marketplace. Several approaches are available, placing different demands on the sales organization. A critical decision for all business strategies is determining the total expenditure for the personal selling function. Research results suggest that salesforce expenditures are positively related to market share increases and gross margin, but negatively related to ROI. The role of personal selling depends upon how an SBU plans to compete in the marketplace. The amount an SBU should spend on personal selling requires careful consideration of the business unit strategy, market share objectives and different cost analyses.

MARKETING STRATEGY AND PERSONAL SELLING

Since SBUs typically market multiple products to different customer groups, separate marketing strategies are often developed for each of an SBUs target markets. These marketing strategies must be consistent with the business strategy. For example, marketers operating in an SBU with a differentiation business strategy would probably not develop marketing strategies that emphasize low price. The marketing strategies for each target market should reinforce the differentiation competitive advantage sought by the SBU.

Figure 5.5 illustrates the major components of a marketing strategy and highlights the position of personal selling within the promotional portion of a marketing strategy. The key components of any marketing strategy are the selection of a **target market** and the development of a **marketing mix**. Target market selection requires a definition of the specific market segment to be served. The marketing mix then consists of a marketing offer designed to appeal to the defined target market. This marketing offer contains a mixture of product, price, distribution, and promotional strategies. The critical task for the marketing strategist is to develop a marketing mix that satisfies the needs of the target market better than competitive offerings.

Personal selling may be an important element in the promotional portion of the marketing mix. The promotional strategy consists of a mixture of personal selling, advertising, sales promotion, and publicity, with most promotional strategies emphasizing either personal selling or advertising as the main communication tool. Sales promotion and publicity are typically viewed as supplemental promotional tools. Thus, a key strategic decision is to determine when promotional strategies should be personal-selling driven or advertising-driven. This decision should capitalize on the relative advantages of personal selling and advertising for different target markets and different marketing mixes.

Figure 5.5 **Marketing Strategy and Personal Selling**

Personal selling is an important element of a promotion strategy. The promotion strategy is one element of a marketing mix designed to appeal to a defined target market. A marketing strategy can be defined in terms of target market and marketing mix components.

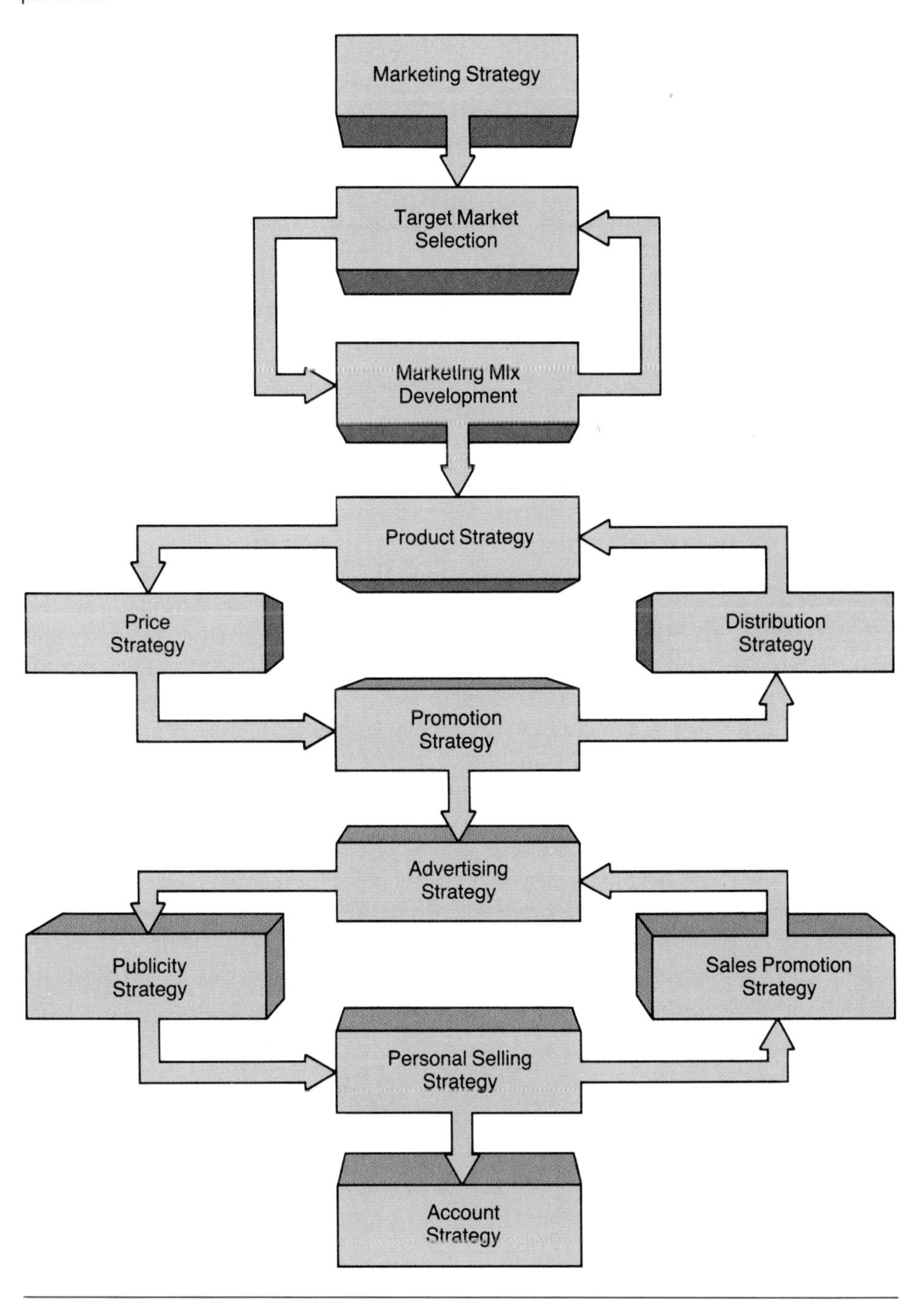

Exhibit 5.6 **Characteristics of Personal Selling and Advertising**

	Impact or Impression	Size of Audience	Cost per Contact	Sales Leads	Message Control	Flexibility	Timing Control	Repetitive Contact	Reaction Speed	Credibility	Closing the Sale
Personal Selling	5	2	1	3	4	5	5	2	5	5	5
Media Advertising	4	5	4	4	5	1	3	5	2	4	2
Publications Advertising	2	4	4	3	5	1	3	3	1	2	1
Direct Mail	4	4	3	4	5	3	3	4	3	3	3

The characteristics of personal selling and different forms of advertising are evaluated on a five-point scale. The higher the score is, the better the evaluation for the promotional tool on a characteristic.

Source: Adapted from George Black, "Why Most Engineers Market Space Age Technology with Low-Tech Mentality," *Business Marketing,* May 1987, 126.

Advantages and Disadvantages of Personal Selling

Personal selling is the only promotional tool that consists of personal communication between seller and buyer, and the advantages and disadvantages of personal selling thus accrue from this personal communication. As indicated in Exhibit 5.6, personal selling possesses major advantages over the different types of advertising: The personal communication between buyer and seller is typically viewed as more credible and has more of an impact (or impression) than messages delivered through advertising media. Personal selling also allows for better timing of message delivery, and it affords the flexibility of communicating different messages to different customers or changing a message during a sales call based on customer feedback. Finally, personal selling has the advantage of allowing a sale to be closed. These characteristics make personal selling a powerful promotional tool.

The major disadvantage of personal selling is the high cost to reach each member of the audience. *Sales and Marketing Management* reported that the median cost of an industrial sales call was $207.21 in 1987.[30] Contrast this with the pennies that it costs to reach an audience member through mass advertising. The benefits of personal selling do not come cheap. They may, however, outweigh its costs for certain types of target market situations and for specific marketing mixes.

Target Market Situations and Personal Selling

The characteristics of personal selling are most advantageous in specific target market situations. As shown in Figure 5.6, personal selling-driven promotional strategies are appropriate when (1) the market consists of only a few buyers that tend to be concentrated in location, (2) when the buyer needs a great deal of information, (3) when

Figure 5.6 **Target Market Characteristics and Promotion Strategy**

Advertising-driven	Balanced	Personal selling-driven
Large	Number and Dispersion of Buyers	Small
Low	Buyers' Information Needs	High
Small	Size and Importance of Purchase	Large
Low	Product Complexity	High
No	Postpurchase Contact Required	Yes

Promotion strategies tend to be advertising-driven or personal selling-driven depending upon the characteristics of the target market being served.

Source: Adapted from David W. Cravens, *Strategic Marketing (Homewood, Ill.: Irwin, 1987), 308.*

the purchase is important, (4) when the product is complex, and (5) when service after the sale is important. The target market characteristics that favor personal selling are similar to those found in most industrial purchasing situations. Thus, personal selling is the preferred promotional tool in **industrial marketing**, while advertising is normally emphasized in consumer marketing situations.

The target market characteristics presented in Exhibit 5.7 are only guidelines and not hard-and-fast rules. Sometimes firms can gain a competitive advantage by developing nontraditional promotional strategies. Take the direct selling industry as an example. Firms such as Avon, Amway, Mary Kay and others market low-priced consumer products. The typical promotional strategy for these types of target markets would be advertising-driven. Yet, the direct selling firms emphasize personal selling and gain much of their competitive advantage from offering the convenience of shopping at home and the personal attention of a salesperson. Retail sales by these direct selling firms reached almost $8.5 billion in 1985.[31]

An effective promotional mix capitalizes on the advantages of each promotional tool. Moreover, characteristics of the target market must be considered, and the promotional mix must also be consistent with the other elements of the marketing mix to ensure a coordinated marketing offer.

Marketing Mix Elements and Personal Selling

One of the most difficult challenges facing the marketing strategist is making sure that decisions concerning the product, distribution, price, and promotion areas result in an effective marketing mix. There are any number of different ways that these elements can be combined to form a marketing mix. However, there tend to be some combinations that represent logical fits. Exhibit 5.6 shows when a personal selling

Exhibit 5.7 **Marketing Mix Elements and Personal Selling**

Marketing Mix Area	Characteristics	Marketing Mix Area	Characteristics
Product or service	Complex products requiring customer application assistance (computers, pollution control systems, steam turbines) Major purchase decisions, such as food items purchased by supermarket chains Features and performance of the product requiring personal demonstration and trial by the customer (private aircraft)	***Channels***	Channel system relatively short and direct to end users Product and service training and assistance needed by channel intermediaries Personal selling needed in "pushing" product through channel Channel intermediaries available to perform personal selling function for supplier with limited resources and experience (brokers or manufacturer's agents)
Price	Final price negotiated between buyer and seller (appliances, automobiles, real estate) Selling price or quantity purchased enable an adequate margin to support selling expenses (traditional department store compared to discount house)		

Source: Cravens, David W., Gerald E. Hills, and Robert B. Woodruff, *Marketing Management* (Homewood, Ill.: Irwin, 1987), 546.

emphasis might fit well with the other marketing elements. Again, these suggestions should be considered only as guidelines, since the development of unique marketing mixes may produce competitive advantages in the marketplace.

An interesting example of a unique promotional strategy exists in the coffee market. The target market characteristics for coffee call for an advertising-driven promotional strategy, since there are a large number of dispersed buyers who are purchasing in small quantities and do not need much information or service. Coffee marketers typically employ indirect distribution channels to reach targeted consumers through various types of retailers. The price to the consumer is normally fixed and sufficiently competitive to produce relatively low margins for the manufacturers. Advertising is used to develop consumer demand and "pull" the product through the channel of distribution. This is the type of marketing mix used by the dominant coffee marketers such as General Foods and Procter & Gamble.

A much smaller, but extremely successful coffee marketer is JFG Coffee Company, which competes in the southeastern United States coffee market. One key to its success is its unique promotional strategy. Although its marketing mix is similar to competitors in the product, distribution, and price areas, its promotional strategy is personal selling-driven rather than advertising-driven. JFG emphasizes personal selling to coffee retailers as a means of "pushing" its products through the distribution channel. Whereas a retailer might see a General Foods or Procter & Gamble salesperson every several months, the JFG salesperson might visit on a weekly or bi-weekly

SALES TECHNOLOGY

INCREASED IMPORTANCE OF PERSONAL SELLING

Scene: Office of a retail chain buyer.
Salesperson: Joe, here are the details of our new promotion. A cents-off coupon, an attractive case allowance, and a heavy schedule of TV spots in your trading area. I think you should order a minimum of 200,000 cases.
Buyer: Wait a second, Frank, let me check my computer. Hmm, your last promotion produced mixed results. It didn't increase overall product category sales or pull new customers into my store. The promotion merely generated a lot of brand churn. I came nowhere near achieving my direct product profitability target. I think I'll order 50,000 cases, unless you can present a stronger argument.

The preceding scenario illustrates the important impact that checkout scanner technology has had in the grocery business. Traditionally, manufacturers have possessed most of the information concerning grocery product sales. The widespread usage of checkout scanners has shifted this information power to the retailer. Retailers can track individual sales by product, category, brand, size, price, flavor, and for causal factors such as coupons, special promotions, or in-store displays.

Manufacturers' salespeople are facing more knowledgeable buyers and must become more information-oriented in planning their sales presentations. Firms are finding it necessary to place more emphasis on the personal selling element of their promotional mix. Although scanner technology has had its greatest impact in the grocery industry, similar situations are expected to face salespeople selling to mass merchandisers, drug stores, discounters, and even department stores in the near future.

Source: Adapted from Thayer C. Taylor, "The Great Scanner Face-Off," *Sales and Marketing Management*, September 1986, 43–46.

basis and spend considerable time arranging shelves, setting up displays, accepting returned merchandise, or addressing other problems. This unique promotional mix has produced strong relationships with retailers and has allowed JFG to compete against much larger firms. Although an emphasis on personal selling in the grocery products business is atypical at this time, changes in technology indicate that personal selling may become more important in nontraditional businesses during the next few years, as commented on in "Sales Technology: Increased Importance of Personal Selling."

Integrating Personal Selling and Advertising

Our discussion to this point has focused on general marketing strategies with an emphasis on when marketing and promotional strategies should be personal selling-driven or advertising-driven. Most firms, however, employ both personal selling and advertising in their promotional mixes. When this is the case, it is important to determine the most effective way to integrate personal selling and advertising efforts.

SALES TREND

BLENDING PERSONAL SELLING AND ADVERTISING IN SPORTS MARKETING

The *Sports Marketing News* estimates that companies spent in excess of $6.2 billion on sports marketing in 1987. These expenditures included advertising on television and radio sports shows, sponsoring sporting events, and hospitality programs at different sporting events. Firms such as 3M Co., MCI Communications Corp., Unisys Corp., and BASF Corp. were big spenders for sports marketing.

The number-one goal of sports marketing is to entertain clients and prospects. Many of the sports marketing programs represent an effective blend of personal selling and advertising in pursuing this goal:

- Konica Business Machines USA Inc. spends 50 to 60 percent of its TV advertising budget on sports shows. It also sponsors the San Jose Golf Classic and invites key dealers to participate in the pro-am tourney. The pro-am tourney provides an opportunity for Konica executives, sales managers, and salespeople to talk informally with dealers in an effort to increase their support for Konica products and cooperative advertising programs.
- Unisys Corp. uses sporting events to demonstrate the performance of its products by providing computerized scoring at the British Open golf tournament, U.S. Tennis Open, and other events. Customers and potential customers are invited to these events, where salespeople in hospitality tents demonstrate how the firm's products can solve complex problems. Sometimes celebrities are used to do the selling. For example, at the U.S. Tennis Open last year, former Wimbledon champion Arthur Ashe demonstrated the Unisys scoring system and the statistical capabilities of Unisys computers to clients and guests. Unisys also advertises on television during these sporting events.

Sports marketing programs are on the increase, and most firms appear to be satisfied with the results from their sports marketing expenditures. According to Gary Tobin of MCI Communications Corp., "Every event contributes many times the revenue over what it costs."

Source: Tom Eisenhart, "Sporting Chances Zap Competitors," *Business Marketing,* January 1988, 92–97.

One typical approach is to use advertising to generate company and product awareness and to identify potential customers. These sales leads are then turned over to the salesforce for personal selling attention. The basic objective is to use low cost-per-contact advertising to identify prospects, while more expensive personal selling efforts are used to turn prospects into customers. The effectiveness of this type of promotional strategy was documented by a study of 2,500 salespeople that found more than 85 percent of the salespeople had received leads from advertising during the past year.[32]

A specific example of effective use of advertising and personal selling is the promotional strategy used by NCR to introduce its Tower computer line into the business market. This promotional strategy had four objectives: (1) to increase brand awareness by 50 percent; (2) to generate high quality leads for the salesforce; (3) to increase sales by 10 percent in six months; and (4) to improve salesforce morale. Although a typical approach would be to advertise in trade publications to increase awareness and generate leads, NCR found these publications to be cluttered with ads from competitors. Therefore, they decided to advertise on television in their largest markets. Ads on programs such as "60 Minutes," "20/20," and major sporting events produced a flood of inquiries, increased brand awareness by more than 50 percent, and improved salesforce morale dramatically. The high quality leads were turned over to a motivated salesforce that then increased sales by 25 percent. NCR Tower computers are now one of the hottest-selling brands.[33]

The NCR story is an example of an effective and unique blend of advertising and personal selling in a marketing strategy. Other such blends of advertising and personal selling in sports marketing have become increasingly popular in recent years. "Sales Trend: Blending Personal Selling and Advertising in Sports Marketing" presents some examples.

Marketing Strategy Summary

Selecting target markets and developing marketing mixes are the key components in marketing strategy development. Marketing strategies must be developed for the target markets served by an SBU and must be consistent with the business unit strategy. One important element of the marketing mix is the promotional mix. The critical task is designing a promotional mix that capitalizes on the advantages of each promotional tool. Personal selling has the basic advantage of personal communication and is emphasized in target market situations and marketing mixes where personal communication is important.

SUMMARY

1. **Define the different strategy levels for multibusiness, multiproduct firms.** Multibusiness, multiproduct firms must make strategic decisions at the corporate, business, marketing, and account levels. Corporate strategy decisions determine the basic scope and direction for the corporate entity through formulating the corporate mission statement, defining strategic business units, setting strategic business unit objectives, and determining corporate growth orientation. Business strategy decisions determine how each business unit plans to compete effectively within its industry. Marketing strategies consist of the selection of target markets and the development of marketing mixes for each product market. Personal selling is an important component of the promotional mix portion of marketing strategies, and a key element in account strategies.
2. **Discuss how corporate strategy decisions affect personal selling.** Corporate strategy decisions provide direction for strategy development at all organizational levels. The corporate mission statement, definition of strategic business units, determination of strategic business unit objectives, and establishment of the corporate growth orientation provide guidelines within which sales managers and

salespeople must operate. Changes in corporate strategy typically lead to changes in sales management and personal selling activities.

3. **Explain the relationships between business strategy and personal selling.** Business strategy decisions determine how each strategic business unit intends to compete. Different business strategies place different demands on the sales organization. Business unit expenditures for personal selling depend upon the specific goals of a strategic business unit.
4. **List the advantages and disadvantages of personal selling as a promotional tool.** Personal selling is the only promotional tool that involves personal communication between buyer and seller. As such, personal selling has the advantage of being able to tailor the promotional message to the specific needs of each customer and to deliver complicated messages. The major disadvantage of personal selling is the high cost to reach individual buyers.
5. **Specify the situations where personal selling is typically emphasized in a marketing strategy.** Marketing strategies tend to be either personal selling-driven or advertising-driven. Personal selling is normally emphasized in industrial markets where there are relatively few buyers, in concentrated locations, who make important purchases of complex products and require a great deal of information and service. Personal selling is also typically emphasized in marketing mixes for complex, expensive products that are distributed through direct channels or through indirect channels using a "push" strategy and when the price affords sufficient margin to support the high costs associated with personal selling.
6. **Describe ways that personal selling and advertising can be blended into effective promotional strategies.** Effective promotional strategies typically consist of a mixture of both personal selling and advertising. Oftentimes, firms use advertising to generate company and brand awareness and to identify potential customers. Personal selling is then used to turn these prospects into customers of the firm's products or services.

Key Terms

- corporate strategy
- business strategy
- marketing strategy
- corporate mission statement
- strategic business unit (SBU)
- business unit portfolio
- intensive growth
- diversification growth
- internal development
- acquisition
- generic business strategies
- low-cost strategy
- differentiation strategy
- niche strategy
- prospectors
- defenders
- analyzers
- Profit Impact of Market Strategies (PIMS)
- target market
- marketing mix
- industrial marketing

Review Questions

1. Discuss how different organizational strategies affect the activities of salespeople and sales managers.
2. How does the corporate mission statement affect personal selling and sales management activities?
3. Explain how SBU expenditures on personal selling could be *negatively* related to ROI and *positively* related to gross margin.
4. How can sales promotion and publicity be used to supplement a personal selling-driven promotional strategy?
5. Why is personal selling typically emphasized in industrial markets and advertising emphasized in consumer markets?
6. What are the critical problems faced by sales managers during and after an acquisition of another firm?
7. Why do most firms employ both personal selling and advertising in their promotional strategies?
8. How would sales management activities differ for an SBU following a differentiation strategy versus an SBU employing a low cost strategy?
9. Explain how changes in the strategic objectives of an SBU might affect the activities of salespeople and sales managers.
10. What are the major sales management problems for firms that are diversifying through internal development?

Application Exercises

1. Identify a recent feature article about a multibusiness, multiproduct corporation from the business press (*Business Week, Forbes, Fortune, Sales and Marketing Management,* etc.). Use the information in the article to describe the firm's corporate strategy, business strategy, marketing strategy, and personal selling operations.
2. Identify three companies that you think employ unique and creative promotional strategies. Explain how each company's promotional strategy is unique and creative. Be sure to highlight the personal selling element in your discussion.
3. Assume that you are the national sales manager for an industrial products firm. Your company's business strategy is to develop a competitive advantage based on excellent customer service. What are five things that you might do as national sales manager to ensure that this competitive advantage is developed throughout the sales organization?
4. The Industrial Products Corporation is in the process of developing budgets for the coming year. As the marketing vice-president, you have been listening to presentations by the firm's national sales manager and advertising manager concerning budget requests for personal selling and advertising activities. As might be expected, the national sales manager argues for more personal selling expenditures, while the advertising manager argues for more advertising expenditures. How would you arrive at the final budget decision? What factors would be most important for you to consider in your decision process?

5. Watch a major sports event with a corporate sponsor on television. Based on advertisements and other information provided during the telecast, describe the corporate sponsor's promotional program. Suggest ways that personal selling might be incorporated into this promotional program.

Notes

[1]David W. Cravens, *Strategic Marketing* (Homewood, Ill.: Irwin, 1987), 12.

[2]John A. Pearce, II, and Fred David, "Corporate Mission Statements: The Bottom Line," *Academy of Management Executive,* May 1987, 109.

[3]See Donald P. Robin and R. Eric Reidenbach, "Social Responsibility, Ethics, and Marketing Strategy: Closing the Gap between Concept and Application," *Journal of Marketing,* January 1987, 44–58, for an interesting discussion concerning the integration of ethical considerations into strategic planning.

[4]Gene R. Laczniak and Patrick E. Murphy, "Incorporating Marketing Ethics into the Organization," *Marketing Ethics: Guidelines for Managers* edited by Gene R. Laczniak and Patrick E. Murphy (Lexington, Mass.: Lexington Books, 1985), 104.

[5]Lawrence B. Chonko and Shelby D. Hunt, "Ethics and Marketing Management: An Empirical Investigation," *Journal of Business Research,* August 1985, 339–359.

[6]Daniel B. Moskowitz and John A. Byrne, "Where Business Goes to Stock Up on Ethics," *Business Week,* October 14, 1985, 66.

[7]Federal Industries, *Corporate Long-Range Plan 1987–1995,* v.

[8]Cravens, *Strategic Marketing,* 52.

[9]National Analysts, *Marketing Organization Structure in Large Multiproduct/Multiservice Companies,* October 1985, 10.

[10]"AT&T's Shotgun Wedding," *Sales and Marketing Management,* November 1986, 25–26.

[11]See Cravens, *Strategic Marketing,* 74–83, for a more complete discussion of these analytical tools.

[12]"The New Breed of Strategic Planner," *Business Week,* September 17, 1984, 63.

[13]Leslie Helm, "Why Kodak is Starting to Click Again," *Business Week,* February 23, 1987, 134–138.

[14]Helm, *Business Week,* 135.

[15]A. J. Magrath, "Are You Overdoing 'Lean and Mean'?", *Sales and Marketing Management,* January 1988, 47–50.

[16]Todd Mason and Geoff Lewis, "Tandy Finds a Cold, Hard World Outside the Radio Shack," *Business Week,* August 31, 1987, 68–70.

[17] Adapted from "Can Goodrich and Uniroyal Keep Each Other Off the Skids?" *Business Week,* February 10, 1986, 28.

[18]Excerpted from "Burroughs Chief on the Road," *Sales and Marketing Management,* July 1986, 32–34.

[19]Kate Bertrand, "When Silence Isn't Golden," *Business Marketing,* February 1987, 62–69; and Kevin E. Carey, "Merging Two Salesforces into One," *Sales and Marketing Management,* March 1987, 102–104.

[20]James H. Huguet, Jr., "Blending Sales Forces After Acquisition," *Mergers and Acquisitions,* Summer 1984, 57.

[21]Al Urbanski, "What Marketers Need to Know," *Sales and Marketing Management,* February 1987, 30.

[22] Michael E. Porter, "From Competitive Advantage to Corporate Strategy," *Harvard Business Review,* May-June 1987, 43–59.

[23]Michael E. Porter, *Competitive Strategy* (New York: The Free Press, 1980), 34–46.

[24]Bill Kelley, "Zenith Labs on a New Product High," *Sales and Marketing Management,* October 1986, 42–45.

[25]Raymond E. Miles and Charles C. Snow, *Organizational Strategy, Structure, and Process* (New York: McGraw-Hill, 1978).

[26]Stephen W. McDaniel and James W. Kolari, "Marketing Strategy Implications of the Miles and Snow Strategic Typology," *Journal of Marketing,* October 1987, 19–30.

[27]Charles Lillis, James Cook, Roger Best, and Del Hawkins, "Marketing Strategy to Achieve Market Share Goals," in *Strategic Marketing and Management,* edited by H. Thomas and D. Gardner (New York: John Wiley, 1985), 181–191.

[28]Robert D. Buzzell and Frederick D. Wiersema, "Successful Share Building Strategies," *Harvard Business Review,* January–February 1981, 135–144.

[29]Douglas J. Dalrymple and Hans B. Thorelli, "Sales Force Budgeting," *Business Horizons,* July-August 1984, 31–36.

[30]"1988 Survey of Selling Costs" *Sales and Marketing Management,* February 22, 1988, 12.

[31]Direct Selling Association, *A Statistical Study of the Direct Selling Industry in the United States: 1980–1985,* Washington, D.C.: Direct Selling Association, October 1986, 3.

[32]Reported in "Salespeople Find Advertising Works," *Sales and Marketing Management,* January 1987, 20–22.

[33]David Perry, "Award-Winning Marketing That Sells," *Business Marketing,* March 1987, 129–131.

CHAPTER 6

PERSONAL SELLING AND ACCOUNT MANAGEMENT AND ACCOUNT COVERAGE STRATEGIES

Learning Objectives

After completing this chapter, you should be able to

1. Discuss the important concepts behind organizational buyer behavior.
2. Explain the different approaches to developing an account management strategy.
3. Describe the different account coverage strategies.
4. Discuss the basic interrelationships between account management strategy and account coverage strategy.

UNIQUE ACCOUNT STRATEGIES FOR THE BANKING INDUSTRY: WELLS FARGO

Wells Fargo is one of the most profitable big banks in the United States, due in large part to its rather unusual account strategies. Its corporate strategy calls for aggressive, decentralized retail and commercial business units. The commercial business unit employs a focused strategy that emphasizes loans to California firms with sales between $2 and $100 million. The marketing strategy for the commercial business unit is the most unique aspect of Wells Fargo's strategy. Since commercial banking products and prices are very similar throughout the industry, bank marketing strategies typically emphasize advertising as a means for differentiation. Wells Fargo, however, does no advertising. Instead, personal selling is the key marketing strategy element. As stated by Bob Hanvey, southern California sales manager: "One of the reasons we don't advertise is that we have people on the streets and no one else does."

The success of this unique strategic approach requires the development and execution of appropriate account strategies. Strategic decisions from the organization's perspective must be translated into effective strategies for individual accounts. This is the essence of account strategies. Let's examine the account strategies used by Wells Fargo.

First, the cornerstone of Wells Fargo's success is an account management strategy that emphasizes the development of profitable, long-term relationships with selected business accounts. The bank employs 29 salespeople at 22 Commercial Banking Group offices throughout California to develop these relationships. As stated by Bob Hanvey: "Their job is to just go out and build relationships."

The second type of account strategy concerns the different methods used to build and maintain account relationships. Initial contacts are made by telephone. This is followed by a personal sales call from a member of the bank's salesforce. After the account's financial needs have been determined, a financial services package is proposed to satisfy the identified needs. The salesperson and a commercial

---

Source: Adapted from Al Urbanski, "Wells Fargo's Sales Force Tames the West," *Sales and Marketing Management,* January 1987, 38–41.

loan officer then make a joint sales call to present the financial services package to the account. As the banking relationship becomes established, account servicing becomes the responsibility of the commercial loan officer. The salesperson is then available to locate new prospects and to establish new relationships. Different account coverage methods are used at different account relationship stages.

Wells Fargo salespeople are limited to calling on middle market companies because of the focused business strategy. However, within this segment the strategy is to identify quickly the best prospects. Expensive selling time is spent only with prospects having high potential for the development of profitable banking relationships. The salespeople attempt to find middle market businesses that already have a satisfactory relationship with a bank. This focuses selling attention on the best types of accounts. The salespeople then spend their selling effort in trying to get the prospect to switch to Wells Fargo for their financial service needs.

The account strategies employed by Wells Fargo have been extremely successful. The bank had a 38 percent increase in earnings for the first three quarters of 1986. Profitability is emphasized in all elements of its account strategies. The focus on long-term relationships and the use of different coverage methods at different stages of relationship development are designed to generate profitable business for Wells Fargo.

Sales management activities are also designed to reinforce this profit emphasis. The sales compensation program provides a good example. Each quarter the bank determines how much profit it has made from each commercial account. The salesperson who brought in this business is paid a percentage of the profit. No profit, no pay. Thus, Wells Fargo emphasizes the quality of account relationships through its sales management activities.

CORPORATE, business, and marketing strategies are developed from the perspective of the organization; customers are viewed as aggregate markets or market segments. The three different types of strategies provide direction and guidance for personal selling activities, but then the sales managers and salespeople must translate these general organizational strategies into specific strategies for individual accounts. As illustrated in the Wells Fargo example, effective account strategies are necessary for successful firm performance.

In most cases, sales managers, who play merely a supporting role in the development of corporate, business, and marketing strategies, are the major players in the development and execution of account strategy. Therefore, this entire chapter is devoted to discussing the key types of account strategy. Account strategy is important for two basic reasons. First, it has a major impact on a firm's sales and profit performance. Second, it influences many other sales management decisions. Salesforce recruiting/selecting, training, compensation, and performance evaluations are all affected by the account strategies employed by a firm.

This chapter is organized in the following manner: First, an account strategy framework is presented for the chapter, showing the close relationship between account strategy and organizational buyer behavior. Next, each element of this framework is examined, beginning with organizational buyer behavior. Then, two basic areas of account strategy are covered: account management strategy and account coverage strategy.

THE ACCOUNT STRATEGY FRAMEWORK

Since personal selling-driven promotional strategies are typical in industrial marketing, our discussion of account strategy focuses on industrial, or organizational, customers. These customers will be referred to as *accounts*. Thus, an account strategy must be based on the important and unique aspects of organizational buyer behavior. A framework that integrates organizational buyer behavior and account strategy is presented in Figure 6.1.

The four critical elements in organizational buyer behavior — buying situation, buying center, buying process, and buying needs — are discussed in detail later in this chapter. Each element must be understood in order to develop an effective account strategy. The key strategic decisions of account management strategy and account coverage strategy are also discussed in depth later in this chapter.

ORGANIZATIONAL BUYER BEHAVIOR

Organizational marketing is typically different from consumer goods marketing. The differences presented in Exhibit 6.1 are largely due to differences in the buying behavior of organizations and consumers. Compared to consumer buyer behavior, the unique aspects of organizational buyer behavior revolve around the buying situation, buying center, buying process, and buying needs.[1] Understanding these concepts in general and being able to apply them to specific accounts is necessary for the development of successful account strategies.

Buying Situation

One of the key determinants of organizational buyer behavior is the buying situation faced by an account. Three major types are possible, each representing its own problems for the buying firm and each having different strategic implications for the selling firm.

Figure 6.1 **The Account Strategy Framework**

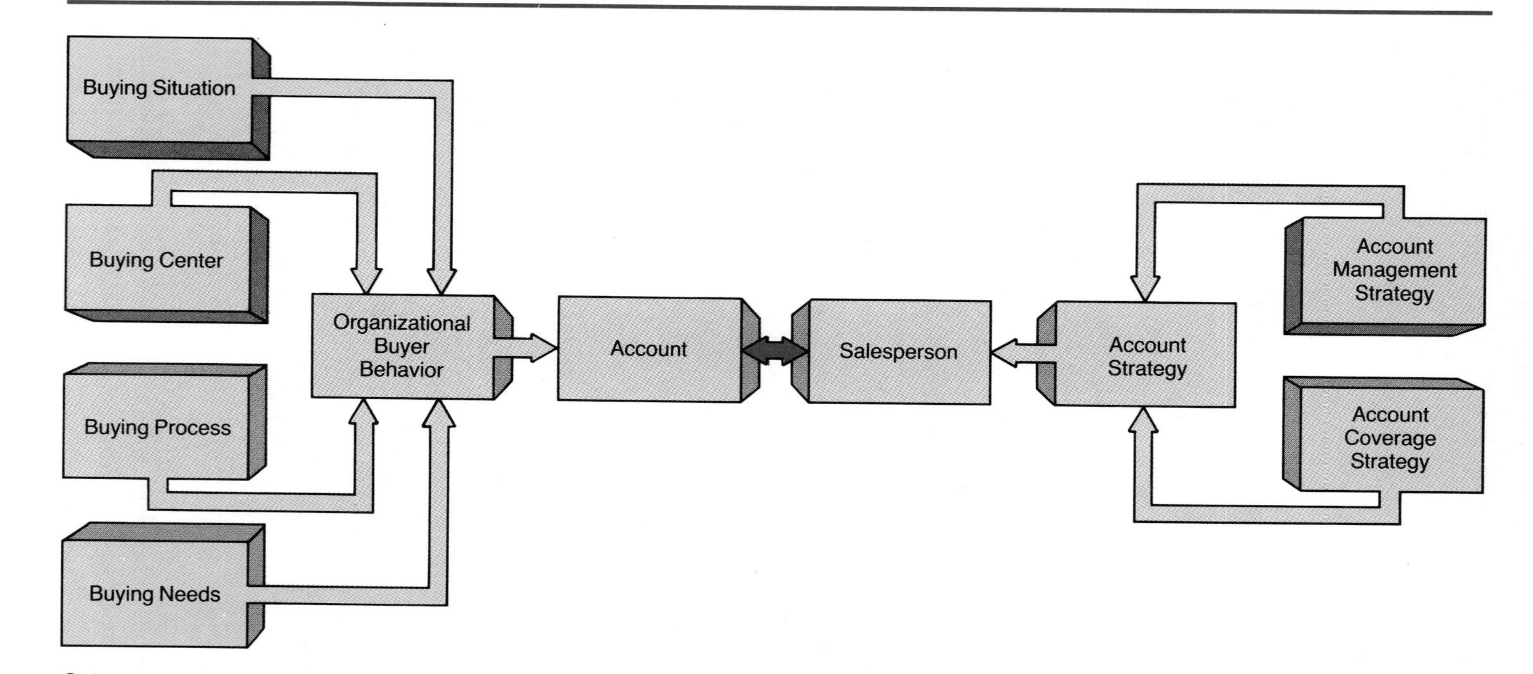

Salesperson interaction with different accounts is directed by an account strategy. The account strategy, which defines how the account is to be managed and how it is to be covered, must be based on an understanding of the buying situation, buying center, buying process, and buying needs of the account.

Exhibit 6.1 **Comparison of Organizational and Consumer Goods Marketing**

	Industrial Marketing	Consumer Marketing
Product	More technical in nature; exact form often variable; accompanying services very important.	Standardized form; service important, but less so.
Price	Competitive bidding for unique items; list prices for standard items.	List prices.
Promotion	Emphasis on personal selling.	Emphasis on advertising.
Distribution	Shorter, more direct channels to market.	Passes through a number of intermediate links en route to consumer.
Customer Relations	More enduring and complex.	Less frequent contact; relationship of a shorter duration.
Consumer Decision-Making Process	Involvement of diverse group of organizational members in decision.	Individual or household unit makes decision.

Source: Michael D. Hutt and Thomas W. Speh, *Industrial Marketing Management* (Hinsdale, Ill.: The Dryden Press, 1985), 12.

A new **task buying situation**, in which the organization is purchasing a product for the first time, poses the most problems for the buyer. Since the account has little knowledge or experience as a basis for making the purchase decision, it will typically use a lengthy process to collect and evaluate purchase information.

A **modified rebuy buying situation** exists when the account has previously purchased and used the product. Although the account has information and experience with the product, it will usually want to collect additional information and may make a change when purchasing a replacement product.

The least complex buying situation is the **straight rebuy buying situation**, wherein the account has considerable experience in using the product and is satisfied with the current purchase arrangements. In this case the buyer is merely reordering from the current supplier.

The buying situation faced by an account affects all aspects of organizational buyer behavior and has important implications for account strategy development. In general, as organizations move from new task buying situations to modified rebuy and straight rebuy situations, fewer members of the organization are involved in the buying process. The buying process itself also becomes less involved. Selling organizations must adjust the account strategy depending upon the account's buying situation. For example, the strategy for selling facsimile machines will differ depending upon whether the account has ever purchased a facsimile machine (new task situation) or whether the account is replacing an existing facsimile machine (modified rebuy situation). The most difficult task for a selling organization is to obtain an order from an account that represents a straight rebuy situation for a competitor.

Buying Center

One of the most important characteristics of organizational buyer behavior to examine is the involvement of the many individuals from the firm that participate in the purchasing process. The term **buying center** has been used to designate these individuals. The buying center is not a formal designation on the organization chart, but rather an informal network of purchasing participants. (However, members of the purchasing department are typically included in most buying centers and are normally represented in the formal organizational structure.) The difficult task facing the selling firm is to identify all the buying center members and to determine the specific role of each.

The possible roles that buying center members might play in a particular purchasing decision are

- *Initiators,* who start the organizational purchasing process.
- *Users,* who use the product to be purchased.
- *Gatekeepers,* who control the flow of information between buying center members.
- *Influencers,* who provide input for the purchasing decision.
- *Deciders,* who make the final purchase decision.
- *Purchasers,* who implement the purchasing decision.

Each buying center role may be performed by more than one individual, and each individual may perform more than one buying center role. Take, for example, the roles for the telecommunications purchase illustrated in Exhibit 6.2. In this example, the corporate telecommunications department and vice-president of data processing both perform influencer roles, while the corporate purchasing and telecommunications departments act as gatekeepers. The telecommunications department is active in this purchasing decision as influencers, gatekeepers, and users.

The strategic implications of the buying center concept are that account strategy must be based on a comprehensive understanding of the buying center for a particular purchasing situation. This includes an identification of all members of the buying center and of the specific purchasing role performed by each member. It is important to define the buying center in terms of departments and individuals within departments; therefore, the buying center description in Exhibit 6.2 provides only a general framework — more information is needed to identify the specific individuals within each department that are involved in the buying center.

Exhibit 6.2 **Buying-Center Roles for Telecommunications Purchase**

Initiator	Division general manager proposes to replace the company's telecommunications system.
Decider	Vice-president of administration selects, with influence from others, the vendor the company will deal with and the system it will buy.
Influencers	Corporate telecommunications department and the vice-president of data processing have important say about which system and vendor the company will deal with.
Purchaser	Corporate purchasing department completes the purchase according to predetermined specifications by negotiating or receiving bids from suppliers.
Gatekeeper	Corporate purchasing and corporate telecommunications departments analyze the company's needs and recommend likely matches with potential vendors.
Users	All division employees who use the telecommunications equipment.

Source: Reprinted by permission of the *Harvard Business Review*. An exhibit from "Major Sales: Who Really Does the Buying?" by Thomas V. Bonoma (May-June 1982). Copyright © 1982 by the President and Fellows of Harvard College; all rights reserved.

Buying Process

Organizational buyer behavior can be viewed as a **buying process** consisting of several phases. Although this process has been presented in different ways, the following phases represent a general consensus:[2]

Phase 1. Initiating the purchase.

Phase 2. Determining the type of product to be purchased.

Phase 3. Developing specifications for the product.

Phase 4. Evaluating supply sources.

Phase 5. Selecting specific suppliers.

Phase 6. Determining the amount of expenditure.

Phase 7. Finalizing purchase authorization.

These buying phases may be formalized for some firms and/or for certain purchases. In other situations, this process may only be a rough approximation of what actually occurs. Nevertheless, viewing organizational buying as a multiple-phase process is helpful in developing account strategy. A major objective of any account strategy is to facilitate an account's movement through this process in a manner that will lead to a purchase of the seller's product.

Using the organizational buying process as a basis for account strategy development requires an understanding of who and what is involved at each phase for a

Exhibit 6.3 **Personal and Organizational Needs**

Personal Goals	Organizational Goals
Want a feeling of power	Control cost in product use situation
Seek personal pleasure	Few breakdowns of product
Desire job security	Dependable delivery for repeat purchases
Want to be well liked	Adequate supply of product
Want respect	Cost within budget limit

Source: David W. Cravens, Gerald E. Hills, Robert B. Woodruff, *Marketing Management* (Homewood, Ill.: Irwin, 1987), 161.

particular account. Although detailed analyses of specific accounts is desirable, there are often general patterns used by similar types of firms. For example, a study in the metalworking industry found that different departments had more influence at different phases. The findings from this study suggested that the typical buying center for firms in the metalworking industry consist of individuals from engineering, purchasing, production, and corporate management. These buying center members do not participate equally throughout the entire decision process. Engineering and production personnel have most influence in the earlier stages, while corporate management and purchasing are most influential at the later stages.[3] From an account strategy perspective, this suggests the need to spend effort on different individuals at different phases of the organizational purchasing process.

Buying Needs

Organizational buying is typically viewed as goal-directed behavior intended to satisfy specific **buying needs**. Although the organizational purchasing process is made to satisfy organizational needs, the buying center consists of individuals who are also trying to satisfy individual needs throughout the decision process. Exhibit 6.3 presents examples of individual and organizational needs that might be important in a purchase situation. Individual needs tend to be career-related, while organizational needs reflect factors related to the use of the product.

Even though organizational purchasing is often thought to be almost entirely objective, subjective personal needs are often extremely important in the final purchase decision. For example, an organization may want to purchase a computer to satisfy data-processing needs. Although a number of suppliers might be able to provide similar products, some suppliers at lower cost than others, buying center members might select the most well-known brand to reduce purchase risk and protect job security.

The personal and organizational needs vary in importance across members of the buying center. A study of the different organizational needs for different buying center members in the heating and air conditioning industry indicated that production engineers and plant managers were most interested in operating cost, corporate engineers with the initial product cost, and top management with state-of-the-art technology.[4]

We discussed how the influence of buying center members varies at different buying phases in the last section. Couple this with the different needs of different buying center members, and the complexity of organization buying behavior is evident. Nevertheless, sales managers must understand this behavior in order to develop account strategies that will satisfy the personal and organizational needs of buying center members.

ACCOUNT STRATEGY

Sales managers and salespeople are typically responsible for strategic decisions at the account level. Although the firm's marketing strategy provides basic guidelines — an overall game plan — the battles are won on an account-by-account basis. Without the design and execution of effective account strategies, the marketing strategy cannot be successfully implemented.

Take, for example, the highly competitive minicomputer industry, where Digital Equipment Corp. has taken market share from IBM in the financial services and data-processing markets. IBM has responded by changing its marketing strategy through the introduction of new products and the addition of services. The success of these strategic changes, however, depends upon IBM's ability to develop, maintain, and expand relationships with individual accounts. Evidence of this ability is suggested by the $200 million contract recently negotiated with Ford Motor Co.[5]

Our framework suggests two basic account strategies: account management strategy and account coverage strategy. We will consider each of these as a separate, but related, strategic decision area. Account strategies are ultimately developed for each individual account; however, the strategic decisions are often made by classifying individual accounts into similar categories.

Account Management Strategy

An **account management strategy** must be developed to ensure the creation of new customers and to maintain and expand business with existing customers. Many firms have taken a rather myopic view of account management and have concentrated entirely on generating sales of individual products.[6] This orientation is changing as technology increases in complexity and service becomes more essential. As a result, the characteristics of organizational exchanges are evolving into closer and longer-lasting relationships (see Exhibit 6.4). Organizational buyers are increasingly purchasing systems and contracts with long lead times for development and usage, bringing

Exhibit 6.4 **Characteristics of Organizational Exchanges**

Category	Past	Present	Future
Item	Product	Augmented product	System contracts
Sale	Unit	System	System/time
Value	Feature advantages	Technology advantages	System advantages
Lead time	Short	Long	Lengthy
Service	Modest	Important	Vital
Delivery place	Local	National	Global
Delivery phase	Once	Frequently	Continuous
Strategy	Sales	Marketing	Relationship

Source: Theodore Levitt, *The Marketing Imagination* (New York: The Free Press, 1984), 116.

more emphasis to the development of long-term relationships between buyers and sellers:

> The sale, then, merely consummates the courtship, at which point the marriage begins. How good the marriage is depends on how well the seller manages the relationship. The quality of the marriage determines whether there will be continued or expanded business, or troubles and divorce. . . Under these conditions, a purchase decision is not a decision to buy an item (to have a casual affair) but a decision to enter a bonded relationship (to get married).[7]

The appropriate account strategy for this type of situation has been termed **relationship marketing.** It consists of developing long-term relationships with individual accounts by producing buyer satisfaction with current purchases and ensuring the capability to satisfy future purchasing needs. Successful relationship marketing requires a firm and often expensive commitment for an extended period from both the seller and the buyer.

Although relationship marketing may be the desirable strategy for most accounts, it is not always possible. Figure 6.2 presents a continuum of purchasing orientations used by organizational buyers and the appropriate account management strategy for each orientation.[8] At one extreme, organizational buyers using this model are commited to one vendor and desire long-term relationships. Sellers must be willing to invest considerable resources to establish and maintain a relationship with these types of accounts. If the account is lost, it is very difficult to win back. Thus, this situation has been termed the *lost-for-good model.* It often applies in industries such as computer mainframes, communications equipment, office automation systems, heavy construction equipment, and aircraft engines. Relationship marketing is the appropriate account management strategy when buyers use the lost-for-good model.

At the other extreme, organizational buyers desire to share patronage among multiple suppliers. Emphasis is short-term and focused on each individual sales transaction. There is little commitment to a long-term relationship between buyer and

Figure 6.2 **Organizational Purchasing Orientations**

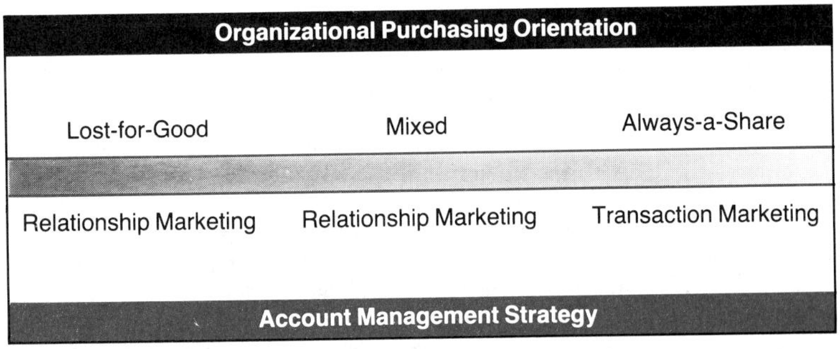

Organizational Purchasing Orientation		
Lost-for-Good	Mixed	Always-a-Share
Relationship Marketing	Relationship Marketing	Transaction Marketing
Account Management Strategy		

The appropriate type of account management strategy depends upon the purchasing orientation of an account. Most situations, however, favor relationship marketing.

Source: Adapted by permission of the publisher from *Winning and Keeping Industrial Customers* by Barbara Bund Jackson (Lexington Books, Copyright 1985, D.C. Heath & Co.) p. 88.

seller. This situation has been referred to as the *always-a-share model.* The always-a-share model typically applies in industries such as commodity chemicals, carbon steel, computer terminals, and shipping services. **Transaction marketing** is the appropriate account management strategy when buyers use the always-a-share model.

Most accounts actually operate somewhere between the lost-for-good and always-a-share extremes. Relationship marketing should be used to try to move these accounts toward the lost-for-good model. The general approach is to attempt to satisfy both short-term and long-term needs and make it difficult and risky for the account to switch to another vendor. An example of the use of technology to build relationships and to move accounts toward the lost-for-good model is presented in "Sales Technology: Computer-to-Computer Ordering."

There appears to be a growing trend toward relationship marketing account strategies. Manufacturers, wholesalers, and even retailers are emphasizing the importance of customer relationships. Consider the following examples:

- Dupont, the large chemical manufacturer, focuses a large portion of sales training efforts on teaching its technical sales representatives the importance of and procedures for developing customer relationships.[9]
- Bergen Brunswig, the pharmaceutical wholesaler, has pioneered the concept of *single supplier* by using computers and various services provided by salespeople to develop long-term relationships with independent, chain, and hospital pharmacies.[10]
- Nordstrom, the soft goods retailer, has been extremely successful by developing customer relationships through exceptional service by retail salespeople. As one salesperson explained, "Nordstrom tells me to do whatever I need to do to make you [the customer] happy. Period."[11]

SALES TECHNOLOGY

COMPUTER-TO-COMPUTER ORDERING

A recent study by the Conference Board identified a growing trend toward computer-to-computer ordering. Advances in computer hardware and software make it possible for a purchase order to originate from a customer's office, be transmitted by telephone cable to the supplier, and processed at the supplier's office. Customers can also check on the status of their order at any time through the computer network.

Since steel is a commodity, customers tend to follow the always-a-share model by using different suppliers for their steel needs. Inland Steel has developed a computer-to-computer ordering system to develop account relationships and move customers toward the lost-for-good model. The system provides an electronic link between the customer and Inland's sales department and steel mills. A customer can place an order electronically and then can check on the status of the order at any time. When the order is shipped, Inland transmits the shipping information directly to the customer.

The computer-to-computer ordering system has helped Inland Steel improve relationships with its accounts. According to William Sanders, general manager of systems, Inland Steel tries to "maintain as strong a customer relationship as we can, and service is a major area of company differentiation. We try to make it as administratively easy to order as we can."

Source: Adapted from Howard Sutton, *Rethinking the Company's Selling and Distribution Channels* (New York: The Conference Board, 1986), 26; and "At Inland Steel, Salespeople are Customers Too," *Sales and Marketing Management*, June 1986, 62.

- Charles F. Terasi has been a direct salesperson for the Fuller Brush Co. for 49 years. He has developed relationships with customers that have lasted over 15 years by providing personalized service and recommending the best products for each customer's specific needs.[12]

Account Coverage Strategy

Account coverage strategy — ensuring that accounts receive selling effort coverage in an effective and efficient manner — is necessary to implement account management strategies. Various methods are available to provide selling coverage to accounts, including a company salesforce, industrial distributors, independent representatives, selling centers, telemarketing, and trade shows. Many firms employ multiple distribution channels and multiple account coverage methods for their products. For example, IBM markets its personal computers directly to larger customers, using its own salesforce, and indirectly to smaller customers through distributors that might use inside and/or outside salesforces as well as telemarketing.

It is also typical to use different account coverage methods at different stages of relationship building. Wells Fargo, as described in the opening vignette, uses telemarketing to open a relationship, its own salespeople to establish a relationship, and commercial loan officers to maintain and build a relationship. Since most of this book is concerned with management of a company field salesforce, our discussion of account coverage strategy will focus on alternatives to the typical company field salesforce.

Industrial Distributors. One alternative for covering accounts is to employ **industrial distributors** — channel middlemen that take title to the goods that they market to end users. These distributors typically employ their own field salesforce and may carry (1) the products of only one manufacturer, (2) related but noncompeting products from different manufacturers, or (3) competing products from different manufacturers. Firms that use industrial distributors normally have a relatively small company salesforce to serve and support the efforts of the distributor.

The use of distributors is prevalent and increasing in the industrial marketplace. One study found that only 24 percent of industrial marketers used direct distribution exclusively, while 76 percent used some type of intermediary to reach end users, with industrial distributors being the most prominent.[13] Another study found that 25 percent of responding firms expect to be more dependent upon industrial distributors during the next five years.[14] Industrial distributors can provide a cost-effective means for covering accounts.

The use of industrial distributors adds another member to the distribution channel. Although these distributors should not be considered as final customers, they should be treated like customers. Developing positive, long-term relationships with distributors is necessary for success. Indeed, the development of a partnership with distributors can be the key to success. As one marketing executive noted,

> If manufacturers develop loyal partnerships with distributors in this country, they probably can hold off or neutralize foreign competition. I'm not sure a lot of manufacturers realize that, but it's a very viable defense.[15]

Black and Decker's U.S. Power Tool Group is one firm that apparently recognizes the importance of distributor relationships as a means to combat foreign competition. Despite intense competition from overseas manufacturers, Black and Decker's sales have grown from $1.1 billion to $1.8 billion during the past four years. Much of this success can be attributed to improved relationships with distributors. Black and Decker has started distributor advisory councils, a formal sales training program for distributors, and is making joint sales calls with distributors' salespeople. The net effect of these efforts is that more than 4,000 distributor salespeople, rather than just the company's 275 salespeople, are actively pushing Black and Decker's products.[16].

Many firms are using advanced technology to strengthen relationships with distributors. For example, Apple Computer has developed AppleLink as a two-way electronic message system between distributors and the corporate office. The system is handling approximately 5,000 inquiries each month.[17] Ford Motor Company uses the Truck Order and Pricing System (TIPS) as an electronic communications program for industrial vehicle distributors to process orders, check the compatibility of orders, and produce price quotes. Training distributor salespeople is also being performed

Exhibit 6.5 **Company Salesforce and Industrial Distributors**

Salesperson and Tasks	Key Skills
Teacher of selling skills; ROI selling; product applications knowledge, market knowledge; display techniques (walk-in business).	Excellent presenter; listener; counselor; coach
Reviewer of sales by product mix; sales vs. forecasted quota; competitive activity in distributor's area; inventory stocking vs. targets; distributor's participation in promotions.	Analyzer; prober; trader of information; forecaster
Working partner on joint "buddy calls" to end-user accounts; sales blitzes at targeted industries; trade show activity at shared booths; lead program follow-up; distributor showroom programs on demo day.	Hands-on demonstrator; leader by showing sales professionalism
Ambassador about terms of sale, credit, warranties, and leasing; promotions, contests, new product launches; co-op plans on advertising; ordering policies and assortments; pricing schedules and margins.	Motivator; selling-in of programs
Ombudsman for distributor complaints on product performance; distributor credit and accounts receivable problems; distributor dissatisfaction about deliveries and back-orders; distributor problems on order mix-ups, policies on assortments, minimums, and nonstandard products.	Negotiator; conciliator; empathetic confidante to distributor

Source: Reprinted by permission of the publisher from Allan J. Magrath and Kenneth G. Hardy, "Factory Salesmen's Roles with Industrial Distributors," *Industrial Marketing Management*, 16, 1987, 165. Copyright 1987 by Elsevier Science Publishing Co., Inc.

effectively using advanced technology with Eastman Kodak sending videotapes to disk-drive distributors and Caterpillar Tractor employing teleconferences to communicate with distributor salespeople.[18]

The use of industrial distributors presents unique challenges for sales managers and company salespeople. As indicated in Exhibit 6.5, company salespeople must play different roles in their interactions with distributors — roles requiring a variety of specific skills. Company sales managers are charged with the responsibility of hiring and developing a company salesforce that can work effectively with industrial distributors.

One area of potential conflict exists when firms employ both industrial distributors and a direct company salesforce. Care must be taken to develop specific policies and procedures that are fair and equitable to both the industrial distributors and direct salespeople. Enormous problems can arise otherwise. For example, distributors for Wang Laboratories protested vigorously and even filed lawsuits when commissions to direct salespeople were lowered for sales made jointly with distributors. This

Exhibit 6.6 Advantages of Independent Representatives

Independent sales representatives offer several advantages over company salesforces:

- Reps provide a professional selling capability that is difficult to match with company salespeople.
- Reps offer in-depth knowledge of general markets and individual customers.
- Reps offer established relationships with individual accounts.
- The use of reps provides improved cash flow since payments to reps are typically not made until customers have paid for their purchases.
- The use of reps provides predictable sales expenses since most of the selling costs are variable and directly related to sales volume.
- The use of reps can provide greater territory coverage since companies can employ more reps than company salespeople for the same cost.
- Companies can usually penetrate new markets faster using reps because of the reps' established customer relationships.

Source: Adapted from Harold J. Novick, "The Case for Reps vs. Direct Selling: Can Reps Do It Better?" *Industrial Marketing*, March 1982, 90–98; and "The Use of Sales Reps," *Small Business Report*, December 1986, 72–78.

put the direct salespeople in competition with the distributors and severely damaged distributor relations.[19] In another situation, Kroy angered distributors of electronic lettering machines by adding a direct salesforce to call on certain customers. A smaller competitor, Varitronics, was able to take advantage of this situation by courting the angry distributors using strong support programs. Varitronics achieved a 15 to 20 percent market share in two years through this industrial distributor network.[20] As suggested by these examples, developing and maintaining positive relationships with industrial distributors is an important and challenging sales management task.

Independent Representatives. Firms employing personal selling can choose to cover accounts with **independent representatives** (also called *manufacturer's representatives* or just *reps*). Reps are independent sales organizations that sell complementary, but noncompeting, products from different manufacturers. In contrast to industrial distributors, independent representatives do not normally carry inventory or take title to the products they sell. Manufacturers typically develop contractual agreements with several rep organizations. Each rep organization consists of one or more salespeople and is assigned a geographic territory. It is compensated on a commission basis for products sold.

Approximately 50,000 U.S. manufacturers use some of the approximately 70,000 reps in the U.S.[21] Why would so many manufacturers use reps instead of company salesforces?[22] As indicated in Exhibit 6.6, reps have certain advantages over company salesforces, especially for small firms or for smaller markets served by larger firms. Since reps are paid on a commission basis, selling costs are almost totally variable, whereas a large percentage of the selling costs of a company salesforce are fixed. Thus, at lower sales levels a rep organization is more cost efficient to use than a

Figure 6.3 **Independent Representatives versus Company Salesforce Costs**

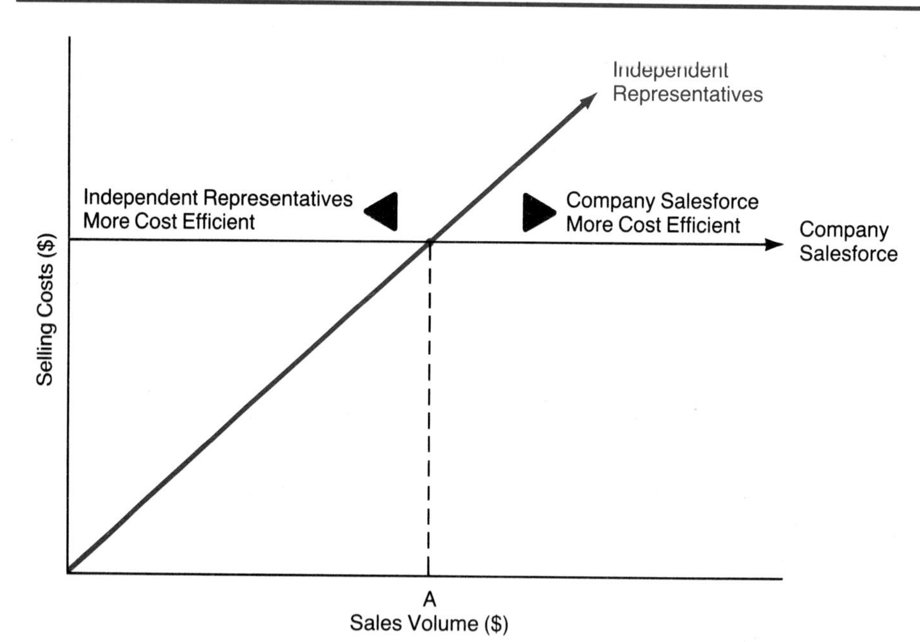

Independent representatives are typically more cost efficient at lower sales levels, since most of the costs associated with reps are variable. However, at higher sales levels (beyond point A) a company salesforce becomes more cost efficient.

company salesforce. However, at some level of sales the company salesforce will become more cost efficient, since reps typically receive higher commission rates than company salespeople (see Figure 6.3).[23]

Although reps may cost less in many situations, management also has less control over their activities. The basic trade-off is cost versus control. There are two aspects to control. First, since reps are paid a commission on sales, it is difficult to get them to engage in activities not directly related to sales generation. Thus, if servicing of accounts is important, reps may not perform these activities as well as a company salesforce. Second, the typical rep represents at least five different manufacturers or principals. Each manufacturer's products will therefore receive 20 percent of the rep's time if it is divided equally. Usually, however, some products receive more attention than others. The biggest complaints that manufacturers seem to have with reps is that they don't spend enough time with their products and thus don't generate sufficient sales.[24] The use of reps limits the amount of control that management has over the time spent selling their products.

The task facing sales management here is similar to the one involving industrial distributors: how to develop successful, long-term relationships. The general approach is to provide reps with support and assistance. Consider Joy Manufacturing's Air Moving Products Division, which has been using reps since 1965 to sell products to the heating, ventilating, and air conditioning market. Stan Harris, manager of marketing administration, describes the company's orientation toward reps as follows:

> We believe that we're faced with a two-edged competitive situation in the field. On the one hand, we compete with other fan manufacturers, but we also compete with the other principals for the rep's time. If we don't make it easy for the rep to make money on our products, Joy becomes a sideline to him and we lose the rep's time and effort.

Joy successfully implements this philosophy by providing training and technical assistance in the field to the reps.[25]

NEC America Inc.'s Broadcast Equipment Division uses independent representatives to sell video broadcast and transmitter products in the United States. Richard Dienhart, national sales manager for NEC, communicates constantly with the independent representatives by telephone, face-to-face communication, and a sales newsletter. He also goes on joint sales calls with reps to build trust and observe the rep's relationship with customers. According to Mr. Dienhart, "Anything that comes under the heading of supporting the sales effort is appropriate and due the manufacturers' rep."[26]

One of the key challenges of sales management is to get independent representatives to spend sufficient time selling the firm's products, as touched on earlier. A recent study found that reps spent more time with a principal's products when (1) they perceived a higher marginal sales return for effort spent, (2) there was a strong partnership between the rep and principal (frequent communication, mutual participation, and frequent feedback), (3) there was synergy between the different principals' products, and (4) the principal was actively involved in the management of the rep agency.[27] Interestingly, higher commission rates were found to have a diminishing effect on reps' time. These results highlight the importance of selecting the appropriate rep agencies and then establishing and nurturing mutually beneficial relationships between reps and principals.

Selling Centers. Our earlier discussion of organizational buyer behavior presented the concepts of buying centers and buying situations. If we move to the selling side of the exchange relationship, we find analogous concepts. Firms often employ multiple-person **selling centers** to deal with the multiple-person buying centers of their accounts. Figure 6.4 illustrates the basic relationships between selling centers and buying centers. A company salesperson typically coordinates the activities of the selling center, while the purchasing agent typically coordinates the activities of the buying center. Both the selling and buying centers can consist of multiple individuals from different functional areas. Each of these individuals can play one or more roles

Figure 6.4 **Exchange between Selling Centers and Buying Centers**

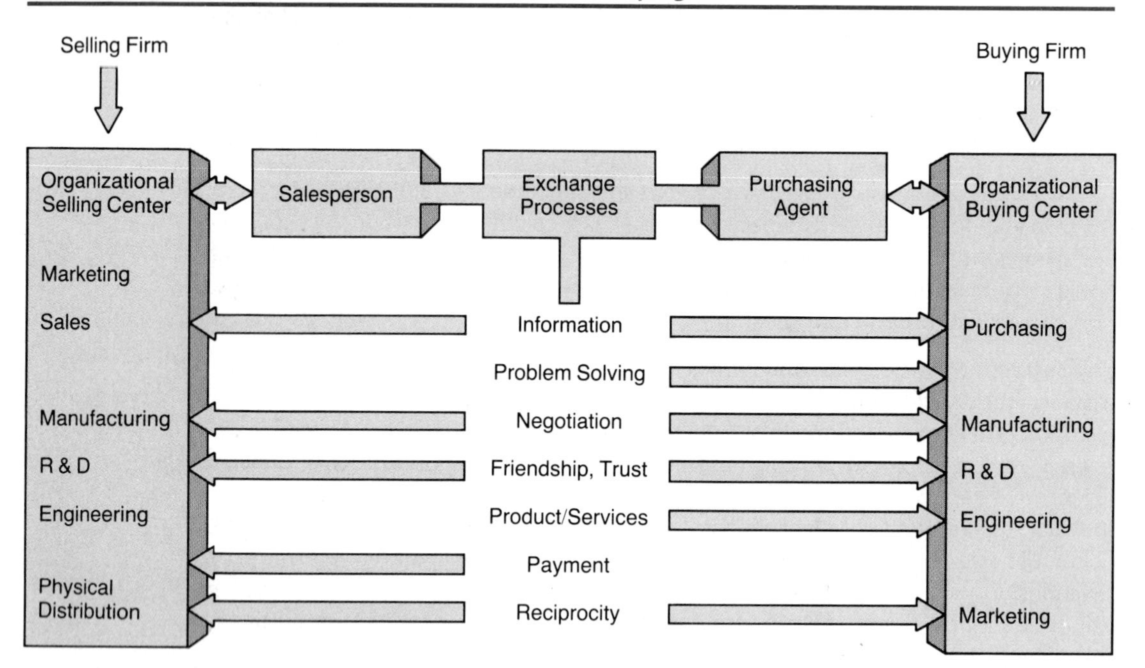

The salesperson coordinates the activities of a selling team to interact with the members of an account's buying center. The size, composition, and activities of the selling center depend upon whether the seller is facing a new task selling situation, modified resell selling situation, or routine resell selling situation.

Source: Michael D. Hutt, Wesley J. Johnston, and John R. Rouchelto, "Selling Centers and Buying Centers: Formulating Strategic Exchange Patterns," *Journal of Personal Selling and Sales Management,* May 1985, 34. Used with permission.

in the exchange process. Just as the type of *buying situation* is a major determinant of size and activities of the buying center, the type of *selling situation* is a major determinant of the size and activities of the selling center. Three different situations are possible, corresponding to the three different buying situations.

From the selling firm's perspective, the **new task selling situation,** in which the seller is either introducing new products or calling on new accounts, is the most difficult and uncertain one. Due to the complexity of this situation, the selling center will typically be large, with participation from many different functional areas. The **modified resell selling situation** has less uncertainty and typically involves a smaller, less involved selling center. The **routine resell selling situation** may consist of interaction only between the salesperson and the purchasing agent.

The design of the selling center is an important account coverage strategy. Developing successful exchanges and relationships with accounts requires the participation of the appropriate individuals from the seller. The account coverage strategy employed by Metaphor Computer Systems is an example. Metaphor markets a specially designed workstation and customized software to help marketing people interpret statistical information. The company employs selling centers consisting of a salesperson, an applications consultant, and a systems engineer. Although this is an expensive approach, chairman David Liddle says it is necessary "because we take responsibility for the whole problem of data use and want to control the situation."[28]

Three different selling center strategies deserve mention. **Team selling** consists of designing a specific selling center for each account. In some cases the selling team will be the same for all accounts, while in other situations the selling center will have to be modified to reflect the unique situation of each account. **Multilevel selling** is a variation of team selling in which the emphasis is to match functional areas between the buying and selling firm. Thus, individuals from a specific functional area or management level in the selling firm deal with their counterparts in the buying firm. Finally, **major account management** may employ team selling or multilevel selling. The unique aspect of this strategy is the emphasis placed on large and important accounts. Specific attention is placed on the selling centers used to serve major accounts, while other accounts typically receive coverage from the regular salesforce. Because of its importance, we will discuss major account management in detail in Chapter 7.

Telemarketing. An increasingly important account coverage strategy is to use **telemarketing**, which consists of using the telephone as a means for customer contact, to perform some or all of the activities required to develop and maintain account relationships. This includes both outbound telemarketing (the seller calls the account) and inbound telemarketing (the account calls the seller). Estimates suggest that business-to-business telemarketing is growing at a rate of 30 to 40 percent each year, with total sales exceeding $100 billion.[29]

Telemarketing can provide a cost-effective way to support or substitute for expensive personal sales calls. Some of its uses include

- Prospecting for customers
- Qualifying customer leads
- Conducting surveys
- Inviting prospects to seminars and trade shows
- Selling to distributors and end users
- Following up for repeat business
- Taking orders
- Checking on order status
- Handling order problems

As illustrated in "Sales Trend: Developing Telemarketing Salesforces," many firms are using telemarketing to replace personal selling for selected accounts. Telemarketing salespeople are able to serve a large number of smaller accounts. This lowers the selling costs to the smaller accounts and frees the field salesforce to con-

SALES TREND

DEVELOPING TELEMARKETING SALESFORCES

The medical and surgical products division of 3M calculated that the average cost of a personal sales call to a hospital was $200. Since it took about 4.3 calls to make a sale, the cost per sale was approximately $860. Analysis of hospital accounts indicated that nearly half of them could be considered low volume in terms of the number of surgical procedures performed each year.

Since the cost of a telephone sales call was approximately $25, 3M established a number of telephone sales representatives (TSRs) to serve the smaller hospital accounts. Each TSR is responsible for about 500 accounts. The TSR's job is to sell. Their performance and compensation is based on how much new business they generate.

According to Virginia Huber, manager of telephone sales, the "major difference between a field rep and a TSR is that one has a company car and has to spend time traveling from one account to the next. The training is the same, the pay scale is the same, the classification is the same. They each have a set of accounts and a quota . . . Telesales is really account management. It is knowing the account, being accessible to the account, and helping them troubleshoot. . . . Our people sell over that phone like I can't believe."

Source: Howard Sutton, *Rethinking the Company's Selling and Distribution Channels* (New York: The Conference Board, 1986), 23–25. Used with permission.

centrate on the larger accounts. For example, Morrell Dow Pharmaceutical found that its cost of a field sales call was $225, but that a telemarketing sales call cost only $20. A telemarketing program was established where each telephone sales rep handles 500 of the smaller independent drug stores. This frees the field salesforce to call on 10,000 new accounts.[30]

Telemarketing is also being integrated with field selling operations. One study of firms that were integrating telemarketing and field salesforces found that the major benefits of this integration were related to improved communication with and service of accounts. The lowering of selling costs was important, but secondary. Surprisingly, 97.6 percent of the firms in this study indicated the use of shared accounts, where telemarketing and field salespeople served the same accounts and actively exchanged information concerning sales and service activity with each account. Telemarketing salespeople were found to be most involved in customer service, order taking, and handling complaints. However, most activities were performed by both the telemarketing and field salesforces, with customer preference often being the deciding factor as to which salesforce performed which activities.[31]

Some of the variety of ways that telemarketing is being used to replace or support field selling operations are illustrated in the following examples:[32]

- Wing-Lynch Inc. markets photographic processing equipment and electronic temperature controls through industrial distributors. Distributor salespeople use the inbound telemarketing line to get product and technical information during

Figure 6.5 **Information from Telemarketing Operations**

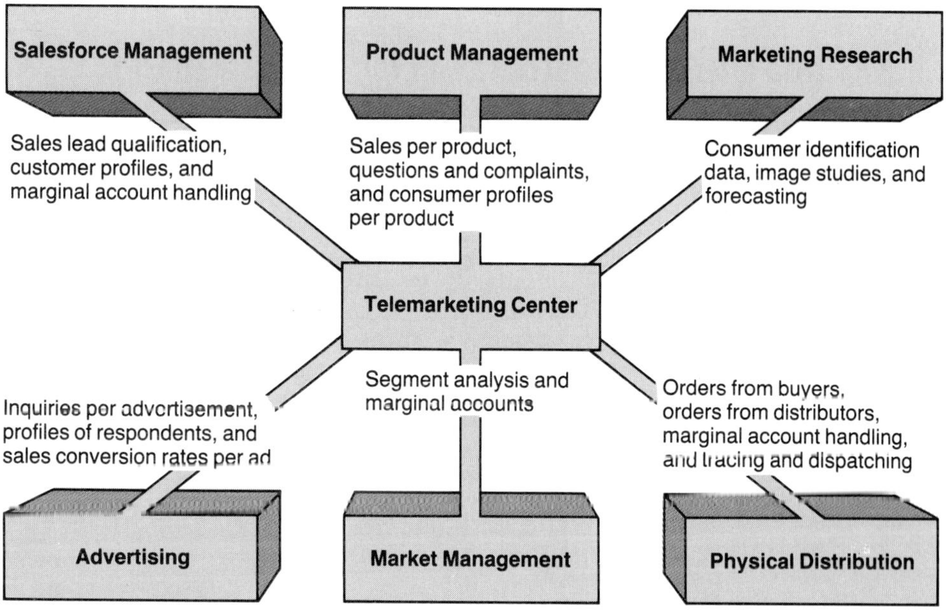

Salesforce Management

Sales lead qualification, customer profiles, and marginal account handling

Product Management

Sales per product, questions and complaints, and consumer profiles per product

Marketing Research

Consumer identification data, image studies, and forecasting

Telemarketing Center

Inquiries per advertisement, profiles of respondents, and sales conversion rates per ad

Advertising

Segment analysis and marginal accounts

Market Management

Orders from buyers, orders from distributors, marginal account handling, and tracing and dispatching

Physical Distribution

Telemarketing operations can provide a great deal of useful information to different functions in the marketing organization.

Source: John C. Coppett and Roy Dale Vorhees, "Telemarketing: A New Weapon in the Arsenal." Reprinted with permission form *The Journal of Business Strategy*, Spring 1983, 81. Copyright © 1983 Warren, Gorham, & Lamont Inc., 210 South Street, Boston, MA 02111. All rights reserved.

sales calls or when equipment is being installed. Customers order replacement parts directly by phone.

- Glendo Corp. markets diamond grinding wheels and engraving equipment. Five years ago the firm had no telemarketers and 70 industrial distributors. Today, the firm has 4 telemarketers and 23 distributors concentrated in large metropolitan areas. Sales have increased 30 percent annually for the past five years due to the fact that the telemarketers typically convert 25 percent of leads into sales, compared to 12.5 percent for the industrial distributors.
- Westinghouse Electric Co.'s Voice Systems Division uses telemarketing to generate and qualify sales leads that are passed on to the field salesforce for on-site demonstrations. Approximately 95 to 99 percent of these qualified leads have been converted into sales.

One of the important benefits from telemarketing is the ability to gather, combine, and disseminate a great deal of useful information. Figure 6.5 illustrates the

INTERNATIONAL SALES

TELEMARKETING FOR INTERNATIONAL MARKETS

As firms expand into international markets, telemarketing is being used as an important element in the account coverage strategy of many firms. A case in point is Wilson Tool International, a manufacturer of tool and die equipment based in Minnesota. After marketing in the United States for 20 years, Wilson expanded into European markets by developing a European salesforce and establishing telemarketing links with the United Kingdom, West Germany, the Netherlands, and Switzerland.

The company's toll-free number appears on sales reps' business cards and all company literature. Customers in Europe can call the Minnesota office to place orders. Each order is sent out by express air carrier and delivered within three days. Billing is done from Minnesota, with the customer being billed in local currency. An in-house telemarketing staff makes calls to international accounts to follow up on customer orders.

The use of international telemarketing allows Wilson to deliver products to customers faster than competitors that are located much closer to the customer. Wilson has used this differential advantage to establish international sales as 10 percent of total sales in only six months.

Source: Adapted from Elaine Santoro, "Telemarketing Globalized," *Direct Marketing*, June 1987, 102–110.

types of information that can be collected by a telemarketing operation and provided to different departments in the marketing organization.

The development of telemarketing salesforces to replace or support field selling operations can be a difficult task for sales managers. One of the keys to success appears to be consistent communication with the field salesforce throughout all stages of telemarketing development. Field salespeople must be assured that the telemarketing operations will help them improve their performance. Specific attention must also be directed toward developing appropriate compensation programs for both salesforces and devising training programs that provide the necessary knowledge and skills for the telemarketing and field salesforces to be able to work effectively together.

As the costs of selling continue to increase and technology develops, the use of telemarketing is likely to expand. The telephone will become a potent and cost-effective tool for communicating with accounts. Many firms will likely develop innovative uses of telemarketing, such as that described in "International Sales: Telemarketing for International Markets."

Trade Shows. The final account coverage method to be discussed here, **trade shows**, are typically industry-sponsored events where companies utilize a booth to display products and services to potential and existing customers.[33] Because a particular trade show is only held once a year and only lasts for a few days, trade shows should be viewed as supplemental methods for account coverage, not to be used by themselves, but integrated with other account coverage methods.

Statistics show that trade shows are popular. Over 90,000 companies participated in more than 9,000 trade shows in 1983, attended by approximately 37,000,000 individuals. One study suggests that 69 percent of a firm's potential market talk with company personnel at a trade show booth and that 82 percent of these qualified buyers would not normally have been contacted by the company's salesforce. The cost of a trade show contact is estimated to be $67.88.[34]

A recent study found that trade shows are used to achieve both selling and nonselling objectives. Relevant selling objectives are to test new products, to close sales, and to introduce new products. Nonselling objectives include servicing current customers, gathering competitive information, identifying new prospects, and enhancing corporate image. Successful trade shows tend to be those where firms exhibit a large number of products to a large number of attendees, where specific written objectives for the trade show are established, and where attendees match the firm's target market.[35]

The use of trade shows places unique demands upon sales managers and salespeople, since they are typically taken out of the field to man company booths at a trade show. Interacting with attendees at a trade show is considerably different than calling on accounts in the field. Therefore, special training is normally required to equip sales managers and salespeople to achieve specific trade show objectives. Many firms also develop specific incentive programs for a trade show. For example, General Electric Silicon Systems Technology Department rewarded the salesperson that garnered the most qualified leads each day with a paperweight decorated with the department's logo. Although the paperweight only cost $10, an elaborate awards ceremony provided recognition that motivated salespeople to double the number of leads that were expected.[36]

Essential to effective use of trade shows is determining the specific results from each show. Firms such as Caterpillar Inc. and Combustion Engineering Inc. conduct multiple-phase studies to pinpoint the specific benefits from trade show participation.[37] The results from their studies and other available evidence suggest that trade shows can be a valuable supplement to other account coverage methods.

SUMMARY

1. **Discuss the important concepts behind organizational buyer behavior.** The key concepts behind organizational buyer behavior are buying situation, buying center, buying process, and buying needs. Buying situations can be characterized as new task, modified rebuy, or straight rebuy. The type of buying situation affects all other aspects of organizational buyer behavior. The buying center consists of all of the individuals from a firm involved in a particular buying decision. These individuals may come from different functional areas and may play the role of initiators, users, gatekeepers, influencers, deciders, and/or buyers. Organizational purchasing should be viewed as a buying process with multiple phases. Different members of the buying center may be involved at different phases of the buying process. Organizational pur-

chases are made to satisfy specific buying needs, which may be both organizational and personal. These concepts are highly interrelated and interact to produce complex organizational purchasing phenomena.

2. **Explain the different approaches to developing an account management strategy.** An account management strategy specifies how the firm plans to develop, maintain, and expand relationships with accounts. The two extremes of account management are relationship marketing and transaction marketing. Accounts that follow the lost-for-good model require a relationship approach, while transaction marketing is appropriate for accounts following the always-a-share model. The account management strategy should attempt to move accounts from the always-a-share orientation toward the lost-for-good end of the spectrum.

3. **Describe the different account coverage methods.** An account coverage strategy consists of decisions as to how to provide selling effort coverage to accounts. The account coverage method depends upon the firm's marketing strategy. If indirect distribution is used, then industrial distributors become the main focus of selling effort coverage. Firms might decide to employ independent representatives instead of having a company salesforce. The concept of selling centers is analagous to the buying center concept. Depending upon whether the seller faces a new task selling situation, a modified resell situation, or a routine resell situation, different individuals will be included in the selling center. Team selling, multilevel selling, and major account management are different types of selling center strategies. Telemarketing is an account coverage method that can be used to replace or support field selling operations. Finally, trade shows can be used to achieve specific objectives and supplement the other account coverage methods.

4. **Discuss the basic interrelationships between account management strategy and account coverage strategy.** Account management strategy and account coverage strategy are separate, but interrelated account strategies. Strategic decisions in one area often have an impact on strategies in other areas. The key is to develop effective and integrated account strategies.

Key Terms

- new task buying situation
- modified rebuy buying situation
- straight rebuy buying situation
- buying center
- buying process
- buying needs
- account management strategy
- relationship marketing
- transaction marketing
- account coverage strategy
- industrial distributors
- independent representatives
- selling centers
- new task selling situation
- modified resell selling situation
- routine resell selling situation
- team selling
- multilevel selling
- major account management
- telemarketing
- trade shows

Review Questions

1. Discuss how the type of buying situation affects the buying center, buying process, and buying needs.
2. How might the personal needs of engineers, purchasing agents, and marketing personnel affect the buying process for a product?
3. What specific activities might be used to move an account from the always-a-share model to the lost-for-good model?
4. How should management decide whether to employ a company-owned salesforce or to use independent representatives?
5. What are the key considerations in developing a telemarketing salesforce?
6. How is the management of relationships with industrial distributors different from the management of relationships with end-user customers?
7. How can trade shows be used to supplement other account coverage methods?
8. When is transaction marketing more appropriate than relationship marketing as an account management strategy?
9. How might telemarketing be used when accounts are covered by distributors?
10. What are the most important organizational buyer behavior trends, and how might these trends affect account strategies in the future?

Application Exercises

1. Contact the purchasing agent of a local manufacturer to investigate how the firm would purchase a microcomputer. Make sure that you determine the type of buying situation, the composition and roles of the buying center, the phases in the buying process, and the buying needs that would be satisfied by the microcomputer purchase. Summarize this buyer behavior information, and suggest how the information would be helpful to a microcomputer manufacturer in developing account strategies.
2. XYZ Food Products markets several food products to retail accounts. The firm's salesforce currently calls on all types of food retailers from small mom-and-pop operations to large superstores. You are considering the establishment of an in-house telemarketing operation to manage the smaller accounts. This would allow the field salesforce to spend more time with larger accounts and reduce the selling costs to smaller accounts. What problems do you foresee in developing the telemarketing operations? What would you do to minimize or solve these problems?
3. ABC Manufacturing markets a small line of industrial products through independent sales representatives. Although your products serve a small market, you are the dominant firm, with over 50 percent market share. Your reps typically represent four other principals. Each of these principals has a relatively small market share but operates in markets much larger than yours. You do not feel that the reps spend enough time trying to sell your products. What would you do to motivate the reps to increase their emphasis on your products?
4. LM Salt Company sells bulk salt to various industrial customers. Some of the accounts purchase all of their salt from LM. However, several accounts want to maintain three

suppliers of salt. For these accounts, LM has only a 33 percent share of their salt business. Since the salt market is experiencing slow overall growth, LM must increase its penetration of existing accounts to achieve sales and profit objectives. As the national sales manager, what account strategies would you use to increase account penetration?

5. Contact the sales manager from a local industrial firm. Ask the sales manager about how his/her firm uses trade shows and about special sales management problems associated with trade shows. Write a report that summarizes the information you have obtained.

Notes

[1]See Frederick E. Webster and Yoram Wind, "A General Model for Understanding Organizational Buyer Behavior," *Journal of Marketing,* April 1972, 12–19; and Jagdish N. Sheth, "A Model of Industrial Buyer Behavior," *Journal of Marketing,* October 1973, 50–56, for more complete presentations of organizational buyer behavior.

[2]The phases presented in this chapter are taken from Gary L. Lilien and M. Anthony Wong, "An Exploratory Investigation of the Structure of the Buying Center in the Metalworking Industry," *Journal of Marketing Research,* February 1984, 3.

[3]Lilien and Wong, 1984, 6.

[4]Michael D. Hutt and Thomas W. Speh, *Industrial Marketing Management* (Hinsdale, Ill.: The Dryden Press, 1985), 12.

[5]Alex Beam and Geoff Lewis, "The IBM-DEC Wars: It's 'The Year of the Customer'," *Business Week,* March 30, 1987, 86–88.

[6]See F. Robert Dwyer, Paul H. Schurr, and Sejo Oh, "Developing Buyer-Seller Relationships," *Journal of Marketing,* April 1987, 11–27, for a more complete discussion of relationship and transaction exchange orientations.

[7]Theodore Levitt, "After the Sale is Over . . . ," *Harvard Business Review,* September–October 1983, 87.

[8]This discussion is adapted from Barbara Bund Jackson, "Build Customer Relationships That Last," *Harvard Business Review,* November–December 1985, 120–128.

[9]"Dupont Turns Scientists into Salespeople," *Sales and Marketing Management,* June 1987, 57.

[10]"Bergen Brunswig Locks in Sales with Service," *Sales and Marketing Management,* June 1987, 48.

[11]Joan Hamilton and Amy Dunkin, "Why Rivals Are Quaking as Nordstrom Heads East," *Business Week,* June 15, 1987, 99–100.

[12]"Fuller Brush Man Uses Soft Sell, Humor to Boost Sales," *Marketing News,* January 18, 1988, 3.

[13]Reported in James A. Narus and James C. Anderson, "Turn Your Industrial Distributors into Partners," *Harvard Business Review,* March–April 1986, 67.

[14]Howard Sutton, *Rethinking the Company's Selling and Distribution Channels* (New York: The Conference Board, 1986), 3.

[15]Reported in Sutton, 1986, 3.

[16]"Black and Decker Rebuilds," *Sales and Marketing Management,* June 1987, 49.

[17]"Apple's Instant Link with Dealers," *Sales and Marketing Management,* June 1987, 23–24.

[18]See Diane L. Kastiel, "Electronic Communications Avoid Short Circuits to Distributors," *Business Marketing,* July 1987, 70–75, for an expanded discussion of these and other examples.

[19]Diane L. Kastiel, "Wang's Retail Hopes Hinge on Plan's Success," *Business Marketing,* April 1987, 43–44.

[20]Sue Kapp, "Face-Off: An Optimist and a Realist Take on an Industry Goliath," *Business Marketing,* May 1987, 12–16.

[21]Reported in Earl Hitchcock, "What Marketers Love and Hate About Their Manufacturers' Reps," *Sales and Marketing Management,* September 10, 1984, 60.

[22]See Thomas L. Powers, "Switching from Reps to Direct Salespeople," *Industrial Marketing Management,* 16, 1987, 169–172, for a systematic method for determining when to switch from independent representatives to a company salesforce.

[23]See Erin Anderson, "The Salesperson as Outside Agent or Employee: A Transaction Cost Analysis," *Marketing Science,* Summer 1985, 234–254, for a thorough discussion and empirical test of using independent representatives versus a company salesforce.

[24]Reported in Hitchcock, 1984, 62.

[25]Adapted from Hitchcock, 1984, 60–65.

[26]Kate Bertrand, "They Don't Get No Respect," *Business Marketing,* June 1987, 38–40.

[27]Erin Anderson, Leonard M. Lodish, and Barton A. Weitz, "Resource Allocation Behavior in Conventional Channels," *Journal of Marketing Research,* February 1987, 85–97.

[28]"Metaphor's High-Cost Sell Pays Off," *Sales and Marketing Management,* April 1987, 25–26.

[29]Reported in William C. Moncrief, Charles W. Lamb, and Terry Dielman, "Developing Telemarketing Support Systems," *Journal of Personal Selling and Sales Management,* August 1986, 43–49.

[30]"Telemarketing Takes the Top Spot," *Direct Marketing,* September 1987, 120.

[31]Geri Gantman, "Exclusive Survey," *Business Marketing,* September 1987, 57, 63–75.

[32]See Kate Bertrand, "The Inside Story," *Business Marketing,* September 1987, 51–62, for a more complete discussion of these and other telemarketing examples.

[33]Joseph A. Bellizzi and Delilah J. Lipps, "Managerial Guidelines for Trade Show Effectiveness," *Industrial Marketing Management,* 13, 1984, 49–52.

[34]These statistics and other statistics concerning trade shows are available in A. J. Farina and J. R. Dickinson, "Trade Show Participation — Importance and Frequency," *Proceedings* (Institute for Decision Sciences, 1985), 527–529.

[35]See Roger A. Kerin and William L. Cron, "Assessing Trade Show Functions and Performance: An Exploratory Study," *Journal of Marketing,* July 1987, 87–94, for a more complete presentation of study results and more detailed discussion of research implications.

[36]Kate Bertrand, "Rewarding Ways to Build Trade Show Sales," *Business Marketing,* April 1987, 104–105.

[37]See Kate Bertrand, "Talking Turkey on Trade Shows," *Business Marketing,* March 1987, 94–103, for a detailed description of these trade-show evaluation methods.

PRIME PLASTICS INC. TELEMARKETING

In May 1982 Hank Naulty, president of Prime Plastics Inc., was trying to decide what action to take with regard to the company's telemarketing program. This program had been initiated early in 1982 in an effort to halt the erosion of sales and profits that Prime Plastics had been experiencing.

Prime Plastics Inc. was a full-service distributor of plastic materials for industrial use. Its product line included a wide variety of plastic sheet, rod and tube. These items were sold either by the pound or by the sheet. The majority of sales consisted of standard items custom cut to customer specifications. These items were sold as follows:

1. To manufacturers of consumer products, i.e., coffee mugs
2. To manufacturers of industrial products, i.e., computer circuit boards and machine parts
3. Directly to end users for windows and storm doors.

Total U.S. manufacturers' shipments of plastics of all types were estimated, in 1982, at over $3 billion annually, of which about 50% was sheet, rod and tube. Direct factory sales to very large users accounted for about 50% of the market. The remaining 50% went through distributors, of which 10% was in the geographic area served by Prime.

The U.S. plastics industry operated on a multi-stage basis, as shown in Exhibit 1. In the first stage petrochemicals and other raw materials were processed into resins from which plastic products could then be made. Resins were made in large, integrated plants by major chemical producers such as Dupont and Monsanto. These resins were then processed into standard size plastic sheet and tube by many smaller companies. Some were subsidiaries of large corporations but most were independents. All processors generally produced products that met industry standards. Prime Plastics bought from more than 30 processors. Only a very small share of the business was for specialized products for which there were only a few suppliers.

Exhibit 1 **PRIME PLASTICS INC.**
Channels of Distribution for Plastics

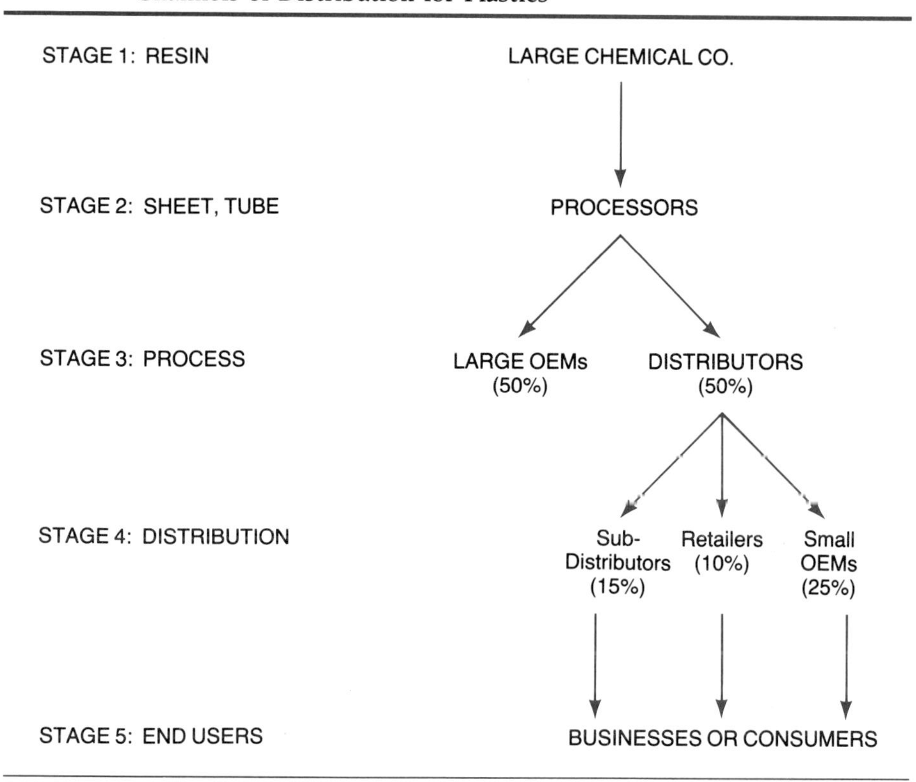

Source: Hank Naulty

The industry included fewer than 10 large national distributors, each of which had a Chicago branch. In addition, there were more than a thousand regional and local distributors in the U.S. of which about 90 served the Chicago market. About 15 Chicago area dealers stocked standard phenolic items, but only four carried full lines of these products. These four accounted for about 60% of the business. Phenolics are a specialty plastic with unique properties of water and acid resistance. Mr. Naulty believed his firm was the third largest phenolics dealer in the area, but the first two firms, Acme and Supreme, had phenolic sales of about $1.8 million and $1.2 million respectively. These two firms were among the top five plastics distributors in the area and both had their own field salesforces. Acme, a leading local firm, had total sales of $7 million in 1981 and a field force of 8 salespeople. Its pre-tax profit were about $300,000. Supreme was a branch of a large national distributor and had sales of $5 million. It had a field force of 7 salespeople. Hank Naulty estimated its profits at about $200,000.

There were few barriers to entry in the distributor market and little or no product differentiation. This stage of the market was very price competitive, and gross margins averaged about 33% of sales to end users. Most customers called two or three distributors for bids before placing orders. Therefore, price, service, and delivery time were key factors in gaining a competitive edge. Each distributor tried to specialize in serving certain types of customers. Instead of carrying large, high-cost inventories of all products, most distributors specialized in certain items. They bought these items in bulk and then sold part of the inventory to other distributors who specialized in other products, to permit them to meet the low-volume needs of their customers for products not in their normal inventories.

Prime specialized in phenolics, which accounted for about 10% of the dollar volume of all sheet rod and tube sales in the U.S. Phenolics provided higher than average contribution margins because they were more difficult than most plastics to cut or shape to precision standards. Because they were so difficult to work, Mr. Naulty referred to them as "the dirty side of the plastics business." About 30% of Prime's sales were made to other distributors, at a 20% gross margin on sales, as compared to its 30% gross margin on phenolic sales to other customers. Phenolics comprised almost all its sales to distributors.

The national economic slowdown that had started in 1979 had adversely affected Prime, as it had other companies in the plastics industry. Increasing competition was further eroding profit margins. Mr. Naulty believed that the only way the company would return to profitability would be to change its strategy. For the past several years, Naulty had been directing the company toward greater specialization in phenolics, his highest-margin items. Despite this concentration, however, profits had continued to decline, and Naulty was looking for new ways to increase profits.

In addition to carrying a full line of phenolic products, Naulty maintained a relatively large inventory of other standard plastic items. This inventory was much larger than was common in the industry and included polyolefins, PVC, Delvin, Teflon and nylon. In early 1982 about 65% of Prime Plastics sales, and one-third of its inventories, were phenolics. Until early 1982 Prime Plastics sales of non-phenolics had been over 50% of its business. But Mr. Naulty had then decided to stop quoting uneconomically low prices on these items after receiving a study from his accountant showing that sales of non-phenolic items barely covered their variable costs. When Naulty decided to raise minimum prices and margins on non-phenolic items by 10%, sales of these items had fallen nearly 50%. As a result, the average cost of handling these items had also increased, and contribution from them remained essentially zero. Prime Plastics' inventory of non-phenolic items had also been inflated by Mr. Naulty's decision, over the 1978–1981 period to keep profits up by buying all products in lots large enough to qualify for maximum discounts. He estimated that this practice had increased Prime Plastics' gross margin by about 3% of sales over this period. About 50% of the non-phenolic inventory consisted of items for which Prime Plastics was currently experiencing no significant demand. But Mr. Naulty had recently been contacted by a distributor who had offered to buy $130,000 book value of this slow-moving inventory for $100,000 cash. Naulty intended to accept this offer, as the cash would provide the means to reinvigorate his business.

Prime Plastics' entire operation was located in a pre-World War II, three-story warehouse building in Chicago. The first floor of the building was divided between 4,000 square feet of office space and a 2,200 square foot warehouse and cutting area. The two upper floors were rented out as office space. Income from this space offset the taxes and some other out-of-pocket costs of the space occupied by the company. The company's workforce consisted of 18 people, in addition to Naulty. There were two telemarketing representatives, three customer service representatives (CSR), five clerical/bookkeeping employees, and 8 warehouse/shipping employees.

Prime was established in 1957 by Hank's father, Bill Naulty. After the Korean war, the U.S. government had a huge surplus of plastics, and Bill seized the opportunity to capitalize on the excess plastic. Over the course of several years he bought large quantities of this surplus from the government for about 10¢ on the dollar and resold it at excellent markups. By the time this opportunity had ended, he had established a good reputation and a large customer base.

By 1972 Bill Naulty had developed this plastics distributorship into a profitable operation with annual sales of $650,000, and profits of $65,000. But tragedy struck in December 1972 as a storm ravaged Prime Plastics' Chicago warehouse, destroying the business. Faced with the task of rebuilding, Bill Naulty decided to retire. He turned the limited remaining assets of the business over to his son Hank, a 1970 graduate of a leading business school. He also loaned Hank the $200,000 fire insurance proceeds. Hank Naulty used these assets to repair the building, replace some of the ruined inventory, and attempt to recapture Prime Plastics' former customers. 1973 sales were just $400,000. But in 1974 sales skyrocketed to $1.4 million as plastics prices nearly quadrupled during the Arab oil embargo. Profits rose to $400,000 in 1974 as low-cost inventory was sold off at high prices. When petrochemical prices stabilized somewhat, sales for the company fell off to about the $1,000,000 level in 1975. Profits fell to $100,000 in 1975 and had been declining ever since. Exhibits 2-1, 2-2, and 2-3 provide excerpts from 1978 to 1981 profit and loss statements, balance sheets, and an analysis of 1982 expenses. In Mr. Naulty's view, other companies in the industry were experiencing similar pressures, and he estimated that more than 30% of the plastics distributors active in 1974 had left the business or failed by 1982.

Until late 1981 Naulty had utilized a single field salesperson to call on existing accounts, open new accounts, and take field orders. Most orders were taken over the telephone by the customer service representatives (CSRs). While Naulty would have preferred to have enough field sales people to call on the firm's 5,000-plus prospects in the Midwest market, he did not believe they could generate enough volume to make such an approach viable. Naulty himself occasionally spoke by phone with a few larger accounts, but he generally concentrated his efforts on home office administration and he approved all significant price reductions quoted to customers. In making pricing decisions, both the CSRs and Naulty utilized a computer report, pro-

Exhibit 2-1 **PRIME PLASTICS INC.**
Profit and Loss Statements*
($000)

	1978	1979	1980	1981	1982 (projected)
Sales	$1,300	$1,450	$1,420	$1,600	$1,200
Cost of Goods Sold	910	1,085	1,095	1,275	958
Gross Margin	$ 390	$ 365	$ 325	$ 325	$ 242
Operating Expenses**	240	260	280	300	282
Mr. Naulty's Salary	80	60	40	25	25
Profit before Taxes	70	45	5	-	(65)
Taxes	10	5	-	-	(15)
Profit after Taxes	$ 60	$ 40	$ 5	$ -	$ (50)
Dividends Paid to Hank Naulty	$ 30	$ 20	$ 20	$ 10	-
Price Index for Prime Products (1974 = 100)	80	84	88	92	90

* All figures have been rounded off.
** Net of Rental Income from office space in company building.

Exhibit 2-2 **PRIME PLASTICS INC.**
Balance Sheet (12/31)
($000)

Assets	1978	1979	1980	1981	1982 (projected)
Cash	$ 15	$ 5	$ 5	$ 5	$ 5
Accounts Receivable	240	210	210	220	250
Inventory	200	300	310	350	390
Plant & Equipment*	140	200	220	240	250
Other	20	20	20	25	25
Total	$615	$735	$765	$840	$920

Liabilities	1978	1979	1980	1981	1982 (projected)
Accounts Payable	$180	$270	$290	$360	$450
Notes Payable*	210	180	165	160	180
Other Current Debt	30	40	50	80	110
Long Term Mortgage Debt***	60	90	120	110	100
Equity	135	155	140	130	80
Total	$615	$735	$765	$840	$920

* Net of Depreciation.
** Principally to Bill Naulty.
*** Of which $50,000 was guaranteed by Bill Naulty.

Exhibit 2-3 **PRIME PLASTICS**
Operating Cost
Monthly Average, 1982

Personnel		
Warehouse/Shipping (8)	$ 6,000	
Clerical/Bookkeeping (5)	4,000	
Customer Service (2)	1,800	
Telemarketing (3)	2,000	
Subtotal		$13,800
Space and Equipment		
Mortgage	$ 800	
Insurance/Utilities	2,000	
Equipment Rental/Repair	400	
Depreciation	1,000	
Subtotal		$4,200
Other		
Freight In and Out	$ 1,300	
Telephone/Postage	2,000	
Interest	1,200	
Telemarketing Consultant	1,000	
Subtotal		$ 5,500
TOTAL		$23,500

duced weekly, that showed inventory on hand for each of the 2,000 stock keeping units. (SKUs) in Prime Plastics' inventory. This report showed the average unit cost at which this inventory had been purchased. The company also had available recent price lists from suppliers, and it knew it could call suppliers for up-to-date quotes on items not in stock or to help price large orders. Price lists became outdated quickly when oversupply or undersupply caused rapid fluctuations in the prices of plastic products. Such fluctuations had been common since 1973.

In late 1981, Naulty was approached by Peter Marksman, a telemarketing consultant. Marksman proposed to Naulty that telephone selling might well be a more cost-effective way to gain new accounts and renew old ones than expensive field sales calls. He spent several weeks studying Prime Plastics' sales and marketing records and determined that of the 5,000 potential customers the company had identified in the Midwest, Prime Plastics had at some time received orders from 2,110. Of these, 771 (37%) had placed orders with Prime Plastics in the second half of 1981, an additional 648 (31%) had purchased in 1980 or the first half of 1981, and 691 (32%) had not purchased within the past two years.

It was estimated that 30% of Prime Plastics' business had come from its 30 distributors' accounts. Fifty large nondistributor accounts represented 20% of sales,

Exhibit 3 **PRIME PLASTICS INC.**
New Account Program for Telemarketers

Within five (5) work days after acquisition, mail a "Thank You" for your business letter.

- Attempt to remit directly to decision maker.
- Allows a degree of continuity and general goodwill.
- Letter will be basic form letter.
- Until such time as it can be automated, all new accounts will be noted on New Accounts List for subsequent follow-up.

Thirty (30) days from point of acquisition, conduct telemarketing campaign:

- Reintroduce company
- Inquire about our service, etc.
- Inquire about new quotes
- Thank for being Prime customer

Sixty (60) days from point of acquisition, mail a "Special Customer Offer."

- Introduce offer
- Inquire for business

Place in normal call pattern.

and 50% of the sales came from more than 691 other nondistributor accounts. The remaining 70% was from nondistributor accounts, 50% from manufacturers, and 20% from plastic retailers, hardware stores, and building supply retailers.

Based on these findings, Marksman recommended that Prime should

- Hire three home office telemarketers and fire the field salesperson.
- Commence an awareness campaign.
- Activate a "customer service" approach that would better meet customer needs for quick quotes and on-time shipments.
- Evaluate customer segments for potential.
- Prepare and introduce measurement standards and controls to monitor the telemarketing activity.
- Base telemarketer compensation on customer retention and reactivation.

Naulty was impressed with this proposal and retained Marksman to implement it. For some time he had been unconvinced of the value of Prime's field sales effort. Three telemarketers were hired, none of whom had had prior experience in either plastics or telemarketing. They therefore received one day of introductory training from Marksman in telemarketing techniques and two days training in plastics and plastic pricing procedures. They were to implement the New Account Program outlined in Exhibit 3. They were also to follow up on requests for quotes that had come to the customer service representatives but had not turned into sales, and to develop and carry out an Account Reactivation Program.

By early May, two of the original three telemarketers had quit. Only one had been replaced and trained, but another was being sought. Every two months Marksman reported progress of the program to Naulty. Data from Marksman's report on March and April activity are shown as Exhibit 4. The telemarketers worked 35 hours per week and were paid a base salary of $600 per month each. In addition, they could earn commissions computed on a sliding scale basis, as follows:

Monthly Orders Taken	
$0–$5,000	0
$5,000–$10,000	3%
Over $10,000	5%

Marksman was also asked to evaluate CSR activity. CSRs received incoming requests for information and quotes. In many instances, they gave quotes on the spot, using standard or minimum markups over costs. Most quotes tended to be at the minimum. Special orders and requests for discounts were referred to Mr. Naulty, and the CSRs then telephoned accounts with the quotes. Exhibit 5 is Marksman's summary of March 1982 CSR activity. Mr. Naulty estimated that about one incoming call in five resulted in an order and that the Prime Plastics average order size was about $300. Only about one order in 100 was from a customer not sold in the past six months. Marksman developed the order process flow found in Exhibit 6. Orders were filled out on the sales sheet, also designed by Marksman, shown in Exhibit 7. Exhibit 8-1 depicts the process flow used on call-back orders, with the accompanying script found in 8-2. Marksman also developed a script, shown in Exhibit 9, which was used by the telemarketers to call inactive accounts or new potential customers. This script offered a special discount to the perspective clients to encourage them to try Prime.

Although the telemarketing system had been in place for less than three months, Hank Naulty was anxious to determine whether it was likely to turn out to be successful. To date, total sales had continued to decline and margins were smaller than ever. If this approach was not working, it was important that Naulty make an immediate change as losses were mounting and cash was running out.

Exhibit 4 **PRIME PLASTICS INC.**
Telemarketing Group Call Analysis
March–April, 1982

	Completed Calls	Number Days Worked	Av. No. Calls/ Day	No. of Quotes	% To Calls	Dollar Sales	No. Orders	% Orders To Calls	Av. Ord.	Av. $ Per Day	Av. # Ord./Day
Frank	639	36	17.8	65	10%	$ 6.2K	26	4 %	$238	$172	.7
Cathy	1307	44	30.0	80	6%	$ 5.5K	40	3 %	$138	$125	.9
TOTAL	1946	80	243	145	7%	$11.7K	66	3.3%	$177	$146	.8

Exhibit 5 **PRIME PLASTICS INC.**
Customer Service Group
Inbound Call Analysis
March 1982

CSR	# Calls	No. Days Worked	Av. No. Calls/Day	Av. No. Calls/Week	Est. Min. Per Call	Est. Phone Hrs./Day	% Of Day	# Orders	$ (000)
John	588	15	39	196	4	2.6	33%	98	26.1
Al	526	20	28	132	4	1.9	24%	104	31.4
Sue	416	15	28	139	4	1.9	24%	101	36.5
TOTAL	1530	50	30.6	153	4	2.04	26%	303	94.0

Exhibit 6 **PRIME PLASTICS INC.**
Telemarketing Order Flow Procedures

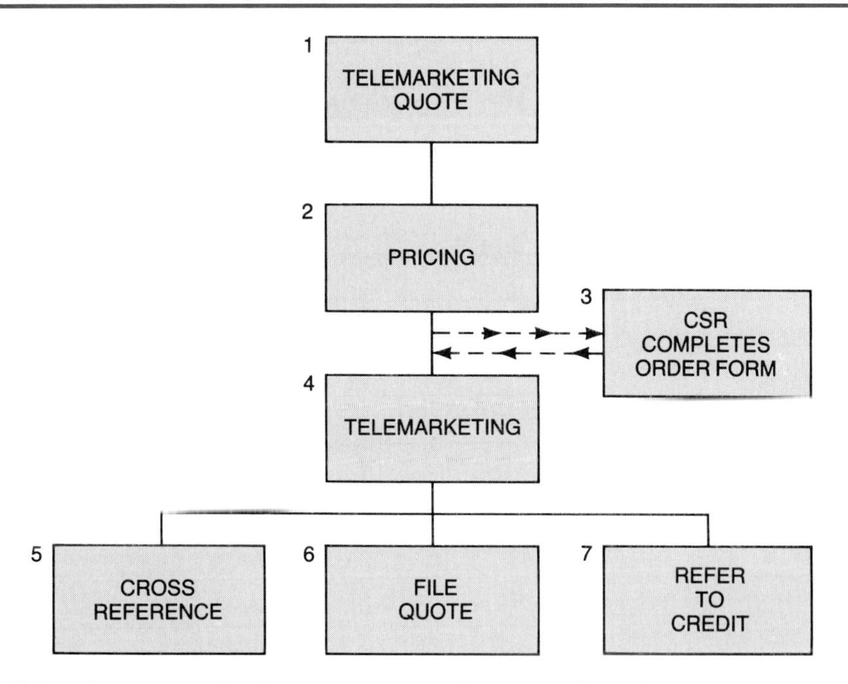

1-2 Telemarketers currently refer quotes to appropriate person for pricing, and maintain a copy for follow-up. When returned contact customer with quote and either close order or place in follow-up cycle—if order follow step 3.

3-4 Customer Service Representative completes order and refers directly back to telemarketing with all appropriate materials.

5-7 Telemarketing cross references order form to original quote. Files quote and refers completed order form to credit.

Exhibit 7 **PRIME PLASTICS INC.**
Telemarketing
Sales Sheet

SHIP TO: ______________ DATE ______________

COMPANY NAME: ______________

ADDRESS: ______________

CITY: ______________ STATE: ______ ZIP: ______________

TELEPHONE: (3#) ______________ SIC ______ TM ______

CONTACT: ______________

LAST PRODUCT PURCHASED: ______________ 1st ACTIVE DATE: ______

DATE LAST PURCHASED: ______________ $ ______________

PRODUCT NUMBER	DESCRIPTION	QTY	PRICE

SPECIAL INSTRUCTIONS: ______________

____

____

Exhibit 8-1 **PRIME PLASTICS INC.**
Follow-up Quote Procedure **for Customer Service Representatives**

OBJECTIVE: To call back quoted jobs and obtain orders or initiate future order activity.

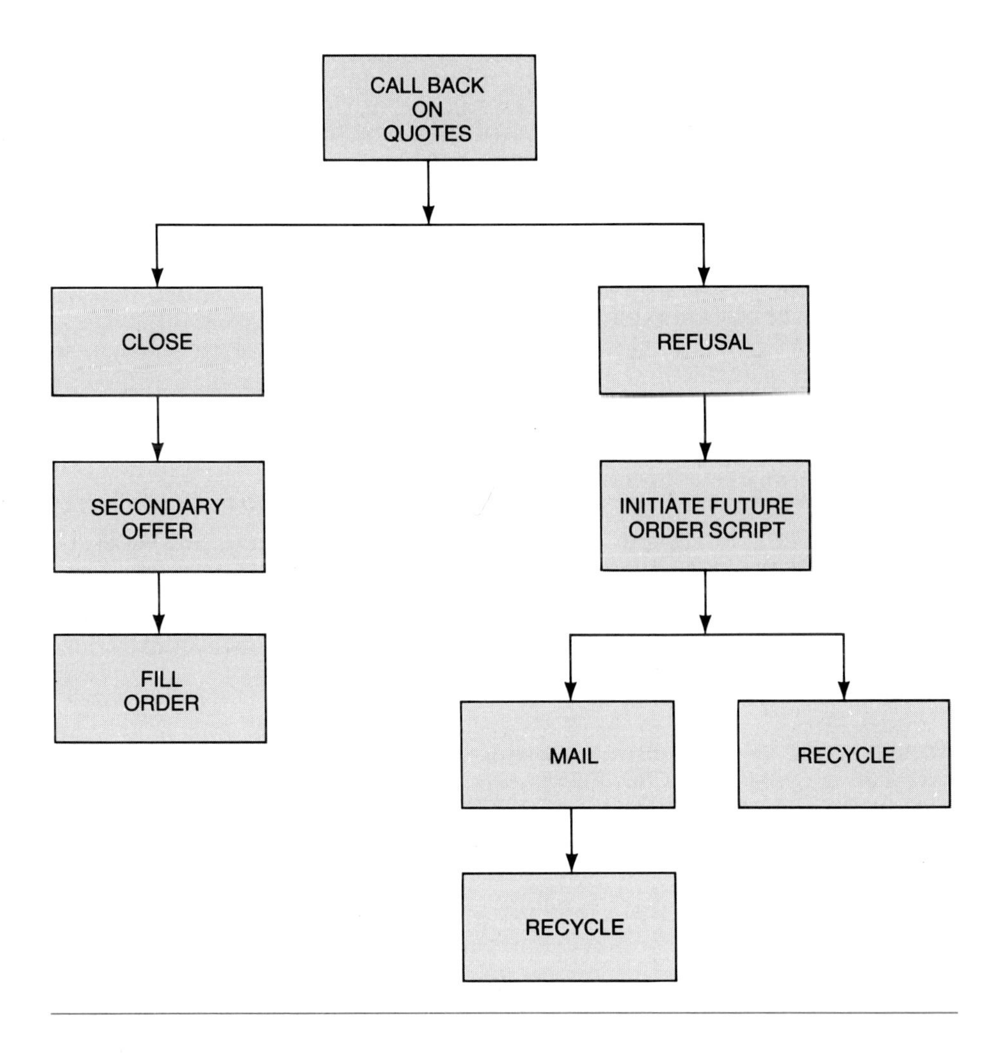

Exhibit 8-2 PRIME PLASTICS INC. Future Order Script for Customer Service Representatives

GOOD ______________, THIS IS ______________, FROM PRIME PLASTICS IN CHICAGO.
MAY I SPEAK WITH (NAME) PLEASE?
(NAME), (YOUR NAME), FROM PRIME PLASTICS IN CHICAGO.
I'M CALLING REGARDING THAT QUOTE WE GAVE YOU (time period, i.e., last week) ON (material).

[RESPONSE:]

(NAME), COULD YOU TELL US WHY YOU DIDN'T PURCHASE FROM PRIME? . . . .

[RESPONSE:]

OVERALL (NAME), WE ARE ONE OF THE MORE COMPETITIVE FIRMS IN THE AREA IN (material). WE HOPE THAT YOU'LL GIVE US ANOTHER OPPORTUNITY TO QUOTE ON A JOB IN THE FUTURE.

[OBJECTIONS]

IS THERE A GOOD TIME I COULD CALL YOU BACK ON A QUOTE?

[RESPONSE]

FINE, WE BELIEVE WE ARE COMPETITIVE. WE'LL CALL YOU IN (approximate time period). IN THE MEANTIME AS SPECIALS BECOME AVAILABLE WE'LL GIVE YOU A CALL . . . . . AND KEEP YOU IN OUR BROCHURE MAILINGS . . . . . ! THANKS AGAIN FOR YOUR TIME.

Exhibit 9 PRIME PLASTICS INC. Telemarketer Special Pricing Script

GOOD __________________________, THIS IS __________________________ FROM PRIME PLASTICS IN CHICAGO. MAY I SPEAK WITH THE PURCHASING MANAGER PLEASE! (obtain name)
(NAME), (your name), OF PRIME PLASTICS IN CHICAGO. WE'RE CALLING SHOPS IN THE (city) AREA TODAY TO INTRODUCE PRIME PLASTICS CO. ARE YOU FAMILIAR WITH OUR COMPANY?

(YES) . . . AS YOU KNOW . . .
(NO)

WE'RE DISTRIBUTORS OF MOST OF THE MAJOR BRANDS OF PLASTICS IN SHEET, ROD AND TUBE ! . . . AND HAVE ONE OF THE LARGEST INVENTORIES IN THE MIDWEST AS WELL AS ONE OF THE MAJOR MANUFACTURERS OF PHENOLIC ROD!! . . . AND AGAIN OUR PRIMARY PURPOSE IN CALLING IS TO INTRODUCE PRIME PLASTICS AND . . . TO OFFER OUR INTRODUCTORY SPECIAL ON G-10.

(OBJECTIONS)

WITH YOUR FIRST ORDER - WE'LL TAKE 10% OFF THE PURCHASE PRICE . . . . !

(CLOSE)
(OBJECTIONS)

FINE (name), WE WOULD LIKE YOU TO KEEP PRIME PLASTICS IN MIND WHEN YOU NEED G-10 OR ANY OTHER LAMINATES, WE CAN GENERALLY SHIP WITHIN 24 HOURS! AND WE CARRY MOST MAJOR BRANDS . . . FOR EXAMPLE, NYLON, WHICH WE CAN OFFER ON OUR 10% OFF SPECIAL! . . . . . .
FINE, AT LEAST YOU'RE AWARE! AS PART OF OUR CONTINUING SERVICE TO YOU WE'LL CALL FROM TIME TO TIME WITH OUR SPECIALS . . . WHEN WOULD BE THE BEST TIME TO CHECK BACK WITH YOU? . . . ALSO PERIODICALLY WE SEND OUT OUR BROCHURES . . . WOULD YOU LIKE TO BE INCLUDED IN OUR MAILING? . . . (confirm contact name & address) (Name) AGAIN, THANKS FOR YOUR TIME AND REMEMBER PRIME PLASTICS OF CHICAGO ON YOUR NEXT ORDER!

UNITED TIRE COMPANY

Phil Hart, Vice President of Sales for United Tire Company, hung up the phone and heaved a sigh of fatigue. He had just concluded a conversation with Jay Johnson, a regional division sales manager in Atlanta. Johnson had described the growing morale problem among his field sales representatives. Many of them had heard about a new telemarketing program that was being adopted by the company which, in their opinion, would cause significant reductions in the salesforce. Other rumors that were circulating indicated that those salespersons who did keep their jobs would find their compensation reduced significantly as a result of United's use of telemarketing to achieve sales.

Background

United Tire Company, a manufacturer of a full line of automotive tires, sells on a nationwide scale to car manufacturers in the United States as well as retail tire dealers. The number of automotive and tire dealers that United serves is approximately 20,000. Among these retailers are a wide variety of types and sizes of businesses. Some of United's customers are chains like K mart and Target. Others are small garages owned and operated by one person. The customers of United are distributed across the United States in a pattern closely resembling the national population distribution. Sales figures for United Tire Company are listed in Table 1.

The salesforce consists of 340 sales representatives managed by 20 district managers who, in turn, report to 5 division managers whose offices are in White Plains, New York; Atlanta, Georgia; St. Louis, Missouri; Denver, Colorado; and Los Angeles, California. The salesforce is organized on a geographic basis with each person assigned a number of counties, an SMSA (Standard Metropolitan Statistical Area), or a portion of an SMSA that provided each salesperson with an approximately equal sales potential.

Compensation of the sales personnel is a combination salary plus commission. Commissions were calculated on the percentage of a gross dollar volume that a sales representative attains each month. Average compensation for the salesforce is $38,000 per year. The lowest paid sales representative received $25,000 and the highest paid received $70,000. As a result of the above-average compensation and benefits package, the salesforce turnover rate was low. Over the past four years the average was less than 10% a year.

United Tire Company is facing the same forms of pressure that confront other domestic tire manufacturers. Foreign brands such as Bridgestone and Michelin have entered the U.S. market during the past ten years. The foreign marketers have intro-

---

Source: This case was prepared by John I. Coppett, Associate Professor of Marketing, and William A. Staples, Professor of Marketing, University of Houston–Clear Lake. Reprinted with permission.

Table 1 **1986 Gross Sales for United Tire Company**

$50 million	Automotive manufacturers purchasing tires for use on new cars and trucks
$200 million	Sales to retailers which included: $40 million–1,000 of the largest United customers $160 million—sales made to the remaining 19,000 customers
$250 million gross sales	

Table 2 **Average Cost of a Sales Call for a United Tire Representative**

1975	$ 64.14
1977	$ 87.11
1979	$123.32
1981	$160.20
1983	$184.86
1985	$206.73

duced high-quality products while also keeping prices at or below the U.S. tire prices. This factor coupled with rising sales costs (see Table 2) caused United's profits to slump by approximately 3% a year for the past 4 years. United's top management has embarked on a vigorous campaign to cut costs and raise employee productivity.

Mr. Hart sensed the need to adopt significant cost-saving practices that would show that the Sales Department was aggressively attacking the problems of high costs. Therefore, when an invitation to attend a seminar on telemarketing was extended to Hart by the telephone company, he accepted it.

The leaders of the seminar emphasized several points which were new to most of the executives attending the program. First, the audience was told that telemarketing was much more than just selling over the telephone to private consumers. Some of the other telemarketing applications that were of immediate interest to Hart involved the qualification of sales leads prior to turning the leads over to a field representative for a face-to-face visit. One of the many diagrams shown to the audience illustrated how the sales lead qualification program worked (see Figure 1).

The average cost to qualify a lead through the telemarketing program was $5.00, which included all of the costs associated with paying salaries, telephone service, and other overhead costs. An example the seminar leader provided to support her claim about the effectiveness of this program involved an adopter of the program who had improved the ratio of sales-closed to sales-calls-made from 1 out of 10 to 5 out of 10. A .500 batting average is fantastic in the sales world!

In addition to the sales lead qualification possibilities, Hart was also intrigued by another application called "marginal account handling." The seminar example featured a situation in which a well-known greeting card manufacturer used telemarketing to continue to serve the thousands of small retail establishments where greeting

Figure 1 **A Sales Lead Qualification Program Using Telemarketing**

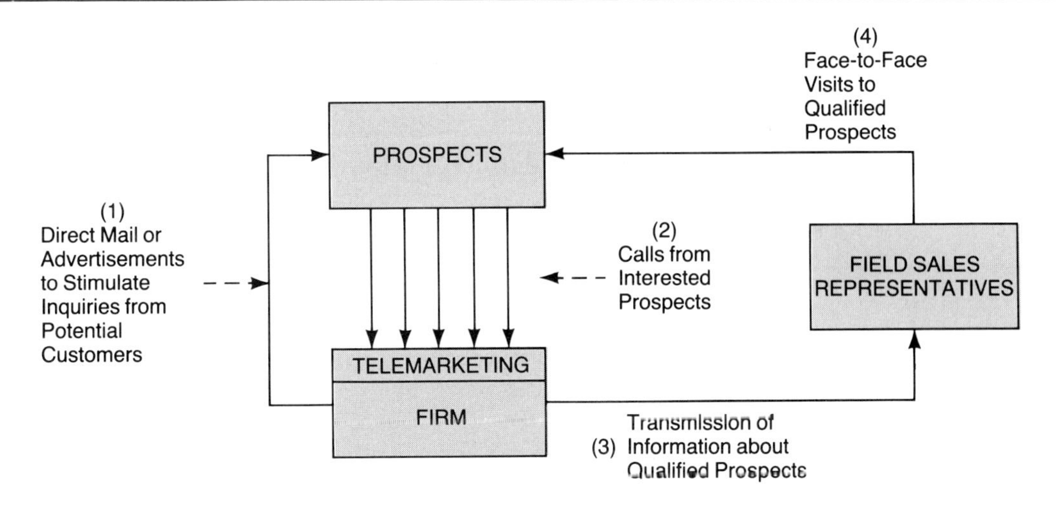

Sequence of Steps in Qualification Process.

1. Firm sponsors advertising of various kinds to stimulate inquiries from people who may be prospective customers.
2. Prospects respond by using (in this case) an 800 number to acquire more information and are then "qualified" by a telemarketing specialist.
3. Prospect's names which have been acquired during the qualification process are passed to field sales.
4. Field sales representatives call on only those consumers or businesses that have been submitted as qualified prospects.

cards were sold. In this situation, the greeting card marketer had realized almost ten years ago that there was no way to economically continue to achieve intensive distribution and serve all of the small accounts through face-to-face contact. By turning the marginally profitable accounts over to the new telemarketing center to handle, more frequent contact was maintained with the small gift shops, drug stores, and grocery stores. Presently, the greeting card marketer served almost 90 percent of its customer base through the telemarketing center. Although Hart's firm sold tires, the parallel to his problem did not escape his attention.

Shortly after attending the seminar, Mr. Hart received a call from a telephone company person who proposed a meeting to discuss the United Tire Company's situation. At the meeting, the telephone representative offered to work with Hart and his people to establish a telemarketing pilot program to test the feasibility of using telemarketing at United Tire Company. The initial test was designated for White Plains, New York. Three people were hired and trained to take in-coming calls from prospects who were making inquiries to various advertisements, brochures, and direct mail (i.e., the "raw material" for sales leads).

In addition, to maximize the productivity of the three telemarketing specialists, each specialist was given 100 dormant accounts to contact. The telemarketing personnel were to attempt to sell tires that had been priced at a very attractive level for this situation. The purpose of this arrangement was to revive the accounts. The offer featured not only low-priced tires but also a two-day maximum delivery time plus a toll-free "hot line" for dealers to get instant service on any problems they were having with the United Tire Company's products or services.

The success of the pilot was apparent within three weeks. After tracking the success of the field salespeople who followed up on the qualified leads furnished to them, Hart discovered that their sales-closed to sales-visits-made ratio exceeded 3.3 out of 10. This was compared to the national average of United's salesforce, which was 2 out of 10. The marginal, or dormant, account situation was also doing quite well. Twenty percent of the accounts contacted had responded favorably, with purchases that averaged $2,000 per customer.

As a by-product of some of the conversations the telemarketing specialists had had with customers, Hart learned that several customers had indicated they had not been contacted by a field salesperson from United Tire in many months. Some of the customers revealed their desire to continue to do business via the telemarketing program rather than having a field representative call on them.

After witnessing the pilot program results in White Plains for two months, Hart submitted a request for $300,000 to develop a telemarketing program in each of the other regional offices. After reviewing the proposal, Hart's superiors approved the request.

During the weekly teleconference Phil Hart had with the regional sales managers, he announced that within the next three months each regional office would have a sales lead qualification program and a marginal account program. The division managers were told to come to White Plains for additional briefing on the telemarketing program that would be implemented at United Tire Company.

It was two weeks after the division managers' meeting in White Plains that Hart received the call from Jay Johnson.

MORGANTOWN INC.

In November 1986 Morgantown Inc. merged with Lea-Meadows Industries, a manufacturer of upholstered furniture for living and family rooms. The merger was not planned in a conventional sense. Charlton Bates' father-in-law died suddenly in August 1986, leaving his daughter with controlling interest in the firm. The merger proceeded smoothly, since the two firms were located on adjacent properties and the general consensus was that the two firms would maintain as much autonomy as was economically justified. Moreover, the upholstery line filled a gap in the Morgantown product mix, even though it would retain its own identity and brand names.

The only real issue that continued to plague Bates was merging the selling effort. Morgantown had its own salesforce, but Lea-Meadows Industries relied on sales agents to represent it. The question was straighforward, in his opinion: "Do we give the upholstery line of chairs and sofas to our salesforce, or do we continue using the sales agents?" Mr. John Bott, Morgantown's sales vice-president, said the line should be given to his sales group; Mr. Martin Moorman, national sales manager of Lea-Meadows Industries, said the upholstery line should remain with sales agents.

Lea-Meadows Industries

Lea-Meadows Industries is a small manufacturer of upholstered furniture for use in living and family rooms. The firm is over seventy-five years old. The company has some of the finest fabrics and frame construction in the industry, according to trade sources. Net sales in 1986 were $3 million. Total industry sales of 1,500 upholstered furniture manufacturers in 1986 were $4.4 billion. Company sales had increased 15 percent annually over the last five years, and company executives believed this growth rate would continue for the foreseeable future.

Lea-Meadows Industries employed fifteen sales agents to represent its products. These sales agents also represented several manufacturers of noncompeting furniture and home furnishings. Often a sales agent found it necessary to deal with several buyers in a store in order to represent all lines carried. On a typical sales call, a sales agent would first visit buyers. New lines, in addition to any promotions being offered by manufacturers, would be discussed. New orders were sought where and when it was appropriate. A sales agent would then visit a retailer's selling floor to check displays, inspect furniture, and inform sales people on furniture. Lea-Meadows Industries paid an agent commission of 5 percent of net company sales for these services. Moorman thought sales agents spent 10 to 15 percent of their in-store sales time on Lea-Meadows products.

Source: This case is used with the permission of its author, Roger A. Kerin, Edwin L. Cox School of Business, Southern Methodist University, Dallas, Texas.

The company did not attempt to influence the type of retailers that agents contacted. Yet it was implicit in the agency agreement that agents would not sell to discount houses. All agents had established relationships with their retail accounts and worked closely with them. Sales records indicated that agents were calling on furniture and department stores. An estimated 1,000 retail accounts were called on in 1986.

Morgantown Inc.

Morgantown Inc. is a manufacturer of medium- to high-priced living and dining room wood furniture. The firm was formed in 1902. Net sales in 1986 were $50 million. Total estimated industry sales of wood furniture in 1986 were $7.1 billion at manufacturers' prices.

The company employed 10 full-time sales representatives who called on 1,000 retail accounts in 1986. These individuals performed the same function as sales agents, but were paid a salary plus a small commission. In 1986 the average Morgantown sales representative received an annual salary of $50,000 (plus expenses) and a commission of 0.5 percent on net company sales. Total sales administration costs were $112,500.

The Morgantown salesforce was highly regarded in the industry. The salesmen were known particularly for their knowledge of wood furniture and willingness to work with buyers and retail sales personnel. Despite these points, Bates knew that all retail accounts did not carry the complete Morgantown furniture line. He had therefore instructed John Bott to "push the group a little harder." At present, sales representatives were making ten sales calls per week, with the average sales call running three hours. Remaining time was accounted for by administrative activities and travel. Bates recommended that the call frequency be increased to seven calls per account per year, which was consistent with what he thought was the industry norm.

Merging the Sales Effort

In separate meetings with Bott and Moorman, Bates was able to piece together a variety of data and perspectives on the question. These meetings also made it clear that Bott and Moorman differed dramatically in their views.

John Bott had no doubts about assigning the line to the Morgantown salesforce. Among the reasons he gave for this approach were the following. First, Morgantown had developed one of the most well respected, professional sales groups in the industry. Sales representatives could easily learn the fabric jargon, and they already knew personally many of the buyers who were responsible for upholstered furniture. Second, selling the Lea-Meadows line would require only about 15 percent of present sales call time. Thus he thought the new line would not be a major burden. Third, more control over sales efforts was possible. He noted that Charlton Bates's father-in-law had developed the sales group twenty-five years earlier because of the commitment it engendered and the service "only our own people are able and willing to give." Moreover, our people have the Morgantown "look" and presentation style that is instilled in every person. Fourth, he said it wouldn't look right if we had our representatives and agents calling on the same stores and buyers. He noted that Morgantown and Lea-Meadows industries overlapped on all their accounts. He said, "We'd be paying a commission on sales to these accounts when we would have gotten them anyway. The difference in commission percentages would not be good for morale."

Martin Moorman advocated keeping sales agents for the Lea-Meadows line. His arguments were as follows. First, all sales agents had established contacts and were highly regarded by store buyers, and most had represented the line in a professional manner for many years. He, too, had a good working relationship with 15 agents. Second, sales agents represented little, if any, cost beyond commissions. Moorman noted, "Agents get paid when we get paid." Third, sales agents were committed to the Lea-Meadows line: "The agents earn a part of their living representing us. They have to service retail accounts to get the repeat business." Fourth, sales agents were calling on buyers not contacted by Morgantown sales representatives. He noted, "If we let Morgantown people handle the line, we might lose these accounts, have to hire more sales personnel, or take away 25 percent of the present selling time given to Morgantown product lines."

As Bates reflected on the meetings, he felt that a broader perspective was necessary beyond the views expressed by Bott and Moorman. One factor was profitability. Existing Morgantown furniture lines typically had gross margins that were 5 percent higher than those for Lea-Meadows upholstered lines. Another factor was the "us and them" references apparent in the meetings with Bott and Moorman. Would merging the sales efforts overcome this, or would it cause more problems? Finally, the idea of increasing the sales force to incorporate the Lea-Meadows line did not sit well with him. Adding a new salesperson would require restructuring of sales territories, potential loss of commission to existing people, and "a big headache."

MEDIQUIP, S.A.

On January 18, 1981, Kurt Thaldorf, a sales engineer for the German sales subsidiary of Mediquip, S.A., was informed by Lohmann University Hospital in Stuttgart that it had decided to place an order with Sigma, a Dutch competitor, for a CT scanner. The hospital's decision came as disappointing news to Thaldorf, who had worked for nearly eight months on the account. The order, if obtained, would have meant a sale of DM 1,580,000 for the sales engineer. He was convinced that Mediquip's CT scanner was technologically superior to Sigma's, and overall a better product.

Thaldorf began a review of his call reports in order to better understand the factors that led to Lohmann University Hospital's decision. He wanted to apply the lessons from this case to future sales situations.

Background

The computer tomography (CT) scanner was a relatively recent product in the field of diagnostic imaging. The medical device, used for diagnostic purposes, allowed examination of cross sections of the human body through display of images. CT scanners combined sophisticated X-ray equipment with a computer to collect the necessary data and translate them into visual images.

When computer tomography was first introduced in the late 1960s, radiologists hailed it as a major technological breakthrough. Commenting on the advantages of CT scanners, a product specialist with Mediquip said, "The end product looks very much like an X-ray image. The only difference is that with scanners you can see sections of a body that were never seen before on a screen—like the pancreas. A radiologist, for example, can diagnose the cancer of pancreas less than two weeks after it develops. This was not possible before the CT scanners."

Mediquip was a subsidiary of Technologie Universelle, a French conglomerate. The company's product line included, in addition to CT scanners, X-ray, ultrasonic and nuclear diagnostic equipment. Mediquip enjoyed worldwide a reputation for advanced technology and competent after-sales service.

"Our competitors are mostly from other European countries," commented Mediquip's Sales Director for Europe. "In some markets they have been there longer than we have and they know the decision makers better than we do. But we are learning fast." Sigma, the subsidiary of a diversified Dutch company under the same name, was the company's most serious competitor. Other major contenders in the CT scanner market were FNC, Eldora, Magna and Piper.

Source: The case was prepared by Professor Kamran Kashani as a basis for class discussion rather than to illustrate either effective or ineffective handling of an administrative situation.

Mediquip executives estimated the European market for CT scanners to be in the neighborhood of 200 units per year. They pointed out that prices ranged between DM 1–2 million per unit. The company's CT scanner sold in the upper end of the price range. "Our equipment is at least two years ahead of our most advanced competition," explained a sales executive. "And our price reflects this technological superiority."

Mediquip's sales organization in Europe included eight country sales subsidiaries, each headed by a managing director. Within each country, sales engineers reported to regional sales managers who themselves reported to the managing director. Product specialists provided technical support to the sales force in each country.

Buyers of CT Scanners

A sales executive at Mediquip described the buyers of CT scanners as follows:

> Most of our sales are to what we call the public sector, the health agencies that are either government-owned or belong to non-profit support organizations such as universities and philanthropic institutions. They are the sort of buyers who buy through formal tenders and who have to budget their purchases at least one year in advance. Once the budget is allocated it must then be spent before the end of the year. Only a minor share of our CT scanner sales goes to the private sector, the profit oriented organizations such as private hospitals or private radiologists.
>
> Between the two markets, the public sector is much more complex. Typically, there are at least four groups who get involved in the purchase decision: the radiologists, the physicists, the administrators and the people from the supporting agency—usually those who approve the budget for purchase of a CT scanner.
>
> Radiologists are users of the equipment. They are doctors whose diagnostic services are sought by other doctors in the hospital or clinic. Patients remember their doctors, but not the radiologists. They never receive flowers from the patients! A CT scanner could really enhance their professional image among their colleagues.
>
> Physicists are the scientists in residence. They write the technical specifications which competing CT scanners must meet. The physicists should know the state of the art in X-ray technology. Their primary concern is the patient's safety.
>
> The administrators are, well, administrators. They have the financial responsibility for their organization. They are concerned with the cost of CT scanners, but also with what revenues they can generate. The administrators are extremely wary of purchasing an expensive technological toy that becomes obsolete in a few years' time.
>
> The people from the supporting agency are usually not directly involved with decisions as to which product to purchase. But since they must approve the

expenditures, they do play an indirect role. Their influence is mostly felt by the administrators.

The interplay among the four groups, as you can imagine, is quite complex. The power of each group in relationship to the others varies from organization to organization. The administrator, for example, is the top decision-maker in certain hospitals. In others, he is only a buyer. One of the key tasks of our sales engineers is to define for each potential account the relative powers of the players. Only then can they set priorities and formulate selling strategies.

The European sales organization of Mediquip had recently put into use a series of forms designed to help sales engineers in their account analysis and strategy formulation. A sample of the forms, called Account Management Analysis, is reproduced in Exhibit 1.

Lohmann University Hospital

Lohmann University Hospital (LUH) was a large general hospital serving Stuttgart, a city of one million residents. The hospital was part of the university's medical school. The university was a leading teaching center and enjoyed an excellent reputation. LUH's radiology department had a variety of X-ray equipment from a number of European manufacturers including Sigma and FNC. Five radiologists staffed the department, which was headed by a senior and nationally known radiologist, Professor Steinborn.

Thaldorf's Sales Activities. From the records he had kept of his sales calls, Thaldorf reviewed the events for the period between June 5, 1980, when he learned of LUH's interest in purchasing a CT scanner and January 18, 1981, when he was informed the Mediquip had lost the order.

June 5, 1980 Office received a call from a Professor Steinborn from Lohmann University Hospital regarding a CT scanner. I was assigned to make the call on the professor. Looked through our files to find out if we had sold anything to the hospital before. We had not. Made an appointment to see the professor on June 9.

June 9, 1980 Called on Professor Steinborn who informed me of a recent decision by university directors to set aside funds next year for the purchase of the hospital's first CT scanner. The professor wanted to know what we had to offer. Told him the general features of our CT system. Gave him some brochures. Asked a few questions which led me to believe other companies had come to see him before I did. Told me to check with Dr. Rufer, the hospital's physicist, regarding the specs. Made an appointment to see him again in ten days' time. Called on Dr. Rufer who was not there. His secretary gave me a lengthy document on the scanner specs.

June 10, 1980 Read the specs last night. Looked like they had been copied straight from somebody's technical manual. Showed them to our Product Specialist who confirmed my own hunch that our system met and exceeded the specs. Made an appointment to see Dr. Rufer next week.

June 15, 1980 Called on Dr. Rufer. Told him about our system's features and the fact that we met all the specs set down on the document. He looked somewhat unimpressed. Left him with technical documents on our system.

June 19, 1980 Called on Professor Steinborn. Had read the material I had left with him. Looked sort of pleased with the features. Asked about our upgrading scheme. Told him we would undertake to upgrade the system as new features became available. Unlike other systems, Mediquip can be made to accommodate the latest technology. There will be no risk of obsolescence for a long time. He was quite impressed. Also answered his questions regarding image manipulation, image processing speed and our service capability. Just before I left he inquired about our price. Told him I would have an informative quote for him at our next meeting. Made an appointment to see him on July 23 after he returned from his vacation. Told me to get in touch with Carl Hartmann, the hospital's general director, in the interim.

July 1, 1980 Called on Hartmann. It was difficult to get an appointment with him. Told him about our interest in supplying his hospital with our CT scanner which met all the specs as defined by Dr. Rufer. Also informed him of our excellent service capability. He wanted to know which other hospitals in the country had purchased our system. Told him I would drop him a list of buyers in a few days' time. Asked about the price. Gave him an informative quote of DM 1,900,000—a price we had arrived at with my boss since my visit to Professor Steinborn. He shook his head saying, "Other scanners are cheaper by a wide margin." I explained that our price reflected the latest technology which was incorporated in it. Also mentioned that the price differential was an investment that could pay for itself several times over through faster speed of operation. He was noncommittal. Before leaving his office he instructed me not to talk to anybody else about the price. Asked him specifically if it included Professor Steinborn. He said it did. Left him with a lot of material on our system.

July 3, 1980 Took a list of three other hospitals of a similar size that had installed our system to Hartmann's office. He was out. Left it with his secretary who recognized me. Learned from her that at least two other firms, Sigma and FNC, were competing for the order. She also volunteered the information that "prices are so different, Mr. Hartmann is confused." She added that the final decision will be made by a committee made up of Hartmann, Professor Steinborn and one other person whom she could not recall.

July 20, 1980 Called on Dr. Rufer. Asked him if he had read the material on our system. He had. But did not have much to say. Repeated some of the key operational advantages our product enjoyed over those produced by others including Sigma and FNC. Left him some more technical documents.

Exhibit 1 **Mediquip, S.A. Account Management Analysis Forms**

Key Account: ______________________________

ACCOUNT MANAGEMENT ANALYSIS

The enclosed forms are designed to facilitate your management of:

1 A key sales account

2 The *Mediquip* resources that can be applied to this key account

Completing the enclosed forms, you will:

- Identify installed equipment, and planned or potential new equipment
- Analyze purchase decision process and influence patterns, including:
  - —Identify and prioritize all major sources of influence
  - —Project probable sequence of events and timing of decision process
  - —Assess position/interest of each major influence source
  - —Identify major competition and probable strategies
  - —Identify needed information/support
- Establish an account development strategy, including:
  - —Select key contacts
  - —Establish strategy and tactics for each key contact, identify appropriate *Mediquip* personnel
  - —Assess plans for the most effective use of local team and headquarters resources

KEY ACCOUNT DATA

☐ Original (Date: ________)	Account No.: ________	Type of Institute: ________
☐ Revision (Date: ________)	Sales Specialist: ________	Bed Size: ________
	Country/Region/District: ________	Telephone: ________

1. CUSTOMER (HOSPITAL, CLINIC, PRIVATE INSTITUTE)

   Name: ________

   Street Address: ________

   City, State: ________

2. DECISION MAKERS—IMPORTANT CONTACTS

INDIVIDUALS	NAME	SPECIALTY	REMARKS
Medical Staff			
Administration			
Local Government			
State Government			

This exhibit presents a condensed version of the forms, which comprised eight 8½ × 11 inch sheets for entry of relevant information.

3. INSTALLED EQUIPMENT

TYPE	DESCRIPTION	SUPPLIED BY	INSTALLATION DATE	YEAR TO REPLACE	VALUE OF POTENTIAL ORDER
X-ray Nuclear Ultrasound RTP CT					

4. PLANNED NEW EQUIPMENT

TYPE	QUOTE		% CHANCE	EST. ORDER DATE		EST. DELIVERY		QUOTED PRICE
	NO.	DATE		1980	1981	1980	1981	

5. COMPETITION

COMPANY/PRODUCT	STRATEGY/ TACTICS	% CHANCE	STRENGTH	WEAKNESS

6. SALES PLAN Product: __________ Quote No: __________ Quoted Price: __________

KEY ISSUES	*Mediquip's* PLAN	SUPPORT NEEDED FROM:	DATE OF FOLLOW-UP/REMARKS

7. ACTIONS—IN SUPPORT OF PLAN

SPECIFIC ACTION	RESPONSIBILITY	DUE DATES			RESULTS/REMARKS
		ORIGNIALS	REVISED	COMPLETED	

8. ORDER STATUS REPORT

REVISION DATE	ACCOUNT NAME AND LOCATION	ISSUES/ COMPETITIVE STRATEGY	ACTIONS/ STRATEGY	RESPON-SIBILITY	% CHANCE	EXPECTED ORDER TIMING	WIN/LOSE

On the way out, stopped by Hartmann's office. His secretary told me that we had received favorable comments from the hospitals using our system.

July 23, 1980 Professor Steinborn was flabbergasted to hear that I could not discuss our price with him. Told him of the hospital administration's instructions to the effect. He was not convinced especially when Sigma had already revealed to him their quote of DM 1,400,000. When he he calmed down he wanted to know if we were going to be at least competitive with the others. Told him our system was more advanced that Sigma's. Promised him we would do our best to come up with an attractive offer. Then we talked about his vacation and sailing experience in the Aegean Sea. He said he loved the Greek food.

August 15, 1980 Called to see if Hartmann had returned from his vacation. He had. While checking his calendar, his secretary told me that our system seemed to be the "radiologists' choice," but that Hartmann had not yet made up his mind.

August 30, 1980 Visited Hartmann accompanied by the regional manager. Hartmann seemed bent on the price. He said, "All companies claim they have the latest technology." So he could not understand why our offer was "so much above the rest." He concluded that only a "very attractive price" could tip the balance in our favor. After repeating the operational advantages our system enjoyed over others, including those produced by Sigma and FNC, my boss indicated that we were willing to lower our price to DM 1,740,000 if the equipment was ordered before the end of the current year. Hartmann said he would consider the offer and seek "objective" expert opinion. He also said a decision would be made before Christmas.

September 15, 1980 Called on Professor Steinborn who was too busy to see me for more than ten minutes. He wanted to know if we had lowered our price since the last meeting with him. I said we had. He shook his head saying laughingly, "Maybe that was not your best offer." He then wanted to know how fast we could make deliveries. Told him within six months. He did not say anything.

October 2, 1980 Discussed with our regional manager about the desirability of inviting one or more people from the LUH to visit the Mediquip headquarter operations near Paris. The three-day trip would have given the participants a chance to see the scope of the facilities and become better acquainted with CT scanner applications. The idea was finally rejected as inappropriate.

October 3, 1980 Dropped in to see Hartmann. He was busy but had the time to ask for a formal "final offer" from us by November 1. On the way out, his secretary told me of "a lot of heated discussions" around which scanner seemed best suited for the hospital. She would not say more.

October 25, 1980 The question of price was raised in a meeting between the regional manager and the managing director. I had recommended a sizeable cut in our price to win the order. The regional manager seemed to agree with me. But the managing director was reluctant. His concern was that too much of a drop in price looked "unhealthy." They finally agreed to a final offer of DM 1,580,000.

Made an appointment to see Hartmann later that week.

October 29, 1980 Took our offer of DM 1,580,000 in a sealed envelope to Hartmann. He did not open it, but commented he hoped the scanner question would be resolved soon to the "satisfaction of all concerned." Asked him how the decision was going to be made. He evaded the question but said he would notify us as soon as a decision was reached. Left his office feeling that our price had a good chance of being accepted.

November 20, 1980 Called on Professor Steinborn. He had nothing to tell me but "the CT scanner is the last thing I like to talk about." Felt he was unhappy with the way things were going.

Tried to make an appointment with Hartmann in November, but he was too busy.

December 5, 1980 Called on Hartmann who told me that a decision would probably not be reached before next January. He indicated that our price was "within the range," but that all the competing systems were being evaluated to see which seemed most appropriate for the hospital. He repeated that he would call us when a decision was reached.

January 18, 1981 Received a brief letter from Hartmann thanking Mediquip for participating in the bid for the CT scanner and informing it of the decision to place the order with Sigma.

PART THREE

DESIGNING THE SALES ORGANIZATION

THE two chapters in Part 3 discuss sales organization design issues. Chapter 7 investigates different approaches for organizing the activities of sales managers and salespeople. The key concepts of specialization, centralization, span of control versus management levels, and line versus staff positions are emphasized as the basic elements of sales organization structure. Special attention is directed toward the increasingly important area of major account management.

Chapter 8 continues the sales organization discussion by addressing issues related to allocating selling effort to accounts, determining the appropriate sales-force size, and designing sales territories. The key considerations in each of these areas are discussed, and different decision making approaches are presented.

CHAPTER 7

ORGANIZING THE ACTIVITIES OF SALES MANAGERS AND SALESPEOPLE

Learning Objectives

After completing this chapter, you should be able to

1. Define the concepts of specialization, centralization, span of control versus management levels, and line versus staff positions.
2. Describe the different ways that salesforces might be specialized.
3. Evaluate the advantages and disadvantages of different sales organization structures.
4. Name the important considerations in organizing major account management programs.
5. Explain how one determines the appropriate sales organization structure for a given selling situation.

CHANGING THE SALES ORGANIZATION: XEROX

The Xerox sales organization had been structured along product lines. The sales organization consisted of several salesforces that each concentrated on selling specific products to many different customers. For example, the largest salesforce included approximately 3,500 sales representatives that sold copier and duplicator products to most customers. There were several other dedicated salesforces of 75 to 200 salespeople for printing systems, office systems, information processing systems, facsimile, and sales engineering. This type of product specialization led to many situations where several different Xerox salespeople called on the same account to sell different products. In some cases, Xerox was competing against itself!

In the mid-1980s Xerox made business and marketing strategy changes. Instead of emphasizing individual products, the new strategies were designed to position Xerox as a marketer of sophisticated business systems. Implementing these new organizational strategies required changes in Xerox's account strategies, aiming them toward developing stronger partnership relationships with accounts. Since it was clear that developing the desired account relationships would be extremely difficult with the sales organization emphasizing individual products, Xerox embarked on a five-year plan (beginning in mid-1985) to redesign the sales organization.

The initial redesign plan consisted of establishing four salesforces:

1. A salesforce of 250 to 300 national account managers to service the largest accounts with national operations.
2. A salesforce of 900 to 1,000 major account managers to service accounts that were large in certain regions.
3. A salesforce of account representatives to service medium-sized businesses.
4. A salesforce of approximately 4,000 marketing representatives to service the remaining accounts, especially smaller businesses.

Source: Adapted from Thayer C. Taylor, "Xerox's Sales Force Learns a New Game," *Sales and Marketing Management,* July 1, 1985, 48–51; and "Xerox's Makeover," *Sales and Marketing Management,* June 1987, 68.

Since this initial reorganization, Xerox has also added a special markets salesforce to service intermediaries in their indirect distribution channels and a custom systems salesforce to service the federal government and other large noncommercial accounts.

Although there are still some product specialists, most of the salespeople in each salesforce sell most of Xerox's products to specific types of accounts. The emphasis has changed from product specialization to specialization by account size. The basic purpose of this reorganization is to facilitate the development of long-term relationships with accounts for their business system needs. According to William Blair, senior vice-president of customer and major account marketing, Xerox is "segmenting the marketplace and is structuring the salesforce to provide the direction, training, and product knowledge to fit each segment."

The advantages of the account-specialized salesforces are several. First, accounts now interface with only one Xerox salesperson for all of their business system needs. Second, since each salesperson can sell most products, the salespeople have a much higher probability of being able to talk with a key decision maker when making a sales call. Xerox's research showed that when a copier salesperson made a sales call, the chances of reaching a key decision maker were only 1 in 25. As the salespeople have been able to sell more products, this ratio has been reduced to less than 1 to 5. Lowering this ratio has greatly increased the sales per salesperson. Finally, as developments in new technology lead to many new business system products, Xerox would have had to add many additional salesforces to maintain the product specialization emphasis. The new sales organization structure can more easily adapt to new product introductions.

Although the benefits of the reorganization are many, it has been and will be very expensive to implement. Compensation plans have been revised to reflect the different selling cycles of the different account groups. A systematic three-tier training program has also been developed to provide the salespeople with the knowledge and skills required to sell a large, complex product line. New computerized information systems are also being developed to provide salespeople with account and competitive information.

Xerox continues to fine-tune its reorganization plans. The company is taking a long-term approach toward implementing the plan and evaluating its success. As David R. Myerscough, vice-president of marketing and planning, suggested, "You can't look at something this ambitious as an overnight affair."

CHAPTERS 5 and 6 discussed the close relationships between corporate, business, marketing, and account strategies. The different strategic levels must be consistent and integrated to be effective. Strategic changes at one organizational level typically require strategic changes at other organizational levels.

The development of effective strategies is one thing, successfully implementing them another.[1] In one sense, the remainder of this book is concerned with the development and management of a sales organization to implement organizational strategies successfully. This chapter begins the journey into successful implementation by investigating the key decisions required in developing a sales organization structure.

The Xerox example in the opening vignette illustrates the close link between strategy and structure. As Xerox changed its strategic focus from the sale of individual products to relationship marketing of integrated business systems, the sales organization structure had to be revised. A product specialized sales organization could not effectively implement the new strategy. An account oriented sales organization was needed to create and nurture the desired customer relationships. Although the organizational changes made by Xerox were drastic, reorganization of this magnitude is not normally required. However, strategic changes almost always necessitate adjustments in sales organization structure.

Our coverage of sales organization structure begins with discussing the basic concepts underlying all sales organization structures. Situational factors that should be considered in making decisions on sales organization structure are then examined. The chapter concludes by presenting and analyzing several different sales organization structures, with special attention to major account organizations.

SALES ORGANIZATION CONCEPTS

The basic problem in sales organization structure can be presented in very simple terms. The corporate, business, marketing, and account strategies developed by a firm prescribe specific activities that must be performed by salespeople for these strategies to be successful. Sales managers are also needed to recruit, select, train, motivate, supervise, evaluate, and control salespeople. In essence, the firm has salespeople and sales managers that must engage in a variety of activities for the firm to perform successfully. A sales organization structure must be developed to help salespeople and sales managers perform the required activities in an effective and efficient manner. This structure provides a framework for sales organization operations by indicating what specific activities are performed by whom in the sales organization. The sales organization structure is the vehicle through which strategic plans are translated into selling operations in the marketplace.

Developing a sales organization structure is difficult. Many different types of structures might be used, and many variations are possible within each basic type. Often the resultant structure is extremely complex with many boxes and arrows. The basic concepts involved are specialization, concentration, span of control versus management levels, and line versus staff positions.[2]

Specialization

Our earlier discussion suggested that a sales organization structure must ensure that all required selling and management activities are performed. In the simplest case, each salesperson could perform all selling tasks, and each sales manager could perform all management activities. Most sales organizations, however, are too complex for this structure and require instead some degree of **specialization**, in which certain individuals concentrate on performing some of the required activities to the exclusion of other tasks. Thus, certain salespeople might sell only certain products or call on certain customers. Some sales managers might concentrate on training, others on planning.

The basic idea behind specialization is that by concentrating on a limited number of activities, individuals can become experts on those tasks, leading to better performance for the entire organization. Though an appealing idea, specialization can produce problems for organizational structure. The more specialization in an organization, the more difficult it is to integrate the efforts of the specialized units.[3] Consider the Xerox situation prior to its recent sales organization changes. Xerox had several salesforces that specialized in selling specific products. The salespeople became experts in the products being sold, but it was extremely difficult to integrate their efforts to satisfy the total business system needs of individual customers. Xerox addressed this problem by reorganizing its sales organization to specialize by account type. Another way some companies integrate their specialized units is through their management structure.

A useful way to view salesforce specialization is from the perspective of the continuum presented in Figure 7.1. At one extreme salespeople act as generalists, performing all selling activities for all of the company's products to all types of customers. Moving toward the right of the continuum, salespeople begin to specialize by performing only certain selling tasks, selling only certain types of products, or calling on only specific types of accounts. There seems to be a trend toward more salesforce specialization. In a recent study, 49 percent of the respondents indicated that they expect to be more dependent upon specialists in the next five years, while only 15 percent indicated more dependency on generalists.[4]

Most firms employ some mixture of generalization and specialization. Salespeople specialize in some areas and are generalists in others. Take the Xerox situation. Under the old sales organization, salespeople were product specialists and account generalists. Under the new sales organization structure, salespeople are product generalists and account specialists. The critical decision facing sales management is determining the type and amount of specialization to use in a particular selling situation.

Centralization

An important characteristic of the management structure within a sales organization is its degree of **centralization** — that is, the degree to which important decisions and tasks are performed at higher levels in the management hierarchy. A centralized structure is one where authority and responsibility are placed at higher management levels. An organization becomes more decentralized as tasks become the responsibility of lower-level managers. Centralization is a relative concept in that no organization is totally centralized or totally decentralized. Organizations typically centralize some activities and decentralize others. However, most organizations tend to have a centralized or decentralized orientation.

Figure 7.1 **Salesforce Specialization Continuum**

There is a broad range of alternatives for specializing salesforce activities.

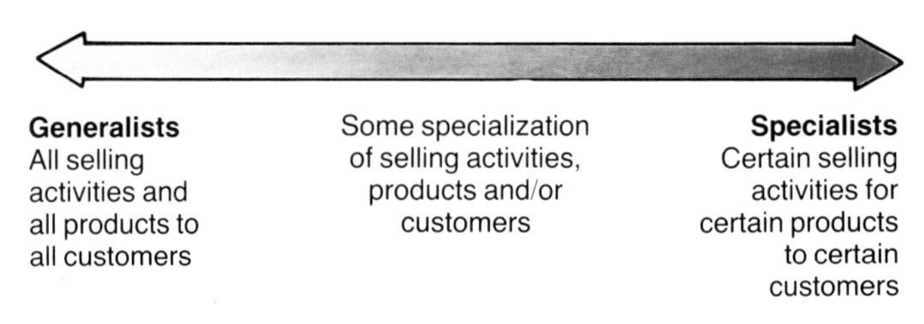

Changing to a more centralized management structure is one way to help integrate the activities of specialized units. A decentralized structure provides less integration capability but promotes more responsive decision making and is usually preferable when there is little salesforce specialization. For example, Herman Miller markets office furniture to different customer types. The salesforce is not specialized, except by geographic area. The company recently added more managers at the sales director and sales district levels. The purpose of these changes was to "decentralize the decision making so you get ownership and accountability in the field."[5] Thus, the centralization and specialization decisions are interrelated and must be considered together in designing a sales organization structure.

Span of Control versus Management Levels

Span of control refers to the number of individuals that report to each sales manager. The larger the span of control, the more subordinates that a sales manager must supervise. **Management levels** define the number of different hierarchical levels of sales management within the organization. Typically, span of control is inversely related to the number of sales management levels. This relationship is illustrated in Figure 7.2.

In the flat sales organization structure, there are relatively few sales management levels, with each sales manager having a relatively large span of control. Conversely, in the tall structure, there are more sales management levels and smaller spans of control. Flat organization structures tend to be used to achieve decentralization, while tall structures are more appropriate for centralized organizations. The span of control also tends to increase at lower sales management levels. Thus, as one moves down the organization chart from national sales manager to regional sales manager to district sales manager, the number of individuals to be supervised directly increases.

Line versus Staff Positions

Sales management positions can be differentiated as to line or staff positions. **Line sales management** positions are part of the direct management hierarchy within the

Figure 7.2 **Span of Control versus Management Levels**

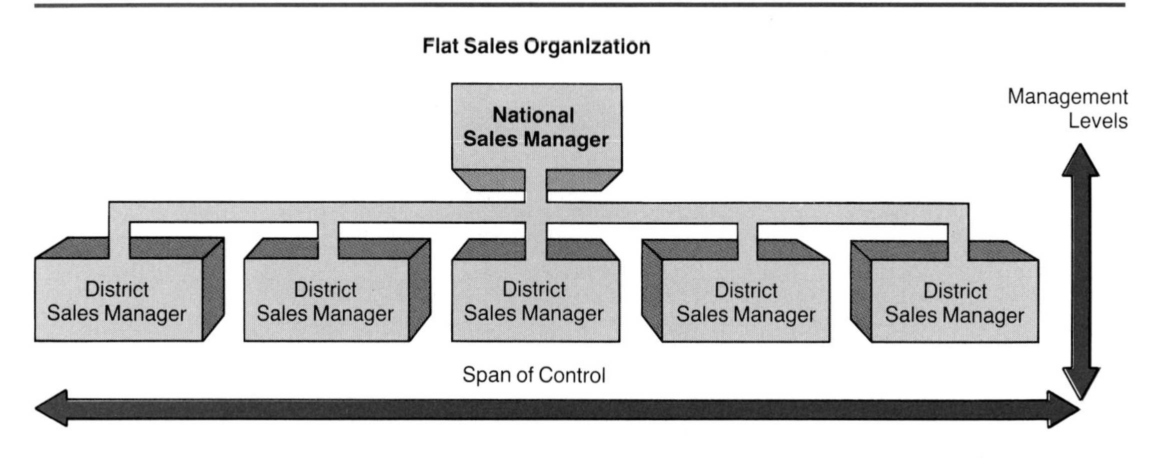

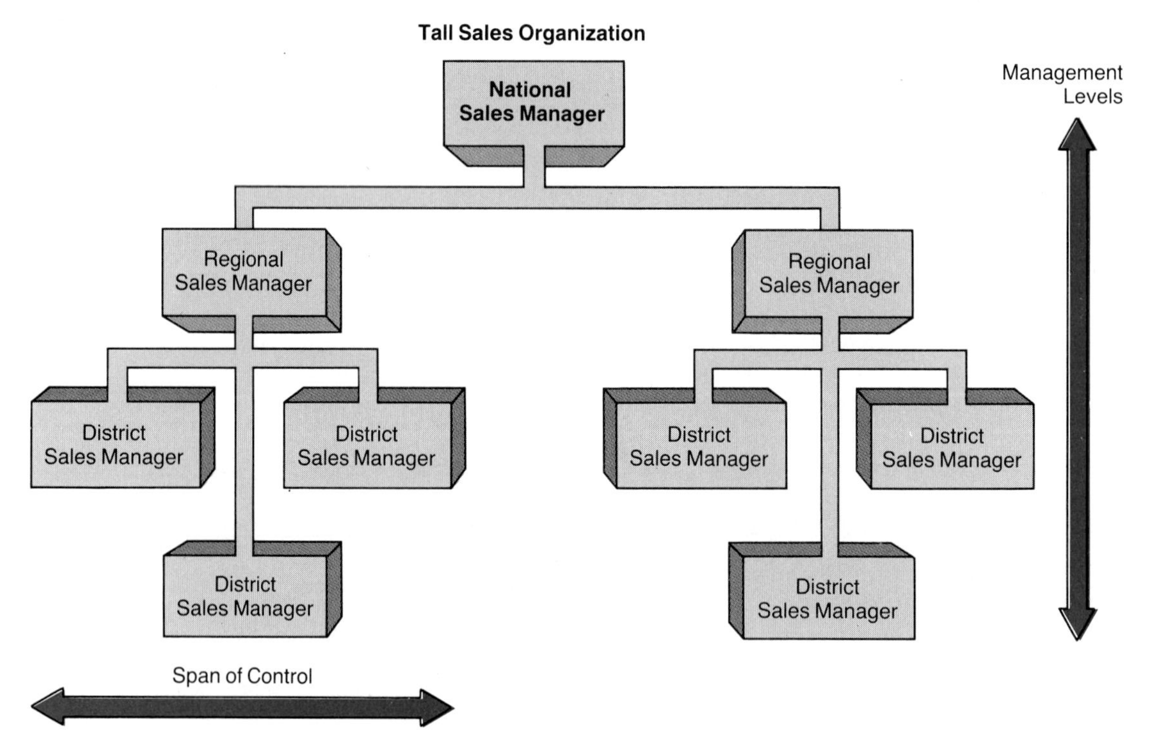

The flat sales organization has only two sales management levels, giving the national sales manager a span of control of 5. The tall sales organization has three sales management levels, giving the national sales manager a span of control of only 2.

Figure 7.3 **Line versus Staff Positions**

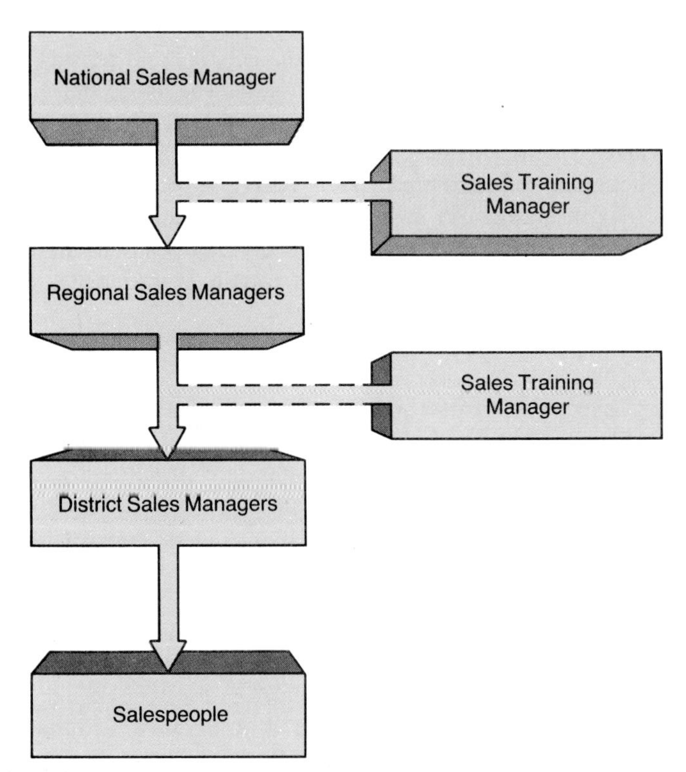

The national, regional, and district sales managers occupy line positions, while the sales training managers represent staff positions.

sales organization. Line sales managers have direct responsibility for a certain number of subordinates and report directly to management at the next highest level in the sales organization. These managers are directly involved in the sales-generating activities of the firm and may perform any number of sales management activities. **Staff sales management** positions, on the other hand, are not in the direct chain of command in the sales organization structure. Instead, those in staff positions occupy management status within the sales organization. They do not directly manage people, but they are responsible for certain functions (e.g., recruiting and selecting, training, etc.) and are not directly involved in sales-generating activities. Staff sales management positions are more specialized than line sales management positions.

A comparison of line and staff sales management positions is presented in Figure 7.3. The regional and district sales managers all operate in line positions. The district sales managers directly manage the field salesforce and report to a specific regional sales manager. The regional sales managers manage the district sales managers and report to the national sales manager. Two staff positions are represented in the figure. These training managers are located at both the national and regional levels and are responsible for sales training programs at each level. The use of staff positions results in more specialization of sales management activities. Staff managers specialize in certain sales management activities.

In sum, designing the sales organization is an extremely important and complex task. Decisions concerning the appropriate specialization, centralization, span of control versus management levels, and line versus staff positions are difficult. These decisions should be based on evaluations of certain characteristics of each selling situation.

SELLING SITUATION CONTINGENCIES

Determining the appropriate type of sales organization structure is as difficult as it is important. There is no one best way to organize a salesforce. The appropriate organization structure depends or is contingent upon the characteristics of the selling situation. As a selling situation changes, the type of sales organization structure may also need to change. The Xerox reorganization provides a good illustration of the way one firm altered its sales organization in response to changes in business and marketing strategies.

One of the key decisions in sales organization design relates to specialization. Two basic questions must be addressed:

1. Should the salesforce be specialized or not?
2. If the salesforce should be specialized, what type of specialization is most appropriate?

The decision on specialization hinges on the relative importance to the firm of selling skill versus selling effort. There is some empirical support for the notion that a generalized salesforce should be used when selling effort is more important than selling skill and a specialized one for the reverse case.[6] Thus, if sales management

Exhibit 7.1 **Selling-Situation Factors and Organizational Structure**

Organization Structure	Environmental Characteristic	Task Performance	Performance Objective
Specialization	High environmental uncertainty	Nonroutine	Adaptiveness
Centralization	Low environmental uncertainty	Repetitive	Effectiveness

Source: Robert W. Ruekert, Orville C. Walker, Jr., and Kenneth J. Roering, "The Organization of Marketing Activities: A Contingency Theory of Structure and Performance," *Journal of Marketing,* Winter 1985, 20–21.

Figure 7.4 **Customer and Product Determinants of Salesforce Specialization**

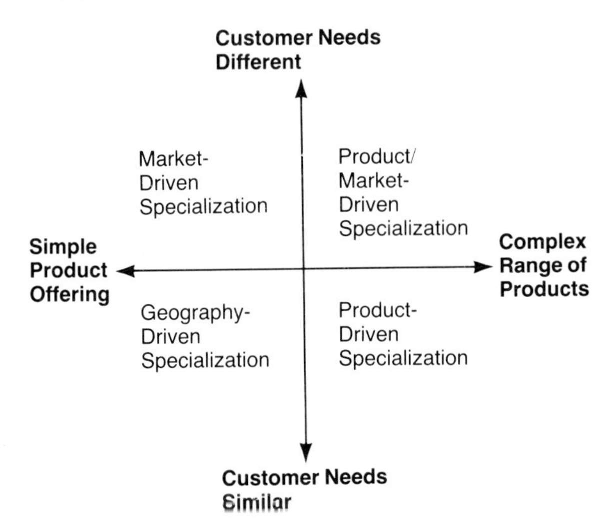

Analysis of the similarity of customer needs and the complexity of a firm's product offering can provide general guidelines for determining the appropriate type of salesforce specialization.

Source: David W. Cravens, *Strategic Marketing* (Homewood, Ill.: Irwin, 1987), 541. Used with permission.

wants to emphasize the amount of selling contact, a generalized salesforce should be used. If sales management wants to focus on specific skills within each selling contact, then a specialized salesforce should be used. Obviously, there must be some balance between selling effort and selling skill in all situations. But sales management can skew this balance toward selling effort or selling skill by employing a generalized or specialized salesforce.

Research results also suggest that environmental characteristics, task characteristics, and performance objectives are important considerations in sales organization design. Some guidelines for sales organization structure and these selling situation factors are presented in Exhibit 7.1. This exhibit suggests that a specialized structure is best when there is a high level of environmental uncertainty, when salespeople and sales managers must perform creative and nonroutine activities, and when adaptability is critical to achieving performance objectives. Centralization is most appropriate when environmental uncertainty is low, sales organization activities are routine and repetitive, and the performance emphasis is on effectiveness.

Two of the most important factors in determining the appropriate type of specialization are the similarity of customer needs and the complexity of products offered by the firm. Figure 7.4 illustrates how these factors can be used to suggest the appropriate type of specialization. For example, when the firm has a simple product offering, but customers have different needs, a market specialized salesforce is recommended. If, however, customers have similar needs and the firm sells a complex range of products, then a product specialized salesforce is more appropriate.

A comprehensive decision making framework is presented in Figure 7.5. This framework suggests that the type of salesforce specialization depends not only upon customer and product factors, but also upon characteristics of the market environment, the professionalism of the salesforce, and the nature of the selling job. Thus, sales management could use this framework as a checklist to analyze many aspects of its selling situation to determine the appropriate type of salesforce specialization.

Figures 7.4 and 7.5 provide guidelines that sales management can use to determine the appropriate type of specialization. Decisions concerning centralization, span of control versus management levels, and line versus staff positions require analysis of similar selling situation factors. Decisions in these areas must be consistent with the specialization decision. For example, decentralized organization structures with few management levels, large spans of control, and the use of staff positions may be consistent with a specialized salesforce in some selling situations, but not in others. The appropriate sales organization structure depends upon the specific characteristics of a firm's selling situation. As selling situation characteristics change, sales organization structures may also need change.

SALES ORGANIZATION STRUCTURES

Designing the sales organization structure requires integration of the desired degree of specialization, centralization, span of control, management levels, line positions, and staff positions. Obviously, there are a tremendous number of different ways that a sales organization might be structured. Our objective is to review several of the basic and most often used ways and to illustrate some variations in these basic structures.

In order to provide continuity to this discussion, each type of sales organization will be discussed from the perspective of the ABC Company. The ABC Company markets office equipment (typewriters, furniture, etc.) and office supplies (paper, pencils, etc.) to commercial accounts and to government accounts. The firm employs 200 salespeople who operate throughout the United States. The salespeople perform various activities that can be characterized as being related either to sales generation or account servicing. Examples of different types of sales organization structures that the ABC Company might use are presented and discussed.

Geographic Sales Organization

Most salesforces use some type of **geographic specialization**. This is the least specialized and most generalized type of salesforce. Salespeople are typically assigned a geographic area and are responsible for all selling activities within the assigned area. There is no attempt to specialize by product, market, or function. For example, Her-

Figure 7.5 Salesforce Specialization Contingencies

Selling-Situation Factors	Specialization Forms: Geographic	Product	Customer	Functional (Task)
I. *Customer*				
1. Distinctiveness and complexity of needs	–	+	+	+
2. Number of people in buying process	–	+	+	+
3. Degree of product knowledge	–	+	+	+
II. *Product*				
4. Consistency of product mix	+	–	–	+
5. Width and depth of product lines	–	+	–	–
6. Technological complexity	–	+	+	+
7. Profitability	–	+	+	+
III. *Market Environment*				
8. Geographic concentration	–	+	+	+
9. Number of potential customers	+	+	+	+
10. Profitable sales potential of each customer in market	–	+	+	+
IV. *Sales Force*				
11. Level of professionalism	–	+	+	+
V. *Nature of Selling Job*				
12. Degree of creative selling demanded in sales job	–	+	+	+

Degree This Factor Characterizes Your Firm and Its Environment

\+ High Degree of This Factor Should Be Present

– Low Degree of This Factor Should Be Present

This framework presents the types of selling situation factors most appropriate for the different types of salesforce specialization.

Source: Adapted from Robert J. Zimmer and Paul S. Hugstad, "A Contingency Approach to Specializing an Industrial Salesforce," *Journal of Personal Selling and Sales Management*, Spring–Summer 1981, 33. Used with permission.

Figure 7.6 **Geographic Sales Organization**

National Sales Manager
Sales Training Manager
Eastern Regional Sales Manager
Western Regional Sales Manager
Zone Sales Managers (4)
Zone Sales Managers (4)
District Sales Managers (20)
District Sales Managers (20)
Salespeople (100)
Salespeople (100)

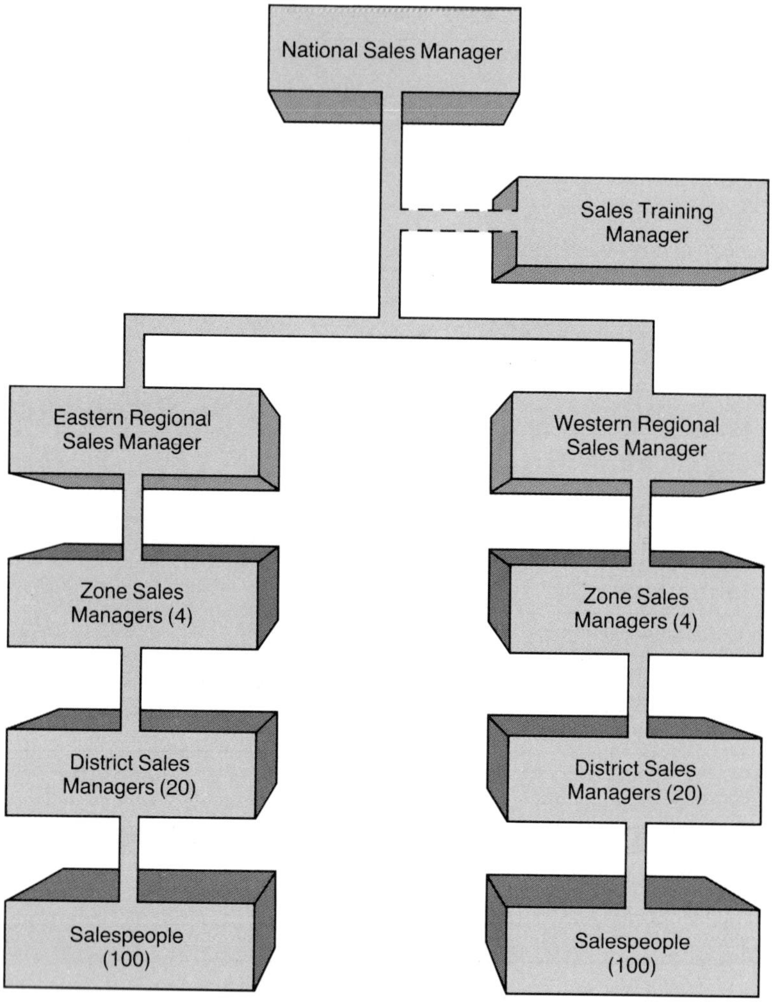

This geographic sales organization structure has four sales management levels, small spans of control, and a staff position at the national level.

man Miller markets office furniture to dealers, specifiers in the architectural and design community, and end users. The company has 245 salespeople who perform all selling functions for all products and accounts within an assigned geographic area.[7] An example of a geographic sales organization for the ABC Company is presented in Figure 7.6. Again, note that this type of organization provides no salesforce specialization except by geographic area. Because of the lack of specialization, there is no duplication of effort. All geographic areas and accounts are served by only one salesperson.

The structure in this example is a rather tall one and thus somewhat centralized. There are four levels of line sales management with relatively small spans of control: national sales managers (2), regional sales managers (4), zone sales managers (5), and district sales managers (5). Note the sales management specialization in the sales training staff position. Since this staff position is located at the national sales manager level, training activities tend to be centralized.

Product Sales Organization

Product specialization has been popular in recent years, but it seems to be declining in importance, at least in certain industries.[8] Salesforces specializing by product assign salespeople selling responsibility for specific products or product lines. The objective is for salespeople to become experts in the assigned product categories. For example, Gillette has separate salesforces for its personal care products and for its writing products.[9] Salespeople might also specialize by brands of the same type of product. This type of product specialization is exemplified by Cooper Tire and Rubber's use of separate salesforces for Cooper brands, Falls brands, and house brands of tires.[10]

An example of a product sales organization for the ABC Company is presented in Figure 7.7. This organization structure indicates two levels of product specialization. There are two separate salesforces: one salesforce specializes in selling office equipment, while the other specializes in selling office supplies. Each of the specialized salesforces performs all selling activities for all types of accounts. The separate salesforces are each organized geographically. Thus, there will be duplication in the coverage of geographic areas, with both office equipment and office supplies salespeople operating in the same areas. In some cases, the salespeople may call on the same accounts.

The example structure in Figure 7.7 is flat and decentralized, especially when compared to the example presented in Figure 7.6. There are only three line management levels with wide spans of control: national sales managers (2), product sales managers (10), and district sales managers (10). This structure has no staff positions and thus no management specialization beyond product specialization. The office equipment and office supplies salesforces are organized in exactly the same manner.

Market Sales Organization

An increasingly important type of specialization is **market specialization**. Salespeople are assigned specific types of customers and required to satisfy all needs of these customers. Market specialization can take several forms:

1. *Broad market specialization*. The Fonda Group, a marketer of disposable paper cups, plates and related products, has separate salesforces for the consumer and organizational markets.[11]

Figure 7.7 **Product Sales Organization**

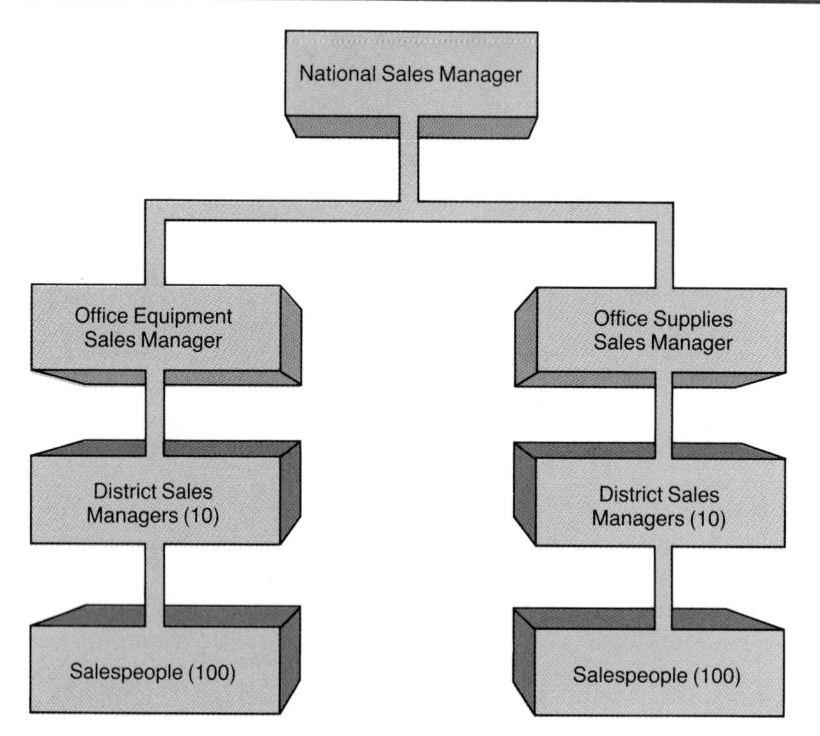

This product sales organization structure has three sales management levels, large spans of control, and no staff positions.

2. *Specific industry specialization.* Data General uses separate salesforces to market minicomputer products to customers in the automotive, financial services, insurance, aerospace, and electronic equipment markets.[12]
3. *Specialization by type of distributor.* Kimberly-Clark's U.S. Consumer Sales Division employs separate salesforces to market diapers, tissues, and feminine products to consumers through grocery stores, mass merchandisers, and Military PXs.[13]
4. *Specialization by account size.* See "Sales Trend: Specialization by Account Size at Pitney Bowes."

The basic objective of market specialization is to ensure that salespeople understand how customers use and purchase their products. Salespeople should then be able to direct their efforts to satisfy customer needs better.

SALES TREND

SPECIALIZATION BY ACCOUNT SIZE AT PITNEY BOWES

Pitney Bowes has diversified into four basic businesses: mailing products, shipping products, copying products, and inserting products. The salesforce had been organized geographically, with each salesperson selling all products to approximately 250 accounts of various sizes. According to George Bradbury, vice-president of sales planning, this type of salesforce organization was not effective since "sometimes we were sending an expert in to sell a $13-a-month postage meter, and we were sending a novice in to our most valuable customers."

The company decided to change from a geographic specialization to specialization by account size. The reorganization created three separate salesforces:

1. A national accounts salesforce of 50 salespeople to service the firm's 400 largest customers.
2. A major accounts salesforce of 100 salespeople to service 1,500 multi-location customers with centralized purchasing.
3. A salesforce of area sales representatives to service the remaining 1,000,000 customers and prospects.

There are also product specialists that can be used to help salespeople with specific accounts.

The reorganization appears to have been successful. Mr. Bradbury feels that "we get more business at a lower cost. The people are more productive . . . the good people get in front of the best customers, and they sell more."

Source: Howard Sutton, *Rethinking the Company's Selling and Distribution Channels* (New York: The Conference Board, 1986), 10–11. Used with permission.

The market sales organization shown for the ABC Company in Figure 7.8 focuses on account types. Separate salesforces have been organized for commercial accounts and for government accounts. Salespeople perform all selling activities for all products, but only for certain accounts. This arrangement avoids duplication of sales effort, since salespeople will never call on the same accounts. They may, however, operate in the same geographic areas.

The example in Figure 7.8 presents some interesting variations in sales management organization. The commercial accounts salesforce is much more centralized than the government accounts salesforce. This centralization is due to more line management levels, shorter spans of control, and a specialized sales training staff position. This example structure illustrates the important point that the specialized salesforces within a sales organization do not have to be structured in the same manner.

Functional Sales Organization

The final type of specialization is **functional specialization**. Most selling situations require a number of selling activities, so there may be efficiencies in having salespeople specialize in performing certain of these required activities. Gillette, for example,

Figure 7.8 **Market Sales Organization**

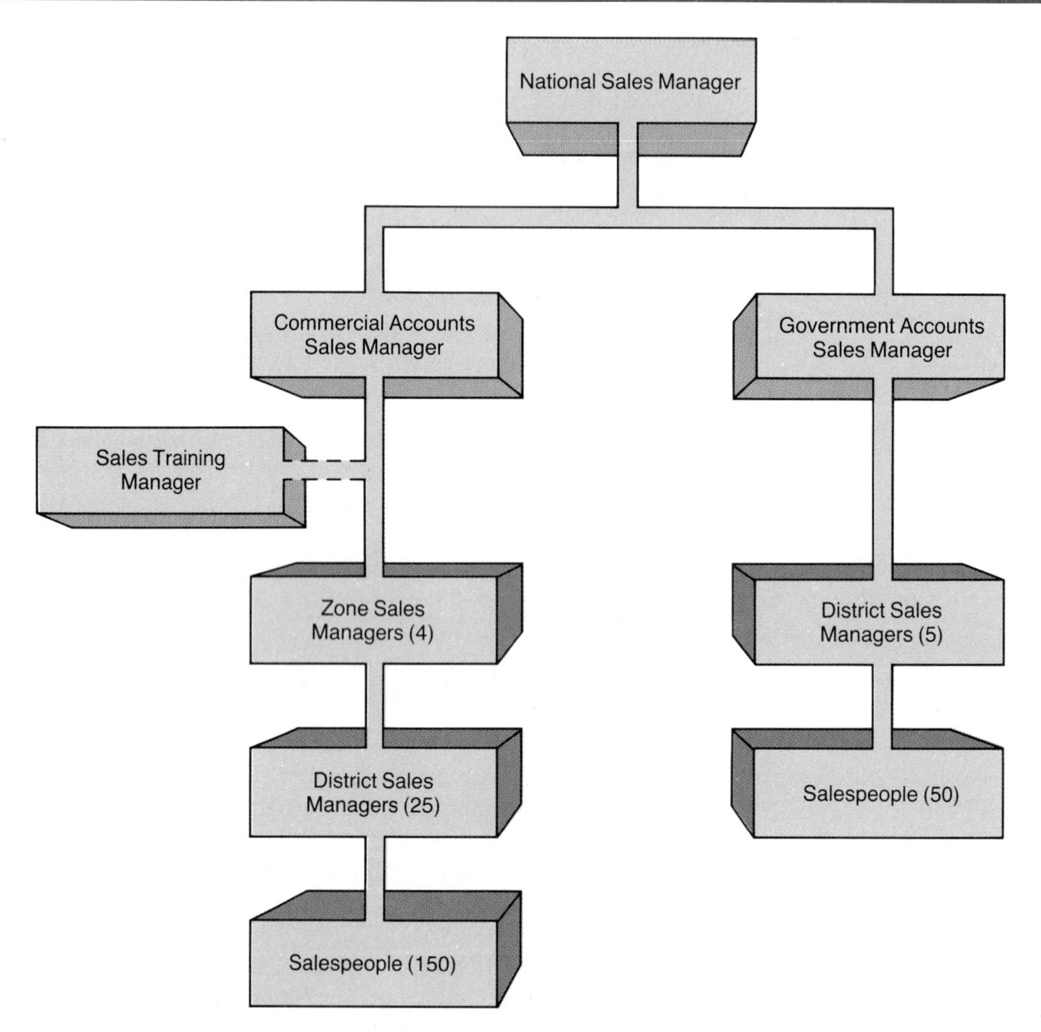

This market sales organization structure organizes its commercial accounts salesforce differently from its government accounts salesforce. The commercial accounts salesforce has three sales management levels, small spans of control, and a staff position. The government accounts salesforce has two sales management levels, large spans of control, and no staff positions.

uses its direct salespeople to sell products and to talk with buyers about pricing, distribution, promotion and display. A separate group of merchandisers is used to make sure that everything goes well at the point of sale by stocking shelves, checking on displays, and performing other in-store activities. As already discussed in Chapter

Figure 7.9 **Functional Sales Organization**

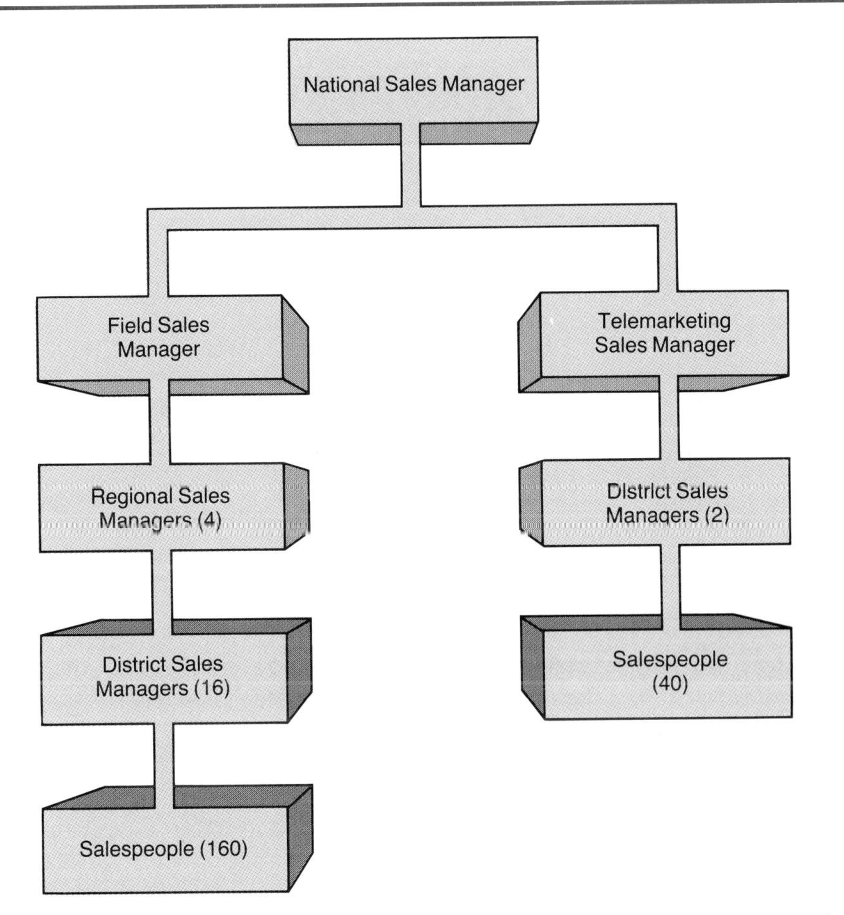

This functional sales organization structure organizes its field salesforce differently from its telemarketing salesforce. The field salesforce has three sales management levels with small spans of control, while the telemarketing salesforce has two sales management levels with large spans of control. Neither salesforce utilizes staff positions.

6, many firms are using a telemarketing salesforce to generate leads, qualify prospects, monitor shipments, and so forth, while the outside salesforce concentrates on sales-generating activities. These firms are specializing by function.

An example of a functional sales organization for ABC Company is presented in Figure 7.9. This is a structure where a field salesforce is used to perform sales-generating activities and a telemarketing salesforce is used to perform account-servicing activities. Although the salesforces will cover the same geographic areas and the same accounts, the use of telemarketing helps to reduce the cost of this duplication of

INTERNATIONAL SALES

EXPANDING MAJOR ACCOUNT PROGRAMS TO INTERNATIONAL MARKETS

Many firms are expanding their major account management programs into international markets. Mr. Jerome A. Colletti, president of The Alexander Group, suggests that international major account marketing "has become a necessity for survival." Many firms seem to agree. Consider the following examples:

- The Moore Business Forms and Systems Division of Toronto-based Moore Corp. has developed major account programs in Japan to serve customers in the automotive, electronic, and financial services industries. One of the goals of the program is to increase the firm's market share among U.S. operations of Japanese-owned companies.
- Occidental Chemical Corp. is using international major account programs to serve its customers that operate globally. The objective is to allow these customers to have continuity in their relationships with Occidental. Major accounts represent 35 percent of total company sales.

Source: Kate Bertrand, "National Account Marketing," *Business Marketing*, November 1987, 48.

effort. The more routine and repetitive activities will be performed by the inside, telemarketing salesforce. The more creative and nonroutine sales-generating activities will be performed by the outside, field salesforce.

The field salesforce is more centralized than the telemarketing salesforce, but both salesforces tend to be decentralized. The cost effectiveness of telemarketing is illustrated by the need for only two management levels and three managers to supervise 40 salespeople. This example does not include any staff positions for sales management specialization.

Major Account Organizations

Many firms receive a large percentage of their total sales from relatively few accounts. These large-volume accounts are obviously extremely important and must be considered when designing a sales organization. The term *major account* is used to refer to large, important accounts that should receive special attention from the sales organization. Some firms use the term *national account* instead. Others use both terms, with national accounts representing large accounts with multiple buying locations, and major accounts representing large customers with single buying locations. We will use the term *major account* to refer to all large, important accounts in this text. A **major account organization** represents a type of market specialization by account size.

Major account organization has become increasingly important in both domestic and international markets (see "International Sales: Expanding Major-Account Pro-

Figure 7.10 **Identifying Major Accounts**

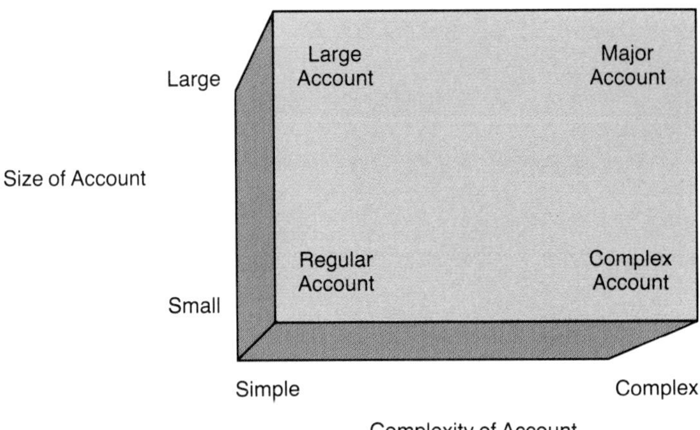

Major accounts are both large and complex. They are extremely important to the firm and require specialized attention.

Source: Adapted from Benson P. Shapiro and Rowland T. Moriarity, *National Account Management: Emerging Insights* (Cambridge, Mass.: Marketing Science Institute, March 1982), 6.

grams to International Markets"). Although major account programs differ considerably across firms, all firms must determine how to identify their own major accounts and how to organize for effective coverage of them.[14]

Identifying Major Accounts. All large accounts do not qualify as major accounts. As illustrated in Figure 7.10, a major account should be of sufficient size and complexity to warrant special attention from the sales organization. An account can be considered complex under the following circumstances:[15]

- Its purchasing function is centralized.
- Top management heavily influences its purchasing decisions.
- It has multi-site purchasing influences.
- Its purchasing process is complex and diffuse.
- It requires special price concessions.
- It requires special services.
- It purchases customized products.

Organizing for Major Account Coverage. Accounts that are not both large and complex are typically served adequately through the basic sales organization structure, but those identified as major accounts pose problems for organization design

Figure 7.11 **Major Account Options**

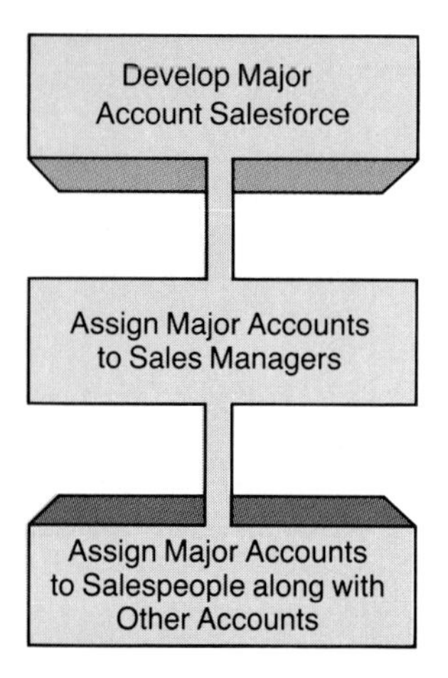

Once identified, major accounts can be served in three basic ways. The development of a major account salesforce is the most comprehensive approach and is being employed increasingly often for customers in domestic and international markets.

Source: Adapted from Benson P. Shapiro and Rowland T. Moriarity, *Organizing the National Account Force* (Cambridge, Mass.: Marketing Science Institute, April 1984), 1–37.

that might be handled in a variety of ways. The basic options are shown in Figure 7.11. In one option, major accounts, although identified, are assigned to salespeople as are other accounts. This approach may provide some special attention to these accounts, but is not a formal major account management program.

Many firms have found that formal major account management programs can strengthen account relationships and improve communications between buyers and sellers.[16] These formal programs are designed in several ways.[17] One approach is to assign major accounts to sales executives, who are responsible for coordinating all activities with each assigned account. This major account responsibility is typically in addition to the executives' normal management activities.

An increasingly popular approach is to establish a separate major accounts salesforce. This approach is a type of market specialization where salespeople specialize by type of account based on size and complexity (recall the Xerox and Pitney Bowes examples presented earlier in this chapter). Another example of this approach is the major account salesforce used by AT&T. Because of the complexity of the major accounts served by AT&T, each major account team consists of a direct marketing specialist, sales specialist, telemarketing account executive, and major account executive. Each member of the major account team focuses on specific activities for specific individuals within the account. AT&T has found this approach to result in more revenue from major accounts at lower selling costs than traditional major account approaches.[18]

One study found that firms tend to use four different major account sales organization structures (see Figure 7.12). Whatever the structure chosen, major account management programs appear to be a trend that will increase in the future. Recent research suggests that firms currently using major account management programs can be profiled in the following manner:[19]

- Total company sales are $1.1 billion.
- Major account program is eight years old.
- Major account revenues represent 30 percent of company sales.
- Major account organization serves 95 customers.
- Major account organization consists of seven salespeople.
- Each major account salesperson is assigned 12 customers.
- A major account salesperson generates $34 million in total sales, or $3 million per customer.

A recent survey of senior marketing executives found that 59 percent saw major account programs as a high priority in the next three years.[20] Although these programs may take different forms, the ultimate objective of all of them is to develop strong and lasting relationships with large and complex accounts. As illustrated in "Sales Technology: Use of High Technology in Major Account Management," technology is being used to maintain long-term relationships with major accounts.

SALES TECHNOLOGY

USE OF HIGH TECHNOLOGY IN MAJOR ACCOUNT MANAGEMENT

Major account management programs are incorporating the use of sophisticated electronic communication and training systems to better serve major accounts. Consider the following examples:

- Dun and Bradstreet Credit Services has developed an electronic information service for major transportation accounts. Called Dun's Transport, the service provides a means for trucking firms to get credit and collection information over the telephone. The major account dials the Dun's Transport phone number, enters a password, and enters the trucking customer's phone number. A computer-simulated voice asks questions about the type of information desired. The major account answers the questions by punching various buttons on the phone and receives the desired information.
- Xerox Corp. is developing a range of computer-based services to enhance major account satisfaction. Services being considered range from electronic invoicing to end-user training. Currently in the pilot stage are an electronic order system for major accounts and an interactive learning system where Xerox can provide training material directly to the computer workstations at a major account.

Source: Kate Bertrand, "High-Tech NAM Treatment," *Business Marketing*, November 1987, 44.

Figure 7.12 Major-Account Sales Organization Structures

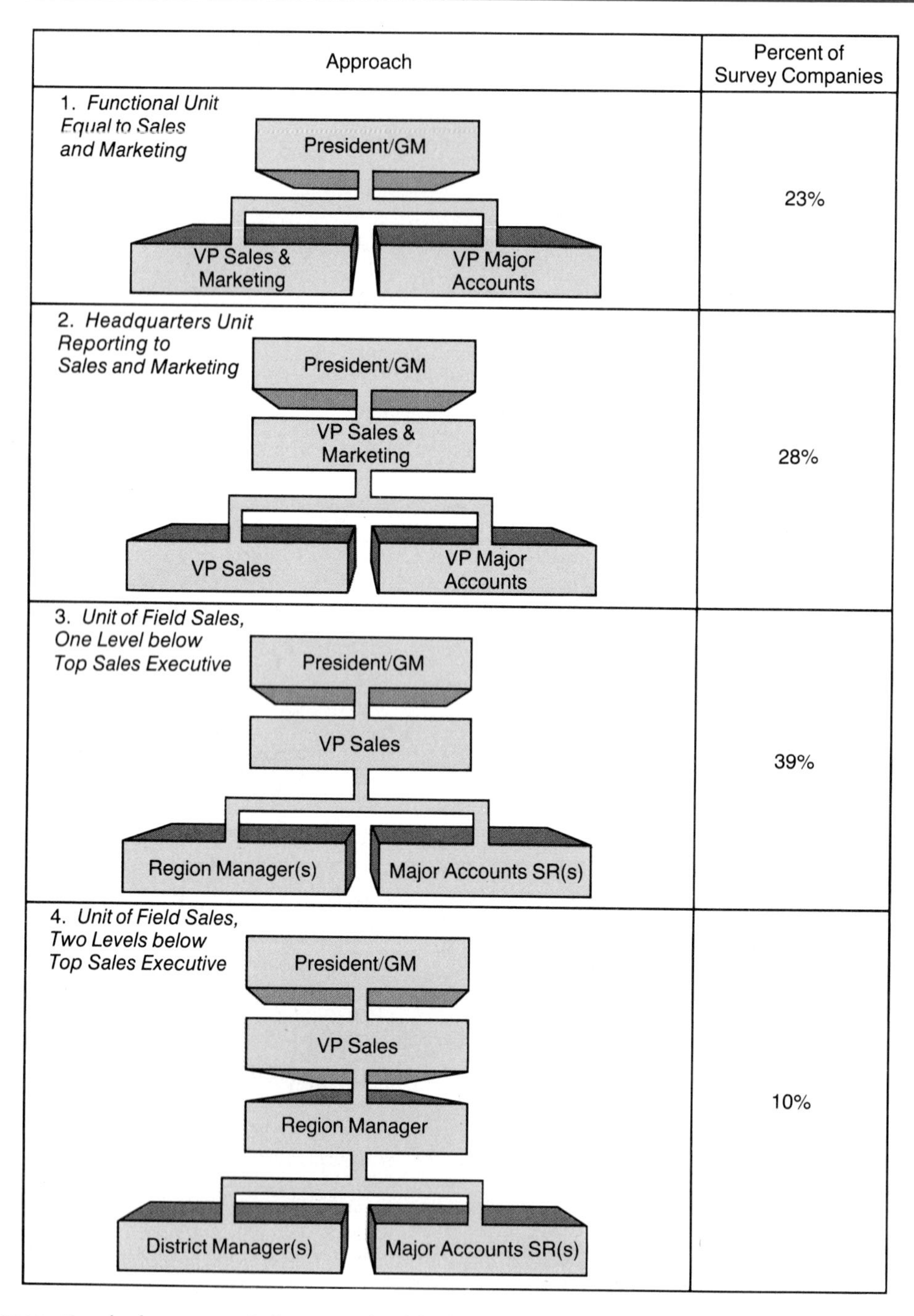

Major account salesforces are being organized in four basic ways today. The most popular is to have the major account organization report to the highest sales management level.[a]

[a]The study producing the results in this figure used the VP Sales title for the highest sales management level. Discussions throughout this textbook use the National Sales manager title in place of VP Sales when referring to the highest sales management level.

Source: Jerome A. Colletti and Gary S. Tubridy, "Effective Major Account Sales Management," *Journal of Personal Selling and Sales Management,* August 1987, 4. Used with permission.

COMPARING SALES ORGANIZATION STRUCTURES

The sales organization structures described in the last section represent the basic types of salesforce specialization and some examples of the variations possible. A premise of this chapter is that there is no one best way to structure a sales organization. The appropriate structure for a given sales organization depends upon the characteristics of the selling situation. Some structures are better in some selling situations than in others. Exhibit 7.2 summarizes much of what has been discussed previously by directly comparing the advantages and disadvantages of each basic sales organization structure.

As is evident from this exhibit, the strengths of one structure are weaknesses in other structures. For example, the lack of geographic and customer duplication is an advantage of a geographic structure, but a disadvantage of the product and market structures. Because of this situation, many firms employ **hybrid sales organization** structures that incorporate several of the basic structural types. The objective of these hybrid structures is to capitalize on the advantage of each type while minimizing the disadvantages.

An example of a hybrid sales organizational structure is presented in Figure 7.13. This structure is extremely complex in that it includes elements of geographic, product, market, function, and major account organizations. Although Figure 7.13 represents only one possible hybrid structure, it does illustrate how the different structure types might be combined into one overall sales organization structure. The example

Exhibit 7.2 **Comparison of Sales Organization Structures**

Organization Structure	Advantages	Disadvantages
Geographic	■ Low cost ■ No geographic duplication ■ No customer duplication ■ Fewer management levels	■ Limited specialization ■ Lack of management control over product or customer emphasis
Product	■ Salespeople become experts in product attributes and applications ■ Management control over selling effort allocated to products	■ High cost ■ Geographic duplication ■ Customer duplication
Market	■ Salespeople develop better understanding of unique customer needs ■ Management control over selling effort allocated to different markets	■ High cost ■ Geographic duplication
Functional	■ Efficiency in performing selling activities	■ Geographic duplication ■ Customer duplication ■ Need for coordination

Figure 7.13 **Hybrid Sales Organization Structure**

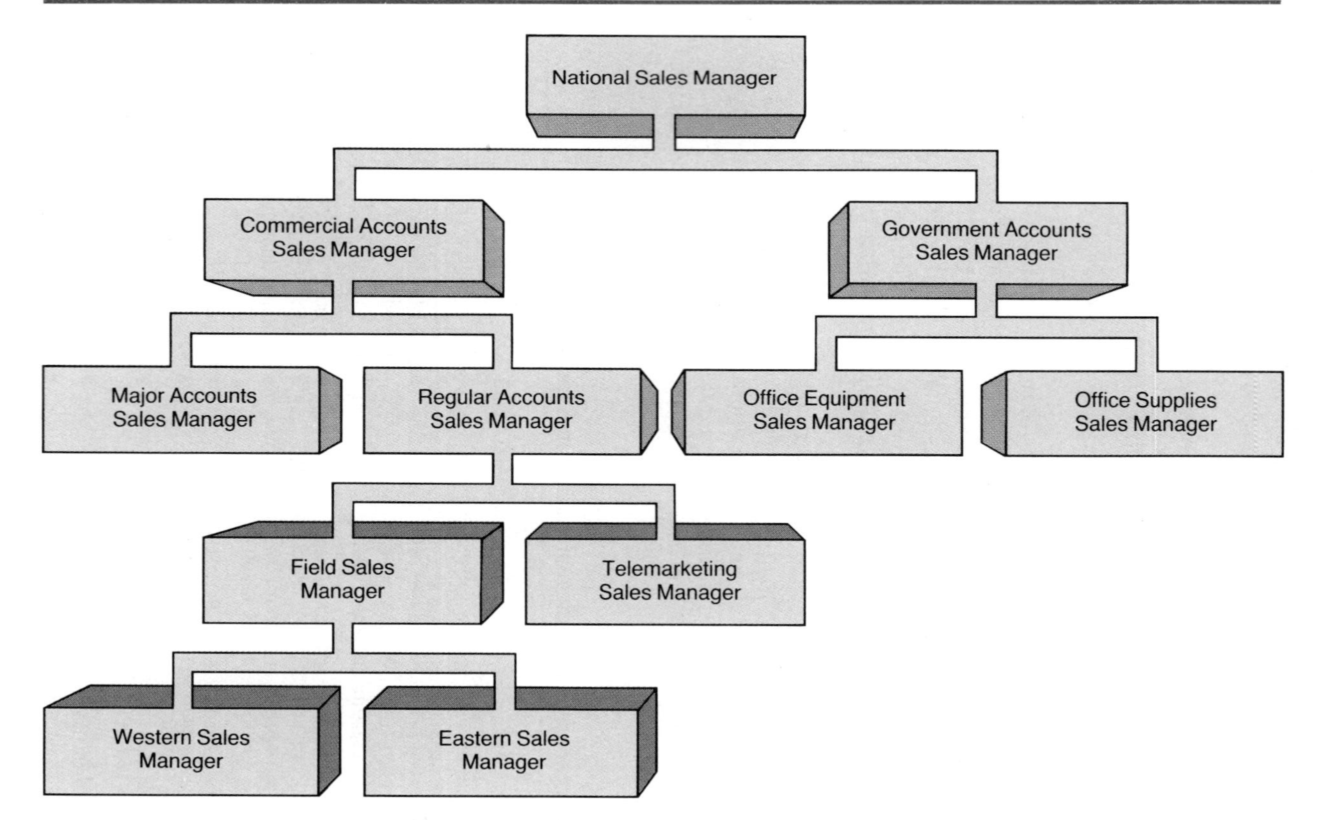

This complex sales organization structure incorporates market, product, functional, and geographic specialization.

also illustrates the complex nature of the task of determining sales organization structure. As noted before, the task is an extremely important one; sales management must develop the appropriate sales organization structure for its particular selling situation to ensure the successful implementation of organizational and account strategies.

SUMMARY

1. **Define the concepts of specialization, centralization, span of control versus management levels, and line versus staff positions.** *Specialization* refers to the division of labor such that salespeople or sales managers concentrate on performing certain activities to the exclusion of others. *Centralization* refers to where in the organization decision-making responsibility exists. Centralized organizations locate decision making responsibility at higher organizational levels than decentralized organizations. Any sales organization structure can be evaluated in terms of the types and degrees of specialization and centralization afforded by the structure. Sales management organization design also requires decisions concerning the number of management levels, spans of control, and line versus staff positions. In general, more *management levels* result in smaller *spans of control* and more *staff positions* result in more sales management specialization.
2. **Describe the different ways that salesforces might be specialized.** A critical decision in designing the sales organization is determining whether the salesforce should be specialized, and if so, the appropriate type of specialization. The basic types of salesforce specialization are geographic, product, market (including major account organization), and functional. The appropriate type of specialization depends upon the characteristics of the selling situation. Important selling situation characteristics include the similarity of customer needs, the complexity of the firm's product offering, the market environment, and the professionalism of the salesforce. The use of different types and levels of specialization typically requires the establishment of separate salesforces.
3. **Evaluate the advantages and disadvantages of different sales organization structures.** Since each type of sales organization structure has certain advantages and disadvantages, many firms use hybrid structures that combine the features of several types. Usually, the strengths of one structure are weaknesses in other structures.
4. **Name the important considerations in organizing major account management programs.** Identifying major accounts (which should be both large and complex) and organizing for coverage of them are the important considerations in major account management.
5. **Explain how one determines the appropriate sales organization structure for a given selling situation.** There is no one best way to structure a sales organiza-

tion. The appropriate way to organize salesforce and sales management depends upon certain characteristics of a particular selling situation. Also, since the sales organization structure decision is dynamic, it must be adapted to changes in a firm's selling situation that occur over time.

Key Terms

- specialization
- centralization
- span of control
- management levels
- line sales management
- staff sales management
- geographic specialization
- product specialization
- market specialization
- functional specialization
- major account organization
- hybrid sales organization

Review Questions

1. Discuss the situational factors that suggest the need for specialization and centralization. Provide a specific example of each factor discussed.
2. What are the basic disadvantages of salesforce specialization?
3. Why do you think there is a trend toward more salesforce specialization in the future?
4. Can sales management be organized with many management levels and large spans of control?
5. Should firms try to incorporate as many sales management staff positions as possible?
6. How should sales organizations be structured to serve accounts that are complex, but small in size?
7. What are the advantages and disadvantages of structuring a sales organization for major account management?
8. What is meant by a contingency approach to sales organization structure?
9. What are some problems that a firm might face when undertaking a major restructuring of its sales organization?
10. What are the important relationships between span of control, management levels, line positions, staff positions, specialization, and centralization?

Application Exercises

1. Assume that you are a sales manager for Xerox. Although you agree that Xerox needed to change from a product to a market organization, you think that salespeople should be specialized by industry type rather than by account size. Prepare a proposal to present to your boss that illustrates your recommended sales organization structure and argues that this structure is better than the account size structure that Xerox is currently using. Make sure that your argument is as forceful as possible.

2. Obtain the formal sales organization structure of any firm. Evaluate this structure in terms of specialization, centralization, span of control, management levels, and line and staff positions. Name any sales organization structural changes your analysis suggests. Be sure to support fully each of your recommended changes.
3. The EMI Corporation markets language labs to secondary schools and colleges/universities. The firm currently employs two salespeople to cover the entire United States. The basic strategy has been to use direct mail to generate requests for proposals and to send salespeople to schools only to present these proposals. The firm is considering the establishment of a field salesforce to call on schools to try to develop more penetration of the market. You have been hired as a consultant to determine the appropriate sales organization structure for EMI. Prepare a proposal that discusses exactly what you would do to arrive at a recommended sales organization structure. Be sure to include all of the factors that you would consider and discuss how these factors will help you determine the most appropriate structure.
4. Figure 7.13 presents a hybrid sales organization structure that includes elements of geographic, product, market, function, and major account structures. Prepare an alternative hybrid sales organization structure that also incorporates the same elements. Compare your hybrid structure to the one presented in Figure 7.13.
5. Identify three firms that use different approaches for major account management. Describe and evaluate each approach. Based on your analysis, make any recommendations that you think are appropriate for any of the firms. Be sure to support fully your recommendations.

Notes

[1]See Thomas V. Bonoma, *The Marketing Edge: Making Strategies Work* (New York: The Free Press, 1985), for a more complete presentation of the importance of and problems in successfully implementing organizational strategies.

[2]See Robert W. Ruekert, Orville C. Walker, Jr., and Kenneth J. Roering, "The Organization of Marketing Activities: A Contingency Theory of Structure and Performance," *Journal of Marketing,* Winter 1985, 13–25, for a more complete presentation of structural characteristics and relationships. The discussion in this section borrows heavily from this article.

[3]See Paul R. Lawrence and Jay W. Lorsch, *Organization and Environment: Managing Differentiation and Integration* (Boston, Mass.: Harvard University, 1967), for the classic discussion of this problem. We are using the term *specialization* instead of *differentiation* in our discussion.

[4]Howard Sutton, *Rethinking the Company's Selling and Distribution Channels* (New York: The Conference Board, 1986), 3.

[5]Rayna Skolnik, "Battling for the Power of the Seats," *Sales and Marketing Management,* April 1987, 46–49.

[6]Ram C. Rao and Ronald E. Turner, "Organization and Effectiveness of the Multiple-Product Salesforce," *Journal of Personal Selling and Sales Management,* May 1984, 24–30.

[7]Skolnik, "Battling for the Power of the Seats," 46–49.

[8]Sutton, 1986, 2.

[9]"Gillette Hones Salespower to a Fine Edge," *Sales and Marketing Management,* June 1987, 59.

[10]"At Cooper Tire, Sales are Rarely Flat," *Sales and Marketing Management,* June 1986, 56.

[11]Rayna Skolnik, "Fonda Gets Feisty," *Sales and Marketing Management,* October 1986, 49–53.

[12]Alex Beam and Barbara Buell, "Who's Breathing Down Whose Neck Now?" *Business Week,* November 25, 1985, 132–136.

[13]"Kimberly-Clark: Do It Right the First Time," *Sales and Marketing Management,* June 1987, 62.

[14]See Michael W. Hunter, "Getting Started in National Account Marketing," *Business Marketing,* November 1987, 61–64, and Kate Bertrand, "National Account Marketing," *Business Marketing,* November 1987, 43–52, for examples of different approaches for major-account organizations.

[15]Benson P. Shapiro and Rowland T. Moriarity, *National Account Management: Emerging Insights* (Cambridge, Mass.: Marketing Science Institute, 1982), 19.

[16]John Barrett, "Why Major Account Selling Works," *Industrial Marketing Management,* 15, 1986, 63–73.

[17]Benson P. Shapiro and Rowland T. Moriarity, *Organizing the National Account Force* (Cambridge, Mass.: Marketing Science Institute, 1983).

[18]Merrill Tutton, "Segmenting a National Account," *Business Horizons,* January–February 1987, 61–67.

[19]See Jerome A. Colletti and Gary S. Turbidy, "Effective Major Account Sales Management," *Journal of Personal Selling and Sales Management,* August 1987, 1–10, for a more complete presentation of these profiles and other research results.

[20]Louis A. Wallis, *Marketing Priorities* (New York: The Conference Board, 1987), 5.

C H A P T E R 8

ALLOCATING SELLING EFFORT, DETERMINING SALESFORCE SIZE, AND DESIGNING TERRITORIES

Learning Objectives:

After completing this chapter, you should be able to

1. Discuss the different areas involved in salesforce deployment.
2. Explain three different analytical approaches for determining allocation of selling effort.
3. Describe three different methods for calculating salesforce size.
4. Explain the importance of sales territories from the perspective of the sales organization and from the perspective of salespeople.
5. List the steps in the territory design process.
6. Describe a method for assigning salespeople to sales territories.
7. Discuss the important "people" considerations in salesforce deployment.

INCREASING SALESFORCE SIZE: IBM

IBM has been in a slump for the past few years. The company has had seven straight quarters of slowing revenue growth. During this period the price of IBM stock has dropped by 25 percent. John F. Akers, chairman of IBM, has taken several steps to return the company to a solid growth path. Changes have been instituted at all organizational levels.

The new corporate strategy is based on a major reorganization of business units into five autonomous product groups. Businesses strategies are developed individually by the general manager and staff of each business unit. The objective of this decentralization is to make the business units more entrepreneurial and to combat competitors in each market more effectively. Many management levels have been eliminated to lower costs, but to also make IBM more adaptive and responsive to industry changes. The marketing emphasis is on developing new and innovative products, especially for the microcomputer, minicomputer, and mainframe markets. IBM's product development has lost ground to key competitors during recent years.

These organizational strategy changes are having a noticeable impact on the IBM sales organization. Account strategies are more concerned with developing long-term customer relationships than with making immediate sales. Salespeople are focusing on solving customer problems and helping customers develop company-wide information networks that use IBM products but also may use competitor's products as well. The sales organization has been structured along industry lines to provide specialized expertise for customers in different industries.

One of the biggest changes has been the tremendous increase in the size of the IBM sales organization. Approximately 5,000 salespeople have been added—an increase of about 25 percent. Although the increase in salesforce size has been company-wide, the company has also targeted specific industries for increased selling attention. For example, a salesforce of 1,300 has been established to serve

---

Source: Adapted from "Computer-Related Firms Focus on Selling," *The Wall Street Journal,* August 14, 1986, 6; "DEC Braces for Rival's Rebound," *Sales and Marketing Management,* October 1986, 27; Gordon Bock, Thane Peterson, and Mark Maremont, "How IBM is Fighting Back," *Business Week,* November 17, 1986, 152–157; and "Big Changes at Big Blue," *Business Week,* February 15, 1988, 92–98.

scientific and engineering accounts. The increase in salesforce size also requires changes in territory design. Existing territories must be revised to accommodate the influx of new salespeople.

Why has IBM chosen to increase the size of its salesforce at a time when it is otherwise cutting costs and eliminating many middle management positions? One reason is that salespeople are the only employees of a firm that are directly involved in generating sales. There is typically a direct relationship between the size of a salesforce and company sales. Since one of IBM's major objectives is to achieve higher levels of sales growth, increasing the size of its salesforce is a logical step.

Another reason is that competitors have been increasing their salesforces to generate more sales even though industry sales have been relatively weak for the past few years. For example, Digital Equipment Corporation has been one of IBM's most successful competitors in the minicomputer market. Digital increased its salesforce by 37 percent in 1986 and expects further increases in the coming years. IBM must put more salespeople in the field to combat the aggressive selling efforts of Digital and other competitors.

There is an obvious downside to increasing salesforce size. The cost of selling increases, often dramatically. The revenue produced by each salesperson is likely to drop as more salespeople fight for shares of the same pie. However, observers and participants in the computer industry think that increasing salesforce size is the way to go for most firms. Frederic G. Withington, a consultant to many of the computer makers, expressed the thinking of many of the firms in the industry when he said that "there are fewer customers and more competitors, so you have to burn more shoe leather." More shoe leather means more salespeople in the field.

THE important sales management decisions involved in allocating selling effort, determining salesforce size, and designing territories are often referred to as **salesforce deployment**. As illustrated in the opening vignette, these decisions are closely related to the organizational strategy and sales organization structure decisions. Changes in strategy and structure often require adjustments in all three areas of salesforce deployment — selling effort allocation, salesforce size determination, and territory design. In the case of international markets, the salesforce deployment task becomes even more difficult (see "International Sales: Salesforce Deployment in Japan").

The size of a salesforce determines the total amount of selling effort that a firm has available. This selling effort must be sufficient to provide adequate selling coverage to all of the firm's accounts and prospects. The use of territories is one way to ensure that selling effort is used effectively. Typically, each salesperson is assigned a specific territory as a basic work unit. Therefore, changes in the allocation of selling effort to accounts often require that salesforce size be increased or decreased and that territories be redesigned. Deployment decisions at IBM reflected a situation where

INTERNATIONAL SALES

SALESFORCE DEPLOYMENT IN JAPAN

American companies trying to develop a salesforce in Japan are often faced with a complex distribution system and long, difficult negotiations. Since many American firms have limited data concerning the Japanese market, there is little information available for determining the appropriate salesforce size, territory design, or allocation of selling effort to accounts.

Matsushita Electric has taken advantage of this problem by creating AMAC Corp. as a part of its Panasonic subsidiary. AMAC Corp. buys products from firms in the United States and sells them to customers in Japan through the 500 member Panasonic salesforce in Japan. AMAC Corp. has signed agreements with approximately 100 U.S. firms marketing a wide range of products. One effect of these agreements is to shift all deployment decisions to management of the Panasonic salesforce. As AMAC Corp. continues to carry more products of different types, Panasonic sales managers will be required to adapt the deployment of its salesforce. Indications are that the size of the Panasonic salesforce will have to be increased, territories redesigned, and selling coverage to accounts altered.

Source: "It Helps to Have a Friend," *Sales and Marketing Management*, December 1987, 25–26.

more selling effort became available due to large increases in salesforce size. This increased selling effort was allocated to specific accounts and salesperson territories redesigned. In other situations, firms might decide to reduce total selling effort by decreasing salesforce size. This also would require changes in allocation of selling effort to accounts and territory redesign.

Since the salesforce deployment decisions are highly interrelated, our discussion will begin by addressing them in an integrated manner. Then, specific discussions of each deployment area will focus on describing the deployment decisions facing sales management and examining different analytical approaches for making these decisions.

SALESFORCE DEPLOYMENT

Salesforce deployment decisions can be viewed as providing answers to three interrelated questions:

1. How much selling effort is needed to cover accounts and prospects adequately so that sales and profit objectives will be achieved?
2. How many salespeople are required to provide the desired amount of selling effort?
3. How should territories be designed to ensure proper coverage of accounts and to provide each salesperson with a reasonable opportunity for success?

Figure 8.1 **Interrelatedness of Salesforce Deployment Decisions**

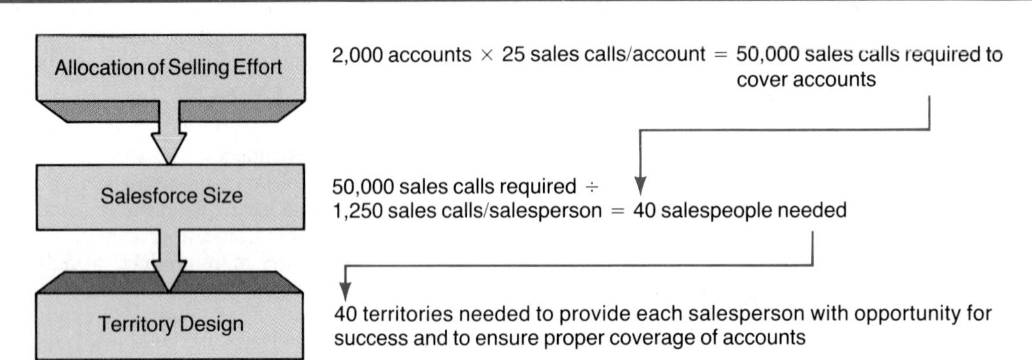

Determining how much selling effort should be allocated to various accounts provides a basis for calculating the number of salespeople required to produce the desired amount of selling effort. The salesforce size decision then determines the number of territories that must be designed. Thus, decisions in one deployment area affect decisions in other deployment areas.

The interrelatedness of these decisions is illustrated in Figure 8.1. Decisions in one salesforce deployment area affect decisions in other areas. For example, the decision of allocation of selling effort provides input for determining salesforce size, which provides input for territory design.

The potential value of addressing the areas of salesforce deployment in an integrated and sequential manner is supported by the results of deployment studies reported in Exhibit 8.1.[1] These studies indicate the impressive sales and profit increases that might be expected from a comprehensive deployment analysis. The development of one such analysis is described in "Sales Trend: A Multi-Decision Support System."

Despite the importance of salesforce deployment and the need to address the deployment decisions in an interrelated manner, many sales organizations use simplified analytical methods and consider each deployment decision in an isolated manner—an approach not likely to result in the best deployment decisions. Even such simplified approaches, however, can typically identify deployment changes that will increase sales and profits. The basic objectives of and approaches for determining selling effort allocation, salesforce size, and territory design are discussed separately in the remainder of this chapter.

Allocation of Selling Effort

The allocation of selling effort is one of the most important deployment decisions, since the salesforce size and territory decisions are based on this allocation decision. Regardless of the method of account coverage, determining how much selling effort

Exhibit 8.1 **Results of Salesforce Deployment Studies**

Study	Type of Product	Deployment Recommendation	Estimated Productivity Improvement
1. Lambert and Kniffin (1970)	Medical x-ray film	Redeployment of salespeople across sales districts	$131,000 increase in gross profits
2. Lodish (1971)	Industry commodity	Redeployment of selling effort	20% sales increase
3. Montgomery, Silk, and Zaragoza (1971)	Ethical drugs	Reallocation of sales call time across products	$85,000 profit improvement for 1 year; $139,000 profit improvement over 2 year period
4. Lodish (1975)	Advertising	Redeployment of selling effort and reassignment of salespeople to accounts	17–21% profit increase
5. Beswick and Cravens (1977)	Appliances	Redeployment of selling effort across trading areas	$830,000 sales increase
		Increase salesforce size and redeployment	$1,400,000 sales increase
6. Fudge and Lodish (1977)	Airline travel and cargo	Redeployment of selling effort to accounts	8.1% sales increase (actual results from implementation)
7. Parasuraman and Day (1977)	Consumer products	Reduction in and redeployment of selling effort to accounts	Maintain current sales levels with nearly 50% reduction in selling effort
8. Zoltners and Sinha (1980)	Consumer products	Redeployment of salespeople across regions and distribution channels	7% sales increase
9. LaForge and Cravens (1985)	Grocery products	Redeployment of selling effort to accounts	8%–30% sales improvement
10. Cravens, Dielman, Lamb, and Moncrief (1986)	Transportation services	Reduction in and redeployment of selling effort	Maintain current sales levels with 10%–20% reduction in salesforce size.

Source: Adapted from Raymond W. LaForge, David W. Cravens, and Clifford E. Young, "Using Contingency Analysis to Select Selling Effort Allocation Methods," *Journal of Personal Selling and Sales Management,* August 1986, 23. Used with permission.

to allocate to individual accounts is an extremely important decision strategically speaking, because selling effort is a major determinant of account sales and a major element of account selling costs. For example, the cost of field sales calls has been estimated to be as high as $452.60 in the computer industry and as low as $99.10 in the petroleum and coal products industry.[2] These selling costs have commanded the attention of top management. A survey of top-level executives found that of 36 activities, improving salesforce productivity was rated as the fourth most important.[3] And the way in which sales calls are allocated to accounts has a major impact on salesforce productivity.

SALES TREND

A MULTI-DECISION SUPPORT SYSTEM

Andris A. Zoltners at Northwestern University and Prabhakant Sinha at Rutgers University have developed a salesforce deployment multi-decision support system. The system addresses selling effort allocation, salesforce size, and territory design. Management can use the decision support system in both an optimization and assessment mode. Both modes require a market behavior model (response functions). In the optimization mode, a computer algorithm (allocation procedure) searches the alternative decisions and determines the best alternative. In the assessment mode, management can evaluate the potential result of any alternative decision.

One application of this decision support system was for the commercial banking services group of a large U.S. bank. The optimization mode was used to determine selling effort allocation, salesforce size, and territory design. Management was then able to use the assessment mode to evaluate "what if" scenarios. The decision support system made it possible for management to consider multiple decisions in an integrated manner and to take advantage of the ability of computer models to perform many, rapid calculations. The incorporation of both an optimization and assessment approach enhances the decision making capability of the system.

Source: Andris A. Zoltners, "MDSS Are More Effective When They Incorporate Both Optimization and Assessment," *Marketing News*.

Although decisions on the allocation of selling effort are difficult, several analytical tools are available to help. The three basic analytical approaches are single factor models, portfolio models, and decision models. These three are compared in Figure 8.2 and discussed in detail throughout the remainder of this section.

Single Factor Models. Easy to develop and use, **single factor models** do not, however, provide a very comprehensive analysis of accounts. The typical procedure is to classify all accounts on one factor, such as market potential, and then to assign all accounts in the same category the same number of sales calls. An example of using a single factor model for sales call allocation is presented in Exhibit 8.2.

Although single factor models have limitations, they do provide sales managers with a systematic approach for determining selling effort allocation. Sales managers are likely to make better allocation decisions using single factor models than when relying totally on judgment and intuition. Because of their ease of development and usage, single factor models are probably the most widely used analytical approach for making these allocation decisions.

Portfolio Models. A more comprehensive analysis of accounts is provided by **portfolio models**, but they are somewhat more difficult to develop and use than single factor models. In a portfolio model each account served by a firm is considered as

Figure 8.2 **Analytical Approaches to Allocation of Selling Effort**

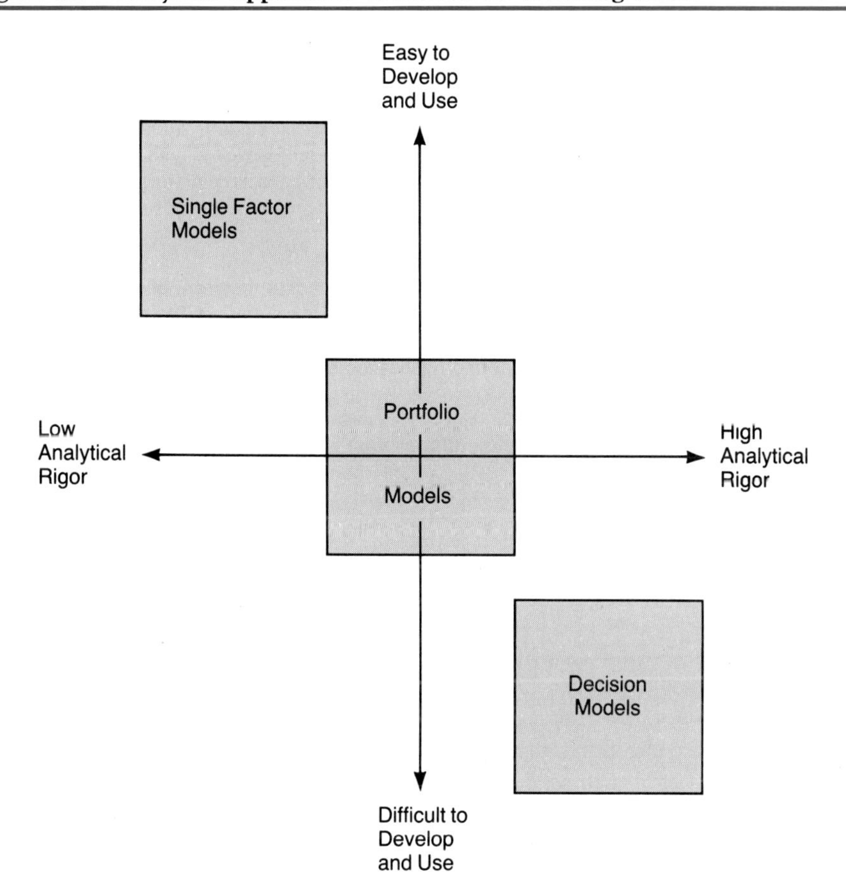

The single factor, portfolio, and decision model approaches for performing a deployment analysis differ in terms of analytical rigor and in ease of development and use. Typically, the more rigorous the approach, the more difficult it is to develop and use.

Source: David W. Cravens and Raymond W. LaForge," Salesforce Deployment," in *Advances in Business Marketing* edited by Arch G. Woodside (JAI Press, 1986), 76.

part of an overall portfolio of accounts. Thus, accounts within the portfolio represent different situations and receive different levels of selling effort attention. The typical approach is to classify all accounts in the portfolio into categories of similar attractiveness for receiving sales call investment. Then, selling effort is allocated so that the more attractive accounts receive more selling effort.[4] The typical attractiveness segments and basic effort allocation strategies are presented in Figure 8.3.[5]

Exhibit 8.2 **Example of Single Factor Model**

The XYZ Company markets a line of food products to ultimate consumers through different grocery wholesalers and retailers. The firm's salesforce calls on the grocery retailers to generate orders, develop sales promotions, and stock shelves. The salespeople are very important to the success of XYZ, and the company's account effort allocation strategy is a major determinant of salesforce productivity. A study was conducted to evaluate the current allocation and to suggest an improved strategy for the future. The study consisted of collecting information on a random sample of accounts, then using portions of the information to provide examples of the use of single factor models (this exhibit), portfolio models (Exhibit 8.3), empirical decision models (Exhibit 8.4), and judgment-based decision models (Exhibit 8.5).

The single factor model was applied to evaluate the market potential of each account and then classify all accounts into A, B, C, and D market potential categories. The average number of sales calls to an account in each market potential category was calculated and evaulated. Based on this analysis, changes in the account effort allocation strategy were made. A summary of the results follows:

Market Potential Categories	Average Sales Calls to an Account Last Year	Average Sales Calls to an Account Next Year
A	25	32
B	23	24
C	20	16
D	16	8

Account attractiveness is a function of account opportunity and competitive position for each account. *Account opportunity* is defined as an account's need for and ability to purchase the firm's products (e.g., grocery products, computer products, financial services, etc.). *Competitive position* is defined as the strength of the relationship between the firm and an account. As indicated in Figure 8.3, accounts are more attractive the higher the account opportunity and the stronger the competitive positions are.

Using portfolio models to develop an account effort allocation strategy requires that account opportunity and competitive position be measured for each account. Based on these measurements, accounts can be classified into the attractiveness segments. The portfolio model differs from the single factor model in that many factors are normally measured to assess account opportunity and competitive position. The exact number and types of factors depend upon a firm's specific selling situation. Thus, the portfolio approach provides a comprehensive account analysis that can be adapted to the specific selling situation faced by any firm. An example of a portfolio model is presented in Exhibit 8.3.[6]

Portfolio models can be valuable tools for helping sales managers improve their account effort allocation strategy. They are relatively easy to develop and use (though more difficult than single factor models) and provide a more comprehensive analysis than single factor models. Also, the portfolio model has been adapted for microcomputer use.[7]

Figure 8.3 **Portfolio Model Segments and Strategies**

Competitive Position

Account Opportunity	Strong	Weak
High	*Segment 1* **Attractiveness:** Accounts are very attractive because they offer high opportunity and sales organization has strong competitive position. **Selling Effort Strategy:** Accounts should receive a heavy investment of sales resources to take advantage of opportunity and maintain/improve competitive position.	*Segment 2* **Attractiveness:** Accounts are potentially attractive due to high opportunity, but sales organization currently has weak competitive position. **Selling Effort Strategy:** Additional analysis should be performed to identify accounts where sales organization's competitive position can be strengthened. These accounts should receive heavy investment of sales resources, while other accounts receive minimal investment.
Low	*Segment 3* **Attractiveness:** Accounts are moderately attractive due to sales organization's strong competitive position. However, future opportunity is limited. **Selling Effort Strategy:** Accounts should receive a sales resource investment sufficient to maintain current competitive position.	*Segment 4* **Attractiveness:** Accounts are very unattractive: they offer low opportunity and sales organization has weak competitive position. **Selling Effort Strategy:** Accounts should receive minimal investments of sales resources. Less costly forms of marketing (for example, telephone sales calls, direct mail) should replace personal selling efforts on a selective basis, or the account coverage should be eliminated entirely.

Accounts are classified into attractiveness categories based upon evaluations of account opportunity and competitive position. The selling effort strategies are based on the concept that the more attractive an account, the more selling effort it should receive.

Source: Raymond W. LaForge, David W. Cravens, and Clifford E. Young, "Improving Salesforce Productivity," *Business Horizons,* September–October 1985, 54. Copyright 1985 by the Foundation for the School of Business at Indiana University. Reprinted by permission.

Exhibit 8.3 Example of Portfolio Model

The portfolio model is applied here to measure the account opportunity and competitive position for each account. Based on these measures, accounts are classified into segments on the portfolio grid (see Figure 8.3). Then the average sales calls and average sales for accounts in each segment are calculated and evaluated according to the portfolio strategies presented in Figure 8.3. Based on this analysis, changes in selling effort allocation are made for next year. Portions of the results follow:

Results for last year:

		Competitive Strength	
		Strong	**Weak**
Account Opportunity	***High***	Segment 1 Average Sales Calls: 27 Average Sales: 2438 cases Number of Accounts: 97	Segment 2 Average Sales Calls: 21 Average Sales: 1248 cases Number of Accounts: 15
	Low	Segment 3 Average Sales Calls: 23 Average Sales: 1017 cases Number of Accounts: 26	Segment 4 Average Sales Calls: 17 Average Sales: 402 cases Number of Accounts: 66

Effort allocation changes for next year:

Portfolio Segment	**Average Sales Calls to an Account Last Year**	**Average Sales Calls to an Account Next Year**
1	27	36
2	21	24
3	23	12
4	17	6

A comparison of the single factor model (Exhibit 8.2) with the portfolio model suggests similarities in the basic approach and reasonably consistent results. However, since the portfolio model incorporates both account opportunity and competitive position, the portfolio results should provide better allocation guidelines than the single factor models.

Decision Models. The most rigorous and and comprehensive method for determining an account effort allocation strategy is by means of a **decision model**. Because of their complexity, decision models are somewhat difficult to develop and use. However, today's computer hardware and software make decision models much easier to use than before. Research results have consistently supported the value of decision models in improving effort allocation and salesforce productivity.[8]

Although the mathematical formulations of decision models can be complex, the basic concept is quite simple — to allocate sales calls to accounts that promise the highest sales return from the sales calls. The objective is to achieve the highest level of sales for any given number of sales calls and to continue increasing sales calls until their marginal costs equal their marginal returns. Thus, decision models calculate the optimal allocation of sales calls in terms of sales maximization.

Decision models consist of two parts. The first, the **response function**, is a mathematical equation that represents the relationship between sales calls and sales to accounts. This mathematical function makes it possible to calculate the expected sales to each account for different numbers of sales calls. For example, a response function allows sales management to forecast sales to each account if 5, 10, 15, or any other number of sales calls were made to the account.

The second part of a decision model, the **allocation procedure**, uses the response function to evaluate the expected sales for many different account effort allocation strategies. Allocation procedures typically are able to rapidly evaluate the total level of sales the firm might expect from all feasible strategies. The net result is usually the specific recommended number of sales calls to each account that will produce the highest level of sales for the firm.

There are two basic types of decision models.[9] They differ in the method used to develop the reponse function. **Empirical models** use account data from the past to develop a regression-type equation that explains previous relationships between sales calls (and other factors) and account sales. This regression-type equation is used to predict what will happen in the future. An example of an empirical decision model application is presented in Exhibit 8.4.

Judgment-based models use estimates from salespeople to develop separate response functions for each account. The typical procedure is to ask salespeople what they think sales to an account would be if they made the same number of sales calls to the account as made last year, if they decreased sales calls by 50 percent, if they increased sales calls by 50 percent, if they made no sales calls, and if they made the maximum possible number of sales calls. These estimates are used to develop a mathematical reponse function for each account that represents the expected relationship between sales calls and sales to the account. An example of a judgment-based decision model application is presented in Exhibit 8.5.

Comparison of Account Effort Allocation Analytical Methods. In sum, sales managers might employ single factor models, portfolio models, or decision models to help them develop an account effort allocation strategy. The approaches differ in the comprehensiveness of the account analysis, the rigor used to evaluate effort allocation alternatives, and the ease with which they can be developed and used. A detailed comparison of the different approaches is presented in Exhibit 8.6. Firms should not always use the most complex approach, but should use the method that best fits their market situation and company capabilities.[10]

Exhibit 8.4 **Example of Empirical Decision Model**

This empirical decision model is applied to measures of the account opportunity, competitive position, territory location, number of sales calls, and length of a sales call for each of the accounts. A regression-type procedure is used to develop an equation (response function) that uses measures of the variables just mentioned to predict sales to a retail account. An allocation procedure is then employed to use the response function to evaluate different effort allocation alternatives and to suggest the specific number of sales calls to each account that promises to produce the highest level of total sales. An example of the output of this procedure for five accounts follows:

Account	Actual Sales Calls Last Year	Actual Sales Last Year	Recommended Sales Calls Next Year From Model	Forecasted Sales Next Year From Model
AAA	25	1,376 cases	38	1,919 cases
BBB	50	1,404 cases	25	1,309 cases
CCC	20	700 cases	14	696 cases
DDD	26	1,213 cases	39	1,988 cases
EEE	20	585 cases	10	506 cases
	141 sales calls	5,278 cases	126 sales calls	6,418 cases

As indicated in this example application, decision models focus on effort allocation to individual accounts, whereas single factor models and portfolio models typically concentrate on effort allocation to groups of accounts. Decision models also provide a sales forecast for the suggested account effort allocation strategy. This is not possible with single factor or portfolio models. It is interesting to note that the portfolio models and empirical decision models use similar types of data. The approaches differ, however, in how this data is processed.

Salesforce Size

Research results have consistently shown that many firms could improve their performance by changing the size of their salesforce (see Exhibit 8.1).[11] In some situations the salesforce should be increased, as was the case for IBM. In other situations, however, firms are employing too many salespeople and could improve performance by reducing the size of their salesforces. Determining the appropriate salesforce size requires an understanding of several key considerations as well as a familiarity with different analytical approaches that might be employed.

Key Considerations. The size of a firm's salesforce determines the total amount of selling effort that is available to call on accounts and prospects. The decision of salesforce size is analogous to the decision on advertising budget. Whereas the advertising budget establishes the total amount that the firm has to spend on advertising communications, the salesforce size determines the total amount of personal selling effort

Exhibit 8.5 Example of Judgment-Based Decision Model

In this judgment-based decision model, salespeople predict what the sales to each account would be for next year if (1) the same number of sales calls are made as last year, (2) 50 percent more sales calls are made, and (3) 50 percent fewer calls are made. These estimates are used to develop a response function for each account. Each response function consists of a mathematical function that represents the relationship between sales calls and sales for a specific account. An allocation procedure is then used to search these response functions for the specific number of sales calls that would produce the highest level of total sales. The results of this procedure for five accounts follow:

Account	Actual Sales Calls Last Year	Actual Sales Last Year	Recommended Sales Calls Next Year From Model	Forecasted Sales Next Year From Model
AAA	25	1,376 cases	44	2,200 cases
BBB	50	1,404 cases	23	1,375 cases
CCC	20	700 cases	10	675 cases
DDD	26	1,213 cases	40	2,050 cases
EEE	20	585 cases	5	475 cases
	141 sales calls	5,278 cases	122 sales calls	6,775 cases

The major difference between the empirical decision model (Exhibit 8.4) and the judgment-based decision model is in the way the response function is developed. Data concerning what has happened in the past provides the basis for response functions in empirical models. Response functions in judgment-based models are based on estimates of what will happen in the future. The results of the two decision models for the same accounts in our example produced reasonably similar results. For example, both decision models suggest that fewer sales calls could produce more sales if changes were made in the account effort allocation strategy to the five accounts in the application example.

that is available. Since each salesperson can make only a certain number of sales calls during any period, the number of salespeople times the number of sales calls per salesperson defines the total available selling effort. For example, a firm with 100 salespeople that each make 500 sales calls per year has a total selling effort of 50,000 sales calls. If the salesforce is increased to 110 salespeople, then total selling effort is increased to 55,000 sales calls. Two of the key considerations in determining salesforce size are productivity and turnover.

Productivity. In general terms, *productivity* is defined as a ratio between outputs and inputs. One way the sales productivity of a salesforce is calculated is the ratio of sales generated to selling effort employed. Thus, productivity is an important consideration for all deployment decisions. However, selling effort is oftentimes expressed in terms of number of salespeople. Exhibit 8.7 presents sales productivity calculations

Exhibit 8.6 **Comparison of Account Effort Allocation Analytical Methods**

Factor	Single Factor Model	Portfolio Model	Judgment-Based Model	Empirical Model
Deployment Decisions	Appropriate for most deployment decisions	Appropriate for most deployment decisions	Best suited for within-territory deployment decisions	Best suited for across-territory deployment decisions
Analytical Rigor	Low	Moderate	High	High
Data Requirements	Minimal	Substantial—multiple factors are evaluated	Substantial—multiple response estimates are required	Substantial—multiple factors are evaluated
Computer Requirements	Minimal—does not require computer analysis	Ideally suited for microcomputer applications	Can be substantial, depending upon the size and complexity of the selling situation	Can be substantial, depending upon the size and complexity of the selling situation
Ease of Implementation	Relatively easy to implement	Moderately easy to implement	Somewhat difficult to implement, but incorporation of model user throughout the process aids implementation	Difficult to implement due to management lack of understanding the complex nature of the analysis
Expenses	Low	Moderate, but depends upon firm's information system	Moderate out-of-pocket costs, but substantial time commitment required to obtain response estimates	Can be substantial, but depends upon firm's information system
Model Output	Classifications based on analysis of one factor	Classifications based on multiple factors and recommended effort deployment based on relative attractiveness	The "optimal" deployment of selling effort which will "maximize" the sales or profit objective	The "optimal" deployment of selling effort which will "maximize" the sales or profit objective

Source: Raymond W. LaForge, David W. Cravens, and Clifford E. Young, "Using Contingency Analysis to Select Selling Effort Allocation Methods," *Journal of Personal Selling and Sales Management,* August 1986, 21. Used with permission.

for the computer industry. It shows IBM with the highest sales productivity and the largest salesforce. This suggests that the critical consideration is the *relationship* between selling effort and sales, not just the total amount of selling effort or the total level of sales.

Interestingly, the figures in Exhibit 8.7 were calculated before IBM increased its salesforce by 25 percent as discussed in the opening vignette. Although the larger salesforce will assuredly increase sales, only time will tell if IBM can maintain its high level of sales productivity in the face of increased selling costs. Sales will generally increase with the addition of salespeople, but not in a linear manner. With some

Exhibit 8.7 **Sales Productivity in the Computer Industry**

Company	1985 Revenue (millions of dollars)	No. of Sales Reps	Revenue per S/R (thousands of dollars)	S/R% of Total Employment
IBM	$50,056	20,000	$2,500	4.9%
Honeywell[a]	1,825	1,000	1,825	6.7
Sperry	3,423	2,000	1,712	5.0
NCR	4,317	3,000	1,439	4.8
Wang	2,352	2,000	1,176	6.3
DEC	6,686	6,000	1,114	8.6
Burroughs	5,038	5,500	916	9.1
Prime	770	860	900	10.6

[a]Information Systems, U.S. only.
Source: "Where IBM Still Leads the Way," *Sales and Marketing Management,* May 1987, 27.

exceptions, costs tend to increase directly with salesforce size. This produces the basic relationship presented in Figure 8.4.

In early stages, the addition of salespeople increases sales considerably more than the selling costs. However, as salespeople continue to be added, sales increases tend to decline until a point is reached where the costs to add a salesperson are more than the revenues that that salesperson can generate. In fact, the profit maximization point is where the marginal costs of adding a salesperson are equal to the marginal profits generated by that salesperson. It typically becomes more difficult to maintain high sales productivity levels at larger salesforce sizes. This makes it imperative that management consider the relationship between sales and costs when making decisions on salesforce size.

Turnover. It has been estimated that when a salesperson quits, the costs associated with recruiting, training, and managing a new salesperson, together with the opportunity costs from lost sales, may be as high as $50,000 to $75,000.[12] **Salesforce turnover** is extremely costly. Of course, rates of turnover vary by industry and firm. For example, the average turnover rate for pharmaceutical salesforces was found to be 12.4 percent,[13] whereas in some firms more than half of the salesforce may have to be replaced each year.

Since some turnover is going to occur for all firms, it should always be considered when determining salesforce size. (Size assessments are normally made on an annual basis.) Once the appropriate salesforce size is determined — that is, one sufficient for salespeople to call on all of the firm's accounts and prospects in a productive manner — this figure should be adjusted to reflect expected turnover. If an increase or maintenance of current salesforce size is desired, excess salespeople should be in the recruiting-selecting-training pipeline. If a decrease is desired, turnover might

Figure 8.4 **Sales and Cost Relationships**

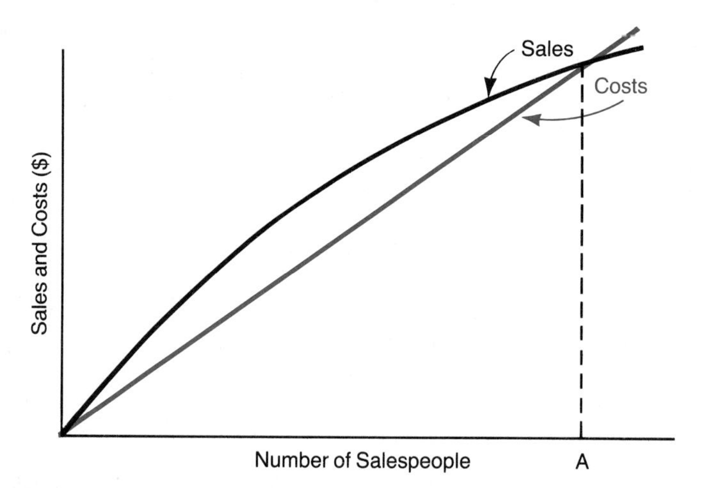

Although costs tend to increase in a linear manner with the addition of salespeople, the associated sales increases are typically nonlinear. In general, the increases in sales tend to decrease as more salespeople are added. A point (A) is reached where the sales from adding a salesperson are not sufficient to cover the additional costs.

be all that is necessary to accomplish it. For example, a grocery products marketer who found that its salesforce should be reduced from 34 to 32 salespeople achieved the two salesperson reduction through scheduled retirements in the near future instead of firing two salespeople.

Analytical Tools. The need to consider sales, costs, productivity, and turnover makes salesforce size a difficult decision. Fortunately, some analytical tools are available to help management process relevant information and evaluate salesforce size alternatives more fully. Before describing these analytical tools, we want to make it clear that there are different types of salesforce size decisions (see Figure 8.5). The most straightforward situation is when a firm has one, generalized salesforce. However, as discussed in Chapter 7, many firms employ multiple, specialized salesforces, in which case both the total number of salespeople employed by the firm and the size of each individual salesforce are important. This is exemplified by the IBM situation described in the opening vignette where IBM increased its total salesforce but also emphasized different areas by changing the size of specific, specialized salesforces. Finally, both generalized and specialized salesforces are normally organized into geographic districts, zones, regions, and so on. The number of salespeople to assign to each district, zone, region, and so on is a type of salesforce size decision.

Figure 8.5 **Different Salesforce Size Decisions**

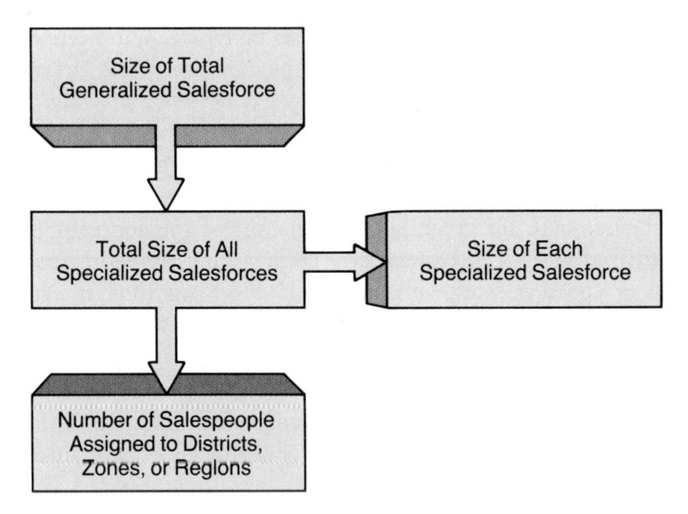

Depending upon the sales organization structure of a firm, sales managers may be faced with several different types of salesforce size decisions. Each requires the same basic concepts and analytical methods.

These different types of decisions are similar conceptually and can be addressed by the same analytical tools, provided that the type of salesforce size decision being addressed is specified. Unless stated otherwise, you can assume the situation of one, generalized salesforce in the following discussion.

Breakdown Approach. A relatively simple approach for calculating salesforce size, the breakdown approach assumes that an accurate sales forecast is available. This forecast is then "broken down" to determine the number of salespeople needed to generate the forecasted level of sales. The basic formula is

Salesforce size = Forecasted sales/Average sales per salesperson

Assume that a firm forecasts sales of $50 million for next year. If salespeople generate an average of $2 million in annual sales, then the firm needs 25 salespeople to achieve the $50 million sales forecast:

Salesforce size = $50,000,000/$2,000,000 = 25 salespeople

The basic advantage of the breakdown method is its ease of development. The approach is very straightforward and the mathematical calculations very simple. However, the approach is very weak conceptually. The concept underlying the calculations is that sales determine the number of salespeople needed. This puts "the cart before the horse," since the number of salespeople employed by a firm is an important determinant of firm sales. A sales forecast should be based on a given salesforce size. The addition of salespeople should increase the forecast, while the elimination of salespeople should decrease it.

Despite this weakness, the breakdown method is probably the most often used for determining salesforce size. It is best suited for relatively stable selling environments where sales change in slow and predictable ways and no major strategic changes are planned, also for organizations that use commission compensation plans and keep their fixed costs low. However, in many selling situations the costs of having too many or too few salespeople are high. More rigorous analytical tools are recommended for calculating salesforce size in these situations.

Workload Approach. The first step in the **workload approach** is to determine how much selling effort is needed to adequately cover the firm's market. Then the number of salespeople required to provide this amount of selling effort is calculated. The basic formula is

$$\text{Number of salespeople} = \frac{\text{Total selling effort needed}}{\text{Average selling effort per salesperson}}$$

For example, if a firm determines that 37,500 sales calls are needed in its market area and a salesperson can make an average of 500 annual sales calls, then 75 salespeople are needed to provide the desired level of selling effort:

$$\text{Number of salespeople} = 37{,}500/500 = 75 \text{ salespeople}$$

The key factor in the workload approach is the total amount of selling effort needed. Several workload methods can be used, depending upon whether single factor, portfolio, or decision models were used for determining the allocation of effort to accounts. Each workload method offers a different way to calculate how many sales calls to make to all accounts and prospects during any time period. When the sales call allocation strategies are summed across all accounts and prospects, the total amount of selling effort for a time period is determined. Thus, the workload approach integrates the salesforce size decision with account effort allocation strategies.

The workload approach is also relatively simple to develop, although this simplicity depends upon the specific method used to determine total selling effort needs. The approach is also sound conceptually, since salesforce size is based on selling effort needs established by account effort allocation decisions. Note, however, we have presented the workload approach in a simplified manner here by considering only selling effort. A more realistic presentation would incorporate nonselling time considerations (e.g., travel time, planning time, etc.) in the analysis. Although incorporating these considerations does not change the basic workload concept, it does make the calculations more complex and cumbersome.

Exhibit 8.8 **Incremental Approach**

Number of Salespeople	Marginal Salesperson Profit Contribution	Marginal Salesperson Cost
100	$85,000	$75,000
101	$80,000	$75,000
102	$75,000	$75,000
103	$70,000	$75,000

The workload approach is suited for all types of selling situations. Sales organizations can adapt the basic approach to their specific situation through the method used to calculate total selling effort. The most sophisticated firms can use decision models for this purpose, while other firms might use portfolio models or single factor approaches.

Incremental Approach. The most rigorous approach for calculating salesforce size is the **incremental approach.**[14] Its basic concept is to compare the marginal profit contribution to the marginal selling costs for each incremental salesperson. An example of these calculations is provided in Exhibit 8.8. At 100 salespeople, marginal profits exceed marginal costs by $10,000. This relationship continues until salesforce size reaches 102. At 102 salespeople, the marginal profit equals marginal cost, and total profits are maximized. If the firm added one more salesperson, total profits would be reduced, because marginal costs would exceed marginal profits by $5,000. Thus, the optimal salesforce size for this example is 102.

The major advantage of the incremental approach is that it quantifies the important relationships between salesforce size, sales, and costs, making it possible to assess the potential sales and profit impacts of different salesforce sizes. It forces management to view the salesforce size decision as one that effects both the level of sales that can be generated and the costs associated with producing each sales level.

The incremental method is, however, somewhat difficult to develop. Relatively complex response functions must be formulated to predict sales at different salesforce sizes (sales = *f*[salesforce size]). Developing these response functions requires either historical data or management judgment. Thus, the incremental approach cannot be used for new salesforces where historical data and accurate judgments are not possible.

Turnover. All of the analytical tools incorporate various elements of sales and costs in their calculations. Therefore, they directly address productivity issues but do not directly consider turnover in the salesforce size calculations. When turnover considerations are important, management should adjust the recommended salesforce size produced by any of the analytical methods to reflect expected turnover rates. For example, if an analytical tool recommended a salesforce size of 100 for a firm that experiences 20 percent annual turnover, the effective salesforce size should be adjusted to 120. Recruiting, selecting, and training plans should be based on the 120 salesforce size.

Designing Territories

As discussed earlier, the size of a salesforce determines the total amount of selling effort that a firm has available to generate sales from accounts and prospects. The effective use of this selling effort often requires that sales **territories** be developed and each salesperson be assigned to a specific territory. A territory consists of whatever specific accounts are assigned to a specific salesperson. The overall objective is to ensure that all accounts are assigned salesperson responsibility and that each salesperson can adequately cover the assigned accounts. Although territories are often defined by geographic area (e.g., the Oklahoma territory, the Tennessee territory, etc.), the key components of a territory are the accounts within the specified geographic area.

The territory can be viewed as the work unit for a salesperson. The salesperson is largely responsible for the selling activities performed and the performance achieved in a territory. Salesperson compensation and success are normally a direct function of territory performance; thus, the design of territories is extremely important to the individual salespeople of a firm as well as to management.

Territory Considerations. The critical territory considerations are illustrated in Exhibit 8.9. In this example, Andy and Sally are salespeople for a consumer durable goods manufacturer. They have each been assigned a geographic territory consisting of several trading areas. The exhibit compares the percentage of their time currently spent in each trading area with the percentages recommended from a decision model analysis. A review of the information provided in the exhibit highlights territory design problems from the perspective of the firm and of each salesperson.

The current territory design does not provide proper selling coverage of the trading areas. The decision model analysis suggests that the trading areas in Andy's territory should require only 36 percent of his time, yet he is spending all of his time there. Clearly, the firm is wasting expensive selling effort in Andy's territory. The situation in Sally's territory is just the opposite. Proper coverage of Sally's trading areas should require more than two salespeople, yet Sally has sole responsibility for these trading areas. In this situation the firm is losing sales opportunities because of a lack of selling attention.

From the firm's perspective, the design of Andy's and Sally's territories limits sales and profit performance. Sales performance in Sally's territory is much lower than it might be, if more selling attention were given to her trading areas. Profit performance is low in Andy's territory, because too much selling effort is being expended in his trading areas. The firm is not achieving the level of sales and profits that might

Exhibit 8.9 **Territory Design Example**

	Trading Area[a]	Present Effort (%)[b]	Recommended Effort (%)[b]
Andy	1	10	4
	2	60	20
	3	15	7
	4	5	2
	5	10	3
Total		100	36
Sally	6	18	81
	7	7	21
	8	5	11
	9	35	35
	10	5	11
	11	30	77
Total		100	236

[a]Each territory is made up of several trading areas.
[b]The percentage of salesperson time spent in the trading area (100% = 1 salesperson). Thus, the deployment analysis suggests that Andy's territory requires only 0.36 salespeople, while Sally's territory needs 2.36 salespeople for proper coverage.
Source: Raymond W. LaForge, David W. Cravens, and Clifford E. Young, "Improving Salesforce Productivity," *Business Horizons*, September/October 1985, 57. Copyright 1985 by the Foundation for the School of Business at Indiana University. Reprinted by permission.

be achieved if the territories were designed to provide more productive market coverage. Thus, one key consideration in territory design is the productive deployment of selling effort within each territory.

From the perspective of Andy and Sally, the poor territory design affects their level of motivation. Andy is frustrated. He spends much of his time making sales calls in trading areas where there is little potential for generating additional sales. Andy's motivational level is low, and he may consider resigning from the company. In contrast, Sally's territory has so much sales potential that she can limit her sales calls to the largest accounts or the easiest sales. She is not motivated to develop the potential of her territory, but can merely "skim the cream" from the best accounts. The situations facing Andy and Sally illustrate how territory design might affect salesperson motivation, morale, and even turnover. These potential effects are important considerations when designing territories.

Procedure for Designing Territories. The general procedure for designing territories is presented in Figure 8.6. Each step in the procedure can be performed manually or by using computer models. We will illustrate the procedure manually using Andy's and Sally's territories as an example application. The basic problem is to organize the 11 trading areas into 3 territories that provide proper market coverage of accounts in

Figure 8.6 **Territory Design Procedure**

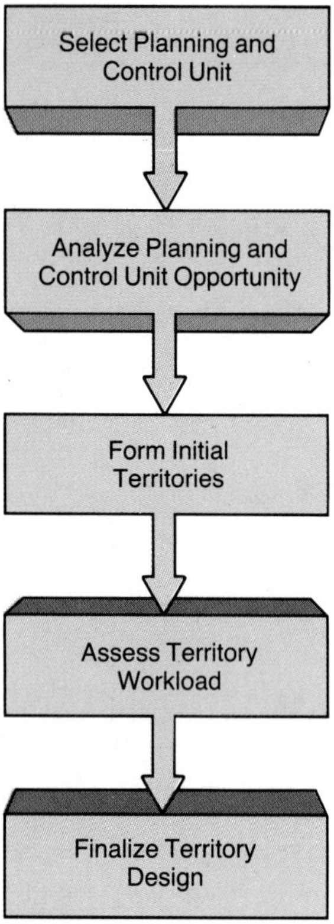

Designing territories requires a multiple-stage approach. Although most territory design approaches follow the stages presented in this figure, the methods used at each stage differ considerably depending upon the analytical tools employed.

each territory and equal performance opportunities for each salesperson. We are developing 3 territories because the decision model results presented in Exhibit 8.9 indicate that two salespeople cannot adequately cover these trading areas. The data needed to design the sales territories is presented in Exhibit 8.10.

Select Planning and Control Unit. The first step in territory design is to select the **planning and control unit** that will be used in the analysis—that is, some entity that is smaller than a territory. The total market area served by a firm is divided into these planning and control units, then they are analyzed and grouped together to form territories.

Exhibit 8.10 **Territory Design Data**

Trading Area	Market Potential	Number of Sales Calls
1	$250,000	25
2	$700,000	100
3	$350,000	35
4	$150,000	15
5	$200,000	20
6	$2,000,000	175
7	$750,000	65
8	$500,000	50
9	$1,000,000	100
10	$500,000	50
11	$1,750,000	175

Examples of potential planning and control units are illustrated in Figure 8.7. In general, management should use the smallest unit feasible. However, data are oftentimes not available for small planning and control units, and the computational task becomes more complex as more units are included in the analysis. The selection of the appropriate planning and control unit therefore represents a trade-off between what is desired and what is possible under the given data or computational conditions. In our example a trading area has been selected as the planning and control unit.

Analyze Opportunity of Planning and Control Unit. First determine the amount of opportunity available from each planning and control unit. Specific methods for performing these calculations will be covered in Chapter 14. However, the most often used measure of opportunity is *market potential.* The market potentials for the 11 trading areas in our example are provided in Exhibit 8.10. Everything else being equal, the higher the market potential is, the more opportunity available.

Form Initial Territories. Once planning and control units have been selected and opportunity evaluated, initial territories can be designed. The objective is to group the planning and control units into territories that are as equal as possible in opportunity. This step may take several iterations as there are probably a number of feasible territory designs. It is also unlikely that any design will achieve complete equality of opportunity. The best approach is to design several different territory arrangements and evaluate each alternative. Each alternative must be feasible in that planning and control units grouped together are contiguous. This can be a cumbersome task when done manually, but is much more efficient when computer modeling approaches are used.

Figure 8.7 **Potential Planning and Control Units**

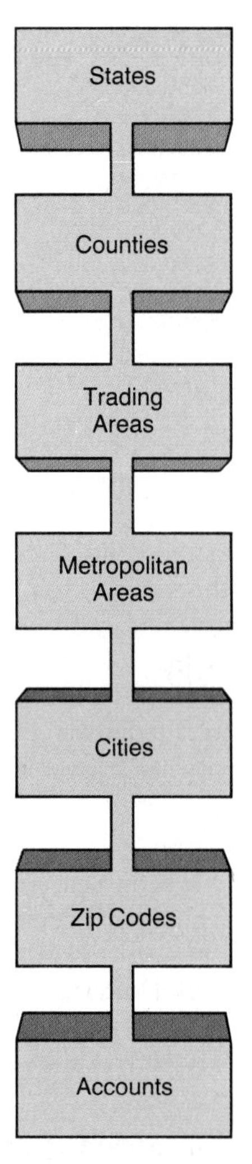

Planning and control units represent the unit of analysis for territory design. Accounts are the preferred planning and control unit. However, oftentimes it is not possible to use them as such, in which case a more aggregate type of planning and control unit is employed.

Exhibit 8.11 **Initial Territory Designs**

	Alternative 1		Alternative 2	
	Trading Area	**Market Potential**	**Trading Area**	**Market Potential**
Territory 1	1	$250,000	1	$250,000
	2	$700,000	2	$700,000
	3	$350,000	5	$200,000
	4	$150,000	8	$500,000
	5	$ 200,000	9	$1,000,000
		$1,650,000		$2,650,000
Territory 2	6	$2,000,000	6	$2,000,000
	7	$750,000	7	$ 750,000
	8	$ 500,000		
		$3,250,000		$2,750,000
Territory 3	9	$1,000,000	3	$350,000
	10	$500,000	4	$150,000
	11	$1,750,000	10	$500,000
			11	$1,750,000
		$3,250,000		$2,750,000

Two alternative territory designs for our example are presented and evaluated in Exhibit 8.11. Although the first design is feasible, the territories are markedly unequal in opportunity. However, a few adjustments produce reasonably equal territories.

Assess Territory Workloads. The preceding step produces territories of equal opportunity. It may, however, take more work to realize this opportunity in some territories than in others. Therefore, the workload of each territory should be evaluated by (1) the number of sales calls required to cover the accounts in the territory, (2) the amount of travel time in the territory, (3) the total number of accounts, and (4) any other factors that measure the amount of work required by a salesperson assigned to the territory. In our example, workload for each trading area and territory is evaluated by the number of sales calls required. This information is presented in Exhibit 8.12.

Finalize Territory Design. The final step is to adjust the initial territories to achieve equal workloads for each salesperson. The objective is to achieve the best possible balance between equal opportunity and equal workload for each territory. Typically, both of these objectives cannot be completely achieved, so management must decide upon the best trade-offs for its situation. Any inequalities in the final territories can be addressed when quotas are established. These procedures will be discussed in Chapter 14.

Exhibit 8.12 **Workload Evaluations**

	Trading Area	Sales Calls
Territory 1	1	25
	2	100
	5	20
	8	50
	9	100
		295
Territory 2	6	175
	7	65
		240
Territory 3	3	35
	4	15
	10	50
	11	175
		275

Exhibit 8.13 **Final Territory Design**

	Trading Area	Market Potential	Sales Calls
Territory 1	1	$250,000	25
	5	$200,000	20
	7	$750,000	65
	8	$500,000	50
	9	$1,000,000	100
		$2,700,000	260
Territory 2	2	$700,000	100
	6	$2,000,000	175
		$2,700,000	275
Territory 3	3	$350,000	35
	4	$150,000	15
	10	$500,000	50
	11	$1,750,000	175
		$2,750,000	275

Achieving workload and opportunity balance for our example is illustrated in Exhibit 8.13. The equal opportunity territories resulted in somewhat unequal workloads (see Exhibit 8.12). The final territory design moved Trading Area 7 to Territory 1 and Trading Area 2 to Territory 2. This produces territories that are reasonably equal in both opportunity and workload.

SALES TECHNOLOGY

COMPUTER MODELING FOR TERRITORY DESIGN

Merrell Dow Pharmaceuticals is using microcomputer mapping software to help it continually adjust its territories to market changes. Management inputs data on market potential, doctor and pharmacy counts, and travel time for zip-code planning and control units. The software combines this data with geographic features to produce optimal territory alignments.

The microcomputer model was especially useful when the company recently replaced its generalized salesforce with two specialized salesforces. One salesforce of 400 sells prescription pharmaceuticals, while the other salesforce of 250 sells over-the-counter drugs. Territories had to be designed for each salesforce.

According to Dan McKee, manager of marketing decision support systems, the old manual system "ordinarily takes a lot of time, hand-drawn maps, grease pencils, and plastic overlays. In addition, hours are consumed in doing the arithmetic. . . . The PC does the arithmetic for a territory in a matter of seconds, and it creates a map of the realigned boundaries in two minutes." The computer modeling approach allows Merrell Dow's sales managers to consider many factors and to evaluate many alternative territory designs in a short time period. The approach has become an integral part of the company's integrated planning activities.

Source: "Merrell Dow Gives Territories a Better Balance," *Sales and Marketing Management*, December 9, 1985, 67–68.

Performing territory design analyses manually is difficult and time-consuming. Fortunately, advances in computer hardware and software make it possible to consider multiple factors and rapidly evaluate many alternatives when designing sales territories. An example of using computer modeling in designing sales territories is illustrated in "Sales Technology: Computer Modeling for Territory Design."

Assigning Salespeople to Territories. Once territories have been designed, salespeople must be assigned to them. Salespeople are not equal in abilities and will perform differently with different types of accounts or products. Some sales managers consider their salespeople to be either *farmers* or *hunters*. Farmers are effective with existing accounts but do not perform well in establishing business with new accounts. Hunters excel in establishing new accounts, but do not fully develop existing accounts. Based on these categories, farmers should be assigned to territories that contain many ongoing account relationships, while hunters should be assigned to territories in new or less developed market areas.

One way to quantify the territory assignment decision is to develop salesperson indices for each territory. Management evaluates the potential effectiveness of each salesperson for each territory, with an index value of 1 for the norm. Values less than 1 indicate poor performance and values greater than 1 superior performance in a

Exhibit 8.14 **Salesperson Indices**

	Territory		
Salesperson	**1**	**2**	**3**
Andy	1.4	1.0	0.8
Sally	0.6	0.9	1.2
Sam	1.2	0.6	1.0

Exhibit 8.15 **Territory Assignment Calculations**

	Sales Potential	**Andy**	**Sally**	**Sam**
Territory 1	$500,000	× 1.4 = $700,000	× 0.6 = $300,000	× 1.2 = $600,000
Territory 2	$475,000	× 1.0 = $475,000	× 0.9 = $427,500	× 0.6 = $285,000
Territory 3	$450,000	× 0.8 = $360,000	× 1.2 = $540,000	× 1.0 = $450,000

territory. The objective is to assign salespeople to territories in a manner that maximizes total firm performance.

As an illustration, let's continue our example. Exhibit 8.13 presents the three territories that have been designed. The task is to assign Andy, Sally, and another salesperson (Sam) to these territories. The first step is for management to develop ability indices for each salesperson and each territory. These indices are presented in Exhibit 8.14. As evident from the exhibit, performance is expected to differ substantially depending upon how the salespeople are assigned to the territories.

The next step is to use the indices to adjust the sales potential for each territory to reflect different salesperson assignments. Whereas the market potential evaluations used to design territories represent assessments of opportunity available to all competing firms, sales potential is an evaluation of the opportunity available to a specific firm. The sales potential figures are smaller than the market potential numbers and change depending upon the salesperson that is assigned to the territory. These calculations are presented in Exhibit 8.15. Since we are performing this task manually, we can calculate the total sales potential for alternative territory assignments. The results of this analysis for three alternatives are shown in Exhibit 8.16. The best alternative is the second one, where Sam is assigned to Territory 1, Andy is assigned to Territory 2, and Sally is assigned to Territory 3. No other alternative will produce a higher total sales potential, so this territory is the one that maximizes total sales potential for the firm.

Two important points should be emphasized. First, assigning three salespeople to three territories is a simplified version of the typical territory assignment task. This

Exhibit 8.16 **Evaluating Territory Assignment Alternatives**

	Alternatives					
	1		2		3	
Andy	Territory 1 =	$700,000	Territory 2 =	$475,000	Territory 1 =	$700,000
Sally	Territory 2 =	$427,500	Territory 3 =	$540,000	Territory 3 =	$540,000
Sam	Territory 3 =	$450,000	Territory 1 =	$600,000	Territory 2 =	$285,000
		$1,577,500		$1,615,000		$1,525,000

manual procedure would be very cumbersome when management has to assign hundreds or thousands of salespeople. However, the procedure is readily adaptable to computerization. Once the salesperson indices and territory sales potentials are established, computer algorithms can rapidly evaluate assignment alternatives to determine the specific assignment of salespeople to territories that will maximize sales potential for the firm.

Second, maximizing the sales potential for individual salespeople will not necessarily maximize sales potential for the firm. As illustrated in Exhibit 8.15, Andy has the highest index for the highest sales potential territory. However, if Andy is assigned to Territory 1, Sally and Sam must be assigned to either Territories 2 or 3. In either case, the total sales potential is less than when Andy is assigned to Territory 2 (see exhibit 8.16). The key implication is that management should consider all salespeople when making territory assignments. Focusing on only one or two salespeople will not normally produce the best decisions.

"PEOPLE" CONSIDERATIONS

Our discussion of salesforce deployment decisions has, to this point, focused entirely on analytical approaches. This analytical orientation emphasizes objective sales and cost considerations in evaluating different allocations of sales calls to accounts, different salesforce sizes, different territory designs, and different assignments of salespeople to territories. Although such analytical approaches are valuable and should be employed by sales managers, final deployment decisions should also be based on "people" considerations.

Statistics are numbers, whereas sales managers, salespeople, and customers are people. Analysis of statistical data provides useful but incomplete information for deployment decisions. Models are only representations of reality and, no matter how complex, no model can incorporate all of the people factors that are important in any salesforce deployment decision. Accordingly, while employing the appropriate analytical approaches, sales managers should temper the analytical results with people considerations before making final deployment decisions.

What are the important people considerations in salesforce deployment? The most important ones concern personal relationships between salespeople and customers and between salespeople and the sales organization. Consider the allocation of selling effort to accounts. The analytical approaches for making this decision produce a recommended number of sales calls to each account based on some assessment of expected sales and costs for different sales call levels. Although these approaches may incorporate a number of factors in developing the recommended sales call levels, there is no way that any analytical approach can utilize the detailed knowledge that a salesperson has about the unique needs of individual accounts. Therefore, an analytical approach may suggest that sales calls should be increased or decreased to a specific account, while the salesperson serving this account may know that the account will react adversely to any changes in sales call coverage. In this situation a sales manager would be wise to ignore the analytical recommendation and not change sales call coverage to the account, because of the existing relationship between the salesperson and customer.

Salesforce size decisions also require consideration of people issues. A decision to reduce the size of a salesforce means that some salespeople will have to be removed from the salesforce. How this reduction is accomplished can affect the relationship between salespeople and the sales organization. Achieving this reduction through attrition or offering salespeople other positions is typically a better approach than merely firing salespeople.

Increasing salesforce size means that the new salespeople must be assigned to territories. Consequently, some accounts will find themselves being served by new salespeople. These changes in assignment can have a devastating effect on the existing customer-salesperson relationship. Not only should that relationship be considered, but also the issue of fairness in taking accounts from one salesperson and assigning them to another. The situation can be a delicate one, requiring careful judgment as to how these people considerations should be balanced against analytical results.

In sum, sales managers should integrate the results from salesforce deployment analysis with people considerations before implementing changes in sales call allocation, salesforce size, or territory design. A good rule-of-thumb is to make salesforce deployment changes that are likely to have the least disruptive effect on existing personal relationships.

SUMMARY

1. **Discuss the different areas involved in salesforce deployment.** Salesforce deployment decisions entail allocating selling effort, determining salesforce size, and designing territories. These decisions are highly interrelated and should be addressed in an integrated, sequential manner. Improvements in salesforce deployment can produce substantial increases in sales and profits.

2. **Explain three different analytical approaches for determining allocation of selling effort.** Single factor, portfolio, and decision models can be used as analytical tools to determine appropriate selling effort allocations. The approaches differ in terms of analytical rigor and ease of development and use. Sales organizations should employ the approach that best fits their particular selling situation.

3. **Describe three different methods for calculating salesforce size.** The breakdown method for calculating salesforce size is the easiest method to use but the weakest conceptually. It uses the expected level of sales to determine the number of salespeople. The workload approach is sounder conceptually, since it bases the salesforce size decision on the amount of selling effort needed to cover the market appropriately. The incremental method is the best approach, although it is often difficult to develop. It examines the marginal sales and costs associated with different salesforce sizes.

4. **Explain the importance of sales territories from the perspective of the sales organization and from the perspective of the salespeople.** Territories are assignments of accounts to salespeople. Each becomes the work unit for a salesperson, who is largely responsible for the performance of the assigned territory. Poorly designed territories can have adverse effects on the motivation of salespeople. From the perspective of the firm, territory design decisions should ensure that the firm's market area is adequately covered in a productive manner.

5. **List the steps in the territory design process.** The first step in the territory design process is to identify planning and control units. Next, the opportunity available from each planning and control unit is determined, initial territories are formed, and the workloads of each potential territory are assessed. The final territory design represents management's judgment concerning the best balance between opportunity and workload.

6. **Describe a method for assigning salespeople to sales territories.** Once territories are designed, each salesperson must be assigned to a specific territory. The basic objective is to assign salespeople to territories in a manner that maximizes total firm performance. Ability indices can be used as a method for determining appropriate territory assignment. The indices are combined with territory sales potentials to calculate the total sales potential from alternative territory assignments. Then the territory assignment alternative that maximizes total sales potential can be selected.

7. **Discuss the important "people" considerations in salesforce deployment.** Although analytical approaches provide useful input for salesforce deployment decisions, they do not address "people" considerations adequately. Sales managers should always consider existing relationships between salespeople and customers and between salespeople and the sales organization before making salesforce deployment changes.

Key Terms

- salesforce deployment
- single factor models
- portfolio models
- decision models
- response function
- allocation procedure
- empirical model
- judgment-based model
- sales productivity
- salesforce turnover
- breakdown approach
- workload approach
- incremental approach
- territory
- planning and control unit

Review Questions

1. How are salesforce deployment decisions related to decisions on sales organization structure?
2. What is sales productivity?
3. How do decisions on allocation of selling effort, salesforce size, and territory design affect salesforce productivity?
4. How can the incremental method be used to determine the number of salespeople to assign to a sales district?
5. How are salesforce size decisions different for firms with one generalized salesforce versus firms with several specialized salesforces?
6. What is a desirable territory from the perspective of a salesperson? From the perspective of a sales organization?
7. Discuss the advantages and disadvantages of the single factor, portfolio model, and decision models for allocating selling effort.
8. How can computer modeling assist sales managers in designing territories?
9. What are the key analytical and people considerations in assigning salespeople to territories?
10. Should firms always try to design equal territories? Why or why not?

Application Exercises

1. The XYZ Corporation is concerned about the productivity of its salesforce. As sales planning manager, you have been asked to prepare a proposal to evaluate current sales productivity and to suggest improvements for increasing sales productivity. Prepare a proposal that describes exactly what you would do and how you would do it. Use a flowchart to illustrate the sequence of steps you would take and how the steps are interrelated.
2. Assume that you are a district sales manager for ABC Company. You supervise six salespeople and are pleased with the performance of your district and the territories assigned to your salespeople. However, your regional sales manager has hired a new salesperson and assigned her to your district. You complain to the regional sales manager that your

district does not need an additional salesperson. The regional sales manager indicates that you must accept this salesperson into your district and assign her to a territory. What would you do? Be sure to address the analyses you would perform and how you would use the new territories that you have designed to incorporate the new salesperson.

3. As regional sales manager for the USA Company, you are concerned about the number of salespeople in each sales district. You are currently responsible for six districts and have compiled the following information:

District	Number of Salespeople in District	District Market Potential	District Sales
1	8	$10,000,000	$2,661.075
2	10	$12,000,000	$3,125,000
3	7	$ 8,000,000	$2,425,025
4	7	$ 7,500,000	$2,133,675
5	12	$15,000,000	$3,925,550
6	9	$11,000,000	$3,375,500

Your firm has developed the following model of district sales based on analysis of historical data:

$$\text{District sales} = 25 \times \text{District market potential}^{.65} \times \text{Number of district salespeople}^{.55}$$

Use this model to help determine if you should shift current salespeople from one district to another, and to determine if your region needs more or fewer salespeople. The average annual costs associated with maintaining a salesperson are $100,000 per year, and the average gross margin for company sales is 40 percent.

4. As a district sales manager for the DEF Corporation you are trying to develop territories for four salespeople in a new market area. You have compiled the following information:

County	Market Potential	Workload
A	$ 600,000	175 sales calls
B	$ 900,000	310 sales calls
C	$ 450,000	150 sales calls
D	$1,250,000	500 sales calls
E	$ 750,000	250 sales calls
F	$ 295,000	90 sales calls
G	$ 850,000	350 sales calls
H	$ 925,000	350 sales calls
I	$ 675,000	200 sales calls
J	$1,050,000	350 sales calls
K	$ 350,000	150 sales calls
L	$ 725,000	250 sales calls
M	$ 475,000	200 sales calls
N	$ 950,000	300 sales calls
O	$ 575,000	200 sales calls
P	$ 425,000	150 sales calls

Using the preceding information, assign counties to salespeople in a manner that equalizes both market potential and workload for each territory (you do not have to consider the geographic location of the country and can assume that any combination of counties is feasible). Evaluate the territories you have designed. In a real territory design situation, what other factors would you consider before finalizing your territory design?

5. As the national sales manager for the PC Corporation, you are concerned about the productivity of your salesforce. You think that an improved account effort allocation strategy would increase sales productivity and have collected the following information:

Account	Account Opportunity	Competitive Position	Sales Calls	Sales
AAA	High	Strong	50	$25,000
BBB	High	Weak	25	$20,000
CCC	High	Weak	35	$5,000
DDD	Low	Strong	50	$10,000
EEE	Low	Strong	20	$10,000
FFF	High	Strong	25	$20,000
GGG	Low	Weak	20	$ 3,000
HHH	Low	Strong	35	$15,000
III	Low	Strong	30	$10,000
JJJ	High	Weak	25	$ 7,500

Assume that this is a large enough sample of accounts to be representative of all accounts. Develop a portfolio model and assess current effort allocation. Based on your analysis, suggest a more productive effort allocation strategy.

Notes

[1]See the following studies for more detailed results from deployment studies: Zarrel V. Lambert and Fred W. Kniffin, "Response Functions and Their Application in Sales Force Management," *Southern Journal of Business,* 5, January 1970, 1–11; Leonard M. Lodish, "CALLPLAN: An Interactive Salesman's Call Planning System," *Management Science,* 18, December 1971, 25–40; David B. Montgomery, Alvin J. Silk, and Carlos E. Zaragoza, "A Multiple-Product Sales Force Allocation Model," *Management Science,* 18, 1971, 3–24; Leonard M. Lodish, "Sales Territory Alignment to Maximize Profit," *Journal of Marketing Research,* 12, February 1975, 30–36; Charles A. Beswick and David W. Cravens, "A Multistage Decision Model for Salesforce Management," *Journal of Marketing Research,* 14, May 1977, 134–144; William K. Fudge and Leonard M. Lodish, "Evaluation of the Effectiveness of a Model Based Salesman's Planning System by Field Experimentation," *Interfaces,* 8, 1977, 97–106; A. Parasuraman and Ralph L. Day, "A Management-Oriented Model for Allocating Sales Effort," *Journal of Marketing Research,* 14, February 1977, 22–23; Andris A. Zoltners and Prabhakant Sinha, "Integer Programming Models for Sales Resource Allocation," *Management Science,* 26, 1980, 242–260; Raymond W. LaForge and David W. Cravens, "Empirical and Judgment-Based Salesforce Decision Models: A Comparative Analysis," *Decision Sciences,* Spring 1985, 177–195; David W. Cravens, Terry Dielman, Charles W. Lamb, Jr., and William C. Moncrief, "Sequential Modeling for Selling Effort Deployment in Reorganized Salesforces," *Working Paper Series,* Texas Christian University, 1986.

[2]"Surprise! Some Call Costs Decline," *Sales and Marketing Management,* November 1986, 24.

[3]Louis A. Wallis, *Marketing Priorities* (New York: The Conference Board, 1987), 5.

[4]See Renato Fiocca, "Account Portfolio Analysis for Strategy Development, *Industrial Marketing Management,* 11, 1982, 53–62 and Alan J. Dubinsky and Thomas N. Ingram, "A Portfolio Approach to Account Profitability," *Industrial Marketing Management,* 13, 1984, 33–41, for slightly different applications of the portfolio concept.

[5]See Raymond W. LaForge, David W. Cravens, and Clifford E. Young, "Improving Salesforce Productivity," *Business Horizons,* September–October 1985, 50–59, for more detailed discussion of the portfolio approach.

[6]See Raymond W. LaForge and David W. Cravens, "Steps in Selling Effort Deployment," *Industrial Marketing Management,* July 1982, 183–194; Raymond W. LaForge, Clifford E. Young, and B. Curtis Hamm, "Increasing Sales Productivity through Improved Sales Call Allocation Strategies," *Journal of Personal Selling and Sales Management,* November 1983, 52–59; and Raymond W. LaForge and Clifford E. Young, "A Portfolio Model for Planning Sales Call Coverage," *Business,* April–June 1985, 10–16, for additional portfolio-model applications.

[7]See Raymond W. LaForge, David W. Cravens, and Clifford E. Young, "Developing Research-Based Selling Strategies," *Proceedings,* 1986 American Marketing Association Winter Educators' Conference, 154–157.

[8]See Raymond W. LaForge, David W. Cravens, and Clifford E. Young, "Using Contingency Analysis to Select Selling Effort Allocation Methods," *Journal of Personal Selling and Sales Management,* August 1986, 23, for a summary of productivity improvements from decision-model applications.

[9]See Raymond W. LaForge and David W. Cravens, "Empirical and Judgment-Based Salesforce Decision Models: A Comparative Analysis," *Decision Sciences,* Spring 1985, 177–195, for a comparative discussion and test of the empirical and judgment-based decision-model approaches.

[10]An approach for determining the appropriate method for a particular firm can be found in LaForge, Cravens, and Young, 1986, 19–27.

[11]See Raymond W. LaForge, David W. Cravens, and Clifford E. Young, "Using Contingency Analysis to Select Selling Effort Allocation Methods," *Journal of Personal Selling and Sales Management,* August 1986, 23, for a summary of these research results.

[12]Reported in George H. Lucas, Jr., A. Parasuraman, Robert A. Davis, and Ben M. Enis, "An Empirical Study of Salesforce Turnover," *Journal of Marketing,* July 1987, 34.

[13]Reported in "Replacement Cost Soars for Reps in Pharmaceuticals," *Marketing News,* September 27, 1985, 18.

[14]See Arthur Beidan, "Optimizing the Number of Industrial Salespersons," *Industrial Marketing Management,* 11, 1982, 63–74, for a detailed presentation of incremental methods for determining salesforce size.

Parke-Davis Professional Health Group

In May 1984 Mr. Marvin Skripitsky, the Marketing Director of the Parke-Davis Professional Health Group, was in the process of preparing the 1985 Strategic Plan recommendations for his group. A formal presentation of his recommendations was to be made to Mr. Robert Serenbetz, the President of Warner-Lambert Canada, at the end of May. As Mr. Skripitsky reviewed the Group's situation, he was convinced that the most pressing problem facing the Group was the lack of detailing capacity in the sales force. The Professional Health Group was planning to introduce a number of new products over the next three years and there appeared to be insufficient salesforce time available to adequately present new and existing products (i.e., to "detail" the products) to the medical community. He viewed this inability to properly promote the Group's pharmaceutical products as the major barrier to meeting the Group's growth objectives. Mr. Skripitsky knew that he, in consultation with Mr. Malcolm Seath the General Manager of the Health Care Division and Mr. Gerry Gibson the Group's Director of Sales, would have to make specific recommendations for dealing with the detailing capacity problem at the presentation to Mr. Serenbetz.

Company

Parke-Davis was the pharmaceutical affiliate of Warner-Lambert, a major U.S.-based multinational. With worldwide sales of over $3.1 billion (U.S.) Warner-Lambert manufactured a wide range of pharmaceutical, personal care, and other products, including such well-known brands as Listerine, Chiclets and Schick. Parke-Davis had been founded in Detroit, Michigan, in 1866, and the company began operations in Canada in 1887, making it the second pharmaceutical company to operate in Canada. Over the years Parke-Davis had pioneered many significant health care products, including the first anti-diptheric serum in 1893, Dilantin, for the control of epilepsy in 1938; Benadryl, the first antihistamine in North America in 1946; and in 1949, Chloromycetin, the first wide-spectrum antibiotic to be discovered. Parke-Davis was acquired by Warner-Lambert in 1970. In 1979 Parke-Davis and Warner-Chilcott, the original pharmaceutical division of Warner-Lambert, were merged into one division to be-

Source: This case was prepared by Professor Adrian B. Ryans, Nabisco Brands Professor of Marketing at the University of Western Ontario, as a basis for class discussion rather than to illustrate either effective or ineffective handling of an administrative situation.

come the pharmaceutical component of Warner-Lambert Canada Inc. In 1983 Parke-Davis was merged with Warner Lambert's Personal Products business unit to form a new Health Care Division. In 1984 the Health Care Division was projected to have sales of $87 million with Parke-Davis accounting for $62 million of these sales.

The mission of the Health Care Division was to be a Canadian leader in developing and providing pharmaceutical and personal care products for health and well being while achieving steady growth in sales and profits. In the five year strategic planning period beginning in 1985 the division was targeting for annual sales growth 4% above the level of inflation to achieve sales of approximately $133 million by 1989. Management of the health care division believed that this objective was attainable, since the division enjoyed a number of major strengths, including a planned stream of major new products during the planning period, a broadly based product line that was not dependent on one or two major products or product categories, and a strong clinical trial and registration capability to expedite the approval of new pharmaceuticals and new claims for existing products. In addition, Parke-Davis had a strong image in the minds of consumers, pharmacists, doctors and government. Most image studies placed Parke-Davis within the top five firms on almost every image criterion. This strong corporate image was useful in gaining access to doctors and the drug trade, and was helpful in developing and maintaining a consumer franchise for smaller non-prescription brands that could not support direct consumer advertising. While the broadly based product line was a strength in many respects, it also represented a weakness in that it made it difficult for the sales force to find the time to adequately detail all the products to the doctors. In addition, many physicians no longer viewed Parke-Davis as an innovator, since the product line was relatively old. A successful introduction of the planned new products was expected to correct this.

In Canada, the Health Care Division was comprised of two major groups: the Consumer Health Group and the Professional Health Group. Because both Warner-Chilcott and Parke-Davis had several big proprietary and OTC pharmaceuticals in 1979, the merger resulted in the Consumer Health Group becoming the largest supplier of self-medication products in Canada including such well known brands as Benylin, Agarol, Sinutab and Gelusil.[1] These products were sold under the Parke-Davis name. The Consumer Health Group also marketed a wide range of personal care products, including Listerine, Bromo, Softsoap, Showermate, Schick, Topol and Lensrins, that were distributed through drug stores and other convenience retail outlets. In addition to its extensive line of prescription ethical pharmaceuticals, the Professional Health Group was responsible for promoting selected Consumer Health Group brands, such as Benylin, a major brand of cough syrup, to physicians. The general manager of the Health Care Division was Mr. Malcolm Seath.

Professional Health Group. The 1984 sales of the Professional Health Group were forecasted to be $33 million and the Group had an objective of increasing sales to over $50 million by 1989. Direct cost of goods sold and freight typically amounted to about 25 percent of selling price. During this period the Professional Health Group

Exhibit 1 Parke-Davis Professional Health Group

GENERAL MANAGER HEALTH CARE DIVISION D. M. SEATH

MARKETING DIRECTOR PROFESSIONAL HEALTH GROUP M. K. SKRIPITSKY

MARKETING DIRECTOR CONSUMER HEALTH GROUP C. CLARK

DIRECTOR OF SALES G. G. GIBSON

GROUP PRODUCT MANAGER

GROUP PRODUCT MANAGER

MANAGER PRICING & PRODUCT SERVICES

MANAGER SALES OPERATIONS

MANAGER MANPOWER DEVELOPMENT

MANAGER SALES ADMINISTRATION

REGIONAL SALES MANAGER WESTERN REGION

REGIONAL SALES MANAGER CENTRAL REGION

REGIONAL SALES MANAGER QUEBEC REGION

DISTRICT MANAGER B.C. ALBERTA

DISTRICT MANAGER MAN. SASK.

DISTRICT MANAGER TORONTO

DISTRICT MANAGER ONTARIO EAST

DISTRICT MANAGER ONTARIO WEST

DISTRICT MANAGER ATLANTIC

DISTRICT MANAGER MONTREAL

DISTRICT MANAGER QUEBEC

1 MEDICAL INFORMATION ASSOCIATE

8 MEDICAL REPRESENTATIVES

6 MEDICAL REPRESENTATIVES

2 MEDICAL INFORMATION ASSOCIATES

7 MEDICAL REPRESENTATIVES

7 MEDICAL REPRESENTATIVES

8 MEDICAL REPRESENTATIVES

6 MEDICAL REPRESENTATIVES

1 MEDICAL INFORMATION ASSOCIATE

8 MEDICAL REPRESENTATIVES

6 MEDICAL REPRESENTATIVES

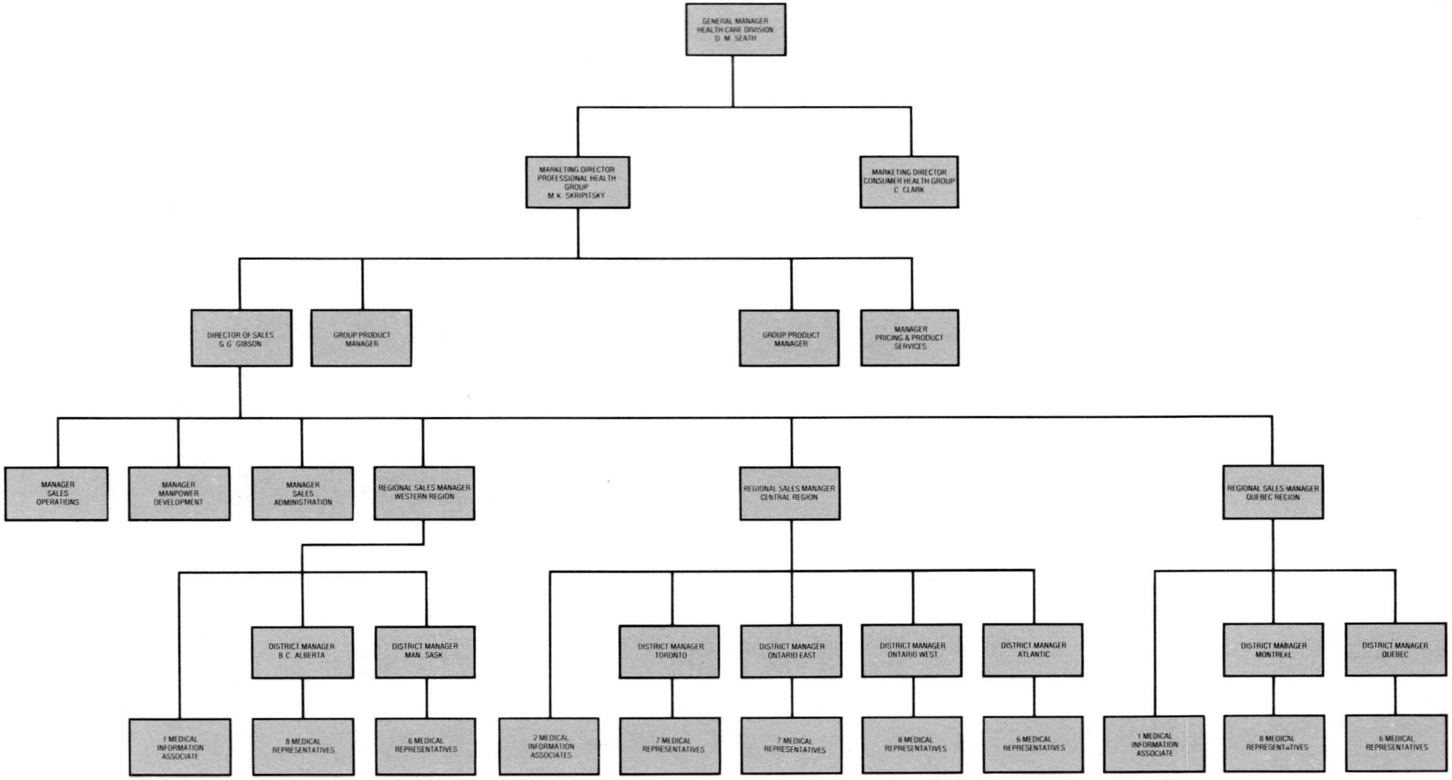

Partial Organization Chart of the Health Care Division

hoped to increase its market share in ethical (prescription) pharmaceuticals from 1.8 percent to 2.2 percent. The Professional Health Group was headed by the marketing director, Mr. Marvin Skripitsky. Reporting to the marketing director were two group product managers and the director of sales, Mr. Gerry Gibson. A simplified organization chart for the Group is shown in Exhibit 1. By 1984 the salesforce consisted of 56 medical representatives, 4 medical information associates, 8 district managers, and 3 regional managers.

The Professional Health Group was responsible for the 24 products or product groups shown in Exhibit 2. The Professional Health Group 15 planned to add 15 additional products to the product line over the next three years with these products having potential sales of over $25 million by 1989.

Industry Environment

Management of the Health Care Division saw both threats and opportunities in the external environment. Health care costs were expected to continue to increase faster than the economy as a whole due to technological developments and an aging population. Although management felt that pharmaceuticals were the most cost-effective part of the health care system, they believed that pharmaceuticals would continue to attract the attention of politicians and others responsible for controlling health care costs. Some provinces had adopted "formularies" in an attempt to control pharmaceutical costs. In these cases the provincial government would pay only for pharmaceuticals listed in the formulary for people who were receiving government assistance in paying for pharmaceuticals. In addition, management believed that the increasing complexity of the the health care system would force politicians to give more power to bureaucrats who would be perceived as "unbiased." In this environment, access to key politicians and bureaucrats would be key.

Insurance companies, which paid at least some drug bills for 70 percent of Canadians, were expected to become increasingly important. Historically they had been passive participants in the health care system, paying whatever pharmacists charged for whatever pharmaceuticals were prescribed by doctors. Some were now attempting to restrict the choice of pharmaceuticals for which they would provide full reimbursement, and in some cases they were attempting to force mandatory substitution of generic drugs.

On the more positive side there was a growing feeling in the industry that the federal government might change Canada's compulsory licensing laws to encourage more innovation in pharmaceuticals in Canada and to encourage more pharmaceutical firms to conduct more of their research in Canada. The compulsory licensing law in Canada required the patent-holding manufacturer to license patented products to other manufacturers.

Parke-Davis executives continued to believe that the keys to growth in the pharmaceutical industry in Canada would be the development of innovative new products and strong marketing of those products.

Exhibit 2 **Parke-Davis Professional Health Group**

Parke-Davis Products

Anticonvulsants	Nardil
Prescription Hemorrhoidals (Anusol)	Nicrostat
Amsa	Oral Contraceptives
Benadryl	Peritrate
Choledyl	Ponstan
Chloro/Vira-A	Tucks
Colymycin	Tedral
Elase	Thrombostat
Eryc	Pyridium
Hose	Mandelamine
Lopid	Beben
Mylanta	Vanquin

Market for Pharmaceutical Products in Canada

The total market for ethical and proprietary pharmaceutical products in Canada was more than $2.5 billion, with 17% of these sales being made to hospitals. The medical community in Canada was comprised of about 43,000 doctors and over 1,000 hospitals. There were also almost 5,000 retail pharmacies in Canada.

Competition. The overall pharmaceutical industry in Canada was highly competitive, with the largest company, American Home Products, having less than 8% market share of the combined ethical and proprietary pharmaceutical market sold through hospitals and drug stores. An additional 14 companies had market shares greater than 2%. The various divisions of Warner-Lambert had a combined market share of over 3%. Most of these companies were broad-line pharmaceutical companies. Competition in the industry seemed to be increasing with the recent entry of major non-pharmaceutical companies through the aquisition of small pharmaceutical companies. Both Procter & Gamble and Dow Chemical had entered the market using this mechanism in the early 1980s.

In total, by the end of 1983 there were 55 pharmaceutical companies with salesforces operating in Canada. The number of medical representatives employed by these companies is shown in Exhibit 3. Some of the major competitors operated under more than one name and corporate structure. American Home Products operated under the Wyeth, Ayerst, and Whitehall names. Johnson and Johnson sold its products under the Ortho, Johnson and Johnson, McNeil, and Janssen names. Several companies, including both American Home Products and Johnson and Johnson, had more than one salesforce. Merck Frosst, the company with the largest number of medical representatives in Canada, had three different salesforces operating under different names, with almost 140 representatives at the end of 1983. When a com-

Exhibit 3 **Parke-Davis Professional Health Group**

Number of Medical Representatives Employed by Competitors in Canada

Size of Salesforce[a]	Number of Companies
0–10	3
11–20	4
21–30	9
31–40	4
41–50	15
51–60	13
61–70	6
71 or greater	1
Total number of salesforces	55

[a] Excludes managers and OTC representatives.

pany had more than one salesforce, it usually operated under the names of different divisions (often the names of predecessor companies). Thus, Johnson and Johnson had two salesforces operating under the McNeil and Ortho names. Earlier in 1984, one relatively small pharmaceutical company, Boehringer-Ingelheim, had added a second salesforce. The two salesforces were using the same name, and the calling cards of the salespersons simply indicated that they were specialists in particular therapeutic classes. It was too early to measure the acceptance of this approach by the medical community. The large number of salesforces meant that the competition for a doctor's time was intense—Mr. Gibson estimated that some doctors could have as many as 40 to 50 medical representatives trying to see them in a given two-month period.

All the major brand-name manufacturers of pharmaceuticals faced competition from generic manufacturers.

The Selling of Ethical Pharmaceuticals in Canada

Medical representatives (over 25,000 of them in North America alone) played a key role in the selling of ethical pharmaceuticals. Often called "detail men" (although they were increasingly women) for the details they provide doctors and pharmacists about pharmaceuticals, they played a key role in trying to convince doctors to prescribe their company's pharmaceuticals to the doctor's patients. Many market research studies concluded that doctors relied very heavily on medical representatives for information on prescribing pharmaceuticals. Some authorities suggested that the success of a new pharmaceutical could depend almost as much on the effectiveness of the medical representatives promoting the new product as on the product itself. The medical profession was faced with the difficult problem of keeping up with the flood of new pharmaceuticals that were continually becoming available. While the pharmaceuticals in major therapeutic product classes, such as those designed to treat heart disease, shared many similarities, the differences could be critical to the patients using the pharmaceutical. Detail men played a crucial role in providing the kind of information that would help a doctor decide whether a particular pharmaceutical was appropriate for a particular patient's condition. Many doctors, particularly harried general practitioners with a diverse practice, found it difficult to keep up with all the literature on the products that they might use in their practice, and they appreciated the information a detail man could provide. A well-trained detail man could provide the doctor with information on the chemical composition of the pharmaceutical, its possible side effects, and how it would interact with other medicines a patient might be taking. From the pharmaceutical company's point of view, detail men provided a valuable feedback channel, sometimes alerting the company to side effects that might not have been noticed before. Detail men also frequently organized symposia for groups of doctors, often bringing in outside medical authorities to help bring doctors up to date on current medical practice and pharmaceuticals. Major pharmaceutical companies regularly had their representatives set up displays in major hospitals in their territories. These displays of products and literature were staffed by the representative, and many doctors dropped by after their morning rounds in the hospital or at the end of the working day.

One of the toughest jobs many detail men faced was getting past the receptionist or the nurse in a doctor's office, particularly when the office was crowded and the doctor was behind schedule. Increasingly, doctors were establishing rules that they would only see one medical representative a day. Parke-Davis representatives tried to make appointments with the doctor ahead of time, when this was possible. Even when the medical representative got into the doctor's office, the doctor might keep the representative waiting and might be interrupted by a nurse or a telephone call during their conversation. The representative typically only had 5 to 10 minutes to make his presentation. During the presentation he might place primary emphasis on one or two products with brief reminders about one or two others. The pharmaceuticals presented to a particular doctor depended on the nature of the doctor's speciality and practice. Doctors frequently asked questions about products or might have questions about the appropriateness of particular products in a given situation.

Parke-Davis sales representatives were expected to make five to six calls per day on doctors, about two calls per day on retail pharmacies and perhaps one call every two days on a hospital. As did many other major pharmaceutical companies, Parke-Davis divided each year into six two-month sales cycles. A major planning issue was the decision as to which one or two products should get primary emphasis in each of these sales cycles for each medical specialty. Each medical representative attempted to call on all the doctors, retail pharmacies, and hospitals targeted by Parke-Davis at least once during each sales cycle. By 1984 Parke-Davis was targeting its sales force at some 18,000 doctors out of the 43,000 in Canada, and at over 80% of the retail pharmacies. The approximate Parke-Davis coverage of physicians and retail pharmacies by province is shown in Exhibit 4.

Exhibit 4 **Parke-Davis Professional Health Group**

Coverage of Physicians and Retail Pharmacies by Parke-Davis Salesforce by Province

	British Columbia	Alberta	Saskatchewan	Manitoba	Ontario	Quebec	Atlantic Provinces	Total Canada
Physicians								
Total Physicans[a]	5,180	3,310	1,410	1,870	15,900	12,470	3,340	43,480
Covered by Parke-Davis	1,750	1,400	700	700	6,300	4,550	1,750	17,500
% Covered by Parke-Davis	33.8	42.3	49.7	37.4	39.6	36.5	52.4	40.2
Retail Pharmacies								
Total Retail Pharmacies	593	559	229	285	1,648	1,079	502	4,965
Covered by Parke-Davis	400	320	160	160	1,440	1,040	400	4,000
% Covered by Parke-Davis	67.5	57.5	53.5	56.1	87.4	96.4	79.7	80.6

[a]This includes all physicians registered in a province. Not all physicians registered in a province were active in a medical practice. For example, some were retired or employed in teaching, research, or administrative postiions.

The Professional Health Group Sales Force

Organization. The field salesforce of 60 persons was divided into two groups: the 56 Medical Representatives and 4 Medical Information Associates (MIAs). The medical representatives were organized into 8 geographical districts, each headed by a district manager, and had responsibility for detailing the full Professional Health Group product line to the medical community in their geographical territories.

In 1983 top management of the Professional Health Group had become very concerned about the ability of the medical representatives to detail their large existing product line and at the same time introduce the large number of sophisticated new products that were planned in the future. The introduction of a sophisticated new pharmaceutical often required that the medical representative focus on key specialists and other potential opinion leaders. Since the medical representatives had largely been trying to maintain sales of existing products rather than introduce new ones over the preceding three or four years, they often were not actively working these key specialists. To overcome this problem, management decided to add a small number of more sophisticated representatives with stronger medical and pharmacological training, and very strong communication skills. These representatives would specialize in launching new products and would do the initial follow-up with doctors after the launch of the product. Given their strong educational background and the fact that at any point in time they would be focusing on a very small number of new products, it would be possible to provide them with more in-depth knowledge about each new product than could be given to the medical representatives.

The company began to add the MIAs in 1983. They were also given geographical territories, but these territories were obviously much larger than those of the medical representatives, since 4 of them had to cover the whole of Canada. The four MIAs reported directly to the Regional Managers. Two were assigned to the Central Region and one each to the Quebec and Western Regions.

Recruiting and Selection. In selecting new representatives, the Professional Health Group sought individuals with a strong background in one of the health sciences. Most recent recruits had bachelors degrees in science, nursing, or pharmacy. Some were recruited directly out of university, but many had worked in the health care industry before joining Parke-Davis. One recent recruit was a registered nurse with several years of nursing experience in a hospital. Another was a pharmacist in his early thirties, who had become bored with the routine of dispensing pharmaceuticals and the long hours associated with operating a retail pharmacy.

Training. After joining Parke-Davis, each medical representative attended two two-week training programs in Toronto. This training included material on Parke-Davis and intensive training on biology and pharmacology, product information on the Parke-Davis product line, and some basic selling skills training. Between the sessions, the representative was in his or her territory under the close supervision of the district manager. Training was a continuing process in any pharmaceutical company, with each representative receiving training in new products as they were introduced. When a major new product was introduced, it was common to provide the representatives with programmed learning materials, followed by an intensive two-day training meeting in Toronto. Many salespersons were also continually trying to update their skills by reading textbooks and a variety of other medical and pharmacological information made available to them by their companies. About every two years all medical representatives came to Toronto for an intensive "refresher" sales training course.

Compensation. Parke-Davis compensated its representatives using a base salary-plus-bonus compensation plan. In 1984 base salaries for representatives varied from $21,000 for a new sales trainee with no experience to $36,000 for a senior sales representative. In addition each representative was eligible for a regional bonus of up to 15% of base salary and an individual merit bonus of up to 10% of base salary. Thus a high-performing medical representative could earn as much as $45,000 plus fringe benefits and the use of a company automobile.

The regional bonus was based on the region's success in meeting sales objectives. For the purpose of calculating the regional bonus, the product line was divided into A, B, and C brands. "A" brands were those that in the opinion of management were the most profitable and had the greatest potential for future growth. "B" brands included high-volume brands with less potential for growth, but whose sales should be maintained. "C" brands included all other brands, which were not typically actively promoted. Management established objectives for each of the three groups of brands for each of the three regions, and performance against these objectives was measured. Approximately 55% of the bonus was applied to the achievement of the A objective, 30% to the achievement of the B objective, and 15% to the achievement of the C objective. If a region met exactly 100% of its objectives for each group of brands each member of the regional team would receive a bonus of 10.5% of base salary. If 102% or more of the objective for each group was met, the full 15% bonus was awarded. Management did not believe it was feasible to do this monitoring at lower than a region level due to the difficulty of establishing exactly which representative or even district was responsible for a given sale. It was not uncommon for a prescription to be written by a doctor in one city, for the prescription to be filled at a retail pharmacy in another city, and for that pharmacy to have its drugs shipped from a warehouse in a different province.

The individual bonus was based on the district manager's judgment of the individual's contribution relative to others in the region. In order to make this judgment, the district manager reviewed territory sales data, call activity, and other activities, such as the number of symposia organized by the representative and the number of physicians who attended these symposia. The individual bonus decisions had to be reviewed and approved by the responsible regional manager and Mr. Gibson. District managers were in a good position to make this subjective judgment, since they spent at least one day every month in the field with each of the representatives they supervised.

Performance Appraisal. Each representative was formally reviewed once a year by his or her manager. In this performance appraisal the district manager carefully reviewed the representative's achievements since the last review and any areas of concern. Particular attention was paid to the employee's skills in managing the work and in dealing with other people. The manager also focused on the individual's promotability and training and development needs. Each performance appraisal was reviewed by the regional manager and Mr. Gibson.

Motivation. A sales meeting was held once during each of the six sales cycles during the year. These meetings played an important role in the training and motivation of the salesforce. Frequently these meetings would be held at the district level, but occasionally regional or national meetings would be held, particularly when a major new program or product was about to be launched.

The Detailing Capacity Problem

In the strategic planning process for the Parke-Davis Professional Health Group in May 1984, Mr. Seath, Mr. Skripitsky, and Mr. Gibson viewed the Professional Health Group's lack of detailing capacity as its most pressing problem. The Group had launched Eryc, a major new antibiotic, in December 1983, with a first-year sales objective of $600,000. While the MIA salesforce had played a major role in pre-launch and launch activities for the product and was actively involved in the follow-up, the medical representatives would have to support it aggressively in their detailing calls for the next eighteen months or so, if it was to achieve its market potential. In May 1984, Lopid, a major new cardiovascular pharmaceutical, was introduced, with a first-year sales objective of almost $500,000. Again, the MIAs were playing a major role in the introduction. With three more new products slated for introduction in 1985, seven more in 1986, and at least five more in 1987, the detailing capacity problem was critical.

The magnitude of the problem was evident to Mr. Skripitsky and Mr. Gibson as they looked at the tentative 1985 Medical Promotion Schedule for the year beginning January 1, 1985, shown in Exhibit 5. Eryc and Lopid, the two new products, would require much of the available primary detailing time. In the case of general practitioners (GPs) six of the twelve available spots were taken up by the two new products, with an additional two of the twelve spots taken up by Choledyl SA, another relatively new product introduced early in 1983. Increasingly the inclusion of new products meant that important "bread and butter" products, many with good growth potential, would have to be dropped from active salesforce promotion.

One brand that would fall in this category was Anusol HC, a pharmaceutically elegant prescription hemorrhoidal preparation that was targeted at general practitioners, family physicians, and surgeons. With projected 1984 sales of $3.1 million, a market share of almost 50% in a market with a real growth rate of over 5%, and a manufacturing contribution margin of over 60%, it was a major contributor to Parke-Davis's sales and profits. In 1984 total advertising and promotional spending on the product was expected to be over $500,000 with about 40% of this for samples. A breakdown of the actual advertising and promotion budget for 1984 and the planned budget for 1985 are shown in Exhibit 6. A projected 34% increase in the budget to support a 10% increase in sales was a partial response to the decreased availability of detailing time for the brand.

Alternatives Under Consideration. As the management team of the Professional Health Group grappled with the problem of insufficient personal medical detailing time, it was apparent that there were several options open to them. The major options open to them were

1. Expand utilization of the MIAs to provide pre-launch, launch, and the entire post-launch responsibility for new products for key specialists. This option would insure that the new products would be very effectively detailed to the key potential prescribing specialists for a particular new product. The major disadvantage of this option was that the MIAs would be of little assistance in detailing the new products to general practitioners.
2. Increase the size of the regular salesforce. This would allow the geographical territories to be smaller, permitting Parke-Davis to reach more doctors. However,

Exhibit 5 **Parke-Davis Professional Health Group**

Planned 1985 Medical Promotion Schedule
Two-Month Sales Promotion Cycle

		1	2	3	4	5	6
General Practitioners (GPs)	Primary	Lopid Benylin	Eryc Choledyl SA	Lopid Benadryl	Choledyl SA Lopid	Lopid Ponstan	Eryc Mylanta
	Reminder	Eryc Mylanta	Mylanta Anusol/Tucks	Ponstan Mylanta	Eryc Ponstan	Eryc Mylanta	Anusol/T Benylin
Surgeons	Primary	Mylanta Thrombostat	Anusol/Tucks	Mylanta Thrombostat	Mylanta	Thrombostat	Ausol/T
	Reminder	Hose	Hose	Anusol/Tucks Hose	Hose	Mylanta Hose	Mylanta Hose
Pediatricians	Primary	Benylin Choledyl Liquid	Benylin Choledyl Liquid	Benadryl Colymycin	Benadryl Vanquin	Choledyl Liquid Benylin	Benylin Choledyl Liquid
Obstetrics/ Gynecology (OB/GYNs)	Primary	Ponstan	Ponstan Mylanta	Ponstan	Ponstan	Mylanta Thrombostat	OC's Ponstan
	Reminder	Mylanta Tucks OC's	Tucks	Tucks OC's	OC's Tucks	Mylanta Tucks	Mylanta Hose
Internal Medicine	Primary	Lopid	Lopid Nitrostat IV Eryc	Lopid Eryc	Lopid Nitrostat IV Eryc	Lopid Nitrostat IV	Lopid Eryc
	Reminder	Mylanta Eryc	Mylanta	Mylanta Benadryl	Mylanta	Mylanta Eryc	Mylanta Benylin
Hospital Staff		Thrombostat Chloromycetin Mylanta	Nitrostat IV Benadryl Elase	Thrombostat Benadryl Mylanta	Nitrostat IV Elase	Thrombostat Chloromycetin Mylanta	Nitro IV Elase
Misc. Samples		Ponstan Hose	Hose Benylin	Hose Colymycin Eryc Anusol/Tucks	Benadryl Hose	Benadryl Hose Benylin	Ponstan Hose

management felt it was unlikely to increase the detailing time a salesperson could spend with key doctors for the Parke-Davis product line, since doctors would be unlikely to be willing to talk to the medical representative more than once during each two-month sales cycle. Thus, the representative's capacity to detail more products to any one physician would not be enhanced.

Exhibit 6 **Parke-Davis Professional Health Group**

Advertising and Promotion Budget for Prescription Anusol in 1984 and 1985 (Planned)

	1984 (Estimated) (in $000)	1985 (Planned) (in $000)	Percentage change from 1984 to 1985
Promotion			
"Loss of Revenue"[a]	221	242	10
Medical Promotion	8	10	25
Mailing of samples	15	15	0
Samples (cost of goods)	224	307	37
Total	468	574	23
Advertising			
Print	78	150	92
Print Production	0	12	—
Agency Fees	24	26	8
Audits and Surveys	6	7	17
Total	108	195	81
Total Advertising and Promotion Budget	574	769	34
As a % of Sales	18	22	

[a]"Loss of revenue" was the estimated cost of price discounts and free-goods (buy 11 and get 1 free) that would be offered to the retail drug trade.

3. Develop a second medical salesforce for the Professional Health Group. The existing product line could be split between the two salesforces, perhaps with one salesforce specializing in the cardiovascular and pulmonary products and the other salesforce specializing in the anti-infective and anti-inflammatory products. If the few miscellaneous products in the Parke-Davis product line were also assigned to the second sales force, the two sales forces would have similar dollar volumes. Of the 15 new products planned for the 1985–87 period, six would be in the first group of products and nine in the second group of products. With this option many physicians, drug stores, and hospitals would be detailed by two Parke-Davis medical representatives, thus doubling the number of products that could be detailed in any two-month sales cycle. However, management was unsure how the medical profession would react to this strategy—would doctors agree to see two different Parke-Davis sales representatives during a given two-month sales cycle, or would they only see one in each sales cycle? Management was also unsure how competition might react to this strategy. While some other competitors did have more than one salesforce, with the exception of the recent move by Boehringer-Ingelheim these different salesforces operated under different names—often the names of predecessor companies.

4. Make no changes in the salesforce, but make adjustments elsewhere to reflect the detailing capacity problem. Some managers felt it would be possible to revamp the detailing schedule to maximize the number of products on promotion. Substantial increases in the advertising and promotion support to brands might also reduce the need for detailing time on some of the products. To handle the large number of anticipated new product introductions, these introductions could be delayed to provide a minimum four to six months interval between the introduction of new brands. The detailing load could also be reduced by licensing the new products with low sales potential to other pharmaceutical manufacturers.

The Second Salesforce Option. By far the most radical of the four options under consideration was the addition of the second salesforce. It was viewed to be quite risky; and if the decision to proceed with it was made, there were several major implementation issues that would need to be addressed.

In "fleshing out" the two-salesforce option for discussion purposes, Mr. Skripitsky and Mr. Gibson thought that they would require 49 representatives for each salesforce organized, as shown in Exhibit 7. Where feasible, district managers would be responsible for medical representatives from only one of the salesforces, although in the more geographically dispersed areas like Manitoba/Saskatchewan, rural Quebec and the Atlantic Provinces, the district managers would have medical representatives from both salesforces reporting to them. Mr. Skripitsky and Mr. Gibson envisioned the continuance of the MIA sales force with five representatives assigned to it. The MIAs would support both salesforces as needed. The 1985 incremental cost of adding salespersons, managers, and support staff and facilities was estimated to average about $57,000 per person in the field; that is, $2.4 million for the 42 incremental persons that would be required to staff the two salesforces. Salesforce costs were expected to rise about 7% per year during the rest of the 1980s.

If a second salesforce were added, the number of detailing slots available would be increased from 24 (four slots in each of the six sales cycles) to 48. In a preliminary look at the potential impact of this doubling of slots, management thought that the 1985 Medical Promotion Schedule for general practitioners might be modified as shown in Exhibit 8. This would allow several more products to be detailed, some of them at high frequencies. In consultation with the product managers for the various products involved, Mr. Skripitsky and Mr. Gibson estimated that under the two-salesforce option, sales might be $1.3 million higher in 1985 than they would be with the continuance of current policies. Incremental sales of $4.6 million, $5.6 million, $7.9 million, and $9.5 million were expected in 1986, 1987, 1988, and 1989, respectively. The sources of these incremental sales are shown in Exhibit 9.

If the decision was made to add a second salesforce there were several major implementation issues that needed to be addressed. A major concern was the naming of the two salesforces. Two major options had been proposed. Some managers thought that both salesforces should operate clearly under the Parke-Davis name with one salesforce being called the Cardiovascular/Pulmonary Sales Group and the other the Anti-Infective/Anti-Inflammatory Sales Group. Others thought that the Parke-

Exhibit 7 **Parke-Davis Professional Health Group**

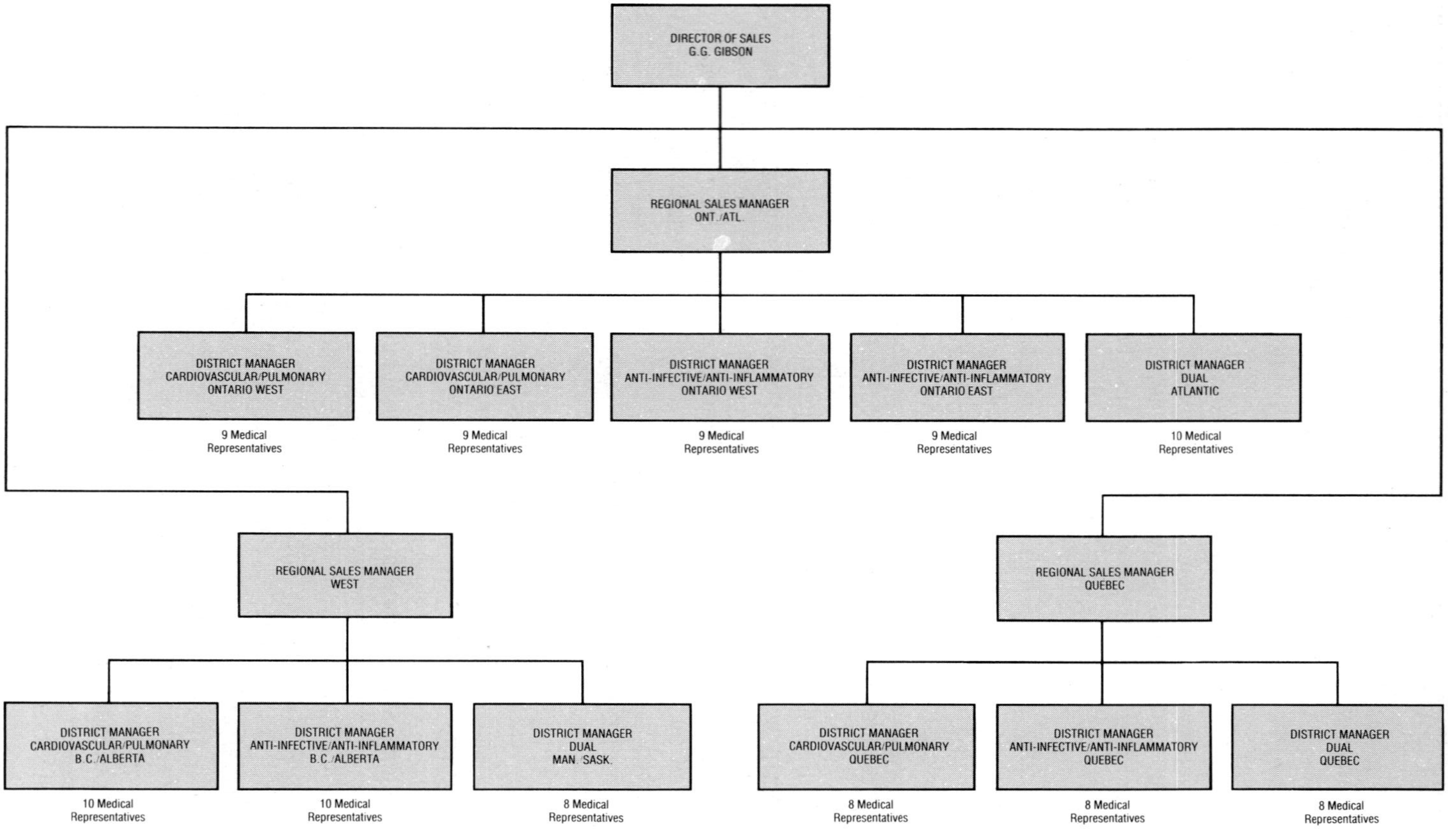

DIRECTOR OF SALES
G.G. GIBSON

REGIONAL SALES MANAGER
ONT./ATL.

DISTRICT MANAGER
CARDIOVASCULAR/PULMONARY
ONTARIO WEST
9 Medical Representatives

DISTRICT MANAGER
CARDIOVASCULAR/PULMONARY
ONTARIO EAST
9 Medical Representatives

DISTRICT MANAGER
ANTI-INFECTIVE/ANTI-INFLAMMATORY
ONTARIO WEST
9 Medical Representatives

DISTRICT MANAGER
ANTI-INFECTIVE/ANTI-INFLAMMATORY
ONTARIO EAST
9 Medical Representatives

DISTRICT MANAGER
DUAL
ATLANTIC
10 Medical Representatives

REGIONAL SALES MANAGER
WEST

DISTRICT MANAGER
CARDIOVASCULAR/PULMONARY
B.C./ALBERTA
10 Medical Representatives

DISTRICT MANAGER
ANTI-INFECTIVE/ANTI-INFLAMMATORY
B.C./ALBERTA
10 Medical Representatives

DISTRICT MANAGER
DUAL
MAN./SASK.
8 Medical Representatives

REGIONAL SALES MANAGER
QUEBEC

DISTRICT MANAGER
CARDIOVASCULAR/PULMONARY
QUEBEC
8 Medical Representatives

DISTRICT MANAGER
ANTI-INFECTIVE/ANTI-INFLAMMATORY
QUEBEC
8 Medical Representatives

DISTRICT MANAGER
DUAL
QUEBEC
8 Medical Representatives

Proposed Sales Organization with Two Sales Forces

Exhibit 8 Parke-Davis Professional Health Group

1985 Product Exposure to General Practitioners (GPs) without and with Second Sales Force (Frequency on Detail Schedule)

Product	Current Plan	Plan with Second Sales Force	Change
Lopid	4	5	1
Benylin	2	4	2
Eryc	5	4	(1)
Mylanta	5	6	1
Choledyl	2	4	2
Anusol/Tucks	2	5	3
Benadryl	1	2	1
Ponstan	3	3	—
Hose	—	3	3
Oral Contraceptives	—	6	6
Colymycin Otic	—	1	1
Procan	—	5	5
	24	48	24

Exhibit 9 Parke-Davis Professional Health Group

Estimated Impact of Second Sales Force on Sales (In Thousands of Dollars)

	1985	1986	1987	1988	1989
Incremental Sales From Existing Ethical Products	615	1,215	1,680	2,440	3,040
Incremental Sales From Consumer Health Group Products[a]	300	350	400	450	500
Incremental Sales From New Products	400	3,000	3,500	5,000	6,000
Total Incremental Sales	1,315	4,565	5,580	7,890	9,540

[a] Consumer Health Group products sold under the Parke-Davis brand, e.g., Benylin and Gelusil.

Davis name should be used, but that the salespersons should be represented as coming from two separate divisions. Suggestions for the division names included Research Laboratories Division of Parke-Davis, the Scientific Laboratories Division of Parke-Davis, and the Warner Laboratories Division of Parke-Davis. The chosen name would appear on the representative's calling card. Another issue was whether all medical representatives should be trained on the full Parke-Davis product line, or just on the part of the product line sold by their sales force. As more new products were introduced, training on the full product line would probably require that the sales training program be lengthened. Perhaps the major implementation issue was how to introduce the idea of two Parke-Davis salesforces to the doctor and his or her receptionist/nurse. A negative reaction on their part could jeopardize the whole two-salesforce plan. A continuing problem would be the need for the two sales representatives serving a particular geographical area to coordinate their activities so that they didn't end up calling on the same doctors at about the same time.

Mr. Gibson also wondered how the salesforce would react if a second salesforce were to be introduced. He could imagine some salespersons being concerned that an additional salesperson in their territory would make it more difficult for them to see their doctors and to gain as frequent access to hospitals. Many would be concerned about how any changes would affect their compensation and would want assurance that they wouldn't be expected to generate the same absolute-dollar increases in sales on a reduced business base.

Possible Test. If the decision were made to add a second salesforce, Mr. Skripitsky and Mr. Gibson wondered if they should first test the concept in one part of Canada prior to introducing it nationally. If they proposed a test, they would have to recommend how it should be conducted, where it should be conducted, and how long it should last. The choice of a test area would not be an easy one. Every province or region of the country had significant drawbacks. British Columbia was geographically large and the Vancouver area had a very high ratio of physicians to people. Alberta had the advantages of being a relatively isolated market with little government intervention and having the Parke-Davis Western Region office in Edmonton. The latter would facilitate monitoring of any test. On the negative side it was a market in which Parke-Davis did extremely well and might not be representative from that point of view. The Alberta economy was also depressed in 1984. Both Saskatchewan and Manitoba were isolated markets, but both provincial governments had very restrictive formularies, making them unrepresentative of the rest of Canada. Ontario's major disadvantage was its size. With over 36% of Canada's population, it seemed too large for a test market. If only part of the province were used, monitoring the results of the test would be extremely difficult and expensive given the potential spillover effects of marketing activity in one part of the province into other areas. Quebec was also large and was a market where Parke-Davis was having some problems in early 1984. In addition, while the company had the capability to train French-speaking representatives, the burden of training people for the test would fall heavily on the shoulders of one individual. The Atlantic Provinces were viewed as being somewhat unique in Canada from a pharmaceutical marketing perspective, and Mr. Skripitsky and Mr. Gibson did not feel that any results obtained there would necessarily be projectable to the rest of the country.

The Situation in May 1984

As Mr. Skripitsky sat down in late May to decide what salesforce recommendations should be included in the five-year plan, he knew that he would have to deal with a number of key issues that Mr. Seath was likely to bring up. Mr. Skripitsky felt that Mr. Seath would have major concerns about the two-salesforce option. One of his concerns would be the large, continuing, fixed costs that would be associated with a second salesforce. Warner-Lambert considered itself a very "people-oriented" company, and there would be no question of dismissing members of the second salesforce if it did not work out. The investment of resources in a new salesperson was also considerable. Mr. Skripitsky felt the company's investment in a new salesperson could add up to $50,000 in the first two years the representative was with the company. Mr. Seath would want to be convinced that any additions to the salesforce head count would be fully warranted and that the additions were meeting a permanent need, not a temporary one. While Mr. Skripitsky expected that the fifteen new products would be introduced, there was always the possibility that some of the introductions might have to be delayed or cancelled, if unforseen problems, such as a failure to get regulatory approval for a product, occurred. Mr. Seath would also want Mr. Skripitsky's assurance that the older products would in fact respond to more detailing time.

Mr. Skripitsky also knew that a key element of Mr. Seath's strategy for the Health Care Division was the continuing establishment of the Parke-Davis name as a highly respected brand name in the medical community. Mr. Seath would need to be convinced that the addition of a second salesforce would not lead to any dilution of the Parke-Davis name.

Before presenting his recommendations, Mr. Skripitsky knew he'd have to develop a detailed set of recommendations for whichever option he chose. If he decided on the two-salesforce option, he would have to have specific recommendations on its size, timing, the naming of the salesforces, whether or not to test market the concept, and a host of implementation issues. He realized he had a lot of work to do within the next week to prepare his recommendations.

Notes

[1] Pharmaceutical products were usually divided into ethical and proprietary categories, depending on how they were marketed by the manufacturer. Ethical products were marketed directly to the medical profession, whereas proprietary products were promoted directly to the consumer. Ethical products were commonly divided into two further categories: prescription pharmaceuticals and over-the-counter (OTC) pharmaceuticals. As the name implies, prescription pharmaceuticals were available only on a prescription written by a physician. OTC pharmaceuticals could be purchased by the consumer without a prescription.

BSI: Manufacturers' Representative Agency—The Dilemma of Expansion

Introduction

With four people and sales of $5.5 million, Barro Stickney Inc. (BSI) had become a successful and profitable manufacturers' representative firm. It enjoyed a reputation for outstanding sales results and friendly, thorough service to both its customers and principals. In addition, BSI was considered a great place to work. The office was comfortable and the atmosphere relaxed but professional. All members of the group had come to value the close, friendly working relationships that had grown with the organization.

Success had brought with it increased profits as well as the inevitable decision regarding further growth. Recent requests from two principals, Franklin Key Electronics and R. D. Ocean, had forced BSI to focus its attention on the question of expansion. It was not to be an easy decision, for expansion offered both risk and opportunity.

Company Background

John Barro and Bill Stickney established their small manufacturers' representative agency, Barro Stickney Inc., ten years ago. Both men were close friends who left different manufacturers' representative firms to join as partners in their own "rep" agency. The two worked very well together, and their talents complemented each other.

John Barro was energetic and gregarious. He enjoyed meeting new people and taking on new challenges. It was mainly through John's efforts that many of BSI's eight principals had signed on with BSI. Even after producing $1.75 million in sales this past year, John still made an effort to contribute much of his free time to community organizations in addition to perfecting his golf score.

Bill Stickney liked to think of himself as someone a person could count on. He was thoughtful and thorough. He liked to figure how things could get done, and how they could be better. Much of the administrative work of the agency, such as resource allocation and territory assignments, was handled by Bill. In addition to his contribution of $1.5 million to total company sales, Bill also had a boy scout troup and

Source: This case was prepared in 1985 by Tony Langan, B. Jane Stewart, and Lawrence M. Stratton, Jr., under the supervision of Assistant Professor Erin Anderson of the Wharton School, University of Pennsylvania. The writing of the case was sponsored by the Manufacturers' Representatives Educational Research Foundation. The cooperation of the Mid-Atlantic Chapter of the Electronic Representatives Association (ERA) is greatly appreciated.

Exhibit 1

Before the meeting, Bill Stickney examined the sources of BSI's revenue and the firm's income for the previous year in addition to estimating the future prospects for each of BSI's lines, considering each line's market potential and BSI's level of saturation in each market. Finally, he estimated the costs of hiring a new employee both in the current sales territory, and in the Washington/Virginia area. Immediately before the meeting, Elizabeth finished compiling Bill's data into four charts.

Return versus Difficulty in Selling

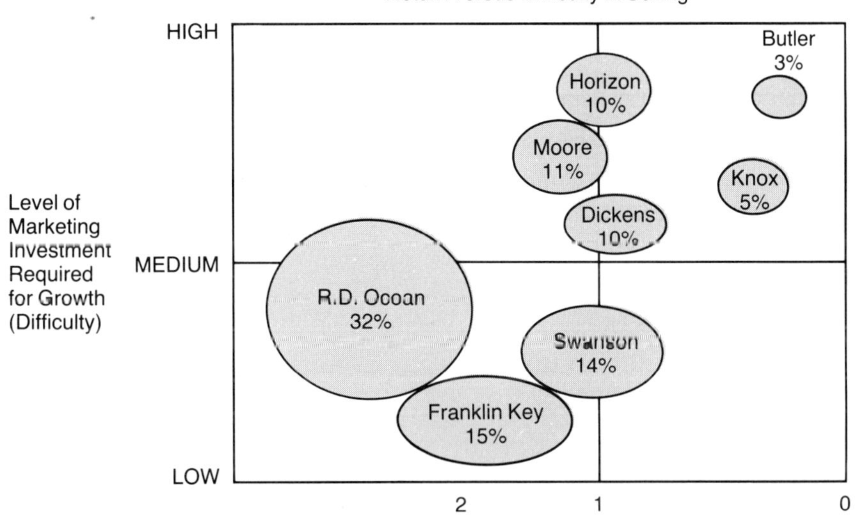

Notes and Explanation

This chart evaluates the amount of sales effort (Difficulty in Selling) necessary in order to achieve a certain percentage of sales in BSI's portfolio (Return). Difficulty in selling is measured by the level of marketing investment required for growth. Stickney's estimate is shown on the vertical axis. Return for this investment is measured by the relative sales commissions as a percent of BSI's portfolio shown on the horizontal axis. If BSI's time were evenly divided among its eight principals, each would receive 12.5 percent of the agency's time. The x-axis shows each principal's time allocation as a proportion of 12.5 percent, the "par" time allocation. The area of each ellipse reflects each principal's share of BSI's commission revenue.

Additional Comments

Swanson's products are being replaced by the competition's computerized electronic equipment, a product category the firm has ignored. As a result, the company is losing its once prominent market position.

Although small amounts of effort are required to promote Ocean's product line to customers in the current sales territory, Ocean is extremely demanding of both BSI and other manufacturer's representative firms.

According to a seminar at the last ERA meeting, the maximum safe proportion of a rep firm's commissions from a single principal should be 25 to 30%. Also, at the meeting, one speaker indicated that if a firm commands 80% of a market, it should focus on another product or expand its territory rather than attempt to obtain the remainder of the market.

The revenue for investment for the Manufacturer's Representative firm comes from one of more of several sources. These sources include reduced forthcoming commission income, retained previous income, and borrowed money from a financial institution. Most successful firms expand their salesforce or sales territory when they experience income growth and use the investment as a tax write-off.

Exhibit 2 Barro Stuckney, Inc.: Estimation of Cost of Additional Sales Representative

Compensation Costs for New Sales Representative

Depending upon the new sales representative's level of experience, BSI would pay a base salary of $15,000 to $25,000 with the following bonus schedule:

0% firm's commission revenue up to $500,000 in sales
20% firm's commission revenue 1st half-million dollars in sales over $500,000
25% firm's commission revenue for the next half-million dollars in sales
30% firm's commission for the next half-million dollars in sales
40% firm's commission sales above $2 million in sales

Estimate of Support Costs[a] for New Representative[b]

Search applicant pool, psychological testing, hiring, training,[c] flying final choice to principals for approval.[d]		$28,000
Automobile expenses, telephone costs, business cards, entertainment/promotion.		$22,000
Insurance, payroll taxes (social security, unemployment compensation)		$16,000
	Total Expenses	$66,000
Incremental expenses for new territory:		
Transportation (additional mileage from Camphill to Virginia)		$ 2,000
Office equipment and rent (same regardless of headquarters location)		$ 4,000
Cost of hiring office manager[e]		$18,000
	Total incremental expenses	$24,000

Notes:
[a]Rounded to the nearest thousand.
[b]In current territory.
[c]Excludes the lost revenue from selling instead of engaging in this activity (opportunity cost).
[d]Although legally rep agencies are not required to show prospective employees to principals, it is generally held to be good business practice.
[e]Discretionary

Exhibit 3 Barro Stickney, Inc.: Statement of Revenue

Total Sales Revenue 1985 $5.5 million

Principal	Estimated Market Saturation	Product Type	Sales/Commission Rate	Share of BSI's Portfolio	Commission Revenue
R.D. Ocean	High	Components	5%	32%	$96,756
Franklin Key	High	Components	5%	15%	$45,354
Butler	Low	Technical/Computer	12%	3%	$ 9,070
Dickins	Low	Components	5%	10%	$30,236
Horizon	Medium	Components	5.5%	10%	$30,237
Swanson	High	Components	5.25%	14%	$42,331
Moore	Medium	Consumer/Electronics	5.25%	11%	$33,260
Knox	Low	Technical/Communications	8.5%	5%	$15,118

Exhibit 4 **Barro Stickney, Inc.: Statement of Income for the Year Ending December 31,1985**

Revenue:	
Commission income	$302,362.00
Expenses:	
Salaries for Sales and Bonuses (includes Barro & Stickney)	$130,250.00
Office manager's salary	$ 20,000.00
Total non-personnel expenses[a]	$128,279.00
Total expenses	$278,529.00
Net Income:[b]	**$23,833.00 (7.9% of revenue)**

Notes:

[a]Includes travel, advertising, taxes, office supplies, retirement, automobile expenses, communications, office equipment, and miscellaneous expenses.

[b]Currently held in negotiable certificates of deposit in a Harrisburg bank.

was interested in gourmet cooking. In fact, he often prepared specialities to share with his fellow workers.

A few years later, as the business grew, J. Todd Smith (J. T.) joined as an additional salesperson. J. T. had worked for a nationally known corporation, and he brought his experience dealing with large customers with him. He and his family loved the Harrisburg area, and J. T. was very happy when he was asked to join BSI just as his firm was ready to transfer him to Chicago. John and Bill had worked with J. T. in connection with a hospital fund-raising project, and they were impressed with his tenacity and enthusiasm. Because he had produced sales of over $2 million this past year, J. T. was now considered eligible to buy a partnership share of BSI.

Soon after J. T. joined BSI, Elizabeth Lee, a school friend of John's older sister, was hired as office manager. She was cheerful and put as much effort into her work as she did coaching the local swim team. The three salespeople knew they could rely on her to keep track of orders and schedules, and she was very helpful when customers and principals called in with requests or problems.

Most principals in the industry assigned their reps exclusive territories, and BSI's ranged over the Pennsylvania, New Jersey, and Delaware area. The partners purchased a small house and converted it into their present office located in Camp Hill, a suburb of Harrisburg, the state capitol of Pennsylvania. The converted home contributed to the family-like atmosphere and attitude that was promoted and prevalent throughout the agency.

Over the years, in addition to local interests, BSI and its people had made an effort to participate in and support the efforts of the Electronics Representative Association (ERA). A wall of the company library was covered with awards and letters of appreciation. BSI had made many friends and important contacts through the organization. Just last year BSI received a recommendation from Chuck Goodman, a Chicago manufacturer's rep who knew a principal in need of representation in the Philadelphia area. The principal's line worked well with BSI's existing portfolio, and customer response had been quite favorable. BSI planned to continue active participation in the ERA.

Each week BSI held a 5:00 meeting in the office library where all members of the company shared their experiences of the week. It was a time where new ideas were encouraged and everyone was kept up to date. For example, many customer problems were solved here, and principals' and members' suggestions were discussed. An established agenda enabled members to prepare. Most meetings took about one to one and one-half hours, with emphasis placed on consensus of the group. It was during this group meeting that BSI would discuss the future of the company.

Opportunities for Expansion

R. D. Ocean was BSI's largest principal, and it accounted for 32% of BSI's revenues. Ocean had just promoted James Innve as new sales manager, and he felt an additional salesperson was needed in order for BSI to achieve the new sales projections. Innve expressed the opinion that BSI's large commission checks justified the additional effort, and he further commented that J. T.'s expensive new car was proof that BSI could afford it.

BSI was not sure an additional salesperson was necessary, but it did not want to lose the goodwill of R. D. Ocean or its business. Also, while it was customary for all principals to meet and tacitly approve new representatives, BSI wanted to be very sure that any new salesperson would fit into the close-knit BSI organization.

Franklin Key Electronics was BSI's initial principal, and it had remained a consistent contributor of approximately 15% of BSI's revenues. BSI felt its customer base was well suited to the Franklin line, and it had worked hard to establish the Franklin Key name with these customers. As a consequence, BSI now considered Franklin Key relatively easy to sell.

A few days previously, Mark Heil, Franklin's representative from Virginia, perished when his private plane crashed, leaving Franklin Key without representation in its D.C./Virginia territory. Franklin did not want to jeopardize its sales of over $800,000, and was desperate to replace Heil before its customers found other sources. Franklin offered the territory to BSI and was anxious to hear the decision within one week.

BSI was not familiar with the territory, but it did understand that there were a great number of military accounts. This meant there was a potential for sizable orders, although a different and specialized sales approach would be required. Military customers are known to have their own unique approach to purchase decisions.

Because of the distance and the size of the territory, serious consideration was needed as to whether a branch office would be necessary. A branch office would mean less interaction with and a greater independence from the main BSI office. None of the current BSI members seemed anxious to move there, but it might be possible to hire someone who was familiar with the territory. There was, of course, always the risk that any successful salesperson might leave and start his or her own rep firm.

In addition to possibilities of expanding its territory and its salesforce, BSI also wanted to consider whether it should increase or maintain its number of principals. BSI's established customer base and its valued reputation put it in a strong position to approach potential principals. If, however, BSI had too many principals, it might not be able to offer them all the attention and service they might require.

Preparation for the Meeting

Each member received an agenda and supporting data for the upcoming meeting asking them to consider the issue of expansion. They would be asked whether BSI should or should not expand its territory, its salesforce, and/or its number of principals. In preparation, they were each asked to take a good hard look at the current BSI portfolio and to consider all possibilities for growth as well as the effect any changes would have on the company's profits, its reputation, and its work environment.

It was an ambitious agenda: one that would determine the future of the company. It would take even more time than usual to discuss everything and reach consensus. Consequently, this week's meeting was set to take place over the weekend at Bill Stickney's vacation lodge in the Pocanos starting with a gourmet dinner served at 7:00 p.m. sharp.

Nebon Medical Products, Incorporated

Nebon Medical Products (NMP) in Milwaukee, Wisconsin, is one of the top manufacturers of life-support medical equipment and surgical pharmaceuticals. In 1980, NMP recorded sales of $230 million (see Exhibit 1). Over the past five years sales have been increasing at an annual rate of 15 percent. The company currently employs 175 sales representatives, including a separate salesforce of 40 that handles the company's pharmaceutical line exclusively. As the result of a recent staff reorganization, a decision was made to realign the sales department to meet the future goals of the company better.

Three years ago Nebon's president retired, and the top position was filled by the executive vice-president, Christopher John. Subsequently, several other major changes occurred in the executive staff hierarchy. The most important were the elimination of the executive vice-president position and the creation of the position of vice-president of marketing and sales. Reporting to the new vice-president would be the current vice-president of sales, service, and distribution; the four marketing managers; the director of market research; and the director of promotion (see Exhibit 2).

The vice-president of marketing and sales, destined to be one of the most powerful positions at NMP, was ultimately filled by Earl Callahan. Callahan had previously held the top marketing job in a firm that manufactured medical products unrelated to those sold by Nebon. Filling this position with an "outsider" generated noticeable discontent among several executives who had been considered as top contenders. Shortly after he began work, Callahan was pressured by John to have a revised sales organization chart completed prior to Nebon's new fiscal year beginning July 1. After reviewing Nebon's current organization charts, sales figures, and marketing plans for new products, Callahan realized there were several major problems.

Marketing Activities

Nebon's marketing function was divided into four separate product areas. The patient care group consisted of anesthesia equipment and disposables, nursing equipment, and infant care supplies. The anesthesia line accounted for the greatest dollar volume with 1980 sales of $60 million. With new products as the primary growth factor, sales were expected to be $115 million by 1985. Product prices ranged from a few cents for disposables to several thousand dollars for equipment.

The respiratory therapy line accounted for $40 million in sales in 1980. The line had experienced only slight growth over the last few years but was expected to generate $58 million by 1985 with the introduction of one major new respirator, priced as high as $35,000 with all accessories. The prime market for this do-everything

Source: Author Bonnie J. Queram, MBA., University of Wisconsin at Madison as it appeared in *Sales Force Management* 2nd Edition by G. A. Churchill, Jr., N. M. Ford, O. C. Walker, Jr.

Exhibit 1 **1980 Sales ($000)**

Patient Care		$ 84,270
Anesthesia equipment	$40,100	
Anesthesia disposables	20,450	
Nursing products	13,720	
Infant care	10,000	
Respiratory therapy		40,418
Architectural products		35,980
Pharmaceuticals		50,055
Other (government, OEM, service, military)		20,000
Total		$230,723

machine was the small to medium-sized hospital. Although Nebon was the leader in the anesthesia field, it did not enjoy the same position in respiratory care. In fact, due to several major failures with new products during the last 10 years, the Nebon name was still associated by many therapists with inferior quality, poor product design, and inadequate service.

The architectural product line, composed of pipelines and gas outlets, had sales of $36 million in 1980, while the pharmaceutical line, sold by a separate sales organization, accounted for $50 million. The major product was a liquid that when converted to gas was used to anesthetize patients for surgery.

Sales Activities

The general-line salesforce, consisting of 135 representatives reporting to 19 district managers, and six regional vice-presidents (see Exhibit 3) were currently expected to call on four major departments in each hospital: anesthesia, respiratory therapy, nursing, and infant care. Additionally they were expected to keep in contact with purchasing and, if one existed, with the biomedical engineering department. The latter, usually present only in larger hospitals, was often responsible for reviewing and testing potential new equipment. Biomedical engineers were becoming instrumental in the purchase of sophisticated electronic devices. Also the salesforce was expected to sell gas and electrical pipeline equipment to new hospitals or those being remodeled. This required that they work very closely with architects and construction contractors, usually a very time-consuming endeavor ranging from several months to over one year. The pharmaceutical salesforce called on the anesthesia staff exclusively. Close and frequent contact was necessary in most cases. The salesforce, all with chemical backgrounds, was expected to keep abreast of technological developments in the field. Some sales representatives were formerly anesthetists.

Although Nebon's products covered a wide variety of medical applications and necessitated sales calls to many different departments, the general-line salesforce had,

Exhibit 2

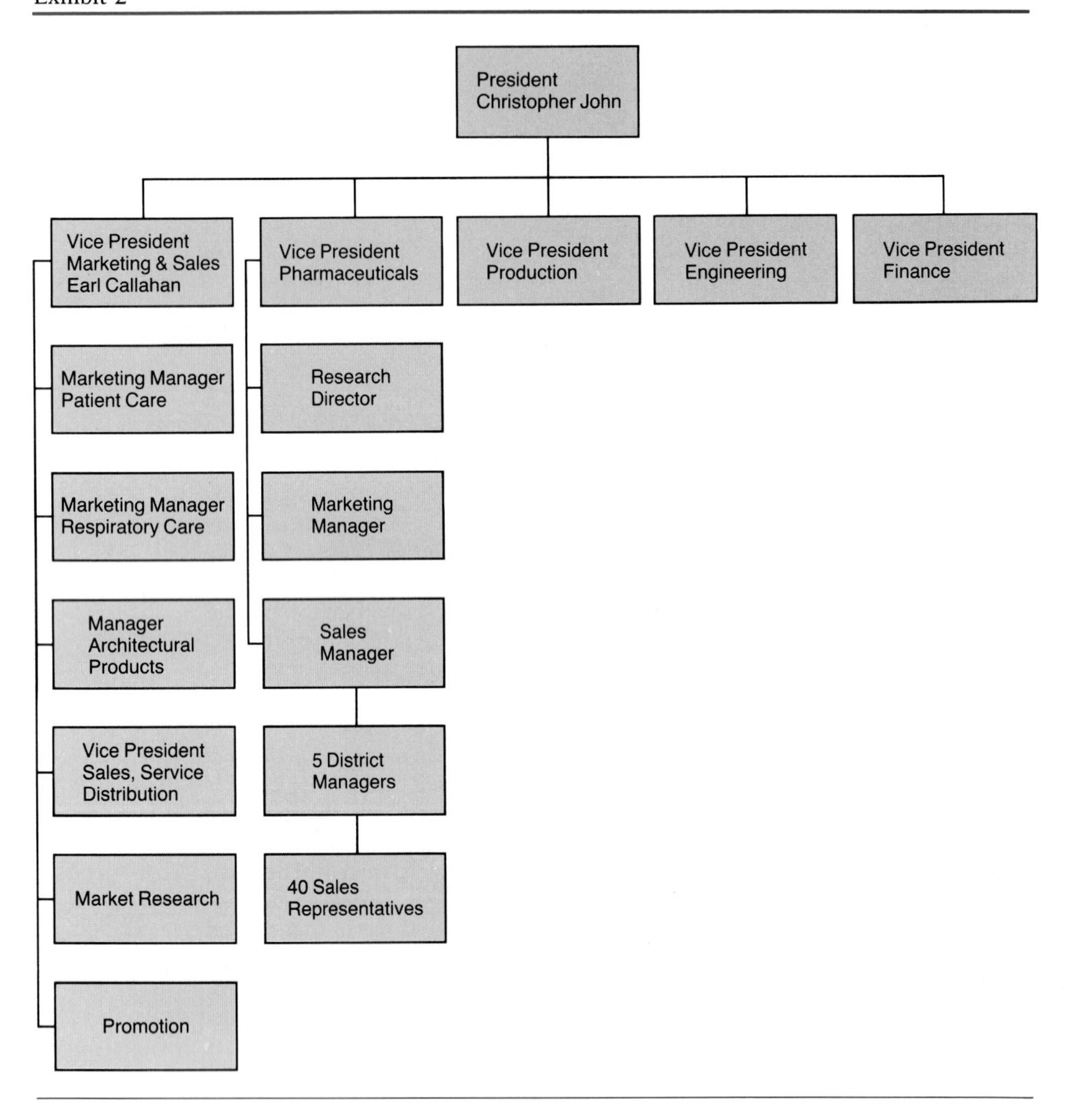
President
Christopher John
Vice President
Marketing & Sales
Earl Callahan
Vice President
Pharmaceuticals
Vice President
Production
Vice President
Engineering
Vice President
Finance
Marketing Manager
Patient Care
Research
Director
Marketing Manager
Respiratory Care
Marketing
Manager
Manager
Architectural
Products
Sales
Manager
Vice President
Sales, Service
Distribution
5 District
Managers
Market Research
40 Sales
Representatives
Promotion

Exhibit 3

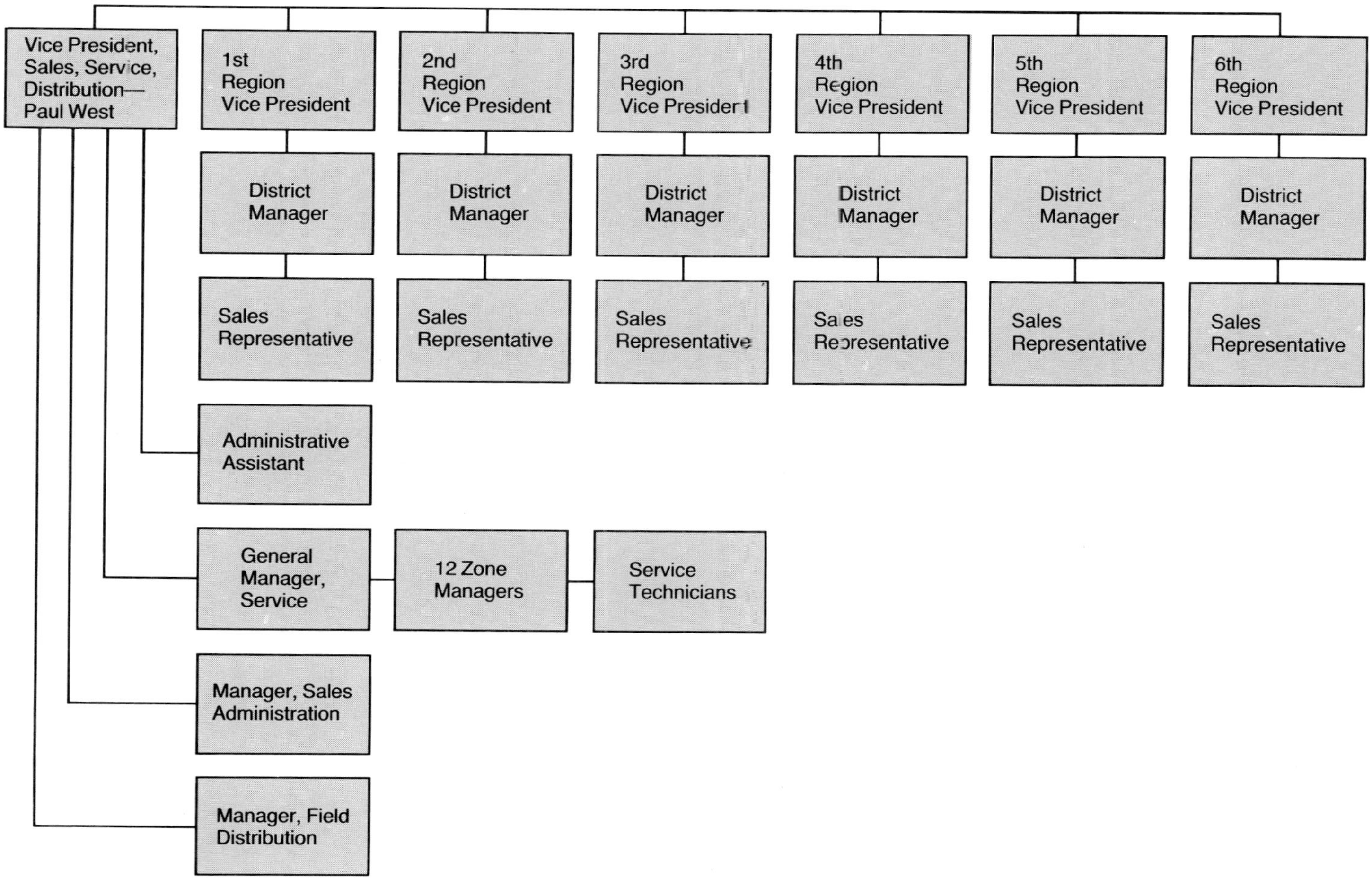

Vice President, Sales, Service, Distribution— Paul West
1st Region Vice President
District Manager
Sales Representative
2nd Region Vice President
District Manager
Sales Representative
3rd Region Vice President
District Manager
Sales Representative
4th Region Vice President
District Manager
Sales Representative
5th Region Vice President
District Manager
Sales Representative
6th Region Vice President
District Manager
Sales Representative
Administrative Assistant
General Manager, Service
12 Zone Managers
Service Technicians
Manager, Sales Administration
Manager, Field Distribution

to date, handled the lines very well. Callahan felt that one primary reason they had done so well was that the majority of Nebon's products were not particularly complicated and the salesforce could be adequately trained by the product managers when new products were introduced. Additionally, although Nebon sold several thousand items, which realistically is a line much too broad for a sales representative to handle effectively, Callahan knew that many products sold with little or no sales effort because of the Nebon name and strong dealer network. Most dealers handled low-cost, easy-to-sell products, although some of the very large dealers sold high-priced equipment. Callahan also felt, however, that this would not continue in the future, because many products planned for market introduction in the next five years were complicated, state-of-the-art electronic pieces of equipment. Most of these products were in the anesthesia line. Nebon's lack of experience in the medical electronics field would mean that an intensive sales effort would be required to enter the market profitably, as there were several formidable competitors controlling the market.

Unfortunately it was generally known that perhaps as many as half of Nebon's sales representatives did not have the training or experience to sell these kinds of products. In view of the need to deal with hospital biomedical engineers on a very technical level, in the long run, Callahan surmised, it would be better to use only sales personnel experienced in selling electronic equipment rather than attempt to train the entire force. Besides, he knew from personal conversations that quite a few representatives had no interest in learning about or selling the new equipment. Thus he wondered about the feasibility of a separate sales group to handle electronic products exclusively.

Other Information

For the last year the marketing manager in respiratory care, Bill Griese, had been attempting to convince Callahan that in spite of the line's history real growth potential existed in respiratory therapy. He wanted the company to spend more time and money pursuing this market. Griese had also indicated that to sell and service the products adequately—particularly the new, very technical respirator—the line should be handled by a separate salesforce. He argued that because most of Nebon's products were in the anesthesia field, the representatives were spending a disproportionate amount of sales time in that area. Thus Nebon's relatively poor sales and image in respiratory therapy were perpetuated.

Callahan knew that Jeff Hardy, marketing manager for patient care, would lobby for a separate sales group for the anesthesia products, since that line represented one-quarter of the company's sales. Apparently this request had been made several times over the past five years. One proposal had included plans for the pharmaceutical salesforce to also handle the anesthesia equipment because both were sold to the same department. Another proposal had called for a separate anesthesia equipment force altogether. Callahan felt that drugs and equipment required substantially different sales techniques and that one force could not adequately handle both. But he also

Exhibit 4 **Sales Compensation Plans**

	General-Line Representatives	Pharmaceutical Representatives
Base salary	$ 1,500–1,850	$ 1,650–2,100
Commission on sales up to quota	¾%	1%
Commission on sales over quota	2%	2%
1980 salary range	$24,200–35,800	$29,800–42,750

had reservations about two different representatives calling on the same customer, as was currently the case. On the other hand, a separate anesthesia force would result in substantially more sales time spent on respiratory products by the general-line force.

Pharmaceutical Sales Organization

Approximately 10 years ago, Nebon's chemical research department discovered a revolutionary new drug to anesthetize patients safely for surgery. Following two years of testing for the Food and Drug Administration, the drug was approved and successfully introduced to the marketplace. It was currently used on 60 percent of all surgical patients, and it continued to capture market share. The drug had a very high gross margin, and in 1980 it had profits of $37 million on sales of $50 million. Its patent would run through 1990.

To develop the surgical drug market fully and lead the marketing and sales activities, a vice-presidential position was created at the time of discovery of the new drug. Ronald Hagen was hired for this position. He in turn put together a separate sales organization with 45 persons by 1980. Most of the sales representatives were hired away from other pharmaceutical companies and thus demanded and were paid salaries and commissions substantially higher than those paid to Nebon's general-line salesmen (see Exhibit 4).

Hagen was very proud of his organization, believing that his sales representatives were a cut above the general-line organization. Consequently he wanted no part of any plans to join the two forces. Besides, another new drug scheduled for introduction in 1983 would provide the drug sales group with a sufficient product load for several years into the future.

General-Line Sales Organization

The general-line sales organization, reporting to Paul West, consisted of 135 representatives, 9 district managers, and 6 regional vice-presidents. The service department, also under West, consisted of a total of 150 technicians reporting to 12 zone managers.

West was initially quite upset about the apparent demotion of his position as a result of the reorganization; he had reported directly to John before Callahan was hired. Knowing that further reorganization was imminent, West felt he would ultimately lose control of the service and distribution areas. Although this would narrow his responsibilities somewhat, West was not particularly concerned. In fact, because of the need to update both the service organization and the distribution organization to handle the new electronic products, those areas had been commanding a disproportionate amount of his time for the last few months. West would have preferred to hire a general manager for service and distribution and have that new individual, reporting to him, handle most of the responsibility in those two crucial areas. He intended to propose this to Callahan.

In the meantime West was most interested in studying the salesforce reorganization and conveying his ideas to Callahan. West had always been interested in developing a separate salesforce for anesthesia equipment and disposables. He felt there was sufficient sales volume to support it and customers would be receptive to the extra attention and service. When selling this equipment, the representative would call on the anesthesia staff, a group typically more difficult to deal with and more technically oriented than personnel from other hospital departments. Often the sale also involved the hospital's biomedical engineers, which was not true of Nebon's other products. A separate force could be more intensely trained, thus ensuring better customer service.

West also felt that a strong case could be made for putting architectural products under the mandate of a small but specialized salesforce. General-line sales representatives tended to ignore architectural products because their sale consumed so much time and involved contact with nonhospital personnel.

If a separate anesthesia force were developed, the remaining general line would be left with nursing, infant care, respiratory therapy, and architectural products. This seemed reasonable because many of these products were sold in the same hospital departments even though they were categorized in different product lines. West also felt that the dealers should be encouraged to handle more low-cost products, giving the general-line salesforce more time for other products.

The real problem with splitting out the anesthesia products, West thought, was that each group would remain responsible for the new electronic products. West thought further, however, that since each force would be responsible for a smaller number of the new products, they could be sufficiently trained to do this work. Since most of the new electronic products were in the anesthesia area, the selection of this group would come from those with the most training and experience with electronics products. Additionally West felt there was a strong case to be made for having "electronic specialists" in both sales groups. These persons would handle all the products of their groups but would place more emphasis on the new equipment and would be available for dual sales calls with their colleagues who were not so well versed in the items.

At a recent convention, West briefly discussed his ideas with Tom Reinke, the western regional vice president and one of West's closest friends. Reinke had at one time worked for a company that manufactured sterilization equipment for hospitals. Following the development of a new, very sophisticated unit, it had divided the sales organization into two groups. One handled the existing line, and the other group specialized in the new equipment. Reinke indicated the sales force division proved disastrous, leading to duplicate sales calls, customer confusion, and increased expenses. He felt the same would occur with West's electronic specialists. He recommended that Nebon should hire more technically qualified personnel for the general-line salesforce. West left the convention somewhat less enthusiastic about his salesforce proposal.

Houston Petroleum Company

"Congratulations, Joe," said Phil Keller, a regional credit manager for the Houston Petroleum Company. "Your new assignment to the Watertown sales district is a good promotion." Joe Smith was the district sales manager of Houston's small River Bend sales district and had recently received word of his promotion to Watertown. "Just think," Phil continued, "old Dick Owen has finally reached retirement age. Forty-two years is a lot of service."

The Houston Petroleum Company, a large and well-established oil distributor, operated in Texas, Oklahoma, and Louisiana. The company's Marketing Division was divided into wholesale and retail departments. Both the River Bend and Watertown districts were part of the wholesale marketing department.

Wholesale distribution involved all customers not buying through service stations of the retail marketing department. Customers included farmers, contractors, truckers, and manufacturing and commercial establishments. The three-state marketing area was divided into regions, which in turn were organized into sales districts. As shown in Exhibit 1, a sales district was a purely line organization; staff support was centralized at the regional headquarters.

District organizations varied depending on the business density and volume of the area served. Typically, however, districts consisted of some 10 bulk plants or depots, a majority of which were operated on a commission basis. Facilities included storage tanks for gasoline and diesel products and a warehouse for lubricating oils, greases, and other packaged materials. Tank trucks distributed Houston products from the local bulk plant to the customer, although certain customers with large requirements and adequate storage were served direct from the refinery or major distribution terminal. The company owned bulk plant facilities and leased them to commission agents.

A sales manager headed each district, but staffing below that level again depended on the size and nature of the area. Assistant sales managers were assigned to larger districts. An average-sized district employed two to three wholesale salespeople, a fuel and lubricant engineer, and the necessary operating personnel to receive, store, and deliver the products. All operating personnel engaged in some way in direct contact with customers. Office personnel sold to walk-in customers, while truck drivers delivered and sold products from tank trucks. Job titles and brief job descriptions of all district positions follow:

> District Sales Manager. Manages the activities of the sales district and administers established policies and procedures relating to sales, delivery, accounting, credit operations, and personnel to secure a representative portion of the available business at maximum realization and minimum operating cost.

Exhibit 1

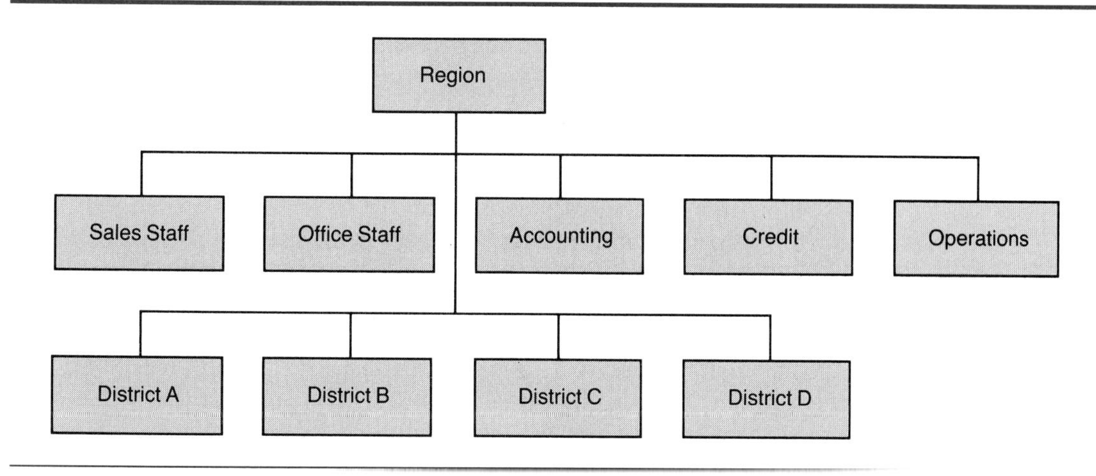

Assistant District Sales Manager. Assists the district sales manager in managing the activities of the sales district and administering established policies and procedures relating to sales, delivery, accounting, credit, plant operations, and personnel to secure a representative proportion of the available business and maximum realization at minimum operating cost.

Fuel and Lubricant Engineer. Provides technical and specialized solicitation and service to accounts which require full engineering help, technical service, and experienced assistance beyond the ability of the general sales organization, through one or a combination of the following activities: (1) solicitation of all product requirements and servicing of accounts requiring constant fuel and lubricant engineering effort beyond the ability of other sales positions; (2) furnishing regularly assigned support to other sales positions on accounts requiring a high degree of fuel and lubricant engineering effort; or (3) providing on-call technical specialized service to accounts requiring fuel and lubricant engineering effort at intermittent or infrequent intervals.

Wholesale Salesperson. Responsible for sale of the full line of products and related services to an assigned group of accounts (both Houston and competitive) within a designated area. Keeps constantly alert to the entrance of new accounts into the field and programs solicitation efforts to best serve such accounts. As appropriate, and when so directed, performs designated administrative and clerical functions closely related to sales and operations.

Office Salesperson. Directs and performs plant sales and clerical work for the district sales manager. In the absence of the district sales manager, acts as a company representative at the station and coordinates station activities. Responsible for meeting standards in the preparation of reports, records, and correspondence; for accurate advice to customers on products, prices, and sales policies; for securing maximum orders from each customer contacting the plant; and for direction of warehouse and delivery functions as required to coordinate station activities.

Assistant Office Salesperson. As a primary function, i.e., at least 25 percent of the time, performs one or a combination of the following duties: (1) taking orders and soliciting business at the counter and over the phone; advising customers on product characteristics, applications, prices and sales, operating or credit policies; (2) performs negotiation-type credit control duties, such as soliciting payments on accounts from customers on the phone or in person; (3) dispatches delivery trucks. Responsible for giving accurate information to customers and for completing assigned clerical and operating duties accurately and expeditiously.

Head Route Salesperson. Operates a small sales office and bulk plant at a location remote from the district sales office to provide service and facilities for the receipt, storage, sale, and delivery of bulk and packaged petroleum products in the area. Performs all functions involved in the receipt, storage, and delivery of packaged and bulk petroleum products. Responsible for plant and operations, safety practices; solicits business of regular and new accounts; collects and arranges for banking of funds; performs accounting functions; prepares sales, stock, credit, personnel and accounting forms, reports, and necessary correspondence.

Route Salesperson. Delivers company products by tank, combination, or package truck to accounts within an assigned area or an assigned route. Loads or assists in loading trucks, drives truck, delivers product from truck, collects for product at the time of delivery or in accordance with established line of credit. Accounts for all products and funds handled. Reports any pertinent competitive activities observed. Services the truck.

The Job of the District Sales Manager

One of Houston's top wholesale marketing executives explained "The job of the district sales manager consisted of three basic functions—to make day-to-day operating decisions to keep the business running smoothly; to plan ahead, setting worthy objectives for each component of the organization, and to follow through to assure that progress actually made was in keeping with goals established; to train, counsel, and motivate the people comprising the organization."

Administering these functions required a number of skills on the part of the district sales manager. He maintained a good deal of the physical plant; he sought out and reported price actions by competitors; he assigned sales territories; he was the company representative in the community; he recommended personnel changes; and so forth. The regional office reserved final approval on price changes, hiring, wage, and salary matters, but the district sales manager initiated such recommendations.

Forms for recording district activity were important to the manager in the effective discharge of basic responsibilities. Several served as the basis for recommenda-

Exhibit 2 Tank Truck Performance Analysis

1	2	3	4	5	6	7	8	9	10	11	12
Truck no.	Capacity	Gals. delv'd	No. of loads	No. of del'ys	Miles run	Loads at 25/min.	Deliveries at 20/min.	Drive at 20 mph	Total (7 + 8 + 9)	Office, plant solic. etc.	Total hours required

The following indicates the source of data entered in columns 1, 2, 3, 4, 5 and 6 and the basis as well as method of computation of figures entered in columns 4, 7, 8, 9, 10, and 11:

Column 1 *Truck Number*
From Statement of Miles Run by Motor Equipment—D123

Column 2 *Capacity*
If the exact truck capacity in gallons is not known, average capacities can be used, i.e., 750 for T1, 950 for T2, 1.250 for T3, and 1.650 for T4

Column 3 *Gallons Delivered*
From Statement of Miles Run—D123

Column 4 *Number of Loads*
Divide gallons delivered (col. 3) by truck capacity (col. 2)

Column 5 *Number of Deliveries*
From Statement of Miles Run—D123

Column 6 *Miles Run*
From Statement of Miles Run—D123

Column 7 *Loading*
Multiply col. 4 by 0.42 (the fractional hour equivalent of 25 minutes per load). For package trucks, full loads, multiply col. 4 by 1 hour

Column 8 *Delivering*
Divide col. 5 by 3 (hourly equivalent of 20 minutes per delivery—a liberal average for all types of deliveries)

Column 9 *Driving*
Divide col. 6 by 20 (average truck speed under normal operating conditions)

Column 10 *Total of Loading, Delivery, and Driving Time*

Column 11 *Office, Plant, Solicitation, Collection, and Miscellaneous*
Multiply col. 10 to 0.28, which is the standard percentage of tank truck work load time allowed for these functions (The office and plant standard allowance to handle daily turn-ins, checking orders, servicing and garaging equipment, etc. is 40 minutes a day. Allowance for solicitation, collection, and miscellaneous is 60 minutes per day. This total, plus 20 minutes for personal time, reduces the average available time for delivery operations to 360 minutes. One hundred minutes is 28 percent of 360 minutes)

tions to regions. For example, Exhibit 2 shows the form used for determining the delivery work load for the route salesperson. The district sales manager used this information periodically to reapportion the work load within the district or to recommend additional personnel to the region.

Sales personnel were expected to record available business information on the customer data sheet, D102 (Exhibit 3). This form provided up-to-date data on the pertinent circumstances surrounding each account, including responsibility for solicitation. Form D105 (Exhibit 4), the account change card, kept the manager informed on sales gains and losses. District managers varied in their insistence on current maintenance of these forms. Some felt that this attention to detail was burdensome and

Exhibit 3 Customer Data Sheet—D102

ASSIGNED TO:	CALLS ASSIGNED
SUPPORTED BY:	

NAME

LOCATION

HEADQUARTERS

TYPE OF BUSINESS

EQUIP OPERATED: PASS. CARS____	TRUCKS____	TRACTORS____	NO. CREDIT CARDS____

OTHER EQUIP:

KEY PERSONNEL—SPECIAL DATA—CONTRACT INFOR.—ETC.

ANNUAL AVAILABLE BUSINESS					
PRODUCT	STGE. TANKS	TOTAL	HOUSTON	COMPETITIVE	CO.
GASOLINE (GALS.)					
DIESEL (GALS.)					
FURNACE (GALS.)					
STOVE/KERO. (GALS.)					
AUTO OILS (GALS.)					
AUTO LUBS/GRS. (LBS.)					
INDUSTRIAL OILS (GALS.)					
INDUSTRIAL GRS. (LBS.)					
THNRS./SOLVS. (GALS.)					
WAXES (LBS.)					
OTHER SPECIAL PRODUCTS (GALS.)					
TOTAL LIGHT PRODUCTS					

CALLS MADE	JAN.	FEB.	MAR.	APR.	MAY	JUNE	JULY	AUG.	SEPT.	OCT.	NOV.	DEC.

Exhibit 4 **Account Change Card—D105**

ACCOUNT CHANGE

DISTRICT ________ OFFICE ________ DATE ________

NAME OF ACCOUNT ____________________

TYPE OF BUSINESS

PRODUCT	ANNUAL REQUIRE-MENTS	VOLUME GAINED LOST	DISTRIBUTION OF REQUIREMENTS AFTER CHANGE		COMPET. GAINED FROM OR LOST TO
			HOUSTON	COMPET.	
Gasoline-gals. Motor Aviation					
Diesel fuel-gals.					
Furnace oil-gals. Stove oil-gals.					
Kerosene-gals.					
Fuel oil-gals.					
Auto oils-gals.					
Auto grease-lbs.					
Ind. oils-gals.					
Ind. grease-lbs.					
Thinners and solvents-gals.					
Liquified pet. gases-gals.					
Other: gals. or lbs.					

REASON FOR GAIN OR LOSS ____________________

Office Manager ____________

Sales Rep. ____________ District Manager ____________

D105

CONTRACTS IN EFFECT (IF GAINED, WHAT TYPE SIGNED: IF LOST, WHAT PAPER IN EFFECT): ____________________

IF ACCOUNT LOST, WHAT ACTION TAKEN TO REGAIN: ____________________

SHOULD APPRECIATION LETTER BE SENT TO ACCOUNT?

Yes ☐ No ☐

CHANGES IN KEY PERSONNEL, SUBSIDIARIES, ETC.: ____________________

not overly productive, while others insisted that the reported information was their only way of keeping aware of district activity.

The commission agents submitted monthly operating and financial statements which the sales managers were to evaluate and use in consultation with the agents. Agents had no formal business training and relied greatly on the supervision of the district sales manager.

The regional office provided the district with information compiled by three staff services. Form R30, for instance, reported cumulative monthly sales results by product for the district and its components. Form R31 showed the number of accounts to which credit had been extended. Form R35 provided expenses per gallon delivered.

The Watertown District

Following several trips to the Watertown District, Joe wondered just what his course of action would be on assuming his new duties. Dick Owen had been at Watertown for 29 years and appeared to be an established part of the community. Joe noted during visits at several service clubs that Dick knew nearly all the town's businesspeople. In fact, at one time or other, Dick had served as president of several of the organizations.

Also going through Joe's mind was the material he had encountered at a recent administrative functions course for district sales managers held at Houston's home office in Dallas. Joe had not been back at River Bend long enough to really apply the material, but he recalled how they had covered the basic management responsibilities of planning, organizing, directing, coordinating, and controlling.

The Watertown district spread over a large area, with a concentration of business activity and population as shown on the map in Exhibit 5. Petroleum and related needs were diversified to the extent that the portion south of the Blue River was highly industrialized, while to the north the mainstay was agriculture. District population figures recorded at 321,000 in 1974 had reached 400,000 in 1978 and were projected to 675,000 in 1990. This growth was based primarily on expected personnel requirements for new business establishments moving into the area. The following figures show new plant construction since 1974:

	Number of New Plants and Expansions (and of Capitalization—000,000)
1974	55 ($10.5)
1975	82 ($12.0)
1976	99 ($15.0)
1977	153 ($24.6)
1978	176 ($35.1)

Fabricated metal products manufacturers ranked first in number of firms, followed by electrical machinery, chemicals, and food and kindred products. Active promotion

Exhibit 5 **Geography of Watertown Sales District**

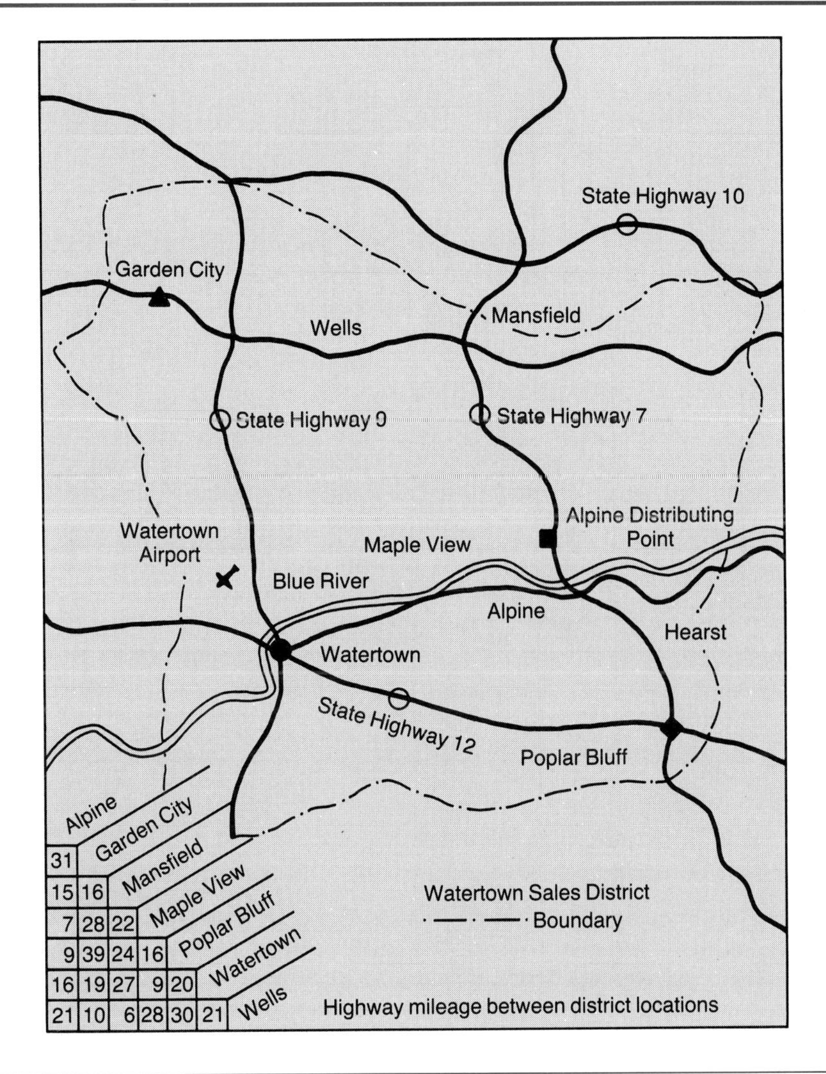

of five major industrial parks promised a continuation of this trend. Navigable waters along the Blue River, adequate rail and trucking facilities, and moderate year-round weather were considered basic attractions to new plant growth.

With the increase in population and industrialization, the area within the district devoted to agriculture had been declining over the past five years. However, mechanical efficiencies in farming and an improved price structure in 1978 helped achieve a

Exhibit 6 **Watertown Sales District Organization Chart**

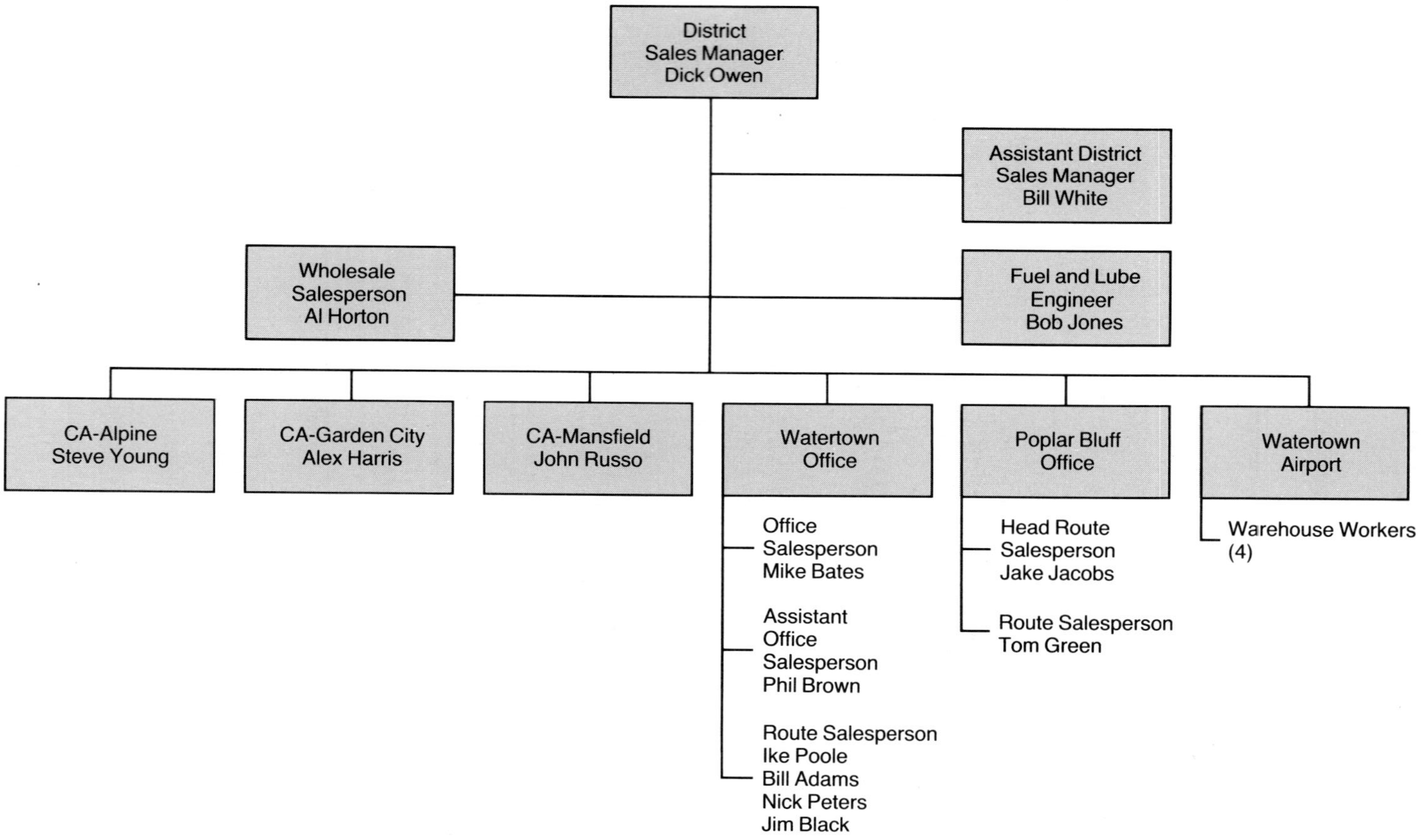

record value of $16.5 million for agricultural production. Flowers, vegetables, and livestock accounted for the major share of the total.

Watertown, the heart of the area's heavy industrial growth, was the home of the district office and main salaried sales office. Encouraged by liberal zoning laws, "smoke-stack" type operations had increased 40 percent over the last five years. A new 300-acre industrial park was to open soon near the city

There were four rather sizable airports in the sales district—located at Watertown, Alpine, Poplar Bluff, and Garden City. The Watertown Airport, five miles outside city limits, was the largest, providing facilities for commercial and private aircraft. The district had been successful in establishing dealerships at each of these airports. Bulk storage facilities at the Watertown Airport were under supervision of the district sales manager and required the services of four warehouse-workers.

A smaller salaried sales office was located 20 miles from Watertown, in the city of *Poplar Bluff.* This was primarily a residential center, but a recently developed light industrial tract had brought 20 new manufacturing firms to the city within the past two years. Commercial establishments, warehousing facilities, and some farming rounded out the activities of the area. Several large accounts were important in maintaining the gallonage position at this station. The light industrial plants, in general, were not large users of petroleum products.

The city of *Alpine,* served by a commission agent, was involved in an overnight transition from an agricultural-commercial economy to one centered around light industry. Electronics and precision-type manufacturing firms were predominant in the area. At the time, industrial sites covering 250 acres were being sold along the Blue River, with reports that actual sales and inquiries had already exceeded expectations. Keeping pace with industrial growth, the city's population, now at 50,000, had doubled in the past five years. Joe was visiting the Watertown office when it was learned that Mac McMurtry, a commissioned distributor for Houston's largest Alpine competitor, was going to retire in several months. McMurtry had always been a leader in Alpine (mayor, city council, etc.) and was held in high esteem by many accounts in the area. A salaried plant was scheduled to replace the old operation.

Garden City and *Mansfield* were both unincorporated farming centers served by commission agents. The total number of agricultural accounts had been declining over the last three years due to the failure of the marginal operators to keep up with new farm innovations. However, those still in business were producing larger quantities through use of more and more mechanized equipment. The Garden City area showed the most promise in terms of agricultural growth, while the future of Mansfield was uncertain. Recent plans for improving Highway 7 and the low cost of land had attracted the interest of several real estate promoters to the Mansfield area. One manufacturing firm had already constructed plant facilities near Mansfield, and from all reports, its management was quite happy with the results.

An organization chart for the Watertown Sales District is shown in Exhibit 6.

Exhibit 7 shows the district's 1978 market position in terms of number of accounts and percent of gallonage for both motor gasoline and diesel sales. These fig-

Exhibit 7 **Houston Petroleum Company Market Position, 1978 (by Number of Accounts and Percent of Gallonage)**

	Motor gasoline				Diesel fuels			
	CA & I		Other		CA & I		Other	
Company	No. of accounts	Percent of gallonage	No. of accounts	Percent of gallonage	No. of accounts	Percent of gallonage	No. of accounts	Percent of gallonage
Watertown district (5,000 gal. per year and over)								
Houston.	244	38.3	8	34.1	69	30.6	2	12.3
Company A	61	14.7	2	11.7	18	15.3	1	5.5
Company B	95	25.7	—	—	20	19.8	—	—
Company C	86	11.3	6	19.0	16	5.6	—	—
Company D	6	1.1	11	25.5	5	20.1	1	54.3
Company E	10	2.4	2	2.3	1	.5	1	27.9
Other	55	6.5	2	7.4	11	8.1		
Accounts available	557		31		140		5	
Total gallonage . . .	8,918,800		1,118,400		2,776,700		107,200	
Watertown office (5,000 gal per year and over)								
Houston.	81	46.1	3	24.3	27	25.7	—	—
Company A	14	15.8	1	16.0	1	7.9	—	—
Company B	56	25.3	—	—	7	20.9	—	—
Company E	5	2.5	—	—	1	1.0	1	34.1
Company C	19	6.4	3	26.4	3	4.1	—	—
Company D	1	.9	6	22.6	3	36.4	1	65.9
Other	16	3.0	1	10.7	2	4.0	—	—
Accounts available	192		14		44		2	
Total gallonage . . .	5,009,000		409,000		1,515,000		88,000	
Poplar Bluff Office (5,000 gal. per year and over)								
Houston.	27	25.6	1	70.8	3	17.0	1	100
Company A	13	14.1	1	26.4	5	49.3	—	—
Company B	3	8.2	—	—	—	—	—	—
Company F.	4	5.4	—	—	1	19.7	—	—
Company G	3	10.8	—	—	1	9.8	—	—
Company C	23	28.5	—	—	3	4.2	—	—
Other	2	7.4	1	2.8	—	—	—	—
Accounts available	75		3		13		1	
Total gallonage . . .	1,980,000		212,000		507,000		12,000	
Alpine (1,200 gal. per year and over)								
Houston.	34	23.0	2	24.0	6	48.5		
Company A	16	13.9	—	—	3	5.3	1	100
Company B	35	38.9	—	—	13	41.3		
Company C	31	12.9	2	20.4	2	3.2		
Company D	5	2.3	5	48.5	2	1.7		
Other	18	9.0	2	92.9	—	—	—	—
Accounts available	139		11		26		1	
Total gallonage . . .	2,391,000		416,000		562,000		13,000	

Exhibit 7 *(continued)*

	Motor gasoline				Diesel fuels			
	CA & I		Other		CA & I		Other	
Company	**No. of accounts**	**Percent of gallonage**	**No. of accounts**	**Percent of gallonage**	**No. of accounts**	**Percent of gallonage**	**No. of accounts**	**Percent of gallonage**
				Mansfield (1,200 gal. per year and over)				
Houston.	49	52.8	—	—	10	62.1	—	—
Company A	5	7.5	—	—	5	12.2	—	—
Company F.	6	10.1	—	—	3	6.2	—	—
Company C	10	29.6	1	100	7	19.5	—	—
Accounts available	70		1		25			
Total gallonage . . .	199,000		4,000		98,000			
				Garden City (1,200 gal. per year and over)				
Houston.	53	76.6	2	100	23	43.3	1	100
Company A	10	8.1			4	12.8		
Company F.	11	8.3			4	6.9		
Company C	3	7.0	—		1	37.0	—	
Accounts available	81		2		32		1	
Total gallonage . . .	239,800		17,400		94,700		1,200	

Source: D-102. Excludes some company activities where minor sales involved.

ures were developed from existing customer data sheets, Form D102, which admittedly had received very little attention from the district sales manager. Comparable figures for prior years had never been developed. Some picture of district growth, however, can be gained from a composite of the $31 credit statements. Quarterly and yearly averages of accounts to which credit had been extended are shown in Exhibit 8 for the last four years.

Sales results for the district and its components are shown in Exhibit 9 for the period covering 1976–78. Dick set the district goals for 1978 at a general increase over the 1977 results. Several large losses, as noted in the exhibit, resulted from situations over which the district had no control. Expenses, as listed in Exhibit 10, showed some improvement for the year. The large decrease per gallon at the Poplar Bluff plant related to the elimination of a route salesperson following a regular workload study.

Exhibit 8 **Number of Accounts to Which Credit Has Been Extended**

	1978	1977	1976	1975
District				
1st qtr.	701	648	730	677
2d qtr.	706	651	705	685
3d qtr.	721	659	680	685
4th qtr.	713	676	689	650
Year avg.	710	659	701	674
Watertown				
1st qtr.	223	177	188	167
2d qtr.	224	172	184	183
3d qtr.	238	173	174	177
4th qtr.	234	220	184	163
Year	230	186	182	172
Poplar Bluff				
1st qtr.	91	78	88	85
2d qtr.	88	83	81	86
3d qtr.	96	93	89	85
4th qtr.	93	81	87	79
Year	92	84	86	84
Alpine				
1st qtr.	123	119	148	121
2d qtr.	131	118	142	129
3d qtr.	132	130	135	129
4th qtr.	133	121	123	129
Year	130	122	137	127
Mansfield				
1st qtr.	93	84	112	104
2d qtr.	96	95	109	104
3d qtr.	94	96	111	104
4th qtr.	86	89	108	102
Year	92	91	110	103
Garden City				
1st qtr.	171	190	194	200
2d qtr.	167	182	189	183
3d qtr.	161	167	171	190
4th qtr.	167	165	187	178
Year	166	176	185	188

Source: R 31 (compiled through averaging obtain data by quarters)

Exhibit 9 **Sales Results by Product, 1976–1978 (gallon)**

District	1978	1977	1976
Motor gasoline			
Agriculture	413,211	410,733	423,592
Construction and contractor	675,031	581,116	634,570
Commercial and industrial	2,316,641	2,187,287	1,973,751
Jobbers	30,264	137,998	25,861
Government	429,345	146,052	179,462
Total	3,864,492	3,400,186	3,237,236
Auto diesel	126,705	114,517	114,100
Truck diesel	695,846*	1,083,705	877,275
Aviation gasoline	18,699,930	18,961,370	16,483,800
Auto oils	113,000	118,899	112,000
Thinners and solvents	2,350,074	2,334,249	2,561,540
Refined wax	476,344	660,778	191,297
Total light products	26,326,937	26,673,704	23,577,248
Watertown Plant			
Motor gasoline:			
Agriculture	141,119	137,365	144,307
Construction and contractor	304,499	287,146	292,250
Commission and industrial	1,876,132	1,832,996	1,559,580
Jobbers	11,014†	125,105†	12,500
Government	209,300	100,105	50,674
Total	2,543,084	2,482,627	2,059,143
Auto diesel	76,443	78,388	82,647
Truck diesel	346,360	454,469	406,284
Auto oils	52,543	54,997	50,674
Thinners and solvents	2,046,644	2,149,941	2,180,938
Refined wax	367,334	264,037	287,653
Total light products	5,314,195	5,386,709	5,071,204
Poplar Bluff Plant			
Motor gasoline:			
Agriculture	8,934	12,699	8,710
Construction and contractor	136,126	94,674	96,852
Commission and industrial	173,003	168,020	164,412
Government	115,884	34,169	36,358
Total	433,547	309,562	306,332
Truck diesel	77,975‡	182,892	92,783
Aviation gasoline	137,859	117,468	100,848
Auto oils	9,245	10,327	9,503
Thinners	48,493	62,564	81,098
Total light products	743,474	694,813	602,564

(continued)

Exhibit 9 *(continued)*

	1978	1977	1976
Alpine			
Motor gasoline:			
Agriculture	29,842	25,315	22,358
Construction and contractor	232,033	121,384	218,095
Commission and industrial	202,618	258,345	282,590
Jobbers	19,250	-0-	-0-
Total	483,743	405,044	523,043
Auto diesel	5,740	7,644	7,534
Truck diesel	191,378	351,600	269,199
Aviation gasoline	136,937	127,613	105,006
Auto oils	20,856	22,447	18,142
Thinners and solvents	253,776	145,227	230,305
Refined wax	10,010	49,737	20,013
Total light products	1,227,232	1,149,630	1,201,038
Mansfield			
Motor gasoline:			
Agriculture	82,455	77,448	87,824
Construction and contractor	311	5,432	15,131
Commission and industrial	28,507	29,228	32,977
Total	111,273	112,108	135,931
Auto diesel	14,961	16,450	10,741
Truck diesel	40,879	49,092	81,668
Auto oils	3,122	3,220	4,720
Bottled gas	58,968	61,969	64,831
Total light products	203,082	211,544	270,628
Garden City			
Motor gasoline:			
Agriculture	150,861	142,304	148,142
Construction and contractor	1,062	-0-	-0-
Commission and industrial	33,650	37,673	44,042
Government	13,800	2,400	2,111
Total	199,373	182,277	194,285
Auto diesel	21,766	3,871	3,377
Truck diesel	39,245	45,644	51,080
Aviation gasoline	28,640	25,844	25,413
Auto oils	4,043	4,274	4,067
Refined wax	99,000	61,600	64,000
Total light products	472,064	447,046	390,532
Watertown Airport			
Aviation gasoline	18,396,500	18,690,445	16,252,433

* Lost (completed) highway contract—nonrecurring business

† Gained and lost jobber—not under district or region control

‡ Loss of large account—moved to other district.

Source: R 30, based on 10-month period.

Exhibit 10 **Expenses per Gallon Delivered, 1977–1978***

	1977 (cents)	1978 (cents)
Total sales district:		
1st qtr	3.34	3.06
2d qtr.	3.00	2.93
3d qtr.	3.20	2.75
4th qtr	3.30	2.94
Year.	3.21	2.92
Supervision solicitation:		
1st qtr	0.64	0.69
2d qtr.	0.57	0.58
3d qtr.	0.49	0.48
4th qtr	0.56	0.57
Year.	0.56	0.57
Plant cost—Watertown sales office:		
1st qtr	1.05	0.71
2d qtr.	0.50	0.75
3d qtr.	0.82	0.86
4th qtr	0.80	0.83
Year.	0.79	0.79
Marketing delivery cost—Watertown sales office:		
1st qtr	2.07	1.90
2d qtr.	1.78	1.72
3d qtr.	2.04	1.47
4th qtr	1.95	1.70
Year.	1.96	1.70
Total cost—Watertown sales office:		
1st qtr	3.12	2.61
2d qtr.	2.28	2.47
3d qtr.	2.86	2.33
4th qtr	2.75	2.53
Year.	2.75	2.49
Plant cost—Poplar Bluff sales office:		
1st qtr	0.78	0.51
2d qtr.	0.76	0.27
3d qtr.	0.72	0.42
4th qtr	0.77	0.40
Year.	0.76	0.40
Marketing delivery costs—Poplar Bluff sales office:		
1st qtr	2.12	2.24
2d qtr.	2.15	2.04
3d qtr.	2.27	1.75
4th qtr	2.17	2.01
Year.	2.18	2.00
Total cost—Poplar Bluff sales office		
1st qtr	2.90	2.75
2d qtr.	2.91	2.31
3d qtr.	2.99	2.17
4th qtr	2.94	2.41
Year.	2.94	2.40
Total cost—commission agents:		
1st qtr	1.99	1.89
2d qtr.	2.35	2.02
3d qtr.	2.35	1.89
4th qtr	2.36	1.91
Year.	2.26	1.93

*Excludes airport gallonage

Source: R-35

Credit collections for the district ran below company objectives of 75 percent current. Figures (dollars and accounts current) for September 1977 and September 1978 are indicative of the yearly results:

	September 1977		September 1978	
	Dollars	Accounts current	Dollars	Accounts current
District	$71	62	66	63
Watertown	77	68	71	70
Poplar Bluff	78	63	68	60
Alpine	75	54	63	60
Mansfield	52	48	53	50
Garden City	54	61	71	59

Source: CD-35

Commission agent operations are outlined in Exhibit 11, which shows the number of employees, major expense items, gross commissions, total expenses, net commissions, commission rates, and equipment. Several monthly statements (Exhibit 12) are included for the operation at Mansfield. Realizing that such earnings would not support the distributorship, John Russo was paid, as a common carrier, for picking up and transporting the product needs for both his own and the Garden City operation. As part of the trucking business, Russo often hauled farm products for other members of the community. Such trips might cover a distance of 200 miles, with fertilizers often making up the load for the return haul. Russo's 22-year-old son tended the CA operations during these absences.

Dick Owen, the retiring district sales manager, had, during his tenure, advanced with the organizational changes of the company. His duties over the past 29 years had changed from agency manager to resident manager and finally district sales manager. He was alert, enthusiastic, and a good personal salesman. As a result of his long association in Watertown, he knew most of the accounts in the immediate area and often supplemented the solicitation efforts of other district employees. To make sure operations continued smoothly, Dick was quite active in checking on clerical details, handling many himself. He insisted on opening all the company mail as a precaution against missing any important correspondence.

The following people were relied upon to carry out district operations:

White-Collar Personnel

Bill White—Assistant District Sales Manager. Age 36, had been with the company 11 years and in his present position 3 years. Held a B.S. degree in engineering and started with Houston as a route salesperson. His ability was obvious,

Exhibit 11 Commission Agent Operations

	Alpine 1976		Alpine 1977		Alpine 1978	
Gross commissions		$24,240		$23,395		$25,193
Expenses						
Salaries	$7,621		$7,986		$8,274	
Gas and oil	1,225		1,091		1,294	
Tires and batteries	195		178		329	
Repairs	923		711		383	
Rental	—		—		—	
Deposits	2,136		637		323	
License and tax	191		145		195	
Insurance	723		769		774	
Business license	56		130		126	
Workman's compensation	103		190		138	
Unemployment compensation tax	—		—		—	
F O A B	201		147		173	
Utilities	137		111		137	
Postage	268		301		307	
Telephone and teletype	572		390		409	
Tool and supply	243		164		228	
Dues and donations	212		231		194	
Advertising	196		—		—	
Dep. P & T	—		—		—	
Storage deductions	—		—		—	
W/D Allowance	739		13		—	
Special allowance	—		—		—	
Entertainment	381		548		680	
Other	64		161		110	
Total expenses		$16,186		$13,903		$14,074
Net commissions		$ 8,054		$ 9,492		$11,119

Commission rates	Cents	Equipment	Full-time employees
Airport and airline	1.10	1972 Dodge—710 gal	1 at $500 per month
All other resale	1.10	1971 Ford—12 bbl.	
Government	.80	1976 Dodge—Pickup	
Other consumer—gasoline and kerosene	1.70		
Diesel/furnace and auto	1.35 + 0.2 = 1.55 cents gas oil		
Stove oil	1.45 + 0.2 = 1.65		

(continued)

Exhibit 11 *(continued)*

	Garden City 1976		1977		1978	
Gross commissions		$15,457		$14,464		$18,222
Expenses						
Salaries	$3,900		$3,900		$5,608	
Gas and oil	650		574		721	
Tires and batteries	394		465		356	
Repairs	1,009		720		550	
Rental	—		—		—	
Deposits	1,320		1,320		1,416	
License and tax	217		175		342	
Insurance	712		1,011		759	
Business license	—		—		—	
Workman's compensation	—		—		—	
Unemployment compensation tax	—		—		—	
F.O.A.B	—		—		—	
Utiltites	144		144		145	
Postage	122		121		144	
Telephone and teletype	562		561		516	
Tool and supply	—		—		—	
Dues and donations	300		275		300	
Advertising	—		—		—	
Dep. P & T	—		—		12	
Storage deductions	87		115		54	
W/D Allowance	—		—		—	
Special allowance	—		—		47	
Entertainment	—		—		—	
Other	—		—		—	
Total expenses		$ 9,417		$ 9,381		$10,970
Net commissions		$ 6,040		$ 5,083		$ 7,252

Commission rates	Cents	Equipment	Full-time employees
Airport and airline*	1.60	1977 Chev—970 gal	1 at $457 per month
Government—all bulk products	1.60	1966 Chev—930 gal.	
All other resale*	1.60	1969 Ford—Pickup	
Other consumer—gasoline and kerosene*	2.10		
Diesel/furnace and auto*	1.95		
Stove oil*	2.05		

Exhibit 11 *(continued)*

	Mansfield					
	1976		1977		1978	
Gross commissions		$7,971		$6,812		$6,986
Expenses						
Salaries	$1,597		$1,812		$1,956	
Gas and oil	690		724		678	
Tires and batteries	506		161		408	
Repairs	1,830		280		270	
Rental	—		—		—	
Deposits	564		564		654	
Licenses and tax	132		150		138	
Insurance	337		458		162	
Business license	10		—		—	
Workman's compensation	—		—		—	
Unemployment compensation tax	—		—		—	
F.O.A.B	—		—		—	
Utilities	54		54		52	
Postage	50		38		43	
Telephone and teletype	110		100		131	
Tool and supply	73		53		29	
Dues and donations	47		42		36	
Advertising	27		—		—	
Dep. P & T	—		—		—	
Storage deductions	22		12		19	
W/D Allowance	—		—		—	
Special allowance	—		—		—	
Entertainment	343		327		387	
Other	114		178		9	
Total expenses		$6,514		$4,961		$4,972
New commissions		$1,457		$1,851		$2,014

Commission rates*	Cents	Equipment	Full-time employees†
All other resale	1.40	1969 Chev.—760 gal.	1 at $163 per month
Consumer—all gasoline and kerosene	2.10	1968 Ford—Stake	
		1972 De Soto—Sedan	
Diesel/furnace and auto	1.95		
Stove oil	2.05		

* Plus 50 cents TSC (temporary supplemental commission)

† Work load shows that TSCs not warranted

‡ Paid to Pete Russo, John's son

Exhibit 12 **Monthly Statement for Mansfield, 1978**

	June	July	August	September
Gross commissions	$607.35	$591.49	$608.06	$533.65
Expenses:	163.13	163.13	163.13	163.13
Wages				
General:	57.03	45.47	75.71	61.76
Gas and oil				
Tire and battery	53.48	156.06	—	—
Repairs	11.53	7.94	52.95	34.06
Depreciation	57.00	57.00	57.00	57.00
Licenses	2.40	2.36	2.61	2.22
Insurance	15.64	15.64	15.64	15.64
Utilities	13.85	24.98	18.82	25.27
Miscellaneous	7.89	—	—	—
Club dues	2.50	2.50	2.50	2.50
Advertising and entertainment	22.20	19.90	32.70	20.95
	$243.52	$331.85	$257.93	$291.40
Total expenses	$406.65	$494.98	$421.06	$382.53
Total net commissions	$200.70	$ 96.51	$187.00	$151.12

as he moved rapidly through the positions of head route salesperson, fuel and lubricant engineer, and regional specialist. As assistant district sales manager, he handled a number of accounts, which greatly relieved the load on the wholesale salesperson. He also took the responsibility for planning the activities of the fuel and lubricant engineer. Joe had formed the impression that Bill was not being used to his full capabilities and was not functioning within the proposed scope of the ADSM position.

Bob Walters—Fuel and Lubricant Engineer. Age 62, had been with the company 35 years and in his present position 16 years. A graduate engineer, he had held a previous position as a home office specialist. He was very conscientious but needed to be told exactly what to do, where to be at a given time. The ADSM had set up certain days when the engineer was to be at stations in the district. He reported to the district office twice a week for instructions.

Al Horton—Wholesale Salesman. Age 60, with the company 35 years and in his present position 12 years. A high school graduate, previously a bottled gas salesman, he was considered to be a good salesperson and was energetic and enthusiastic. While not particularly effective in organizing his own time, once told to do something, he required little follow-up. He reported each day to the district office, left (about 9.30 A.M.) to make his calls, returned in the afternoon to set up appointments on the telephone, and then left again about 3.00 P.M. Al seemed to be left pretty much on his own in terms of planning his sales approach and setting up his calls for the day. Very little of his time was actually spent in the area north of the Blue River. Occasionally, when a problem was heard of through one of the commission agents, Dick would instruct him to take a run out and see what was taking place. According to both Dick and Al, the nature of these accounts did not warrant a more intensive solicitation effort.

Operating Personnel—Watertown Sales Office

Mike Bates—Office Salesperson. Age 32, with the company 10 years and in present assignment for the last 4 years. Had completed two years of college and seemed to possess the necessary qualifications for the job, although it was noted that he was not particularly exacting in his work. There was evidence that he needed training in the clerical aspects of his job, but this seemed to stem from the fact that he had not been delegated the full responsibility called for in this position. Normally Mike should have been the spokesperson for the rest of the operating personnel, but very seldom was he included in problem-solving or planning conferences held by Dick Owen.

Phil Brown—Assistant Office Salesperson. 59 years old, had been with the company 35 years and in his present assignment for the past six months. Previous positions included time as a field salesperson and head field salesperson. There were indications that he didn't work well under pressure and lacked knowledge of many company policies.

Ike Poole—Route Salesperson. 57 years old and had been with the company for 30 years in his present position. Performed his work well.

Bill Adams—Route Salesperson. 59 years old and had been with the company for 40 years as a field salesperson. Performed work well and required a minimum of supervision.

Nick Peters—Route Salesperson. Age 45, with the company as a field salesperson for 20 years. An energetic and enthusiastic worker with real concern for company welfare. Well acquainted with company policy and required little supervision.

Jim Black—Route Salesperson. Age 38, had been a field salesperson for 11 years. Had potential for position of head field salesperson or head office salesperson. Followed directions well.

It was noted that the work done by the above men consisted principally of delivering to accounts, taking orders, truck maintenance, etc. However, in terms of solicitation of new and existing small accounts, all needed development of sales desire and techniques. Few tangible results were being recognized from their efforts to gain new accounts or increase sales from present customers.

Personnel—Poplar Bluff Sales Office

Jack Jacobs—Head Route Salesperson. Age 58, had been with the company 38 years. Very energetic and conscientious. Required a minimum of supervision but did require occasional counseling from the district management. Noted as a good salesperson.

Tom Green—Route Salesperson. 58 years old and with the company 35 of these. Had no formal sales training, but was very alert to duties involving filling orders, maintenance, etc.

Commission Agents

Steve Young—Alpine. 50 years old with eight years as agent. Was at one time a bottled gas salesperson for the company. Steve was sized up as a rather retiring individual and, while effective in selling agricultural accounts, he was not particularly suited to the growing industrial trend of his area. It was felt that he was making little effort to keep the district office posted on potential business that entered the area.

John Russo—Mansfield. Age 59, had been an agent for 15 years. Previously worked 15 years for the company. In addition to the low area potential, his operation was somewhat sloppily run. John did not seem to be particularly concerned with company welfare. Much of the area was of the same nationality and was extremely clannish. Consequently, there was danger that business could well follow the distributor rather than the company, should he become alienated. The present CA agreement was soon due to expire, and regional reports that always preceded renewal of such contracts showed considerable weakness, particularly in the areas of plant maintenance and credit collections.

Alex Harris—Garden City. 58 years old, with 16 years as agent. Was head field salesperson at the same station before it was converted to an agency. Similar to John Russo, he had greatly tied up the area business in an extremely clannish community. Although he needed considerable supervision, the operation had always been independently profitable. Alex had always been very cooperative and receptive to suggestions.

As implied earlier, supervision of district functions was closely held by Dick Owens. Having grown with most of the local accounts, he seemed to feel that he owed personal attention to them. During one of the visits, Dick said to Joe, "I know everything that happens in this district. If I walk into the front office of any of our accounts here in Watertown, they know who I am. Knowing as much as I do about the accounts saves a lot of time in working with my sales personnel. Unless a special problem arises, it's very seldom that we have to sit down and plan an approach to a particular customer."

"One thing I've really limited," continued Dick, "is the use of sales meetings for district personnel. If you ask me, they are a pure waste of time; most people form a negative attitude when they are asked to attend these meetings. I see all of my white-collar people every day, and, believe me, the grapevine takes care of passing on information of interest to the operating personnel."

Apparently Dick was satisfied with the job being done by his sales force, as he spent relatively little time with them observing sales techniques. "If I play nursemaid to these people," he said, "they would never learn to go out on their own. Hell, I'll know anyway when one of them goofs up."

District sales coverage logically broke down into geographical areas, with the wholesale salesperson and fuel and lubricant engineer providing white-collar support to the entire district. Alpine, Poplar Bluff, Garden City, and Mansfield, with their

Exhibit 13 **Route Salesperson Performance, 1977–1978**

Route salesman	Miles run		Light products delivered (gallon)		Number of deliveries		Average gal./del.	
	1977	1978	1977	1978	1977	1978	1977	1978
Jim Black—T2—Capacity 850								
1st quarter	3,146	2,547	78,697	99,554	217	318	312	313
2d quarter	3,473	5,044	89,256	124,525	258	440	344	287
3d quarter	2,899	3,404	58,282	119,132	167	330	304	358
4th quarter	3,133	3,191	62,878	118,005	209	410	292	282
Year	12,651	14,186	289,113	461,216	851	1,498	313	310
Bill Adams—T2—Capacity 977								
1st quarter	2,719	1,963	114,693	141,621	406	431	281	328
2d quarter	2,664	2,113	127,813	157,392	457	484	280	325
3d quarter	2,687	2,182	127,633	176,900	451	629	283	283
4th quarter	2,369	2,023	120,889	177,000	452	590	252	300
Year	10,439	8,281	491,028	652,913	1,766	2,134	274	309
Ike Poole—T2—Capacity 814								
1st quarter	3,225	3,293	168,433	128,564	487	435	342	296
2d quarter	2,813	3,585	162,500	157,624	503	509	329	310
3d quarter	3,317	3,490	156,824	178,958	487	522	322	348
4th quarter	3,050	3,030	133,122	134,368	383	442	366	299
Year	12,405	13,398	620,879	599,514	1,860	1,908	340	313
Nick Peters—T3—Capacity 1,130								
1st quarter	2,360	3,457	157,020	126,627	449	408	351	288
2d quarter	1,970	3,938	166,070	158,651	435	430	375	369
3d quarter	2,178	3,688	162,693	170,154	452	520	339	329
4th quarter	3,033	4,462	152,109	157,885	474	468	299	358
Year	9,541	15,545	637,892	613,317	1,810	1,826	341	336
Composite	45,036	51,410	2,038,912	2,326,960	6,287	7,366	317	317

Source: D-123

relatively limited number of accounts, posed no real problem of area breakdown. Within the Watertown area, the responsibility of the four route salespersons were originally organized by geographical boundries. However, local revisions over a period of time had finally resulted in each route salesperson serving a certain list of accounts. This occurred as account status changed and Dick found it necessary to add or subtract gallonage as a means of maintaining an equal work load for each salesperson. Finally, Jim Black was pulled off regular business and given the responsibility to service contractor accounts only. The net results of the shifting had been a composite of accounts for each salesperson which no longer followed the original geographical breakdown. A two-year record by route salespeople of miles run, gallons delivered, number of deliveries, and average gallons delivered is offered in Exhibit 13.

PART FOUR

DEVELOPING THE SALESFORCE

THE two chapters in Part Four concentrate on the development of a productive salesforce. In Chapter 9, the process of staffing the salesforce through recruitment and selection is reviewed. Standard recruitment and selection tools such as advertising, job interviews, and tests are discussed. Legal and ethical issues are also raised, and the topic of salesforce socialization is introduced.

Chapter 10 focuses on the continual development of salespeople through sales training. A model of the sales training process provides a framework for discussing needs assessment, training objectives, alternatives for training, and the design, performance, and evaluation of sales training.

CHAPTER 9

STAFFING THE SALESFORCE: RECRUITMENT AND SELECTION

Learning Objectives

After completing this chapter, you should be able to

1. Explain the critical role of recruitment and selection in building and maintaining a productive salesforce.
2. Identify the key activities in planning and executing a program for salesforce recruitment and selection.
3. Discuss the legal considerations in salesforce recruitment and selection.
4. Discuss the ethical concerns of salesforce recruitment and selection.
5. Name some additional special issues to be aware of in salesforce recruitment and selection.
6. Describe how recruitment and selection affects salesforce socialization and performance.

RECRUITMENT AND SELECTION: WILKINSON SWORD USA CREATES ITS OWN SALESFORCE

In November 1984 Wilkinson Sword USA consisted of two people: Norman Prolux, president, and Ronald Mineo, vice-president of sales. In less than two years, the U.S. arm of London-based Wilkinson Sword Ltd. had grown to approximately 100 employees, including 34 salespeople. For thirty years prior to establishing its own salesforce, the company had relied on manufacturers' representatives or the salesforces of other companies to sell its line of razors and blades.

The reason for hiring its own salespeople was explained by Mineo as being a need for better control of the salesforce. With independent salespeople, Mineo pointed out, "Wilkinson could not get the kind of focus our product lines require to compete efficiently. All our competitors are out there with their own salesforces." When the decision had been made to establish a direct salesforce, company president Prolux added, "No longer will our products be sixteenth in line in the manufacturers' rep's bag."

Before the first new salesperson was hired, marketing and sales strategy was developed. This was followed by an analysis of existing and potential Wilkinson accounts. The account analysis identified 25 key accounts to be assigned to two key account managers working out of the Atlanta headquarters. Another 400 primary and secondary accounts would be divided among field salespeople and sales managers.

According to Mineo, organizing the salesforce was easy compared to finding the right people to fill the sales positions. The New York area was especially hard to staff, because Wilkinson was looking for two truly exceptional salespeople who could be trusted with its multimillion-dollar territories in the area.

The recruitment and selection process was further complicated by the fact that Wilkinson executives were trying to function as salespeople to maintain the business until permanent salespeople could be hired. Furthermore, Wilkinson was seeking people with five years of experience in the better health and beauty aids

---

Source: Rayna Skolink, "The Birth Of A Sales Force," *Sales and Marketing Management*, March 10, 1986, 42–44.

companies. Their new hires included salespeople with experience at Procter & Gamble, Colgate, and Gillette.

Hiring experienced salespeople can be a costly proposition. Mineo estimates that the 24 salespeople hired during the first year cost the company a half-million dollars in recruitment, training, salaries, bonuses, and related costs. He pointed out that in some cases Wilkinson had paid as much as $15,000 to an employment agency to hire one person.

To be sure it was offering competitive salaries, Wilkinson polled other firms in the field. Its strategy was to offer a package at least as good as the competition and, in some cases, as much as 10 percent better.

It took nine months to hire the first 24 salespeople. In January 1985 Wilkinson began interviewing candidates. The first seven were hired by early February, and by the beginning of April, eight more had been hired. By May 1, 18 of the 24 were on board, and the final six were in place by mid-September. Plans were then approved to hire the last ten salespeople to complete the initial salesforce.

The new Wilkinson salesforce seemed to work out quite well from the beginning, and the future looked bright heading into 1986. The company began hiring retail merchandisers to support sales efforts by reducing out-of-stocks, building incremental facings and displays, and monitoring pricing. Mid-Atlantic area manager Mark Cavalier reflected the optimism at Wilkinson by saying: "We've opened the doors. In 1986, we need to kick the doors down."

As the Wilkinson Sword USA example implies, recruitment and selection is a critical sales management function. It is costly, too; and it is hard to predict the future return on investment for a newly hired salesperson. While other factors also influence sales performance, sales managers cannot survive without doing a competent job in recruiting and selecting salespeople. The vital and complex nature of the job is summarized by Munson and Spivey:

> The process is complicated by various conflicting factors — the need to select applicants with characteristics related to job success, the difficulty of determining these characteristics, inadequacies inherent in the various selection techniques themselves, and the need to simultaneously insure that the selection process satisfies existing governmental regulations pertaining to discrimination in hiring practices.[1]

In the 1990s the recruitment and selection process will have to be adjusted to new demographics of an older salesforce with a higher proportion of women than in the past.[2] Sales managers are expected to face considerable pressure to raise compensation levels for new recruits, retain older salespeople for longer periods, or depend more on raiding their competition for the salespeople they will need to staff their organizations.[3]

Today's sales manager's role in recruitment and selection will be explored in this chapter. Before examining a basic model of the process, the importance of recruitment and selection will be further discussed.

IMPORTANCE OF RECRUITMENT AND SELECTION

In most sales organizations, sales managers with direct supervisory responsibilities for salespeople have the ultimate responsibility for recruitment and selection. They may have the support of top management, or perhaps they coordinate their efforts with human resource personnel or other managers within the firm. But it is the sales manager who generally retains primary recruitment and selection responsibilities. To emphasize the importance of recruitment and selection, consider only a few of the potential problems associated with its inadequate implementation:

1. Inadequate sales coverage and lack of customer follow-up
2. Increased training costs to overcome deficiencies
3. More supervisory problems
4. Higher turnover rates
5. Difficulty in establishing enduring relationships with customers
6. Total salesforce performance is sub-optimal.

Clearly, salesforce performance will suffer if recruitment and selection are poorly executed. Other sales management functions become more burdensome when the sales manager is handicapped by a multitude of "bad hires." The full costs of unsuccessful recruitment and selection are probably impossible to estimate. In addition to sales trainee salaries and employment agency fees, there are hidden costs associated with salesforce turnover and increased managerial problems that defy calculation. To get some perspective on the potential costs that might result from a single hiring mistake, recall from a previous chapter that it costs from $10,000 to $50,000 to hire, train, and supervise a salesperson until he or she has reached productive status. For a bad hire, such an investment represents sunk costs that may be nonrecoverable. And in view of studies that tell us that a significant number of salespeople should not be in sales for one reason or another,[4] it is apparent that recruitment and selection are among the most challenging and important responsibilities of sales management.

A MODEL OF RECRUITMENT AND SELECTION

Figure 9.1 illustrates the steps in the recruitment and selection process. The first step involves **planning activities**: conducting a job analysis, establishing job qualifications, completing a written job description, setting recruitment and selection objectives, and developing a recruitment and selection strategy. These planning activities are con-

Figure 9.1 **Recruiting and Selecting Salespeople**

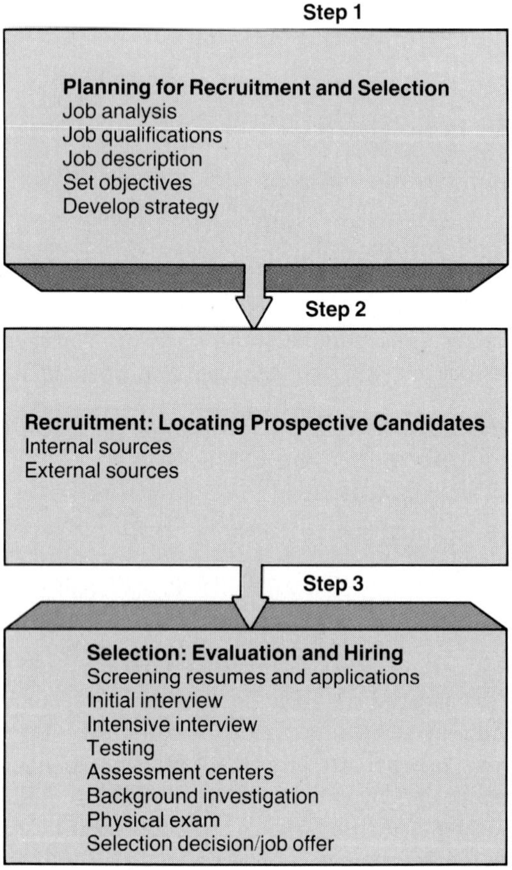

Three main steps are involved in recruiting and selecting salespeople: planning activities are followed by recruiting activities, which are followed by selection activities.

ducted within the overall planning framework of the organization to ensure consistency with the objectives, strategies, resources, and constraints of the organization.

The second step is **recruitment**, which, simply put, is the procedure of locating a sufficient number of prospective job applicants. A number of internal (within the company) and external (outside the company) sources may be utilized to develop this pool of candidates.

The next step in the model is **selection**, the process of choosing which candidates will be offered the job. A variety of screening and evaluation methods are used in this step, including evaluation of resumes and job-application forms, interviews, tests, assessment centers, background investigations, and physical exams. A more detailed discussion of each step in the recruitment and selection process now follows.

Planning for Recruitment and Selection

Given the critical nature of recruitment and selection, it would be difficult to overstate the case for careful planning as part of the process. Sales managers are concerned with the current staffing needs of their organizations; but perhaps more importantly, they are also concerned with future staffing needs, which is what makes planning so essential.

Proper planning provides more time for locating the best recruits. Upper management can be alerted in advance to probable future needs, rather than having to be convinced quickly when the need becomes imminent. Also, training can be planned more effectively when the flow of new trainees into the organization is known. Overall, the main benefit of adequate planning for the recruitment and selection process is that it helps prevent the kind of poor decisions that often prove so expensive in psychic and monetary terms. The key tasks in planning for recruitment and selection will now be reviewed.

Job Analysis. To effectively recruit and select salespeople, sales managers must have a complete understanding of the job for which candidates are sought. Since most sales managers have served as salespeople in their companies prior to entering management, it is reasonable to think that they would have a good understanding of the sales jobs for which they recruit. Some, however, have lost touch with changing conditions in the field and thus have an obsolete view of the current sales task to be accomplished.

To assure an understanding of the sales job, the sales manager may need to conduct, confirm, or update a **job analysis**, which entails an investigation of the tasks, duties, and responsibilities of the job. For example, will the selling tasks include responsibilities for opening new accounts as well as maintaining existing accounts? Will the salesperson be responsible for collecting accounts receivable or completing administrative reports? The job analysis defines the expected behavior of salespeople, indicating which areas of performance will be crucial for success. In most larger companies, the job analysis is completed by human resource managers or other corporate managers, but even then, the sales manager may have input into the job analysis.

Job Qualifications. The job analysis indicates what the salespeople are supposed to do on the job, while **job qualifications** refer to the aptitude, skills, knowledge, personal traits, and willingness to accept occupational conditions necessary to perform the job. For example, is there a need for computer salespeople to possess technical aptitude? The answer could be yes or no, depending on a particular company's approach to personal selling.[5] A few years ago, Apple Computer decided to diminish the importance of computer expertise as a job qualification in favor of knowledge of retail selling practices.[6]

Common sales job qualifications address sales experience, educational level, willingness to travel, willingness to relocate, and ability to work independently. Consistent with our earlier discussion of the diversity of personal selling jobs, there is a corresponding variance in job qualifications for different sales jobs. For this reason, each sales manager should record the pertinent job qualifications for each job in the salesforce. A generic list of job qualifications for all the salespeople in the organization may not be feasible.

Job Description. Based on the job analysis and job qualifications, a written summary of the job, the **job description**, is completed by the sales manager, or in many cases, human resource manager. Job descriptions for salespeople could contain any or all of the following elements:

1. Job title (for example, sales trainee, senior sales representative)
2. Duties, tasks, and responsibilities of the salesperson
3. Administrative relationships indicating to whom the salesperson reports
4. Types of products to be sold
5. Customer types
6. Significant job-related demands such as mental stress, physical strength or stamina requirements, or environmental pressures to be encountered.

Job descriptions are an essential document in sales management. Their use in recruitment and selection is only one of their multiple functions. They are used to clarify duties and thereby reduce role ambiguity in the salesforce, to familiarize potential employees with the sales job, to set objectives for salespeople, and, eventually, to aid in evaluating performance. A typical job description for a sales representative is shown in Exhibit 9.1.

Recruitment and Selection Objectives. To be fully operational, recruitment and selection objectives should be specifically stated for a given time period. For example, the objective of the Wilkinson Sword program described at the outset of the chapter was to hire 34 salespeople within a year. The following general objectives of recruitment and selection could be converted to specific operational objectives in a given firm:

- Determine present and future needs in terms of numbers and types of salespeople.
- Meet the company's legal and social responsibilities regarding composition of the salesforce.
- Reduce the number of underqualified or overqualified applicants.

Exhibit 9.1 Sales Representative's Job Description (Stanley Electric Tools Division, the Stanley Works)

Position Title: Sales Representative

Reports to: Regional Manager

Function: Within the limits of corporate policies, to promote sales of specified products and to attain sales and profit objectives in assigned territory.

Responsibilities

1. Devises all necessary plans to accomplish sales objectives established for each account
2. Plans travel and other expenses to cover assigned territory and service customer needs satisfactorily and in most economical way
3. Plans sales presentations to customers and prospects
4. Promotes and solicits business by personal calls on assigned accounts and new prospects to develop maximum profitable business potential
5. Develops a thorough knowledge of the problems of his customers and prospects and provides assistance in accomplishing their solution
6. Requests sales management assistance through regional manager in planning and conducting direct customer contacts with important key accounts and target accounts
7. Follows up any reported customer complaints and requests immediate action to provide prompt equitable disposition and recommends approval for justifiable returns and allowances
8. Maintains complete customer and prospect record cards
9. Submits itineraries weekly in advance
10. Submits a weekly call report promptly on personal visits
11. Makes special reports and recommendations concerning market requirements and competitive conditions in his territory
12. Attends national meetings, conventions, and exhibitions as directed by sales management
13. Maintains a thorough and current knowledge of Stanley Electric Tool Product lines, sales policies, prices, procedures, and merchandising techniques
14. Maintains a thorough and current knowledge of competitors' product lines, prices, and methods of distribution

Relationships

1. *Customers.* Promotes and maintains good relations with customers
2. *Regional Manager.* Reports on progress toward total sales accomplishment as compared to objective and by specific account as requested and consults regularly concerning policy and future planning
3. *Other Company Personnel.* Represents the interests of customers with other company personnel by reflecting customer requirements clearly and following closely their fulfillment
4. *Corporate and Divisional Staff.* Understands the functions of the various corporate staff organizations so that their help can be solicited as determined by the regional manager
5. *Public.* Promotes and maintains good relations with the public in general and the local community

Source: Kenneth R. Davis, *Marketing Management,* 5th ed. (New York: John Wiley, 1985), 477.

- Increase the number of qualified applicants at a specified cost.
- Evaluate the effectiveness of recruiting sources and evaluation techniques.

By setting specific objectives for recruitment and selection, sales managers can channel resources into priority areas and improve organizational and salesforce effectiveness.

Recruitment and Selection Strategy. After objectives have been set, a **recruitment and selection strategy** can be developed. Formulating this strategy requires the sales manager to consider the scope and timing of recruitment and selection activities, as follows:

- When will the recruitment and selection be done?
- How will the job be portrayed?
- How much time will be allowed for the candidate to accept or reject an offer?
- What are the most likely sources for qualified applicants?
- How will efforts with intermediaries such as employment agencies and college placement centers be optimized?

Recruitment and selection are perpetual activities in some sales organizations but in others are conducted only when a vacancy occurs. Most sales organizations could benefit by ongoing recruitment to facilitate selection when the need arises. Some recruit seasonally. For example, large companies often concentrate their efforts to coincide with spring graduation dates on college campuses.

A strategic decision must be made in terms of how the job will be portrayed, particularly in advertisements. Initial descriptions of the job in the media are necessarily limited. Should earnings potential be featured, or perhaps the opportunity for advancement? Or is this job correctly portrayed as ideal for the career salesperson? Consider how the magazine advertisement in Exhibit 9.2 portrays the life insurance salesperson's job.

Another strategic decision is the length of time a candidate will be given to accept an offer. This time element is important because other recruitment and selection activities may be temporarily suspended until the decision is made. Strategy also involves identifying the sources that look most promising for recruitment. This subject will be discussed in detail in the following section.

Recruitment: Locating Prospective Candidates

As Figure 9.1 showed, the next step in recruitment and selection is to locate a pool of prospective job candidates. This step, the actual recruiting, may utilize a variety of sources. Some of the more popular ones are shown in Exhibit 9.3.

Exhibit 9.2 **Example of an Individual Company's Advertisement to Recruit Salespeople**

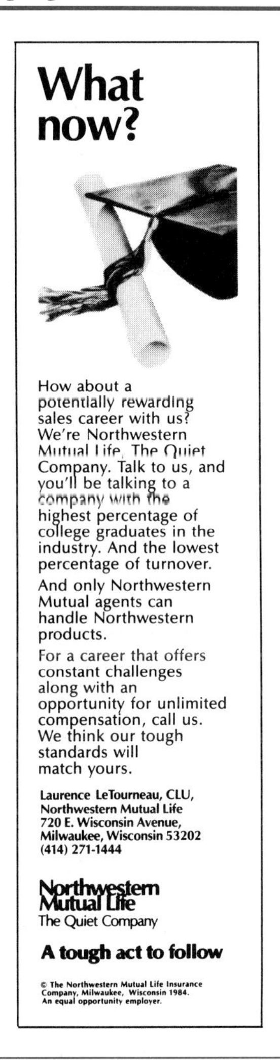

Source: Reprinted with permission from Northwestern Mutual Life Insurance Company.

Internal Sources. As indicated in Exhibit 9.3, one of the most popular methods of locating sales recruits is through **employee referral programs**. These programs are relatively quick and inexpensive compared to other recruiting methods such as newspaper advertising, utilizing employment agencies, and visiting college campuses. While the employee who furnishes the referral may be paid a "finder's fee," the cost

Exhibit 9.3 **Sources of Sales Recruits**

Source	Percentage of Firms Using Source
Employee referrals	74
Newspaper advertising	75
Private employment agencies	63
Colleges/universities	48
Advertising in special publications	43
Career conferences/job fairs	19
Professional societies	17

Source: *Personnel Policies Forum,* Survey no. 126, Recruiting Policies and Practices, (Washington, D.C.: The Bureau of National Affairs, Inc., 1979), 4–5.

is usually nominal. Existing salespeople are obviously good sources for referral programs, since they have a good understanding of the type of person sought for a sales position. Purchasing agents within the company may also be helpful in identifying prospective sales candidates.

Other internal methods include announcing sales job openings through newsletters, in meetings, or on the bulletin board. Internal transfers or promotions may result from announcing an opening on the salesforce, as was the case with IBM in recent years, when many of its employees were transferred into marketing and sales to bolster its field efforts.

External Sources. While it is a good idea to include internal sources as part of a recruitment and selection program, there may not be enough qualified people inside the organization to meet the human resource needs of the salesforce. This is when the search is expanded to the external sources listed in Exhibit 9.3.

Newspaper Advertisements. One way to produce a large pool of applicants in a short period of time is by newspaper advertising. On a cost-per-applicant basis, newspaper advertising is generally inexpensive. A large number of the applicants, however, may not be qualified for the job, even when the ads carefully dictate job qualifications. As a result, newspaper advertising usually requires extensive screening procedures to identify a reasonable number of prospective candidates. Exhibit 9.4 offers sound advice on how to use the newspaper to recruit salespeople.

Private Employment Agencies. A frequently used source is the **private employment agency**. The fee charged by the agency may be paid by the employer or the job-seeker, as established contractually before the agency commences work on behalf of either party. Fees vary, but typically amount to 15 to 20 percent of the first-year earnings of the person hired through the agency. The higher the caliber of salesperson being sought, the greater the probability the employer will pay the fee.

Exhibit 9.4 Writing Help-Wanted Ads for Salespeople

THE SALES RECRUITING ads you run depend on the job, speed needed to fill it, availability of this applicant, and competition. If you want specific experience in your industry, business publications are effective. However, need for speed may rule this avenue out. For faster results, advertise in newspapers. Sundays are effective for classified. Provide a telephone number the reader can call on Sunday, if possible. Answer inquires right away before they cool off. Display ads in the business pages are good for sales management and top selling posts. If the newspaper groups sales ads, don't start your ad with SALES. Flag them down with the experience required:

APPLIANCES

Major nationally advertised firm seeks salesperson for established territory to sell electrical appliances to department and discount stores. Experience required. Salary plus expenses plus company car plus commission. Call OX 7-3700.

If you are more interested in markets sold to than product sold, play that up in the headline:

VARIETY CHAINS

If you have sold to variety chains and have merchandising, POP, co-op advertising experience, here's opportunity to take over growing territory. Heavy travel. Company car. Draw against high commissions. Phone Mike Thomas at 800-222-3456 for appointment this week.

If you estimate earnings, do not exaggerate. Puffed-up estimates cause distrust.

If inexperienced applicants are fair game, advertise for sales trainees:

SALES TRAINEE:
WE WILL TRAIN

In sales techniques and product knowledge if you are college graduate with some technical or mechanical background. Nationally known manufacturer of valves and fittings sold to original equipment manufacturers offers $18,000 starting salary plus expenses and bonus. Send resume to Sales Manager, Acme Valve Co., 111 Second Street, Mineola, N.Y. 11501.

This ad shows you want someone interested in learning sales. Copy shows established, well-known firm, starting salary, bonus opportunity. Restrictor—college grad with technical or mechanical background—prevents you from being flooded with unqualified trainees.

Here's how to attract trainees from another field:

ACCOUNTANTS

Tired of working with figures? If you have accounting background or education and prefer dealing with people rather than ledgers, we will train you to sell business forms and systems.

Our training program includes a step-by-step approach to mastering selling of our products which will lead to high earnings on a commission basis. Salary $1000 per month during training period. Phone Rod Mathews at 212-789-0987.

Using a box number allows you to screen unwanted applicants. They won't be able to bother you with phone calls or surprise visits. Disadvantage: many employed people won't answer box number ads.

Source: Arthur Pell, *Marketing Times* 30 (May–June 1983): 27.

Many agencies, such as Salesworld and Sales Consultants, specialize in the placement of salespeople and have offices across the country. Such agencies can be extremely useful in national searches, particularly if the sales manager is seeking high-quality, experienced salespeople. This is true because high-performing salespeople are usually employed but may contact an agency just to see if a better opportunity arises.

Employment agencies usually work from a job description furnished by the sales manager and can be instructed to screen candidates based on specific job qualifications. The professionalism of private employment agencies varies widely, but there are a sufficient number of good ones that a sales manager should not tolerate an agency that cannot refer qualified candidates. The concern for professionalism and ethical conduct is featured in the magazine ad shown in Exhibit 9.5. Notice that the agency in this case requires that all fees be paid by the employer.

Colleges and Universities. A popular source for sales recruits, especially for large companies with extensive training programs, are the colleges and universities. College students usually can be hired at lower salaries than experienced salespeople, yet they have already demonstrated their learning abilities. Companies seeking future managers often look here for sales recruits.

Campus placement centers can be helpful in providing resumes of applicants, arranging interviews, and providing facilities for screening interviews. Most placement centers also provide access to alumni in addition to the current student body. In some instances, contacts with faculty members may provide sales recruits. Another campus recruiting method is to offer sales internships, which allow both the company and the student an opportunity to see if a match exists. The internship as a recruiting vehicle is gaining in popularity as major companies such as Procter and Gamble, McGraw-Hill, and Automatic Data Processing are joined by hundreds of other large and small firms in sales internship programs.[7] College campuses are also frequent sites for career conferences in which multiple companies participate in trade show fashion to familiarize students with sales job opportunities.

On the international scene, college campuses are gaining in popularity as a source of sales recruits. College students in foreign countries are beginning to see U.S.-based firms as viable alternatives to home-country firms. The recruiting experience of Digital Equipment Corporation in Japan is recounted in "International Sales: Recruiting Salespeople in Japan."

Advertising in Special Publications. Advertisements in trade publications can attract those already in a specified field. In the case of trade magazines, lead time to have an advertisement included in the next issue is longer than with newspapers — typically six to eight weeks. Other specialty publications are nationally distributed employment listings such as the one published by *The Wall Street Journal.*

Job Fairs. Several employers are brought together in one location for recruiting purposes by **job fairs**. Candidates visit the booths of employers they are interested in, or companies request a meeting with a candidate based on a favorable reaction to the

Exhibit 9.5 **Example of a Private Employment Agency's Advertisement to Recruit Salespeople**

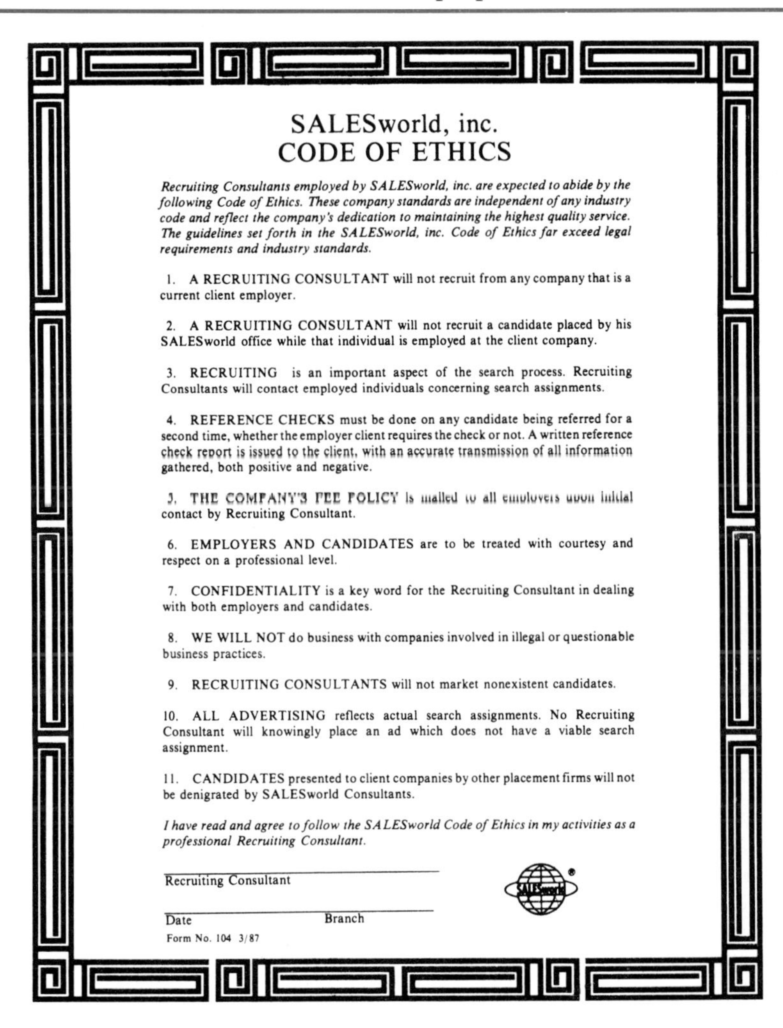

SALESworld, inc.
CODE OF ETHICS

Recruiting Consultants employed by SALESworld, inc. are expected to abide by the following Code of Ethics. These company standards are independent of any industry code and reflect the company's dedication to maintaining the highest quality service. The guidelines set forth in the SALESworld, inc. Code of Ethics far exceed legal requirements and industry standards.

1. A RECRUITING CONSULTANT will not recruit from any company that is a current client employer.

2. A RECRUITING CONSULTANT will not recruit a candidate placed by his SALESworld office while that individual is employed at the client company.

3. RECRUITING is an important aspect of the search process. Recruiting Consultants will contact employed individuals concerning search assignments.

4. REFERENCE CHECKS must be done on any candidate being referred for a second time, whether the employer client requires the check or not. A written reference check report is issued to the client, with an accurate transmission of all information gathered, both positive and negative.

5. THE COMPANY'S FEE POLICY is mailed to all employers upon initial contact by Recruiting Consultant.

6. EMPLOYERS AND CANDIDATES are to be treated with courtesy and respect on a professional level.

7. CONFIDENTIALITY is a key word for the Recruiting Consultant in dealing with both employers and candidates.

8. WE WILL NOT do business with companies involved in illegal or questionable business practices.

9. RECRUITING CONSULTANTS will not market nonexistent candidates.

10. ALL ADVERTISING reflects actual search assignments. No Recruiting Consultant will knowingly place an ad which does not have a viable search assignment.

11. CANDIDATES presented to client companies by other placement firms will not be denigrated by SALESworld Consultants.

I have read and agree to follow the SALESworld Code of Ethics in my activities as a professional Recruiting Consultant.

Recruiting Consultant

Date Branch

Form No. 104 3/87

Source: Courtesy of SALESworld, Inc.

candidate's resume. One organizer of job fairs, Career Concepts, usually arranges them for about 15 to 25 companies and hundreds of applicants. Career Concepts has conducted job fairs in eleven cities, charging a fee of $2,500 per company, paid whether or not a salesperson is hired as a result of the fair. Job fairs are best conducted in the evening hours so that currently employed salespeople can attend.[8]

INTERNATIONAL SALES

RECRUITING SALESPEOPLE IN JAPAN

For decades, U.S. firms have thought that Japanese people could not be effectively recruited. Few U.S. firms can offer the secure, paternalistic environment or prestige that comes with working for a Japanese firm. Conditions are changing, however; and some firms, such as Digital Equipment Corporation, are successfully recruiting Japanese as professional salespeople.

Digital has made considerable headway by recruiting heavily on Japanese college campuses. It has fully staffed its subsidiaries' salesforce with highly qualified Japanese college graduates. Digital recruiters call on professors and placement personnel and also contact parents, who are quite influential in deciding where students will work. Surveys show that Digital has improved its position with college students as a preferred place to work, ranking number thirteen among all employers.

When job qualifications include sales experience, Digital works through executive-search firms, which can be described as private employment agencies specializing in higher-level jobs. The Digital experience clearly illustrates that new sources for sales recruits should be considered in developing recruitment and selection strategy.

Source: Vernon R. Alden, "Who Says You Can't Crack Japanese Markets?" *Harvard Business Review* 65 (January–February 1987): 52–56.

Professional Societies. Another worthwhile source of sales recruits are professional societies. A primary reason why sales executives join professional organizations is to establish a network of colleagues who have common interests. Organizations such as Sales and Marketing Executives International meet regularly and provide the opportunity to establish contacts with professional sales executives, who may provide the names of prospective salespeople. Some professional organizations publish newsletters or operate a placement service, which could also be used in recruiting.

Computer Rosters. Locating prospective salespeople through **computerized matchmaking** services is becoming a more important recruiting method as each day passes. Computer technology is being used by an increasing number of college placement centers and employment agencies. Independent computer recruiting services are also widely available. An example of recruiting with the help of the computer is given in "Sales Technology: Recruiting via Computer." This example also illustrates how recruiting data can be matched with subsequent salesperson performance data so that the process of recruitment and selection can be improved over time.

Selection: Evaluation and Hiring

The third step in the recruitment and selection model shown in Figure 9.1 is selection. As part of the selection process, various tools are employed to evaluate the job candidate in terms of job qualifications and provide a relative ranking compared to

SALES TECHNOLOGY

RECRUITING VIA COMPUTER

New England Mutual Life Insurance (NEL) is using computerized database techniques and psychological prediction strategies to help recruit and select salespeople. NEL is also analyzing salesperson-performance data to attempt to predict salesperson characteristics that are associated with future sales success. The recruiting task at NEL involves locating thousands of candidates in multiple locations each year. The field managers can record data on personal computers about each candidate. This information is processed, stored, and analyzed in the facilities of Tracom Corporation, a Denver consulting firm.

From the database, NEL and Tracom have developed a recruitment and selection model that identifies the characteristics of the salespeople to be hired. The model is constantly updated, and changes in the recruitment and selection process may occur with updates in the model.

The capacity to adapt to change is a strong point of the NEL/Tracom model. Indeed, it was the need to change recruitment and selection methods at NEL in the mid-1980s that led to the current version of the model. NEL management recognized that new political directions, shifting economic priorities, and evolving social expectations were dictating a need to rethink its procedure of recruitment and selection. NEL management is now convinced it has improved the ratio of successful salespeople to the total number hired.

Source: "New England Life Takes Steps to Insure Its Future," *Sales and Marketing Management*, August 12, 1985, 74–77.

other candidates. In this section, we will present commonly used evaluation tools and discuss some of the key issues in salesforce selection.

Screening Resumes and Applications. The pool of prospective salespeople generated in the recruiting phase must often be drastically reduced prior to engaging in time-consuming, expensive evaluation procedures such as personal interviews. Initially, sales recruits may be screened based on a review of a resume or an application form.

In analyzing resumes, sales managers check job qualifications (for example, education or sales experience requirements), the degree of career progress by the applicant, and the frequency of job change. Depending on the format and extensiveness of the resume, it may be possible to examine salary history and requirements, travel or relocation restrictions, and reasons for past job changes. Also, valuable clues about the recruit may be gathered from the appearance and completeness of the resume.

A job-application form can be designed to gather all pertinent information and exclude unnecessary information. There are three additional advantages of application forms as a selection tool. First, the application form can be designed to meet antidiscriminatory legal requirements, whereas resumes often contain such information. For example, if some applicants note age, sex, race, color, religion or national origin on their resumes while others do not, a legal question as to whether or not this information was used in the selection process might arise. A second advantage of application forms is that the comparison of multiple candidates is facilitated since the information on each candidate is presented in the same sequence. This is not the case with personalized resumes. Finally, job applications are usually filled out in handwriting, so the sales manager can observe the attention to detail and neatness of the candidate. In some sales jobs, these factors may be important for success.

Interviews. Interviews of assorted types are an integral part of the selection process. Since interpersonal communications and relationships are a fundamental part of sales jobs, it is only natural for sales managers to weigh interview results heavily in the selection process. One survey found that the top-ranked factor in making a selection decision is the interview — more specifically, the candidate's personality and demeanor during the interview stage.[9] Another survey reported that over 90 percent of large and small companies use interviews extensively in the salesforce selection process.[10]

While sales managers agree that interviews are important in selecting salespeople, there is less agreement on how structured the interviews should be and how they should be conducted. For example, some sales managers favor unstructured interviews, which encourage the candidates to talk freely about themselves. Others favor a more structured approach in which particular answers are sought, in a particular sequence, from each candidate.

Initial Interviews. Interviews are usually designed to get an in-depth look at the candidate. In some cases, however, they merely serve as a screening mechanism to support or replace a review of resumes or application forms. These **initial interviews** are typified by the on-campus interviews conducted by most sales recruiters. They are brief, lasting less than an hour. The recruiter clarifies questions about job qualifications and makes a preliminary judgement on whether or not a match exists between the applicant and the company.

During this phase of selection, sales managers should be careful to give the candidate an accurate picture of the job and not oversell it. Candidates who are totally "sold" on the job during the first interview only to be rejected later suffer unnecessary trauma.

Intensive Interviews. One or more **intensive interviews** may be conducted to get an in-depth look at the candidate. Often, this involves multiple sequential interviews by several executives or several managers at the company's facilities. Another variation on the theme, employed less often, is to interview several job candidates simultaneously in a group setting.

When a candidate is to be interviewed in succession by several managers, planning and coordination are required to achieve more depth and to avoid redundancy. Otherwise, each interviewer might concentrate on the more interesting dimensions of a candidate and some important areas may be neglected. An interviewing guide such as the one in Exhibit 9.6 could be utilized with multiple interviewers, each of

Exhibit 9.6: **Interview Guide**

Meeting the Candidate

At the outset, act friendly but avoid prolonged small talk—interviewing time costs money.

- Introduce yourself by using your name and title.
- Mention casually that you will make notes. (You don't mind if I make notes, do you?)
- Assure candidate that all information will be treated in confidence.

Questions:

- Ask questions in a conversational tone. Make them both concise and clear.
- Avoid loaded and/or negative questions. Ask open ended questions which will force complete answers: "Why do you say that?" (Who, what, where, when, how?)
- Don't ask direct questions that can be answered "Yes" or "No."

Analyzing:

- Attempt to determine the candidate's goals. Try to draw the candidate out, but let him/her do most of the talking. Don't sell—interview.
- Try to avoid snap judgments.

Interviewer Instructions:

You will find two columns of questions on the following pages. The left hand column contains questions to ask yourself about the candidate. The right hand column suggests questions to ask the candidate.

During the interview it is suggested that you continually ask yourself "what is this person telling me about himself or herself? What kind of person is he/she?" In other parts of the interview you can cover education, previous experience and other matters relating to specific qualifications.

Ask Yourself	Ask the Candidate
I. Attitude	
• Can compete without irritation? • Can bounce back easily? • Can balance interest of both company and self? • What is important to him/her? • Is he/she loyal? • Takes pride in doing a good job? • Is he/she cooperative team player?	1. Ever lose in competition? Feelings? 2. Ever uncertain about providing for your family? 3. How can the American way of business be improved? 4. Do you feel you've made a success of life to date? 5. Who was your best boss? Describe the person. 6. How do you handle customer complaints?
II. Motivation	
• Is settled in choice of work? • Works from necessity, or choice? • Makes day-to-day and long-range plans? • Uses some leisure for self-improvement? • Is willing to work for what he/she wants in face of opposition?	1. How does your spouse (or others) feel about a selling career? 2. When and how did you first develop an interest in selling? 3. What mortgages, debts, etc., press you now? 4. How will this job help you get what you want? 5. What obstacles are most likely to trip you up?
III. Initiative	
• Is he or she a self-starter? • Completes own tasks? • Follows through on assigned tasks? • Works in assigned manner without leaving own "trademark"? • Can work independently?	1. How (or why) did you get into (or want) sales? 2. Do you prefer to work alone or with others? 3. What do you like most, like least about selling? 4. Which supervisors let you work alone? How did you feel about this? 5. When have you felt like giving up on a task? Tell me about it.

continued

Exhibit 9.6: *(continued)*

Ask Yourself	**Ask the Candidate**
IV. Stability	
• Is he or she excitable or even-tempered? • Impatient or understanding? • Does candidate use words that show strong feelings? • Is candidate poised or impulsive; controlled or erratic? • Will he or she broaden or flatten under pressure? • Is candidate enthusiastic about job?	1. What things disturb you most? 2. How do you get along with customers (people) you dislike? 3. What buyers' actions irritate you? 4. What were your most unpleasant sales (work) experiences? 5. Most pleasant sales (work) experiences? 6. What do you most admire about your friends? 7. What things do some customers do that are irritating to other people?
V. Planning	
• Ability to plan and follow through? Or will he depend on supervisor for planning? • Ability to coordinate work of others? • Ability to think of ways of improving methods? • Ability to fit into company methods? • Will he or she see the whole job or get caught up in details?	1. What part of your work (selling) do you like best? Like least? 2. What part is the most difficult for you? 3. Give me an idea of how you spend a typical day. 4. Where do you want to be five years from today? 5. If you were Manager, how would you run your present job? 6. What are the differences between planned and unplanned work?
VI. Insight	
• Realistic in appraising self? • Desire for self-improvement? • Interested in problems of others? • Interested in reaction of others to self? • Will he or she take constructive action on weaknesses? • How does he/she take criticism?	1. Tell me about your strengths/weaknesses. 2. Are your weaknesses important enough to do something about them? Why or why not? 3. How do you feel about those weaknesses? 4. How would you size up your last employer? 5. Most useful criticism received? From whom? Tell me about it. Most useless? 6. How do you handle fault finders?
VII. Social Skills	
• Is he/she a leader or follower? • Interested in new ways of dealing with people? • Can get along best with what types of people? • Will wear well over the long term? • Can make friends easily?	1. What do you like to do in your spare time? 2. Have you ever organized a group? Tell me about it. 3. What methods are effective in dealing with people? What methods are ineffective? 4. What kind of customers (people) do you get along with best? 5. Do you prefer making new friends or keeping old ones? Why? 6. How would you go about making a friend? Developing a customer? 7. What must a person do to be liked by others?

Source: "Interviewing The Candidate," Sales Consultants International, Inc., Cleveland, Ohio.

whom would delve into one or more of the seven categories of information about the candidate.

Interviews, like any other single selection tool, may fail to adequately predict applicants' future success on the job.[11] **Interviewer bias**, or allowing personal opinions, attitudes, and beliefs to influence judgments about a candidate, can be a particularly acute problem with some interviewers. Sales managers, like other human beings, tend to have preferences in candidates' appearances and personalities — and any number of other subjective feelings that may be irrelevant for a given interview situation.

Research confirms the subjective nature of interviewing, concluding that different interviewers will rate the same applicant differently unless there is a commonly accepted stereotype of the ideal applicant.[12]

Testing. To overcome the pitfalls of subjectivity and a potential lack of critical analysis of job candidates, many firms use tests as part of the selection process. Selection tests may be designed to measure intelligence, aptitudes, personality, and other interpersonal factors.

Historically, the use of such tests has been controversial. In the late 1960s, it appeared that testing would slowly disappear from the employment scene under legal and social pressure related to the lack of validity and possible discriminatory nature of some testing procedures. Instead, selection tests have changed, and perhaps managers have learned more about how to utilize them as a legitimate part of the selection process. Therefore, they are still used today. A 1984 survey found that approximately one-quarter of the large, industrial firms in the survey used tests in selecting salespeople.[13]

Those who remain reluctant to use tests ask three interacting questions: (1) Can selection tests really predict future job performance? (2) Can tests give an accurate, job-related profile of the candidate? (3) What are the legal liabilities arising from testing? In addressing the first question, one must admit it is sometimes difficult to correlate performance on a test at a given point in time with job performance at a later date. For example, how can sales managers account for performance variations caused primarily by changes in the uncontrollable environment, as might be the case in an unpredictable economic setting?

Question 2 is really concerned with whether or not the tests measure the appropriate factors in an accurate fashion. The precise measurement of complex behavioral variables such as motivation is difficult at best, so it is likely that some tests do not really measure what they purport to measure.

Answers to Question 3 depend largely on the complete answers to questions 1 and 2. The capsule response to the third question is that unless test results can be validated as a meaningful indicator of performance, there is a strong possibility that the sales manager is in a legally precarious position.

Suggestions to improve the usefulness of tests to sales managers as selection tools follow:[14]

1. Do not attempt to construct tests for the purpose of selecting salespeople. Leave this job to the testing experts and human resource specialists.
2. If psychological tests are used, be sure the standards of the American Psychological Association have been met.
3. Utilize tests that have been based on a job analysis for the particular job in question.
4. Select a test that minimizes the applicant's ability to anticipate desired responses.
5. Use tests as part of the selection process, but do not base the hiring decision solely on test results.

Tests can be useful selection tools if these suggestions are followed. In particular, tests can identify areas worthy of further scrutiny if they are administered and interpreted before a final round of intensive interviewing.

Assessment Centers. The concept of an **assessment center** refers to a set of well-defined procedures for utilizing multiple techniques such as group discussion, business game simulations, presentations, and role-playing exercises for the purpose of employee selection or development. The participant's performance is evaluated by a group of assessors, usually members of management within the firm. Though somewhat expensive due to the high cost of managerial time to conduct the assessments, such centers are being used more often in the selection of salespeople.

An interesting report of the use of an assessment center to select salespeople comes from the life insurance industry, which is notorious for a continual need for new salespeople. Traditional selection methods used in this industry apparently leave something to be desired, as turnover rates are among the highest for salespeople. An assessment-center approach was used by one life insurance firm to select salespeople based on exercises simulating various sales skills such as prospecting, time management, and sales-presentation skills. Results of the study indicated that this program was superior to traditional methods of selecting salespeople in the insurance industry in terms of predicting which salespeople would survive and which would drop out within six months of being hired.[15]

Background Investigation. Job candidates who have favorably emerged from resume and application screening, interviewing, testing, and perhaps an assessment center may next become the subjects of **background investigations**. These may be as perfunctory as a reference check or quite comprehensive if the situation warrants it. In conducting background investigations, it is advisable to request job-related information only, and to obtain a written release from the candidate before proceeding with the investigation.

If a reference check is conducted, two points should be kept in mind. First, persons listed as references are biased in favor of the job applicant. As one sales manager puts it, "Even the losers have three good references — so I don't bother checking them." Second, persons serving as references may not be candid or may not provide the desired information. This reluctance may stem from a personal concern (i.e., will I lose a friend or be sued if I tell the truth?) or from a company policy limiting the discussion of past employees.

Despite these and other limitations, a reference check can help verify the true identity of a person and possibly confirm his or her employment history. With personal misrepresentation and resume fraud being very real possibilities, a reference check is recommended.[16]

Physical Exam. Requiring the job candidate to pass a physical exam is often a formal condition of employment. In many instances, the insurance carrier of the employing firm requires a physical exam of all incoming employees. The objective is to discover any physical problem that may inhibit job performance.

In recent years, drug and communicable-disease testing has made this phase of selection controversial. While the courts will undoubtedly have a major role in determining the legality of testing in these areas in the future, the current rules, at least in the case of drug testing of potential employees, are fairly simple. A company can test for drug use if the applicant is informed of the test prior to taking it, if the results are kept confidential, and if the need for drug testing is reasonably related to potential job functions.[17]

Selection Decision and Job Offer. After evaluating the available candidates, the sales manager may be ready to offer a job to one or more candidates. Some candidates may be "put on hold" until the top candidates have made their decisions. Another possibility is that the sales manager may decide to extend the search and begin the recruitment and selection process all over again.

In communicating with those offered jobs, it is now appropriate for the sales manager to "sell" the prospective salesperson on joining the firm. In reality, top salespeople are hard to find, and the competition for them is intense. Therefore, a sales manager should enthusiastically pursue the candidate once the offer is extended. As always, an accurate portrayal of the job is a must.

The offer of employment should be written but can be initially extended in verbal form. Any final contingencies, such as passing a physical exam, should be detailed in the offer letter. Candidates not receiving a job offer should be notified in a prompt, courteous manner. A specific reason for not hiring a candidate need not be given. A simple statement that an individual who better suits the needs of the company has been hired is sufficient.

LEGAL CONSIDERATIONS IN RECRUITMENT AND SELECTION

Key Legislation

The possibility of illegal discrimination permeates the recruitment and selection process, and a basic understanding of pertinent legislation can be beneficial to the sales manager. Some of the most important legislation is summarized in Exhibit 9.7. The legislative acts featured in Exhibit 9.7 are federal laws, applicable to all firms engaged in interstate commerce. Companies not engaging in interstate commerce are often subject to state and local laws that are quite similar to these federal laws.

Guidelines for Sales Managers

The legislation reviewed in Exhibit 9.7 is supported by various executive orders and guidelines that make it clear that a sales manager, along with other hiring officials in a firm, have legal responsibilities of grave importance in the recruitment and selection

Exhibit 9.7 **Legislation Affecting Recruitment and Selection**

Legislative Act	Purpose
Civil Rights Act (1964)	Prohibits discrimination based on age, race, color, religion, sex, or national origin.
Fair Employment Opportunity Act (1972)	Founded the Equal Employment Opportunity Commission to ensure compliance with the Civil Rights Act.
Equal Pay Act (1963)	Requires that men and women be paid the same amount for performing similar job duties.
Rehabilitation Act (1973)	Requires affirmative action to hire and promote handicapped persons if the firm employs 50 or more employees and is seeking a federal contract in excess of $50,000.
Vietnam Veterans Readjustment Act (1974)	Requires affirmative action to hire Vietnam veterans and disabled veterans of any war. Applicable to firms holding federal contracts in excess of $10,000.
Age Discrimination in Employment Act (1967)	Prohibits discrimination against people of ages 40 to 70.
Fifth and Fourteenth Amendments to the U.S. Constitution	Provides equal-protection standards to prevent irrational or unreasonable selection methods.

process. In Step 1 of the process, planning for recruitment and selection, sales managers must take care to analyze the job to be filled in an open-minded way, attempting to overcome any personal mental biases. For example, in the 1980s, many sales organizations have overcome biases against women in sales positions. These organizations are practically unanimous in reporting that women have performed as well as, and in some cases better than, their male counterparts.

Job descriptions and job qualifications should be accurate and based on a thoughtful job analysis. The planning stage may also require that the sales manager consider fair-employment legislation and affirmative action requirements before setting recruitment and selection objectives.

In Step 2 of the process, recruitment, the sources that serve as intermediaries in the search for prospective candidates should be informed of the firm's legal position. It is also crucial that advertising and other communications be devoid of potentially discriminatory content. For example, companies that advertise for "young, self-motivated salesmen" may be inviting an inquiry from the EEOC.

Finally, all selection tools must be related to job performance. Munson and Spivey summarize legal advice for selection by stating, "At each step in the selection process, it would be advisable to be as objective, quantitative, and consistent as possible, especially since present federal guidelines are concerned with all procedures suggesting employment discrimination."[18]

To more fully appreciate the sensitivity necessary in these matters, consider the following list of potentially troublesome information often found on employment applications:[19]

- Age or date of birth
- Length of time at present address
- Height and/or weight
- Marital status
- Ages of children
- Occupation of spouse
- Relatives already employed by the firm
- Person to notify in case of an emergency
- Type of military discharge

Not only are these topics open to charges of discrimination, but so is a request for a photograph of the applicant, a birth certificate, or a copy of military discharge papers. Further questions to avoid are those concerning the original name of the applicant, race or color, religion (including holidays observed), nationality or birthplace of the applicant, and memberships in organizations that may suggest race, religion, color, or ancestral origin of the applicant.[20]

SPECIAL ISSUES IN RECRUITMENT AND SELECTION

Some additional topics related to recruitment and selection are:

- Ethical issues
- Use of part-time salespeople
- Extra employment incentives offered to job candidates
- Assistance to cooperative channel members

Ethical Issues

Two ethical issues of particular importance are (1) how the job to be filled is represented and (2) how interviews are conducted. **Misrepresentation** of the job does not always extend into the legal domain. For example, earnings potential may be stated in terms of what the top producer earns, not expected first-year earnings of the average salesperson. Or perhaps the opportunities for promotion are somewhat overstated, but no actually false statements are used. As simple as it may sound, the best policy is a truthful policy if the sales manager wants to match the applicant to the job and avoid later problems from those recruited under false pretenses.

Some ethical issues also arise in interviewing, especially regarding the **stress interview**. This technique is designed to put job candidates under extreme, unexpected, psychological duress for the purpose of seeing how they react. A common tactic for stress interviewing in the sales field is to demand an impromptu sales presentation for a convenient item such as a ballpoint pen or an ashtray. Such requests may seem unreasonable to a professional salesperson who is accustomed to planning a presentation before delivering it.

Sales managers who use stress interviewing justify its use by pointing out that salespeople must be able to think on their feet and react quickly to unanticipated questions from customers. While this is true, there would seem to be better ways of assessing a candidate's skills. The stress interview may create an unfavorable image of the company, and it may alienate some of the better candidates. It appears to be a risky, and ethically questionable, approach.

Part-Time Salespeople

In recent years, there has been an explosion in the number of firms utilizing **part-time salespeople** to support or supplant the full-time salesforce. In most cases, part-time salespeople are not eligible for fringe benefits, so the cost of sales coverage can be reduced by using them. Further, there is virtually no pressure from part-time salespeople to be promoted into management, which may be an advantage in administering some salesforces. The recruitment and selection process is not different for

SALES TREND

PART-TIME SALESPEOPLE

As a result of several interacting trends, another trend is emerging — the increased use of part-time salespeople.[a] Large retailers are becoming more dominant in the channel of distribution for many packaged products. At the same time, sales promotion in the form of in-store merchandising is gaining popularity. These developments, when coupled with tightening of sales budgets in quest of improved salesforce productivity, have fueled the rapid growth of part-time salesforces and part-time sales support personnel working for manufacturers.

Colgate-Palmolive was one of the first major companies to utilize part-time salespeople, beginning in the mid-1970s. Today, other large sales organizations such as Ligget & Myers, Scripto, and Blistex have followed suit. Federal regulations require benefit coverage for part-timers working more than 1,000 hours a year (20 hours a week), so many firms are contracting with staffing organizations to hire, train, supervise, and if necessary, terminate the employment of part-timers. One such contractor, Powerforce, charges 9.5 percent of payroll costs to provide these services. Powerforce supplies approximately 75,000 part-time salespeople per year to its clients.

An alternative is to set up the part-time salesforce on an in-house basis. Whether they hire their own part-timers or contract with a specialty firm, a growing number of companies are finding part-timers to be valuable additions to the salesforce.

[a]Arthur Bragg, "Temporaries: The New Look in Sales," *Sales and Marketing Management*, August 1987, 39–41.
Source: Kevin T. Higgins, "Extras Come to Aid of Merchandisers," *Marketing News*, June 6, 1986, 22.

part-time salespeople, except that the sales manager may want to use an employment agency that specializes in part-timers. This subject is explored further in "Sales Trend: Part-Time Salespeople."

Incentives in Recruitment and Selection

In addition to standard enticements such as salary, performance bonuses, company car, and fringe benefits, certain extra incentives are sometimes offered to prospective salespeople. Bonuses for relocation are one type of incentive, especially with today's sentiment for less mobile lifestyles. Another is the **market bonus** paid upon hiring to salespeople having highly sought after skills and qualifications. This one-time payment recognizes an existing imbalance in supply and demand in a given labor market. Using a market bonus could be a reasonable alternative if the supply-demand imbalance is thought to be temporary, since the bonus is a one-time payment and not a permanent addition to base compensation. Limited research into the effectiveness of market bonuses when recruiting for sales positions has indicated that the bonus is not particulary effective.[21] This could change, however, if the demand for salespeople continues to intensify.

Figure 9.2 **A Proposed Model of Salesforce Socialization**

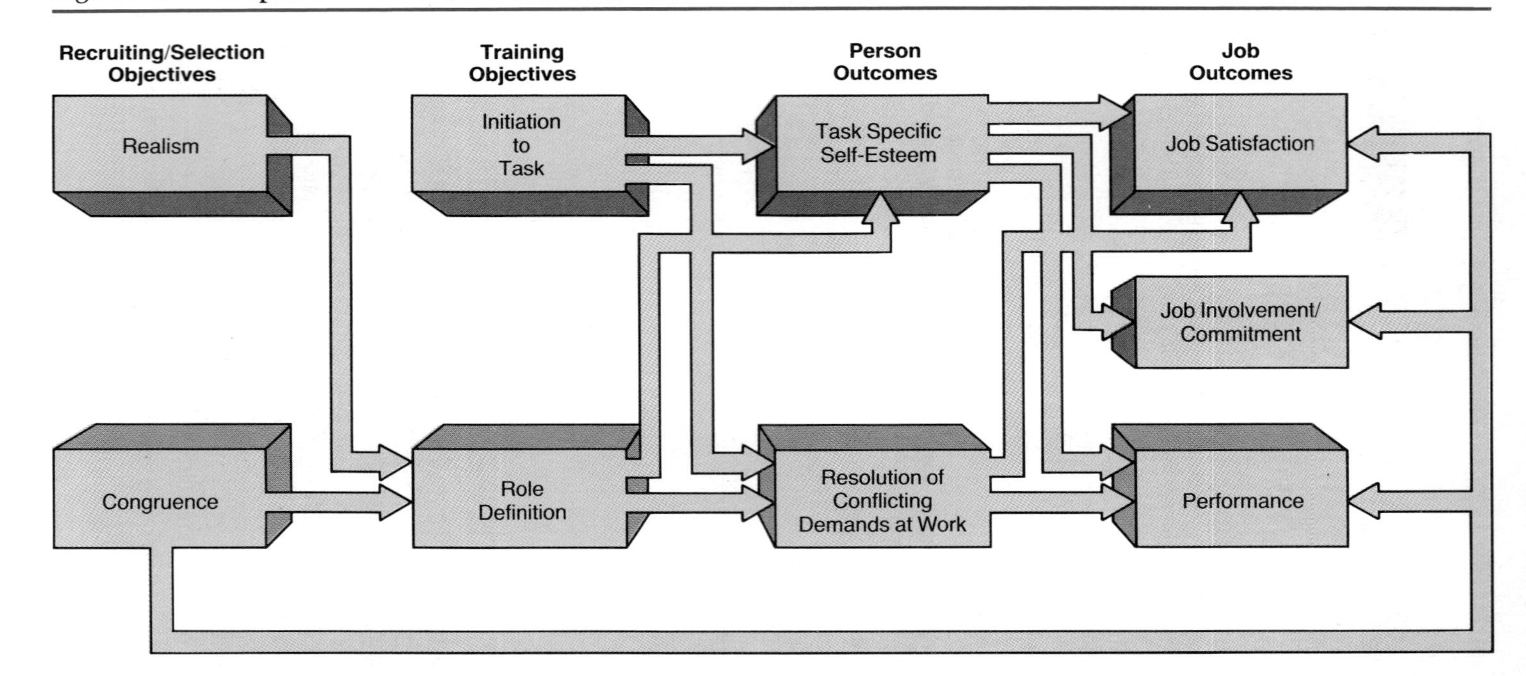

Sales organizations must present accurate portrayals of the sales job (achieving realism) to sales recruits, who must possess skills and needs compatible with the needs and offerings of the organization (achieving congruence). If these objectives of recruiting and selection are met, salesforce socialization is enhanced, and, ultimately, salesforce performance, job satisfaction, and job involvement and commitment are improved.

Source: Alan J. Dubinsky, Roy D. Howell, Thomas N. Ingram, and Danny N. Bellenger, "Salesforce Socialization." Reprinted from *Journal of Marketing* 50 (October 1986): 203, published by the American Marketing Association. Used with permission.

Assisting Cooperative Channel Members

An interesting extension of recruitment and selection is for the sales manager to become involved in these activities on behalf of cooperative channel members such as distributors, wholesalers, and retailers. This strategy has helped increase sales for General Automation, manufacturers of Zebra, an IBM-compatible computer. General Automation has arranged for national recruiting firms to assist their dealers in locating prospective salesforce members, and in some cases, has assisted dealers in selecting salespeople.[22]

RECRUITMENT, SELECTION, AND SALESFORCE SOCIALIZATION

Salesforce socialization refers to the process by which salespeople acquire the knowledge, skills, and values essential to perform their job. The process begins when the sales recruit is first exposed to the organization and may extend for several years thereafter. A model of salesforce socialization is shown in Figure 9.2. This model suggests that important job outcomes such as job satisfaction, job involvement and commitment, and performance are directly and indirectly affected by recruitment and selection procedures.

The socialization process will be discussed again in subsequent chapters. For now, accept the idea that socialization affects salesforce performance, and that recruitment and selection procedures play a major role in the socialization process. The two stages of socialization relevant to recruitment and selection are (1) **achieving realism,** which is giving the recruit an accurate portrayal of the job, and (2) **achieving congruence,** which is matching the capabilities of the recruit with the needs of the organization. Accurate job descriptions, matching candidates to the job, and perhaps offering a **job preview** through a field visit with a salesperson are suggested for achieving realism and congruence in recruitment and selection.

Bristol-Meyers has an interesting approach to achieving realism and congruence in its recruiting efforts on college campuses. The company uses a videocassette to show the day-to-day activities of a Bristol-Meyers salesperson and to illustrate company policies in areas such as compensation, promotion, and expense reimbursement.[23] The videos are shown by sales managers and campus recruiters, who then respond to student questions raised by the videos.

SUMMARY

1. **Explain the critical role of recruitment and selection in building and maintaining a productive salesforce.** Recruitment and selection of salespeople can be an expensive process, characterized by uncertainty and complicated by legal consid-

erations. If the procedures are not properly conducted, a multitude of managerial problems can arise, the worst of which being that salesforce performance is suboptimal. The sales manager is the key person in the recruitment and selection process, although other managers in the hiring firm may share responsibilities for staffing the salesforce.

2. **Identify the key activities in planning and executing a program for sales force recruitment and selection.** Figure 9.1 depicts a model of the recruitment and selection process. There are three steps in the process: planning, recruitment, and selection. Planning consists of conducting a job analysis, determining job qualifications, writing a job description, setting objectives, and formulating a strategy. Recruitment involves locating prospective job candidates from one or more sources within or outside the hiring firm. The third step, selection, entails an evaluation of the candidates culminating in a hiring decision. Major methods of evaluating candidates include resume and job-application analysis, interviewing, testing, assessment centers, background investigation, and physical examinations.

3. **Discuss the legal considerations in salesforce recruitment and selection.** Every step of the recruitment and selection process has the potential to illegally discriminate against some job candidates. Federal laws and guidelines provide the basic anti-discriminatory framework, and state and local statutes may also be applicable. The most important legislation that applies are the Civil Rights Act and the Equal Employment Opportunity Act.

4. **Discuss the ethical concerns of salesforce recruitment and selection.** Two primary ethical concerns are (1) misrepresentation of the job to be filled and (2) utilizing stress interviews in the selection stage.

5. **Name some additional special issues to be aware of in salesforce recruitment and selection.** Some special issues in recruitment and selection are (1) the increasing usage of part-time salespeople, (2) the use of market bonuses, and (3) assisting cooperative channel members in recruiting and selecting their salespeople.

6. **Describe how recruitment and selection affects salesforce socialization and performance.** Socialization, the process by which salespeople adjust to their jobs, begins when the recruit is first contacted by the hiring firm. Two stages of socialization should be accomplished during recruitment and selection: achieving realism and achieving congruence. Realism means giving the recruit an accurate portrayal of the job. Congruence refers to the matching process that should occur between the needs of the organization and the capabilities of the recruit. If realism and congruence can be accomplished, future job satisfaction, involvement, commitment, and performance should be improved. These relationships are shown in a model of the socialization process in Figure 9.2.

Key Terms

- recruitment
- selection
- job analysis
- job qualifications
- job description
- recruitment and selection strategy
- employee referral programs
- employment agencies
- job fairs
- computerized matchmaking
- job-application form
- initial interviews
- intensive interviews
- interviewer bias
- assessment centers
- background investigations
- misrepresentation
- stress interview
- part-time salespeople
- market bonus
- salesforce socialization
- achieving realism
- achieving congruence
- job preview

Review Questions

1. What are some of the problems associated with improperly executed recruitment and selection activities?
2. Describe the relationship between conducting a job analysis, determining job qualifications, and completing a written job description.
3. What are the advantages of using employee referral programs to recruit salespeople? Can you identify some disadvantages?
4. How can private employment agencies assist in the recruitment and selection of salespeople? Who pays the fee charged by such agencies, the hiring company or the job candidate?
5. What can be learned about a job candidate from analyzing a job application that cannot be learned from the candidate's resume?
6. What advice would you offer to a sales manager who is contemplating the use of a generic sales aptitude test to select salespeople?
7. Summarize the primary legislation designed to prohibit illegal discrimination in the recruitment and selection process.
8. What factors are contributing to the growth in the number of part-time salespeople?
9. To enhance salesforce socialization, recruitment and selection should assure realism and congruence. How can this be accomplished?
10. What is stress interviewing? How do some sales managers justify using stress interviews?

Application Exercises

1. Examine the newspaper advertisements in Exhibit 9.4, noting the different emphasis for each advertisement. Using a Sunday edition of a newspaper, locate an example of each of the following types of advertisements for salespeople:
   - An ad that emphasizes product-specific sales experience
   - An ad that emphasizes customers sold to, rather than products sold

- An ad for sales trainees without sales experience
- An ad designed to attract trainees from another field

What suggestions would you make for improving each of these advertisements?

2. Assume you are the regional manager for the Stanley Electric Tool products salespeople described in Exhibit 9.1. You are in the process of filling a vacancy in your salesforce and have contacted a private employment agency to help locate prospective job candidates. Other than the job description shown in Exhibit 9.1, what information would the agency need to do a competent job in locating candidates?
3. Examine the following generic sales aptitude test. Can you dispute the appropriateness of the designated correct answers?

Sales Aptitude Questions
What's Their/Your Sales Intelligence?

How well would you do on a test that is aiding sales executives in selecting salespeople? Take the test to find out.

Presented here are 10 questions adapted from the 40-question Diagnostic Sales Intelligence Test being used by Sales Aptitude Corp., a division of Personnel Sciences Center of New York, for recruiting salespeople. The company has evaluated over 27,000 salespeople for such companies as Emery Air Freight, E. F. Hutton, Almay, Inc., Sun Chemical, Hilti., and Melville Corp. and its Thom McAn division.

The best score is 11 (the final question requires a double answer); the worst possible score is 0.

Preparation

1. As a salesman of complex industrial equipment, which of the following would be most important to you?

- **a.** a full understanding of the equipment
- **b.** an ability to cite exact figures about the equipment's efficiency, life span, production capacity, etc.
- **c.** information about companies that have used this equipment
- **d.** memorizing a standard sales presentation covering all important features of the equipment

2. The salesman should try to understand his prospect in order to (check the *worst* answer)—

- **a.** show that he is interested in the prospect
- **b.** make the sale as fast as possible
- **c.** see the prospect's viewpoint regarding the product
- **d.** quickly establish rapport with the prospect

Opening

3. Prior to your presentation, your prospect, whom you have just met, is talking to you about something not related to your product. While this is going on, the worst thing you could do is—

- **a.** listen attentively
- **b.** mentally review your presentation but appear attentive
- **c.** attempt to politely interrupt so that you can start your presentation
- **d.** try to get some clues about his personality

4. You have found out that your prospect wants very much to impress his boss. The best way of establishing your relationship with your prospect would be to—

- **a.** mail him a news clipping in which his boss is mentioned
- **b.** put in a good word for him to his boss

c. give him ideas he can present to his own management
d. ask him what you can do to help him impress his boss

Presentation

5. When presenting information about your product, advertising material is best used—
a. as an initial attention-getter
b. in the middle of the presentation to break up whatever boredom there may be
c. as a visual aid, to be referred to from time to time
d. at the end of the presentation, and left with the prospect

6. During the course of a presentation, a prospect inquires about his competitor's plans, with which you are familiar since the competitor is also one of your customers. Which would be the worst course to take?
a. show how ethical you are by refusing to answer such a question
b. help the sale along by telling what you have learned
c. avoid answering by saying that you are not aware of the plans
d. impress your prospect with the idea that he wouldn't want you to divulge such information about his organization

Overcoming Objections

7. When a prospect points out that in certain areas your competitor's product is better, the worst thing you can do is—
a. show how your competitor's product is lacking in other areas
b. point out that this is only a very minor advantage compared with the advantages of your product
c. point out the benefits of your own product
d. subtly deny that his statement is valid

8. Your prospect is a "yes" man who agrees with every point you make. However, when the close is attempted he says that he needs more time to think it over. When you call on him again, the same situation occurs. What should you do on the third call?
a. continue your presentation, but inform him that you can't call again
b. attempt to close the sale, but if this is not successfull leave and forget this prospect for the time being
c. make a far-fetched claim about your product to see if your prospect is listening
d. ask your prospect directly why he is not giving you the order

Closing

9. What should you do if the buyer of a company constantly refuses you?
a. alter your presentation
b. study the methods of your competition
c. don't call on him for a while
d. attempt to influence his subordinate personnel

10. After completing a rather lengthy presentation which included most benefits and features of your product, you should (check both the best *and* the worst action)—
a. summarize the features in which the person has shown interest
b. suggest that he think a minute before making a decision
c. ask him when he thinks he can make a decision
d. ask him how much of your product he wants to order

Source: Reprinted by permission of Sales Aptitude Corp.

4. Executives at Acme Fabrications estimate they lose approximately $25,000 on each fired sales representative in salary, training costs, and lost sales. They hire 100 people a year of the 500 they interview. On the average, 20 are fired per year, at a cost of $500,000. Acme recently contracted with an assessment service, who will analyze 200 "finalists" for the 100 jobs at a cost of $150 per candidate. How much reduction in the average turnover rate is necessary to recoup the costs of utilizing the assessment center?
5. Analyze the following three resumes. Assume you are a sales manager for a Fortune 500 consumer goods company whose customers include grocery chains, discount stores, and drug stores. Your product line is health and beauty aids. For each candidate, develop questions to be asked in the interview. Exhibit 9.6 may be helpful in planning the interviews.

THOMAS WILLIAM GROGAN

Current Address	Permanent Address
212 Parkview Dr. Lexington, Ky. 40503 (606) 555-1302	1121 Bath Avenue London, Ky. 41101 (606) 555-3340

JOB OBJECTIVE: Entry level sales position leading to advancement based on performance.

EDUCATION: University of Kentucky, Lexington, Kentucky
Bachelor of Business Administration, May 1987
Major: Marketing Minor: Economics
GPA 3.51/4.00

HONORS & ACTIVITIES:
American Marketing Association: President
Beta Gamma Sigma Honorary: President
Academic Excellence Scholarship
Sigma Alpha Epsilon Fraternity: Rush Chairman, Assistant Treasurer
President of Pledge Class, Editor of Summer Newsletter
Lances Junior Men's Honorary
Omicron Delta Kappa Leadership Honor Society
Mortar Board Senior Honor Society
Student Agencies Incorporated

EXPERIENCE:

Manager/Internship
Copy Cat Print Shop, Lexington Kentucky
Hire, schedule, and supervise employees. Develop sales promotions and make personal sales calls. Conduct inventory and order supplies. Maintain financial records.
January 1986 to present

Servicing Clerk
First Security Mortgage Co., Lexington, Kentucky
Made deposits and daily journal entries. Filed and copied loan information.
May 1986 to August 1986

Sales Clerk
Copy Cat Print Shop, Lexington, Kentucky
Operated printing machine. Sold supplies to customers. Handled cash/credit transactions.
September 1985 to December 1985

Ophthalmic Assistant
Raymond V. Mecca, M.D., Ashland, Kentucky
Recorded patients' general medical history. Measured visual acuity. Operated eye computer.
Summers of 1981 to 1985

REFERENCES: Available upon request.

LINDA A. BLACKBURN

School Address	Permanent Address
378 Summertree Road	730 Hemingway Road
Lexington, Kentucky 40802	Circleville, Ohio 43113
(606) 555-9842	(614) 555-9301

CAREER OBJECTIVE: A competitive position in the realm of marketing, customer service or sales with career opportunities conducive to personal and professional growth.

EDUCATION. University of Kentucky Lexington, Kentucky
B.B.A. to be awarded in May 1987
Major: Marketing
G.P.A.: 3.2 (A = 4.0)
G.P.A. in major field of study: 3.83

RELATED COURSEWORK:

Sales Force Management	Computer Science
Retail and Distribution Management	Managerial Accounting
Marketing Research	Business Statistics
Promotion Management	Industrial Communication
Behavioral Systems in Marketing	Strategic Management
Marketing Strategy and Planning	Corporation Finance

EMPLOYMENT:

Office for Experiential Education — Lexington, KY
September 1986–Present

Marketing Intern: Responsibilities involved development of marketing strategies to increase awareness of the services offered by the Office for Experiential Education.

RCA Corporation — Circleville, OH
Summers 1986, 1985

Assisted in the production of television picture tube parts on the production line.

Container Corporation of America — Circleville, OH
Summer 1984

General labor pool which included training in the woodyard and work on a forklift truck.

McDonald's Restaurant — Circleville, OH
Summer 1983

Operated cash register and assembled orders.

ACTIVITIES AND HONORS:
Dean's Honor List
Scholarship member of women's varsity track and cross country teams
1986 All-American Honors in track
1986 Academic All-Southeastern Conference
Member of American Marketing Association
Member of Phi Beta Lambda
Member of the Fellowship of Christian Athletes

REFERENCES: Furnished upon request.

STEVEN J. WICKHAM

Campus Address
Box 642 Killian Hall
Lexington, KY
40526-0149
Phone: (606) 555-9165

Permanent Address
358 Mandino Circle
Edgewood, KY 41017
Phone: (606) 555-7891

Objective To obtain an entry-level position in corporate sales/advertising/marketing, with potential advancement to sales management.

Education University of Kentucky, Lexington, KY
Bachelor of Business Administration (concentration in marketing)
Cumulative GPA: 3.45/4.0
Graduation: May 1987

Graduated with honors from Covington Catholic High School, Park Hills, KY

Work Experience

August 1986-Present

Kentucky Kernel, University of Kentucky's student newspaper
Advertising Sales-Responsibilities include sales, servicing existing accounts, making cold calls, handling invoices, ad contracts, credit applications, and ad layouts. Requires salesperson who is a self-starter, aggressive, and self-motivated with commission based pay.

August 1986-Present

Resident Advisor, using leadership skills to aid in student development of 30 men. Coordinating service, charity and intramural programs. Also development of tournament activities for 640 men.

May 1981-Present

Summit Hills Country Club. Responsibilities include retail sales, supervising and maintaining club storage. Strong membership service required.

Leadership Activities

Resident Advisor
Collegians for Academic Excellence 1985-'87
American Marketing Association
Haggin Hall's House Council Representative
Charity Fundraising
Christian Awakening Program-team leader
Intramural Sports

Honors

Academic Excellence Scholarship
Beta Gamma Sigma Business Honorary
Dean's List
Business Award, C.C.H.S.

(References available on request)

Notes

[1]J. Michael Munson and W. Austin Spivey, "Salesforce Selection That Meets Federal Regulation and Management Needs," *Industrial Marketing Management* 9 (February 1980): 12.

[2]"Hiring Plans Face Serious Bottlenecks," *Sales and Marketing Management,* September 1987, 124.

[3]Thayer C. Taylor, "Meet the Sales Force of the Future," *Sales and Marketing Management,* March 10, 1986, 59–60.

[4]Herbert M. Greenberg and Jeanne Greenberg, "Job Matching for Better Performance," *Harvard Business Review,* 58 (September-October 1980): 128–133.

[5]Joseph A. Bellizzi and Paul A. Cline, "Technical or Nontechnical Salesmen?" *Industrial Marketing Management* 14 (May 1985): 69–74.

[6]Thayer C. Taylor, "Apple-Polishing the Dealer," *Sales and Marketing Management,* September 10, 1984, 47–50.

[7]See Arthur Bragg, "Persistent Demand Keeps Sales Hires Steady," *Sales and Marketing Management,* August 12, 1985, 70; and Christine Dempsey, "Students Get a Foot in the Door," *Sales and Marketing Management,* August 13, 1984, 64–65.

[8]"A Matchmaker for Sales Managers," *Sales and Marketing Management,* December 9, 1985, 52–53.

[9]Arthur Bragg, "Interviews That Rate A 10," *Sales and Marketing Management,* August 17, 1981, 58–60.

[10]Alan J. Dubinsky and Thomas E. Barry, "A Survey of Sales Management Practices," *Industrial Marketing Management* 11 (April 1982): 136.

[11]Richard Nelson, "Maybe It's Time to Take Another Look at Tests as a Selection Tool?" *Journal of Personal Selling and Sales Management* 7 (August 1987): 33–38.

[12]Wesley J. Johnston and Martha C. Cooper, "Industrial Sales Force Selection: Current Knowledge and Needed Research," *Journal of Personal Selling and Sales Management* 1 (Spring–Summer 1981): 49–57.

[13]Richard Nelson, *The Use of Psychological Tests in Selecting Sales Representatives* (monograph), National Society of Sales Training Executives, NSSTE Library, Center for Research and Management Services, Indiana State University, Terre Haute, Ind.

[14]Based on Samuel J. Maurice, "Stalking the High-Scoring Salesperson," *Sales and Marketing Management,* October 7, 1985, 63–64; George B. Salsbury, "Properly Recruit Salespeople To Reduce Training Cost," *Industrial Marketing Management* 11 (April 1982): 143–146; Richard Kern, "IQ Tests for Salesmen Make A Comeback," *Sales and Marketing Management,* April, 1988, 42–46.

[15]E. James Randall, Ernest F. Cooke, and Lois Smith, "A Successful Application of The Assessment Center Concept to The Salesperson Selection Process," *Journal of Personal Selling and Sales Management* 5 (May 1985): 53–61.

[16]Liz Murphy, "Did Your Salesman Lie to Get His Job?" *Sales and Marketing Management,* November, 1987, 54–58.

[17]Kenneth H. Richman, "Laws Differ For Testing Potential, Present Employees," *Marketing News,* November 21, 1986, 9.

[18]Munson and Spivey, "Salesforce Selection," 15.

[19]Adapted from "Employment Application Forms: Avoiding Discrimination Problems," The Research Institute of America, Inc., in *Marketing for Sales Executives* 4 (May 11, 1978): 1–3.

[20]John H. Rose, *How to Recruit, Interview, Select Productive Sales Representatives* (Orlando, Florida: National Society of Sales Training Executives, 1981), 9.

[21]Alan J. Dubinsky, Charles H. Fay, Thomas N. Ingram, and Marc J. Wallace, "Market Bonuses: How Effective Are They? *Business Horizons,* May–June, 1983, 11–14.

[22]"GA Helps Dealers Hire the Best," *Sales and Marketing Management,* May 19, 1986, 26.

[23]"What You See Is What You Get at Bristol-Meyers," *Sales and Marketing Management,* July, 1987, 22.

CHAPTER 10

CONTINUAL DEVELOPMENT OF THE SALESFORCE: SALES TRAINING

Learning Objectives

After completing this chapter, you should be able to

1. Explain the importance of sales training and the sales manager's role in training.
2. Describe the sales training process as a series of six interrelated steps.
3. Discuss five methods for assessing sales training needs and identify typical sales training needs.
4. Name some typical objectives of sales training programs, and explain how setting objectives for training is beneficial to sales managers.
5. Identify the key issues in evaluating sales training alternatives.

CONTINUAL DEVELOPMENT: SALES TRAINING AT MERCK, SHARP & DOHME

A recent survey proclaimed Merck Sharp & Dohme, a division of Merck & Co., to have the best salesforce in the highly competitive pharmaceutical industry. Jerry Keller, division vice-president of sales, offers a one-word explanation for Merck's exalted status: training. According to Keller, "We have the best-trained reps in the industry. We have an obsession about it. Training drives the whole salesforce and it separates us from everybody else."

Merck's philosophy is that a highly trained salesperson is required to build a relationship of trust with the customer, and that this relationship is the "absolute key" to marketing in the pharmaceutical industry. There is no question that training is paying handsome dividends at Merck, where sales have been rising at a spectacular rate in recent years.

All Merck salespeople go through three levels of instruction. First, they learn the basics of medicine such as anatomy, physiology, and diseases. Next comes a six-month to one-year course on how to present Merck products in a sales territory. The third phase of training is a medical summary concentrating on how Merck products are used to treat various diseases and maladies.

This training is supplemented on a continual basis every year or two, when each of Merck's 1,500 salespeople is sent to medical school to learn the latest developments in the field. Further, each salesperson receives individualized training from a physician-mentor in a course that includes on-site hospital training. District meetings are also on the training agenda every two months to focus on specific topics, such as diseases of unknown origin or progress in the treatment of arthritis.

Keller believes that physicians rely on Merck salespeople because of the intense training the salesforce receives. He says that physicians depend on Merck salespeople for a balanced, fair sales presentation that includes disadvantages as well as advantages of Merck products.

Source: "Merck's Grand Obsession," *Sales and Marketing Management,* June 1987, 65.

Pharmacists comprise another important customer group served by Merck, and Merck gets high marks from this group as well. Says Larry Braden, an Atlanta pharmacist and owner of several drugstores, "Too many companies still think the physician is their prime customer, and they treat the pharmacist with anything from benign neglect to disdain." Braden adds that Merck is among the best at recognizing and supporting the key role of the pharmacist in the channel of distribution.

Future sales training at Merck will undoubtedly be challenged to stay abreast of a rapidly changing environment. One current development is that nurses and ancillary personnel are becoming more important in the purchase decision, and this may require changes in the Merck training program.

LIKE Jerry Keller of Merck, many sales executives invest heavily in salesforce training and expect a lot in return. The National Society of Sales Training Executives emphasizes the training-performance link in this passage:

> You are a sales manager. You and you alone are accountable for the performance of your salespeople. You select or help select them, and you motivate and train them. Although your company may help you by providing formalized training programs, in the final analysis it is you, the sales manager, who must provide the day-to-day training and development experiences. If you look closely at your position description, you will most likely find a statement such as: "responsible for the continuous training and development of field salespeople." Naturally, your final evaluation will depend on bottom-line results, but if you have done a good job in training your people, the bottom line should take care of itself.[1]

In this chapter, we will discuss a number of sales training issues and methods. First, we will consider the importance of sales training. Then a model of the sales training process will be discussed.

IMPORTANCE OF SALES TRAINING

Experts point out that training has long been considered a key element in the development and implementation of marketing and sales strategies.[2] A comprehensive review of sales management research concludes that whom one recruits is important, but probably not as important in determining salesforce performance as what sales managers do with the recruits — and to the recruits — after they have been hired.[3] The general need for sales training is reflected in a study of training practices in U.S. firms, which discovered that the type of employee likely to get the greatest amount of formal training is the salesperson.[4]

While there is a general need for sales training, other factors affect its relative importance in a given sales organization, namely, the size of the company, technological orientation, level of competitiveness, and whether or not the company sells a tangible product or a service.

General Need for Sales Training

Most organizations have a need for sales training of some type. This enduring need for sales training exists in part due to inadequacies of current training programs and in part because new salespeople join the organization on a regular basis. The inadequacies of existing sales training programs are exposed in surveys such as the following:

- A study of salespeople from 42 industries found that they were less prepared in the critical steps of the sales process (prospecting, coping with questions and objections, and confirming the sale) than in other steps in the sales process.[5]
- A survey of sales executives found that 29 percent felt their salespeople were not doing an effective job in giving customers specific product information.[6]
- A study of the computer industry, where sales training is commonplace, concluded that sales representatives are inadequately trained. According to the author of the study, "It is a credit to the learning ability of the people on the job — and to the adaptability of computer users — that systems solve user problems as well as they do."[7]

These examples indicate an ongoing need to conduct sales training to improve salesforce performance. It should be stressed that the need for sales training is continual, as was illustrated in the Merck example at the beginning of the chapter. The need for continual training was dramatized in a study by the Xerox Corporation that found that 87 percent of the skills learned in a classroom are lost unless the training is reinforced.[8]

Further evidence of the need for sales training comes from the customer side of the buyer-seller relationship. As we have previously mentioned, customers appreciate, and sometimes demand, a well-trained salesforce from their vendors. It is also interesting to note that professional purchasing agents put a premium on sales-related topics in their own training programs. One survey of purchasing personnel found the most important topics covered in their training programs to be vendor relations and negotiation techniques.[9] At a minimum, this indicates a need to stay abreast of customers through sales training.

Company Size and Sales Training

As shown in Exhibit 10.1, there is a positive relationship between company size and whether or not the company offers *formalized* sales training (which is structured in some way) as opposed to *informal on-the-job* training. Approximately 60 percent of

Exhibit 10.1 **Sales Training by Size of Organization**

No. of Employees	Percent Offering Formal Sales Training
50–99	41.7
100–499	44.8
500–999	43.6
1,000–2,499	43.3
2,500–9,999	48.7
10,000 or more	60.0

Source: Jack Gordon, "Where the Training Goes," *Training*, October 1986, 62.

companies with 10,000 or more employees, and slightly over 40 percent of companies with 50 to 100 employees, offer formalized sales training. Large companies are more likely to have sales training programs, in part because they have outgrown the alternative of hiring skilled, capable salespeople from other firms. Smaller companies may choose to minimize training by hiring salespeople from other firms known for their excellent training programs. For example, the competition among smaller firms to hire salespeople from IBM, Procter & Gamble and Xerox can be intense.

Technological Orientation and Sales Training

High technology companies place considerable emphasis on sales training to correspond with their often hectic pace of new-product or new-service development. The importance of sales training to high-technology companies is illustrated in the case of AT&T, when the company moved into the computer business in the mid-1980s. The 6,000 AT&T salespeople were well equipped to sell telephone systems, but not computers. They had not been trained in tailoring computer systems to customer needs. When results were disappointing, a new sales training program was implemented to make the salesforce more competitive. Customers reacted favorably, as indicated by a J.C. Penney vice-president who commented, "I am impressed with the quality of the people I am seeing now. They understand they have to sell, and if they get some better products, they can do it."[10]

Level of Competitiveness and Sales Training

Sales organizations in highly competitive markets, especially newly competitive markets, have a strong need for sales training. For example, the direct-sales industry, with companies such as Tupperware, Mary Kay, and Avon, has become a lot more competitive in recent years. To survive in this increasingly competitive market, many firms are upgrading their training methods. Avon has decided to push for improved salesforce productivity rather than continuing a strong reliance on simply increasing salesforce size.[11] Another example of the importance of sales training in newly competitive industries is offered by a General Telephone executive:

> With some people, utilities were always considered a real safe place to work. What we needed were people who had the ability to move from selling to captive customers to competitive sales. We had to teach them how to sell in a direct sales environment. Typically in our industry, they're called salespersons but they didn't really sell anything. They rented phone equipment and had someone sign a contract.[12]

Product or Service and Sales Training

A trend in corporate training is that service organizations are becoming more involved in intensive training, and that customer-contact personnel such as salespeople are among those most likely to receive training.[13] The interest in sales training in service industries was clearly revealed in a survey of bank marketing executives that concluded, "Far and away the most important priority for increasing selling effectiveness in sample banks was sales training."[14] Alan Jenkins, an account officer at Bank of America, further noted that the emphasis today on sales techniques and client relationships has changed sales training to the point of being unrecognizable compared with the sales training of the past.[15]

Until quite recently, service organizations lagged behind industrial and consumer product companies in the amount of time and money dedicated to training new salespeople. As shown in Figure 10.1, this is no longer the case, as service organizations now spend more time and money on sales training than do consumer and industrial product companies.[16] Apparently, service organizations are beginning to see that sales training is just as important for them as it is for product companies, and that, in addition, they require training which focuses on the unique challenges of selling intangibles.

INVESTMENT IN SALES TRAINING

The importance accorded sales training by most firms is not always matched by their investment in it. Recall from Exhibit 10.1 that although a majority of large firms (10,000 or more employees) offer formalized training, a majority of smaller firms do not; and when firms of all sizes are considered, it is estimated that only 30 percent of all salespeople receive formalized training.[17] In firms where sales training is offered, the investment in time and money is often considerable, however. Training periods for new salespeople commonly run from three to twelve months at an average cost per salesperson in excess of $20,000.[18]

Figure 10.1 **Time and Money Spent on Sales Training**

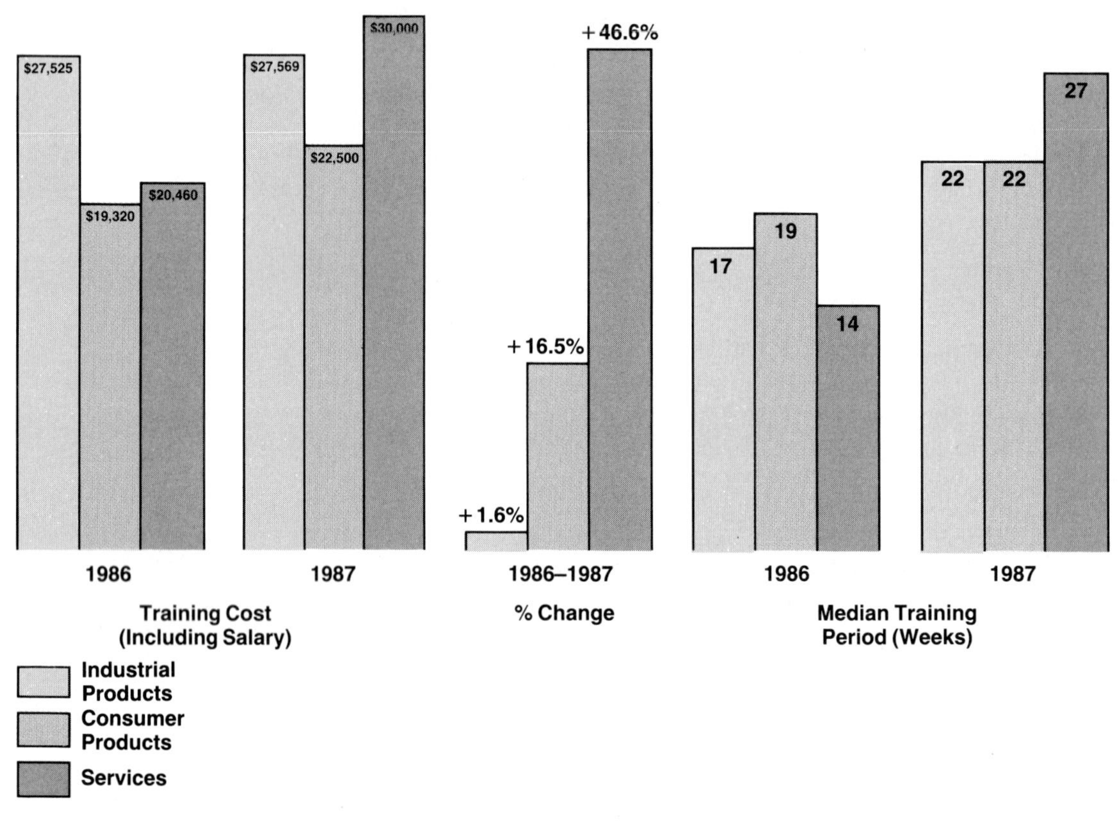

The substantial amount of time and money invested in sales training is increasing, particularly in service industries.

Source: "Survey of Selling Costs," *Sales and Marketing Management,* February 22, 1988, 49.

One aspect of the investment in sales training is the amount of time required of the sales manager. Usually, sales managers are involved not only in the "big picture" of planning, but also in the time-consuming details of implementing training, such as the following:[19]

- Arranging for salespeople to work with key personnel in various departments in the firm in order to familiarize them with the functions of those departments.
- Selecting literature, sales aids, and materials for study.

- Enrolling salespeople in professional workshops.
- Accompanying salespeople in the field to critique their sales behavior and reinforce other training.
- Conducting periodic training meetings and personal training conferences.

The significant time investment required from sales management is, unfortunately, not always well spent. Said one well-known sales training executive, "Millions of dollars are spent each year to teach salespeople what they already know."[20] With these thoughts in mind, let us examine a model for the judicious analysis, planning, and implementation of a sales training program.

A MODEL OF THE SALES TRAINING PROCESS

The sales training process is depicted as six interrelated steps in Figure 10.2: assess training needs, set training objectives, evaluate training alternatives, design sales training program, perform sales training, and conduct follow-up and evaluation.

Assess Training Needs

The purpose of sales training **needs assessment** is to compare the specific performance-related skills, attitudes, perceptions, and behaviors required for salesforce success to the state of readiness of the salesforce. Such an assessment usually reveals a need for changing or reinforcing one or more determinants of salesforce performance.

All too often, the need for sales training becomes apparent only after a decline in salesforce performance manifested by decreasing sales volume, rising expenses, or perhaps low morale. Sales training for correcting such problems is sometimes necessary, but the preferred role of sales training is to prevent problems and improve salesforce productivity on a proactive, not reactive, basis.

Needs assessment requires that sales managers consider the training appropriate for both *sales trainees* and regular salespeople. A sales trainee is an entry-level salesperson who is learning the company's products, services, and policies in preparation for a regular sales assignment. Another factor worth considering during needs assessment is each salesperson's career stage as explained in Chapter 4. For example, salespeople in the exploration stage may need basic training in sales techniques, while the salespeople in the maintenance stage could benefit from training in advanced sales techniques.

Methods of Needs Assessment. Proactive approaches to determining sales training needs include a salesforce audit, performance testing, observation, salesforce survey,

Figure 10.2 **Sales Training Process**

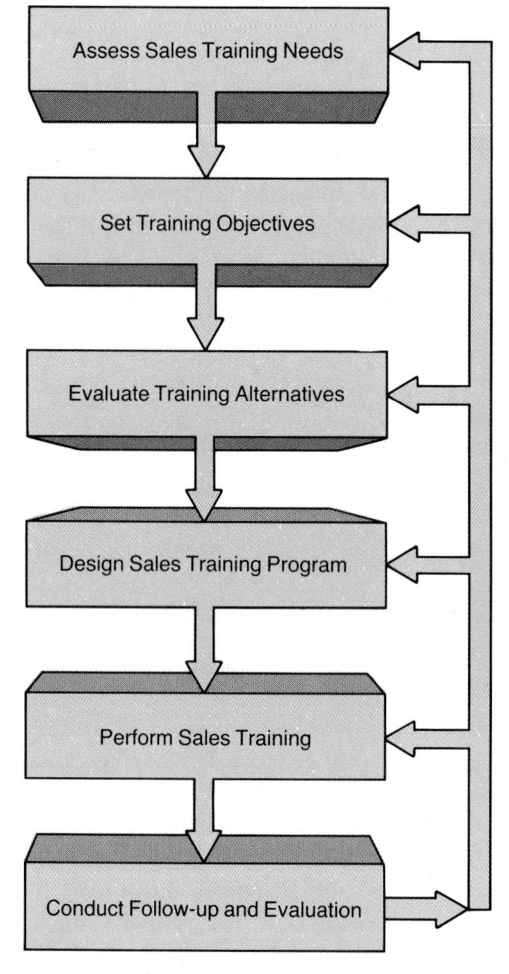

The sales training process is performed in six steps, beginning with an assessment of training needs. The process is continual, with the follow-up and evaluation step providing feedback that may alter the other steps in future sales training activities.

customer survey, and a job analysis.[21] A reactive approach (see Exhibit 10.2) could suggest other training needs if performance deteriorates.

Salesforce Audit. A comprehensive definition of **salesforce audit** is "a systematic, diagnostic, prescriptive tool which can be employed on a periodic basis to identify and address sales department problems and to prevent or reduce the impact of future

Exhibit 10.2 **Assessing Sales Training Needs (Reactive Approach)**

How XYZ Co. determined its training needs

At XYZ Co., the problem of declining market share had been obscured by rising sales volume. But the slow start of two new products prompted a study of sales-training needs. Management hired a training consultant to investigate those needs and recommend training priorities. The following are the steps he took:

1. **Interviewed key members** of management to ask, "What changes are needed in the performance of the sales force? Be specific. Concentrate on results, not methods."
2. **Sent an anonymous questionnaire** to customers and prospects, asking:
   - ☐ What do you expect of a salesperson in this industry?
   - ☐ How do salespersons disappoint you?
   - ☐ Which company in this industry does the best selling job?
   - ☐ In what ways are its salespersons better?
3. **Sent a confidential questionnaire** to each salesperson asking:
   - ☐ What information do most of our salespersons need?
   - ☐ What information do you want to learn better?
   - ☐ What skills do most of our salespersons need to improve?
   - ☐ What skills do you want to improve?
   - ☐ Other suggestions for ongoing training?
4. **Did field audits** with 20% of the salesforce.
5. **Interviewed sales supervisors.**
6. **Analyzed the information** gathered in steps 1 through 5 to determine trainable topics and separate them.
7. **Discussed and agreed** on training priorities with management.

Source: *Sales Training and Motivation: A Special Report* (New York: Sales and Marketing Management, 1977).

problems."[22] The salesforce audit (discussed fully in Chapter 15) includes an appraisal of all salesforce activities and the environment in which the salesforce operates. In the sales training area, the audit examines questions such as

- Is the training program adequate in light of objectives and resources?
- Does the training program need revision?
- Is there an ongoing training program for senior salespeople?
- Does the training program contribute in a positive manner to the socialization of sales trainees?

To be effective, a salesforce audit should be conducted annually. More frequent audits may be warranted in some situations, but the comprehensive nature of an audit requires a considerable time and money investment. As a result, other periodic assessments of sales training are suggested.

Performance Testing. Some firms use **performance testing** to help determine training needs. This method specifies the evaluation of particular tasks or skills of the salesforce. For example, salespeople may be given periodic exams on product knowledge to check retention rates and uncover areas for needing retraining. Salespeople may be asked to exhibit particular sales techniques such as demonstrating the product or using the telephone to set up sales appointments while the sales trainer evaluates their performance.

Observation. First-level sales managers spend a considerable amount of time in the field working with salespeople. They also may have direct responsibility for some accounts, acting as a salesperson or as a member of a sales team. Through these field selling activities, sales managers often *observe* the need for particular sales training. In some instances, the training need is addressed instantaneously by critiquing the salesperson's performance after the sales call has been completed. In other situations, frequent observation of particularly deficient or outstanding sales behavior may suggest future training topics.

Salesforce Survey. Exhibit 10.2 includes a section on surveying the salesforce in an attempt to isolate sales training needs. Such **salesforce surveys** may be completed as an independent activity or combined with other sales management activities such as field visits, or even included as part of the routine salesforce reporting procedures. The reports submitted by many salespeople on a weekly basis to their sales managers frequently have sections dealing with problems to be solved and areas in which managerial assistance is requested. For example, a faltering new-product introduction may signal the need for more product training, additional sales technique sharpening, or perhaps training needs specific to an individual salesperson.

Customer Survey. Also illustrated in Exhibit 10.2 is a **customer survey**, which is intended to define customer expectations and help determine how competitive the salesforce is compared to other salesforces in the industry. If personal selling is prominent in the firm's marketing strategy, some sort of customer survey to help determine sales training needs is highly recommended.

Job Analysis. The job analysis, defined in Chapter 9, is an investigation of the task, duties, and responsibilities of the sales job. In a well-run sales organization, a job analysis will be part of the recruitment and selection process and then will continue to be used in sales training and other managerial functions. Since the job analysis defines expected behavior for salespeople, it is a logical tool to be employed in assessing training needs. Since sales jobs may vary within the same salesforce, job analyses may also help in determining individualized sales training needs or the needs of different groups of salespeople.

Typical Sales Training Needs. As the preceding discussion implies, the need for sales training varies over time and across organizations. The need for salesforce training on certain topics, however, is widespread. Some of the more popular sales training topics will now be discussed.

Orientation and Socialization. Newly hired salespeople usually receive a company orientation designed to familiarize them with company history, policies, facilities, procedures, and key people with whom salespeople interact. Some firms go well beyond a perfunctory company orientation in an effort to enhance salesforce *socialization,* a concept introduced at the conclusion of Chapter 9. By referring to Figure 9.2 in that chapter, you can see how sales training can affect salesforce socialization. During initial sales training, it is hoped that each salesforce member will experience a positive **initiation to task** — the degree to which a sales trainee feels competent and accepted as a working partner — and satisfactory **role definition** — an understanding of what tasks are to be performed, what the priorities of the tasks are, and how time should be allocated among the tasks.[23]

The need for socialization as part of the training process is supported by expected indirect linkages between socialization and beneficial job outcomes. As suggested in Figure 9.2, trainees who have been properly recruited and trained tend to be more confident on the job and have fewer problems with job conflicts, leading to higher job satisfaction, involvement, commitment, and performance.

Newly hired salespeople should be extremely interested in learning about their jobs, peers, and supervisors. A basic orientation may be insufficient to provide all the information they desire, so more extensive socialization may be indicated. One company that emphasizes salesforce socialization as part of its training program is Apple Computer. A few years ago, Apple hired 400 new salespeople to sell direct to computer retailers. The initial training meeting contained an overview of the upcoming training, and the trainees were told what was expected of them. The next step involved allowing the sales trainees to go wherever they chose in the Apple headquarters building, visiting with whomever they chose, talking about whatever topic interested them. According to Apple's manager of sales training and development, the purpose was "to get them into the organization right from the beginning. That way, they find out, first hand, from people in various departments what it means to work for a company like Apple, what Apple means to them, and what it takes to succeed at Apple."[24]

The need for salesforce socialization is especially likely to extend past the initial training period. This is particularly true if salesforce members have limited personal contact with peers, managers, and other company personnel.

Sales Techniques. There is a universal ongoing need for training on "how to sell." Research has indicated that salespeople sometimes sell in spite of themselves; that is to say, many salespeople do not competently execute fundamental sales techniques.[25] Common mistakes identified in this research include

- Poor job of prospecting for new accounts
- Lack of preplanning of sales calls
- Reluctance to make cold calls (without an appointment)
- Lack of sales strategies for different accounts

SALES TREND

TRAINING SALESPEOPLE IN CUSTOMER-ORIENTED SELLING

Increasingly, marketers are seeking long-term partnerships with their customers. This phenomenon, called *relationship marketing,* was discussed in Chapter 6. It requires a skilled salesforce with a true customer orientation. According to Jim Cathcart, a well-known sales trainer, relationship marketing has spurred radical changes in sales training. Cathcart says that the new service-oriented, "get close to the customer" approach has caused the most notable change in sales training in decades.

The customer-oriented selling practiced by firms such as Ciba-Geigy, Digital Equipment, IBM, and Union Carbide requires that salespeople back away from old high-pressure methods. But salespeople in these companies are hardly passive in their sales approaches. They must be capable of eliciting a statement of needs from customers and of promptly responding to buyer requests for information and ideas for product applications.

The manager of Forum, one of the nation's largest training firms, reporting on 12 blue-chip companies in a variety of industries, identified customer-oriented selling as the key to each firm's success. She said that these firms make it "their business to know the companies, the industries, and what's happening in them." In fact, she suggested that customer-oriented selling could involve suggesting that a customer contact a competitive supplier rather than trying to force a fit with the buyer.

Source: Arthur Bragg, "Turning Salespeople Into Partners, *Sales and Marketing Management,* August 1986, 82.

- Failure to match call frequency with account potential
- Spending too much time with old customers
- Over-controlling the sales call
- Failure to respond to customer needs with related benefits
- Giving benefits before clarifying customer needs
- Ineffective handling of negative attitudes
- Failure to effectively confirm the sale.

This rather lengthy list of common shortcomings is remarkable in that proper training could erase these problems entirely. In fact, most formal sales training programs do spend a considerable amount of time on sales techniques. It appears that sales technique training is becoming more prevalent, as indicated in "Sales Trend: Training Salespeople in Customer-Oriented Selling."

Product Knowledge. Salespeople must have thorough **product knowledge** including the benefits, applications, competitive strengths, and limitations of the product. Product knowledge may need updating in the event of new-product development, product modification, product deletions, or the development of new applications for the product.

Generally speaking, product knowledge is the most frequently covered topic in sales training programs. As expected, the more complex the product or service, the higher the likelihood that detailed knowledge about the offering will be stressed in the training program.

Customer Knowledge. Sales training may include information relating to customer needs, buying motives, buying procedures, and personalities. Faced with situational and individual differences among customers, some firms use classification methods to categorize buyers according to personality and the buying situation. An example of different types of buyers and suggested sales training topics is presented in Exhibit 10.3

Competitive Knowledge. Salespeople must know competitive offerings in terms of strengths and weaknesses to effectively plan sales strategy and sales presentations and be able to respond effectively to customer questions and objections. This area is extremely important for salespeople who are new to the industry, as the competitor's salespeople may have years of experience and be quite knowledgeable. Further, customers may exploit a salesperson's lack of competitive knowledge to negotiate terms of sale that may be costly to the selling firm. For example, salespeople who are not familiar with a competitor's price structure may unnecessarily reduce their own price to make a sale, thereby sacrificing more revenue and profits than they should have.

Time and Territory Management. The quest for an optimal balance between salesforce output and salesforce expenditures is a perennial objective for most sales managers. For this reason, training in time and territory management (TTM), introduced in Chapter 3 of this text, is often included in formal sales training programs. Essentially, the purpose of TTM training is to teach salespeople how to use time and efforts for maximum work efficiency.

TTM training is important for all sales organizations, but especially for those in declining or stagnant industries or highly competitive industries. In such situations, salespeople are often overworked, and there comes a point when working harder to improve results is not realistic. Such circumstances call for "working smarter, not harder," an idea that is receiving considerable discussion in sales management circles.[26]

Ethical and Legal Issues. Ethical and legal issues are being included in sales training programs more frequently than in the past. One catalyst for this change has been product-liability litigation that has awarded multimillion-dollar judgments to plaintiffs who have suffered as a result of unsafe products. Research has found that salespeople face a number of ethical and legal dilemmas on the job, and that salespeople want more direction from their managers on how to handle such dilemmas.[27]

Training in the legal area is extremely difficult, since laws are sometimes confusing and subject to multiple interpretations. Training salespeople in ethics is even

Exhibit 10.3 **Sales Training for Different Types of Buyers**

Kind of Buyer	Sales Training Topic
1. The Hard Bargainer (a difficult person to deal with)	1. Teach psychologically-oriented sales strategies (such as transactional analysis). 2. Teach sales *negotiation* strategies (such as the use of different bases of power) 3. Teach listening skills and the benefits of listening to the prospect. 4. Emphasize how to handle objections. 5. Emphasize *competitive* product knowledge.
2. The Sales Job Facilitator (attempts to make the sales transaction go smoothly)	1. Teach importance of a *quid pro quo.* 2. Communicate advantages of having a satisfied customer base. 3. Show how customers can assist salespeople (e.g., by pooling orders, providing leads).
3. The Straight Shooter (behaves with integrity and propriety)	1. Teach importance of selling the "substance" of the product offering and not just the "sizzle." 2. Teach straightforward techniques of handling objections (e.g., a direct denial approach).
4. The Socializer (enjoys personal interaction with salespeople)	1. Communicate company policy information about giving gifts and entertaining and socializing with customers. 2. Discuss ethical and legal implications of transacting business. 3. Emphasize importance of salespeople maintaining an appropriate balance between socializing with customers and performing job responsibilities.
5. The Persuader (attempts to "market" his or her company)	1. Communicate importance of qualifying prospects. 2. Teach techniques for qualifying customers.
6. The Considerate (shows compassion for salesperson)	1. Communicate importance of obtaining market information from customers. 2. Teach importance of a *quid pro quo.*

Source: Alan J. Dubinsky and Thomas N. Ingram, "A Classification of Industrial Buyers: Implications For Sales Training, *Journal of Personal Selling and Sales Management* 2 (Fall–Winter 1981–1982): 49.

more difficult, as ethical issues are often "gray," not black or white. Companies who address ethics and legal issues in their sales training programs usually rely on straightforward guidelines that avoid complexity. Salespeople are given basic training on applicable legal dimensions and advised simply to tell the truth and seek management assistance should problems arise. This may sound simplistic, but such training can greatly reduce salesperson conflict on the job, help develop profitable long-term

Exhibit 10.4 Example Items from General Dynamics Code of Ethics

1. If it becomes clear that the company must engage in unethical or illegal activity to win a contract, that business will not be further pursued.
2. All information provided relative to products or services should be clear and concise.
3. Receiving or soliciting gifts, entertainment, or anything else of value is expressly prohibited.
4. In countries where common practice might indicate conduct lower than that to which General Dynamics aspires, salespeople will follow the company's standards.
5. Under no circumstance may an employee give anything to a customer's representative in an effort to influence him.

Source: Arthur Bragg, "Ethics in Selling, Honest!" *Sales and Marketing Management,* May 1987, 44.

Exhibit 10.5 Legal Reminders for Salespeople

1. Use factual data rather than general statements of praise during the sales presentation. Avoid misrepresentation.
2. Thoroughly educate customers before the sale on the product's specifications, capabilities, and limitations.
3. Do not overstep authority, as the salesperson's actions can be binding to the selling firm.
4. Avoid discussing these topics with competitors: prices, profit margins, discounts, terms of sale, bids or intent to bid, sales territories or markets to be served, rejection or termination of customers.
5. Do not use one product as bait for selling another product.
6. Do not try to force the customer to buy only from your organization.
7. Offer the same price and support to all buyers who purchase under the same set of circumstances.
8. Do not tamper with a competitor's product.
9. Do not disparage a competitor's product without specific evidence of your contentions.
10. Avoid promises that will be difficult or impossible to honor.

relationships with customers, and reduce the liability of the salesperson and the organization.

Interestingly, some of the stronger ethical and legal training programs are being conducted in firms that previously engaged in some unethical and illegal sales methods. One such firm is General Dynamics, which was charged with overbilling the government on defense contracts but now has a 20-page code of ethics telling salespeople how to conduct themselves.[28] Examples from this code of ethics are shown in Exhibit 10.4.

The legal framework for personal selling is quite extensive. Some of the key components of this framework are antitrust legislation, contract law, local ordinances governing sales practices, and guidelines issued by the Federal Trade Commission dealing with unfair trade practices. A partial listing of important legal reminders that should be included in a sales training program is shown in Exhibit 10.5.

Set Training Objectives

Having assessed the needs for sales training, the sales manager moves to the next step in the sales training model shown in Figure 10.2: setting specific **sales training objectives**. Since training needs vary from one sales organization to the next, so do the objectives. In general, however, one or more of the following are included:

1. Increase sales or profits.
2. Create positive attitudes and improve salesforce morale.
3. Assist in salesforce socialization.
4. Reduce role conflict and ambiguity.
5. Introduce new products, markets, and promotional programs.
6. Develop salespeople for future management positions.
7. Ensure awareness of ethical and legal responsibilities.
8. Teach administrative procedures (i.e., expense accounts, call reports).
9. Ensure competence in the use of sales and sales support tools such as portable computers.
10. Minimize salesforce turnover rate.
11. Prepare new salespeople for assignment to a sales territory.

These objectives are interrelated. For example, if salespeople gain competence in the use of a new sales tool, sales and profit may improve, salesforce morale may be positively affected, and other beneficial outcomes may occur. By setting objectives for sales training, the manager avoids the wasteful practice of training simply for training's sake. Further, objectives force the sales manager to define the reasonable expectations of sales training rather than to view training as a quick-fix panacea for all the problems faced by the salesforce. Additional benefits of setting objectives for sales training are[29]

- Written objectives become a good communications vehicle to inform the salesforce and other interested parties about upcoming training.
- Top management is responsive to well-written, specific objectives and may be more willing to provide budget support for the training.
- Specific training objectives provide a standard for measuring the effectiveness of training.
- By setting objectives, the sales manager finds it easier to prioritize various training needs, and the proper sequence of training becomes more apparent.

Evaluate Training Alternatives

In the third step of the sales training process, the sales manager considers various approaches for accomplishing the objectives of training. Certainly many more alternatives exist today than in the past, thanks to technologies such as computer-assisted instruction, videotape, and videotext. The number of sales training professionals for hire also seems to be increasing, or perhaps such trainers are just doing a better job of promoting their services. Even a casual examination of a typical shopping mall bookstore will reveal a number of titles related to building sales skills, along with audiotapes and videotapes on the subject.

Critiquing all these alternatives is a monumental job, so it is recommended that fairly stringent criteria be established for preliminary screening, including cost, location of the training, flexibility of prepackaged materials, opportunity for reinforcement training, and time required to implement an alternative.

The evaluation of alternatives for training inevitably leads to three key questions. First, who will conduct the training? An answer to this question will require the consideration of internal (within the company) and external (outside the company) trainers. The second question deals with location for the training. Sales training may be conducted in the field, in the office, at a central training location, hotels and conference centers, or other locations. The third question is, which method (or methods) and media are best suited for conducting the training?

Selecting Sales Trainers. In general, companies rely most heavily on their own personnel to conduct sales training. In this endeavor, the sales manager is the most important **sales trainer**. Senior salespeople are also frequently involved as trainers. In larger companies, a full-time sales trainer is often available. According to surveys of training practices, only a small percentage of firms use outside training consultants, and these are primarily larger firms.[30]

What factors lead to the dominance of internal sources in sales training? First, and perhaps most importantly, sales managers and senior salespeople are intimately aware of job requirements and can communicate in very specific terms to the sales trainee. On the other hand, outside consultants may be only superficially informed about a specific sales job, and frequently offer generic sales training packages. Second, sales managers are the logical source for training to be conducted in the field, where valuable learning can occur with each sales call. It is extremely difficult to turn field training over to external trainers. Finally, using internal trainers simplifies control and coordination tasks. It is easier for sales managers to control the content of the program, coordinate training for maximum impact, and provide continuity for the program when it is the sales manager who does the training or who designates other company personnel to do the training.

At some point, a sales manager's effectiveness may be improved by using external trainers. Internal resources, including time, expertise, facilities, and personnel may be insufficient to accomplish the objectives of the sales training program. Also, outside trainers might be looked to for new ideas and methods. One sales manager who strongly supports the use of external trainers is Sherry Collins, sales manager of radio station KSLM/KSKD in Salem, Oregon. Referring to sales consultants, she says, "If you don't use them, you can't sell to your full potential . . . it's somebody else giving them some excitement, some proof that radio sales are OK; that radio is a great

INTERNATIONAL SALES

CONDUCTING SALES TRAINING

Melvin Kallett, manager of marketing education of the Dresser Leadership Center in Dallas, has trained salespeople in England, Belgium, Switzerland, and Brazil. He finds the salespeople in foreign countries to be eager to learn, and more receptive and appreciative of sales training than salespeople in the United States. However, he also finds that foreign salespeople are sometimes skeptical, and even hostile, to his group, feeling that, as Americans, Kallett and his co-workers may be trying to impose their cultural views and values on their non-American audience.

Sales training in the uncertain international arena requires thorough preparation aimed at reducing culture shock and building the credibility of the trainers. For example, translators may be necessary. Kallett uses two translators who work from a specially equipped soundproof booth to provide simultaneous translation during the training sessions. The translation task is so demanding that translators alternate in 20-minute shifts. Translators can also help trainers become acquainted with local customs and help them avoid blunders. In Brazil, for example, a gesture that signals "okay" in the United States is considered obscene.

Mr. Kallett also likes to spend a day or two in the field, observing salespeople, before conducting training in a foreign country. He looks for differences in the sales practices in different countries, knowledge of which further builds his credibility as a trainer.

Source: Melvin W. Kallett, "Conducting International Sales Training," *Training and Development Journal* 35 (November 1981): 30–33.

medium."[31] The use of an external sales trainer is illustrated in "International Sales: Conducting Sales Training."

Evaluating Sales Training Locations. As shown in Figure 10.3, the large majority of sales training is conducted in home, regional, or field offices of the sales organization. Manufacturing plants are also popular training sites, and some firms use non-company sites such as hotels or conference centers to conduct training.

Central training facilities are another possibility, used extensively by Xerox, IBM, General Electric, Armstrong World Industries, and scores of other large firms. The manager of General Electric's training facility in New York says, "Hotels tend to be set up for banquets and weddings and rah-rah sales meetings where people are just geared up for a big party."[32] In contrast, central training facilities can focus on learning in a controlled environment.

As video broadcasting and teleconferencing becomes more prevalent, many firms are enjoying some of the benefits of a centralized training facility without incurring the travel costs and lost time to transport the salesforce to and from training. Field offices arrange for video hook-up, either in-house or at video equipped conference hotels, and trainees across the country share simultaneously in training emanating

Figure 10.3 **Sites Most Frequently Used for Sales Training**

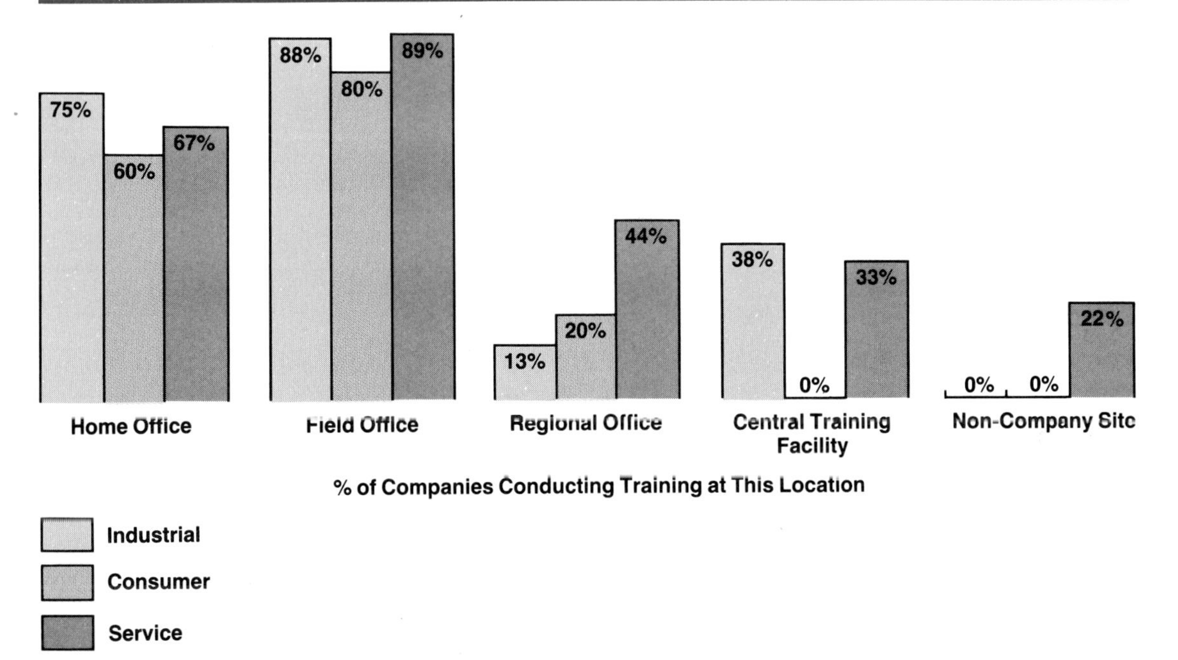

Most sales training is conducted in company facilities. The field office is the most popular location for sales training, followed by the home office.

Source: "Survey of Selling Costs," *Sales and Marketing Management*, February 22, 1988, 49.

from a central location. Training with broadcast technology is also available from sales training consultants, as described in "Sales Technology: Sales Training via Satellite."

Selecting Sales Training Methods. A variety of methods can be selected to fit the training situation. Indeed, the use of multiple methods is encouraged over the course of a training program to help maintain trainee attention and enhance the learning experience. There are four categories of training methods: classroom/conference, on-the-job, behavioral simulations, and absorption.

Classroom/Conference Training. The classroom or conference setting features lectures, demonstrations, and group discussion with expert trainers serving as instructors. This method is frequently used for training on basic product knowledge, new-product introductions, administrative procedures, and legal and ethical issues in personal selling. The format often resembles a college classroom, with regularly

SALES TECHNOLOGY

SALES TRAINING VIA SATELLITE

As competitive activity in the automotive market continues to intensify, dealers are searching for better ways to train their salespeople. Sales training on the local level can be supplemented by training from the Automotive Satellite Television Network (ASTN), a subscription broadcast service aimed at the country's 22,000 independent dealers. ASTN is the first business-to-business television network, and it provides training on a daily basis to its subscribers.

Dealers accustomed to spending $300 to $400 per salesperson for training seminars have been fast to sign up for ASTN's programming, which costs the dealer $385 per month. According to ASTN founder and Dallas car dealer Carl Wescott, "We're not teaching tricks or gimmicks; we're raising the level of salespeople's professionalism so they can make a career of this. Understand that at your typical dealership, 50 percent of the salesforce wasn't there the year before. And our fee is lunch money when you're talking monthly operating budgets of $150,000 and up. If we help you sell one more car per month, we're worth it."

ASTN has negotiated a deal with General Motors to provide specialized training for its dealers. There is a possibility that Mr. Wescott will expand the video training concept to other industries, such as the hotel industry.

Source: "Automatic Transmission," *INC.*, January 1987, 11.

scheduled exams and overnight homework assignments. In addition to using internal facilities and personnel, some companies send their salespeople to seminars sponsored by the American Management Association, American Marketing Association, Sales and Marketing Executives International, and local colleges and universities. These organizations offer training on practically any phase of selling and sales management, and there is even a graduate school of sales management co-sponsored by Syracuse University and Sales and Marketing Executives International.

On-The-Job Training. In the final analysis, salespeople can only be taught so much about selling without actually experiencing it. Consequently, **on-the-job training (OJT)** is extremely important. OJT puts the trainee into actual work circumstances, under the observant (it is hoped) eye of a supportive mentor or sales manager. Other OJT methods approximate a "sink or swim" philosophy, and often produce disastrous results when the trainee is overwhelmed with unfamiliar job requirements.

Common OJT assignments include the trainee filling in for a vacationing salesperson, working with a senior salesperson/mentor, working with a sales manager who acts as a "coach," and job rotation. When senior salespeople act as mentors, they too are undergoing continual training as their ideas and methods are reassessed, and sometimes refined, with each trainee. The sales manager's role as *coach* will be discussed in a later chapter on supervision and leadership of the salesforce. **Job rotation**, the exposure of different jobs to the sales trainee, may involve stints as customer service representatives, distribution clerks, or perhaps other sales positions. Job rotation is frequently used to groom salespeople for management positions.

Behavioral Simulations. Methods that focus on behavioral learning by means of business games and simulations, case studies, and role playing, where trainees portray a specified role in a staged situation, are called **behavioral simulations**. They focus on defining desirable behavior or in correcting behavioral mistakes.

An example of a business game for salespeople has been developed by Management Campus, Inc., in Atlanta. The game uses a "day in the life of a salesperson" approach to teach salespeople to develop selling strategies and skills. Salespeople compete with each other on prospecting, routing, and how well they execute necessary sales tasks.[33] Another game, in this case featuring product knowledge, is being used by Chase Manhattan Bank, BMW's Motorcycle Division, Caterpillar, and Ford's Heavy Truck Division. The competitive nature of this game is intended to generate the kind of enthusiasm for learning that was reported by a winner from Caterpillar, who said the game "forced me not only to read about the technical aspects of the Caterpillar engines, but to study and learn that material thoroughly. All of us who entered the competition had absolutely no idea of how really good a product we had to sell."[34]

Along with OJT, **role playing** is extremely popular for teaching sales techniques. Typically, one trainee plays the role of the salesperson, and another trainee acts as the buyer. The role playing is videotaped or performed live for a group of observers who then critique the performance. This can be an extremely effective means of teaching personal selling, without the risk of a poor performance in the presence of a live customer. It is most effective when promptly critiqued with emphasis on the positive points of the performance as well as suggestions for improvement. A good way to maximize the benefits of the critique is to have the person who has played the role of the salesperson offer opinions first and then solicit opinions from observers. After role playing, the "salesperson" is usually quite modest about his or her performance, and the comments from observers may bolster this individual's self-confidence. In turn, future performance may be improved.[35]

Absorption Training. As the name implies, **absorption training** involves furnishing trainees or salespeople with materials that they peruse (or "absorb") without opportunity for immediate feedback and questioning. Product manuals, direction-laden memoranda, and sales bulletins are used in absorption training. This method is most useful as a supplement to update salesforce knowledge, reinforce previous training, or to introduce basic materials to be covered in more detail at a later date.

Selecting Sales Training Media. Communications and computer technology have expanded the range of sales training media dramatically in the past decade. Sales trainers warn against the tendency to be overly impressed with the glamorous aspects of such training media, but they agree that it is advisable to evaluate new media on a continual basis to see if it should be incorporated into the sales training program. The most promising new media are found at the communications/computer technology interface.

An example of how video technology can improve sales training comes from Medtronics, Inc., manufacturer of a prosthetic heart valve. Videotape of live surgery using the valve is used as a training film, replacing printed materials as the preferred training medium. Noting that live surgery cannot be conducted on a sales call, the training film is also promoted as an effective adjunct to the sales presentation to doctors.[36]

Computer and communications equipment are combined for training purposes in the Simulation System Trainer developed by Performax, Inc. This system features a personal computer, videodisc player, videotape camera and recorder, video monitor, equipment interfaces, and computer programs that enable the trainee to "talk" to a customer on the screen. Realistic dialogues are accomplished, and the trainee has the opportunity to analyze the outcomes of sales behaviors and improve presentation skills.[37]

There is also a growing supply of sales training software available for a few hundred dollars per program or less. Programs cover time and territory management, sales analysis, and the entire sales process. Popular programs include the Sales Edge and Sell! Sell! Sell![38]

Design Sales Training Program

The fourth step in the sales training process is a culmination of, and condensation of, the first three steps shown in Figure 10.2. Working toward selected objectives based on needs assessment, and having evaluated training alternatives, the sales manager now commits resources to the training to be accomplished. At this point in the process, sales managers may have to seek budget approval from upper management.

In this step of designing the training program, the necessary responses to what, when, where, and how questions are finalized. Training is scheduled, travel arrangements made, media selected, speakers hired, and countless other details attended to. Certainly this can be the most tedious part of the sales training process, but attention to detail is necessary to ensure successful implementation of the process.

Perform Sales Training

The fifth step in the process, actually performing the training, may only take a fraction of the time required by the previous steps. This is particulary true in better sales training programs. As the training is being conducted, the sales manager's primary responsibility is to monitor the progress of the trainees and to ensure adequate presentation of the training topics. In particular, sales managers should assess the clarity of training materials. It is also recommended that some assessment of the trainees' continuing motivation to learn be made. Feedback from the trainees might be solicited on everything from the effectiveness of external trainers to the adequacy of the physical training site.

Exhibit 10.6 **Sales Training Evaluation Practices In Large Companies**

Types/Methods	Percentage Using This Method
Trainee Reaction	
Written critique: content	77%
Written critique: methods	63%
Written critique: trainers	66%
Discussion of training program	46%
Knowledge	
Testing	55%
Behavior	
Field evaluation: attitude	35%
Results	
Field evaluation: performance	73%

* Multiple responses were allowed.

Source: Earl D. Honeycutt Jr., Clyde E. Harris, Jr., and Stephen B. Castleberry, "Sales Training: A Status Report," *Training and Development Journal,* May 1987, 44.

Conduct Follow-up and Evaluation

It is always difficult to measure the effectiveness of sales training. This is a long-standing problem, due in some cases to a lack of clearly stated sales training objectives. Even with clearly stated objectives, however, it is hard to determine which future performance variations are a result of sales training. Other factors such as motivation, role perceptions, and environmental factors may affect performance more or less than training in different situations.

Although scientific precision cannot be hoped for, a reasonable attempt must be nevertheless made to assess whether current training expenditures are worthwhile and whether future modification is warranted. Evaluations can be made before, during, and after the training occurs.[39] For example, the pre-training evaluation might include an exam for sales trainees to assess their level of knowledge, corroborate or deny the need for training, and further define the objectives of the training. As suggested earlier, training can be evaluated while it is being conducted, and adjustments may be made at any point in the delivery of training. Post-training evaluations might include reactions or critiques of the trainees, "final exams," retention exams at later dates, observations by sales managers as they work in the field with salespeople, and in some cases an examination of actual performance indicators such as sales volume. Exhibit 10.6 summarizes the sales training evaluation practices of 155 large companies.

An interesting case dealing with the measurement of the effectiveness of sales training is provided in the life insurance industry. Graduates from a seminar sponsored by the School of Life Insurance Marketing reported increased sales of more than 40 percent nine weeks after completing the seminar. Three years later, this same group exhibited significantly lower turnover rates than life insurance industry averages.[40] Did this mean the training was a success? While it would be difficult to prove conclusively that training alone produced these outcomes, most managers would agree that unless the training in this case was prohibitively expensive, it proved itself worthwhile.

In essence, this thinking pervades this entire chapter. A reasonable approach to sales training is to ensure that it is not prohibitively expensive by carefully assessing training needs, setting objectives and evaluating training alternatives before designing the training program and performing the training. Further, the sales training process is incomplete without evaluation and follow-up.

SUMMARY

1. **Explain the importance of sales training and the sales manager's role in sales training.** Most organizations have a continual need for sales training as a result of changing business conditions, the influx of new salespeople into the organization, and the need to reinforce previous training. Sizable investments in training are likely in larger companies, and those companies involved in high technology industries and highly competitive industries. The investment in sales training in service organizations lags behind the training investment in product firms but is growing at a faster rate that it is in product organizations. The sales manager has the overall responsibility for training the salesforce, although other people may also conduct sales training.
2. **Describe the sales training process as a series of six interrelated steps.** Figure 10.2 presents the sales training process in six steps: assess sales training needs, set training objectives, evaluate training alternatives, design sales training program, perform sales training, and conduct follow-up and evaluation. The time spent to perform sales training may be only a fraction of the time spent to complete the other steps in the process, especially in well-run sales organizations.
3. **Discuss five methods for assessing sales training needs and identify typical sales training needs.** Sales managers may assess needs through performance testing, observation, a salesforce survey, customer survey, or a job analysis. It is recommended that salesforce training needs be assessed in a proactive fashion; that is, needs should be assessed before performance problems occur rather than after problems occur. Typical sales training needs include orientation and socialization of the salesforce; product, customer, and competitive knowledge; sales techniques; time and territory management; and ethical and legal issues.
4. **Name some typical objectives of sales training programs, and explain how setting objectives for sales training is beneficial to sales managers.** The objec-

tives of sales training vary over time and across organizations, but they often include preparing sales trainees for assignment to a sales territory, improving a particular dimension of performance, aiding in the socialization process, or improving salesforce morale and motivation. By setting objectives, the sales manager can prioritize training, allocate resources consistent with priorities, communicate the purpose of the training to interested parties, and perhaps gain top management support for sales training.

5. **Identify the key issues in evaluating sales training alternatives.** The evaluation of alternatives is a search for an optimal balance between cost and effectiveness. One key issue is the selection of trainers, whether from outside the company (external) or inside the company (internal). Another is the potential location or locations for training. Still another important factor is the method or methods to use for various topics. Sales training methods include classroom/conference training, on-the-job training (OJT), behavioral simulations, and absorption training. The sales manager must also consider whether to use various sales training media such as printed material, videotape, and computer-assisted instruction.

Key Terms

- needs assessment
- salesforce audit
- performance testing
- salesforce survey
- customer survey
- initiation to task
- role definition
- product knowledge
- sales training objectives
- sales trainer
- central training facility
- on-the-job training (OJT)
- job rotation
- behavioral simulations
- role playing
- absorption training

Review Questions

1. What factors contribute to a general need for sales training?
2. What conditions would suggest a particularly strong need for sales training?
3. What are five methods of assessing sales training needs? Can each of these methods be used in either a proactive or reactive approach to determining training needs?
4. How is sales training related to recruiting and selecting salespeople? How can sales training contribute to salesforce socialization?
5. What are some of the important ethical and legal considerations that might be included in a sales training program?
6. How is the process of setting objectives for sales training beneficial to sales managers?
7. When the sales manager is evaluating sales training alternatives, what four areas should he or she consider?

8. When might external consultants be used in sales training?
9. Discuss four methods for delivering sales training.
10. What is the purpose of the follow-up and evaluation step in the sales training process? When should evaluation take place?

Application Exercises

1. Assume you are a sales manager for a large manufacturer of gasoline-powered portable generators and that your firm sells directly to building contractors. As part of the initial training program for 50 newly hired salespeople, you are planning a week-long session on product knowledge. The director of human resources in your firm has suggested that the effectiveness of the product-knowledge training be evaluated, and has asked you for suggestions on how this may be accomplished. She has suggested testing the trainees before and after the training, which would be a departure from past practices. Historically, new trainees have taken a "final exam" on product knowledge, but have not been tested prior to receiving product training. The director has also suggested experimenting with different training methods and media to try to determine which is most effective. What ideas do you have for evaluating the effectiveness of the product-knowledge training?
2. You are a sales manager for a regional distributor of fresh and frozen seafood. You have a salesforce of eight people, none of whom have ever had formal training on sales techniques. Recently you have been contacted by several sales training consultants who offer a variety of printed materials, videocassettes, seminars, and software for training salespeople in sales techniques. You are considering whether or not to give your salespeople formal training on sales techniques. To help guide your efforts, develop a list of questions to ask each of the consultants about their offerings.
3. Visit the business section of an off-campus bookstore and locate the paperback books on selling. Select one of the books, read it, and answer the following questions:
   a. How effective do you think the book would be in teaching a novice how to sell?
   b. Does the book suggest any ethically questionable sales techniques? If so, cite examples.
   c. How could the book be incorporated into a formalized sales training program for professional salespeople?
4. Refer to Exhibit 10.2, which suggests different types of sales techniques for different customer personality types. Companies who use this approach train their salespeople to observe their customer's office, dress, verbal and nonverbal behavior, and the content of their communications for the purpose of classifying them as one personality type or another. Once the customer has been classified, the salesperson proceeds with predetermined sales tactics. What are the benefits of such training? What are its shortcomings and potential problems?
5. This chapter presented four sales training methods: classroom/conference, on-the-job, behavioral simulations, and absorption. Which methods would you recommend for each of the following training needs?
   a. To communicate a change in the company's pricing strategy.
   b. To give the salesforce refresher training in time and territory management.

c. To provide a historical overview of the company history to new sales trainees.
d. To acquaint the salesforce with ethical and legal responsibilities.
e. To teach salespeople how to use a personal computer for sales activity reporting.

Notes

[1] Jared F. Harrison, ed., *The Sales Manager as a Trainer,* (Orlando, Fl.: National Society of Sales Training Executives, 1983), vii.

[2] Lawrence Olson, "Training Trends: The Corporate View," *Training and Development Journal* 40 (September 1986): 33.

[3] Gilbert A. Churchill, Jr., Neil M. Ford, Steven W. Hartley, and Orville C. Walker, Jr., "The Determinants of Salesperson Performance: A Meta-Analysis," *Journal of Marketing Research* 22(May 1985): 117.

[4] Chris Lee, "Training Magazine's Industry Report 1987," *Training,* October 1987, 35.

[5] Alan J. Dubinsky and William A. Staples, "Sales Training: Salespeople's Preparedness and Managerial Implications," *Journal of Personal Selling and Sales Management* 2 (Fall-Winter 1981–1982): 29.

[6] "Salespeople Not Doing the Job?" *Sales and Marketing Management,* December 1986, 36.

[7] Efrem G. Mallach, "The Truth about Training for Computer Sales," *Training and Development Journal* 40 (November 1986): 59.

[8] William T. Finn, "Keep Your Eye on the Sales Training Manager," *Training and Development Journal* 38 (July 1984): 65.

[9] Earl Naumann, "Purchasing Training Programs," *Journal of Purchasing and Materials Management* 18 (Summer 1983): 21.

[10] "AT&T Makes a Second Stab at the Computer Market," *Business Week,* April 1, 1985, 92.

[11] Amy Dunkin, "Big Names Are Opening Doors for Avon," *Business Week,* June 1, 1987, 96.

[12] "GTC in a Brave New World," *Sales and Marketing Management,* April 2, 1984, 32.

[13] Olson, "Training Trends," 33.

[14] Charles M. Futrell, Leonard L. Berry, and Michael R. Bowers, "An Evaluation of Sales Training in the U.S. Banking Industry," *Journal of Personal Selling and Sales Management* 4 (November 1984): 46.

[15] William J. Birnes and Gary Markham, *Selling At the Top* (New York: Harper & Row, 1985), 24.

[16] "Survey of Selling Costs," *Sales and Marketing Management,* February 22, 1988, 49.

[17] Gordon, Where the Training Goes," 49.

[18] "Survey of Selling Costs," 62.

[19] Jack Cohen, "Old-Style Sales Management No Longer Works in A Contemporary, Market-Driven Corporate Culture," *Marketing News*, February 15, 1985, 6.

[20] "Creating Sales," *Personal Selling Power,* January-February, 1982, 1.

[21] See: Alan J. Dubinsky and Richard W. Hansen, "The Sales Force Management Audit," *California Management Review* 24 (Winter 1981): 86–95; and Harrison, *The Sales Manager as a Trainer,* 9–10.

[22] Dubinsky and Hansen, "The Sales Force Management Audit," 86.

[23] Alan J. Dubinsky, Roy D. Howell, Thomas N. Ingram, and Danny N. Bellenger, "Salesforce Socialization," *Journal of Marketing* 50 (October 1986): 195.

[24] Thayer C. Taylor, "Apple-Polishing the Dealer," *Sales and Marketing Management,* September 10, 1984, 50.

[25] See Ron Zemke, "What Sales Managers Say about Their Training and Development Needs," *Training/HRD* 16 (March 1979); and Mike Radick, "Training Salespeople to Get Success on Their Side," *Sales and Marketing Management,* August 15, 1983, 63–65.

[26] Harish Sujan, "Smarter versus Harder: An Exploratory Attributional Analysis of Salespeople's Motivation," *Journal of Marketing Research* 23 (February 1986): 41–49.

[27] Alan J. Dubinsky and Thomas N. Ingram, "Correlates of Salespeople's Ethical Conflict," *Journal of Business Ethics* 3 (1984): 343–353.

[28] Arthur Bragg, "Ethics in Selling, Honest!" *Sales and Marketing Management,* May, 1987, 44.

[29] Harrison, *The Sales Manager as a Trainer,* 7.

[30] See Gordon, "Where the Training Goes," 50; and Dubinsky and Barry, "A Survey of Sales Management Practices," 137.

[31] William H. Dunlap, "Does Radio Need Sales Consultants?" *Sound Management,* September, 1985, 8.

[32] Mary Williams Walsh, "Company-Built Retreats Reflect Firms' Cultures and Personalities," *Wall Street Journal*, August 16, 1984, 25.

[33] "Learning Sales Tactics Is Like Playing a Game," *Marketing News,* May 23, 1986, 9.

[34] Christopher Payne-Taylor and Henry G. Berszinn, "Sales Reps Win with Product Knowledge," *Marketing News,* May 8, 1987, 9–10.

[35] For an application of role playing in sales training, see Larry J. B. Robinson, "Role Playing as a Sales Training Tool," *Harvard Business Review* 65 (May-June 1987): 34–35.

[36] "Videos Assist in Medical Product Sales, Training," *Marketing News,* October 10, 1986, 14.

[37] "Training System Lets Sales Rep Talk Back to the Customer," *Marketing News,* February 27, 1987, 10; and Al Urbanski, "Electronic Training May Be in Your Future," *Sales and Marketing Management,* March 1988, 46–47.

[38] For reviews of these software packages, see Robert H. Collins, "Sales Training: A Microcomputer-Based Approach," *Journal of Personal Selling and Sales Management* 6 (May 1986): 71–76; and Robert H. Collins, "Artificial Intelligence in Personal Selling," *Journal of Personal Selling and Sales Management* 4 (May 1984): 58–66.

[39] Jon M. Hawes, Stephen P. Huthchens, and William F. Crittenden, "Evaluating Corporate Sales Training Programs," *Training and Development Journal* 36 (November 1982), 44–49.

[40] Laura L'Herison, "Teaching the Sales Force to Fail," *Training and Development Journal* 35 (November 1981): 79.

Shaklee Corporation

Shaklee Corporation is the leading U.S. seller of vitamins and nutritional products, having achieved this position primarily because of its two-million member direct sales organization. Members of this "Shaklee Family" do not only sell Shaklee products: they live and breathe the whole Shaklee philosophy of good nutrition and health. The importance of the field sales force is recognized by Shaklee president, Gary Shansby, who boasts, "Many people from industry don't understand direct selling. Someone else could copy our products and our sales plan, but they couldn't copy our salespeople."

The company's only advertising is product ads in its monthly publication, *Shaklee Survey*. These ads are directed at its salespeople, who are continually reminded that they must use the products before they can sell them, since they cannot sell any products in which they do not believe. This emphasis on the sales force, making sure morale is high and the salespeople motivated, claims Shansby, has gotten Shaklee Corporation where it is today and will take it where it plans to be tomorrow: "What IBM is to computers, what General Motors is to cars, what Procter and Gamble is to soap, Shaklee will be to nutrition."

History of Shaklee

As a boy, Forrest Shaklee was fascinated by carnivals and touring shows. Intrigued by the audience appeal and the message of the touring sideshow artists, Shaklee took to heart the showmanship techniques he saw demonstrated, as well as the occasional wisdom he heard expounded. He soon became an assistant for some of these traveling showmen. There was "Professor" Santinelli, a well-known hypnotist, who frequently lectured Shaklee on the power of positive thinking: "What you think, you look; what you think, you do, what you think, you are." There was also the physical fitness and nutritionist "expert," Bernarr MacFadden, who toured the country entertaining audiences with awesome weightlifting feats and promoting his health magazine. Shaklee assisted in the feats of strength show by hoisting a hollow ball purportedly weighing 500 pounds.

Shaklee's philosophy of life, good mental and physical health, gradually crystallized, and he became convinced of the effectiveness of salesmanship and showman-

---

Exhibit 1 **Code of Ethics**

As a Shaklee Distributor,

(1) I will operate by, and fully support, Shaklee's philosophy of doing business by the Golden Rule.

(2) I pledge not to misrepresent Shaklee products or the Shaklee Corporation. I will present products, information about the Sales Plan and the Shaklee Corporation in an honest, truthful and straightforward manner to my customers and to potential Shaklee Distributors.

(3) I will stand behind the Shaklee Corporation Unconditional Guarantee of product quality and performance and customer satisfaction. I will provide my customers with service reflecting the highest intent of the Golden Rule and Shaklee philosophy.

(4) I will strive to reflect the highest standards of integrity, honesty and responsibility in dealing with my customers and with other Shaklee Distributors.

(5) I will accept and carry out all responsibilities that come with my advancement to various levels of earned honorary rank.

(6) I recognize and support the efforts of the Direct Selling Association of America to establish, implement and maintain the highest standards and practices of truth in selling for all companies in the Personal Selling profession. Shaklee Corporation has been recognized as an active and supportive member of the national organization since 1964, helping to set the standards for the entire industry.

ship. Besides carnivals, Shaklee tried several other careers. He was a film distributor, an inventor, a chiropractor (who once had a Davenport, Iowa, parade in his honor featuring a fifty-foot replica of a human spine), and a lecturer (whose favorite topic was "Thoughtmanship"—"The trouble with most people is that they emulate the humble sheep . . . blah, blah").

During this time, Shaklee continued to develop his interest in nutrition; it grew as he noticed improvement in his own health by taking food supplements. Shaklee even claims to have cured himself of tuberculosis and terminal cancer by proper nutrition. As a chiropractor, he not only recommended food supplements to his patients, but also developed his own supplements. He soon discovered that he was spending more of his time developing his food supplements and emphasizing this part of his chiropractic business. In 1956, the sixty-two-year-old Shaklee, with his two sons, Forrest, Jr., and Raleigh, decided to form the Shaklee Corporation.

From the beginning, Shaklee planned to develop products that were designed to work "in cooperation with nature." This theme is carried through in Shaklee products today: household cleaning products that are biodegradable and nonpolluting, cosmetics and toiletries that are intended to promote healthy, attractive skin and hair, rather than follow fashion fads, and the vitamins and food supplements that use natural ingredients that are low in potency, as they are found in nature.

Another underlying principle of the Shaklee Corp. is "Dr." Shaklee's belief that a business should be based on the Golden Rule; the company still stresses integrity and fairness in the code of ethics which salespeople are expected to follow (see Exhibit 1). Company literature is sprinkled with sayings like, "An unselfish desire to help others is more effective than just a sales pitch."

Exhibit 2 Shaklee Corp. Income Statement

In thousands, except per share amounts

Year ended September 30	*1979*	*1980*	*1981*
Sales revenues	$314,149	$411,331	$454,522
Costs and expenses:			
Cost of goods sold	84,874	115,587	116,200
Volume incentives	131,410	171,540	189,569
Selling, general and administrative expenses	62,970	83,719	100,883
	279,254	370,846	406,652
Operating income	34,895	40,485	47,870
Other income (expense):			
Interest income	3,034	3,530	3,895
Interest expense	(545)	(3,218)	(2,208)
Provision for plant closings and discontinued products	—	(16,000)	(1,000)
Foreign exchange gains (losses)	(16)	163	(635)
Miscellaneous, net	(14)	(208)	(1,191)
	2,459	(15,733)	(1,139)
Income before income taxes	37,354	24,752	46,731
Provision for income taxes	16,066	12,681	22,188
Net income	21,288	12,071	24,543
Retained earnings, beginning of year	54,850	71,605	78,723
Cash dividends ($1.00, $.80 and $.74 per share)	(4,533)	(4,953)	(6,228)
Retained earnings, end of year	$ 71,605	$ 78,723	$ 97,038
Net income per share	$ 3.43	$ 1.92	$ 3.85

Source: Annual Reports

The Company

Shaklee Corporation has a long history of growth. In 1981 the company achieved sales of over $454 million, a 10 percent increase over 1980. Although domestic sales were up only 4 percent, international sales, primarily from Japan, were up 51 percent to $83.3 million. Income Statements and Balance Sheets are shown in Exhibits 2 and 3.

The president and chief operating officer of Shaklee is forty-four-year-old J. Gary Shansby. Before coming to Shaklee in 1976, Shansby was a senior officer and marketing consultant with Booz, Allen, and Hamilton, a consulting firm, and before that, he had been with Colgate-Palmolive, Clorox, and American Home Products. When he came to Shaklee, he was faced with declining profitability of the company, due primarily to the company's unsuccessful entry into the European market. He imme-

Exhibit 3 **Shaklee Corp. Balance Sheet**

	1977	*1978*	*1979*	*1980*	*1981*
Cash	$ 1.4	$ 4.8	$ 2.1	$ 7.0	$ 4.7
Short-term investments	53.4	9.2	24.2	19.4	21.6
Receivables	2.3	1.8	2.8	5.9	8.0
Inventories	25.7	42.6	32.6	42.9	51.3
Other	1.9	3.1	8.9	10.0	12.7
Total current assets	$ 84.8	$ 61.5	$ 70.6	$ 85.3	$ 98.3
Automobiles	$ 18.8	$26.5	$ 30.8	$27.9	$ 14.6
Machinery improvements and building	16.8	33.6	74.6	69.8	91.3
Gross plant	$ 35.6	$ 60.1	$105.3	$ 97.8	$108.0
Less depreciation	(8.9)	(12.6)	(17.6)	(15.5)	(19.5)
Net property, plant and equipment	$ 27.1	$ 47.5	$ 87.7	$ 82.3	$ 88.5
Land	0.4	0.4	1.9	1.6	2.0
Other	3.3	3.7	4.5	4.0	4.8
Total assets	$115.3	$113.0	$164.7	173.2	$191.7
Debt currently due	$ 5.6	$ 0.9	$ 8.8	—	—
Payables	7.3	5.2	10.9	12.4	10.6
Advance sales deposits	7.6	0.2	5.5	2.3	0.7
Accrued volume incentives	7.6	7.1	6.4	10.0	11.1
Accrued liabilities and taxes	21.1	16.3	17.5	28.2	28.9
Total current liabilities	$ 49.2	$ 29.6	$ 49.2	$ 52.9	$ 51.3
Long-term debt	$ 16.3	$ 14.9	$28.0	$ 22.6	$20.2
Deferred taxes	4.6	6.8	8.7	10.7	14.5
Common equity	45.2	61.7	78.9	87.0	105.6
Total liabilities and equity	$115.3	$113.0	$164.7	173.4	$191.7

Source: Annual Reports

diately consolidated European operations and took a foreign loss of $3 million for that year. Concentrating on the U.S. market, Shaklee's sales and profits rose in 1977, thanks to the huge demand for Shaklee's Instant Protein®, a meal replacement product that benefitted from widespread consumer interest in liquid protein diets.

About this time some pricing problems developed. Shaklee had always sold its products for a premium price, claiming that its "natural" vitamins were better than "synthetic" vitamins. In keeping with this pricing strategy, Shaklee's prices increased 35 percent between 1974 and 1977, with an increment of 10 percent posted in November, 1977 (unfortunately just as the company reported record profits). Discount health food stores, such as General Nutrition, were growing rapidly, and Shaklee distributors and customers began complaining about excessive prices. Morale of the sales force was dampened not only by the consumer price resistance, but also by

Shaklee's voluntary move to post all ingredients on its labels; this change divulged that certain formulations were not as completely natural as distributors and customers thought. While Shaklee remained a premium-priced, largely natural product, the concept of natural vitamins was being questioned. For example, the chairman of the American Institute of Nutrition's Committee on Public Information was quoted as saying that Shaklee's claims of superiority for its natural vitamins, as opposed to synthetic vitamins, were "pure drivel and utter nonsense." A further blow to field morale came in 1977, when the FDA issued an advisory opinion warning of the dangers of a liquid protein diet. In the wake of adverse publicity, Shaklee's sales of Instant Protein®, its largest seller, dropped 40 percent. After the initial panic, sales did improve over the next few years.

Shansby made several strategic decisions to correct some problems. He instituted a price freeze to be in effect for several years, even at the sacrifice of gross margins, so that the company could reestablish the price/value relationship for its products. He decided the company should have more modern, more centrally located manufacturing facilities; so, in 1980, it built a $50 million plant in Norman, Oklahoma. The 250,000 square foot facility enabled the company to produce its products at a much lower cost than it was able to do in its older and less efficient facilities in California. Also in April, 1981, Shaklee purchased a manufacturing plant in Fort Worth, Texas. With these two facilities, it can now manufacture over 90 percent of its own nutritional products and distribute all its products through the five field service centers located in various parts of the U.S. (see Exhibit 4).

Beginning in early 1978, Shansby brought several key executives into the company to strengthen the company's research, marketing, finance, budgeting, and forecasting.

James Scala, Vice President of Science and Technology, was previously a nutritionist with General Foods. He joined Shaklee in early 1978 to strengthen Shaklee's research effort, which at the time was primarily a quality control program. With a research budget now totaling $7 million, clinical testing was begun in an effort to better document product claims.

Robert Walter, Vice President of Operations had been with Heinz. He is in charge of operations for manufacturing and distribution and orchestrated the start-up of the Norman plant. He is now examining the five regional distribution centers to economize on shipping costs.

Allan Nagle, Senior Vice President, International, joined Shaklee from Brown & Williamson, and has been instrumental in developing the sales literature and marketing aids for each product. This was part of a concerted change in the nature of the selling message delivered by Shaklee distributors and leaders. No longer is the message an individualistic, emotional, and often personal product endorsement, but a more unified, scientifically-based message, with a well documented product benefit story.

Barry Roach, Chief Financial Officer, joined the company from McKinsey. He is improving the reporting of financial information from the field.

Exhibit 4 **Headquarters, Manufacturing Facilities, and Service Center Locations**

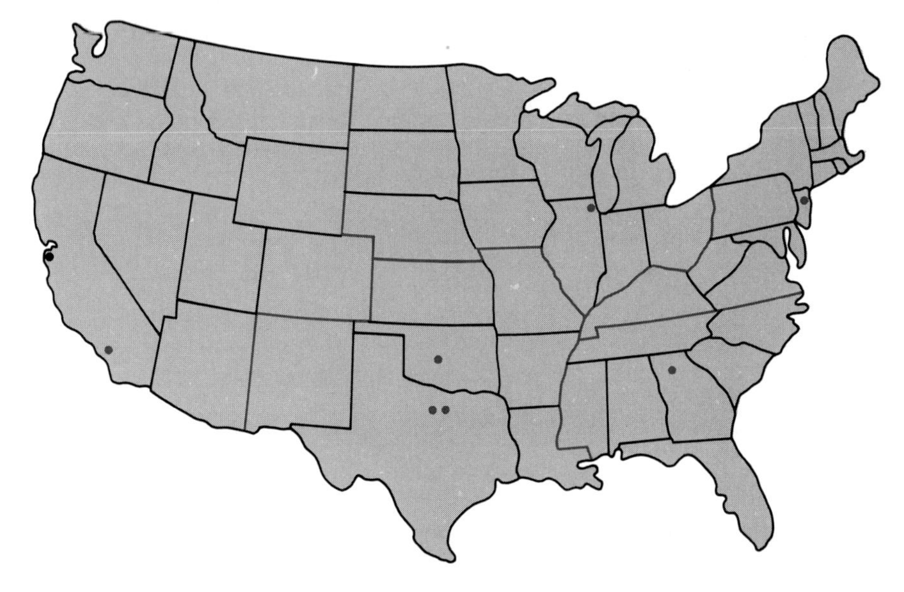

• **Headquarters**
San Francisco, California

• **Manufacturing Facilities**
Norman, Oklahoma
Ft. Worth, Texas

Region	• Field Service Center	Sales Leaders at September 30, 1981	% of 1981 Domestic Sales
Far West	La Palma, California	1,900	21.0%
North Central	Chicago, Illinois	3,200	31.1
South Central	Ft. Worth, Texas	1,800	15.4
Northeast	Dayton, New Jersey	1,900	19.1
Southeast	Atlanta, Georgia	1,400	13.4

Source: Shaklee Corporation 1981 Annual Report

Jack Wilder, Vice President, Sales, had previous experience at Mary Kay Cosmetics. He has restructured the sales organization to consist of five regional managers who interact with sales leaders and coordinators. Additionally, thirty to forty counselors handle service requests from distributors and sales leaders. He installed a computerized phone-ordering system in 1980 to expedite shipments to sales leaders, so that the order turnaround is now only one week. Sales promotion, conventions, and promotional planning are handled by about fifty people under his direction.

The Shaklee Customer

Shaklee Corp. has a unique situation in that its prime customer base consists of its more than 2 million distributors, or salespeople. Generally, these distributors buy for their family and one or two friends, finding that buying direct to eliminate the retail markup is desirable. It is estimated that 90 percent of all Shaklee sales are made in this manner.

According to company research, Shaklee customers, as well as distributors, tend to be highly educated, family-oriented, somewhat religious, and usually suburban. Their alcohol consumption is low and they watch a minimal amount of television. The company has also found that use of Shaklee products is frequently accompanied by a change in life style that includes greater emphasis on proper nutrition and increased exercise.

Current research studies by outside organizations indicate widespread interest in the U.S. in physical fitness and nutrition. For example, a Lou Harris public opinion poll conducted in 1978 revealed that 67 percent of Americans thought they would be healthier if they were more active physically. In that year, 90 million Americans (or 59 percent of those 18 years of age or older) participated in some form of regular exercise. Also, 93 percent of parents wanted their children to develop a deep concern about physical fitness.

As pointed out by a recent stock analysis of Shaklee Corporation, there are several other factors at work in society at this time that should encourage future consumer demand for nutritional products:

- As the U.S. population gets older, the demand for vitamins should increase. Children of the post-war baby boom are now in their early- to mid-thirties, and concerned about preserving their youth and active life styles.
- It is estimated that one of three Americans is overweight. Since weight control is a constant preoccupation for a large segment of the population, products such as Shaklee's Instant Protein® (a "meal replacement" product) should continue to be in great demand.
- It is estimated that one of three meals is consumed away from home. Because of this, and of the fact that snack foods often displace meals, there is concern about a possible lack of nutrition.
- There is a significant segment of the population that believes that vitamins generally promote health. Specifically, vitamins B, C, and E are desired by many who believe they can enhance their resistance to colds, promote their ability to withstand stress, and even aid their sexual function. Additional clincal research on the effectiveness of vitamins, as well as the circulation growth of such nutrition-related periodicals as *Prevention,* is expected to encourage this health-conscious trend.

Exhibit 5 **Major Vitamin Producers in the United States**

	Approximate 1980 Vitamin Sales
Shaklee	$230 million
General Nutrition	140 million
Miles Labs: "One a Day"	35 million
Ledoile: "Stress Tabs" and "Centrum"	30 million
Squibb's: "Theragram"	30 million

Competition

Shaklee's major competitor is General Nutrition, a retailer of vitamins and health foods, with 800 stores across the U.S. In 1980, General Nutrition had total sales of $242 million, of which approximately $140 million were vitamins and other nutrients (compared with Shaklee nutrition sales that year of $220 million). Typically, General Nutrition's strategy has been to discount vitamins, promote those discounts widely, and then improve its gross margin with higher margin impulse items such as health foods or personal care items. Shaklee executives feel that vitamins/food supplement sales of the company have been hurt somewhat by General Nutrition's discount pricing strategy. There are also approximately 5,000 independent health food stores in the U.S. These have not been as threatening to Shaklee since their focus is on personal service rather than price.

Exhibit 5 lists the leading vitamin producers in the U.S. It is expected that future manufacturing competition will come from smaller manufacturers such as Hudson and Richard Vicks; future competition may also come from such proprietary companies as Bristol Myers. Each of these companies have both substantial marketing skills and resources, and product experience in the food supplements or meal replacement market (e.g., Metrecal). Experts do not expect the major ethical drug companies to enter the vitamin market very heavily, since the profit margins on mainstream vitamins are not very high. However, there may be tougher competition for some of the higher-margin food supplement/vitamin lines like Shaklee's Sustained Release Vita-C.

Products

Shaklee sells three different product lines: nutritional products (twenty-four items), household products (nine items), and personal care products (twenty-two items). All Shaklee products are premium-priced. A list of these Shaklee products, along with prices for two of the lines, is shown in Exhibit 6.

In May, 1980, the company decided to reduce the number of household and personal care items to concentrate more heavily on nutritional products. The household line was cut from 13 products to 9, while reducing the number of stockkeeping units from 37 to 14. In personal care, the line was cut from 56 products to 22, while the number of stockkeeping units was reduced from 141 to 28. According to President Shansby, this change occurred to:

> refocus the company on nutritional products—the area we feel offers our Sales Leaders the greatest potential for growth. We planned this strategic direction in response to our Sales Leaders' desire to emphasize nutritional products in their individual businesses. Shaklee nutritional products are both door openers and business builders for our own independent distributors. Moreover, the higher turnover of the line helps Sales Leaders better manage their cash flows, thus further strengthening their businesses. The product line rationalization was, therefore, an important strategic advance for them—and, as a result, for us.

Relative breakdowns of sales for the different product lines over the past four years are shown in Exhibit 7.

Shaklee's nutritional products are primarily natural, packaged in glass or polystyrene, with all ingredients listed on the bottle. Among consumers, Shaklee has a reputation for product quality because of its use of natural ingredients, and the amount, variety, and balance of nutrients included in its products. Among many nutrition enthusiasts, Shaklee vitamins have a certain mystique because of their ingredient formulations. This has led to some belief that Shaklee products can even cure gout, cancer, diabetes, and many other diseases. With Shaklee's transition from an entrepreneurial company to a professionally managed company, and due to pressure from the Food & Drug Adminstration, the company has tried to tone down these claims by salespeople. In fact, company literature directed to its salespeople now warns: "For your own protection and for the integrity of the Shaklee name, NEVER make any claims for a product or recommend any product uses other than those specified in official Shaklee Corporation publications and literature." In spite of these warnings the mystique remains.

The company introduced eight new products in 1980 and five in 1981. A few of these are Sustained Release Vita-C™, Vita-E™ Tablets Plus selenium, Fiber Wafers, Instant Protein® Convenience Packs, Brown 'N Oats™ bar, and Fruit Bar.

Public Relations

Large corporations are traditionally prone to public relations problems and Shaklee is no exception. For example, the company recently was accused of using improper sterilization techniques on one of its products. In 1973 the company began treating its alfalfa tablets, which were prone to infection with salmonella bacteria, with ethylene oxide (ETO), a suspected carcinogen. Shaklee continued the treatments until

Exhibit 6 **Shaklee Products**

		Distributor Net Price
Nutritional Products	Vita-Lea Tablets, 240 or 480 tablets	$7.75-$14.40
	Vita-Lea Chewables, 125 or 250 tablets	5.95-11.30
	Liquid-Lea, 8 fluid oz.	5.20
	Instant Protein Drink Mix, regular & cocoa	7.95-15.00
	Instant Protein Convenience Pack, regular & cocoa	8.50
	Sustained Release Vita-C 500 mg. 70 or 180 tablets	3.95-9.40
	Chewable Vita-C 100mg. 100 or 500 tablets	3.60-15.40
	400 I.U. Vita-E Plus Selenium Tablets, 100 tablets	10.60
	400 I.U. Vita-E Capsules, 100 or 250 tablets	10.90-25.75
	Chewable 100 I.U. Vita-E Plus Selenium Tablets, 100 or 500 tablets	6.30-28.45
	100 I.U. Vita-E Capsules, 180 or 480 capsules	9.70-24.50
	B-Complex, 120 or 320 tablets	6.45-16.50
	Calcium Magnesium, 260 tablets	4.00
	Chewable Vita-Cal, 200 & 425 tablets	5.95-11.90
	Vita-Cal Plus Iron, 100 tablets	4.50
	Zinc, 130 tablets	3.10
	Alfalfa Tabs, 330 or 700 tablets	5.90-11.50
	Bran 'N Oats Bar	0.75
	Pro-Lecin Nibblers, 200 or 390	7.80-14.95
	Fiber Wafers, 120 wafers	5.00
	Energy Bar, cocoa & peanut	0.65
	Herb-Lax, 120 tablets	2.95
	Lecithin, 190 capsules	6.80
	Baking Enricher, 28 oz.	12.20
Personal Care Products	Meadow Blend Soap-Free Cleansing Bar	2.50
	New Concept Organic Dentifrice	1.85
	Desert Wind Deodorant	2.05

1977, when the company discontinued the ETO process and substituted an innovative technique that did not require ETO. In 1982 an investigative report in *The Wall Street Journal* made this information public, leading critics to charge "cover-up," since the company never notified anyone that the sterilization procedures involved the use of a suspected cancer-causing chemical. Shaklee responded, "ETO was a major process used in the mid-70s to sterilize products and is still being used in sterilization of medical devices and certain foods, particularly seasonings and botanicals." The company also claimed that it should be praised for its pioneering efforts in developing a safer sterilization procedure. Because of the importance of good relations with distributors and customers, Shaklee must successfully resolve similar problems that may occur.

Exhibit 6 *(continued)*

		Distributor Net Price
Personal Care Products	Foot Cream	$ 3.85
	Deodorant Cream	5.30
	Apricot Hand & Body Lotion	3.90
	Bath Essence	5.55
	Tioga Men's Skin Conditioner	6.45
	Deuvies Body Creme	6.45
	Proteinized Shampoo	3.10
	Arrange Hair Spray	3.50
	Rainsilk Shampoo, 8 fluid oz. or 1 gallon	3.10-30.20
	Rainsilk Clear Conditioning Rinse, 8 fluid oz. or 1 gallon	3.10-30.20
	Ester Droplets Replenishing Oil	7.80
	Under-Makeup Moisturizer	4.20
	Beauty Masque	4.75
	Cream Cleanser	4.05
	Lotion Cleanser	3.80
	Proteinized Cleanser	3.60
	Proteinized Velva Dew Moisturizer	5.55
	Fluid Foundation	3.25
	Gel Blush	3.25
Household Products	Basic H. quart, gallon or 5 gallons or 30 gallons	
	Basic L Laundry Concentrate, 10 or 21 lbs.	
	Liquid L Laundry Concentrate, gallon	
	Softer Than Soft Fabric Conditioner, gallon	
	Basic-I Heavy Duty Cleaner, quart or gallon	
	Basic-G Germicidal Cleaner	
	At-Ease Scouring Cleaner	
	Basic-D Automatic Dishwashing Concentrate	
	Satin Sheen Dishwashing Liquid	

Source: Salomon Brothers, Company analysis, May 26, 1981

Exhibit 7 **Shaklee Corporation Breakdown of Product Mix**

Product Line	1978	(% of sales revenues) 1979	1980	1981
Nutritional products	70%	68%	69%	76%
Household products	16%	17%	18%	16%
Personal care products	14%	15%	13%	8%

Source: Salomon Brothers. Company analysis, May 26, 1981

Exhibit 8 **Shaklee Corporation Selling Organization**

	Distributor	**Assistant Supervisor**
All who join the Shaklee Family begin as Distributors, sponsored by someone who is already a Distributor or Sales Leader. Distributors buy Shaklee products from the Sales Leader in this sponsorship group for resale to retail customers and for personal and family consumption. Although the Company suggests retail prices for its products, Distributors may sell at any price they wish. There are no territories or franchises; Shaklee Distributors in each country may sell anywhere in their country. In 1981, the Company received an average of over 2,000 Distributor applications every business day.	Each new Distributor purchases a New Distributor Kit for $12.50. Distributors have no minimum purchase requirements, and generally do not maintain significant amounts of inventory, relying on their Assistant Supervisor or Sales Leader to supply them with the products their customers order. Distributors may receive monthly cash bonuses from their Sales Leaders, based on the volume of products they purchase.	Distributors whose purchase volume reaches $1,000 per month may be appointed by their Sales Leaders as Assistant Supervisors. Although they do not buy directly from the Company, they often maintain some inventory to supply the Distributors in their groups, and assist their Sales Leader in training and motivating Distributors.

Selling Organization

The backbone of Shaklee Corporation is its selling organization. With an incentive-oriented compensation structure that is one of the most attractive in the direct selling industry, Shaklee's selling organization is critical to the company's success. Exhibit 8 summarizes each level in Shaklee's six-step pyramidal selling organization.

At the bottom of Shaklee's selling organization are the more than two million Shaklee distributors who pay a fee of $12.50 to purchase a New Distributor Kit, and which entitles them to buy Shaklee products for "distributor net," basically a wholesale price of approximately 25 to 30 percent less than suggested retail. When a distributor has achieved and maintained $1,000 in monthly sales (i.e., $735 distributor's net), he or she may be appointed assistant supervisor. This person still buys products from a member of the selling organization, rather than directly from the company.

The first significant jump in the organization comes when the distributor or assistant supervisor has attained a monthly sales volume of $3,000 (or $2,200 on distributor net sales). This person is then classified as a "sales leader," a term used for any of the top four levels in the organization. There are presently about 13,000 sales leaders in the organization. Each sales leader is able to purchase products directly from Shaklee, and also receives cash bonuses each month from the Company. Sales

Exhibit 8 (continued)

Supervisor 11,700*	Coordinator 1,000*	Key Coordinator 150*	Master Coordinator 75*
Distributors who demonstrate leadership abilities, and whose purchase volume reaches $3,000 per month, may be appointed by the Company as Supervisors, the first rank of Sales Leader. Supervisors buy directly from the Company, receive Shaklee cash bonuses, and may qualify for bonus cars and convention attendance. In addition, by sponsoring and training other Distributors who become Sales Leaders, they can earn special leadership bonuses.	Supervisors who in turn develop and maintain four Supervisors from Distributors in their own Sales Group may be designated as Coordinators, making them eligible for additional conventions, a Coordinator Bonus, and other recognition.	Key Coordinators are Coordinators who have developed, trained and maintained a minumum of nine Sales Leaders from Distributors in their Sales Group, making them eligible for more prestigious bonus cars and recognition from the company.	The highest sales rank in Shaklee is attained by developing a minimum of fifteen Sales Leaders. Master Coordinators receive top-of-the-line bonus cars and additional rewards, and recognition as guest speakers at conventions and as featured success stories in company publications.

Source: Shaklee Corporation 1981 Annual Report.
*approximate figures

leaders who maintain monthly purchase volume of $5,000 ($3,700 distribution net) for six months qualify for free use of a rental car. At the end of fiscal 1981, over 6,000 sales leaders were driving bonus cars, accounting for one of the largest corporate auto fleets in the country. There are twelve different car models available.

A beginning sales leader earns more than $10,000 a year; the typical sales leader, who may have one or more other sales leaders under him or her, earns about $14,000. To encourage development of new management, a sales leader receives 5 percent of the purchase volume of the sales leaders he or she develops, 2 percent of second-generation sales leaders' business, and 1 percent of third-generation sales leaders' business.

When a supervisor has developed four first-level supervisors, he or she may qualify for promotion to coordinator; there are approximately 1,000 coordinators, each earning approximately $50,000 annually. At the top of the selling organization are the key coordinators and master coordinators. These individuals earn over $100,000 annually; a handful are presently making over $400,000.

The potential for top earnings, accumulated primarily from bonuses or commissions, is a powerful motivating factor for people rising in the Shaklee selling organization. Additional motivational devices include the international and regional conferences and conventions, which were attended by over 60,000 people last year (at a cost to the company of over $10 million). Shaklee is convinced that company success depends on this selling organization. As stated in the company's *1981 Annual Report:*

> The distributors and Sales Leaders who are the Shaklee family share a common bond of interest in nutrition and health. It is an appreciation of the importance of high-quality nutritional products as part of an all-around self improvement program that motivates a person to become a Shaklee distributor.
>
> Because members of the Shaklee sales force are consumers first, it easy for them to share their enthusiasm for the products they trust. Shaklee distributors are not just out plugging some company's line of merchandise—they are telling people about products that have a place in their homes and in their lives. They share their personal commitment to health, and their appreciation for good nutrition. This sharing of products and information with relatives, friends and neighbors leads many distributors to develop their own individual business enterprises by participating in the Shaklee sales plan.
>
> Of the hundreds of thousands of Shaklee distributors, 12,900 have been appointed by the Company as Sales Leaders. These are individuals who have displayed leadership abilities and whose businesses have reached such a size that they are qualified to buy their products directly from the Company. Sales Leaders build their businesses by making Shaklee products available to a wider audience and by encouraging other consumers to become distributors. As enthusiasm about the products and the business opportunity spreads to more and more people, additional consumers become distributors and the sponsoring Sales Leaders' business sales volume expands.
>
> The Shaklee Sales Plan is truly democratic, allowing an individual to go as far as he or she wishes and is able. The Plan provides business-building incentives and benefits-cash bonuses, bonus cars, travel to conventions, and participation in insurance programs.
>
> But every successful Sales Leader from Supervisor to Master Coordinator must take the same steps. And each begins a Shaklee business the same way—as a consumer and distributor.
>
> As Sales Leaders build their businesses, our business will grow. We depend on the motivation, direction and hard work of our sales force to maintain our position as one of the world's leading nutritional products companies. While corporate staff and resources, R&D, and manufacturing and distribution efficiencies are important for our business, ultimately it is the individual in the field—the independent entrepreneur who is building a business—that is the foundation of the Shaklee Corporation.

Exhibit 9 **Four Direct Selling Companies—A Comparison of U.S. Operations**

	Avon	Tupperware	Mary Kay	Shaklee
Sales				
Retail (millions)	$1,950.0	$800	$303.0	$509
Factory (millions)	$1,170.0	$360	$151.5	$356
Factory as percent of retail	60%	45%	50%	70%
Sales force				
Number of salespeople	425,000 representatives	85,000 dealers	105,000 consultants	2 million distributors who are primarily consumers
Retail sales per salesperson	$4,600	$9,400	$2,900	$255
Factory sales per salesperson	2,900	$4,200	1,450	$178
Earnings per salesperson	$1,800	$3,300	$1,450	$77 in product savings
Commission	40% of retail sales	35% of retail sales	50% of retail sales	30% of retail sales

Source: Salomon Brothers, Company analysis, May 26,1981

A comparison of the Shaklee selling organization with that of three other leading direct selling companies is given in Exhibits 9 and 10.

The Future

Shaklee's long-term objective is to be "the world's leading nutritional products company." To accomplish this, the company wants to increase its international thrust, as Shaklee's long-term objective is to be "the world's leading nutritional products company." To accomplish this, the company wants to increase its international thrust, as well as continue to improve its domestic marketing efforts. Internationally, the company has been very cautious since its disastrous international results of the mid-1970s. It appears that some countries such as Japan and Canada are enthusiastic about nutritional products. However, in countries where confectionery consumption is high (such as England), concern about vitamins is lower. Less developed countries, such as Brazil, may be promising markets in the future since other direct-sale companies (such as Avon and Mary Kay) have been very successful here.

The primary concern at the moment for Shaklee executives is to improve the company's marketing efforts in the United States. They are particularly aware of the fact that growth for any direct selling company is largely a function of growth in the sales force—both the number of salespersons as well as the revenue per salesperson. It is this area of company operations that Shaklee executives feel can be most dramatically improved in the near future.

Exhibit 10 **Comparison of Sales Force Management**

	Avon	Tupperware	Mary Kay	Shaklee
First level				
Number of managers	2,800 district managers	8,000 managers	2,100 directors	10,100
Salespeople per manager	150	11	50	198
Retail sales per manager	$695,000	$100,000	$144,000	$50,400
Compensation	$15,000 salary + 3% of sales increase + leased car	3%–5% of retail sales or $4,000 + rental car worth $7,000 every 2 years.	12% of retail sales or $17,300 + avg. bonus of 3% of sales ($4,300) rental car worth $8,000 every 2 years.	22% of purchases volume + 5% of sales leaders he develops + 2% of second generation sales + 1% of third generation + rental car program $14,000 average
Second level				
Number of managers	159 division managers	365 distributors	21 national sales managers	1,000 coordinators with five sales leaders
Retail sales per manager	$12.2 million	$2.2 million	$14.4 million	$509,000
Compensation	$35,000	$80,000–$100,000 + net or 20% of retail sales less expenses	12%–15% of 1st-generation retail sales. Smaller percent of 2nd-generation retail sales. $14,000 avg.	$50,000
Duties	Supervise district managers	Purchase inventory and ship product to unit managers		
Third level				
Number of managers	7 national sales managers	12 regional vice presidents		200 coordinators
Compensation	$50,000 salary	$40,000—$60,000 salary-incentive		$100,000 plus

Source: Salomon Brothers, Company analysis, May 26, 1981.

Allied Food Distributors

In April 1987, Ms. Elizabeth Ramsey, the district sales manager for the upper Midwest district of Allied Food Distributors, was preparing to hire a new salesperson for the southwest Indiana sales territory. The current salesperson in this territory was leaving the company at the end of June. Ms. Ramsey had narrowed the list of potential candidates to three. She wondered which of these applicants she should select.

Company Background

Allied Food Distributors was one of the largest food wholesalers in the United States. The company carried hundreds of different packaged food items (fruits, vegetables, cake mixes, cookies, powdered soft drinks, and so on) for sales to supermarkets and grocery stores. Allied carried items in two different circumstances. First, some small food companies had Allied carry their entire line in all areas of the United States. Allied was in essence their sales force. Second, some large good companies had Allied carry their lines in less populated parts of the country. These areas were not large enough to sustain a salesperson for each food company.

Allied operated in all 50 states. The country was divided into 20 sales districts. Ms. Ramsey's sales district included Michigan, Indiana, and Illinois. Each district was divided into a number of sales territories. A salesperson was assigned to each territory.

The Southwest Indiana Territory

The sales territory for which Ms. Ramsey was seeking a salesperson was located in the southwest corner of Indiana. Exhibit 1 presents a map of the territory. It was bordered on the south by the Ohio River and the state of Kentucky, on the west by the Wabash River and the state of Illinois, and on the east by the Hoosier National Forest. The northern boundary ran a few miles north of Highways 50 and 150 that ran from Vincennes in the west through Washington to Shoals in the east. Evansville was the largest city in the area with a population of about 140,000. The salesperson for the territory was expected to live in Evansville, but would spend about three nights a week on the road. The only other reasonably large population concentration was in Vincennes with a population of about 20,000. Vincennes was located about 55 miles straight north of Evansville on Highway 41. Interstate Highway 64 ran the

---

Source: This case was written by Thomas C. Kinnear.

Exhibit 1 **A Map of the Southwest Indiana Territory**

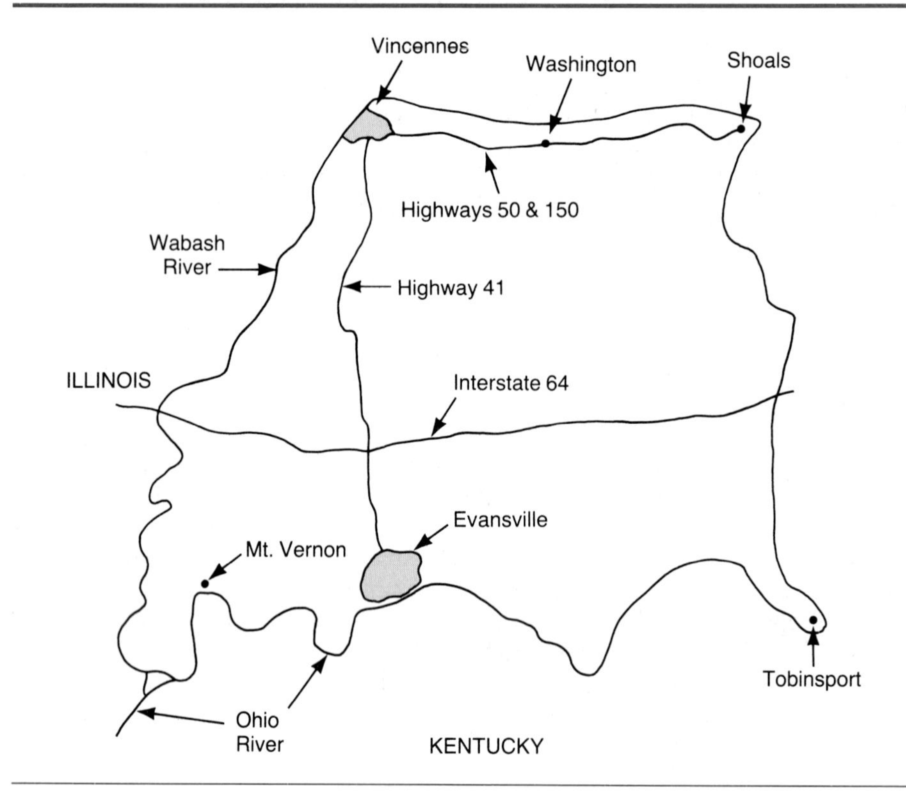

80 miles east-west through the territory about 15 miles north of Evansville. Evansville was 165 miles southwest of Indianapolis, 170 miles east of St. Louis, Missouri, and 115 miles southwest of Louisville, Kentucky. The territory was very rural in character with agriculture being the dominant industry. The terrain was quite hilly, with poor soil. As a result, the farms in the area tended to be economically weak. There were many small towns and villages located throughout this basically rural environment.

The Selling Task

Allied maintained 75 active retail accounts in the southwest Indiana territory. About 10 of these accounts were medium- to large-sized independent supermarkets located in Evansville and Vincennes. The rest of the accounts were small, independent general food stores located throughout the territory.

The salesperson was expected to call on these accounts about every three weeks. The salesperson's duties included: checking displays and inventory levels for items already carried, obtaining orders on these items, informing retailers about new items, attempting to gain sales orders on these items, setting up special displays, and generally servicing the retailers' needs. Often, the salesperson would check the level of inventory on an item, make out an order, and present it to the retailer to be signed. The salesperson generally knew the store owner on a first name basis. The ordered goods were sent directly to the retailer from a warehouse located in Indianapolis.

The Selection Process

The responsibility for recruiting salespersons for the territories within a district was given to the district sales manager. The process consisted of the following steps:

1. An advertisement for the job was placed in newspapers in the state in question.
2. Those responding to the ad were sent job application forms.
3. The returned application forms were examined and certain applicants were asked to come to the district sales office for a full day of interviews.
4. The selection was then made by the district sales manager, or all applicants were rejected and the process started again.

Training

Allied did all its salesperson training on the job. The salesperson on the territory to which a new person would be assigned was given the task of training. Basically, this involved having the new person travel the territory to meet the retailers and to be shown how to obtain and send in orders. The district sales manager usually assisted in this process by traveling with the new salesperson for a few days.

Compensation

The current salesperson on the southwest Indiana sales territory was earning a straight salary of about $37,000 per year plus fringe benefits. Ms. Ramsey indicated that she was willing to pay between $19,000 and $40,000 for a new person depending on the qualifications presented.

The Choices

On the basis of application forms and personal interviews, Ms. Ramsey had narrowed the field of applicants down to three. A summary of the information on their application forms along with the comments she had written to herself are contained in Exhibits 2, 3, and 4. She wondered which person she should select for the position.

Exhibit 2 **Information on Mr. Michael Gehringer**

Personal information

Born July 15, 1945; married; three children ages 14, 16, and 19; height 5 feet, 10 inches; weight 205; excellent health; born and raised in Indianapolis.

Education

High school graduate; played football; no extracurricular activities of note.

Employment record

1. Currently employed by Allied Food Distributors in the warehouse in Indianapolis; two years with Allied; job responsibilities include processing orders from the field and expediting rush orders; current salary $2,200 per month.
2. In 1984–85 employed by Hoosier Van Lines in Indianapolis as a sales agent; terminating salary was $550 per month; left due to limits placed on salary and lack of challenge in the job.
3. In 1982–84 employed by Main Street Clothiers of Indianapolis as a retail salesperson in the men's department; terminating salary $1,500 per month; left due to boring nature of this type of selling.
4. Between 1965 and 1982 held six other clerical and sales type jobs, all in Indianapolis.

Applicant's statement

I feel that my true employment interest lies in selling in a situation where I can be my own boss. This jobs seems just right.

Ms. Ramsey's comments

Seems very interested in job as a career.
Well recommended by his current boss.
Reasonably intelligent.
Good appearance.
Moderately aggressive.

Exhibit 3 Information on Mr. Carley Tobias

Personal information

Born February 12, 1957; married; two children ages 1 and 4; height 6 feet, 2 inches; weight 170; excellent health; born in San Francisco; raised in Cleveland, Ohio.

Education

High school and Community College graduate in business administration; student council president at Community College; plus belonged to a number of other clubs.

Employment record

1. Currently employed by The Drug Trading Company in Cincinnati as a salesperson; job responsibility involves selling to retail drugstores; seven years with Drug Trading; current salary $3,300 per month.
2. In 1979–81 U.S. Army private; did one tour of duty in Germany.

Applicant's statement

I am seeking a new position because of the limited earning potential at Drug Trading, plus my family's desire to live in a less populated city.

Other information

He is very active in civic and church organizations in Cincinnati; he is currently president of the Sales and Marketing Executives of Cincinnati.

Ms. Ramsey's comments

Very personable.
Reasonably intelligent.
Good appearance.
He seems to like Cincinnati a lot.
Good experience.

Exhibit 4 Information on Mr. Arthur Woodhead

Personal information

Born May 26, 1965; single; height 6 feet; weight 180; excellent health; born and raised in Chicago.

Education

Will graduate in May 1987 from the University of Illinois, Chicago, with a B.B.A. Active in intramural athletics and student government.

Employment record

Summer jobs only; did house painting and gardening work for his own company. Earned $1,400 per month in summer of 1986.

Applicant's statement

I really like to run my own affairs, and selling seems like a good position to reach this objective.

Ms. Ramsey's comments

Well dressed and groomed.
Very intelligent.
Management potential, not career salesperson.
Not very aggressive.

Golden Bear Distributors

John Gray, president and owner of Golden Bear Distributors (GBD), had been pleased by his firm's progress and by the growth in sales and profits. Only 10 years old, GBD had grown to be generally regarded as number three in its area and was definitely a marketing force to be reckoned with. But there were some storm clouds on the horizon:

1. The rate of growth for GBD (in sales and profits) had decreased in the past two years—in fact, Gray suspected his firm may have lost market share (there were no hard data by which to accurately measure this surmise).
2. Mass merchandisers and other volume retailers were beginning to dominate the markets, and GBD's traditional independent dealers were hard pressed to survive.
3. For the first time, Gray was experiencing a worrisome increase in salesman turnover.
4. The dealers were increasingly vocal in asking the GBD provide ever greater sales and promotional help.
5. The largest competitor, a national distributor, had recently installed an expensive and extensive sales training program.

Gray decided therefore to launch a study intended to reassess the firm's selling strategy. His first step was to engage a local consulting firm with the charge of "evaluating GBD's sales strategy and, in particular, the training needs of the sales force."

The Company and Its Lines

GBD carried a wide line of consumer products including refrigerators and kitchen ranges, TVs and radios, home video players, and a limited line of medium- to low-priced computers. All told, there were over 2,000 different items in inventory. Sales in 1983 exceeded $55 million with the bulk of the dollar volume centered in home appliances. Computer volume, although small, was expanding at a 45 percent annual rate.

Sales were made to 500 independent retailers as well as to a growing number of small chain operators and about 35 industrial accounts (i.e., contractors and local manufacturers primarily). The large chains, as implied earlier, preferred to purchase direct from the manufacturers and from the distributors for small, fill-in orders. Increasingly, these direct buyers purchased their product requirements on a bid basis. Not all dealers carried all the GBD lines.

Exhibit 1 **Organizational Chart**

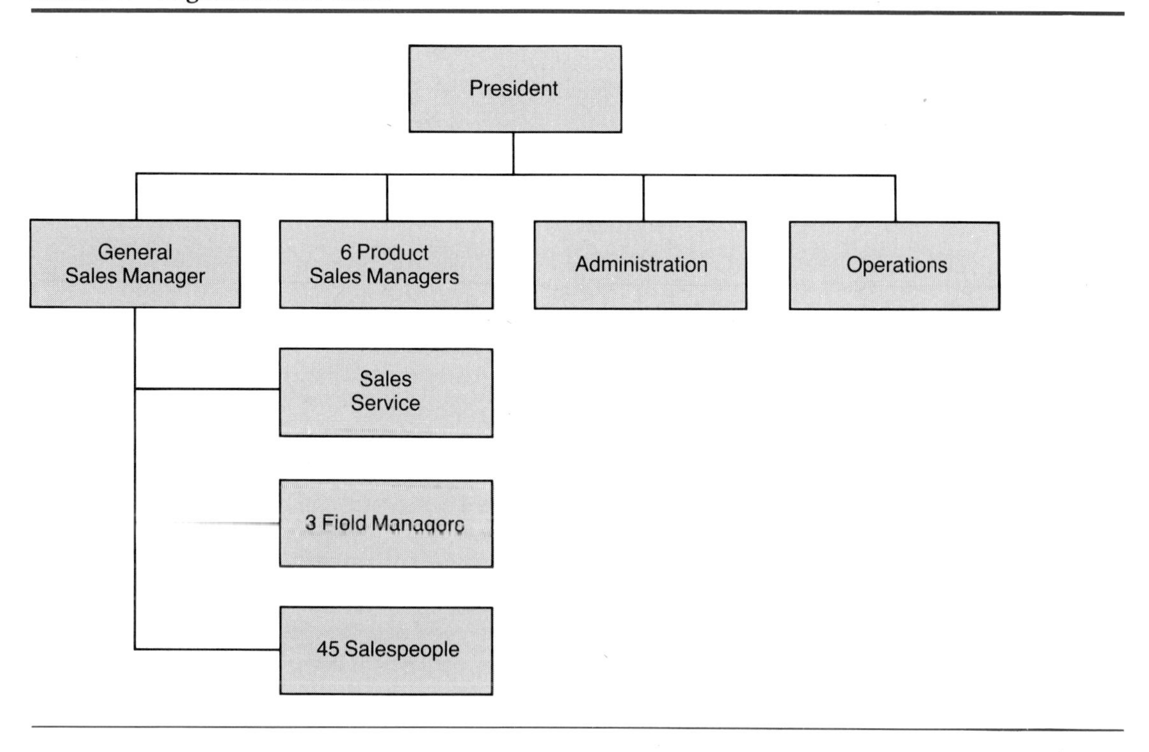

GBD had a number of distribution arrangements with its suppliers. The great bulk of the products represented merchandise in open distribution. However, one third of GBD's business represented products that were either exclusively handled or distributed on a selective basis. GBD made considerably more profits in these specialty items.

The firm's sales organization included six product sales managers who reported to the president. (See Exhibit 1.) Each product sales manager was assigned a number of the company's lines and was held responsible for sales and profits.

The sales force consisted of 45 individuals supervised directly by three field managers and indirectly by the product sales managers. Each salesperson was assigned a specific geographic territory made up of approximately 1/45 of the total Retail Distribution Index of GBD's trading area (calculated from the Survey of Buying Power). Each time a new person was hired, he or she was assigned a territory equal in potential to the others.

There was little formal sales training. The field managers and product sales managers took turns "going the rounds" with the new hire to acquaint him or her with the territory and to introduce the customers. Each salesperson sold all of the products in the company's line; if sales fell off in one product area, that product sales manager usually discussed at regular bi-weekly meetings any problems the sales rep had encountered.

Each sales individual received a draw of $300 a week against commissions. Since the average commission rate was 3 percent, each salesperson had to sell slightly over $500,000 per year in order to cover the draw. Net annual commissions for the different members of the sales force varied between $15,000 and $65,000. All selling expenses were paid by the company.

The sales force filled out individual detailed weekly route sheets describing all planned activities for the following week. In addition, they made out a dialy call report which was mailed to the home office at the end of each workday as well as a "special attention" memorandum for unusual situations.

Selling to independents was quite different than selling to chains and large operators. The latter, as stated preferred to buy direct and expected a considerable amount of promotional and advertising support. They were, by and large, reasonably able merchandisers and put a great deal of pressure on their suppliers for deals, special prices, and point-of-sale assistance. There wasn't much demand by these big oeprators for selling assistance, though they did welcome abundant product informatio and unique product features.

The independents were much more dependent upon their suppliers for credit terms, selling assistance, product availability, and service. Although they talked price, they were eually concerned with ongoing support and service. In recent months, however, there was a noticeable increase in retail price cutting.

The Consultant's Interviews

The consulting firm assigned the GBD account to one of its top young men, Kevin Murphy. Murphy had received an MBA from a leading western business school in 1975 and, upon graduation, had taken a job with the General Electric Company. He left his sales management job there four years later to join the consulting group.

Shortly after John Gray's initial discussion with the consultants, Murphy contacted GBD's general sales manager, Harry Overstreet, at the home office in Oakland. After getting some background data on the sales organization, Murphy asked Overstreet for his views on sales training at GBD. He responded:

> As far as I'm concerned, the training job has to be twofold; retail salesclerks need training just as much as our field salespeople. Right now we have a poilicy whereby we invite dealer personnel to our home office in small groups for meetings to demonstrate and discuss all of the products that we carry. On the other hand, as I mentioned earlier, our salesmen's only on-the-job training is the initial joint calling by the product sales managers and the field sales managers. Such limited training probaly isn't suffiecient, but I'm not sure what kind of training they do need. That's what I expect you to tell me after you spend some time with them.

Overstreet then arranged for Murphy to "make the rounds" with several of the GBD salesmen. Murphy first met Bob Benton, who serviced part of Monterey County south of San Francisco. Bob was 34 years old and had been with GBD over 7 years. His initial reaction to Murphy was one of suspicion. "I never hear from the office unless my sales are down." But when Murphy explained that he was merely interested in learning how he sold as part of a general study on sales training, Bob talked more freely:

> You have to learn to sell like a retailer sells. New salesmen should be given all kinds of product information, and the company should demonstrate the operation of our products to them.
>
> Next, you need to follow up on the new people so they tell their story to the retailer every time they go into a store. The idea is to get them to give the story to the retailer and his floor people so many times that when a customer walks in the store and asks about a recorder or TV, the retailer goes into "the pitch" on our equipment automatically.
>
> According to management, we're supposed to be "sales consultants" to the dealers, but I think that's a lot of baloney. I tried to help out a couple of small retailers once by showing them how I'd sell our product line, but they both thought I was trying to run their business. I think the best training is to bring the retail salesmen into the home office every once in awhile and show them how to operate our equipment and explain it thoroughly—just like we do now. That's how to train.

Bob's first stop was at the Mission Home Center, a successful San Francisco retailer. Before he and Murphy went in, Bob explained his sales approach:

> I go in and say hello to the salespeople first because, if there's any service problem with our products, they're sure to know about it. That way, the boss won't surprise me if something's gone wrong. Next, if I have a chance, I slip back into the stockroom to see how many of our items they have in stock. Mission is a good operator and sells a pretty good mix of our products. Incidentally, most of my sales are TV and appliances—I can't sell many computers down in this part of town.
>
> Well, after that, I check with the service manager to make certain that anything I've promised him in the last week or so has been taken care of. Then, of course, I tip my hat to the secretary and ask to see the boss.

When Bob entered the store, he greeted the two retail clerks, walked over to a quiet corner and conversed with one of them in low tones. Shortly thereafter, he and the consultant went downstairs to the storeroom for about 40 minutes. When they came back, Benton headed for a desk at the back and motioned for Murphy to follow. He greeted the service manager and introduced Murphy as his helper. The service manager was apparently mad at GBD and Bob in particular because Bob had promised him some special software for the computers which had not yet been delivered. After Bob stated that he had relayed the information to GBD's service department a week or so ago, he phoned the GBD service manager and a short, heated argument ensued. When Bob finished the call, he informed Mission's service manager that he would have to "check further." Although the service manager was not satisfied, Bob explained that he wanted to see the boss first and that he would talk later.

Bob then knocked on a door marked "Private" and waved Murphy to follow. As they entered, a man on the telephone looked up and motioned them to a seat. After he hung up, Bob introduced Murphy to the owner and proceeded to ask if there was anything he needed. The owner answered by questioning Bob about the missing software. When Bob assured him that he was following it up, the owner stated: "That's OK for me, Bob."

The salesman then began to explain a new TV floor display GBD had designed for its dealers for the Christmas holidays. The owner turned down the offer because "Panasonic pays me $250 bucks a year to put their line on special display during the first three weeks of December, so you can forget about it."

Bob glanced at his note pad and informed the owner that he was running low on a couple of popular models. The owner replied, "I'm OK for now, but I'll give you an order next week." After leaving the office, Bob stopped by the service manager's desk and reviewed the software situation. He concluded by stating that he would check on the material the following morning when he reported to the home office. He promised to call the service manager with a report.

As they left the store, the salesman remarked. "The owner evidently wasn't in a buying mood today, but I'll definitely get an order from him next week." Since it was then nearly 4:30 P.M., Bob wanted to call it a day, but he offered to take Murphy to visit other stores on Monday if he wished.

The following week, Murphy spent most of one day with Grace Adams. She was a divorcee, about 35 years old, who had been selling for GBD for almost three years. She had left a sales job with the J. C. Penney organization because she preferred the relative freedom of an outside position. Grace had a large territory north of San Francisco which covered a number of small towns. Murphy met her about 9 A.M., and they chatted over a cup of coffee before beginning their calls.

When Murphy explained that he was helping to do a study for GBD on methods of training salesmen, Grace evidently interpreted this to mean that she should talk about her job, for she started explaining her daily call routine. Her suggested approach to the retailer was much the same as that of Bob Benton.

Grace and Murphy first visited the Petaluma TV and Radio store, which sold additionally a broad line of home appliances. Adams quickly introduced Murphy to Mrs. Smith (the owner's wife), listened to a complaint about a scratched cabinet on a television set, and checked the company's inventory. After discussing with Mrs. Smith the aggressive price cutting initiated by a local discounter, Grace took an order for two home video units. The call lasted about 20 minutes.

As they walked toward the second stop several blocks away, Grace confided:

I always try to get on a first-name basis with my retailers as soon as I can because it helps me establish rapport. We all like to do business with our friends. Another secret to calling in a territory that you haven't visited for a week or so is to walk along the main street and window shop and see who's got what bargains displayed. I also buy a local paper most every time I come into these little towns to see who's advertising what. I think that helps me to get a feel for my competition too.

The second call, which lasted about 45 minutes, was at a large home service center. As soon as they entered the store, Grace introduced Murphy to Joe, the owner. The following conversation took place:

Adams: I see you're featuring a couple of our home computer systems, Joe. Great—that should help to boost your sales.
Joe: Yeah, that's true. But the reason I'm promoting them is that I can't sell them at full retail. As long as I make some profit, though, I should care.
Adams: Joe, that business should be picking up pretty soon now—Christmas, you know. Over half of these sales should come in November and December.
Joe: What's good in the rest of your lines?
Adams: Everything, Joe.
Joe: *(Looking at some promotional material)* I've got some Sonys here, got them at a special price. But the last I sold was about three months ago.

Adams began to talk about a new warranty program on the food mixer. Joe explained he was aware of it.

Adams: Well, we do have a nice gift promotion on the mixers.
Joe: I don't need all that stuff. I've got plenty now.
Adams: We can send it to you prepaid you know, Joe, plus a 10 percent dating. These mixers will really go well . . .
Joe: I just don't need any.
Adams: Well, anything else? How about taking an ad in your local paper on the video player? I've never seen your newspaper feature any of our products. What's the cost over there anyway?
Joe: $2.60 a line.
Adams: Well, of course, we'd split the cost 50-50 with you, Joe, on any ads you'd like to run.
Joe: 50-50?
Adams: Yes, on all the lines you run with our mats.
Joe: On everything?
Adams: Thats right. Just send us the tear sheets.

Joe: Why don't you mail me some mats then? I can use them.

Adams: OK. Now, how about the TVs, Joe?

Joe: Send me a couple of those new Sony portables—you know the ones I mean?

Adams: The FM-36B? A good choice. That's the popular one, Joe.

Joe: OK. I'll see you next week.

Adams: Fine, Joe, see you.

As they left the store, Grace remarked, "Gee, sure looks like a good day. You know, the personal approach means everything in this business. I'm trying to build goodwill so that when I leave a store, those retailers will want to sell GBD because of me. Now Joe there thinks that I'm a pleasant person, so he tries to sell my line. Incidentally, the reason I pushed some advertising is that he's got to advertise if he wants to sell. These dealers often look upon advertising as a cost instead of an investment. Or they think the manufacturer should do it all."

The next stop was a new TV dealer. Grace had taken an order from the dealer for a new combination stereo TV and home recording system on the promise that it would be delivered in two days. Three days after taking the order, she had received a phone call from the dealer who stated that unless the set was delivered that very day, Grace was to cancel the order. She commented to Murphy, "I checked with our people yesterday after I got the call, and they weren't sure the set would go out. If it isn't there now, I'll be in trouble with him. Seeing as how he's a new dealer, I don't want to rock the boat."

In the TV dealer's window was the system distributed by GBD. "Well," remarked Grace, "I guess it's safe to go in." As soon as they entered the store, a thin man greeted her with, "The set arrived just as I was closing last night." Grace explained some of the features of the set to the dealer and gave him some literature on several other models. Then she inquired about what other sets the dealer was planning to install. The dealer replied that he wouldn't carry any others until he had sold this one. After a few more words, Grace and Murphy left the store. Several minutes later she remarked, "You know, bringing people around with you hurts your sales . . . but he's a tough dealer to sell, anyway."

Murphy and Adams then drove 20 miles to another town further north. During the trip, Grace talked about why she had left the retail business and why she liked selling. When they arrived at the next stop, Grace explained, "I have to try to collect a check from the dealer and report my results back to the home office by telephone." Since the man she wished to see was not in, she made arrangements to call back later that afternoon.

During lunch at a small diner, Grace talked more about the retail business. She also expressed a desire to obtain a territory closer to the city. After lunch, as they began walking toward the next call, they passed a newly renovated electronics store. Grace paused, "This is a new store. I haven't gotten them for an account. It's just possible they don't have a computer line. I think I'll go in cold and see what I can do." They entered the store and looked around for a clerk. A woman came out, and Grace explained the purpose of her call, stating that her company had just started up with a new line of complete computer systems. When she mentioned the brand names, the worman remarked that the store carried one well-known brand and added that she could show it to them. In a corner of the store, a special display was devoted to the computer and peripherals. The shopkeeper explained that she and her husband had recently purchased the store, didn't know much about personal computers, and were in the process of rethinking the business. Grace noted the inventory that she had and explained that, on her next call, she would supply some promotional materials. She also added that the distributor who formerly handled the line had gone out of business and that GBD would gladly provide the components from now on. The woman thanked her, and they left the store.

After similar experiences traveling with three other salespeople, Kevin Murphy felt that he had a good feeling for the GBD selling job and its requirements. Since two men were retiring soon from GBD's sales force, John Gray was very anxious that Murphy complete his recommendations for a sales training program before new recruits had to be hired to take over the territories. Thus, Murphy began outlining a training program for GBD which would include recommendations for training dealer sales personnel as well as the firm's own sales force.

Questions

1. What is the basic role of the distributors' salesmen in this situation?
2. What skills do these salesmen need?
3. What specific training program (coverage, subjects) do you recommend?
4. Elaborate upon one particular training subject in your program that you consider important—points to be covered, specific training technique to be used, measurement objectives, etc.

Plastic Piping Systems: Employee Turnover (A)

Introduction

In March 1983, Mr. George C. Mammola, Vice President of Sales of Plastic Piping Systems (PPS), was conducting a review of the company's performance for previous years. During the last three years, PPS has undergone significant expansion, increasing their number of sales offices from five to eight. The combination of the poor economy and high employee turnover has had a negative impact on PPS over the past six months; with sales even with the same period in 1981, PPS went from 5% profit to a 2% loss. Mr. Mammola will be meeting with the Board of Directors next week to discuss the situation and recommend a course of action. PPS is a distributor of plastic pipe, valves, and fittings to the industrial marketplace.

History

PPS was started in 1969 in Newark, New Jersey. Sales spiraled upward for the first four years with branches in 7 cities by 1975. The rapid expansion of PPS resulted in an overextension of both assets and management. Consequently, in 1977 and 1978 management was changed and consolidated. Mr. Ted Vagell bought out the other partners and initiated the following actions: The Maryland branch was sold off with a restrictive agreement that PPS would not enter that marketplace for 10 years. Two other branches were closed, leaving PPS with branches in South Plainfield, New Jersey; Cleveland, Ohio; Charlotte, North Carolina; and Chicago, Illinois. The turnaround was successful.

PPS's sales and earnings grew at a rate of 25% per year from 1978 to 1981. This rapid increase is the result of PPS's concentration on the industrial marketplace, the talents of each branch manager, and the strict attention to asset management.

Product

PPS distributes plastic pipe, valves, and fittings used in manufacturing plants to transport fluids. These products are made from a variety of materials such as polyvinyl chloride, chlorinated polyvinyl chloride, polypropylene, and polyvinylidene flouride. The advantage of plastic pipe is its exceptional chemical resistance to nearly all acids, alkalis, alcohols, halogens and other corrosive materials up to temperatures of 280°F. Industrial plastic pipe is different from the plastic pipe used in residential construc-

---

 Prepared by Hubert D. Hennessey. Interviews of past and present salespeople were conducted by Kim Koehler and Anne Timson.

tion, with industrial pipe, valves, and fittings being thicker, therefore more durable and more expensive.

First introduced in 1935 for piping applications, plastic piping profited from intensive R&D during WW II. Since 1948, the plastic piping industry has sustained a remarkable growth rate of 25% per year in both industry and residential construction. PPS carries other products such as plastic pumps, tanks and fans, but 90% of sales are from pipe, valves, and fittings.

Industry Structure

Plastic pipe, valves, and fittings are manufactured by a variety of companies. There are eight companies which manufacture industrial plastic pipe of which three of these companies also manufacture valves and fittings. There are another four companies which only manufacture valves and fittings. These 12 manufacturers sell their products to industrial plants using distributors and/or reps. Historically, the manufacturers have not sold direct due to the large number of potential customers and the need for local inventory.

The three types of distributors are plastic piping specialists, plumbing supply houses and mill supply houses. Plastic piping specialists are smaller distributors, usually with less than twenty employees, which represent 2 or 3 manufacturers and sell to local plants. Plumbing supply houses sell primarily to local plumbers items used in residential construction such as water, sewer, and drain pipe, tubs, sinks, toilets, etc. Occasionally plumbing supply houses also carry industrial plastic pipe. Mill supply houses are usually large distributors specializing in metal pipe, valves and fittings for industrial use. In most cases the mill supply houses look at plastic pipe as a low cost alternative to metal pipe. Some mill supply houses carry plastic, others do not.

Over the past twenty years there has been a trend toward the use of plastic specialty distributors to sell industrial plastic pipe. The basis for this trend is, first, the technical knowledge needed to select which type of plastic pipe should be used and, second, the fact that the traditional metal pipe suppliers such as the mill supply house view plastic pipe as competition and prefer not to offer it.

Distributor Operations

Plastic piping specialists provide an important function in the distribution channel. They maintain an inventory of plastic pipe, valves, and fittings from various manufacturers in a local location. The plastic piping specialist is technically competent to select a particular type of pipe based on the corrosive being carried, the temperature, and the pressure of the fluid.

The distributor fills a large volume of small and medium-sized orders which would be uneconomical for a manufacturer to supply from regional warehouses.

Distributors purchase from manufacturers based on price, availability, and credit terms. While most distributors carry competitive lines, each normally carries one main line, filling in with complementary lines. The distributor makes annual purchase agreements with manufacturers based on expected demand.

In addition to serving the needs of current customers, distributor salespeople are continually calling on plant engineers, plant maintenance supervisors, and consulting engineers to persuade them to recommend or use plastic pipe instead of the traditional metal piping such as stainless steel.

How Customers Buy

Industrial plastics are used in manufacturing plants. There are two different buying situations which will result in the sale of plastic piping products. Larger expansions to manufacturing plants are normally designed by consulting engineers and bid through mechanical contractors. These contractors will get prices from distributors to be used in their bids. The mechanical contractor with the lowest price is normally awarded the bid. Small additions to current facilities or maintenance and repair situations are normally handled by the maintenance staff; therefore, the buying is done by the plant purchasing agent. Piping products purchased directly by the plant personnel are normally less price competitive than piping products purchased by the mechanical contractors.

Customers normally purchase plastic piping based on performance requirements of the situation, i.e., material being handled, temperature, and pressure. In most cases the customer will not specify a particular manufacturer except in the case of some specialized valves which are perceived to be significantly different than other valves.

The purchase decisions for most small purchases is usually a function of availability. If a processing line is shut down because of a leaking valve or fitting, the cost of the item is insignificant to the cost of the line being shut down. Local suppliers are preferred for these situations, since someone from the plant will be sent to pick up the item.

Larger purchases are normally purchased based on price and availability. Two or more distributors are normally contacted to compare prices and availability with the order going to the lowest price.

PPS Long-Term Strategy

PPS's primary objective is to maintain itself as a privately managed distributor organization providing quality products at competitive prices, serving industrial end users and contractors. Prior to the economic downturn in 1982, PPS had planned to double sales and profit between 1981 and 1985. To achieve these objectives, PPS implemented the following programs during 1981 and 1982: (1) geographic expansion, (2) selection and training of sales personnel, (3) annual branch planning, and (4) computerization.

(1) Geographic Expansion: To expand geographically, PPS opened a new office in Tampa, Florida. The office was opened in August, 1982. John Camp, formerly the branch manager for Charlotte, North Carolina, was promoted to Southeast Divisional Manager and given the responsibility for both North Carolina and Florida. Al Rubens, a seasoned pipe salesperson, was hired as the Florida branch manager, reporting to Camp. An inside salesperson was hired in August 1981 and is still located at the

branch. Three outside salespeople have been hired to work out of the Florida branch. As of December 1982 all three have left.

In July of 1981 Plastic Piping Systems acquired Plastic Fluid Systems with offices in Houston and Austin for a reasonable price to be paid over a seven-year period. PFS's president was the founder and former owner of PPS and in 1978 sold his interest in PPS to Ted Vagell.

The Texas offices report to George Mammola, the Vice President of Sales. The Houston office was managed by Mr. Matthews when acquired. Matthews was given the responsibility of sales manager, and Patricia Minter, a recent graduate of Babson and PPS's 8-week training program, was appointed operation manager. Six months after the acquisition, Matthews left, and Rob Vernon, a star salesperson in the North Carolina office, was promoted to Sales Manager of the Houston office. Rob Vernon and Patricia Minter were married on February 5, 1983.

The Austin branch is managed by John Nevin, formerly a salesperson for PFS. He was promoted to branch manager just before the acquisition.

(2) Selection and Training: Since it is a distributor organization, the lifeblood of PPS is its salespeople. In 1980, PPS initiated a comprehensive training program. The first group of six trainees was given a four-week indoctrination and training in the summer of 1980. The second group of 14 was given an eight-week program in the summer of 1981. Before 1980, most of the salespeople who were hired had some sales experience and limited college education. They received their training at the branch level. The new program was oriented toward hiring undergraduates, training them in a location, then sending them to their respective branches. Out of the first six trainees, two are left, and out of the second fourteen trainees, seven remain at PPS. No training program was held in the summer of 1982.

(3) Annual Branch Planning: Prior to 1980, much of the planning was superficial. In 1980, PPS initiated a detailed planning and control system which established objectives for each employee in the company, based on individual and branch performance. All salespeople received a salary plus commission, but the commission does not kick in until you meet a minimum gross profit for the month. The branch managers also participate in the bonus program, receiving up to 100% of their base salary, based on the profit of the branch.

(4) Computerization: The computerization of all invoicing, inventory, payables, accounts receivables, and mailing lists started in 1981. As of February 1983, most of the systems are up and running with the last of the sales offices just being connected with the home office in Cranford, New Jersey.

PPS Management

The home office staff consists of Ted Vagell, the President; George Mammola, the Vice President of Sales; Doug Sebesky, Manager of Corporate Accounting; Charles Windruff, Director of MIS; and approximately seven other accounting, computer, and secretarial people. The tone of the home office is dominated by Mr. Vagell and Mr. Mammola, both major stockholders who are concerned about the short- and long-

Exhibit 1 **PPS—Organizational Chart**

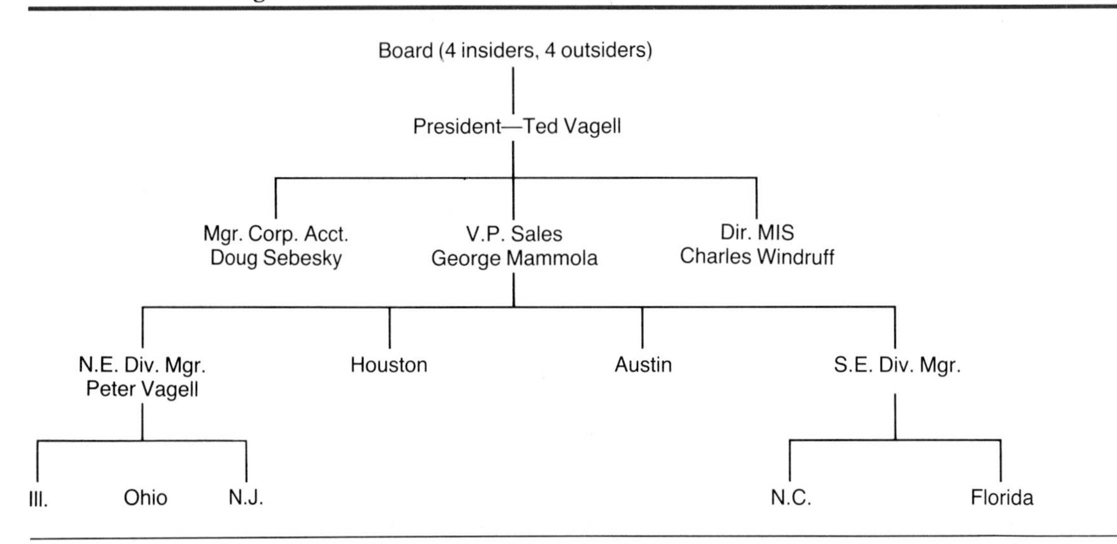

term future of PPS. Both have a friendly ongoing relationship with the home office employees.

The tone of the branch operations is set by the individual manager and in most cases the division manager—John Camp or Peter Vagell. John Camp has been with the company eight years. He opened the Charlotte, North Carolina branch, trained most of the current employees, and had a major input on its success. The Charlotte branch has grown every year since it started until 1982, which was the first year sales did not increase and profits were down. Peter Vagell, brother of the President, has also been with PPS for eight years. Mr. Peter Vagell has been the branch manager of the South Plainfield, New Jersey office for six years. Sales growth in New Jersey has been steady with an especially good performance expected this year. Both Peter Vagell and John Camp are shareholders in the corporation.

The organizational structure of PPS is shown in Exhibit 1.

Responsibilities of Fieldforce

The salesforce consists of telemarketing customers service respresentatives and outside salespeople. The customer service representative is responsible for handling incoming calls, entering and processing orders, checking credit and selling via the telephone to low-volume customers. The telemarketer calls other distributors and accounts not assigned to outside salespeople. The outside salesperson handles personal calls to current and potential customers, mostly through visits but occasionally by phone.

Exhibit 2 contains a summary of interviews conducted of salespeople currently employed at PPS.

Exhibit 2 **Interviews with Current PPS Salespeople**

Frank Bower: New Jersey
College Degree: B.S. Marketing
Prior Sales Experience: No formal sales
Time with PPS: 3 years
Training Received: 3 months in Chicago upon graduation from college.

Initial Perceptions: Frank knew about PPS through Ted Vagell. Upon graduating from college, Ted had asked Frank to come in for an interview. Frank was hired and went through the three-month intensive training program which he felt was accurate. After training he went into telemarketing. He felt that the telemarketing gave him a firm understanding of the product line and he also learned how to allocate his time.

Present Position: After four months doing telemarketing, Frank moved into outside sales where he calls on regular customers and follows up on leads. He likes this position because it allows him to meet his customers face-to-face, and he enjoys the personal contact.

Frank realizes that PPS does not have the manpower to provide the technical expertise that is occasionally needed, but he feels the company does a good job given its size. On a scale from 1 to 10, Frank rates the technical support given to him by PPS as an 8.

Frank is quite content working for a small distributor and while he realizes that the other branches might have problems, his main objective is to better his branch. He feels that the product line is sufficent and the key to being good in this industry is to know what you can and cannot deliver.

Frank sees his primary responsibility as providing the best service to the customer. He feels the one area in which PPS can help him to enhance his service capabilities is to improve the delivery system. Frank feels that by adding trucks (instead of using common carriers and couriers), delivery will improve.

All in all, Frank is satisfied with his position at PPS and enjoys his work.

Contact: Alice Kopp
Office: Cleveland
College Degree: (Major) Marketing
Prior Sales Experience: Sold ski equipment in high school
Time with PPS: Started in June 1981
Training: 3 months in Chicago

Initial Perceptions: Alice had heard about PPS from a friend who had interviewed with the company. The friend was very enthusiastic about the job opportunity but wanted to live in Chicago. Prior to the interview, Alice attempted to research the company but could not find anything published on PPS. Although Alice did not know anything about pipes, valves, and fittings, she was assured that she could sell anything.

Present Status: Alice spent her first year in telemarketing. While she became well-versed in the product lines, she was discouraged by the rejections she received. She had originally been told that she would get established accounts, but found herself calling on dormant accounts and inquiries. She was further discouraged about telemarketing because she felt that as a female she did not have the credibility over the phone that her male counterparts had. She felt that the customers she called on perceived her as a secretary/clerk and not as a trained sales representative.

In her second year, Alice became a customer service representative. She enjoys this position, primarily because she has established accounts and receives incoming calls. Alice has received a tremendous amount of technical support from the home office and says the computer is a great asset for operations. She, however, is under time pressure to get out bids. Larger orders must go through the home office to get approved, and this takes longer than the 2 days most clients need. On smaller orders, which do not need home office approval, Alice must check into the financial background before she issues the bid. If the client company defaults on its payments, then the representative's salary is docked. While Alice realizes it is important to check up on the financial positions, she feels that it detracts both from her selling time and potential bids she can issue.

(continued)

Exhibit 2 *(continued)*

Alice has been out of the office to make calls. She would like to do more of this. Her office, however, has done so well in telemarketing, PPS is discouraging the representatives from making outside calls. As a result, Alice does not see herself in this position forever and would like to move into an outside sales career. She feels that there is limited potential for her to move into outside sales within PPS and might eventually leave the company for such a position.

Name: John Murphy

College Degree: Business Economics

Prior Sales Experience: None

Time with PPS: 3 years

Training Received: 3 months

Initial Perceptions: John heard about PPS through the placement service at his college in Illinois. He turned down the job offer he received from PPS because he would not be able to stay in the Chicago area. PPS later called informing him that he could work in the Chicago office. John feels the training program definitely helped him and was of great value in gaining product knowledge. After his training program, John spent six months in telemarketing, then six months in customer service. He then spent a year in telemarketing.

Present Position: John is now in customer service. He says that telemarketing and customer service were both easier the second time around, as telemarketing was, at first, hard and took getting used to. He has received a great deal of technical support from his office and while he does not deal regularly with the home office, he says that when he does, they are extremely helpful. He has had no major problems with PPS since he has been there.

Name: David Flynn, North Carolina

College Degree: B.S. Marketing

Prior Sales Experience: No prior

Time with PPS: 5 years

Training: 3 months

Initial Perceptions: David was interviewed by Ted Vagell at the placement office through his school. He wanted a sales position and had interviewed mostly with large computer companies. He, however, was impressed with the opportunities PPS offered. During David's training he learned the technical expertise required to sell the product but had no hands-on experience with respect to selling. He was very impressed by a sales seminar held in 1983 for the representatives at PPS.

Present Status: The first 2½ months David worked in the home office in North Carolina doing telemarketing, after which he was transferred to South Carolina. He works mostly in his home and is left on his own. Until just recently, David worked in the field five days a week, but now spends two days telemarketing. Although he is under the North Carolina office, he has been basically on his own since his move to South Carolina.

He finds the company to be supportive in fulfilling his needs. Because of its size, he feels free to call his boss at home if there is a problem, and/or the home office.

David almost left the company two years ago as a result of his branch manager who was extremely difficult to work with. He started to look for other jobs, but then found out his manager was leaving. David, therefore, decided to stay. He presently feels the company does not have any clear objectives (or they have not been communicated to the sales representatives). He also feels that the company has lost touch with what has been happening in the marketplace.

Exhibit 3 **Summary of Salespeople Having Left the Company**

	College Degree	Sales Experience	Time at PPS	New Job When Left Company	Training	Money Reason For Quitting	Office
Pat Owen	yes BS Bus. Ad	no	18 mos.	no	Chicago (classroom)	no	N.J.
Mark Sands	no	no		yes	general	yes	Cleveland
Steve Robertson	yes BS Biology	yes	18 mos.	yes	California	no	Houston
Warren Smith	no 1 yr. college	yes	4 mos.	yes	California	no	Houston
Tim Neeley	yes Liberal Arts	no	16 mos.	yes	Chicago	no	North Carolina

Note: Names are fictitious.

Salesperson Turnover

There was a major turnover of salespeople at each branch in 1982, ranging from 300% in Florida to 40% in New Jersey, with a company average of 50% turnover. According to branch managers it takes 1 to 2 years for a new salesperson to be productive for PPS. The long lead time is required to learn the technical knowledge, develop the sales skills, and locate, identify, and sell new accounts. During this start-up period, the salesperson earns a straight salary, and receives a bonus commission only when the monthly gross margin minimum is reached.

The turnover of salespeople is a serious problem for PPS, due to the start-up cost of salespeople who leave and the cost of hiring and training new people. To help understand this problem, a graduate student interviewed via telephone four salespeople who left PPS in the last 5 months. A summary of the four salespeople who were interviewed is shown in Exhibit 3. The summary of each interview is shown in Exhibit 4. Exhibit 5 includes a letter written by an ex-salesperson in Chicago to the Branch Manager.

Exhibit 4 **Interviews with Former P.P.S. Salespeople**

Mark Sands, Cleveland
No college degree
First sales job

Initial Perception of Company: Mark was flown to New Jersey to get a tour of the company. He was impressed with the company's senior management. During his training he was flown around the country to view different offices of the company and vendors. Mark would have preferred some formal training in addition to this.

Problems on the Job: Mark said that PPS on the local level is vastly different from the company as a whole. He had trouble meeting obligations he made to his customers due to poor management in the lower level of the company. He said he was encouraged to make sales promises and then given no support in the follow through.

(continued)

Exhibit 4 *(continued)*

Mark claims that he would have stayed at PPS if he had not been approached by a competitor who offered more benefits and a much better base salary. He claims that some firefighting between salesmen and management is to be expected in industrial sales, and it didn't bother him too much at PPS; however, it did contribute to his leaving the company.

Mark said he would recommend a sales career at PPS, but not above others in the industry. He did emphasize that PPS is the leader in corrosive piping, and that the problems are localized at the branch management levels. He felt that as a first job, PPS was a good place to learn the business.

Pat Owen, New Jersey
BS Business Administration
18 months with PPS

Initial Perception of Company: Pat saw the sales job advertised in the classified section of the New York Times. He did not research the company or the industry before his interview. He believed that the company had a good reputation. In the interview he was given salary expectations that he claims were not lived up to.

Pat spent eight weeks in a training program for PPS salesmen in Chicago. The experience was interesting and fun, with a party-like atmosphere after hours. Pat said that the training program could have easily been half as long. He would have preferred some office and field training in addition to the classroom instruction.

Problems on the Job: Pat's biggest problem was with his immediate superior. Pat did not believe him to be ethical. His boss's policy was to get an order and worry later if the company could fill it. Pat could not keep the deadlines he promised to his customers because sales quotas were being rammed down his throat. Pat was caught between a boss he claims would have wrung his neck if he didn't get the order, and many angry customers. In one instance, a contractor (over the phone) threatened to beat Pat up because of an order that was not delivered on time.

In spite of this, Pat claims that he was a very good salesman and that he exceeded his quota regularly.

Besides his discontent with work, Pat did not like the geographic area he moved to. He said that if only one of these aspects was positive, he might have stayed with PPS longer. After 18 months he was tired of being miserable at work, and then going home and being miserable. Pat left the company to move back with his parents, and look for a job in the area he grew up in.

Steve Robertson, Houston
BS Biology
Sales Experience with two companies
18 months with PPS

Initial Perception of Company: Steve had learned about PPS from a friend. At the time of his interview Steve believed that PPS was a good, aggressive company. He decided to work there based on the money, benefits, and promotion opportunity he was promised.

Steve participated in the Chicago training program, which he believed was good but could have been shortened.

Problems on the Job: Steve said that PPS tried to keep their incentive promises but couldn't due to personality conflicts that developed at the office. This resulted in a system that lacked incentives and was poor overall. Steve said that 80% of his time with the company was enjoyable while 20% he hated very much.

Steve had hoped to be promoted to sales manager some time in the future. But, when two of the middle managers (one his sales manager) made plans to marry each other, he expected that neither would be leaving the company soon, thereby leaving no room for promotion. This situation was 40% of the reason he left. His biggest sore spot was the animosity between the salesmen and their superiors, particularly the engaged couple at his office. Steve said that a large salary increase might have kept him at PPS for a while, but he would have left eventually. He now sells protective coatings to the same customer base. Steve, like all the salesmen, was often contacted by headhunters.

(continued)

Exhibit 4 *(continued)*

Steve would recommend a job at PPS as a learning experience. He would not recommend a career there, because the incentive system is poor.

Warren Smith, Houston

1 year college

8 years sales experience

4 months with PPS

Initial Perception of Company: Warren saw an employment ad for PPS in a large city newspaper. He had interviewed with PPS one year previous. Warren was leaving his job due to personality conflicts, and it was convenient to take the job at PPS. Warren said he was promised a lucrative job with good opportunities. At the time of the interview he thought the commission was good.

Warren participated in the California training program which he thought was very adequate.

Problems on the Job: Once he started selling, Warren realized that the company had colored things up in the interview. On a ten-point scale he rated PPS's honesty in hiring at 5, and most other companies at 7 to 8.

His main complaint was with the sales manager whom he described as young and unprofessional. Warren was adamant that the whole system from the bottom up needed to become more professionalized. He claimed his manager was a back-stabber who was afraid to call his boss, or give support to his salespeople. His perception was that the bosses were always pointing fingers at each other.

At one time the people in Warren's office tried to go to the sales manager's boss for a confidential meeting. The meeting was not held in confidence, and the sales manager knew which individuals had gone over his head.

Besides company politics, Warren resented that salesmen were expected to spend one day each week in the office doing telemarketing duties. He believed this hurt the income of both the salesmen and the company. Warren would have liked for other personnel to have the responsibility for telemarketing.

Warren views himself as a small sales business person and his top priority is to generate orders for the company. He did not think the system at PPS allowed for a professional salesman to do his job. Warren started looking for a new job after his second week at PPS.

Tim Neeley, North Carolina

4 year college degree

First Industrial Sales Job

16 months with PPS

Initial Perception of Company: Tim spoke with a PPS recruiter on campus before graduation. Although PPS was not his first choice, he thought the company had strong potential and very good market penetration. He also liked the fact that he would be able to work in the southern part of the U.S. He believed the salary and benefits at PPS to be about equal to that offered by other companies. Tim received his sales training in Chicago. His main criticism was that the training did not prepare him for the managers with whom he would be working.

Problems on the Job: Tim said that there was a lot of friction between the branch manager and the sales manager. He elaborated that the branch manager was very secretive about what went on at the different offices. The salesmen were not really free to communicate with their counterparts at different PPS sales offices. Tim would have liked to have contacted salesmen he had trained with but was afraid of repercussions from his superiors.

Tim would not recommend a sales career at PPS unless the lower management system was changed. He said that upper management was not aware of what went on below the branch level of the company. He thought that the problem was due to a few people, who, for greed or other reasons, did not back up the salespeople.

Tim has taken another sales job that he describes as a very satisfying team effort, for a very good company.

Exhibit 5 Exit Letter from Salesperson Who Left PPS

Dear Sales Manager,

Plastic Piping Systems is a profitable company which obviously does many things correctly from the standpoint of its customers, vendors, managers and employees. For those reasons I am grateful to the company for having me as an employee. Upon resignation you asked me to comment in writing about the negative things which occurred at PPS rather than make a lot of patronizing comments. Following is the information you wanted. I sincerely hope that it is used in a positive manner to improve corporate relations and profits.

Commitments

Corporate commitments, to me, have never been taken seriously by the company or its managers. That is the most frustrating thing I have experienced at PPS. Before joining PPS the following commitments were made:

- Product and sales training was promised to prepare me for an outside sales territory after six months when it was available within the company. Training was a joke after my first three weeks. Requests for 20 minutes per day during my first year to review questions and problems were ignored. Organized product training was forgotten after the first three weeks with the exception of several days at AO-Smith. Outside sales training and preparation was non-existent during my first year.
- Quarterly reviews during my first year were promised to insure growth and progress. The second, third, and fourth reviews were never arranged.
- An inside sales commission program was supposed to be implemented early in the spring during my first year with the company. Nothing was implemented until the fall after the busy season. When it was implemented, we could not obtain anything in writing. What happened is that a program was set up to run for three months after which time it would be reviewed to make sure it was fair to the salesman and the company. The program was not given a chance. When we started earning some decent sales commissions the rules were unilaterally changed. Twice!

After six months a couple of outside sales territories were available. Instead of me being prepared to manage one, there were new, young, and less mature people hired and trained for the position.

During my first year at PPS I was already interviewing for sales positions at other companies. When management at PPS discovered that I would be gone within two months, they offered me a geographical sales territory in Chicago with a fair car allowance and a review scheduled for July 1, 1981.

Sales efforts and progress during my first year in Chicago were excellent despite the recession and limited inside sales support. (During the past one-and-a-half years the personnel responsible for inside support changed ten (10) times. This made it difficult to establish effective communication and teamwork.)

After I called on a diversity of accounts in my territory as advised by management, the commissions in the territory grew. Without financial compensation, the company stopped giving me credit for two-hundred (200) + accounts that I had worked with because they did not fit on an arbitrary list number of 100 which was now established.

When the new sales program was implemented we did not even understand the basic mechanics, such as how to add or subtract an account or get an engineering credit. *Before* changing the sales programs there should have been communication with the salesmen. Changes in base salary, minimum gross margin, etc., should have been clear. There was no increase in my base salary or decrease in the bogie—only less accounts from an existing territory to receive credit for.

July first, I was scheduled to have a salary and performance review. At this point I was the most profitable salesman in the midwest. Logic dictated that I would be rewarded and encouraged to achieve more. During the month of *October* my review was still not granted despite constant reminders and requests. When the review was given, it offered a modest increase in salary and a greater increase in minimum gross margin. This would have lowered my income based upon past average sales performance by almost $150.00 per month. A new package was then offered which increased my annual salary $3,000.00 per year and increased my minimum gross margin total $45,000.00 per year. What this means is that I am standing still at PPS. When a good salesman earns less than $30,000 per year in industrial sales he should consider changing companies. (My projected income this year is less than $25,000.)

Although Plastic Piping Systems has intelligent, hard-working people at all levels of operation, it is my opinion that positive reinforcement is severely lacking. For example, the bonus check earned by a warehouse worker was withheld by the office for more than three months. These actions develop negative attitudes in the company.

Better communication and teamwork should be encouraged.

Respectfully submitted,

Donald Larson

Plastic Piping Systems: Employee Turnover (B)

Ted: Well, George and Peter, it looks as if 1984 is shaping up to be a good year. I was just examining our 1st quarter results and sales are up 14% over 1983, gross profit is up 13%, and net income is up.

George: Everything seems to be up!

Peter: Except the turnover among our field force.

Ted: I know, and that is because of your hard work.

Peter: Thanks, Ted, but quite honestly I think it was a result of a lot of internal changes.

George: The computer was sure a big help.

Ted: (Turns to a computer screen in his office) You're right. Let's see what Cleveland sold this morning. (Types on keyboard) They just sold a shipment of $42,000 to a contractor in Columbus.

George: Have we sold to him before?

Ted: (Punches some more keys) Yes, back in September 1982. Seems he basically deals in residential construction.

Peter: This computer system is our best asset. It provides us with a great deal of information and saves on excessive paperwork, which enables our field force to perform more effectively and efficiently.

George: It does so much that it allowed us to virtually eliminate middle management.

Peter: And consequently, the friction between the field-force and middle management no longer exists.

Ted: I like the new organizational structure that we have created. (Exhibit 1).

George: And Peter is doing a fine job in his new position of overseeing all the branches.

Ted: I've got to hand it to you Peter, you have a difficult task, especially with those branches that do not have managers.

Peter: Well, because of the computer system it's easier for me to monitor those branches.

George: Under our old system, the branch managers spent 50% of their time managing the inventory to insure that it was at the appropriate levels.

Peter: Now with centralized purchasing and inventory management our remaining managers have more time to focus on key accounts and help their people with the selling function.

Ted: I'm also glad we stopped promising everyone in the world that they could all become branch managers. It seemed like some of the previous people we hired were disappointed when they didn't take over the branch after 3 months.

Exhibit 1 **Organization Structure**

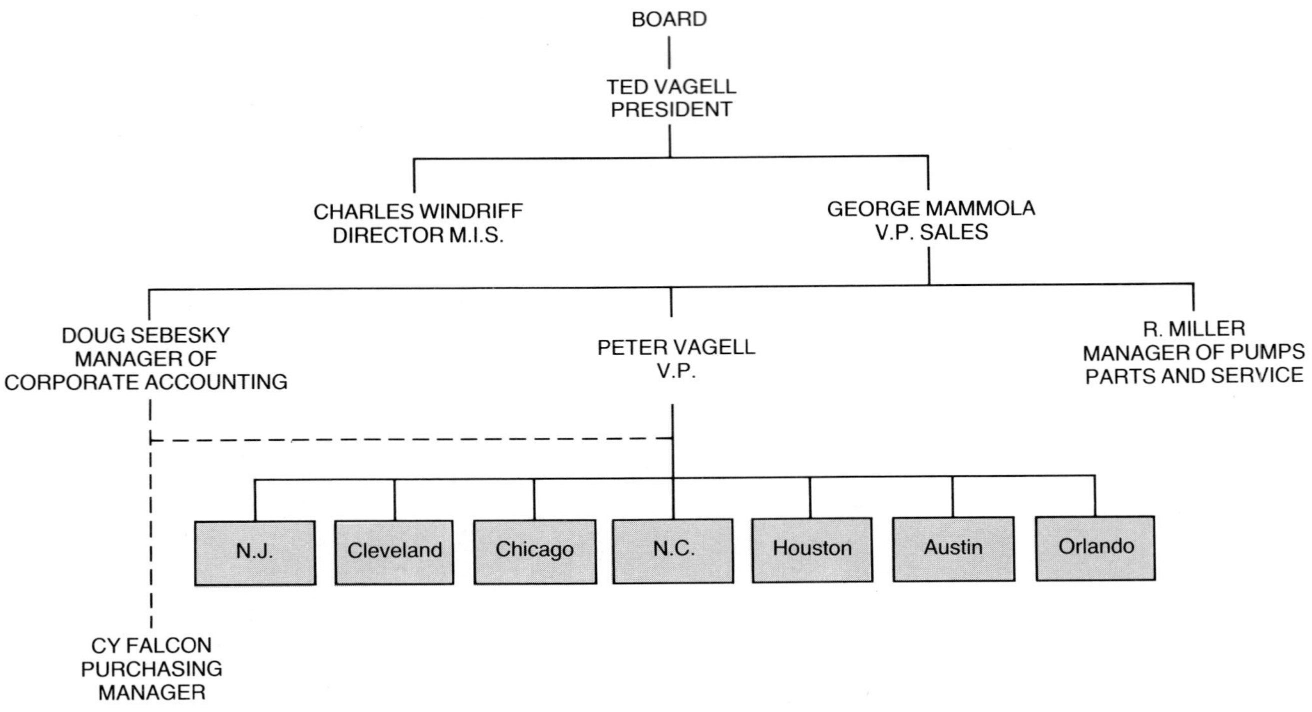

BOARD

TED VAGELL
PRESIDENT

CHARLES WINDRIFF
DIRECTOR M.I.S.

GEORGE MAMMOLA
V.P. SALES

DOUG SEBESKY
MANAGER OF
CORPORATE ACCOUNTING

PETER VAGELL
V.P.

R. MILLER
MANAGER OF PUMPS
PARTS AND SERVICE

N.J.
Cleveland
Chicago
N.C.
Houston
Austin
Orlando

CY FALCON
PURCHASING
MANAGER

George: That's true, but to get and maintain good people we need to establish some sort of career path. Our present structure is tight, and rapid advancement is hard to provide.

Peter: Well, George, despite a lack of a lot of upward mobility we were able to hire three solid outside salesmen. We have an engineer, who was previously with a consulting firm in Tampa, and two men in Texas and New Jersey with a proven track record in outside sales, one with a college degree.

Ted: Sounds like a qualified group. How did we lure them to PPS?

George: Don't forget, Ted, we have an extensive product line and we've increased our compensation package so we are competitive within the industry.

Peter: I'm also pleased with the three people from the warehouse we promoted to inside sales. All six of the new recruits are getting on-the-job training.

Ted: With what you said before, George, about career mobility, I hope everyone in the warehouse doesn't think they will automatically be promoted to inside sales. Especially since we have been able to stabilize turnover.

George: I guess we never fully analyzed the various sales functions and the appropriate people for each position, but when you have good people you want to keep them.

Peter: Yea, take Alice Kopp for example. We could tell she was anxious to move to outside sales and had offers from other companies. We hated to lose Alice so we were able to accommodate her.

George: And from the first quarter results, we might have some more openings in sales.

Ted: I guess it's not too early to start thinking about beginning our college recruitment program and reinstituting our formal training classes. What do you guys think about hiring more salespeople, one for each location? How should we hire and train them?

PART FIVE

DIRECTING THE SALESFORCE

THIS part contains three chapters dealing with the direction of the activities of the salesforce. Chapter 11 provides a summary of relevant salesforce motivation theories and examines several current issues related to motivating the salesforce. Guidelines for managing the motivation component are also presented.

Chapter 12 discusses the management of salesforce reward systems, with an emphasis on financial and nonfinancial compensation. Sales expenses and sales contests are among the other topics covered in this chapter.

Chapter 13 presents a model of sales management leadership. Important leadership functions such as coaching are discussed, and the always important topic of ethics in leadership is investigated. Problems that challenge sales managers as leaders are also treated in this chapter.

CHAPTER 11

SALESFORCE MOTIVATION: THEORIES AND CURRENT ISSUES

Learning Objectives

After completing this chapter, you should be able to

1. Define motivation in terms of intensity, persistence, and direction.
2. Discuss motivation as a process that begins with a perceived need deficiency.
3. Discuss the basic points of four content theories and four process theories of motivation.
4. Identify key issues in salesforce motivation.
5. Cite managerial guidelines for salesforce motivation.

A CLASSIC CASE IN SALESFORCE MOTIVATION: THE DASHER

The "Dasher," a fixture in salesforces everywhere, is a bright, articulate, sociable whirlwind of activity—sometimes. The rest of the time, Dasher works on his or her own clock, which often seems to stand still as company deadlines and priorities are ignored in favor of personal affairs. Sales managers tend to be perplexed with a Dasher's off and on approach to work. They cannot predict when Dasher will embark on an enthusiastic burst, or, conversely, need prodding out of a seemingly inevitable slump in performance.

The Dasher is out of step with the rest of the salesforce. Though he or she may be a top producer, sales results are not consistent, and the sales manager must spend an inordinate amount of time puzzling over the Dasher. Other members of the salesforce are likely to share the sales manager's frustration. Uncommitted to the concept of team effectiveness, the Dasher all too often takes one of his (or her) unofficial vacations from work just when everyone's individual contributions are most sorely needed.

A sales manager need not be a psychologist to realize that the Dasher is afraid of failure. Years of people experience tell the sales manager that this kind of behavior indicates low self-esteem, matched by low expectations of personal performance. People like the Dasher see risk as a road to failure, so they only occasionally can overcome their fear of failure and charge boldly ahead. Even after a success, the power of negative thinking soon catches up with them, and fear again pushes them back into the safe web of inactivity.

Obviously, Dashers somehow manage to perform satisfactorily, even if well below their potential. No company could afford to spend so much time on a poor performer. But salespeople with this problem are always on shaky ground, no matter how brilliant an occasional performance might be, since they add a fair measure of instability to the management of the salesforce and they make the sales manager's job very difficult. Weekly sales reports become a chore, marked so by

Source: Leon A. Wortmann, *Sales Manager's Problem Solver* (New York: John Wiley and Sons, 1983), 63–65.

uncertainty, and the suspense builds as the end of each fiscal year approaches. The sales manager is bound to feel pressure from his or her own boss and from the rest of the salesforce to do something about the Dasher. Several options are available.

The sales manager can try pressure and reinforcement to even out the Dasher's performance — perhaps even old-fashioned discipline. Or the sales manager can prop up the Dasher's performance in some way. Another possibility is that the Dasher might respond to an open discussion of the problem and take corrective action himself or herself — but it is unlikely that the Dasher is capable of doing so. No doubt about it, the Dasher represents a complex motivation and supervisory challenge.

THE case of the Dasher illustrates a typical scenario in salesforce motivation. This type of salesperson meets overall performance expectations — but only barely — and is not working up to full capability. The sales manager must struggle with the problem as an amateur psychologist, relying on intuition about observed behavior to suggest corrective action. The complex nature of the Dasher's problem is hidden deep in his or her psyche. In fact, the Dasher may not be aware of any problem at all. It's probably too difficult a psychological problem for the sales manager's level of expertise in such matters; yet, some action must be taken.

In this chapter, we provide a foundation for understanding the sales manager's role in salesforce motivation. Motivation will be defined, motivational theories discussed, and current issues in salesforce motivation will be presented. Guidelines for managerial actions regarding motivation will also be suggested.

MOTIVATION DEFINED

Defining **motivation** has been a tedious job for psychologists, sales management researchers, and sales managers. After decades of study, the most commonly used definitions of motivation include three dimensions — intensity, persistence, and direction.[1] **Intensity** refers to the amount of mental and physical effort put forth by the salesperson. **Persistence** describes the salesperson's choice to expend effort over a period of time, especially when faced with adverse conditions. **Direction** implies that salespeople choose where their efforts will be spent among various job activities.[2]

Since salespeople are often faced with a diverse set of selling and nonselling job responsibilities, their choice of which activities warrant action is just as important as how hard they work or how well they persist in their efforts. The motivation task is incomplete unless salespeople's efforts are channeled in directions consistent with the overall strategic role of the salesforce within the firm. Further, a truly "motivated" salesforce does not need constant reminders to work hard on the right job dimensions and to persevere in the face of adversity. Rather, the ideal salesforce is self-motivated and requires only periodic direction from the sales manager.

Motivation is an unobservable phenomena, and the terms intensity, persistence, and direction are explanatory concepts that help managers explain what they expect from their salespeople. It is important to note that although sales managers can observe salespeople's behavior, they can only infer their motivation. Indeed, it is the personal, unobservable nature of motivation that makes it such a difficult area of study.

Motivation can also be viewed as intrinsic or extrinsic. If salespeople find their job to be inherently rewarding, they are **intrinsically motivated**. If they are motivated by the rewards provided by others, such as pay and formal recognition, they are **extrinsically motivated**. Certainly it is conceivable that a salesperson's overall motivation could be a function of both intrinsic and extrinsic motivation.

MOTIVATION AND BEHAVIOR

As shown in Figure 11.1, the motivation process begins when the salesperson feels a deficiency in one or more needs. These needs may be economic, social, or self-actualizing.[3] In the salesforce context, **economic needs**, or *existence needs,* could relate to the pay, fringe benefits, and security offered by the job. **Social needs** are relationship-oriented. They could be associated with the salesperson's interactions with the sales manager, co-workers, and customers or be affected by the nature of company policy and support. **Self-actualization needs** are essentially personal-growth needs such as interesting work and opportunities for job advancement.

The process shown in Figure 11.1 suggests several key points. First, normal human behavior is not a random process. It is **goal-directed behavior**, though, not necessarily rational. Second, rewards and punishment contribute to an individual's learning experience, and needs-satisfaction typically results from learned, not instinctive, behaviors. Third, consider how much the sales manager can influence salespeople at each step in the process. To some degree, sales managers have the opportunity to stimulate felt needs, identify ways to satisfy the need, direct the behavior of the salesperson, evaluate performance, reward or punish, and counsel the salesperson during the reassessment stage.

THEORIES OF MOTIVATION

A considerable number of sales managers are skeptical of theoretical approaches to salesforce motivation, as expressed in this review of standard motivation training for sales managers:

> Typically it has consisted of lengthy exposure to the motivational theories of Maslow, Herzberg, and others. In such sessions, almost everything presented is either theory or unrelated to the field manager's business and the realities of their organizations' cultures and policies. So nothing really changes.[4]

Figure 11.1 **A Basic Model of the Motivational Process**

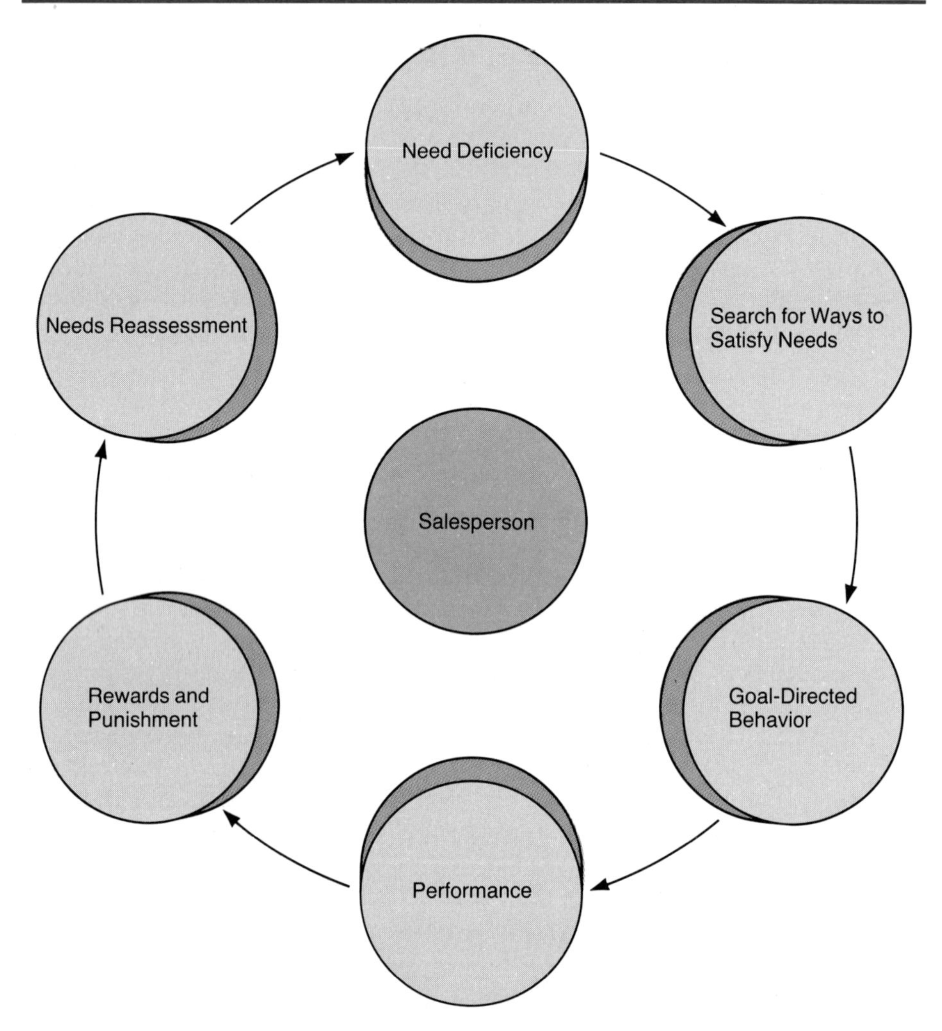

The motivational process begins when an individual perceives an unfulfilled need and begins to search for ways to meet the need. When people feel that needs can be partially or fully met through job behavior, they will set goals and direct their efforts accordingly. Subsequent performance is evaluated and perhaps reinforced through rewards or punishment. This may lead to reassessment of the need and the means for satisfying the need.

Source: Adapted from James L. Gibson, John M. Ivancevich, and James H. Donnelly, Jr., *Organizations: Behavior, Structure, Precesses*, 5th ed. (Plano, Texas: Business Publications, Inc., 1985), 101.

Such opinions indicate the misapplication of motivational theories by those who expect simple answers to complex questions. Theories do not purport to provide wide-sweeping prescriptions for motivating a salesforce, but rather a basic understanding of the complex processes of motivation.

In fairness to sales managers who reject the inputs of motivation theories, it should be stressed that motivation theories focus on the individual, and that the realities of the workplace often dictate a group orientation. Further, these theories were developed by psychologists who have specialized expertise in the application of the theories. Sales managers have expertise in running a sales organization, not in uncovering obscure dimensions of an individual's motivation.

As we proceed with our discussion of motivation theories, remember two cautionary points. First, none of the theories offers a universally accepted explanation of human behavior, either in or out of the salesforce setting. Second, the complexity of the human mind assures us that "theories will continue to be created, expounded, tried, revised, accepted, and rejected."[5] In other words, the theories to be discussed are obviously not infallible, but they are presented as tools useful for gaining a basic understanding of salesforce motivation.

Motivation theories can be classified as content theories or as process theories. **Content theories of motivation** are more concerned with inferring the factors that influence behavior and less concerned with how these factors influence behavior.[6] Content theories try to describe the types of needs people have, the rewards they seek, and which incentives will have the greatest impact on their behavior. Sales managers can benefit from a basic understanding of content theories in that these approaches emphasize the importance of understanding individual differences when trying to motivate a salesforce.

Process theories of motivation concentrate on the mental processes people go through in deciding on alternative courses of action and how much effort should be expended.[7] These theories attempt to explain how different variables interact to influence the expenditure of effort and behavior. Clearly, sales managers need to try to understand the processes of motivation and how salespeople make choices.

Content Theories of Motivation

Four content theories of motivation will be reviewed: Maslow's need hierarchy theory, Alderfer's ERG theory, Herzberg's hygiene-motivation theory, and McClelland's learned-needs theory.

Maslow's Need Hierarchy. First presented over 50 years ago, **Maslow's need-hierarchy theory** has endured as a popular way to study salesforce motivation, despite a lack of convincing empirical support.[8] As shown in Figure 11.2, Maslow's theory proposes that people have five basic sets of needs:[9]

1. *Physiological needs.* The basic needs or drives that are satisfied by such things as food, water, and sleep.

Figure 11.2 **Maslow's Hierarchy of Needs**

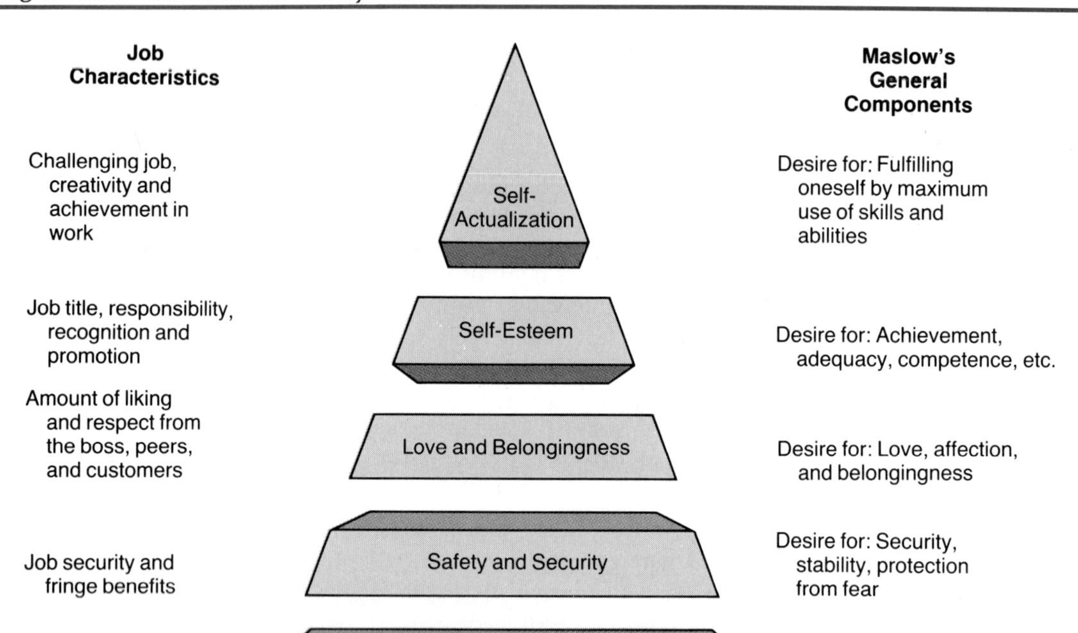

Self-actualization is the highest-order need in Maslow's hierarchy of needs and is achieved by the fewest number of people.

Source: Robert L. Berl, Nicholas C. Williamson, and Terry Powell, "Industrial Salesforce Motivation: A Critique and Test of Maslow's Hierarchy of Need," *Journal of Personal Selling and Sales Management* 4 (May 1984): 33. Used with permission.

2. *Safety and security needs.* The needs associated with producing a secure environment free of threats to continued existence.
3. *Love and belongingness needs.* Concerned with interpersonal factors; reflect a desire to have peer acceptance.
4. *Self-esteem needs.* Needs for self-respect and respect by others. Needs for strength, achievement and recognition by others.
5. *Self-actualization.* Need for self-fulfillment; need for the individual to maximize potential.

According to Maslow, these basic needs are arranged in a hierarchy of prepotency such that the lower-order needs are of primary importance until they are satisfied. As the lower-order needs are satisfied, the higher-order needs become more important to the individual. When needs are met at the highest level, self-actualization, these

INTERNATIONAL SALES

MOTIVATION IN A COMMUNIST-BLOC COUNTRY

If asked to describe the typical salesperson in Yugoslavia, your immediate thoughts probably would not include the term "highly motivated." But, according to American sales trainer Beau Toskich, the Yugoslavian salespeople he has worked with are extremely motivated now that competitive business practices are becoming more commonplace in Yugoslavia.

Recently, he has been working with salespeople at Zavodi Crvena Zastava, manufacturer of Iveco trucks and the Yugo automobile. He finds that Zastava salespeople are hungry for knowledge about Western sales techniques. Toskich reports, "People had told me Yugoslavs are not interested in breaking records or being successful, but it's just not true." He claims that Yugoslavian salespeople are a lot more motivated than their American counterparts, despite the lack of incentive pay for exceptional sales performance. Toskich notes, "The Zastava salespeople are full of pent-up energy that's dying to be unleashed and directed. Yugoslavs have never been exposed to anything like this."

Toskich believes motivation could be further enhanced if he could convince Zastava management to change the salespeoples' compensation plan. He plans to recommend incentive pay for superior performance, but admits it will be hard to gain acceptance for such a thoroughly capitalistic idea.

Source: Al Urbanski, "American Abroad: Iveco's Man in Yugoslavia," *Sales and Marketing Management*, June 1987, 76–78.

needs become even more important to the individual. In summary, behavior is motivated by the need that is most important at a particular time. The strength of a need is a function of its position in the hierarchy and whether or not lower-ranked needs in the hierarchy have been satisfied.

Recent research indicates that of the five categories in Maslow's hierarchy, esteem needs may more important in the motivation of salespeople than previously thought. Bagozzi found self-esteem to be a key determinant of sales performance, suggesting that sales managers should put a high priority on enhancing salesperson self-esteem through positive reinforcement in the form of recognition programs and monetary rewards.[10] Other researchers have suggested that esteem needs could be partially met through giving salespeople more prestigious job titles.[11] It would be interesting to speculate on which needs are the strongest for the salespeople described in "International Sales: Motivation in a Communist-Bloc Country."

Alderfer's ERG Theory. In contrast to Maslow's theory, Alderfer's ERG theory presumed that people have three sets of needs:[12]

1. *Existence needs.* Includes various forms of material and physiological desires; satisfied by environmental factors such as food, water, pay, and working conditions.
2. *Relatedness needs.* Needs concerning maintenance of interpersonal relationships with significant others such as co-workers, family and friends.
3. *Growth needs.* Needs related to an individual's attempt to seek opportunities for unique personal development and full utilization of his or her capacities.

Alderfer's hierarchy differs from Maslow's hierarchy in the number of need categories it identifies and in the content of those categories, but both theories propose that higher-order needs become more important when lower-order needs have been satisfied. An important distinction between the two theories revolves around the issue of frustration in satisfying higher-order needs. Maslow says an individual will continue to "swim upstream" in the quest for unmet higher-order needs, while Alderfer contends that some people might decide to drop back down the hierarchy and attempt to maximize a lower-order reward. For example, a career salesperson may have unmet growth or self-actualization needs as a result of having been continually passed over for promotion into sales management. Maslow would argue that such a person will continue to be motivated by the unmet need to be promoted, while Alderfer would say that he or she might give up on the prospect of promotion and perhaps try to maximize a lower-order reward such as pay.

Herzberg's Hygiene-Motivation Theory. Another content theory, Herzberg's **hygiene-motivation theory** postulates that the job environment can be separated into two dimensions: hygiene factors and motivation factors.[13] **Hygiene factors** are those which, if insufficient, can cause dissatisfaction on the job. Examples are pay, company policies, working conditions, and relationships with co-workers and supervisors. A sales manager may alleviate dissatisfaction by improving a hygiene factor, but the effects are thought to be temporary and lacking in lasting motivational benefit. For example, dissatisfaction with pay could be eliminated with a pay raise, but this might not motivate better performance or assure satisfaction beyond the short term. To gain some idea of the challenge associated with providing sufficient hygiene factors, consider that one survey found 80 percent of salespeople to be dissatisfied with company policy.[14]

Motivation factors in Herzberg's theory include achievement, recognition, challenging work, and opportunity for growth and advancement. These factors correspond to the esteem and self-actualization categories in Maslow's hierarchy, and are thought to be related to long-term motivation, job satisfaction, and performance.

Although recent studies have reported a lack of support for Herzberg's theory among salespeople,[15] the hygiene-motivation concept offers a solid principle of salesforce motivation. Pay and other hygiene factors are only partially sufficient to motivate the salesforce, and their effects are often fleeting.

McClelland's Theory of Learned Needs. Another theory, McClelland's **learned-needs theory**, holds that people learn to strive for achievement, affiliation, and power.[16] It attributes the individual differences in motivation to whichever of these three needs is dominant at a given point in time. Salespeople who are high in the need for *achievement* may prefer higher-order rewards such as feelings of accomplishment and opportunities for personal growth. Further, they may avoid tasks where they believe the probability of failure is high.[17] The need for achievement has received considerable attention as a determinant of overall salesperson motivation. One study appearing in the *Harvard Business Review* identified *personality,* particularly the need to achieve, as one of the key determinants of motivation, along with the sales job itself and type of compensation plan.[18]

Salespeople whose need for *affiliation* dominates their behavior are motivated by being a part of a group or company organization. They may value friendships with established customers but show reluctance to call on new prospects, unless they have reason to believe the prospect will be friendly. Interestingly, the stereotypical high-producing salesperson is often depicted as a loner who wants as little direction as possible. The vice-president of sales and general manager of Mohr Development of Stamford, Connecticut, believes the image of the top salesperson/loner is mythical, and that affiliation needs are strong among salespeople. He says the most dissatisfied, low-performing salespeople are found in companies where managers do not spend enough time in the field to give adequate guidance.[19]

Some salespeople covet *power* and are extremely motivated in their pursuit of it. According to McClelland, a need for power is a need to influence other's behavior, and it can be a positive characteristic for successful sales management. Salespeople who seek promotion into management might be extremely motivated to sharpen their interpersonal sales skills, thinking that such skills will be a positive attribute in future management assignments.

Overlap of Content Theories. The content theories of motivation, while different, have considerable overlap. Since each has been derived in part from a preexisting theory, such overlap is to be expected. The similarities among the content theories discussed in this chapter are summarized in Figure 11.3.

Process Theories of Motivation

Four process theories of motivation will be briefly reviewed: expectancy theory, equity theory, attribution theory, and reinforcement theory.

Expectancy Theory. Building on the work of Vroom[20] and others, Walker, Churchill, and Ford introduced the **expectancy theory** of salesperson motivation over a decade ago.[21] According to expectancy theory, a salesperson's motivation to expend effort on a given task is a function of three interrelated factors: expectancies, instrumentalities, and valences.

Expectancies are the salesperson's perceptions of the linkages between effort and job performance. For example, one salesperson may perceive a strong connection between total hours worked and job performance. Conversely, another salesperson might see very little connection between incremental effort and improved performance. An illustration of how salesforce expectancies can be altered is given in "Sales Technology: Motivational Effects of Computerizing."

Figure 11.3 **Summary of Content Theories of Motivation**

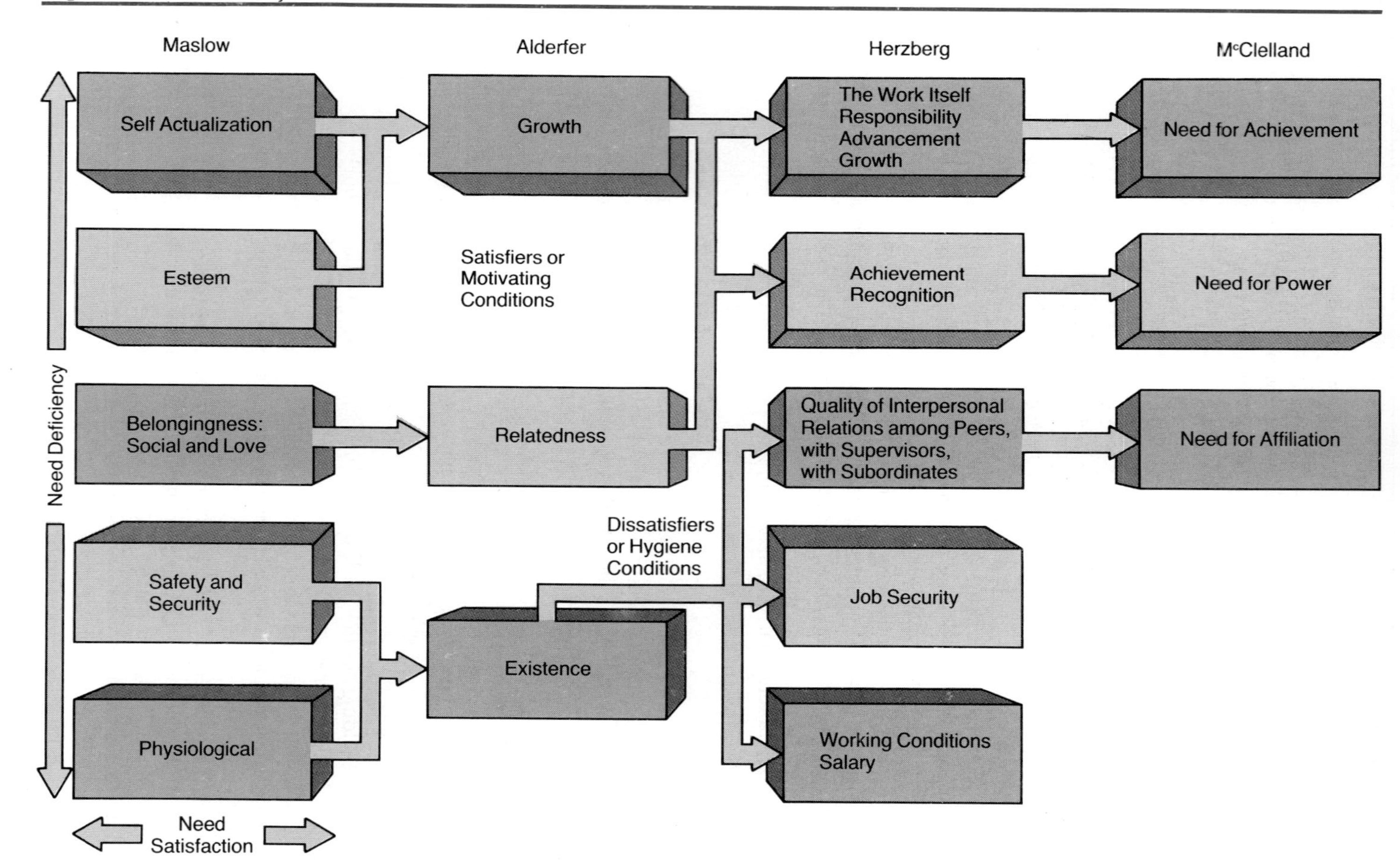

Each of the four content theories of motivation attempts to explain behavior from similar but not identical perspectives. By following the arrows from left to right, you can compare the components of these theories.

Source: James L. Gibson, John M. Ivancevich, and James H. Donnelly, *Organizations: Behavior, Structure, Processes,* 5th ed. (Plano, Texas: Business Publications, Inc., 1985), 123. Used with permission.

SALES TECHNOLOGY

MOTIVATIONAL EFFECTS OF COMPUTERIZING

When Hewlett-Packard furnished its salesforce with portable computers, to save time on nonselling chores, the primary goal was to increase sales productivity as measured in terms of customer-contact time. The result was a 27 percent increase in customer-contact time. The computerization of the salesforce brought some interesting motivational side effects.

Paperwork became less onerous. One sales rep who used to spend half his weekends on paperwork said, "Now my weekends are spent with my family, and my work at home has been cut to three or four hours a month because I do my work on the portable whenever I have free time." The internal communications system has been improved, and HP salespeople can send and receive messages without making a trip to the office as was required in the past.

Overall job motivation among the HP salespeople has improved since computerization. Project manager Ben Menold says, "A salesperson must feel proud about his products. If the portable gives him firsthand knowledge in solving business productivity problems, he can sell office automation benefits to the customer with more integrity. That makes him feel important and more professional." Clearly, the HP computerization project affected the effort/performance perceptions (expectancies) of its salesforce, and achieved other motivating effects as well.

Source: Thayer C. Taylor, "Hewlett-Packard Gives Sales Reps A Competitive Edge," *Sales and Marketing Management,* February 1987, 36–40.

Instrumentalities are the salesperson's perceptions about the correlation of performance and various rewards. For example, a salesperson can easily see that increasing sales volume leads to a financial reward if he or she is paid a commission on sales. A straight-salary salesperson, however, will probably be less certain of the nature of the reward, if any, for increased sales volume.

The **valence for rewards**, the third dimension of motivation according to expectancy theory, is the salesperson's perception of the desirability of receiving increased rewards for improved performance. While it is generally assumed that all rewards are desirable, in fact some rewards are only marginally effective, and some can actually have a negative effect on a salesperson's motivation. For example, we know of a high-performing sales representative who tried not to win a sales contest, since the grand prize was a trip to Hawaii, and he had a true fear of flying. His valence for the available reward was actually negative.

Expectancy theory holds that behavior is "purposeful, based on conscious behavior, and goal-directed."[22] By perceiving expectancies, instrumentalities, and valences for rewards, salespeople look into the future and adjust behavior based on what they expect to happen and how much they value the outcomes of their performance. This "future-gazing" can influence motivation positively, negatively, or leave it unchanged.

Figure 11.4 **Key Salesperson Questions in Expectancy Theory**

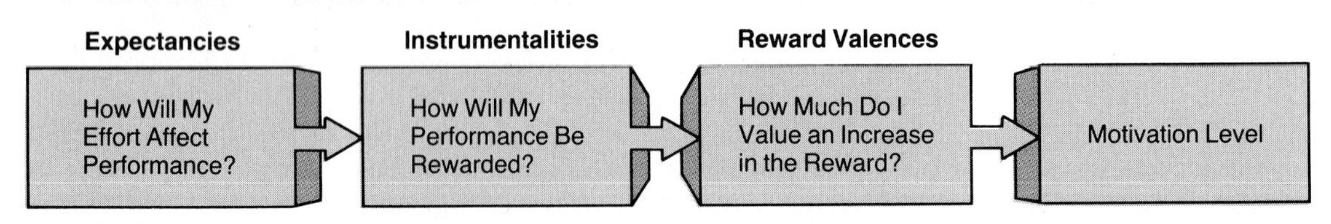

Salespeople's motivation level may be affected by their perceptions of the linkages between effort and performance and between performance and rewards. Motivation can also be affected by how much the salesperson values the reward being offered.

The key questions asked of themselves by salespeople who behave according to the expectancy model of motivation are summarized in Figure 11.4.

Equity Theory. Introducing the concept of fairness into sales force motivation, **equity theory** proposes that salespeople may evaluate their treatment as compared to "relevant others" in the salesforce and if they perceive inequitable treatment, suffer detrimental motivational effects. Equity theory was developed by Adams, who proposed that employees use input/output ratios to determine relative equity.[23] Inputs to the organization might include educational level, job experience, or perhaps hours worked, while typical outputs would be pay, promotion opportunities, and other rewards. A salesperson sensitive to equity issues might say, "I don't mind making less money than Joe for doing basically the same job, since he has twice the sales experience that I do, but I really don't think it is fair for me to make less money than Bill just because he has a MBA and I don't."

According to Adams, individuals who perceive inequity may take one of several courses of action to rectify the situation. They may rationalize the situation by distorting their own perceptions (maybe a MBA is worth more after all), or they may alter their job inputs (I will cut down on the number of hours worked, since it doesn't really pay to work extra hours). They may also try to influence the "relevant other" person to alter his or her inputs or outcomes, select another person for comparison purposes, or perhaps leave the job. All of these actions could have negative effects on overall salesforce motivation and performance. The primary processes in equity theory are illustrated in Figure 11.5.

Sales managers can expect that job-related equity issues will become more important in the future. Employee expectations are being influenced by widespread discussions on topics such as providing comparable pay for comparable jobs and curtailing sexual harassment. The fair treatment of employees is viewed not only as a motivational tool, but also as a basic responsibility of sales managers.

Figure 11.5 **Equity Theory and Salesforce Motivation**

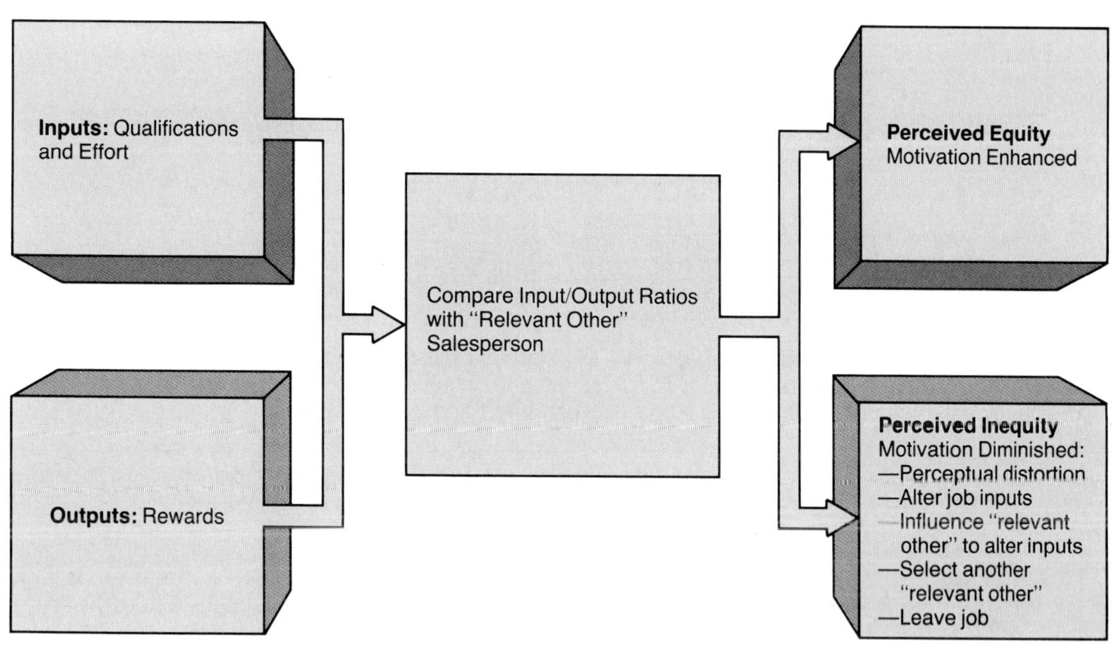

Equity theory suggests that salespeople will compare their efforts, performance, and rewards to others in the salesforce. If they feel they have been treated unfairly, their motivation may be diminished.

Attribution Theory. Based on the notion that people are motivated to understand the causes of their performance, **attribution theory** concentrates on the mental processes people utilize to understand why events occur as they do. In a review of attribution theory, Teas and McElroy reiterate the basic assumptions underlying the theory:[24]

1. Individuals will try to assign causes for important instances of behavior, sometimes seeking additional information to do so.
2. Individuals will assign causes in a systematic manner.
3. The particular cause that an individual attributes to a given event will affect subsequent behavior.

The attribution process might be initiated if a salesperson achieves an unexpected result or fails to perform satisfactorily on a well-defined routine task. The self-analysis

Figure 11.6 **Attribution Theory and Expectancy Estimates**

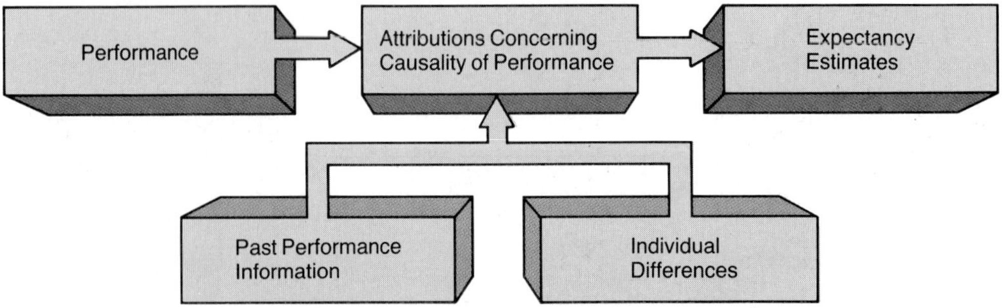

Attribution theory suggests that salespeople try to determine the causes of their successes and failures. After attributing performance results to a set of factors and circumstances, salespeople may change their expectancy estimates (the perceived linkage between effort and performance).

Source: R. Kenneth Teas and James C. McElroy, "Causal Attributions and Expectancy Estimates: A Framework for Understanding the Dynamics of Salesforce Motivation." Reprinted from *Journal of Marketing* 50 (January 1986): 76, published by the American Marketing Association. Used with permission.

will utilize past performance information and perhaps an assessment of how the salesperson differs from other salespeople. Further, future behavior and perceptions, including the effort-performance linkage (*expectancy*) may be altered. For example, a salesperson may attribute failure to poor strategy rather than to poor effort. In these situations, salespeople may be motivated to change their strategy, perhaps by using a different sales approach or asking more questions during the sales presentation. When failure is attributed to a lack of effort, salespeople may be motivated to work longer hours, but still following the same strategies and tactics.[25]

As the sales job becomes more sophisticated and competition intensifies, sales managers and salespeople will become more involved in the use of post-hoc analysis consistent with attribution theory to attempt to uncover the causes of success and failure. Attribution theory is summarized in Figure 11.6.

Reinforcement Theory. Reinforcement theorists are not interested in explaining behavior by studying unobservable personality traits, inner drives and needs, or mental processes. In contrast to the other motivation theories we have discussed to this point, **reinforcement theory**, pioneered by B. F. Skinner, never moves its focus from behavior. Moreover, Skinner believes that behavior can be explained solely on the principle of reinforcement.[26]

Basically, reinforcement theory proposes that specific behaviors can be initiated, encouraged, modified, or eliminated by utilizing the specific reinforcement strategies of positive reinforcement, negative reinforcement, punishment, and extinction. As

Exhibit 11.1 **Behavior Modification through Reinforcement**

I. Behavior Modification Strategies to Increase Desired Behavior		
Problem:	Desirable behavior does not occur frequently enough	
Behavior modification strategies:	1. Positive reinforcement	2. Negative reinforcement
Method:	When desirable behavior occurs, follow it with a pleasant consequence.	When desirable behavior occurs, allow the salesperson to avoid an unpleasant consequence.
Example:		
1. Desirable behavior	Gain a new customer.	Turn in expense accounts on time.
2. Consequence	Bonus for gaining new customer.	If expense account on time, allow salesperson to *avoid* a downgrading in performance review.

II. Behavior Modification Strategies to Decrease Undesirable Behavior		
Problem:	Undesirable behavior occurs too frequently	
Behavior modification strategies:	1. Punishment	2. Extinction
Method:	When undesirable behavior occurs, follow it with an unpleasant consequence.	When undesirable behavior occurs, no positive reinforcement.
Example:		
1. Undesirable behavior	Sales order not complete.	Salesperson turns in incomplete expense reports.
2. Consequence	Loss of part of the commission on the order.	Sales manager stops correcting the reports for the salesperson and returns them to the salesperson for completion.[a]

[a] By correcting incomplete reports, the sales manager was inadvertently providing positive reinforcement for undesirable behavior.

Source: Robert A. Scott, John E. Swan, M. Elizabeth Wilson, and Jenny J. Roberts, "Organizational Behavior Modification: A General Tool for Sales Management," *Journal of Personal Selling and Sales Management* 6 (August 1986): 63–64. Used with permission.

shown in Exhibit 11.1, **positive reinforcement** provides a pleasant consequence for desirable behavior. **Negative reinforcement** allows the salesperson to avoid an unpleasant consequence if desirable behavior has occurred. **Punishment**, the provision of an unpleasant experience, or **extinction**, the withholding of positive reinforcement, may be used following undesirable behavior.

Reinforcement theory's critics contend that it places too much reliance on "carrot and stick" dimensions of motivation. They charge that adherents to this theory may mistakenly believe that motivation is simply a matter of meting out rewards and punishments and thus ignore other important dimensions of motivation such as job design and providing necessary job training. Nevertheless, reinforcement theory has been used in several major corporations to motivate specific employee behaviors. A large national chemical sales organization, for example, offered a bonus as a positive reinforcement for increasing sales volume and forecasting accuracy.[27]

Comment on Content and Process Motivation Theories

We would encourage any sales manager to become familiar with the basic concepts of all the motivation theories we have discussed. An experienced sales manager reflected on the usefulness of theoreticians such as Maslow, Vroom, Herzberg, and McClelland as follows:

> Although we will never know whether these famous scientists could ever have been as effective as you are in meeting a sales quota, the probability is they could identify your people-problems and guide you in a way that could help you develop highly effective solutions. Therefore, a good comprehension of their theories of human behavior can be quite valuable as you attempt to bring order to your potentially chaotic situations, provide incentives and motivation, and satisfy your own needs at the same time. After all, the title "manager" does not mean you are also not a human being.[28]

Sales managers and theorists would agree that there is still a lot to learn about what motivates salespeople, but at least some insights into the subject are offered by the major theories reviewed here. For a summary of how the thought-provoking suggestions of these theorists can be applied to salesforce motivation, refer to Exhibit 11.2.

CURRENT ISSUES IN SALESFORCE MOTIVATION

Issues of particular interest in salesforce motivation today are usually phrased as questions, indicating that the answers are yet to be determined:

1. How individualized should motivation be?
2. What will be the effects of an aging population on salesforce motivation?
3. How should the expectations of today's emerging salesforce concerning the future be addressed in motivational programs?
4. Are traditional motivational practices still effective?

Motivation: Individual or Group Orientation

Motivation theories stress the individual nature of motivation and contend that group approaches to motivation will be sub-optimal. Yet, in practice, it is rare to find individualized motivational programs, especially in large organizations. In fact, there is a fair amount of resistance to individualized programs, partly due to the inescapable fact that it is easier to implement one motivational program for the entire salesforce than to design individual ones for every salesperson. In some cases, greater overall productivity can be achieved through standardization. Furthermore, the utilization of a single program for everyone can reduce the firm's legal liabilities with regard to employee treatment.

Exhibit 11.2 **Sales Motivation Implications of Motivation Theories**

Theory	Selected Managerial Implications
Maslow's need-hierarchy theory	Recognize that different people are motivated by different needs; consider individual needs when designing motivational programs; offer a variety of rewards if individual needs cannot be explicitly considered.
Alderfer's ERG theory	Recognize that salespeople may become frustrated if they cannot fulfill higher-order needs and may seek instead to maximize a lower-order reward related to lower-order need fulfillment.
Herzberg's motivation-hygiene theory	Recognize that pay and other job hygiene factors, though important in salesforce motivation, may be insufficient to sustain high levels of motivation in the long run.
McClelland's learned-needs theory	In some cases, it may be worthwhile to attempt to increase a salesperson's need for achievement through training or counseling; teach salespeople to exercise self-control and demonstrate maturity to balance their need for power when dealing with customers.
Expectancy theory	Clearly communicate the linkages between (1) job effort and performance and (2) performance and rewards.
Equity theory	Offer rewards valued by the salesforce; reward each salesperson on an equitable basis compared with other salespeople.
Attribution theory	Help salespeople understand the cause-and-effect relationships between their behavior and performance; consider the importance of direction of effort along with intensity and persistence of effort.
Reinforcement theory	Be consistent in reinforcing desirable behavior and discouraging undesirable behavior.

There has been some discussion of developing a compromise approach to motivation that falls between the extremes of individual and mass approaches. The concept, called **salesforce segmentation**, suggests dividing the salesforce into groups based on motivational needs, then developing motivational programs for each group (which, of course, would share some common parts). This idea was first proposed by Professors Moissen and Fram and has continued to spur discussion.[29]

One study of salespeople identified three segments for motivational purposes called: **comfort seekers, spotlight seekers, and developers.**[30] The *comfort seekers* sought job security, a sense of accomplishment, and liking and respect from their sales jobs. The *spotlight seekers* wanted highly visible rewards such as pay and recognition awards. The *developers* valued opportunities for personal growth as a job reward. This study demonstrated that salespeople can be effectively segmented for motivational purposes, and it recommended that more organizations consider such segmentation for motivational purposes.

Demographics: An Aging Workforce

By 1995 nearly three-fourths of the nation's workforce will be in the 25–54 age range, compared to approximately two-thirds in this range in 1984.[31] For sales managers, this demographic development is a mixed blessing. According to the research on salesperson career cycles (briefly reviewed in Chapter 4), older, more experienced salespeople are among the most satisfied with their jobs. Further, they are among the highest performers in the salesforce.

On the other hand, there are some concerns related to aging salesforces. For the younger salespeople in the 25–54 group, opportunities for promotion into management are expected to be limited. Salespeople who have limited opportunities for future promotion may be facing what researchers call a **career plateau.** In a study of two large salesforces, approximately 65 percent of the salespeople were considered plateaued, that is, these salespeople had not received a promotion in the past five years.[32] Among the plateaued group, over half were considered "deadwood" in that their current performance was low. Motivating such salespeople would indeed be a challenge.

Even though the demand for salespeople and sales managers is expected to be strong, the number of new sales management positions will not accommodate all those who seek promotion. This problem could worsen if the current trend toward downsizing corporations continues.

Another issue related to motivating the maturing sales forces is job-related stress, which has been called the primary mental problem among salespeople.[33] While all age groups are potential victims of stress, there is some thought that career salespeople may be particularly vulnerable to it. Job pressures and increasingly competitive conditions can lead to **job burnout** (see Exhibit 11.3) or to undesirable coping behaviors such as alcohol and drug abuse. In a recent survey, over 50 percent of responding sales managers reported that alcohol abuse was at least a minor problem in their salesforce.[34] While this finding cannot be strictly attributed to job stress, it does suggest the possibility that stress-reduction programs will become a more important part of salesforce motivation programs in the future.

Salespeoples' Job Expectations

There is a general feeling that the job expectations of today's salespeople differ from those of generations past. Certainly this is a natural process, as new generations often bring new values and norms to the workplace. Evidence of changing work values among salespeople come from several sources:

1. A survey of 264 salespeople in a national firm found that older salespeople place greater emphasis on the moral importance of work and have more pride in their work than do younger salespeople.[35]

Exhibit 11.3 Salesperson Burnout Self-Test

Burnout Signals

Are you burning out?

At the heart of burnout is increasing disability to handle stress and mounting dissatisfaction with your job and yourself. While all of us, on occasion, have been unhappy with our lives or jobs, the problem of burnout goes much deeper and is more prolonged.

After three years of conducting burnout and stress management workshops for sales representatives and others in the work force, we have found the following self-test useful in determining just who may be burning out. Ask yourself these questions:

	Yes	No
■ Do you feel you're working harder and accomplishing less?	☐	☐
■ Are you unhappy during work hours and irritated with fellow workers?	☐	☐
■ Do you feel powerless or helpless to change the situation?	☐	☐
■ Are you using more of your sick leave or other kinds of leave to stay away form work?	☐	☐
■ Do you find yourself frequently saying, "I don't give a damn anymore," "I just can't keep up," or "It doesn't ever really matter what I do, it will turn out the same anyway"?	☐	☐
■ Do you find your relationships with others—family and friends—more agitated because of the frustrations of the job?	☐	☐
■ Do you find you're ignoring or angry at your buyers because of your work-related tensions?	☐	☐

If you're answering "yes" more often than "no," you may be a candidate for burnout. Some people are able to cope with their job frustrations and stress, but this might be the time for you to take stock of where you are in your job, where you're heading, and what you would like to change for the better.

A person has to decide what is creating stress and how best to handle it. While you may try to change your organization or company, it might be easier and better if you change your attitudes, work habits, values, goals and how you spend your time.

Source: Charles Larson, Ph.D., "Help! My Job Is Killing Me! Burnout among Sales Reps," *Personal Selling Power* 1 (no. 4, 1981): 2. © by Personal Selling Power. Reprinted by permission of the publisher.

2. A sales executive asserts that "motivational techniques that used to be effective have lost much of their impact." He does not believe that traditional motivation and leadership methods will improve sales productivity.[36]
3. Speaking about "baby boomers," one motivation expert has said, "Homes, cars, vacations, and free time are not considered luxuries. They are, in fact, not only desired but expected and are recognized as rewards to be gained by working in an economy based on free enterprise. The acquisitive qualities of human nature are up front."[37]

What do these changes mean to sales managers? They strongly suggest that sales managers must make genuine efforts to understand the legitimate needs of today's salespeople, who happen to be among the most highly educated, achievement-oriented occupational groups. Traditional viewpoints must be reevaluated and discarded if necessary.

SALES TREND

REDEFINING THE ROLE OF THE MOTIVATIONAL SPEAKER

Motivational speakers, or so-called "evangelists of inspiration," have long been a tradition in salesforce motivation. A *Fortune* magazine article notes that "the market for motivational speakers is no more measurable than the effectiveness of their work, but there is no doubt it has exploded in the 1980s." Speakers like Zig Ziglar, Don Hutson, Tom Peters, and Dennis Waitley are often booked years in advance, earning handsome fees for their work. For example, Ziglar, who usually addresses salespeople, earns $10,000 for a one-hour motivational talk.

While the demand for motivational speakers is strong, sales executives frequently want more substance to go along with the uplifting, but often only temporarily motivating, message offered by speaker superstars. Don Beverage notes that when he began in the speaking business in 1971, motivation was the hot topic. Today, he says, hype and sermonizing have become obsolete; a more practical content in the message is sought by corporate trainers. Jack Cohen of the Sales Dynamic Institute reports that he used to be a rah-rah speaker, but is now spending more time on business strategy in his talks.

Jerry Porras, a Stanford professor, summarized the dominant current thinking on motivational speakers in *Fortune:* "Having a motivational speaker is worthwhile as part of a bigger process, but many organizations rely on them to do much more than that. It won't work."

Source: Compiled from: Jeremy Main, "Merchants of Inspiration," *Fortune,* July 6, 1987, 69–74; and Kevin T. Higgins, "Motivating the Sales Force: Does Rah-Rah Talk Translate into Action?" *Marketing News,* July 4, 1986, 10.

Reevaluating Traditional Practices

As previously mentioned, there has been a historical reliance on rewards and punishment in salesforce motivation. While both rewards and punishment have important places in the motivational program, other dimensions are emerging as being at least as important as these traditional tools. For example, **job enrichment**, which involves designing the sales job to include more variety, responsibility for completing the entire job, feedback, and meaningful work experiences, can be used to stimulate motivation.[38] **Career pathing** is another practice that is becoming more useful as a motivational tool. It involves acquainting the salesperson with potential routes for career development in the organization, being as specific as possible regarding the skills, behavior, and performance necessary to pursue various paths. Perhaps the use of job enrichment and career pathing will ultimately redefine the role of traditional rewards and punishment in salesforce motivation.

Another traditional practice undergoing evaluation is the use of "rah-rah" motivational speakers. While motivational speakers are still an integral part of the salesforce motivation programs of many firms, the role of these performers is being reevaluated, and often redefined. The motivational speaker phenomenon is explored in "Sales Trend: Redefining the Role of the Motivational Speaker."

GUIDELINES FOR MOTIVATING SALESPEOPLE

Sales mangers should realize that practically everything they do will influence salesforce motivation one way or another. The people they recruit, the plans and policies they institute, the training they provide, and the way they communicate with and supervise salespeople are among the more important factors. In addition, sales managers should realize that environmental factors beyond their control may also influence salesforce motivation. Like other managerial functions, motivating salespeople requires a prioritized, calculated approach, rather than a futile attempt to address all motivational needs simultaneously. If for no other reason, the complexity of human nature and changing needs of salesforce members will prohibit the construction of motivational programs that run smoothly without periodic adjustment. Guidelines for motivating salespeople follow:

1. Recruit and select salespeople whose personal motives match the requirements and rewards of the job.
2. Attempt to incorporate the individual needs of salespeople into motivational programs.
3. Provide adequate job information and assure proper skill development for the salesforce.
4. Use job design and redesign as motivational tools.
5. Concentrate on building the self-esteem of salespeople.
6. Take a proactive approach to seeking out motivational problems and sources of frustration in the salesforce.

Recruitment and Selection

The importance of matching the abilities and needs of sales recruits to the requirements and rewards of the job cannot be overstated. This is especially critical for sales managers who have little opportunity to alter job dimensions and reward structures. Investing more time in recruitment and selection to assure a good match is likely to pay off later in terms of fewer motivational and other managerial problems. A regional manager for a business products company echoes these sentiments: "Our motivational program is built around goals, evaluations, and hiring the right people. It is not unusual for an applicant to visit our office six or seven times before a hiring decision is made. I want to get to know each person as thoroughly as possible before I make a commitment."[39]

Incorporation of Individual Needs

At the outset of this chapter, motivation was described as complex personal process. At the heart of the complexity of motivation is the concept of individual needs. While there is considerable pressure and, in many cases, sound economic rationale, for supporting mass approaches to salesforce motivation, there may also be opportunities to incorporate individual needs into motivational programs. As researchers learn more about the salesperson's career cycle, it is likely that more intra-salesforce diversity in motivational programs will occur. Salesforce segmentation offers some of the benefits of individualized approaches and may be a logical alternative in large salesforces.

Information and Skills

The importance of providing adequate job information is well documented in expectancy theory. If sales managers equip their salespeople to make accurate expectancy and instrumentality estimates, a major motivational task is accomplished. If the salespeople's estimates are accurate and in agreement with the sales managers, reasonable goals can be set that allow performance worthy of rewards. Providing adequate information to the salesforce and nurturing skill development can also enhance salesforce socialization (discussed in earlier chapters), thereby reducing role ambiguity and role conflict.

Job Design

Some of the more promising research into salesforce motivation is in the area of job design and redesign. For example, two studies found job skill variety, task significance, job autonomy, and job feedback to be significantly related to the intrinsic motivational levels of salespeople.[40] **Job skill variety** is the extent to which salespeople get a chance to use skills and abilities in a wide range of job behaviors. **Task significance** is the degree to which the salesperson feels the job makes a meaningful contribution and is important to the organization. **Job autonomy** is the ability of the person in a given job to determine the nature of the tasks and to chart a course of action. **Feedback** refers to the degree to which salespeople receive clear information concerning the effectiveness of their performance.

Given the nature of sales jobs, one would expect good opportunities to stimulate intrinsic motivation without major changes in the job. Job skill variety is already present in many sales jobs. And given the unique contributions of personal selling to the organization as discussed in Chapter 2, imparting a feeling of task significance to salespeople should be feasible. Certainly, time and territory management as practiced in many sales organizations contributes to a feeling of job autonomy. Finally, feedback from sales managers or through self-monitoring is fairly easy to arrange. In many ways, the motivational task of sales managers is much easier than for some of their managerial counterparts in the organization. The sales job itself can be a powerful motivator.

Building Self-Esteem

Researchers have emphasized the importance of building self-esteem to enhance motivation and performance of salespeople.[41] Practitioners have agreed. One sales executive who believes that nothing is more important than money in motivating salespeople adds,

> Equally important is helping salespeople meet their needs for self-esteem. Fewer occupational groups have stronger needs in this area . . . . Our experience shows that even where financial incentives are extraordinary, turnover is high when sales managers erode salespeople's self-esteem. There are limits to the financial incentives that can be offered. The supply of self-esteem incentives is unlimited, however, and sales managers would do well to use them more often.[42]

Sales managers can use the insights of reinforcement theorists to build self-esteem in the salesforce. Positive reinforcement for good performance should be standard procedure. This may be done with formal or informal communications or recognition programs designed to spotlight good performance. When performance is less than satisfactory, it should not be overlooked, but addressed in a constructive manner.

Proactive Approach

Sales managers should be committed to uncovering potential problems in motivation and eliminating them before they develop. For example, if some members of the salesforce perceive a lack of opportunity for promotion into management, and are demotivated as a result, the sales manager might take additional steps to clearly define the guidelines for promotion into management and review the performance of management hopefuls in light of these guidelines. If promotion opportunities are indeed limited, the matching function of recruitment and selection again shows its importance.[43]

SUMMARY

1. **Define motivation in terms of intensity, persistence, and direction.** Motivation has been defined in a variety of ways. The definition we use incorporates the qualities of intensity, persistence, and direction. Intensity is the amount of mental and physical effort the salesperson is willing to expend on a specific activity. Persistence is a choice to expend effort over time, especially in the face of adversity. Direction implies that, to some extent, salespeople choose the activities on which effort is expended.
2. **Discuss motivation as a process that begins with a perceived need deficiency.** As shown in Figure 11.1, motivation begins when the individual perceives a need deficiency. Needs are classified differently by different theorists, but three rather generic types of human needs are economic, social, and self-actualizing needs. When a need deficiency is perceived, people search for ways to satisfy the need and then engage in goal-directed behavior. Their performance on the job is usually followed by some form of reward or punishment, after which needs are reassessed.
3. **Discuss the basic points of four content theories and four process theories of motivation.** The four content theories of motivation discussed in this chapter were Maslow's need-hierarchy theory (Figure 11.2), Alderfer's ERG theory, Herz-

berg's hygiene-motivation theory, and McClelland's learned-needs theory. The four process theories of motivation presented were expectancy theory (Figure 11.4), equity theory (Figure 11.5), attribution theory (Figure 11.6), and reinforcement theory (Exhibit 11.1).

4. **Identify key issues in salesforce motivation.** One important issue deals with the question of how individualized motivational programs can be. While there are obvious advantages to incorporating individual needs into such programs, there are also strong arguments for a mass approach. Salesforce segmentation can compromise between individualized and mass approaches. Other important issues are the aging workforce, the incidence of job burnout among salespeople (Exhibit 11.2), and the expectations of today's emerging salesforce, including an apparently increasing desire for material possessions. Still another issue is the current trend to reevaluate traditional practices of salesforce motivation, including a strong reliance on rewards and punishment and the use of motivational speakers.
5. **Cite managerial guidelines for salesforce motivation.** Six managerial guidelines for motivating salespeople are as follows: First, match the recruit to the requirements and rewards of the job. Second, incorporate individual needs into motivational programs when feasible. Third, provide salespeople with adequate information and ensure proper skill development to facilitate job performance. Fourth, cultivate salespeople's self-esteem. Fifth, take a proactive approach to uncovering motivational problems. Sixth, try to eliminate problems before they become serious.

Key Terms

- motivation
- intensity
- persistence
- direction
- intrinsic motivation
- extrinsic motivation
- economic needs
- social needs
- self-actualization needs
- goal-directed behavior
- content theories of motivation
- process theories of motivation
- Maslow's need-hierarchy theory
- Alderfer's ERG theory
- Herzberg's hygiene-motivation theory
- McClelland's learned-needs theory
- expectancy theory
- expectancies
- instrumentalities
- valence for rewards
- equity theory
- attribution theory
- reinforcement theory
- positive reinforcement
- negative reinforcement
- punishment
- extinction
- salesforce segmentation
- career plateau
- job burnout
- job enrichment
- career pathing
- job skill variety
- task significance
- job autonomy
- feedback

Review Questions

1. Explain motivation in terms of intensity, persistence, and direction.
2. Explain the motivation process in terms of events that follow a perceived need deficiency.
3. How are the need hierarchies of Maslow and Alderfer alike? How do they differ?
4. Explain how McClelland's learned needs (achievement, power, and affiliation) correspond to dimensions of the other three content theories of motivation.
5. Explain the meanings of these terms: expectancies, instrumentalities, and valence for rewards.
6. How does attribution theory differ from the other three process theories of motivation?
7. Why should sales managers be concerned with theoretical approaches to motivation?
8. What is meant by salesforce segmentation? When might segmentation work for motivational purposes?
9. What role, if any, should motivational speakers have in salesforce motivation?
10. What opportunities are there to motivate the salesforce through job design and redesign?

Application Exercises

1. You are a national sales manager, with 150 salespeople in your organization. Your salespeople range in age from 22 to 67, with the average age being 36. Average earnings, including salary and bonuses, is $40,000 per year. Recently, you hired a consulting firm to assess the motivational level and reward preferences of your salesforce. You are now interpreting the findings of the consulting firm, and you are puzzled by one conclusion in particular.

   According to the consultants, the older salespeople voiced stronger preferences for increased pay than did the younger salespeople. Since the older salespeople generally earn more money than do their younger counterparts, and you subscribe to the concepts of Maslow's need hierarchy, you find this surprising. You had always reasoned that since older salespeople earned more money, they probably placed more value on higher-order needs such as esteem and self-actualization. What are the possible explanations for this unexpected finding?

2. In his book, *Sales Manager's Problem-Solver,* Leon Wortman introduces us to a character called "no-no."[44] No-no is a malcontent, who never has a positive thing to say to other company personnel. He is a chronic complainer, but there is one good thing about him—he does a great job with his customers and regularly achieves high sales performance levels. When anyone suggests he adopt a more positive approach, he screams that he is not a robot and that he has a right to question the way things are done. Though highly intelligent, he has no idea of the disruptive effects he is having on his co-workers. At this point, assume you are no-no's sales manager, and your boss, having become aware of the problem, has asked you to present some options for dealing with no-no. You have come up with five options:

   a. Talk with the other salespeople and try to get them to be more tolerant of no-no.
   b. Ask one of his friends, or maybe someone from personnel, to take him aside and explain how his behavior is detrimental to the company.

c. Apply some gentle pressure, much like a parent who tries to manage an unruly child.
d. Assume someone else (family, peers, the company, or maybe you) are to blame for his behavior, and try to have a friendly conversation to uncover the underlying problem.
e. Consider the possibility that he might be too intelligent for the job, and provide job enrichment to give him more challenging assignments.

Now that you have come with these options, identify the advantages and disadvantages of each one.

3. It is Monday morning, and Bill Jackson, the sales manager for a major-league baseball team, has the 15 members of the group ticket salesforce assembled for what promises to be an explosive meeting. Jackson is unhappy with last week's sales report, and he fully intends to do something about it. After a few preliminary announcements, he addresses the salesforce as follows:

   The numbers from last week are in, and I've got to wonder what you people did last week. I know one thing — you didn't sell enough to be called salespeople! How many of you sold at least 500 tickets last week? [A few hands go up, and Jackson continues]

   Well, big deal! I could probably sell 500 tickets without getting out of bed. How many of you so-called salespeople sold 1,000 tickets last week — I know the answer, I just want to see if any of you know just how lousy you are. [This time, no one raises a hand, and Jackson concludes the meeting with these comments]

   This week better be different. You get out there and call on every civic organization, corporation, and social club in town, and I mean *sell, sell, sell* huge blocks of tickets! Bat day is coming up, and I want a full house. Let me make one thing crystal clear — if you do not personally sell 1,000 tickets this week, don't bother to come to work next Monday. Now, hit the streets!

   How would you react to Mr. Jackson's exhortations if you were one of the salespeople? What type of person would react most negatively? Most positively?

4. For this exercise, you should assume you have graduated from college and have begun work as a sales representative. Your employer is assessing the motivational needs of the salesforce according to Maslow's hierarchy of needs. After everyone in the class has assessed his or her individual needs, it might be interesting to see how many motivational groups there are in the class and then discuss how sales managers might motivate each group.

An Exercise to Determine Your Motivational Needs

To perform the exercise, read through the following statements . . . check those which are most important in motivating you to do your best work. Select the ten most important statements. Your instructor will be able to discuss the results with you.

Job security because of seniority or employment contract arrangements

Being trusted to do my job the way I think it should be done

Participating in work group conversations

Including other people in what I do

Being selected for an exclusive award

Being involved with work associates in social and recreational activities

Being sexually satisfied

Having adequate shelter to protect from the elements
Having a job which allows me time with my family
Having an opportunity for personal growth
Socializing with my friends
Being considered for an advancement opportunity
Working with other people
Having children
Doing something meaningful with my life
Being in a position to contribute new ideas
Having an associate that looks out for my interests
Not having to do exhausting work or do extra work at home
Having steady work
Being able to express my full potential
Knowing that I will always have a job
Having rest breaks with nourishment available
Having a healthful working environment
Being given a new interesting job
Having the opportunity for self-improvement
Having protection from physical harm
Being able to learn and grow in my work
Having a responsible person tell me when I've done a good job
Having an active part in work-related social activities
Knowing that other people respect me and my work
Acceptance as a work group member
Having insurance or other protective benefits
Having others recognize the importance of my job
Having a new and exciting job challenge
Having enough food to eat each day
Not having to be responsible to other people
Having personal comfort in my working environment
Knowing what is expected of me in my work
Having the opportunity to express myself fully and creatively
Having good air to breathe
Working with persons I want to associate with
Having a position of authority
A guaranteed income
The personal satisfaction of a job well done
Assurance that I will have adequate clothing to protect from the elements

Source: Dick Berry and Ken Abrahamsen, "Three Types of Salesman to Understand and Motivate," *Industrial Marketing Management* 10 (July 1981): 211.

5. Refer to the salesperson's career cycle, which was discussed in Chapter 4. What motivational practices are likely to be most important in each of the four stages (exploration, establishment, maintenance, and disengagement) to assist salespeople in meeting their personal challenges and psychosocial needs?

Notes

[1] Orville C. Walker, Jr., Gilbert A. Churchill, Jr., and Neil M. Ford, "Where Do We Go From Here? Selected Conceptual and Empirical Issues Concerning the Motivation and Performance of the Industrial Salesforce" in *Critical Issues in Sales Management: State-of-the Art and Future Research Needs* edited by Gerald Albaum and Gilbert A. Churchill, Jr. (Eugene, Ore.: Division of Research, College of Business Administration, University of Oregon, 1979), 25.

[2] Barton A. Weitz, Harish Sujan, and Mita Sujan, "Knowledge, Motivation, and Adaptive Behavior: A Framework for Improving Selling Effectiveness," *Journal of Marketing* 50 (October 1986): 180–181.

[3] Z.S. Demirdjian, "A Multidimensional Approach to Motivating Salespeople," *Industrial Marketing Management* 13 (February 1984): 25–32.

[4] Robert Whyte, "So You Think You're Motivating," in *Sales Training and Motivation: A Special Report* (New York: Sales and Marketing Management, 1977), 2.

[5] Leon A. Wortman, *Sales Manager's Problem-Solver* (New York: John Wiley and Sons, 1983), 208.

[6] Walker, Churchill, and Ford, "Where Do We Go From Here?" 40.

[7] Ibid.

[8] Robert L. Berl, Nicholas C. Williamson, and Terry Powell, "Industrial Salesforce Motivation: A Critique and Test of Maslow's Hierarchy of Need," *Journal of Personal Selling and Sales Management* 4 (May 1984): 33–39.

[9] Abraham H. Maslow, "A Theory of Human Motivation," *Psychological Review* 50 (July 1943): 370–396.

[10] Richard P. Bagozzi, "Performance and Satisfaction in an Industrial Sales Force: An Examination of Their Antecedents and Simultaneity," *Journal of Marketing* 44 (Spring 1980): 65–77.

[11] Robert T. Adkins and John E. Swan, "Increase Salespeople's Prestige With a New Title," *Industrial Marketing Management* 9 (February 1980): 1–9.

[12] Clayton P. Alderfer, "An Empirical Test of a New Theory of Human Needs," *Organizational Behavior and Human Performance* 4 (May 1969): 142–175.

[13] Frederick Herzberg, Bernard Mauser, and R. Snyderman, *The Motivation to Work* (New York: John Wiley and Sons, 1959).

[14] Leon Winer and J. S. Schiff, "Industrial Salespeople's Views on Motivation," *Industrial Marketing Management* 9 (October 1980): 319–323.

[15] See Robert Berl, Terry Powell, and Nicholas C. Williamson, "Industrial Salesforce Satisfaction and Performance with Herzberg's Theory," *Industrial Marketing Management* 13 (February 1984): 11–19; and David D. Shipley and Julia A. Kiely, "Industrial Salesforce Motivation and Herzberg's Dual Factor Theory: A UK Perspective," *Journal of Personal Selling and Sales Management* 6 (May 1986): 9–16.

[16] David C. McClelland, "Business Drive and National Achievement," *Harvard Business Review* 40 (July-August 1962): 99–112.

[17] Walker, Churchill, and Ford, "Where Do We Go?" 44–45.

[18] Stephen X. Doyle and Benson P. Shapiro, "What Counts Most in Motivating Your Sales Force?" *Harvard Business Review* 58 (May-June 1980): 133–140.

[19] Nicholas H. Ward, "Drop Those Salesman Psychology Myths," *Industrial Marketing*, July 1981, 91.

[20] Victor H. Vroom, *Work and Motivation* (New York: John Wiley and Sons, 1964).

[21] Orville C. Walker, Jr., Gilbert A. Churchill, Jr., and Neil M. Ford, "Motivation and Performance in Industrial Selling: Present Knowledge and Needed Research," *Journal of Marketing Research* 14 (May 1977): 156–168.

[22] Kenneth R. Evans, Loren Margheim, and John L. Schlacter, "A Review of Expectancy Theory Research in Selling," *Journal of Personal Selling and Sales Management* 2 (November 1982): 34.

[23] J. Stacy Adams, "Toward an Understanding of Inequity," *Journal of Abnormal and Social Psychology* 67 (November 1963): 422–436.

[24] R. Kenneth Teas and James C. McElroy, "Causal Attributions and Expectancy Estimates: A Framework for Understanding the Dynamics of Salesforce Motivation," *Journal of Marketing* 50 (January 1986): 75–86.

[25] Weitz, Sujan, and Sujan, "Knowledge, Motivation, and Adaptive Behavior," 181–182.

[26] B. F. Skinner, *Beyond Freedom and Dignity* (New York: Alfred Knopf, Inc., 1971).

[27] I. M. Miller, "Improving Sales and Forecast Accuracy in a Nationwide Sales Organization," *Journal of Organizational Behavior Management* 1 (1977): 39–51.

[28] Wortman, *Sales Manager's Problem-Solver*, 229.

[29] Herbert Moissen and Eugene H. Fram, "Segmentation for Sales Force Motivation," *Akron Business and Economic Review* (Winter 1973): 5–12.

[30] Thomas N. Ingram and Danny N. Bellenger, "Motivational Segments in the Salesforce," *California Management Review* 24 (Spring 1982): 81–88.

[31] Thayer C. Taylor, "Meet the Sales Force of the Future," *Sales and Marketing Management*, March 10, 1986, 59–60.

[32] John W. Slocum, Jr., William L. Cron, Richard W. Hansen, and Sallie Rawlings, "Business Strategy and the Management of Plateaued Employees," *Academy of Management Journal* 28 (March 1985): 133–154.

[33] Henry Lavin, "How Next Generation of Managers Sees Future," *Marketing News*, April 7, 1978, 3.

[34] W. E. Patton, III, and Michael Questell, "Alcohol Abuse in the Sales Force," *Journal of Personal Selling and Sales Management* 6 (November 1986): 39–51.

[35] Charles Futrell and Jeffrey K. Sager, "Value Analysis of a Sales Force," *Industrial Marketing Management* 2 (April 1982): 147–150.

[36] Ward, "Drop Those Salesman Psychology Myths," 91.

[37] Richard I. Henderson, "Designing a Reward System for Today's Employee," *Business*, July-September 1982, 2.

[38] John M. Ivancevich and Michael J. Etzel, "Job Enrichment in Marketing," *California Management Review* 22 (Fall 1979): 88–95.

[39] Doyle and Shapiro, "What Counts Most in Motivating Your Sales Force," 136.

[40] See Richard C. Becherer, Fred W. Morgan, and Lawrence M. Richard, "The Job Characteristics of Industrial Salespersons: Relationship to Motivation and Satisfaction," *Journal of Marketing* 46 (Fall 1982): 125–135; and Pradeep K. Tyagi, "Relative

Importance of Key Job Dimensions and Leadership Behaviors in Motivating Salesperson Work Performance," *Journal of Marketing* 49 (Summer 1985): 86–86.

[41] See Alan J. Dubinsky, Roy D. Howell, Thomas N. Ingram, and Danny N. Bellenger, "Salesforce Socialization," *Journal of Marketing* 50 (October 1986): 192–207; and Bagozzi, "Performance and Satisfaction in an Industrial Sales Force."

[42] Ward, "Drop Those Salesman Psychology Myths."

[43] Alan J. Dubinsky and Mary E. Lippit, "Managing Frustration in the Sales Force," *Industrial Marketing Management* 8 (July 1979): 200–206.

[44] Wortman, *Sales Manager's Problem-Solver,* 41–46.

CHAPTER 12

MANAGING SALESFORCE REWARD SYSTEMS

Learning Objectives

After completing this chapter, you should be able to

1. Explain the difference between compensation rewards and non-compensation rewards.
2. Describe the primary financial and nonfinancial compensation rewards available to salespeople.
3. Describe salary, commission, and combination pay plans in terms of their advantages and disadvantages.
4. Explain the fundamental concepts in sales-expense reimbursement.
5. Discuss issues associated with the use of sales contests, pay secrecy versus pay disclosure, equal pay for equal work, and changing a reward system.
6. List the guidelines for managing a reward system.

MANAGING SALESFORCE REWARDS: COMPENSATION CHANGES ON WALL STREET

In the mid-1980s a stockbroker earning $80,000 before taxes ranked among the top 1 percent to 2 percent of wage earners in the country. But he or she would not have succeeded at Merrill Lynch. Along with other top brokerage firms, Merrill Lynch was instructing its salespeople to produce more or leave the firm to make room for those who could. To improve salesforce productivity, stock brokerage firms linked compensation to sales volume, utilizing stringent quotas to push for more volume. Unfortunately, this sometimes led to high-pressure sales techniques and a lack of concern for the true needs of the customer.

Despite potential problems with customers, the brokerage houses felt strong pressure to curb escalating costs of selling. Dean-Witter estimated that the average salesperson cost it $111,700 per year. Industry profits were declining, and all of the firms quite naturally wanted to employ only the most productive salespeople. At Merrill Lynch, brokers with six or more years on the job were expected to bring in a minimum of $250,000 per year in gross commissions, which could easily translate into an income of $80,000 for the broker. If the $250,000 minimum was not met, the broker faced termination of employment. When market conditions worsened, Merrill Lynch backed off the minimum, but only temporarily.

Paine-Webber reduced commission rates for low-performing salespeople to 25 percent as compared to the typical 35–40 percent rate earned by other brokers. This action was taken after determining that sales expenses had grown 35 percent during the past year, while broker-generated revenues had grown only 26 percent. Similar commission cutbacks were also announced at Prudential-Bache and at Dean-Witter.

Brokers were understandably upset. Some felt their employers were changing their compensation to encourage resignations. Others felt they were being forced to sacrifice compensation in order for their firms to improve short-term profits. Many quit. Some of those who remained began to avoid opening small "embryo"

Source: Scott McMurray, "Brokerage Firms Push Salespeople to Produce More or Face Penalties," *The Wall Street Journal,* June 19, 1984, 31.

accounts. In the long term, such accounts can become the key to the industry's growth and survival, but low commissions in the short term make them unattractive to the pressured stockbroker.

Another consequence of the changed compensation practices was that small investors were shuffled off to salaried employees of the brokerage firms, who were not as well-trained as professional brokers. Merrill Lynch has 220 salaried customer service representatives who handle small accounts.

Pressuring brokers to produce more volume may also have caused an increase in abusive sales practices and fraud. Regulatory officials reported that such an increase followed the changes in compensation practices, although they could not tie the incidents directly to those changes.

THE opening vignette introduces several topics in the management of salesforce job rewards. The question of overall compensation levels for salespeople is raised. The merits of different compensation methods such as salary and commissions are briefly implied, and the trauma associated with changing reward structures is suggested. In this chapter, we will discuss this often delicate subject of managing salesforce reward systems.

To illustrate the challenges inherent in managing salesforce reward systems, consider the findings of national consulting firms. Russell Roberts of Sibson & Company, a major consulting firm, asserts that most major companies fail to maximize salesforce productivity due to shortcomings in their reward systems. He says that some of the reward systems are too complex, some are too simple and narrow in scope, and that many are not coordinated with the company's marketing and financial objectives.[1]

Another consultant, Suzanne Minken of A.S. Hansen Inc., points out that 60 percent of large companies surveyed are using a single performance measure — overall sales growth — in incentive programs, when they should be using a variety of criteria, including new accounts and mix of products sold, that reflect the firm's marketing plan.[2]

In the first section of this chapter, the characteristics of an effective reward system will be discussed along with the reward preferences of salespeople in general. The next section will concentrate on financial rewards such as salaries, commissions, and bonuses. Expense reimbursement will also be covered. As illustrated in Figure 12.1, expenditures for financial rewards are quite substantial, often being the largest component of the sales organization's budget.

Nonfinancial rewards such as opportunities for growth, recognition, and promotion will be reviewed. Current issues in reward system management such as the use of sales contests, pay secrecy versus pay disclosure, equal pay for equal work, and changing reward systems will be presented. The chapter will conclude with summary guidelines for managing salesforce reward systems.

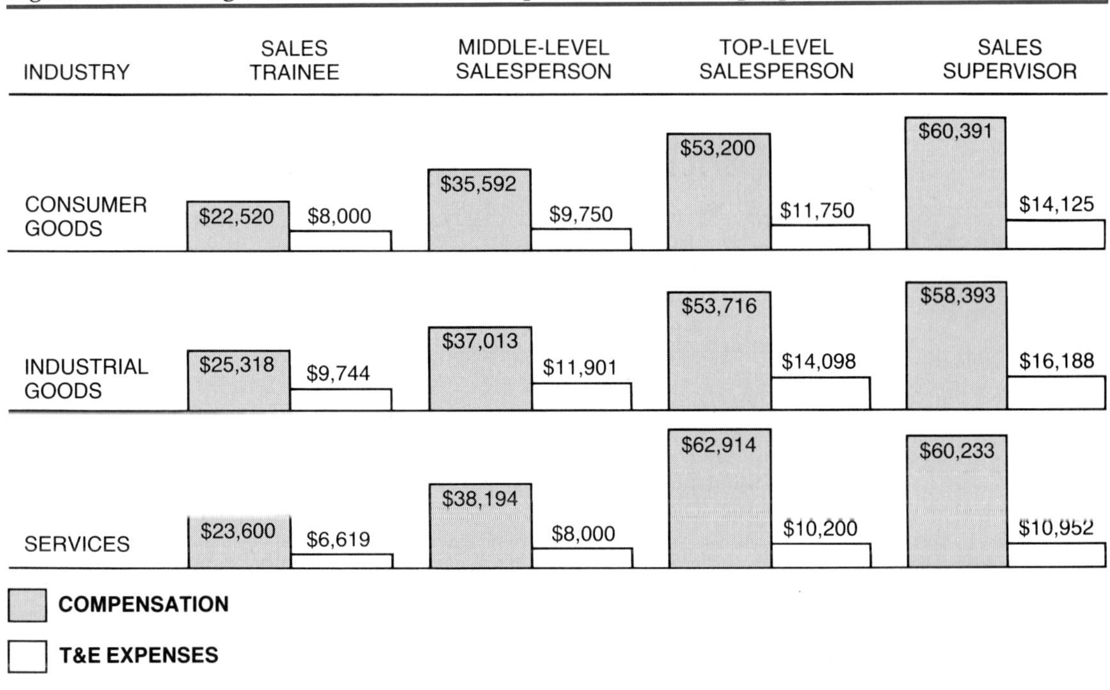

Figure 12.1 **Average Costs of Financial Compensation for Salespeople, 1987**

Notes: Financial compensation includes base salary, commission, and bonus. T&E Expenses include travel, entertainment, food, and lodging costs.

Source: "Survey of Selling Costs," *Sales and Marketing Management,* February 22, 1988, 39.

Before addressing these topics, we should explain that **reward system management** involves the selection and utilization of organizational rewards to direct salespeoples' behavior toward the attainment of organizational objectives. An organizational reward could be anything from a $5,000 pay raise to a pat on the back for a job well done.

Organizational rewards can be classified as compensation and non-compensation rewards. **Compensation rewards** are those that are given in return for acceptable performance or effort. It is important to note that compensation rewards can include nonfinancial compensation such as recognition, and opportunities for growth and promotion.

Non-compensation rewards include factors related to the work situation and well-being of each salesperson. Job-design factors as discussed in Chapter 11 (skill variety, task significance, autonomy, and feedback) can certainly be viewed as non-compensation rewards when properly utilized. Other examples of non-compensation rewards are (1) providing adequate resources so that salespeople can accomplish their jobs and, (2) practicing a supportive sales management leadership style. In this chapter, the focus is on compensation rewards, including financial and nonfinancial compensation.

OPTIMAL SALESFORCE REWARD SYSTEM

The optimal reward system balances the needs of the organization, its salespeople, and its customers against one another. From the organization's perspective, the reward system should help accomplish these results:

1. Provide an acceptable ratio of costs and salesforce output in volume, profit, or other objectives.
2. Encourage specific activities consistent with the firm's overall, marketing, and salesforce objectives. As examples, the firm may use the reward system to encourage selling particular products or to conduct important follow-up after the sale.
3. Attract and retain competent salespeople, thereby enhancing long-term customer relationships.
4. Be clear, and be flexible enough to allow the kind of adjustments that facilitate administration of the reward system.

On the surface, these characteristics sound reasonable, logical, and feasible for most sales organizations. Recall, however, the remarks of consultants in the opening part of this chapter indicating that many companies are struggling with their reward systems. Consider environmental pressures that sometimes cause pay freezes, pay reductions, cutbacks in formal recognition programs, and limited opportunities for promotion into management. Further consider the seemingly insatiable desires of even the best-paid salespeople. For example, one survey found only 60 percent of salespeople in smaller firms and 70 percent of salespeople in larger companies held favorable views of their compensation plans.[3] Obviously, the management of salesforce reward systems is a difficult job.

From the perspective of the salesperson, reward systems are expected to meet a somewhat different set of criteria than from the sales manager's perspective. As indicated in the previous chapter, salespeople expect to be treated equitably, with rewards comparable to those of others in the organization doing a similar job—and to the rewards of competitors' salespeople. Most salespeople prefer some stability in the reward system, but they simultaneously want incentive rewards for superior performance. The desire for stabilizing and incentive components was borne out by a study that found 89 percent of salespeople preferred to be paid by a combination of a salary plus incentives in commission or bonus.[4] Since the most productive salespeople have

Exhibit 12.1 **Salesforce Rewards Ranked in Order of Preference**

Pay

Promotion

Sense of Accomplishment

Personal Growth Opportunities

Recognition

Job Security

Source: Compiled from two studies: Thomas N. Ingram and Danny N. Bellenger, "Personal and Organizational Variables: Their Relative Effect on Reward Valences of Industrial Salespeople," *Journal of Marketing Research* 20 (May 1983): 198–205; and Neil M. Ford, Gilbert A. Churchill, Jr., and Orville C. Walker, Jr., "Differences in the Attractiveness of Alternative Rewards Among Industrial Salespeople: Additional Evidence," *Journal of Business Research* 13 (April 1985): 123–138.

the best opportunities to leave the firm for more attractive work situations, the preferences of the salesforce regarding compensation must be given due consideration.

In recent years, the needs of the customer have become more important than the needs of the salesforce in determining the structure of reward systems in sales organizations. Recognizing the strength of long-term alliances with customers as a key to survival, some firms have reacted by changing salesforce reward systems. For example, some automobile dealers have tried to reduce customer dissatisfaction stemming from high-pressure sales techniques by paying their salespeople a salary instead of a commission based on sales volume. A few years ago, Metropolitan Insurance converted a portion of its salesforce to straight salary in order to better control follow-up activities, which had been neglected in favor of selling new policies.

Meeting the needs of customers, salespeople, and the sales organization simultaneously is indeed a challenging task. As you might suspect, compromise between sometimes divergent interests becomes essential for managing most salesforce reward systems.

TYPES OF SALESFORCE REWARDS

For discussion purposes, the countless number of specific rewards available to salespeople will be classified into six categories (ranked in order of salespeoples' preferences) as shown in Exhibit 12.1: pay, promotion, sense of accomplishment, personal growth opportunities, recognition, and job security. Each of these reward categories will be discussed in the next two sections of this chapter. The financial-compensation section will focus on pay, and the nonfinancial-compensation section on the other rewards shown in Exhibit 12.1.

Exhibit 12.2 **Types of Financial Compensation for Salespeople**

Description	Percentage of Companies Using
Salary and bonus (combination plan)	45.9%
Salary and commission (combination plan)	45.9%
Commission only (straight commission)	3.5%
Salary only (straight salary)	4.7%

Source: "Survey of Selling Costs," *Sales and Marketing Management,* February 16, 1987, 57.

FINANCIAL COMPENSATION

In many sales organizations, financial compensation is composed of current spendable income, deferred income or retirement pay, and various insurance plans that may provide income when needed. Our discussion will be limited to the current spendable income, as it is the most controllable, and arguably most important, dimension of a salesforce reward system. The other components of financial compensation tend to be dictated more by overall company policy rather than by sales managers.

Current spendable income includes money provided in the short term (weekly, monthly, and annually) that allows salespeople to pay for desired goods and services. It includes salaries, commissions, and bonuses. Bonus compensation may include noncash income equivalents such as merchandise and free-travel awards. A comprehensive study of salesforce financial compensation practices found salaries, commissions, and bonuses to be widely used to pay salespeople. The study concluded that financial-compensation plans including a salary and one or more incentive (commission and/or bonus) are the most popular among consumer and industrial firms.[5] These conclusions were supported in another survey of financial-compensation practices, as summarized in Exhibit 12.2.

The three basic types of salesforce financial-compensation plans are straight salary, straight commission, and a salary plus incentive, with the incentive being a commission and/or a bonus. A discussion of each type follows (summarized in Exhibit 12.3).

Straight Salary

As indicated in Exhibit 12.2, less than 5 percent of all salespeople are paid **straight salary** (exclusively by a salary). Though rarely employed, salary-only plans are sometimes the optimal choice. For example, they are well suited for paying sales support and existing-business salespeople, those in seasonal or high-technology industries, those involved in team selling, and sales trainees.[6]

Exhibit 12.3 **Summary of Financial-Compensation Plans**

Type of Plan	Advantages	Disadvantages	Common Uses
Salary	Simple to administer; planned earnings facilitates budgeting and recruiting; customer loyalty enhanced; more control of nonselling activities	No financial incentive to improve performance; pay often based on seniority, not merit; salaries may be a burden to new firms or to those in declining industries	Sales trainees; team selling; sales support; seasonal sales
Commission	Income linked to results; strong financial incentive to improve results; costs reduced during slow sales periods; less operating capital required	Difficult to build loyalty of salesforce to company; less control of nonselling activities	Real estate; insurance; wholesaling; securities; automobiles
Combination	Flexibility allows frequent reward of desired behavior; may attract high-potential but unproven recruits	Complex to administer; may encourage crisis-oriented objectives	Widely used — most popular type of financial pay plan

Sales support personnel, including missionaries and detailers, are involved in situations where it is difficult to determine who really makes the sale. Since missionaries and detailers are primarily concerned with dissemination of information rather than direct solicitation of orders, a salary can equitably compensate for effort. Compensation based on sales results would not be fair.

Salespeople who specialize in maintaining existing business, such as order-takers and route salespeople, are frequently paid by salary. These salespeople are not engaged in creative selling to a significant degree, and they are not usually expected to influence the size of the orders they are taking. Advertising may be more important in the sale of their products than personal selling, and incentives paid to these salespeople are likely to be an inefficient use of funds.

One example of a salesperson who specializes in maintaining existing business is the Exxon Dealer Sales Representative who sells to independent service station operators. Although some creative selling is required, the emphasis is on order-taking and performing a number of nonselling activities as detailed in Exhibit 12.4. A straight-salary compensation plan is appropriate in such cases.

Salespeople who sell highly seasonal products such as college graduation rings make the large majority of their sales in the spring and spend the rest of the year developing new accounts. If these salespeople were paid by commission instead of salary, they would suffer a prolonged absence of income.

Sales engineers working in high-technology industries are another type of candidate for a salary plan, since they are frequently involved in advising customers,

Exhibit 12.4 **Primary Duties of a Exxon Dealer Sales Representative**

Company: Exxon Company, USA
Position: Dealer Sales Representative
Customers: Independent Service Station Operators

Primary Duties:

1. Achieve sales quota for gasoline, motor oil, tires, batteries, and automotive accessories by taking dealer orders on a regular basis.
2. Recruit new dealers on an as-needed basis.
3. Prepare documents to arrange financing for new dealers.
4. Provide training for service station personnel.
5. Provide business counseling for service station operators in the areas of merchandising and retail accounting practices.
6. Ensure that appearance standards of service stations are maintained, including having necessary repairs completed by outside contractors.
7. Maintain financial vigilance to ensure that dealers promptly remit proper lease payments to Exxon.

installing systems, training the customer's employees, and assisting in the diffusion of innovative products to the marketplace, sometimes over a period of years, making it difficult to assess their short-term sales performance.

Salary plans are also warranted when group, or team, selling is utilized. For example, if a field salesperson locates prospective customers, then works in concert with a team of financial, technical, and training specialists to confirm the sale, it is impossible to assess the relative contribution of each team member for incentive-pay purposes. Instead, each team member should receive a salary.

Finally, salaries are appropriate for sales trainees, who are involved in learning about the job rather than producing on the job. In most cases, a firm cannot recruit sales trainees on a college campus without the lure of a salary to be paid at least until training is completed.

Advantages of Salary Plans. One advantage of using salary plans is that they are the simplest ones to administer, with adjustments usually occurring only once a year. Since salaries are fixed costs, **planned earnings** for the salesforce are easy to project, which facilitates the salesforce budgeting process. The fixed nature of planned earnings with salary plans may also facilitate recruitment and selection. For example, some recruits may be more likely to join the sales organization when their first-year earnings can be clearly articulated in salary terms rather than less certain commission terms.

Salaries can provide control over salespeople's activities, and reassigning salespeople and changing sales territories is less a problem with salary plans than with other financial-compensation plans. There is general agreement that salesforce loyalty to the company may be greater with salary plans, and that there is less chance that high-pressure, non-customer-oriented sales techniques will be used.

Salaries are also used when substantial developmental work is required to open a new sales territory or introduce new products to the marketplace. Presumably, the income stability guaranteed by a salary allows the salesperson to concentrate on job activities rather than worry about how much the next paycheck will be. In general, salary plans allow more control over salesforce activities, especially nonselling activities.

Disadvantages of Salary Plans. The most serious shortcoming of straight-salary plans is that they offer little financial incentive to perform past a merely acceptable level. As a result, the least productive members of the salesforce are, in effect, the most rewarded salespeople. Conversely, the most productive salespeople are likely to think salary plans are inequitable.

Differences in salary levels among salespeople is often a function of seniority on the job instead of true merit. Even so, the constraints under which many salary plans operate may cause **salary compression**, or a narrow range of salaries in the salesforce. Thus, sales trainees may be earning close to what experienced salespeople earn, which could cause perceptions of inequity among experienced salespeople.

Salaries represent fixed overhead in a sales operation. If the market is declining or stagnating, the financial burden of the firm is greater with salary plans than with a variable expense such as commissions based on sales.

Straight Commission

Unlike straight-salary plans, commission-only plans, or **straight commission**, offer strong financial incentives to maximize performance. They also limit control of the salesforce, however. According to Exhibit 12.2, straight-commission plans are the least popular of all salesforce financial-compensation plans. Commission-only salespeople, however, are the highest paid salespeople. They earned approximately $100,000 per year, or twice that of salaried salespeople, in a survey conducted by consulting firm A. S. Hansen.[7]

Some industries — real estate, insurance, automobiles, and securities — have traditionally paid salespeople by straight commission. In these industries, the primary responsibility of the salespeople is quite simply to close sales; nonselling activities are less important to the employer than in some other industries.

Manufacturer's representatives, who represent multiple manufacturers, are also paid by commission. Wholesalers, many of whom founded their businesses with limited working capital, also traditionally pay their salesforces by commission.

The huge direct-sales industry, including companies such as Mary Kay Cosmetics, Tupperware, and Avon, also pays by straight commission. The large number of salespeople working for these organizations makes salary payments impractical from an overhead and administrative standpoint. Avon, for example, has over 400,000 salespeople and simply could not afford to pay each of them a salary.[8]

Commission Plan Variations. There are several factors to be considered in developing a commission-only plan:

1. **Commission base** — volume or profitability.
2. **Commission rate** — constant, progressive, regressive, or a combination.
3. **Commission splits** — between two or more salespeople, or between salespeople and the employer.
4. **Commission payout event** — when the order is confirmed, shipped, billed, paid for, or some combination of these events.

Commissions may be paid according to sales volume or some measure of profitability such as gross margin, contribution margin, or in rare instances, net income. In recent years, there has been more experimentation with profitability-oriented commission plans in an effort to improve salesforce productivity. The practice of paying commissions based on sales volume, however, is still dominant, and it has yet to be established that profit-oriented commission structures are superior to volume-oriented commission plans.[9]

Commission rates vary widely, and determining the appropriate rate is a weighty managerial task. The commission rate, or percentage paid to the salesperson, may be a **constant rate** over the pay period, which is an easy plan for the salespeople to understand and does provide incentive for them to produce more sales or profits (since pay is linked directly to performance). A **progressive rate** increases as salespeople reach prespecified targets. This provides an even stronger incentive to the salesperson, but it may result in overselling and higher selling costs. A **regressive rate** declines at some predetermined point. Regressive rates might be appropriate when the first order is hard to secure, but reorders are virtually automatic. Such is the case for many manufacturer salespeople who sell to distributors and retailers.

Some circumstances might warrant a combination of a constant rate with either a progressive or regressive rate. For example, assume that a manufacturer has limited production capacity. The manufacturer wants to fully utilize capacity (i.e., sell out) but not oversell, because service problems would hamper future marketing plans. In such a case, the commission rate might be fixed, or perhaps progressive up to the point where capacity is almost fully utilized, then regressive to the point of full utilization.

When salespeople are paid on straight commission, the question of splitting commissions is of primary concern. To illustrate this point, consider a company with centralized purchasing such as Eastern Airlines. Eastern may buy from a sales representative in Miami, where its headquarters are located, and have the product shipped to various hubs across the country. The salespeople in the hub cities are expected to provide local follow-up and be sure the product is performing satisfactorily. Which salespeople will receive how much commission? Procedures for splitting commissions are best established before such a question is asked.

There are no general rules for splitting commissions; rather, company-specific rules must be spelled out to avoid serious disputes. A company selling to Eastern Airlines in the situation just described might decide to pay the salesperson who calls on the Miami headquarters 50 percent of the total commission and split the remaining 50 percent among the salespeople who service the hub cities. The details of how commissions are split depend entirely on each company's situation.

Another issue in structuring straight-commission plans is when to pay the commission. The actual payment may be at any time interval, although monthly and quarterly payments are most commonplace. The question of when the commission is earned is probably just as important as when it is paid. The largest proportion of companies operating on the basis of sales-volume commissions declare the commission earned at the time the customer is billed for the order, rather than when the order is confirmed, shipped, or paid for.

Advantages of Commission Plans. One advantage of straight-commission plans is that salespeople's income is linked directly to desired results and therefore may be perceived as more equitable than salary plans. In the right circumstances, a strong financial incentive can provide superior results, and commission plans provide such an incentive.

From a cost-control perspective, commissions offer further advantages. Since commissions are a variable cost, operating costs are minimized during slack selling periods. Also, working capital requirements are lessened with commission-only pay plans. Before choosing a straight commission plan, however, the disadvantages of such plans should be considered.

Disadvantages of Commission Plans. Perhaps the most serious shortcoming of straight-commission plans is that they contribute little to company loyalty, which may mean other problems in controlling the activities of the salesforce, particularly nonselling and administrative activities. A lack of commitment may lead commission salespeople to leave the company if business conditions worsen or sales drop. Another potential problem can arise if commissions are not limited by an earnings cap, in that salespeople may earn more than their managers. Not only do managers resent this outcome, but the salespeople may not respond to direction from those they exceed in earnings.

Performance Bonuses

The third dimension of current spendable income is the **performance bonus**, either group or individual. Both types are prevalent, and some bonus plans combine them. As an example, the Plastics Division of Mobil Chemical pays a cash bonus of 10 percent of salary to any salesperson achieving his or her sales-volume target. If the

INTERNATIONAL SALES

TRAVEL AND TERRORISM

Central States Health & Life, an Omaha-based insurance company, was three weeks away from taking 150 people to London and Montreux, Switzerland, as a performance bonus when terrorists hijacked a TWA airliner en route from Rome to Athens. At this point, Central States reevaluated its European junket plans. Several questions were addressed. Was it possible to avoid cancellation of the trip, which had been planned for and promoted for months? Would management appear to be irresponsible if it continued as planned? Could a suitable alternative be arranged on such short notice? The key issue was how to assure the safety of salespeople, spouses, and other employees who were to make the trip.

The possibility of terroristic activity had existed when Central States began planning the trip; thus, the relatively safe destinations of England and Switzerland had been chosen. In light of recent news reports, travel to any part of the Europe seemed to bear some risk. After reviewing the options, the company decided to change its destinations to Boston and Bermuda. Boston was chosen because, like London, it is rich in history and culture. Bermuda was picked since available accommodations were comparable to the luxury facilities available in Montreux.

Many of the salespeople were disappointed at the change, but management worked hard to explain the necessity for the change and to build enthusiasm for the substitute locations. As it worked out, the decision to alter plans was a good one. Within days, the American bombing of Libya and the Chernobyl nuclear disaster in the Soviet Union made travel to Europe even less attractive.

Source: "A Quick Switch Saves Central States," *Sales and Marketing Management*, September 1986, 144–154.

operating group achieves its overall profit objectives, the salesperson receives another percentage point in bonus for every percentage point by which he or she exceeds the sales-volume target.

Bonuses are typically used to direct effort toward relatively short-term objectives such as introducing new products, adding new accounts, or reducing accounts receivable. They may be offered in the form of cash or income equivalents such as merchandise or free travel (see "International Sales: Travel and Terrorism," for an example of free travel as a bonus). While commissions or salary may be the financial-compensation base, bonuses are used strictly in a supplementary fashion.

Combination Plans (Salary plus Incentive)

The limitations of straight-salary and straight-commission plans have led to an increasing usage of plans that feature some combination of salary, commission, and bonus — in other words, **salary plus incentive**. Exhibit 12.2 indicates that salary-plus-bonus and commission-plus-bonus plans are extremely popular. Another combination not shown in Exhibit 12.2 is salary-plus-commission-and-bonus, which is used in less than 10 percent of sales organizations.[10]

Exhibit 12.5 **Conditions Influencing the Proportion of Salary to Total Pay for Salespeople**

Condition	Proportion of Salary to Total Pay should be	
	Lower	Higher
1. Importance of salesperson's personal skills in making sales	Considerable	Slight
2. Reputation of salesperson's company	Little known	Well known
3. Company's reliance on advertising and other sales promotion activities	Little	Much
4. Competitive advantage of product in terms of price, quality, etc.	Little	Much
5. Importance of providing customer service	Slight	Considerable
6. Significance of total sales volume as a primary selling objective	Greater	Lesser
7. Incidence of technical or team selling	Little	Much
8. Importance of factors beyond the control of salesperson which influence sales	Slight	Considerable

Source: Amiya K. Basu, Rajiv Lal, V. Srinivasan, and Richard Staelin, "Salesforce Compensation Plans: An Agency Theoretic Perspective," *Marketing Science* 4 (Fall 1985): 270.

When properly conceived, combination plans offer a balance of incentive, control, and enough flexibility to reward important salesforce activities. The most difficult part of structuring combination plans is determining the financial-compensation mix, or the relative amounts to be paid in salary, commission, and bonus. Exhibit 12.5 enumerates a number of factors related to the determining the appropriate ratio of salary to total financial compensation.

As indicated in Exhibit 12.5, the compensation mix should be tilted more heavily toward the salary component when individual salespeople have limited control over their own performance. When well-established companies rely heavily on advertising to sell their products in highly competitive markets, the salesforce has less direct control over job outcomes. Then a salary emphasis is quite logical. Further, if the provision of customer service is crucial as contrasted with maximizing short-term sales volume, or if team selling is utilized, a compensation mix favoring the salary dimension is appropriate. As suggested in Exhibit 12.5, conditions contrary to those favorable to a high salary-to-total-compensation ratio would dictate an emphasis on commissions in the compensation mix.

Combination pay plans usually feature salary as the major source of salesperson income. Studies have indicated that the most popular plans contain approximately 80 percent salary and 20 percent incentive (commission and/or bonus) pay, with a 70/30 salary/incentive split being a close second.[11]

Advantages of Combination Plans. The primary advantage of combination pay plans is their flexibility. Sales behavior can be rewarded frequently, and specific behaviors can be reinforced or stimulated quickly. For example, bonuses or additional commissions could be easily added to a salary base to encourage activities such as selling excess inventory, maximizing the sales of highly seasonal products, introducing new products, or obtaining new customers. In California, an office supply firm redesigned its commission structure to encourage its salespeople to increase the customer base of 3,800. Within a month, 100 new customers had been added, and gross profits had improved 4 percent. By changing the components of its compensation plan, it added as many new customers in a month as it had previously obtained in two and one-half years.[12]

Combination pay plans are attractive to high-potential, but unproven, candidates for sales jobs. College students nearing graduation, for example, might be attracted by the security of a salary and the opportunity for additional earnings from incentive-pay components.

Disadvantages of Combination Plans. As compared to straight-salary and straight-commission plans, combination plans are more complex and difficult to administer. Their flexibility sometimes leads to frequent changes in compensation practices to achieve short-term objectives. While flexibility is desirable, each change requires careful communication with the salesforce and precise coordination with long-term sales, marketing, and corporate objectives. A common criticism of combination plans is they tend to produce too many salesforce objectives, many of which are of the crisis-resolution, "fire-fighting" variety. Should this occur, the accomplishment of more important long-term progress can be impeded.

NONFINANCIAL COMPENSATION

As indicated early in this chapter, compensation for effort and performance may include nonfinancial rewards. Examples of these types of **nonfinancial compensation** include career advancement through promotion, a sense of accomplishment on the job, opportunities for personal growth, recognition of achievement, and job security. Sometimes nonfinancial rewards are coupled with financial rewards — for example, a promotion into sales management usually results in a pay increase — so one salesperson might view these rewards as primarily financial, while another might view them from a nonfinancial perspective. The value of nonfinancial compensation is illustrated by the considerable number of salespeople who knowingly take cuts in financial compensation to become sales managers. The prevalence of other nonfinancial rewards in salesforce reward systems also attests to their important role.

Opportunity for Promotion

As shown in Exhibit 12.1, **opportunity for promotion** ranks second only to pay as the most preferred reward among salespeople. Among younger salespeople, it often eclipses pay as the most valued reward.[13] Given the increasing number of young to middle-age people in the workforce, the opportunities for promotion may be severely limited in non-growth industries. (Growth industries, such as financial services and direct sales, offer reasonably good opportunities for advancement through promotion.) Since opportunities for promotion are not easily varied in the short run, the importance of matching recruits to the job and its rewards is again emphasized.

It should be noted that a promotion need not involve a move from sales into management. Recall from Chapter 4 that some career paths may extend from sales into management, while others progress along a career salesperson path.

Sense of Accomplishment

Unlike some rewards, a **sense of accomplishment** cannot be delivered to the salesperson from the organization. Since a sense of accomplishment emanates from the salesperson's psyche, all the organization can do is to facilitate the process by which it develops. While organizations cannot administer sense-of-accomplishment rewards as they would pay increases, promotions, or formal recognition rewards, the converse is not true — they do have the ability to withhold this reward, to deprive individuals of feeling a sense of accomplishment. Of course, no organization chooses this result; it stems from poor management practice.

To facilitate a sense of accomplishment in the salesforce, several steps can be taken. First, assure that the salesforce members understand the critical role they fulfill in revenue production and other key activities within the company. Second, personalize the causes and effects of salesperson performance. In expectancy-theory terms, this means that each salesperson should understand the linkages between effort and performance (expectancies) and between performance and rewards (instrumentalities). Third, strongly consider the practice of management by objectives and/or goal setting as a standard management practice. Finally, reinforce feelings of worthwhile accomplishment in communications with the salesforce.

Opportunity for Personal Growth

Opportunities for personal growth are routinely offered to salespeople. For example, college-tuition reimbursement programs are commonplace, as are seminars and workshops on topics such as physical fitness, stress reduction, and personal financial planning. Interestingly, many sales job candidates think the major reward available from well-known companies is the opportunity for personal growth. This is particularly true of entrepreneurially oriented college students who hope to "learn then earn" in their own business. In a parallel development, many companies showcase their training program during recruitment and selection as an opportunity for personal growth through the acquisition of universally valuable selling skills.

Recognition

Recognition, both informal and formal, is an integral part of most salesforce reward systems. Informal recognition refers to "nice job" accolades and similar kudos usually delivered in private conversation or correspondence between a sales manager and a

Exhibit 12.6 Guidelines for Formal Recognition Programs

A Program that Will Do the Job

Regardless of its size or cost, any recognition program should incorporate the following features, says consultant Dr. Richard Boyatiz of McBer and Co.:

- The program must be strictly performance-based with no room for subjective judgments. If people suspect that it is in any way a personality contest, the program will not work. Says Boyatiz: "It should be clear to anyone looking at the data that, yes, these people won."
- It should be balanced. The program should not be so difficult that only a few can hope to win, or so easy that just about everyone does. In the first case, people will not try; in the second, the program will be meaningless.
- A ceremony should be involved. If rings are casually passed out, or plagues sent through the mail, a lot of the glamour of the program will be lost.
- The program must be in good taste. If not, it will be subject to ridicule and, rather than motivate people, leave them uninspired. No one wants to be part of a recognition program that is condescending or tacky. Says Boyatiz: "The program should make people feel good about being part of the company."
- There must be adequate publicity. In some cases, sales managers do such a poor job of explaining a program or promoting it to their own salespeople that no one seems to understand or care about it. Prominent mention of the program in company publications is the first step to overcoming this handicap.

Source: Bill Kelley, "Recognition Reaps Rewards," *Sales and Marketing Management,* June 1986, 104.

salesperson. Informal recognition is easy to administer, costs nothing, or practically nothing, and can reinforce desirable behavior immediately after it occurs.

Long a tradition in most sales organizations, formal-recognition programs are becoming even more popular.[14] Examples include the Million Dollar Roundtable designation in the insurance industry, Stroh Brewery's Top Performer award for sales improvement, and numerous 100% Clubs for those who reach or exceed 100 percent of their sales quota. One particularly successful 100% Club program has been reported by Norwest Corp., a Minneapolis-based bank.[15] Stephen Byrnes, Norwest's Director of Marketing and Product Management commented, "Much to our surprise, the element of recognition became more important than anything else we did" to spur sales.

Formal-recognition programs are typically based on group competition, or individual accomplishments representing improved performance. Formal recognition may also be associated with monetary, merchandise, or travel awards but are distinguished from other rewards by two characteristics. First, formal recognition implies public recognition for accomplishment in the presence of peers and superiors in the organization. Second, there is a symbolic award of lasting psychological value such as jewelry or a plaque.[16] Sound advice for conducting formal recognition programs is offered in Exhibit 12.6.

SALES TREND

UPSCALE RECOGNITION CEREMONIES

Leading companies in direct sales such as Dallas-based Mary Kay Cosmetics have long been renowned for their annual seminars that combine training and recognition for their field salespeople. Choreographed stage productions, state-of-the-art audiovideo equipment, and well-prepared speakers are used to enhance the excitement surrounding awards ceremonies featuring top salespeople. Salespeople are honored in the spotlight on stage in front of thousands of Mary Kay salespeople, and they receive awards ranging from small pieces of jewelry to fur coats and automobiles.

Industrial firms, perhaps taking a cue from Mary Kay and others, have begun to pour more time, money, and effort into their formal recognition programs. For example, Standard Register, supplier of business forms, gathers the top third of its 1,000-member salesforce for an annual awards ceremony. The setting is strictly first-class, with fine china, linen tablecloths, and tuxedos being standard accoutrements. An outside consulting producer works with the director of corporate communications to accomplish the overall purpose of the ceremony, making the winners feel special.

During the awards ceremonies, the band plays music to match the home state of each winner, and the spotlight is used liberally to single out winners. Top salespeople are designated as members of the President's Committee, and they receive rings from the president of the company. Everything is done with fanfare. Then, during the business sessions that follow in the next few days, speakers again highlight the accomplishments of the winners. By the end of the week, the foundation for the following year's recognition program has been laid.

Source: Personal observation of Mary Kay Cosmetics "Success Express 1987" seminar, July 1987, in Dallas, Texas; and Heidi A. Waldrop, "An Event To Remember," *Sales and Marketing Management,* June 3, 1985, 88–93.

As formal-recognition programs grow in popularity, there seems to be an accompanying trend toward lavish awards banquets and ceremonies to culminate the program and set the stage for future recognition programs. Since lavish expenditures for any salesforce activity must ultimately be well justified in this era of emphasis on productivity improvement, it is evident that many companies believe that money spent on recognition is a good investment. A closer look at extravagant recognition ceremonies is provided in "Sales Trend: Upscale Recognition Ceremonies."

Job Security

Job security, though valued highly by salespeople nearing retirement age, is the least valued reward among those shown in Exhibit 12.1. High-performing salespeople may sense they have job security, if not with their present employer then with another employer. According to Maslow's need hierarchy, these salespeople may value some other reward higher in the hierarchy. Low performers may not enjoy their sales jobs and thus place a low premium on job security.

With the current wave of mergers, acquisitions, and general downsizing of corporations, it is becoming more difficult to offer job security as a reward. In the past, job security was easier to assure, at least as long as performance contingencies were met. Another factor that will make it difficult to offer job security with a given company is the lack of unionization of salespeople in most fields.

SALES EXPENSES

A large majority of sales organizations provide full reimbursement to their salespeople for legitimate **sales expenses** incurred while on the job. One survey found that 85 percent of small firms and over 90 percent of large firms provide full reimbursement for sales expenses.[17] As shown in Exhibit 12.7, typical reimbursable expenses include travel, lodging, meals, entertainment of customers, telephone, and incidentals such as tips. Some companies also reimburse laundry and dry cleaning expenses if the salesperson is required to be away from home for prolonged periods.

Sales expenses can be substantial. According to compensation expert Bill Ryckman, "Eliminating the extremes, we feel safe in suggesting that expenses can average between 20 and 30 percent of compensation."[18] A review of the data in Figure 12.1 confirms Ryckman's conclusion. Given the magnitude of sales expenses, it is easy to understand why most companies impose tight controls to ensure judicious spending by the salesforce.

Controls used in the sales-expense reimbursement process include (1) a definition of which expenses are reimbursable, (2) the establishment of expense budgets, (3) the use of allowances for certain expenditures, and (4) documentation of expenses to be reimbursed.

Covered expenses vary from company to company, so it is important for each company to designate which expenses are reimbursable and which are not. For example, some firms reimburse their salespeople for personal entertainment such as the cost of movies and reading material while traveling, and others do not.

Expense budgets may be used to maintain expenses as a specified percentage of overall sales volume or profit. Expenditures are compared regularly to the budgeted amount, and expenditure patterns may change in response to budgetary pressures.

Allowances for automobile expenses, lodging, and meal costs are sometimes used to control expenditures. For example, one common practice is to reimburse personal automobile usage on the job at a cents-per-mile allowance. Many firms use a per-diem allowance for meals and lodging. In an unusual use of allowances, Timex reimburses its salespeople for two-thirds of their clothing expenditures as long as the clothing conforms to corporate standards of attire.[19]

Documentation in the form of receipts and other information concerning the what, when, who, and why of the expenditure is required as a matter of standard procedure. Salespeople whose companies do not reimburse expenses must also provide such documentation in order to deduct sales expenses in calculating their income taxes.

Exhibit 12.7 Sales Expense Report Form

TRAVEL EXPENSE REPORT

NAME:________________ FOR WEEK ENDING:__________ DEPT.__________

	SUNDAY	MONDAY	TUESDAY	WEDNESDAY	THURSDAY	FRIDAY	SATURDAY	TOTAL FOR WEEK
FROM								
TO								
TO								
TOTAL AUTO MILES								
MILEAGE MI.								
GAS—OIL—LUBE								
PARKING & TOLLS								
AUTO RENTAL								
LOCAL—CAB/LIMO								
AIR—RAIL—BUS								
LODGING								
BREAKFAST								
LUNCH								
DINNER								
LAUNDRY—CLEANING								
PHONE & TELEGRAM								
TIPS								
OTHER								
ENTERTAINMENT*								
TOTAL PER DAY								

*DETAILED ENTERTAINMENT RECORD

DATE	ITEM	PERSONS ENTERTAINED / BUSINESS RELATIONSHIP	PLACE NAME & LOCATION	BUSINESS PURPOSE	AMOUNT

PURPOSE OF TRIP:____________________

REMARKS:____________________

DATE:__________ SIGNATURE:________________

SUMMARY

TOTAL EXPENSES	
LESS CASH ADVANCED	
LESS CHARGES TO CO.	
AMOUNT DUE ☐ ME ☐ CO.	

Source: *Easy to Make Sales and Marketing Forms* (Caddylak Systems, Inc., 1982), Westbury, New York 11590. Used with permission.

The area of expense reimbursement is the cause of some ethical and legal concern in sales organizations. Certainly **expense account padding**, in which a salesperson seeks reimbursement for ineligible or fictional expenses is not unknown. There are countless ways for an unscrupulous salesperson to misappropriate company funds. A common ploy of expense account "padders" is to entertain friends rather than customers, then seek reimbursement for customer entertainment. Another tactic is to purchase equipment such as video players or slide projectors for personal use by applying company-paid rental fees in a lease-to-buy agreement with the dealer.

Tight financial controls, requirements for documentation of expenditures, and periodic visits by highly trained financial auditors help deter expense account abuse. While it may sound extreme, many companies have a simple policy regarding misappropriation of company funds — the minimum sanction is termination of employment, and criminal charges are a distinct possibility. For an interesting ethical scenario involving questionable sales management action in the area of expense accounts, see Application Exercise 2 at the end of the chapter.

ADDITIONAL ISSUES IN MANAGING SALESFORCE REWARD SYSTEMS

In addition to the managerial issues raised thus far, four other areas of salesforce reward systems are currently receiving considerable attention: sales contests, pay secrecy versus disclosure, equal pay for equal work, and changing an existing reward system.

Sales Contests

Sales contests are temporary programs that offer financial and/or nonfinancial rewards for accomplishing specified, usually short-term, objectives. Contests may involve group competition among salespeople, individual competition whereby each salesperson competes against past performance standards or new goals, or a combination of group and individual competition. Sales contests can be instituted without altering the basic financial-compensation plan.

Despite the widespread use of sales contests and the sizable expenditures for them, very little is known about their true effects. In fact, many contests are held to correct bad planning and poor sales performance, and others are held with the belief that contests must have positive effects, despite the difficulty in pinpointing these effects. While some researchers have found sales contests to be positively related to sales and profitability,[20] others have pointed out the great number of questions that remain unanswered about them.[21] For example, the optimum duration for a contest, the desired number of contest winners, whether or not spouses should be included in the contest, the relationship between contest expenditures and effectiveness, and which prizes and awards are most effective remain largely undecided.[22]

Though not supported by conclusive research, several guidelines for conducting sales contests have emerged from experienced practitioners:[23]

1. Minimize potential motivation and morale problems by allowing multiple winners. Salespeople should compete against individual goals and be declared a winner if those goals are met.
2. Recognize that contests will concentrate efforts in specific areas, often at the temporary neglect of other areas. Plan accordingly.
3. Consider the positive effects of including nonselling personnel in sales contests.
4. Use variety as a basic element of sales contests. Vary timing, duration, themes, and rewards.
5. Ensure that sales contest objectives are clear, realistically attainable, and quantifiable to allow performance assessment.

It is hard to design a sales contest that will maximally motivate every member of the salesforce. It is even more difficult to precisely measure the effectiveness of most sales contests. Even so, sales contests will doubtless continue to be a frequently used tool. By following the five guidelines previously mentioned, sales managers can improve the odds of making justifiable investments in sales contests.

Secrecy versus Disclosure

Most companies use **closed pay systems**, meaning that critical financial-compensation information is kept secret from the employees. They are not told how much other salespeople earn, nor the amount of pay raises received by others. Even the way that pay raises are determined might not be revealed to the employees. In contrast, **open pay systems** are characterized by disclosure of pay information, including earnings of other employees and explanations of how pay levels are determined.

Closed pay systems presumably reduce tension among employees and keep petty complaints to a minimum. As a result, sales managers spend less time explaining financial-compensation decisions than with an open pay system. In recent years, however, a growing number of companies have opened their pay systems to some degree.[24]

For sales organizations where there is a strong correlation between performance and pay, open pay systems may be preferable. Salespeople paid a straight commission on sales volume may find it to be extremely motivating to know how much their peers earn. A study of pharmaceutical salespeople found that an open pay system was positively related to salesforce performance, as well as satisfaction with pay, company promotional policies, and the job itself.[25]

Another argument for open pay systems is rooted in the equity-theory concepts discussed in Chapter 11. If a sales manager believes that overall equity in the financial-compensation system contributes to motivation, performance, and retention of salespeople, then strong consideration should be given to implementing an open system. With a closed system, the necessary comparisons with relevant other salespeople is extremely difficult or impossible, and the information used for comparisons is likely to be inaccurate.

Equal Pay

In addition to the motivational aspects of equity in financial-compensation systems, there is a legal responsibility to assure that salespeople are paid on an equitable basis. The Equal Pay Act, mentioned in Chapter 9, requires that equal pay be given for jobs requiring the same skills, efforts, responsibilities, and working conditions.

Sad to say, some sales managers attempt to pay female salespeople less than males because they think women's family responsibilities will cause them to leave the salesforce, or they think women will be less willing to travel or relocate than male salespeople. The dangers of such thinking are not limited to legal ramifications, but the Equal Pay Act of 1963 does provide a strong reminder for those who consider paying one group of people less than another.

Changing the Reward System

In 1986 the president of Digital Equipment Corporation reiterated the company's commitment to its long-time policy of paying DEC salespeople a straight salary. He believed that commission-paid salespeople would place more emphasis on making sales quotas than on ensuring customer satisfaction.[26] Less than one year later, DEC announced the payment of bonuses for the first time to its top salespeople.[27] Why the change? DEC had decided to attack IBM directly, and one part of the attack was to increase the salesforce size 30 percent, to a total of 6,000. To attract such a sizable number of highly qualified salespeople (many of the new hires were ex-IBM salespeople), DEC probably had no choice but to change its reward system. Further, it is likely that the bonuses were meant to generate more aggressive, market-share-oriented sales activities.

The DEC situation is not uncommon for sales managers — the need to change the reward system when conditions warrant it. Minor adjustments in reward systems can be made relatively painlessly, and sometimes even pleasurably, for all concerned parties. For example, the sales manager might plan three sales contests this year instead of the customary two, or he (or she) might announce a cash bonus instead of a trip to Acapulco for those who make quota.

Making major changes in reward systems, however, can be traumatic for salespeople and management alike if not properly handled. Any major change in financial-compensation practices is likely to produce a widespread fear among the salesforce

SALES TECHNOLOGY

USING THE COMPUTER TO FACILITATE CHANGE

The task of selling the salesforce on a major change in the reward system is a difficult one. A computer-generated personalized pay statement such as the one shown below can help each salesperson assess the impact of the change.

Computer-generated pay statements can easily accommodate multiple performance criteria without causing confusion. The statements reduce the need for a meeting of the entire salesforce to explain the change, and they give each salesperson the opportunity to carefully analyze the change before asking questions of the sales manager. A stronger version of such statements is an interactive software package that lets salespeople calculate their own earnings with different assumptions regarding their performance.

Source: Robert Freedman and Martin Lapidus, "Selling the Pay Plan Is a Tough Sale," *Sales and Marketing Management,* May 1987, 82–84.

Personalized Pay Statement for Salespeople

Name:
Annual salary: $30,000
Target bonus %: 25%
Target quantitative bonus: $7,500
Expected annual revenues: $1,000,000

Actual Revenues	% of Expected Annual Revenues	% of Quantitative Bonus	Amount of Quantitative Bonus
Less than $600,000	less than 60%	0%	$ 0
600,000	60	25	1,875
700,000	70	38	2,815
800,000	80	50	3,750
900,000	90	75	5,625
1,000,000	100	100	7,500
1,100,000	110	125	9,375

that their earnings will decline. Since many changes are precipitated by poor financial performance by the company or inequitable earnings among salesforce members, this fear is often justified for at least part of the salesforce.

To implement a new or modified reward system, sales managers must, in effect, sell the plan to the salesforce. To do this, the details of the plan must be clearly communicated well in advance of its implementation. Feedback from the salesforce should be encouraged and questions promptly addressed. Reasons for the change should be openly discussed, and any expected changes in job activities should be detailed. An example of how computer-generated material can help sell a salesforce on a change in the reward system is given in "Sales Technology: Using the Computer to Facilitate Change."

If possible, it is recommended that major changes be implemented to coincide with the beginning of a new fiscal year or planning period. It is also preferable to institute changes during favorable business conditions, rather than during recessionary periods.

The dynamic nature of marketing and sales environments dictates that sales managers constantly monitor their reward systems. It is not unreasonable to think that major changes could occur every few years, or even more frequently.

GUIDELINES FOR MANAGING SALESFORCE REWARD SYSTEMS

Several guidelines have been proposed for managing salesforce reward systems.[28] First, the reward system should be a direct reflection of corporate, business-unit, and marketing department priorities. The example of the change in the reward system at Digital Equipment illustrates this thinking.

The reward system should be based on what a particular company wants to accomplish, not necessarily what has been the industry tradition. Success stories are circulating about automobile dealers who have changed from straight-commission to salary-based compensation to improve customer-oriented sales behavior.

Strong consideration should be given to rewarding teamwork rather than relying solely on individual effort. While some internal competition can be healthy, the notion of building a strong sales team may serve long-term purposes better, especially if some of the top performers leave the organization.

There should be a strong emphasis on pay for performance, rather than paying according to competitive pay levels or seniority. This suggests the importance of incentive pay in the form of bonuses and/or commissions for paying salespeople in most situations.

SUMMARY

1. **Explain the difference between compensation rewards and non-compensation rewards.** Compensation rewards are those given by the organization in return for the salesperson's efforts and performance. They may include both financial and nonfinancial rewards. Non-compensation rewards are related to job design and work environment. The opportunity to be involved in meaningful, interesting work is an example of a non-compensation reward. The provision of adequate resources to do the job and a supportive management system are other examples. The focus in this chapter is on the management of compensation rewards.

2. **Describe the primary financial and nonfinancial compensation rewards available to salespeople.** As shown in Exhibit 12.1, there are six major rewards available to salespeople: pay (or financial compensation), opportunity for promotion, a sense of accomplishment, personal growth opportunities, recognition, and job security (the last five being nonfinancial). Pay is usually current spendable income generated by salary, commissions, and bonuses.

3. **Describe salary, commission, and combination pay plans in terms of their advantages and disadvantages.** Straight-salary plans and straight-commission plans represent the two extremes in financial compensation for salespeople. Straight salary offers maximum control over salesforce activities, but does not provide added incentive for exceptional performance. The opposite is true for straight-commission plans. The limitations of both plans have made combination plans the most popular with sales organizations. Although such plans can become too complex for easy administration, when properly conceived they offer a balance of control and incentive.

4. **Explain the fundamental concepts in sales-expense reimbursement.** Job-related expenses incurred by salespeople are reimbursed by a large majority of sales organizations. Sales expenses are usually substantial, averaging 20 to 30 percent of total financial compensation paid to salespeople. Companies use budgets, allowances, and documentation requirements to control sales expenses.

5. **Discuss issues associated with the use of sales contests, pay secrecy versus pay disclosure, equal pay for equal work, and changing a reward system.** Sales contests are widely used to achieve short-term results, but little is known about their true effects. Some sales organizations disclose the particulars of their pay policies and the earnings of all the salespeople as part of an open pay system. Open systems can have positive effects on motivation and performance if there is a strong link between performance and pay, such as in straight-commission selling. The Equal Pay Act of 1963 reinforces an ethically desirable behavior—paying those who do equal work an equal amount of money. Changing a reward system is a delicate procedure, requiring careful communication to the salesforce, who must "buy" the new system much like a customer would buy a product.

6. **List the guidelines for managing a reward system.** Guidelines for the effective management of reward systems are as follows: The reward system should be a direct reflection of all pertinent organizational goals. This may require procedures that deemphasize industry traditions. Strong consideration should be given to rewarding teamwork, at least in part, rather than rewarding only individual effort. Finally, there should be a strong correlation between performance and pay, rather than relying too heavily on seniority and competitive pay levels to determine the earnings of salespeople.

Key Terms

- reward system management
- compensation rewards
- non-compensation rewards
- current spendable income
- straight salary
- planned earnings
- straight commission
- commission base
- commission rate
- commission splits
- commission payout event
- constant rate
- progressive rate
- regressive rate
- performance bonus
- salary plus incentive
- financial-compensation mix
- nonfinancial compensation
- opportunity for promotion
- sense of accomplishment
- opportunity for personal growth
- recognition
- job security
- sales expenses
- expense account padding
- sales contests
- closed pay systems
- open pay systems

Review Questions

1. Distinguish between compensation rewards and non-compensation rewards.
2. Describe an optimal salesforce reward system.
3. What are the nonfinancial compensation rewards discussed in this chapter? What suggestions can you make for administering recognition rewards?
4. Evaluate straight-salary, straight-commission, and combination pay plans in terms of their advantages and disadvantages. When should each be used?
5. Describe the conditions that indicate a high proportion of salary to total compensation in combination pay plans.
6. What concerns should a sales manager have regarding the use of sales contests?
7. Describe an open pay system. What are the possible effects of an open pay system?
8. Most organizations use a closed pay system. Why?
9. What should a sales manager do to facilitate a major change in the reward system?
10. Discuss several guidelines to improve the effectiveness of reward system management.

Application Exercises

1. Refer to Exhibit 12.4, "Primary Duties of an Exxon Dealer Sales Representative." Assume you want to change the financial-compensation package by adding performance bonuses to the straight-salary component. How can bonuses be added without altering the basic responsibilities and activities of the sales representative?
2. Assume you are a newly hired salesperson, and you have just turned in your first expense account for reimbursement. Your sales manager has called you in to question the overall

total of your expenses. The sales manager tells you that your expenses are "out of line" with the rest of the salesforce. You are surprised, as you kept accurate records and have provided all required documentation for your expenses. As the discussion progresses, the sales manager makes it clear that your expenses are much lower than average, and that it will look suspicious to upper management if your expense account is compared to those of other salespeople. You begin to get the feeling that the other salespeople pad their expense accounts by claiming expenses they did not incur. Exasperated, you ask the sales manager if he wants you to increase the amount of expenses you are claiming. His reply is, "I can't say that, but it is going to be a hassle explaining why you are so much lower than the others." What would you do?

3. Describe the type of salesperson that you think would be most motivated by each of the six rewards shown in Exhibit 12.1. To do this, it might be helpful to think of the salesperson in terms of age, marital status, and stage in the career cycle.
4. Assume you are the national sales manager for a large manufacturer of petroleum-based chemical compounds. Your salesforce of 150 sells directly to other manufacturers in a variety of industries. For the past decade, the sales force has been paid on a salary-plus-bonus arrangement. A 10 percent bonus is paid at year end if the salesperson achieves 100 percent of his or her sales quota. In addition, if the company reaches its profit goals for the year, salespeople receive an additional percentage point in bonus for every percentage point achieved in excess of 100 percent of quota — up to a limit of 25 percent. Thus, a salesperson can earn up to 35 percent of his or her salary in annual bonuses.

    If the company does not meet its profit goals, salespeople still receive a 10 percent bonus for making quota, but the incremental bonus for exceeding quota is cut in half. In an unprofitable year, therefore, a salesperson can earn a total of 22.5 percent of salary in bonus.

    The company's situation has changed drastically, however. It is the middle of the fiscal year, and limited warfare in the Middle East has curtailed shipments of petroleum products to this country. Prices for finished products are escalating as supplies drop. You are considering a rationing program for your customers, as current production is only 75 percent of the normal rate. You are also considering changing the financial-compensation package, as you foresee windfall earnings for your salespeople. What are your recommendations?
5. Refer to Exhibit 12.5. For each of the following sales jobs, indicate whether the salary component should be relatively high (70 percent or more) or not compared to total compensation.
    a. Life insurance agent
    b. Computer sales representative for IBM
    c. Sales representative for a textbook publisher

Notes

[1] "Labor Letter," *The Wall Street Journal,* July 15, 1986, 1.

[2] Ibid.

[3] "Satisfaction and Job Class: The INC. 500 At a Glance," *INC.*, November 1987, 67.

[4] Ibid.

[5] Anne T. Coughlan and Subrata K. Sen, "Salesforce Compensation: Insights from Management Science," (Cambridge, Mass.: Marketing Science Institute, Report No. 86–101, March, 1986): 32.

[6] W. G. Ryckman, *Compensating Your Sales Force* (Chicago: Probus Publishing Company, 1986), 15–17.

[7] Gregg Cebrzynski, "Sales Compensation Survey Shows Some 'Dramatic' Findings," *Marketing News,* November 7, 1986, 32.

[8] Ryckman, *Compensating Your Sales Force,* 28.

[9] Douglas J. Dalrymple, P. Ronald Stephenson, and William Cron, "Gross Margin Sales Compensation Plans," *Industrial Marketing Management* 10 (July 1981): 219–224.

[10] "1986 Survey of Selling Costs," *Sales and Marketing Management,* February 17, 1986, 57.

[11] Cebrzynski, "Sales Compensation Survey," 32.

[12] "New Account-ing of Commissions," *Sales and Marketing Management,* March 11, 1985, 27.

[13] See William L. Cron, Alan J. Dubinsky, and Ronald E. Michaels, "The Influence of Career Stages on Components of Salesperson Motivation," *Journal of Marketing* 52 (January 1988): 78–92; Gilbert A. Churchill, Jr., Neil M. Ford, and Orville C. Walker, Jr., "Personal Characteristics of Salespeople and the Attractiveness of Alternative Rewards," *Journal of Business Research* 7 (June 1979): 25–50; Neil M. Ford, Gilbert A. Churchill, Jr., and Orville C. Walker, Jr., "Differences in the Attractiveness of Alternative Rewards among Salespeople: Additional Evidence," *Journal of Business Research* 13 (April 1985): 123–138; and Thomas N. Ingram and Danny N. Bellenger, "Personal and Organizational Variables: Their Relative Effect on Reward Valences of Industrial Salespeople," *Journal of Marketing Research* 20 (May 1983): 198–205.

[14] Bill Kelley, "Recognition Reaps Rewards," *Sales and Marketing Management,* June 1986, 101.

[15] Kate Bertrand, "Recognition Keeps Them Selling," *Business Marketing,* January 1988, 107.

[16] Jerry McAdams, "Rewarding Sales and Marketing Performance," *Management Review,* April 1987, 33–38.

[17] Alan J. Dubinsky and Thomas E. Barry, "A Survey of Sales Management Practices," *Industrial Marketing Management* 2 (April 1982): 137.

[18] Ryckman, *Compensating Your Sales Force,* 110.

[19] "Timex Subsidizes Suits and Ties," *Sales and Marketing Management,* November 1986, 26.

[20] See Albert R. Wildt, James D. Parker, and Clyde E. Harris, Jr., "Assessing the Impact of Sales-Force Contests: An Application," *Journal of Business Research* 15 (April 1987): 145–155; and Thomas R. Wotruba and Donald J. Schoel, "Evaluation of Salesforce Contest Performance," *Journal of Personal Selling and Sales Management* 3 (May 1983): 1–10.

[21] Albert R. Wildt, James D. Parker, and Clyde E. Harris, Jr., "Sales Contest: What We Know and What We Need To Know," *Journal of Personal Selling and Sales Management* 1 (Fall-Winter 1980–1981): 57–64.

[22] Ibid., 60.

[23] See Heinz Goldmann, "Unrewarding Rewards," *Sales and Marketing Management,* April 1986, 136–138; and Maria Conte, "Motivating Your Market," *Business Marketing,* April 1987, 92–97.

[24] Robert L. Mathis and John H. Jackson, *Personnel: Contemporary Perspectives and Applications* (St. Paul, Minn.: West Publishing Company 1982): 317.

[25] Charles M. Futrell and Omer C. Jenkins, "Pay Secrecy Versus Pay Disclosure for Salesmen: A Longitudnal Study," *Journal of Marketing Research* 15 (May 1978): 214–219.

[26] Arthur Bragg, "Turning Salespeople into Partners," *Sales and Marketing Management,* August 1986, 84.

[27] Alex Beam and Geoff Lewis, "The IBM-DEC Wars: It's 'The Year of the Customer'," *Business Week,* March 30, 1987, 88.

[28] Jay R. Schuster and Patricia Zingheim, "Sales Compensation Strategies at the Most Successful Companies," *Personnel Journal* 65 (June 1986): 112–116.

CHAPTER 13

SALES MANAGEMENT LEADERSHIP AND SUPERVISION

Learning Objectives

After completing this chapter, you should be able to

1. Distinguish between salesforce leadership and supervision.
2. List the six components of a sales leadership model.
3. Discuss five bases of power that affect leadership.
4. Explain five influence strategies used in leadership.
5. Describe the style of sales management preferred by salespeople.
6. Discuss issues related to coaching the salesforce, holding integrative meetings, and practicing ethical management.
7. Name some problems encountered in leading and supervising the salesforce.

SALES MANAGERS AS SUPERVISORS AND LEADERS: TWO CONTRASTING APPROACHES

The vice-president of sales for a large pharmaceutical firm hired Rocky to improve sales productivity in the midwest region, where results had been inconsistent. Rocky's experience, sales record, and reputation as a "tough manager" made him the perfect person to straighten things out, or at least the vice-president thought so. Rocky immediately instituted a ranking system to foster competition among the salespeople. Sales results were posted, and salespeople were put on a "you bet your job" alert — produce or lose your job. At the end of his second year, Rocky was honored as top district manager in the company, and his district was the highest-performing district in the country. By the end of the third year, however, results had leveled off, and four of the seven salespeople in Rocky's district had requested transfers. What led to this decline?

Interviews with the salespeople provided insight. Rocky's strict, coercive methods, while initially effective, had violated existing group norms. In a district characterized by deep midwestern roots, cooperative attitudes, and friendly interactions both on and off the job, Rocky imposed isolation and competition on the salesforce. Salespeople reacted by falsifying call reports and other information. When Rocky worked with them in the field, salespeople would call ahead to customers to prompt them on what to say in his presence. Eventually, the situation deteriorated further, and Rocky was demoted to the position of product specialist.

Another newly appointed sales manager in a telecommunications company faced the same situation that Rocky had faced — low morale and declining results. Within 18 months, morale was substantially improved, as were sales results. He described his approach thusly:

> Some people call me lazy . . . I don't do the selling for my people . . . It's their job to get the results and my job to be of assistance when needed. I

Source: Stephen X. Doyle, Charles Pignatelli, and Karen Florman, "The Hawthorne Legacy and the Motivation of Salespeople," *Journal of Personal Selling and Sales Management* 5 (November 1985): 1–6.

know that this is a radical departure for this district, because in the past the sales manager was the goliath who closed all the tough sales and the territory salespeople often functioned as administrators or assistants.

Pleased with the changes brought about by the new sales manager, one of the salespeople commented,

> At first we were very surprised . . . He asked what our sales goals should be and then helped us develop a plan to sell to our major accounts . . . He then let us do it . . . We often worked in district teams, refining our account plans together . . . We all feel that we are in charge of our own destiny . . . He can be described in two ways: accessible and helpful.

This sales manager's formula for success was straightforward. He used the informal group to motivate and manage sales activities, and he provided support by building an atmosphere of trust and open communication.

THIS chapter deals with the leadership and supervisory roles of sales managers. **Leadership** involves the use of influence with other people through communications processes to attain specific goals and objectives. Even though sales managers have a fair amount of authority by virtue of their positions in the organizational hierarchy, it is their skill to influence rather than dictate the actions of others that determines whether or not they are effective leaders. For example, in the previous chapter, we discussed the necessity to "sell" the salesforce on major changes in the financial-compensation system. A poor leader would ignore the need to gain the support of the salesforce and would simply dictate the terms of the new system and hope for the best.

Supervision is the day-to-day control of the salesforce under routine operating conditions. It is obviously an integral part of leadership; however, it is not the sum total of leadership. For one thing, supervision is only concerned with the sales manager–salesperson relationship, whereas leadership extends to all interpersonal relationships in which the sales manager is engaged. Further, leadership requires more foresight and intuition than supervision. This is true because supervision deals more with maintenance and improvement of the status quo, while leadership often requires redefinition of major objectives and operations of the salesforce.

This chapter is organized into three sections. In the first, a leadership model is discussed. The second section deals with three important leadership functions: coaching, holding integrative meetings, and practicing ethical sales management. The last section addresses some problems in leading and supervising a salesforce — namely, conflicts of interest; chemical abuse and dependency; disruptive, rule-breaking salespeople; and termination of employment.

A LEADERSHIP MODEL FOR SALES MANAGEMENT

Figure 13.1 shows a leadership model for sales management with six components:

1. *Power* — of the salesperson, salespeople, or other party with whom the sales manager is interacting.
2. *Power* — of the sales manager.
3. *Situation* — including time constraints, nature of the task, organizational history, and group norms.
4. *Needs and wants* — of the salesperson, salespeople, or other people with whom the sales manager is interacting.
5. *Goals and objectives* — of the individuals and the organization.
6. *Leadership skills* — anticipation, diagnostic, selection and matching, and communications.

Power and Leadership

In most job-related interpersonal situations, sales managers and the parties with whom they interact hold power in some form or another. As the model in Figure 13.1 suggests, the possession and use of this power will have a major impact on the quality of leadership achieved by a sales manager. To simplify discussion, we will focus on the sales manager–salesperson relationship, but keep in mind that sales managers must use their leadership skills in dealing with other personnel in the firm, as well as outside parties such as employment agencies, external trainers, customers, and suppliers.

The power held by an individual in an interpersonal relationship can be one or more of the following five types.[1] For each type, a sample comment from a salesperson recognizing the sales manager's power is shown in parentheses.[2]

1. *Expert power* — based on the belief that a person has valuable knowledge or skills in a given area. ("I respect her knowledge and good judgment because she is well-trained and experienced.")
2. *Referent power* — based on the attractiveness of one party to another. It may arise from friendship, role modeling, or perceived similarity of personal background or viewpoints. ("I like him personally and regard him as a friend.")
3. *Legitimate power* — associated with the right to be a leader, usually as a result of designated organizational roles. ("She has a legitimate right, considering her position as sales manager, to expect that her suggestions be followed.")
4. *Reward power* — stems from the ability of one party to reward the other party for a designated action. ("He is in good position to recommend promotions or permit special privileges for me.")

Figure 13.1 **A Leadership Model for Sales Management**

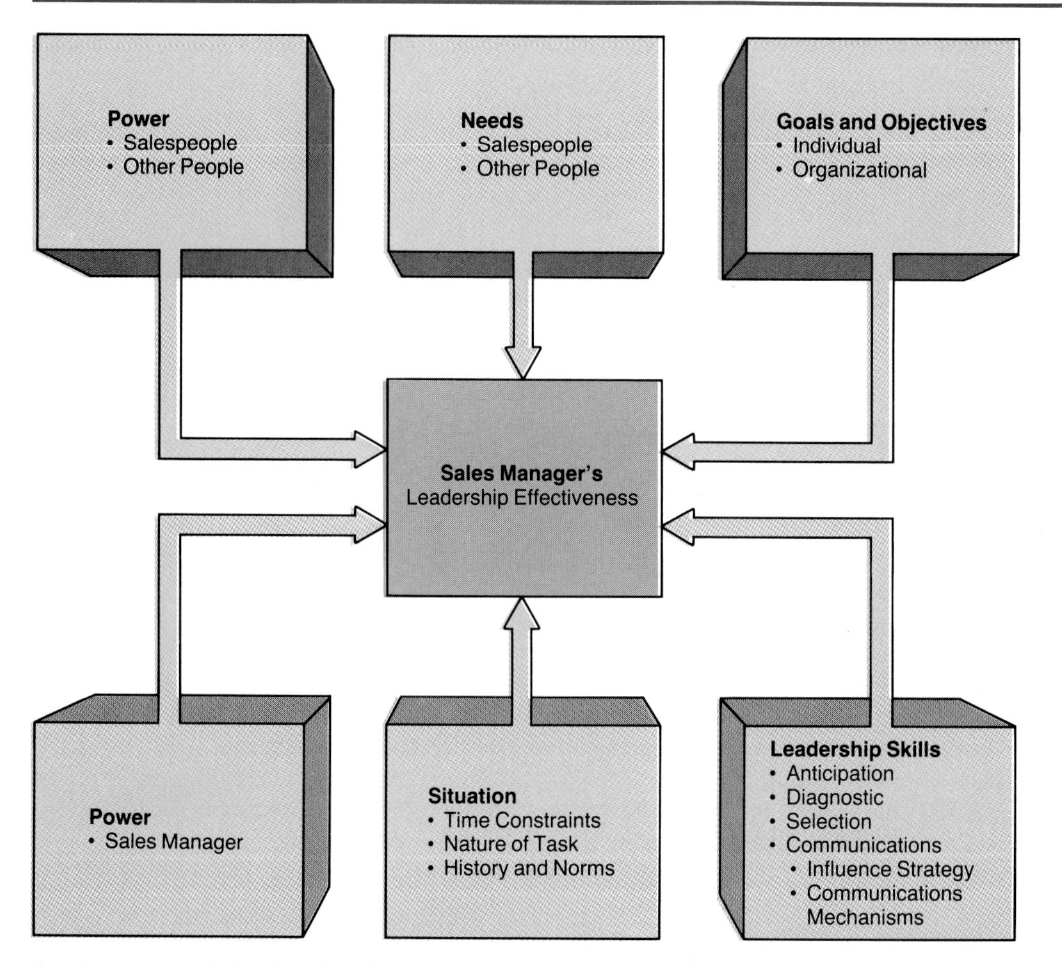

A sales manager's leadership effectiveness is a function of six factors: the power of the salesperson and other people, the power of the sales manager, the situation, human needs and wants, individual and organizational goals and objectives, and the leadership skills of the sales manager.

5. *Coercive Power*—based on a belief that one party can remove rewards and provide punishment to affect behavior. ("She can apply pressure to enforce her suggestions if they are not carried out fully and properly.")

It should be stressed that it is the various individuals' perceptions of power, rather than a necessarily objective assessment of where the power lies, that will determine the effects of power in interpersonal relationships. For example, a newly appointed district sales manager may perceive the legitimate power associated with being a manager to be extremely high, while the salespeople may not share this perception in the least. Such differences in perceptions regarding the nature and balance of power are frequently at the root of the problems that challenge sales managers.

Many sales managers have been accused of relying too much on reward and coercive power. This is disturbing for three reasons. First, coercive actions are likely to create strife in the salesforce and may encourage turnover among high-performing salespeople who have other employment opportunities. Second, as salespeople move through the career cycle, they tend to self-regulate the reward system. Senior salespeople are often seeking intrinsic rewards that cannot be dispensed and controlled by sales managers. As a result, rewards lose some of their impact. Third, research has demonstrated that other power bases (expert and referent) are positively related to salespeople's satisfaction with supervision and with sales managers.[3] Thus, it is recommended that sales managers who wish to become effective leaders develop referent and expert power bases.

At times, salespeople have more power in a situation than the sales manager. For example, senior salespeople may be extremely knowledgeable and therefore have dominant expert power over a relatively inexperienced sales manager. Or a sales manager with strong esteem needs may be intent on winning a popularity contest with the salesforce, which could give salespeople a strong referent power base. When a sales manager senses that the salesperson is more powerful in one of these dimensions, there is a strong tendency to rely on legitimate, coercive, or reward power to gain control of the situation. Again, it is suggested that these three power bases be used sparingly, however, and that the sales manager instead work toward developing more expert and referent power.

Situational Factors

Scores of studies have tried to uncover what makes an effective leader. One popular category of this research is called the **trait approach**, which attempts to determine the personality traits of an effective leader. To date, trait research, however, has not been enlightening. The **behavior approach**, which seeks to catalog behaviors associated with effective leadership, has likewise failed to identify what makes an effective leader. As the behavior and trait studies continue inconclusive, it has become increasingly apparent that the *situation* could have a strong impact on leadership. The model in Figure 13.1 of a **contingency approach** to leadership recognizes the importance of the interaction between situational factors and other factors. Situational factors include time constraints, the nature of the task, and the history and norms of the organization. When time is at a premium, crisis management is called for, which requires totally different leadership behaviors than usual. For example, a sales manager might rely on legitimate power, or even coercive power, to get immediate, undisputed support of the salesforce if time is constrained. Recall in the opening vignette for this chapter that Rocky used coercive power to remedy a crisis situation, and he had positive sales results for a limited time. It is only speculation, but if Rocky had changed his leadership methods over time to adapt to a changing situation, he might have survived as a sales manager.

Certainly the nature of the task is an important part of the situation. If the situation is concerned with the top priority of the sales organization, a more calculated approach to leadership may be called for than when the situation is of minor importance.

The norms established either formally or informally in the workplace are another situational factor. Recall from the opening vignette how Rocky violated informal group norms and thus was an ineffective leader over the long run. Research on work groups indicates that groups will form on the job, that the norms of the group will exert a strong influence on group members, and that managers must be aware of group processes to be effective leaders.[4]

The history, culture, and policies of the company may also affect a particular situation and thus the leadership action that would be most suitable. For example, Oscar Mayer has a long-standing history as a market leader offering high-quality products at premium prices. Despite intense competitive pressures to reduce prices, Oscar Mayer sales leadership is bolstered by the tradition of high-quality products, and what might be viewed as a crisis in price competition by another firm is hardly worthy of managerial attention at Oscar Mayer.

Needs and Wants of Salespeople

Continuing the discussion of the model shown in Figure 13.1, it should be stressed that leadership is an interactive process requiring one or more individuals to assume the role of followers or constituents. If coercive power-based behavior is cast aside, the needs and wants of salespeople must be given due consideration to ensure a supporting constituency for effective sales management leadership. Obviously, the needs and wants of salespeople cannot be met on a carte blanche basis. Further, a sales manager cannot become overly sensitive to the point of paranoia or managerial paralysis brought on by the fear that necessary actions will alienate the salesforce. But, on balance, the needs and wants of salespeople must be constantly weighed as an important determinant of leadership behavior.

The wisdom of considering the needs and wants of individual salespeople has been expressed as follows:

> Sexist or not, many people think men and women tend to work differently. Among sales managers, that thinking isn't limited to men. Most of the female sales managers we spoke with agree that the growing ranks of women in the profession have special strengths and weaknesses . . . . For example, female reps may not have "quite the self-confidence that men tend to exude," says Colleen Owens, national sales training manager with Kraft Inc.'s Dairy Group, Philadelphia.[5]

The trade magazine article from which the preceding quotation was taken points out that a female salesperson's "expressions of self-doubt are not the same red flag they are with men," and that encouragement from sales managers is usually effective in helping women overcome their self-doubt (whereas the same problem in a male salesperson may not be so easily corrected).[6] Whether or not men and women differ on the job is not the crucial point here, but rather that sales managers should attempt to consider the needs and wants of individual salespeople, as well as those of other people, if they hope be effective leaders.

Goals and Objectives

If salespeople's needs and wants are consistent with the organization's goals and objectives, leadership is an easier task for sales managers. To this end, some companies hold extensive training and development sessions on "life planning" for their salespeople. In these sessions, salespeople define their short-term and long term personal goals. In subsequent sessions, company management attempts to show how the salespeople's personal goal achievement can also assist in organizational goal achievement.

One firm that uses life planning is Combustion Engineering, a large industrial company. Combustion Engineering conducts these sessions on college campuses such as MIT with the assistance of industrial psychologists. The sessions are taken seriously. Company management feels that such goal clarification is beneficial not only to the personal development of their employees, but also because it helps produce a supportive constituency for the leaders of the firm.

Leadership Skills

As previously suggested, no one has been able to identify the exact personality traits or leadership behaviors that make an effective sales management leader. Likewise, there is no magic combination of skills that assures effective leadership. In this section, several skill areas will be reviewed that may be related to effective leadership; but keep in mind that possession of a particular skill is no more important than knowing when to employ it. The skill areas to be covered include anticipation and seeking feedback, diagnostic skills, selection and matching, and communications skills.

Anticipation and Seeking Feedback. The business press is full of examples of leadership crises that could have been avoided by *anticipation* of a potential problem. As mentioned in Chapter 5, Tandy has experienced extreme difficulty in trying to establish an outside salesforce to sell to business customers. While its Radio Shack retail stores are flourishing, the non-store salesforce is plagued with high turnover and a flat sales curve. Some observers feel that a major part of the problem is that Tandy took a "bargain basement" approach to developing its outside salesforce, which meant low salaries for the salespeople. Presumably, Tandy management did not anticipate the problems that could arise from such a stringent, budget-driven approach. It had a hard time attracting knowledgeable salespeople, and apparently those who did go to work for Tandy were ineffective against IBM and Apple. Many of these salespeople left, and Tandy faced a sales leadership crisis.[7]

The Tandy case illustrates how even the best-run companies can benefit from better anticipation of problems to avert leadership crises. It is not fair to expect unerring clairvoyance of sales managers, but it is reasonable to expect that responsible leaders will try to extend their vision into the future. One way they can do this is to *seek feedback* from customers, salespeople, and other important sources on a regular basis. An application of this idea that has become popular in recent years is called "management by wandering around" (MBWA).[8] Key concepts of MBWA include listening, empathizing, and maintaining contact with customers and salespeople. As one executive puts it, MBWA helps to "uncover problems before they become major irritants" and to "give management a daily reminder of where the real world is — with our field reps and our customers."[9]

Feedback can also be regularly gathered through field visits, salesforce audits, and conscientious reviews of routine call reports submitted by salespeople. Exhibit 13.1 provides several questions that could be explored with salespeople for the purpose of giving sales managers valuable feedback to facilitate leadership activities. These questions could be addressed as part of the salesperson reporting system or in conversations with the sales manager.

Diagnostic Skills. Effective leaders must be able to determine the specific nature of the problem or opportunity to be addressed. While this sounds simple, it is often difficult to distinguish between the real problem and the more visible symptoms of the problem. Earlier it was noted that sales managers have relied too heavily on reward and coercive power to direct their salesforces. A primary reason for this is a recurring tendency to attack easily identified symptoms of problems, not the core problems that need resolution. Reward and coercive power are also expedient ways to exercise control, and they suit the manager who likes to react without deliberation when faced with a problem.

For example, a sales manager may react to sluggish sales volume results by automatically assuming the problem is motivation. What follows from this hasty conclusion is a heavy dose of newly structured rewards, or just the opposite, a strong shot of coercion. Perhaps motivation is not the underlying problem, and other determinants of performance are actually the source of the problem. But a lack of *diagnostic skills* (discussed further in Chapter 16) has led the sales manager to attack the easiest target, the symptom of the problem, rather than fully examine the root cause of the problem. As we all know from our experiences with the common cold, treating the symptoms will not permanently solve the problem.

Selection and Matching. As we have already mentioned, no specific inventory of skills exists for effective leadership. Rather, there is a range of behaviors that should be matched to a particular situation. For example, we have cast dispersions on the

Exhibit 13.1 **Questions Providing Feedback from the Salesforce**

1. In your own words, what are your major job responsibilities?
2. Have you ever been uncertain as to what is expected of you on the job? If so, describe the situation.
3. How can we improve the overall effectiveness of the sales operation?
4. What are your personal goals in the short term and in the long term?
5. What can you do to achieve your goals? How can management help you to achieve your goals?
6. What factors cause stress on the job? How do you cope with stress? How can sales management help reduce stress?
7. Are there significant factors within the organization, but outside the sales department, that affect your performance? Can improvements be made in these areas?
8. Do you feel you have sufficient input into decisions that affect your job?
9. What major obstacles must be overcome during the next year for you to reach your job-related objectives?
10. How can your sales manager improve his or her performance?

use of coercive power in sales management, but its use may be entirely appropriate in some situations. In the case of a problem employee whose insubordination is creating morale problems for the remainder of the salesforce, for example, a "shape up or ship out" ultimatum may be the best response.

The importance of *selecting* appropriate leadership responses to *match* the situation is highlighted in the research dealing with salespeoples' concerns as they move through career stages. A study of one company's salespeople found those in the exploration stage to be unhappy with their sales managers and the aspects of the sales jobs over which the manager had considerable control.[10] For example, they did not perceive their sales managers to be open and supportive, and they felt they had little opportunity to make important decisions. Salespeople in the other career stages (establishment, maintenance, and disengagement) in this company held positive perceptions toward their sales managers and toward aspects of their jobs heavily influenced by management. Obviously, either a change in managerial behavior toward the discontented salespeople in the exploration stage was called for in this case, or the company's recruitment and selection methods should have been changed. Either way, being able to match managerial actions to the situation, rather than responding within a narrowly defined range of behaviors, would be a big advantage to effective leadership.

Communications

Recall the definition of leadership from the beginning of this chapter. At the heart of the definition is the phrase "the use of influence through communications processes." In this section, we will discuss various influence strategies and communications mechanisms involved in leadership and supervision. Effective leaders deliver clear, timely information through appropriate media or interpersonal communications. In contrast, the best plans and intentions can be destroyed by faulty communications. All too often, sales operations are damaged by premature leakage of information, inconsistent and conflicting communications, tardy messages, or poorly conceived strategies for influencing the salesforce.

Influence Strategies. Since sales managers have power from different sources to use in dealing with salespeople, peers, and superiors, they have the opportunity to devise different **influence strategies** according to situational demands. Influence strategies can be based on threats, promises, persuasion, relationships, and manipulation.[11] All are appropriate at some time with some salespeople but not necessarily with superiors or peers.

Threats. In a strategy based on **threats**, a manager might specify a desired behavior and the punishment that will follow if the behavior is not achieved. "If you do not call on your accounts at least once a week, you will lose your job," is an example. Since threats are used only in cases of noncompliance to operational guidelines, their use requires a monitoring system to see if the threatened person is engaging in the desired behavior. This can be time-consuming and annoying for the manager. Threats should be viewed as a last resort, but they should not be eliminated as a viable influence strategy. Research has indicated that salespeople, contrary to common wisdom, do not appear to react unfavorably to appropriate punishment and that managers "need to overcome their own reluctance in meting out punishment."[12]

Promises. Sales managers can utilize reward power as a basis for developing influence strategies based on **promises**. Research has indicated that promises produce better compliance than threats.[13] This would seem to be especially true for well-educated, mobile employees as typified by a large portion of professional salespeople. Further, influence strategies based on promises as opposed to threats help foster positive feelings among salespeople and boost salesforce morale.

Persuasion. An influence strategy based on **persuasion** can work without the use of reward or coercive power. Since persuasive messages must be rational and reasonable, however, expert and referent power bases are necessary to make them effective. Persuasion implies that the target of influence must first change his or her attitudes and intentions in order to produce a subsequent change in behavior. For example, a sales manager might persuade the salesforce to submit weekly activity reports by first convincing them of the importance of the reports in the company's marketing information system.

Sales managers are almost always former salespeople and therefore are quite comfortable with influence through persuasion. Generally speaking, persuasion is preferred to threats and promises, but it does require more time and skill.

THE HUB CONCEPT AND SALESFORCE COMMUNICATIONS

THE LINEAR VS THE HUB

Traditional Linear Approach
Information flowing predominantly in one direction. What you tend to achieve is a series of bottlenecks.

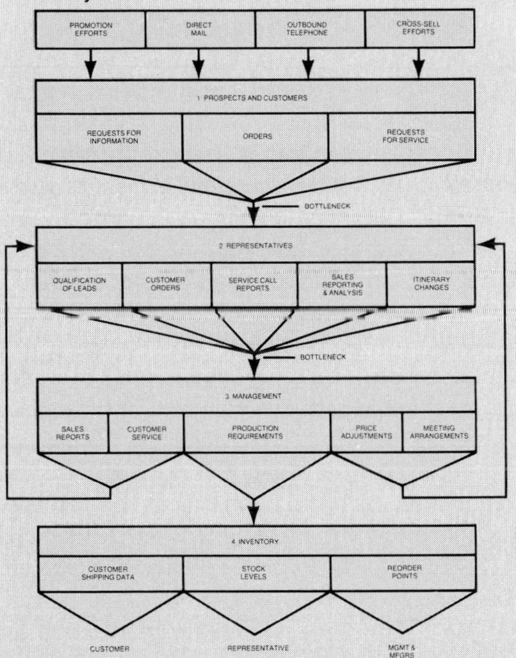

The Hub Concept
Example of the efficiencies: One call to the hub from management can distribute messages to many reps.

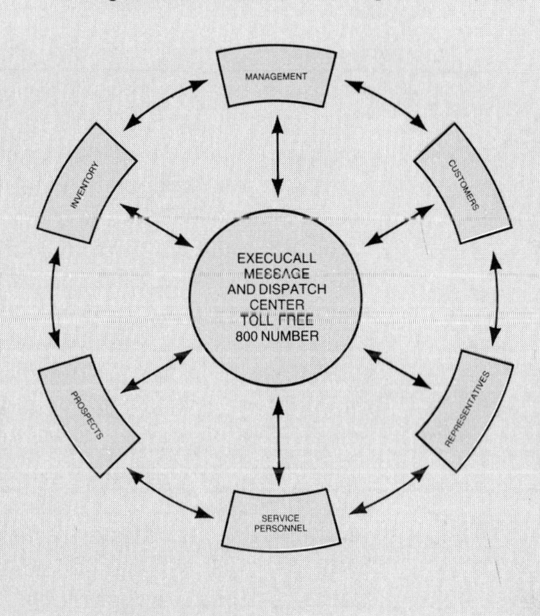

The hub concept establishes a central access and dispatch point with a toll-free number for communications with a variety of parties, including salespeople, customers, sales managers, and other company personnel. To visualize the benefits of the hub concept, imagine that a company with 100 salespeople and 3,000 customers was planning a price increase in the near future. Think about how many phone calls and memos would be necessary to communicate the planned price increase if traditional linear communications flows were followed. Further imagine the chaos if the price increase had to be rescinded a week later. When contrasted with the instantaneous communication via the computerized telephone hub, traditional methods seem slow and awkward.

While the installation of a communications system featuring a hub may be costly in absolute terms, the relative cost may be quite reasonable. For example, the Philadelphia office of Control Data Corporation's business services division reports a 17 percent savings in telephone bills through the elimination of collect and credit card calls after implementing a hub system. Further, Control Data feels that faster responses to customers more than justify the cost of the system.[a] In addition to speeding communications and offering constant access, hub systems may also reduce preparation and postage costs of mailing.

[a] Thayer C. Taylor, "Eliminating Telephone Tag," *Sales and Marketing Management*, April 1988, 80.

Source: ExecuCall Incorporated, Cincinnati, Ohio. Used with permission.

Relationships. Two types of **relationships** can affect influence processes. The first type is based on referent power. It builds on personal friendships, or feelings of trust, admiration, or respect. In short, one party is quite willing to do what the other party desires, simply because the former likes the latter. The second type of relationship is where one party has legitimate power over the other party by virtue of position in the organizational hierarchy. Sales managers have legitimate power in dealing with salespeople. As a result, they can influence salespeople in many situations without the use of threats, promises, or persuasion.[14]

Manipulation. Unlike the other influence strategies, **manipulation** does not involve direct communications with the target of influence. Rather, circumstances are controlled to influence behavior. For example, a salesperson lacking self-confidence might be assigned to work on temporary assignment with a confident senior salesperson. In team selling, the sales manager might control the group dynamics within teams by carefully selecting compatible personality types to compose the teams. Manipulation might also involve "office politics" and the use of third parties to influence others. For example, a sales manager might use the backing of his or her superior in dealing with peers on the job.

Communications Mechanisms. A critical part of using communications in leadership processes is knowing how to effectively use appropriate **communications mechanisms**. It is beyond the scope of this book to fully discuss fundamental business communications topics such as letter and memo writing and report writing. Instead, consider how a recently developed communications mechanism called the *hub concept* could contribute to effective leadership. This concept is contrasted to the traditional linear approach to communications in "Sales Technology: The Hub Concept and Salesforce Communications."

The hub concept is only one example of how communications mechanisms can facilitate leadership functions. All communications with the salesforce must be carefully planned to ensure accuracy and clarity. And, remember, while the latest developments such as the hub offer exciting features, the simple spoken word between a sales manager and a salesperson is still of prime importance in effective leadership.

MANAGEMENT STYLE

The combination of two highly visible facets of leadership, power and communications, are sometimes referred to as **management style**. We have suggested that management style may vary according to the dictates of the situation, which contradicts the notion that a singular management style could be optimal. It is possible, however, that a sales manager might have a *primary management style* that is appropriate for a large number of situations — perhaps a majority of the situations typically encountered by sales managers.

Exhibit 13.2 **Sales Management Styles**

DOMINANCE

Quadrant 1

Planning: Rarely involves salespeople ("Why should it? Planning is my prerogative. I make the plans, they carry them out. That's as it should be.")

Organizing: Tight organization. Patterns of relationship emphasize one-to-one interaction ("I make sure everyone knows what to do and how to do it. I call the shots.")

Controlling: Very close supervision ("Any sales manager who isn't vigilant is asking for trouble. Salespeople must know they're being closely scrutinized.")

Leading: Pushes, demands, drives ("Most people want a strong leader to tell them what to do. My people know who's boss.")

Quadrant 4

Planning: Consults salespeople whenever their thinking might help ("I want the best plans possible. That frequently requires ideas from others. I don't have all the answers.")

Organizing: Patterns of relationship designed to stimulate collaboration and interdependence ("I try to get synergism through pooling of resources.")

Controlling: Tries to develop salespeople who control themselves ("Get people committed to their goals, and they'll supervise their own efforts.") Provides more structure for those who can't.

Leading: Tries to make salespeople aware of their potential ("Leadership is helping people do what they have in them to do. A leader develops people.")

HOSTILITY ← → WARMTH

Quadrant 2

Planning: Relies heavily on own manager ("I prefer to pass along her plans. That way, my people know they'd better follow through.") Or leans heavily on tradition ("It's worked before; it should work again.")

Organizing: Patterns of relationship vague, indefinite. Doesn't encourage interaction ("Just do your own job and stay out of trouble.")

Controlling: Sees self mainly as a caretaker ("I'm paid to keep things stable. I exert enough control to make sure nobody disrupts routines. There's no point in doing more.")

Leading: Passive, indifferent. Downplays own influence ("Don't kid yourself. No matter how hard you try to lead people, they'll end up doing pretty much as they please.")

Quadrant 3

Planning: More concerned with generalities than details ("If you fence people in with too much planning, you'll demoralize them. I'm flexible; I give my people plenty of leeway.")

Organizing: Patterns of relationship emphasize loosely structured sociability ("If people feel good about their jobs, they'll do their best without lots of regulation. My job is to make sure they feel good.")

Controlling: Relies on high morale to produce hard work ("Control is secondary. What salespeople need most is a good feeling about their jobs.")

Leading: Believes optimism and encouragement get results ("Being a sales manager is like being a cheerleader. You can't let your people get discouraged.")

SUBMISSION

Source: Reprinted by permission of the publisher from Robert E. Hite and Joseph A. Bellizzi, "A Preferred Style of Sales Management," *Industrial Marketing Management* 15 (August 1986): 217. Copyright 1986 by Elsevier Science Publishing Co., Inc.

Some interesting research has explored the type of management style preferred by salespeople.[15] This research classified sales managers' use of power according to whether the manager was dominant or submissive in dealing with salespeople. Communications methods used by sales managers were also divided into two categories, hostile and warm. Exhibit 13.2 shows the characteristics of each of the resultant four management styles: dominant-hostile, submissive-hostile, submissive-warm, and dominant-warm.

Salespeople who participated in a national survey preferred the dominant-warm management style shown in Quadrant 4 of Exhibit 13.2. The type of leader described in this quadrant seeks feedback from salespeople and realizes the importance of goal setting in controlling salesforce efforts. There is also evidence in Exhibit 13.2 that this type of sales manager adapts to the situation in that he or she provides more structure for those salespeople who cannot supervise their own efforts.

A valid question that arises from this research is, to what extent should a sales manager's style be determined by the desires of the salesforce? Since research has shown that salespeople prefer a dominant sales manager who provides fairly close supervision rather than a submissive sales manager,[16] it does not appear that sales management would be compromised by adopting salespeople's generally preferred management style. And in terms of communications, it is hard to argue against warm, open communications with the salesforce instead of hostile communications as general operating procedure.

SELECTED LEADERSHIP FUNCTIONS

In this section, three particularly important leadership functions of sales management will be discussed: coaching the salesforce, planning and conducting integrative sales meetings, and striving for ethical (or moral) leadership behavior.

Coaching

In the **coaching** role, a sales manager concentrates on continuous development of salespeople. Although coaching may entail the sales manager's interactions with a group of salespeople, its most crucial activities are those conducted with individual salespeople. Coaching sessions may take place in the office or during the sales manager's field visits with salespeople. In the field, such sessions often take the form of "curbstone conferences" immediately prior to or following each sales call.

Coaching is especially important for sales managers, as compared to other managers in a given company. As Peters and Austin have concluded, "Perhaps surprisingly, the more elbowroom a company grants to its people, the more important on-the-job coaching becomes."[17] Since salespeople often have considerable latitude to plan and execute work activities, coaching is extremely important for most sales managers. Further, the boundary-role demands of sales jobs, and the frequent geographic isolation of salespeople from other company personnel, adds to the significance of coaching activities.

The essence of coaching is providing guidance and feedback in close time proximity to the occurrence of an appropriate event related to developing salespeople's skills, attitudes, or behaviors. By assuring a close link between the coaching session and the appropriate event (for example, a sales call), the sales manager is using the principle of *recency* to assist the developmental, or learning, process. Essentially, this

Exhibit 13.3 **Coaching Suggestions**

1. Instead of criticizing salespeople during coaching, help them improve by giving "how to" advice. Repeatedly tell them what you like about their performance.
2. Ask questions to maximize the salesperson's active involvement in the coaching process.
3. Insist that salespeople evaluate themselves. Self-evaluation helps develop salespeople into critical thinkers regarding their work habits and performance.
4. Reach concrete agreements about what corrective action is to be taken following each coaching session. Failure to agree on corrective action may lead to the salesperson's withdrawal from the developmental aspects of coaching.
5. Keep records of coaching sessions specifying corrective action to be taken, objectives of the coaching session, and a timetable for accomplishing the objective. Follow up to ensure objectives are accomplished.

Source: "First Train Them, Then Coach Them," *Sales and Marketing Management,* August 1987, 64–65.

is the principle that learning is facilitated when it is immediately applied. By making a practice of holding coaching sessions before and after each sales call, sales managers are also using *repetition,* another powerful learning tool.

In addition to using repetition and recency to facilitate learning, sales managers should consider the type of feedback they offer to salespeople during coaching sessions. Feedback can be described as either outcome feedback or as cognitive feedback.[18] **Outcome feedback** is information on whether or not a desired outcome is achieved. In contrast, **cognitive feedback** is information on how and why the desired outcome is achieved. Post-sales-call coaching focusing on outcome feedback might feature comments such as, "Your response to the question on pricing was totally inadequate," while cognitive feedback might focus on why the pricing question was poorly handled, how a better response could have been made, and how the proper handling of the question could have facilitated the desired outcome for the sales call.

Researchers have suggested that the use of cognitive feedback can be helpful to salespeople, and that outcome feedback can be dysfunctional in the complex dynamic environments faced by many salespeople.[19] The importance of cognitive feedback is reaffirmed in the first point of Exhibit 13.3, which contains coaching suggestions from a sales management consultant whose clients include Foster-Grant and Textron.

Planning and Conducting Integrative Meetings

One of the best opportunities for sales managers to demonstrate leadership ability comes when they plan and execute an **integrative meeting**, one in which several sales and sales management functions are achieved. Although multiple objectives are accomplished at such meetings, their overall purpose is to unite the salesforce in the quest for common objectives, a key part of the leadership model discussed earlier in the chapter. Such meetings may combine training, strategic planning, motivational programs, recognition of outstanding sales performance, and recreation and entertainment for the attendees. In large sales organizations, the entire salesforce may attend

Exhibit 13.4 **Suggestions from Salespeople on Conducting Meetings**

1. Keep technical presentations succinct, and use visual aids and breakout discussion groups to maintain salespeoples' interest.
2. Keep salespeople informed of corporate strategy and their role in it.
3. Minimize operations reviews unless they are directly related to sales. Use a combination of face-to-face exchanges and written handouts to introduce key people in advertising and customer service.
4. Set a humane schedule. Overscheduling can deter learning. Allow time for salespeople to share experiences so they learn from each other.
5. Let salespeople know what's planned. Be sure they are briefed on the purpose and content of the meeting.
6. Ask salespeople for their ideas of topics, speakers, and preferred recreational activities, if applicable.

Source: Rayna Skolnik, "Salespeople Sound Off On Meetings," *Sales and Marketing Management,* November 1987,108.

a major integrative sales meeting each year to review the past year's performance and unite for the upcoming year. As is true with all leadership functions, the needs and wants of the salesforce should be given some consideration in the planning and execution of integrative meetings. Some suggestions from salespeople are given in Exhibit 13.4

Planning and conducting an integrative sales meeting involves creative, sometimes glamorous activities such as selecting a theme for the meeting, arranging for the appearances of professional entertainers, or even assisting in the production of special films and other audiovisual materials. The ultimate success of all meetings, however, depends on the planning and execution of rather mundane activities such as those shown in the meeting planner's checklist in Exhibit 13.5. As you review the items listed in the checklist, imagine the consequences if these details are improperly handled.

To get a better idea of the importance of attention to detail in assuring a successful meeting, consider the case of Saab-Scania Canada Ltd., a subsidiary of the Swedish automaker. The complications arising from differences in European and Canadian technologies and logistical details are explained in "International Sales: Saab-Scania's Integrative Meeting Experience."

Meeting Ethical/Moral Responsibilities

In recent years, there has been increased attention paid to the subject of ethical responsibilities of business leaders. As pointed out in a prize-winning *Harvard Business Review* article, "Most business decisions involve some degree of ethical judgment; few can be taken solely on the basis of arithmetic."[20] In previous chapters, ethical concerns have been highlighted to stress their importance in practically every sales management function. In this section, we will discuss three approaches to management ethics: immoral management, amoral management, and moral management. The

Exhibit 13.5 **Sales Manager's Meeting Review List**

Attendees

- ☐ notified in writing, date, location, hours
- ☐ told what to bring
- ☐ have directions to meeting site
- ☐ meeting schedule conflicts?

Meeting Site

- ☐ sleeping rooms reserved
- ☐ meeting room reserved
- ☐ meeting room seen or know dimensions
- ☐ meeting room setup arranged
- ☐ meeting supplies arranged
- ☐ meeting equipment arranged
- ☐ meal functions arranged
- ☐ coffee breaks arranged
- ☐ meeting room location posted
- ☐ material shipped or taken to site
- ☐ estimate cost of meeting
- ☐ how to handle messages

Preparing Myself

- ☐ agenda complete
- ☐ prepared opening remarks
- ☐ written speech or made notes
- ☐ practiced what I will say
- ☐ anticipated questions & remarks
- ☐ visuals prepared, films, slides, etc.
- ☐ handout material prepared
- ☐ samples, sales aids ready
- ☐ meeting evaluation form
- ☐ prepared case study
- ☐ prepared for adequate participation

Equipment

- ☐ video equipment
- ☐ slide projector, slide tray, remote extension
- ☐ 16mm projector, take-up reel
- ☐ overhead projector
- ☐ tape recorder
- ☐ screen
- ☐ chalkboard
- ☐ easel with paper pad
- ☐ lectern
- ☐ spare projector bulbs
- ☐ sound amplification

Supplies

- ☐ markers, chalk, eraser
- ☐ paper for note-taking
- ☐ pens, pencils (sharpened)
- ☐ badges
- ☐ table name cards
- ☐ masking, scotch tape
- ☐ gaffer's tape
- ☐ extension cord(s)
- ☐ 3-prong adapter plug
- ☐ blank tape, cassettes
- ☐ blank overhead transparencies
- ☐ 3-hole punch
- ☐ stapler
- ☐ pocket knife

Source: Jim Rapp, *How To Get Participation in Sales Meetings* (Orlando, Fla.: National Society of Sales Training Executives, 1981). Used with permission.

key points distinguishing these three approaches are shown in Exhibit 13.6. The author of the material shown in the exhibit contends that the majority of managers fit into the amoral category, and that the number of moral managers roughly equals the number of immoral managers.[21]

As you review the information in Exhibit 13.6, examples of immoral management may come to mind quite easily, while examples of amoral and moral management are probably harder to recall. This is partially a function of what types of business practices have been deemed most topical by the business and popular press. However,

Exhibit 13.6 **Approaches to Management Ethics**

Organizational Characteristics	Immoral Management	Amoral Management	Moral Management
Ethical Norms	Management decisions, actions, and behavior imply a positive and active opposition to what is moral (ethical). Decisions are discordant with accepted ethical principles. An active negation of what is moral is implied.	Management is neither moral nor immoral, but decisions lie outside the sphere to which moral judgments apply. Management activity is outside or beyond the moral order of a particular code. May imply a lack of ethical perception and moral awareness.	Management activity conforms to a standard of ethical, or right, behavior. Conforms to accepted professional standards of conduct. Ethical leadership is commonplace on the part of management
Motives	Selfish. Management cares only about its or the company's gains.	Well-intentioned but selfish in the sense that impact on others is not considered.	Good. Management wants to succeed but only within the confines of sound ethical precepts (fairness, justice, due process).
Goals	Profitability and organizational success at any price.	Profitability. Other goals are not considered.	Profitability within the confines of legal obedience and ethical standards.
Orientation toward Law	Legal standards are barriers that management must overcome to accomplish what it wants.	Law is the ethical guide, preferably the letter of the law. The central question is what we can do legally.	Obedience toward letter and spirit of the law. Law is a minimal ethical behavior. Prefer to operate well above what law mandates.
Strategy	Exploit opportunites for corporate gain. Cut corners when it appears useful.	Give managers free rein. Personal ethics may apply but only if managers choose. Respond to legal mandates if caught and required to do so.	Live by sound ethical standards. Assume leadership position when ethical dilemmas arise. Enlightened self-interest.

Source: Archie B. Carroll, "In Search of the Moral Manager," *Business Horizons* 30 (March–April 1987): 12. Copyright 1987 by the Foundation for the School of Business at Indiana University. Reprinted by permission.

INTERNATIONAL SALES

SAAB-SCANIA'S INTEGRATIVE MEETING EXPERIENCE

Saab-Scania Canada Ltd. had planned a 4½-minute multimedia extravaganza with the theme of "hands across the ocean" to demonstrate the strength of the Swedish parent company and build the confidence and pride of its sales organization. The presentation was to be the dramatic opening for the meeting, but with only 48 hours remaining until the scheduled opening of the meeting, problems and questions were in abundance.

The materials for the opening presentation had been shipped from Stockholm in plenty of time to arrive for the meeting but were lost in the Toronto airport for three days, cutting into the time needed to make sure that the show would look the same in Canada as it did in Sweden. It was possible that the projector commonly used in Europe, the German-produced Kodak SAV, would have different lamp-filament characteristics than the Elmo Omnigraphic projector to be used in Toronto. Also, the European lamp required 24 volts, while the Canadian model ran on 110 volt circuitry.

Either of these factors could affect the rate at which the lamps would brighten and dim. This could play havoc with the seven-slides-per-second sequences in the presentation. For example, a scene meant to appear on the screen in staccato images might be smoothed out. Correcting this problem would require reprogramming the computer used to control the slide projectors used in the presentation.

The total show required 3,005 computerized cues during the 4½ minutes. Necessary revisions took less than 2 hours. After the presentation was fine-tuned, videotapes were produced for use by dealers in point-of-purchase promotions. The night before the meeting, a number of details remained to be completed, including a final check of the staging area, which featured a replica of a Saab showroom.

During the night a fire alarm sounded in the area where the meeting was to be held, and Saab personnel envisioned the worst— total destruction of their efforts and loss of $400,000 in sunk meeting expenses. After a half hour in suspense, a false alarm was declared. The next morning, final technical details were attended to moments before the multimedia kickoff. The presentation played flawlessly to an appreciative, enthusiastic audience who could not possibly have conceived of all the detail work necessary to make the entire meeting a success.

Source: Don Sutherland, "The Sales Meeting Show-Biz Convincer," *Business Marketing,* March 1987, 84–93.

that press coverage could also indicate a deep concern throughout society about ethics in management.

Before discussing the features of moral, or ethical, sales management, some examples of seemingly immoral management (as described in Exhibit 13.6) might be helpful:

- KIS, seller of a film-processing machine, was sued by customers and former employees for fraud, coercive sales tactics, and poor service. While KIS executives claimed they were only selling equipment, not franchises, their promotional brochures promised "all the advantages of a franchise without the inconvenience." The top executive of the firm blamed any problems on excessive zeal, saying, "We wanted to grow too fast and didn't have the structure for it."[22]

- Insurance agents misrepresented life insurance policies as savings accounts that would pay high interest rates, preserve estates for heirs, and allow withdrawal of money at any time. Targeted buyers were elderly people who feared their estates would be severely diminished by inheritance taxes. In many cases, refunds were ordered to rectify sales abuses.[23]
- A salesperson contends he was fired so the company could avoid paying him earned commissions. He won the suit and recovered lost income.[24]
- A sales manager for a division of Congoleum lost his job after it was discovered that he received bribes under the guise of a consulting agreement with one of his customers.[25]
- Through a West German middleman, sensitive defense-related equipment manufactured by U.S. firm Tektronix ended up in Soviet-bloc countries in violation of the Export Administration Act. Tektronix claimed no wrong had been intended, but government officials said the firm should have been more diligent in checking into the likely final destination of the equipment.[26]

These examples are in sharp contrast to moral management as described in Exhibit 13.6. Corporate training can help sensitize managers to ethical issues and may be able to convert amoral, and even immoral, managers to the moral school of thought. For example, Phillip Morris USA has trained 500 field managers in its salesforce on issues dealing with sexual harassment in a series of workshops involving group discussions and a video entitled "Shades of Gray."[27]

Tighter financial controls and closer supervision of sales activities may help achieve ethical sales management practices. Bribery, for example, is hard to commit when sales expenditures are closely monitored. Many sales organizations are adopting a **code of ethics**. An example of a company-specific code of ethics, that of General Dynamics, was presented in Chapter 10. Associations also develop ethical codes and urge members to adhere to standards of ethical business behavior. Sample items from the American Marketing Association's code of ethics for sales managers and salespeople are shown in Exhibit 13.7.

Those interested in achieving moral management will undoubtedly face some challenges, since competitive pressures and the premium placed on expedient action often encourage unethical behavior. As one observer puts it, "In the short run, strategically developed manipulation and coercion will help us faster to accomplish our goals."[28] Moreover, ethical issues are sometimes muddied by the complexity of a decision. For a long-term horizon for success, however, we urge you to use a framework for moral, ethical management as described in the last column of Exhibit 13.6 and to embrace, where available, codes of ethics, training to sensitize salespeople and their managers to ethical issues, and legal instruction. Those who become sales managers will have the added responsibility of providing ethical leadership by setting an example.

Exhibit 13.7 **Excerpts from the American Marketing Association's Code of Ethics**

1. Reject the use of high-pressure manipulations or misleading sales tactics.
2. Disclose the full price associated with any purchase.
3. Disclose all substantial risks associated with product or service usage.
4. Do not manipulate the availability of a product for the purpose of exploitation.
5. Do not use coercion in the marketing channel.
6. Refrain from exerting undue influence over the reseller's choice to handle a product.
7. Prohibit selling under the guise of conducting research.
8. Communicate in a truthful and forthright manner.
9. Avoid manipulation to take advantage of situations to maximize personal welfare in a way that unfairly deprives or damages the organization or others.

Source: "AMA Adopts New Code of Ethics," *Marketing News,* (September 11, 1987): 1, published by the American Marketing Association. Used with permission.

PROBLEMS IN LEADERSHIP

Any managerial position involving the direct supervision of employees will require periodic handling of personnel management problems. As indicated earlier, personnel problems can be minimized through proper recruitment and selection, training, motivation and compensation, and the establishment of clearly stated salesforce plans, policies, and procedures.

Examples of the problems that sales managers may have to deal with include conflicts of interest, chemical abuse and dependency, salespeople who will not conform to guidelines, and salespeople whose employment must be terminated.

Conflict of Interest

Since salespeople assume a boundary-role position, they cannot help but encounter **conflicts of interest**. Such conflicts are part of the job, and problem-solving skills are often tested. In some cases, meeting customer demands could violate company policy. In an even more serious vein, the salesperson could have a vested interest or ownership in a customer's business, or even in a competitor's business. The use of confidential information for individual profit, as in the case of Wall Street insider trading, is also an example of serious — in fact, criminal — conflict of interest. Many companies require that employees periodically sign an agreement not to engage in specified situations that may represent conflicting interests.

Chemical Abuse and Dependency

Salespeople may be no more susceptible to chemical dependency than any other occupational group, nor is there any hard evidence that chemical abuse and dependency are worse among their ranks now than in the past. However, awareness of this

SALES TREND

SALES MANAGEMENT RESPONDS TO CHEMICAL ABUSE

Travel, lack of constant supervision, and job pressure may contribute to chemical abuse and dependency among salespeople. As a Xerox executive says, "Job pressure dictates the need for something outside oneself. Some salespeople may require a bit of euphoria before the big sales call." The costs of chemical abuse are staggering in dollar and human terms. Federal studies indicate that through absenteeism, accidents, and sub-par performance, a company loses a quarter of an individual's pay for every year that a dependency problem goes undetected. A spokesperson for Digital Equipment notes the financial concern: "When you have a heavy front-end investment in training a salesman and additional training as he moves up to senior sales level, you face substantial costs in replacing that person."

According to the director of occupational programs for Hospital Corporation of America, sales managers have been inclined to avoid the problems in a "tolerate-to-terminate" cycle in which "they are inclined to cover up for someone in the hope that the problem will go away. When it doesn't, they end up firing him." Things may be changing as the negative consequences of chemical abuse become better understood. Many firms, including Xerox, Litton, and Campbell's Soup, have instituted employee assistance programs to address chemical-abuse problems.

Source: Martin Everett, "Drugs Can Bust Your Sales Force," *Sales and Marketing Management,* March 1987, 44–50.

problem is increasing, and sales managers are taking a more active role in identifying individuals with problems and in assisting rehabilitative efforts.

A recent survey found that over 40 percent of the policies for dealing with alcohol abuse in the salesforce were set by the sales manager, not someone else in the company. The same survey found that the most common response to alcohol abuse was counseling by the sales manager, and the next most frequent response was referral to a formal alcohol-abuse program outside the firm.[29] A overwhelming majority (75 percent) of the sales managers in the survey felt that, in general, alcohol abuse was at least a "somewhat serious" problem. For a closer look at problems associated with chemical abuse and dependency, read "Sales Trend: Sales Management Responds to Chemical Abuse."

Problem Salespeople: A Disruptive Influence

Perhaps the most infamous of the "problem salespeople" is the nonconforming "maverick" who breaks all the rules in the quest for sales results. While mavericks often are high achievers, their flaunting of the rules can be disruptive to sales managers and adversely affect the remainder of the salesforce. A maverick who fails to produce will not survive in most sales organizations, but a rule-breaker who can produce often thrives as the center of attention. Why is this true?

Perhaps, as one observer puts says, "people who can produce results shouldn't be tied down to organizational restraints."[30] A director of national account marketing for Dell Computer adds, "mavericks are needed on every salesforce; they illustrate that multiple styles are successful."[31] If, however, mavericks are allowed to ignore the rules the other salespeople abide by, the morale of the other salespeople may suffer. One recommended action for sales managers is to explain to the maverick why the rules cannot be broken while also freely praising his or her good performance.[32]

Termination of Employment

In some cases, problems cannot be overcome, and it is necessary to terminate the employment of a salesperson. When performance consistently fails to meet standards, and coaching, training, and retraining are unsuccessful, termination or reassignment may be the only remaining alternatives. Also, a salesperson's insubordination or lack of effort may damage the overall effectiveness or morale of the salesforce, in which case termination could be justified.

The current environment dictates that sales managers pay close attention to the legal ramifications of terminating a salesperson's employment. A permanent record of performance appraisals, conditions of employment, and any deviations from expected performance or behavior should be carefully maintained throughout the salesperson's term of employment. Attempts to correct performance deficiencies should be noted and filed when they occur.

Before firing the salesperson, the sales manager should carefully review all relevant company policies to ensure his or her own adherence to appropriate guidelines. Finally, the actual communication of termination should be written, and any verbal communication of the termination should be witnessed by a third party. At all times, sales managers should respect the dignity of the person whose employment is being terminated while firmly communicating the termination notice.

The examples of conflicts of interest, chemical dependency, rule-breaking salespeople, and the need to terminate employment of unsatisfactory salespeople are offered here to remind the reader of the complex human issues of managing a salesforce. Realities dictate that sales managers be able to confront and handle personnel problems as adeptly as strategic sales management issues in order to be effective leaders of their salesforces.

SUMMARY

1. **Distinguish between salesforce leadership and supervision.** Supervision is part of leadership. It deals with the day-to-day operations of the salesforce and is primarily concerned with the maintenance and improvement of the status quo. Leadership requires more foresight and intuition than mere supervision, however,

and may involve major changes in salesforce objectives and operations. Leadership involves the sales manager's interactions with a variety of parties, including salespeople, customers, other company personnel, external trainers, and employment agencies. Supervision, on the other hand, is concerned only with the relationships between the sales manager and the salesforce.

2. **List the six components of a sales leadership model.** A model for sales leadership, shown in Figure 13.1, identifies six components: power of the sales manager, power of salespeople, situational factors, needs and wants of salespeople and other parties, goals and objectives, and leadership skills.

3. **Discuss five bases of power that affect leadership.** Five power bases are coercive, reward, legitimate, referent, and expert. Coercive power is associated with punishment and is the opposite of reward power. Legitimate power stems from the individual's position in the organizational hierarchy. Referent power is held by one person when another person wants to maintain a relationship with that person. Expert power is attributed to the possession of information. A sales manager and those with whom he or she interacts may utilize one or more power bases in a given situation.

4. **Explain five influence strategies used in leadership.** Influence strategies used by sales managers could be based on threats, promises, persuasion, relationships, or manipulation. Unlike the other four strategies, manipulation does not involve face-to-face interactions with the target of influence. Threats utilize coercive power, while promises stem from the reward power base. Persuasion employs expert and referent power. Legitimate and referent power are used when influence strategy is based on interpersonal relationships.

5. **Describe the style of sales management preferred by salespeople.** Although leadership requires adapting to varying situational demands, research suggests that salespeople prefer a style of management described as dominant (as opposed to submissive) in terms of power utilization and warm (as opposed to hostile) in communications with the salesforce. Four management styles are summarized in Exhibit 13.2.

6. **Discuss issues related to coaching the salesforce, holding integrative meetings, and practicing ethical management.** Coaching involves the continual development of the salesforce. A most critical part of coaching is one-on-one sessions with a salesperson. Coaching relies on the learning principles of recency and repetition, and is often conducted in the field before and after sales calls. Integrative meetings accomplish multiple sales management functions. Sales managers are involved in creative aspects of planning integrative meetings, but paying attention to mundane details is the key to successful meetings. Meeting ethical responsibilities is not necessarily easy but is essential to long-term success in a sales career.

7. **Name some of the problems encountered in leading and supervising a salesforce.** Some of the problems encountered in salesforce management are conflicts of interest; chemical abuse and dependency; disruptive, rule-breaking salespeople; and salespeople whose employment must be terminated.

Key Terms

- leadership
- supervision
- expert power
- referent power
- legitimate power
- reward power
- coercive power
- trait approach
- behavior approach
- contingency approach
- MBWA
- influence strategies
- threats
- promises
- persuasion
- relationships
- manipulation
- communications mechanisms
- management style
- coaching
- outcome feedback
- cognitive feedback
- integrative meeting
- immoral management
- amoral management
- moral management
- code of ethics
- conflict of interest

Review Questions

1. Briefly describe the six components of the sales leadership model shown in Figure 13.1.
2. Describe five types of power that affect leadership. What are the problems associated with overreliance on reward and coercive power?
3. How does the contingency approach to leadership differ from the trait approach and the behavior approach?
4. What are four categories of skills that could be useful in leadership?
5. Which power base (or bases) is important to practice "management by walking around"?
6. Describe five influence strategies, including the power bases related to each strategy.
7. What is the difference between outcome feedback and cognitive feedback? Which is most important in coaching?
8. From salespeople's point of view, what is the preferred sales management style? Can a sales manager use this style without abdicating his or her management responsibilities?
9. What can a company do to encourage ethical, or moral, management?
10. Could you suggest other points to be included in the American Marketing Association code of ethics that would be particularly relevant for salespeople?

Applications

1. Bill Holman, district sales manager, was involved in a heated face-to-face confrontation with Larry Martin, a senior sales representative. Martin was angry with his sales manager because Holman had called one of Martin's customers to deny a request for a lower price. The customer had threatened to change suppliers unless the price concession was granted, and it now appeared that indeed this could occur. Despite Holman's attempts to cool Martin down, it seemed the senior sales representative was interested only in telling his sales manager off. In progressively louder tones, he told Holman,

   > I can't believe you called the customer without my knowledge! I don't care if the customer did call you for an answer instead of calling me. You should have stalled for time and waited to talk with me. I just wish you would stick to playing your silly management games and leave the real work — selling — to those of us who know what we are doing!

   How would you react if you were Holman?

2. Assume you are a newly appointed sales manager, responsible for eight salespeople in a ten-state area. You have completed your initial field visits with each of the salespeople and are now beginning your second month on the job. In yesterday's mail, an anonymous letter arrived, charging one of your salespeople with a conflict of interest. The letter claimed that Fred, a 55-year-old senior salesperson, was a silent owner in a newly established wholesaler in his territory. The letter also alleged that Fred was giving the new wholesaler preferential treatment on pricing. You suspect the letter must have come from another wholesaler or from a disgruntled competitor. How would you proceed in this matter?

3. Which power base is in evidence in the following statements from a sales manager to a salesperson?

   a. "If you come through with the Holiday Inn account, I guarantee you will be the next person promoted."
   b. "Don't ask me why — just do it, please."
   c. "You have always been one of my favorites, and I am depending on you to hit it big in the new territory. As a personal favor, will you accept the transfer?"
   d. "There are some logistics of the situation that will not allow me to accept your proposal. I will be glad to lay out the details if you wish."
   e. "If you don't improve your sales volume by the end of the year, your friends are going to be asking you how you liked being a sales rep for us."

4. Ron Tabor, sales manager, has just received a letter from Mack Wides, an experienced salesperson. Mack has heard through the grapevine that an opportunity for a management position is opening up in another division, and he is anxious to get the job. In his letter, Mack points out that he has always exceeded his sales quotas and received excellent performance reviews. He states that he is ready to be promoted into sales management and concludes his letter by saying, "If this company can't use my talents I will have only one choice to make. What do you say?" Tabor believes the letter is basically an ultimatum — promote Mack Wides or he will resign. While Wides is a good performer as a salesperson, Tabor does not view him as management material at the present time.

Further, contrary to the grapevine, there is no sales management opening at the present time.

Identify at least three options for dealing with this situation. Discuss the advantages and disadvantages of each option you identify.

5. October 19, 1987, was a disastrous day for stockbrokers as Wall Street experienced its worst crash since the Great Depression. The day following the crash was even worse, as investors and brokers experienced a sense of loss and confusion. Uncertainty about the future threatened to paralyze the sales organizations of many brokerage firms. In others, the demoralizing effects of the crash had simply left the brokers in a daze. What could a sales manager of a brokerage firm have done to provide leadership to the salesforce immediately following the crash?

Notes

[1] Based on John French, Jr., and Bertram Raven, "The Bases of Social Power," in *Studies in Social Power*, edited by D. Cartwright (Ann Arbor, Mich.: The University of Michigan Press, 1959).

[2] Paul Busch, "The Sales Manager's Bases of Social Power and Influence upon the Sales Force," *Journal of Marketing* 44 (Summer 1980): 95.

[3] Ibid., 98–99.

[4] Stephen X. Doyle, Charles Pignatelli, and Karen Florman, "The Hawthorne Legacy and the Motivation of Salespeople," *Journal of Personal Selling and Sales Management* 5 (November 1985): 1–6.

[5] Kate Bertrand, "Women Break the Sales 'Glass Ceiling," *Business Marketing,* November 1987, 38.

[6] Ibid.

[7] Todd Mason and Geoff Lewis, "Tandy Finds a Cold, Hard World Outside the Radio Shack," *Business Week,* August 31, 1987.

[8] Tom Peters and Nancy Austin, *A Passion for Excellence* (New York: Random House, 1985): 8–33.

[9] Ibid., 9.

[10] William L. Cron and John W. Slocum, Jr., "Career Stages Approach to Managing the Sales Force," *Journal of Consumer Marketing* 3 (Fall 1986): 11–20.

[11] This discussion of influence strategies is largely based on Madeline E. Heilman and Harvey Hornstein, *Managing Human Forces in Organizations* (Homewood, Ill.: Irwin, 1982): 116–126.

[12] Ajay K. Kohli, "Some Unexplored Supervisory Behaviors and Their Influence on Salespeople's Role Clarity, Specific Self-Esteem, Job Satisfaction, and Motivation," *Journal of Marketing Research* 22 (November 1985): 424–433.

[13] Ibid., 118.

[14] For an interesting discussion, see Stephen B. Castleberry and John F. Tanner, Jr., "The Manager-Salesperson Relationship: An Exploratory Examination of the Vertical-Dyad Linkage Model," *Journal of Personal Selling and Sales Management* 6 (November 1986): 29–37.

[15] Robert E. Hite and Joseph A. Bellizzi, "A Preferred Style of Sales Management," *Industrial Marketing Management* 15 (August 1986): 215–223.

[16] In addition to the Hite and Bellizzi study discussed in the text, see Gilbert A. Churchill, Jr., Neil M. Ford, And Orville C. Walker, Jr., "Organizational Climate and Job Satisfaction in the Salesforce," *Journal of Marketing Research* 13 (November 1976): 323–332.

[17] Peters and Austin, *A Passion For Excellence*: 329.

[18] Barton A. Weitz, Harish Sujan, and Mita Sujan, "Knowledge, Motivation, and Adaptive Behavior: A Framework for Improving Sales Effectiveness," *Journal of Marketing* 50 (October 1986): 183.

[19] Ibid.

[20] Sir Adrian Cadbury, "Ethical Managers Make Their Own Rules," *Harvard Business Review* 65 (September-October 1987): 70.

[21] Archie B. Carroll, "In Search of the Moral Manager," *Business Horizons* 30 (March-April 1987): 7–15.

[22] Linda Bernier, Frank J. Comes, and Charles Gaffney, "Is the KIS Instant Empire Headed for a Fall?" *Business Week*, December 22, 1986, 36–37.

[23] Alix M. Fridman, "How Insurance Agents Exploited Those Who Fear Inheritance Taxes," *The Wall Street Journal*, January 1, 1985, 1.

[24] Steven A. Meyerowitz, "Sales Incentives: A Two-Edged Sword," *Business Marketing*, April 1986, 6.

[25] "A Legal Tangle over a Tale of Bribery," *Sales and Marketing Management*, November 11, 1985.

[26] "Defense vs. Tektronix," *Sales and Marketing Management*, December, 1986, 20–21.

[27] Cathy Trost, "With Problem More Visible, Firms Crack Down on Sexual Harassment," *The Wall Street Journal*, August 28, 1986, 17.

[28] Hugh E. Kramer, *The Moral Dilemma of Salesmanship: Sources, Modes, and Moral Hierarchies of Purposeful Communication*, Academy of Marketing Science Monograph Series 1, no.2, 1980, 15.

[29] W. E. Patton, III, and Michael Questell, "Alcohol Abuse in the Sales Force," *Journal of Personal Selling and Sales Management* 6 (November 1986): 39–51.

[30] Jack Falvey, "Rebels with a Cause," *INC.*, September 1987, 118.

[31] Kate Bertrand, "Rounding up the Mavericks," *Business Marketing*, January 1988, 48.

[32] Ibid.

WESTERN INDUSTRIAL SUPPLY COMPANY

Western Industrial Supply Company, located in Los Angeles, distributed janitorial supplies—waxes, cleaners, paper toweling, and the like—to industrial and institutional users in California from San Diego to Fresno and east as far as Needles. Salesmen called mainly on custodians who, if sold on the product(s), requisitioned the purchase through the firm's purchasing department. Western was one of the larger companies of its type in the state and, within its sales area, competed with some 30 to 40 other companies—many of which were small, local distributors. In both the Los Angeles and San Diego metropolitan areas, competition came mainly from distributors of a size similar to Western.

Population and industrial growth had increased the demand for janitorial supplies substantially during the early and mid-1970s. In more recent years, market growth had slowed, and competition had become more intense with the result that profits had declined when measured in real dollar terms. Mr. Randy Cross, the company's president and chief executive officer, felt that a new sales strategy was needed which included a different way of compensating the sales force.

In the past, Western had tried to minimize competition by emphasizing proprietary products through aggressive selling. Over the years, the company had increased the number of its proprietary products which yielded a gross margin considerably higher than did jobbed items. Such products were manufactured under contract by a variety of small manufacturers located in southern California. The company had a laboratory which developed the product's specifications, tested it against competitive products under a variety of use conditions, and made certain that it was produced to specification. Proprietary products represented about 18 percent of total sales but nearly 35 percent of total gross margin.

Western Industrial salesmen were expected to call regularly on their accounts, although their call frequency by account type and size was not known, since salesmen did not make out call reports. Once on the premises, they were expected to demonstrate items—especially proprietary ones—whenever possible in an effort to call attention to those features which made the product unique. This required them to have

Source: This case was written by Professor Harper Boyd, College of Business Administration, University of Arkansas. Included in *Stanford Business Cases 1983* with permission. Reprinted with permission of Stanford University Graduate School of Business

a good technical knowledge of the product and a willingness to "get their hands dirty." Salesmen were trained to work with custodians to show them how to make their jobs easier and at the same time to improve the hygiene and cleanliness of the facilities they maintained.

The company employed 14 salespersons working under a vice-president in charge of sales. Each salesperson had an assigned territory the size of which depended upon the number, size, and density of accounts. Outside salespersons were paid on a commission basis backed by a monthly guarantee based on the individual's earnings record. In addition, each member of the sales force received either a $250 or $150 monthly car allowance (depending upon the size of the territory) plus fringe benefits. Three members of the sales force were "insiders" in that they handled phone orders and service requests. These persons were paid on a salary basis. Of the 11 outside salespersons, 4 were still on monthly guarantee, having been with the company less than one year. An average salesperson earned $1,500 per month while the better ones exceeded $2,000. Most of the better salespersons had been with the company a long time.

A number of trends had conspired to make the industry increasingly competitive. One was the growing consolidation of supply distributors. The small local distributor was fast becoming extinct. Cost of capital associated with inventories and accounts receivable coupled with high inflation had forced many small firms to exit the industry. A second trend was that an impressive number of medium to large customers had contracted out their cleaning activities, thereby reducing their direct purchases of janitorial supplies substantially. The larger contract cleaning firms either bought direct from manufacturers or acquired their supplies from distributors on a bid basis. A third trend was the increased importance of the purchasing department in the purchase of janitorial supplies. This tended to downplay the role of the custodian in the purchasing decision. Yet another trend was that more and more of the larger accounts were requesting bids on major supply items.

In view of the above, Mr. Cross thought that Western had to make some important decisions near term if the company was to survive and prosper. In commenting on the situation he said:

> The basic trends have dried up a number of our larger accounts since our company has never learned how to bid successfully. We really do very little bidding, but we've got to start learning how soon. Also, we're stuck with an increasing number of small accounts which means lots of small orders. These have increased our sales, order processing and fulfillment, delivery, and bad debt costs to a point where something signficant has to be done. And we're having trouble holding our better salesmen. Our turnover here is not good.

Mr. Cross outlined his tentative corrective plan as follows:

1. Price the company's proprietary products more competitively. This meant that prices on present proprietary products would be reduced by as much as 10 to 20 percent through the use of quantity discounts.

2. Increase the number of new products. To accomplish this, two new technicians would be added to the company laboratory.
3. Divest in the very small accounts by using a minimum order size requirement in an effort to lower costs and allocate more resources to the larger accounts. These actions would likely result in a substantial shift in the composition and size of the sales territories.
4. Undertake aggressive bidding which would be accomplished by establishing a special inside unit to work with the sales force in the preparation of bids.
5. Better service to a point "where it is at least as good as any competitor and better than most." The plan called for all orders to be shipped within 72 hours after receipt. This was to be made possible mainly by a computerized order processing system which prepared all necessary documents and identified the exact warehouse location (bin number) of each invoice line item. In addition, a computerized inventory model would be installed which would hopefully reduce out-of-stocks to less than 2 percent of all items stocked.
6. Professionalization of the sales force. Given the actions cited above, it seemed clear that a different kind of salesperson would be needed. Some of the present sales force could be retrained, but it was anticipated that probably half would need to be replaced. It was likely that a new sales manager would have to be hired; further, that the infrastructure within the sales department would have to be improved (e.g., addition of the estimating unit and an increase in the number of inside salesmen).

Mr. Cross recognized that considerable fact-finding had to take place before he could make his plan operational. He also recognized that he should move slowly in this regard, perhaps taking several years to implement it. He thought the place to start was with the sales force. In this regard, he reasoned that since several salespersons needed replacing in the near future, the first step would be to draw up a new compensation plan which would retain the loyalty of those asked to stay while attracting the caliber of person desired. If a satisfactory plan could be developed which could accomodate both the present and the future, Mr. Cross was willing to install it for the next fiscal year, which started some five months hence.

The present outside sales force was paid a 10 percent commission on the sales of all proprietary items and a 5 percent commission on all jobbed items. In addition, each had a car allowance and received fringe benefits mostly in the form of health and life insurance and social security. Each had a monthly guarantee which was expected to be equaled or bettered by commissions. The company paid no bonus to the sales force, although all other workers received one in those years when before-tax profits exceeded a certain percent of sales. This was distributed on the basis of an employee's annual wages. Typically, this amounted to a week's salary.

The new compensation plan called for the setting of a dollar quota for each outside salesperson in three product categories—proprietary, high-margin jobbed products, and low-margin jobbed products. The quotas would be based on an extrapolation of sales from the three previous years with the last year carrying a double weight. This result would then be subject to adjustment based on the forecast for the coming year. The forecast would take into account new products, price changes, general economic conditions in the territory, and any change in competition. Adjustments would also need to be made to accommodate territorial shifts or realignments.

All salespersons would be paid a monthly salary in the future. This would be calculated by applying the present commission system to the quota for proprietary products and a total of the high- and low-margin jobbed items. Every effort would be made to approximate the present remuneration of a salesperson, although it was recognized that this could prove difficult when substantial territorial adjustments had to be made. In addition to salaries, salespersons would receive car mileage and the company's fringe benefit package and participate in the annual bonus plan. Quotas were to be set for each month of the year.

In addition to the base compensation plan, salespersons had the opportunity of earning an "improvement over standard bonus" each quarter for the three product categories as follows:

Percent improvement over standard (quota)	Commission rate to be paid
Category A—proprietary (18 percent of sales):	
0 and under 5	8%
5 and under 10	9
10 and under 15	10
15 and under 20	11
20 and over	12
Category B—high-margin jobbed items (26 percent of sales):	
0 and under 5	4.0
5 and under 10	4.5
10 and under 15	5.0
15 and under 20	5.5
20 and over	6.0
Category C—low-margin jobbed items (56 percent of sales):	
0 and under 5	2.0
5 and under 10	2.5
10 and under 15	3.0
15 and under 20	3.5
20 and over	4.0

To ensure that the sales force did not neglect the high-volume but low-margin items completely, the plan provided that *no* improvement over standard bonus would be paid unless the quotas were met in each of the three product categories. This seemed critical, given the relatively high fixed costs associated with the company's warehouse and delivery operations.

A possible alternative to the above was to set up a point system whereby an underage in one category could be offset by an overage elsewhere. Points would be assigned to each category based on its percent of the total quota which equaled 100 points. In the case of Category A, any deficit would be translated into a gross margin dollar figure which would have to be equaled by some combination of gross margin overages from the other two categories. A deficit in Category B could only be made up from a gross margin overage in Category C, while a deficit in the latter could only be accommodated by an overage in Category B. Average margins would be used to calculate overages and underages and were expected to be approximately 54 percent for Category A, 26 percent for Category B, and 16 percent for Category C.

While quota by product category was to be set monthly, commissions would be based on a quarterly basis, thereby enabling the salesperson to make up for a bad month; i.e., there would be four chances during the year for a salesperson to earn extra compensation in the form of a commission bonus since a failure to meet or exceed quota for any one quarter would not be cumulative.

Bidding posed a special problem. Since the company had little experience here, there was some question as to how best to handle it in terms of the new compensation plan. Sales from successful bidding activities could be large, but margins would be reduced. Thus, if successful, the sales force could meet the sales quotas but at a considerably lower average gross margin. One possibility was to credit sales on the basis of gross margin; e.g., if the company made a successful bid by cutting its margins by half, then the salesperson would receive credit for 50 percent of the dollar sales involved. The objection here was that, under such conditions, salesmen would shy away from bidding situations. Much the same would happen if quotas were established on the basis of gross margin dollars and not sales dollars. Once the company had developed a history of bidding, then the problem would be less acute.

Another problem was whether the new compensation plan would in any way inhibit the motivation of the inside sales force. A smart outside salesperson would likely use the insiders to do as much of his/her follow-up work as possible and would set high service standards. This could generate the feeling by the inside sales personnel that they were making a significant contribution to company sales and profits and yet did not participate in the rewards.

THE GOLDMAN CHEMICAL COMPANY

"A substantial growth in sales and a shift in market strength from the Northeast to the South and Southwest have knocked our sales territories completely out of line," said Bill King, sales manager of the Goldman Chemical Company. "The morale of the sales force is low," he continued, "because some of the salespeople feel that the present territories don't afford an equal opportunity to earn commissions."

The Company

Goldman Chemical was a wholesale chemical house supplying specialized chemicals to paper processors throughout the country. The several thousand potential users of the company's products ranged in size from small operators to giants such as International Paper and Crown Zellerbach. Competition was intense, with sales going to the firms offering the best combination of quality, service, and price.

The company's sales increased significantly between the years 1976 and 1979. A continuation of this trend was expected in 1980, although there was some concern about general economic conditions. The company started in the East and extended operations westward after 1960. Twenty-four states were serviced in 1979.

The Sale

The typical Goldman customer purchased $17,000 in chemicals yearly, although the range was from $50 to over $120,000. Some sales were contracted but most were solicited directly by the company's ten-man sales force. About 70 percent of the Goldman line consisted of standard items for which purchasing agents made the final buying decision. The remaining items were specialized "brand" products and required the approval of production personnel. The chemical companies, in 1979, faced a buyers' market; thus the demands for service were heavy. A purchasing agent from one of the larger paper firms recently said to a Goldman salesman, "We might as well get one thing straight. You know as well as I do that your competitors can meet you in price and quality, so if you want our business we had better see some real service."

Salespeople, during their calls, checked the performance of products sold previously, followed up delivery promises, and sought to introduce the customer to new uses for existing products as well as to new products. Goldman salespeople were expected to have a chemical engineering background because of the technical orientation of their customers.

Salesmen/women averaged five calls daily in metropolitan centers and four in non-metropolitan areas. Typically they spent four days in each week on metropolitan calls. Accounts were classified by purchases as A, B, or C: the limits for A accounts being "over $50,000;" for B accounts, "between $10,000 and $50,000;" and for C accounts, "below $10,000." A accounts were called on weekly, B accounts monthly, and C accounts quarterly. About 10 percent of a salesperson's time was devoted to "service call-backs."

The Salesmen

The Goldman Company employed ten salesmen/women ranging in experience from six months to twenty-five years. Mr. King was generally satisfied with his sales force and thought them technically qualified to sell the full lines.

Each salesperson had a monthly drawing account of between $1,000 and $1,200. "This," said Mr. King, "is justification for the missionary work that they are required to do." Above the draw, compensation was by straight commission. Commission rates varied with the profitability of products and, according to the sales manager, there was no apparent tendency for salespeople to overlook the full-line in favor of higher-margin items. "The nature of our selling is such," said Mr. King, "that the salesperson first has to establish him/herself with the account. Once this is done, full-line selling is no problem."

Mr. King was convinced that differences in compensation (see Exhibit 1) arose from the distribution of territories rather than the individual abilities of the salespeople. Of this he said, "I would expect some variations in commissions earned, but not to the extent we've experienced. I don't see that much difference among the members of our sales force."

Mr. King gave the following appraisal of his ten salespeople:

Phil Haney is our "old timer," having been with us since 1955. He is one year from our mandatory retirement age of 65 and he likes to remind people of his twenty-odd years of seniority. He hasn't been particularly easy for me to work with. Phil has strong personal ideas about selling, many of which are "academically" outdated but are apparently accepted by his customers. He has what you might call an old-time personality and has been tremendously successful over the years. I often wonder what kind of volume could be generated by combining Phil's personality with some of our new merchandising techniques. Phil has always worked Manhattan, although initially he sold to all of New York City.

Mary Whalen is in her sixth year with the company and sells to accounts in the New Jersey Pennsylvania area. Whalen is an excellent saleswoman who is obviously aware of the "smoothness" of her sales approach. She carries this self-assurance to the extent that she often becomes very indifferent whenever I offer a few suggestions for improvement in her sales techniques.

Norman Ives is probably the most ambitious, aggressive, and argumentative salesman we have. He has been with the company since 1966 following his discharge

Exhibit 1 Performance of Salespeople, 1978–1979

Salesman	Territory	Terr. #	Sales Record[2] 1978	Sales Record[2] 1979[1]	Number of Accounts Metro	Number of Accounts Non-Metro	Number of Accounts Total	Compensation	Cost % to Sales 1979[1]	Planned Sales 1980[2]	Planned Accounts 1970	Estimated Share of Market 1969[1]	Estimated Share of Market 1970	Selling Cost % to Planned Sales
Ives	Me., N.H., Ver.	1	not covered under present territory arrangement							$ 82	7	—	26.0%	
	Mass.		$ 972	$ 816	54	13	67			648	54	24.0%	18.6	
	R.I.		240	160	13	—	13			82	7	39.7	49.6	
	Conn.		240	240	13	7	20			160	13	21.2	19.9	
	Total terr.		$ 1,452	$ 1,216	80	20	100	$ 25,200	2.1%	$ 972	81	23.2	19.9	2.6%
Gordon	N.Y. State	2	488	408	27	7	34	13,200	3.2	324	27	50.2	50.3	4.1
Haney	Manhattan	3	4,054	3,888	162	—	162	37,200	0.96	3,408	142	18.7	18.6	1.1
Richards	Other N.Y. City & L.I.	4	1,452	1,608	61	7	68	28,800	1.8	1,784	74	25.3	25.2	1.6
Whalen	New Jersey	5	324	406	27	7	34			488	40	10.6	16.5	
	Pennsylvania		2,592	2,424	88	13	101			2,112	88	18.2	17.0	
	Total terr.		$ 2,916	$ 2,830	115	20	135	$ 30,000	1.1	$ 2,600	128	16.9	17.0	1.2
Ericson	Del., Md., Wash., D.C.		not covered under present territory arrangement							160	13	—	20.0	
	Va., W.Va.,	6	240	324	13	13	26			324	27	19.9	16.2	
	N. Carolina		240	324	20	7	27			408	34	16.5	16.3	
	S. Carolina		82	160	7	7	14			324	27	11.0	16.5	
	Georgia		240	240	7	13	20			240	20	18.5	14.9	
	Florida		160	324	27	0	27			408	34	20.2	16.1	
	Total terr.		$ 962	$ 1,372	74	40	114	$ 20,400	1.5	$ 1,864	155	16.3	16.4	1.1
Davey	Mississippi	7	82	160	7	7	14			160	13	16.7	16.6	
	Alabama		240	324	13	13	26			324	27	18.3	18.3	
	Kty. & Tenn.		—	82	7	—	7			82	7	16.5	16.5	
	Total terr.		$ 322	$ 566	27	20	47	$ 16,800	3.0	$ 566	47	17.4	17.4	3.0

[1]Projected
[2]000's omitted

Exhibit 1 *continued*

Salesman	Territory	Terr. #	Sales Record[2] 1978	Sales Record[2] 1979[1]	Number of Accounts Metro	Number of Accounts Non-Metro	Number of Accounts Total	Compensation	Cost % to Sales 1979[1]	Planned Sales 1980[2]	Planned Accounts 1970	Estimated Share of Market 1969[1]	Estimated Share of Market 1970	Selling Cost% to Planned Sales
Owens	Ohio & Ind.	8	not covered under present territory arrangement							160	13	—	14.1	
	Illinois		$ 1,534	$ 1,370	51	7	58			1,214	51	16.2	16.2	
	Michigan		564	564	40	7	47			480	40	15.1	15.1	
	Wisconsin		not covered under present territory arrangement							82	7	—	16.6	
	Total terr.		$ 2,098	$ 1,934	91	14	105	$ 27,600	1.4	$ 1,936	111	15.1	15.7	1.4
Billings	Minn., Iowa, N. Dak, S. Dak, Nebraska		not covered under present territory arrangement							240	20	—	18.6	
	Missouri	9	160	564	40	7	47			730	61	11.4	15.1	
	Kansas		—	82	7	—	7			160	13	8.3	16.6	
	Ark., La., Okla.		not covered under present territory arrangement							160	13	—	16.7	
	Texas		160	324	20	7	27			816	67	6.6	14.6	
	Total terr.		$ 320	$ 970	67	14	81	$ 18,000	1.9	$ 2,106	174	7.9	15.5	.85
Sharp	Mont., Wyo., Idaho		not covered under present territory arrangement							—	—	—	—	
	Utah, Col., Az., N.M.		not covered under present territory arrangement							240	20	—	18.7	
	Wash., Ore.	10	$ 160	$ 240	7	13	20			324	27	18.9	16.6	
	California		564	648	38	7	45			816	67	11.3	14.3	
	Nevada		not covererd under present territory arrangement							—	—	—	—	
	Total terr.		$ 724	$ 888	45	20	65	$ 18,000	2.0	$ 1,380	114	15.2	15.4	1.3
GRAND TOTAL-United States			$14,788	$15,680	749	162	911	$235,200	1.5	$16,940	1,053	16.6	17.8	1.4

[1]Projected
[2]000's omitted

from the Army. He reached the rank of Lt. Colonel at the age of 30 but had no interest in a military career. Norman really stormed into his present territory in 1969 and, in the first year, doubled its volume. He's extremely independent but will work hard to implement any sales program that he agrees with. If he doesn't agree, though, I get absolutely no cooperation. In 1976, Norman's territory began to slip—primarily, I think, because of a shift in market strength. Moreover, his compensation fell from $30,000 in 1976 to $25,000 in 1979.

Bob Ericson has been with the company three years now and I still get the feeling that he is unsure of himself. He seems somewhat confused and over-worked, probably beause he's trying to serve too many accounts in too large an area. Suprisingly enough, though, the general growth in the territory has given Bob a significant increase in sales in 1979.

Dick Richards is the "mystery man" of the sales force. Neither the other salespeople nor I know very much about Dick's personal life. He's quiet and unassuming and knows the Goldman line amazingly well. I've often wondered why Dick chose sales over research work. Sales in his territory have continued to grow, which is unusual considering an opposite trend in neighboring territories.

Warren Sharp is the guy on the sales force who keeps the rest of us going. Warren is slightly rotund and always good-natured. His accounts seem genuinely happy to see him when he makes a call. He worked the New York State territory for his first two years and then moved into the West Coast when we took on Joe Gordon. At first I worried about Warren's ability to get serious long enough to make a sale. However, this has not proved to be a problem.

Gus Billings joined the company in 1973 after four years with a competitor. Gus is easygoing, eventempered, and very popular with his customers. Despite his even temperament, Gus was somewhat upset the last time I saw him. We plan to activate five more states in his territory during 1980. This would make Gus responsible for a geographic area covering roughly one fourth of the United States. He is already calling on eighty-one accounts in six states, and this keeps him away from home much of the time.

Barbara Owens joined us in 1975 after receiving an M.S. degree in Chemistry from the University of Pennsylvania. After the normal three-month training program, during which time Barbara travelled with Mary Whalen, she stepped into her territory and was immediately successful. Barbara is earnest and conscientious, and has increased her sales volume each year. She's not what you would call the "sales type" but she is always exceedingly successful in using the merchandising techniques that I try to implement.

Joe Gordon is the youngster of our sales force at twenty-three. Joe went into New York State in the spring of 1978. The territory is relatively inactive and we usually try to assign it to new salespeople. Sales have dropped from the time that Joe took over and he is very apologetic about the situation. I've told him that he would have to expect some tough moments and I think his determination to "make a go of it" will be realized because of his conscientiousness. He's always receptive to any help

Exhibit 2 **Number of customers by $ volume for the year 1979**

Salesperson	0 to 1,999	2,000 to 4,499	4,500 to 9,999	10,000 to 19,999	20,000 to 29 999	30,000 to 49,999	50,000 to 99,999	100,000 to 199,999	TOTAL
Ives	32	30	15	10	5	5	2	1	100
Gordon	10	5	4	12	1	2	—	—	34
Haney	26	30	20	31	22	20	10	3	162
Richards	9	3	13	15	15	8	4	—	67
Whalen	16	40	30	10	10	21	6	2	135
Ericson	34	32	21	8	8	7	4	—	114
Davey	14	10	6	7	9	—	1	—	47
Owens	33	11	19	13	15	9	3	2	105
Billings	30	6	13	14	16	2	—	—	81
Sharp	10	12	24	8	10	—	—	—	65
Total	214	179	165	128	[illegible]11	74	30	9	910
$ Volume totals (000)	256	730	1,488	2,304	3,328	3,552	2,700	1,620	15,978
Cumulative $ total (000)		986	2,474	4,778	8,[illegible]06	11,658	14,358	15,978	
Cumulative % of $ volume	1.6	6.2	15.5	29.9	50.7	73.0	89.8	100	
Cumulative % of accounts	23.5	43.2	61.8	75.4	87.6	95.7	99.0	100	

that is offered and tries hard to put suggestions to use. That territory has always been a "dog."

Jim Davey is in his third year and I'd say he's good at selling. Jim always dresses impeccably in ivy league fashion and he has good bearing. He responds well to any suggestion that I make to him. It's a funny thing, but whenever I travel with Jim the sales in the territory increase for the next several months. After that, right back to the previous level. Accounts within the territory are scattered, which keeps Jim on the road most of the time.

Aside from the morale problem, Bill King had other reasons for wanting to change the territories. "We expect continued growth," he said, "and at least for the time being I plan to add no new people. I'm positive that by redistributing the sales territories we can get more sales effort from the sales force as a group and thus handle our growth."

SIERRA CHEMICAL COMPANY

Jay Rossi, recently appointed as marketing vice president for the Sierra Chemical Company, was troubled about his firm's ability to execute an effective sales program. As he summarized, "Good sales management requires sales forecasts and reasonable cost estimates. Otherwise you can't price to value or control your profits. To do this you've got to get hold of your sales force." His reservations were based on the fact that even though sales growth seemed reasonable in dollars, unit volumes almost always fell short of forecasts. Moreover there was a primitive, at best, sales information system and almost no formal control mechanism. Hence, Jay really didn't know what sales to anticipate, what level of effort to require, what standards and evaluation criteria to apply. He was literally starting from ground zero. His task was complicated further by the fact that he was new to the industry and had no related market experience.

Sierra Products and Markets

Sierra produced and sold slow-release fertilizers, Osmocote and Agriform by name.[1] Pellet-like in form, similar to B-Bs, the products were coated with a patented rosin material. This coasting had tiny pores which allowed small amounts of water to seep into the fertilizer ingredients, which then seeped out at a predictable rate (i.e., over two months, four months, six months, etc.). Product uniqueness was in the coating (the manufacturing process) and product form, not in the fertilizer. Fertilizer is primarily a standard commodity, consisting of varying proportions of nitrates, phosphates, and potassium. Growers buy different combinations, depending upon individual needs.

Growers could apply fertilizer three ways: by liquid feeding, dry application to the soil, or by slow release. The greatest tonnage of fertilizer was sold in dry form to agricultural markets and consisted of the three essential ingredients named above. Prices per ton were in the $100–$150 range.

Slow-release products were designed for specialty markets, not the huge field crops such as corn and wheat. There were four specialty markets: (1) nursery, (2) landscape, (3) row crops or agricultural (such as strawberries and tomatoes), and (4) retail. It was estimated that slow-release fertilizers were distributed in these four markets in the proportions 60 percent, 10 percent, 30 percent and negligible.

Source: This case was written by Professor Robert T. Davis, Graduate School of Business, Stanford University. It is based in part on his 1977 case of the same title. Reprinted with permission of Stanford University Graduate School of Business,

Slow-release fertilizers, needless to say, were not without competition in these markets. Growers often used dry and liquid alternatives, sometimes in combination. Most growers were convinced that they were experts at growing their particular product(s). Whether they used dry, liquid, or slow-release fertilizers was a function of their particular plants, prejudices, soil and weather conditions, and timing problems (i.e., did they want to "force bloom" roses for Mother's Day). It was not unusual, therefore, to find use of all three application techniques within a single establishment.

Liquid systems normally made use of local fertilizer ingredients. The problem with liquid systems was that they were continuous and many of the nutrients were washed or leached away. Dry fertilizers were limited by the fact that release was not controlled and application might be required several times during the season.

There were quite a few large companies in the dry, liquid, and slow-release fertilizer business. For example, firms like International Chemical, Scott, Swift, DuPont, and Hercules were important Sierra competitors. Urea Formaldehyde was a controlled-released product, as were some of Scott's items. Osmocote was the only product, however, which controlled the release of all three fertilizer ingredients.

It was estimated by Sierra management that slow-release products were gaining share in the total specialty markets and accounted for almost 30 percent of the nursery market in 1976. One out of four nursery plants was grown on Osmocote, and it was the only national label in its segment.

There were many reasons why growers accepted or rejected Osmocote. On the positive side:

1. It produced better plants—greener, healthier, faster, more consistently.
2. It was safer—reduced the chance of error (human or environmental).
3. It saved money—primarily in labor savings (compared to dry types) and in less raw material waste (compared to liquid feeds).

And on the negative side:

1. Its initial price was high—four times normal fertilizers and two times most slow-release types.
2. It was inflexible—once applied, it went! There was no way to slow it down, speed it up, or stop it.

Growers tended to be concentrated in southern California, northern California, and the Seattle-Portland belt; Florida, North Carolina, and Connecticut; and Texas, Wisconsin, and Ohio. Growers were reached through approximately 200 distributors, who carried thousands of items and regularly serviced their accounts. Manufacturers' salespeople, such as Sierra's, were supposed to establish and maintain distribution and do missionary selling among nurseries. For instance, in creating a new grower-user, it was essential that the grower be induced to set up some test plantings, measure the results, and compare these results with alternative fertilizing techniques. Distributor salespeople rarely were effective in this kind of selling; they were, essentially sources of supply for already established users. Moreover, test plantings took time and effort.

The nursery business was heavily populated with "cottage type" operators. Large, 100-plus acre nurseries were important, but Sierra's real expansion has been among "start-ups" with one to five acres under shade but planning to add more each year. As a rule of thumb, each new acre was a potential one-ton sale for Sierra. There were several thousand such small operators.

Osmocote, by 1976, was the single most important specialty fertilizer on the market and was well known and well regarded among commercial growers and state extension agents. The agents were important product endorsers, since they were the acknowledged experts. Their "stamp of approval" was virtually mandatory, though approval by no means guaranteed purchase. A summary of the product lines and markets is contained in Exhibit 1 (company brochure)

Sales, by 1976, had reached 247,494 units or $4 million for the domestic market. The table below summarizes the Company's unit sales for 1976 and the previous five years, with 1977 forecasted:

Sales in Units (50-pound bags)*

	1971	1972	1973	1974	1975	1976	1977 (est.)
Domestic	111,290	147,639	214,043	233,666	211,315	247,494	305,956
Foreign.........	6,932	6,659	22,900	47,834	36,028	82,600	104,000

*Included were sales of about $300,000 in small bags through professional nurseries to homeowners.

The Company

The Company traced its history to Agriform of Woodland, which was later acquired by Leslie Salt. In 1967, a new venture capital team purchased the company from Leslie and established it as the Sierra Chemical Company in Newark, California, after combining its Agriform technology with a fertilizer rosin coating process developed by Archer Daniel Midland (Osmocote). A final series of transactions resulted in a new management takeover in 1971 under Robert Severns as president.

By the middle of 1976, Sierra was beginning to generate a healthier cash position, although funds were not plentiful by any means. Jay Rossi estimated that the company could probably borrow $500,000 from banks if it had to. Current assets exceeded current liabilities in the ratio of 1.3 to 1.0. The company had moved to a new

Exhibit 1

Osmocote® is the most economical, efficient controlled release fertilizer available.

Osmocote® provides a steady, continuous metering of N-P-K nutrients corresponding closely to the requirements of all nursery stock. This prolonged, constant feeding helps ensure an ideal level of nutrients for optimum plant growth

One application of Osmocote® lasts for an entire crop cycle.

Osmocote® is available in a variety of formulations; 3 to 4 months, 8 to 9 months and 12 to 14 months. This offers the grower a nutrient release rate based on individual crop cycles.

Osmocote® is safe and efficient.

There is virtually no risk of burning plants with Osmocote® when used at recommended rates. Nutrients are released approximately 1% per day with the 3 to 4 month formulations, 0.4% per day with the 8 to 9 month formulations, and 0.25% per day with the 12 to 14 month formulation.

Osmocote® is economical.

There is less labor cost and management concerns involved with the use of Osmocote® because one application is sufficient for an entire crop cycle. And, since Osmocote® is resistant to leaching loss, the grower also saves on materials.

Osmocote® releases nutrients as plants need them.

The rate of nutrient release from Osmocote® is *not* significantly affected by:
•Soil moisture levels
•Total volume of water applied
•External salt concentration of the soil
•Soil pH
•Soil bacteria

Nutrient release from Osmocote® is *only* affected by changes in soil temperature. The release rate increases as the soil warms, and decreases as the soil cools, therefore corresponding to plant needs.

Osmocote®

Product	Longevity	General Use	Specific Use
Osmocote 14-14-14	3-4 mo.	Greenhouse Nursery	Pot plants, bedding plants, foiliage plants, nursery stock. For use in growing media containing no soil.
Osmocote 19-6-12	3-4 mo.	Greenhouse Nursery	For plants requiring high nitrogen. For use in growing media containing 25% soil or more.
Osmocote 18-6-12	8-9 mo.	Nursery	For all nursery stock. For propagation and establishment of young transplants. Spring, summer, or fall application.
Osmocote 18-6-12 Fast Start	8-9 mo.	Nursery	For use only with established, rapidly growing plants that require nutrients immediately. Spring, summer, or fall application
Osmocote 18-5-11	12-14 mo.	Greenhouse Nursery	For mild climate, long season areas, spring and summer use on long term crops. Not generally used for fall feeding. For long term greenhouse crops (roses, carnations).
Osmocote 14-14-14 Retail Pack	3-4 mo.	Home & Garden	House plants, flowers, and vegetables.
Osmocote 18-6-12 Retail Pack	8-9 mo.	Home & Garden	House plants, flowers, and vegetables.

Agriform™

Product	Longevity	General Use	Specific Use
Agriform 16-7-12-1 iron	5-6 mo.	Landscaping	Turf, hydroseeding, flowers and ground covers, trees and shrubs.
Agriform 21-8-8	3-6 mo.	Lanscaping	Maintenance of turf, ground cover and landscape plants.
Agriform 18-18-6	3-6 mo.	Landscaping	Establishment of turf, ground cover and landscape plants
Agriform Planting Tablets			
Planting Tablets 20-10-5	24 mo.	Lanscaping	New tree and shrub plantings, established trees and shrubs, liners, ground covers, and perennials.
Agriform retail pack 20-10-5	24 mo.	Home Landscaping	New tree and shrub plantings, established trees and shrubs, ground covers, perennials.
Container Tablets 14-4-6	3-4 mo.	Nursery Greenhouse	Pot plants, retail nursery stock.
Orchard Starter Tablets 28-8-4	24 mo.	Orchards	New plantings or young established trees.
Grape Starter Tablet 28-8-4	24 mo.	Vineyard	New plantings or young established vines.
Forest Starter Tablet 22-8-2	24 mo.	Tree farms	Xmas trees, reforestation, land reclamation.
Forest Starter Tablet 18-8-3	24 mo.	Tree farms	Xmas trees, reforestation, land reclamation. This formulation used in magnesium deficient areas as in S.E. U.S.

plant in Milpitas, California, during 1973, and in 1976, the plant was operating at 50 percent of capacity.

Rossi Hired

By 1975, Sierra had experienced a slow but acceptable growth. Dollar sales were steadily rising, and business was beginning to develop in Europe. In the United States, penetration of particular markets was encouraging, such as tomatoes and strawberries, but the overall situation was deceptive. Between 1973 and 1975, the potential market grew an estimated 30 percent, but Sierra's unit sales were fairly flat. Inflation and European dollar sales had disguised the domestic unit sales problem.

Then suddenly, in October of 1974, Sierra sales growth ground to a halt for six to eight months. The economy was bad, but that didn't seem to be the entire explanation. Growers were still in business; they just appeared to be turning away from Osmocote and its higher prices, and substituting alternative fertilizer. In an attempt to better understand the real problem, the company president made a number of field visits. He was appalled at the level of sales performance. The salespeople were not aggressive, appeared to consider themselves as advisors and horticulture experts to the growers, and blamed the distributors for all their selling problems. While it had been true that this type of advisory selling was desirable in the early introduction of the controlled-release fertilizer, this innovation stage of the selling cycle had been over by 1970.

Some indication of the firm's lack of sales aggressiveness could be inferred from the existing job desciption of regional managers, i.e., salespeople (Exhibit 2), and one typical sales call report (Exhibit 3). The decision was made to bring in an experienced and professional marketing executive. Continued success, it seemed, would require a new look in both sales and marketing.

Jay Rossi was offered the job. Not only had he enjoyed a successful career in marketing, but he had been a consultant to Sierra. Bob Severns and his management team knew and respected Jay. And Jay knew enough about the Sierra products and markets to be optimistic about the future. There were some short-term problems of immediate concern. For half of the previous six quarters, for example, Sierra had experienced losses in operations. Cash itself was tight. Not only were all sales factored, but projections for 1975 indicated that cash flow would barely be enough to cover a bank repayment due in January.

Jay Rossi had graduated from one of the top universities on the West Coast and earned an MBA at its business school. He spent four years at Maxwell House in product management; seven years at Basic Vegetable Products Company (San Francisco) as marketing manager; 18 months as an independent consultant; and 6 months as vice president of Marketing for Saga Corporation. He left Saga with no ill feelings, since Saga management recognized that the Sierra offer was "one in a lifetime."

Exhibit 2 Job Description—Regional Manager (i.e., Salesman)

The regional manager is responsible for the representation of the company, its products, and policies to customers, distributors, dealers, and the general public within his area. The manager is reponsible for maintaining contact with universities, experiment stations, corporate research facilities, and other areas where technical interest may be expressed in controlled-release fertilizers. He strives to maintain a favorable public relations image for the company in his territory and works in conjunction with the advertising and sales promotion manager as required.

He is responsible for the securing, training, and supervision of distributors for Sierra products within his territory. The following specific responsibilties apply:

1. Selection and evaluation of candidate distributors
2. Recommendation of distributor appointments to home office
3. Training of distributor salesmen to acceptable levels of product knowledge and proficiency.
4. Establishment of goals and programs with the distributor to provide acceptable sales levels for our products.
5. Maintain overview of distributor's operations to be certain that they are conducted on a businesslike and creditworthy basis.
6. Maintain distributor interest in our programs, products, and activities so that vigorous representation of our products to the trade is maintained.

The manager will be responsible for a knowledge of the market within his territory. This knowledge shall include:

1. The major users and customers within the area.
2. The size, location, and trends of the various markets within the region.
3. Advice to the home office on business opportunities requiring development of new products or adapation of existing products to new opportunities.
4. Investigation of new crops or uses or industries as may be requested and directed by the main office.

The manager is responsible for securing and maintaining an acceptable sales level within his region:

1. An annual sales plan will be prepared and presented to management for acceptance.
2. Quotas for distributors will be assigned and discussed with the responsible distributor personnel.
3. Adequate representation of our products to meet sales plan throughout the region by dealers or distributors is required.
4. Performance of distributors and dealers in compliance with the distributor agreements is the responsibility of the regional manager.
5. Development of sales programs specifically tailored to an area or region as may be required to develop and maintain sales.
6. Giving advice to dealers and distributors on the most profitable ways for them to handle Sierra Chemical Company's product line is also within the regional manager's area.

The regional manager is responsible for the investigation and evaluation of complaints registered by customers:

1. A report of the situation as determined by personal investigation will be made to the home office, attention technical director.
2. A recommendation on the disposition of the complaint will be made by the regional manager to the operating vice president.
3. A complaint settlement up to $200 invoiced cost may be made by the regional manager at his own discretion.

The regional manager is further responsible for the following activities:

1. Preparation of an expense budget for the operation of the region each year and operation within the accepted budget level.
2. Recommendations for attendance at regional trade shows.
3. Maintaining office complete with necessary records for distributor follow-up, correspondence with customers, and activity reports to sales management.

Exhibit 3

To David Martin
From: George Parker
Subject: Call Report for the Week of May 25

Harvey Blake Poinsettia Ranch, Sonoma, California

We were able to confirm this morning that the problem in the stock bench area at the ranch was twofold, as George and I suspected, but previously were unable to confirm.

1. The rooted cuttings were slightly infected with Pythium when they were set out in the stock benches. Mr. Metkin at Soil & Plant Laboratory had earlier confirmed this point and further indicated that poinsettia plants could, in fact, recover from a slight infection Pythium.
2. The workers assigned to apply Osmocote to the surface of the test benches were using a drop-type spreader, the result being that several of the particles of the Osmocote were crushed. Sally Jones, their in-house technical advisor, further stated that when the Osmocote granules would clog up the applicator, the workers merely lifted the spreader and forced the wheels around until they again moved freely. The Osmocote was substantially worked in the top six inches of planting bed with a rototiller, which would tend to erase any severely turned areas across the bench.

Dave, we understand that all of the principals of the Blake organization are away on their annual selling trip, but when they return, I will make sure that they are aware of the cause of the earlier damage.

B & D Wholesale Nursery

I left a sample of our Osmocote 18-5-11 with Mr. Bill Ramsey, who is the head grower for their container division. We outlined a trial for Bill similar to the one we have set out at Valborg's Nursery, and I'll be checking back with Bill in three to four weeks to make sure that the trial was set out in a proper manner.

Mr. John Liddicoat, who is in charge of their rose breeding program, is also the man we'll have to talk to about setting up Osmocote trails in their field-grown roses. John is already aware, as previously reported, of the benefits derived from using Osmocote, and there is a good chance we can get him to begin using the product in certain sandy fields this next February.

Our first meeting with John was rather brief, due to a previous commitment on his part, and John is now away on a six-week business trip through Europe. I plan to see him as soon as he returns from his trip and will keep you posted as to the progress we make.

Willamette Chemical, Eugene

The recent 10-ton (approximately) order from this company should have been a full truckload and reflects a continuing desire on the part of our major distributor to carry a reduced inventory in the hope that prices on all fertilizer products will eventually come down.

I'm having a meeting the week of June 16th with Steve Lookabill, who is in charge of specialty sales programs through the various branch offices. I told Steve that we would shortly be selling some of the major accounts on a direct basis in the Salem basin, but there was still a huge potential in that area that was not being tapped by any of our present distributors.

I feel this company has a place in our chain of distributors, even though they did not sell their initial truckload as quickly as we would have liked. I feel that Steve in his new position will certainly enhance our total sales program.

Eureka Plant Growers

I reported earlier that Eureka had placed a small initial order for Osmocote through Willamette Chemical, and I was supposed to meet him at the Summit growing grounds this morning to instruct the workers on the proper amount of Osmocote to apply to each can. Little did we know that the Immigration Department was going to raid their field yesterday, so they are without help for two or three weeks until workers can get back up and begin working again.

continued

Exhibit 3 *continued*

I reported earlier that George is having middle management problems and has a new grower in charge of the Summit growing grounds, so it may be a while until we really get the program started here, even though we have sold the merchandise and made the initial delivery.

Butler's Mill, Crescent City

Open house was a tremendous success, both in terms of general interest in our product line and the number of people who attended. Between 200 and 300 people came to the exhibit area (outside) between 10 A.M. and 2 P.M., and it seemed that most of them either knew about Osmocote or were using one of our products, and I was extremely grateful for Dick Spray's assistance during this time.

We picked up several good leads of people who deserve a follow-up call, and we'll certainly sell a lot more merchandise as a result of being at this meeting.

The dealers only portion of the open house was held in the evening between 5 and 7 P.M. Approximately 36 dealers showed up, and although many of them were from the various chain store garden departments, we did sell three new Green Green accounts. In addition, there was a great deal of interest in Green Green on the part of both Sears Roebuck and Handyman, so we should begin to see real movement of this product in the Del Norte County area. Dick Spray was going to spend all day Friday, the 30th, detailing some of the region accounts in the Crescent City area and will be anxious to hear how well he is able to do.

Jay arrived at Sierra in May 1975 and took immediate stock of his situation. In terms of people, he inherited the following:

1. *David Martin—Sales Manager.* Age 62, highly competent and experienced—a slow-release fertilizer salesman since 1957 (in the predecessor company) and sales manager since 1973. Dave had earlier owned a small chain of greenhouses and three retail outlets in Wisconsin and was a well-known and respected member of the industry. He was an active participant on many industry committees.
2. *William K. McFarland—Marketing Manager.* Age 53, very strong in advertising and publicity. A frequent writer for trade magazines and the "book editor" of *Nursery Business* magazine. He admittedly had no interest in profit and loss statements, nor did he enjoy his management responsibilities.
3. *Beverly James—Regional Manager or Saleswoman.* Age 32, a horticultural graduate from Ohio. Work experience with Procter & Gamble, Horticultural Division. She was an excellent saleswoman but weak on administration; i.e., paper work, reports.
4. *George Parker—Salesman.* Age 45, one of Martin's first hires in the predecessor company (early 1960s). He had an excellent understanding of horticulture matters.
5. *Dick Smith—Salesman.* Age 45, with Sierra since 1972. Smith previously sold insurance and fertilizer on the East Coast. An "old time, stand up and tell you what you have to do" salesman.

6. *James Van Horn—Salesman.* Age 26, a former plant superintendent, who asked for a field-selling assignment and seemed to be floundering.
7. *George Schwartz—Technical Director.* Age 52, the "dean" of slow-release fertilizer technology and the company's best asset "as a spokesman." Schwartz was a sought-after speaker, respected scientist, and friend of many major growers. He had a master's degree in horticulture.

For complete organization chart, see Exhibit 4.

What Rossi Found

It didn't take Jay Rossi long to discover that his sales manager, David Martin, was right in his diagnosis of the problem. Here was a selling group with little marketing direction, strategy, controls, or leadership. Forecasts were useless (as much as 50 percent off), and there were no records that indicated how the company was doing with its various lines in the separate markets. Field reports were filled in sporadically, and weekly reports were sometimes backed up in the system for two weeks by the two typists. Phone calls were used to get things accomplished, since reports were useless. Penetration rates were rarely known, and most sales efforts seemed to be reactive. There was no professional selling. Servicing old accounts and distributors was the focus—prospecting was given little attention. In short, management was entirely reactive. All information was after the fact. "We were always putting out fires," was a common complaint. Quotas were ignored, and compensation was by straight salary.

An extended field trip confirmed Jay Rossi's fears about the sales force. The first person he contacted criticized his "dumb distributors," complained about the tough market conditions, and never even talked about Osmocote's advantages to a new customer because "he didn't ask." The second salesman evidenced reasonable activity but had neither a sense of urgency nor any apparent professional selling skills. The third was a great saleswoman but terrible at managing her time. She would spend hours driving between calls and averaged only two calls per day (which was below the company average of 2.9).

Each seemed to blame problems on the distributors, and their visits to users were courtesy calls. They didn't feel they were supposed to "sell." It was apparent, furthermore, that the group believed strongly in a number of "principles":

1. You can't do much about sales in the short run. After all, growers are reluctant to try a new technique until they have been conditioned, educated, and made confident that the new supplier is reliable. And this takes time.
2. Salespeople have to be horticulturists first. Because controlled-release fertilizers are a technical innovation and commercial growing a scientific endeavor, it is obvious that horticultural skill is the most important prerequisite for selling. Advice and counsel are crucial if the salesperson is to successfully convert growers into Osmocote users.

Exhibit 4 **Table of Organization as of July 1976**

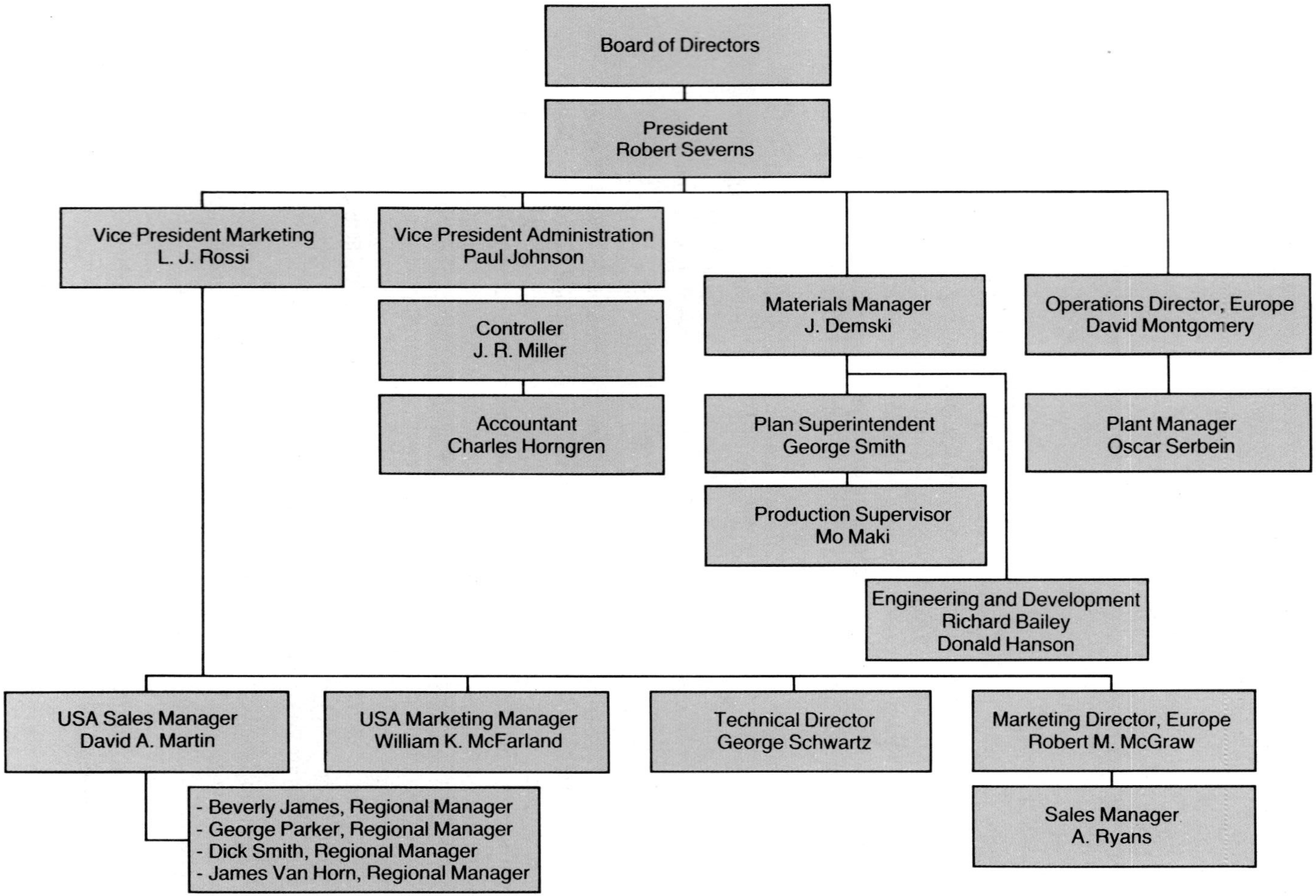

Board of Directors

President
Robert Severns

Vice President Marketing
L. J. Rossi

Vice President Administration
Paul Johnson

Controller
J. R. Miller

Accountant
Charles Horngren

Materials Manager
J. Demski

Plan Superintendent
George Smith

Production Supervisor
Mo Maki

Engineering and Development
Richard Bailey
Donald Hanson

Operations Director, Europe
David Montgomery

Plant Manager
Oscar Serbein

USA Sales Manager
David A. Martin

- Beverly James, Regional Manager
- George Parker, Regional Manager
- Dick Smith, Regional Manager
- James Van Horn, Regional Manager

USA Marketing Manager
William K. McFarland

Technical Director
George Schwartz

Marketing Director, Europe
Robert M. McGraw

Sales Manager
A. Ryans

3. The product is expensive and therefore hard to sell (a typical price is $650 per ton to the user).
4. Quality is irregular and a complication for the sales personnel.
5. Comparison between salespeople and regions is not possible because of the great differences between various parts of the market.
6. Distributors are not on "our team" but rather are "our customers." And you can't ask your customers to do things for you!

New Product Possibilities

There was a second pressure on Jay to bring the sales force under rapid control; namely, the firm's plans for new product and market opportunities. He had first read some information from one of Sierra's new product groups:

> OSMOCOTE 14[3] and urea-only products have been undergoing recent trial work in mushroom cultivation. At this time, it seems that our products may be able to prove their value and gain acceptance in this high-value market.
>
> During trial . . . it has been found that one-quarter pound of OSMOCOTE increases mushroom yields from 4.15 to 4.69 pounds per square foot, an obvious economic advantage.
>
> Another potential market where extensive work with our products is being done is in British Columbia stream fertilization. It has been found that nitrogen and potassium increase algae populations in streams and this, via several food steps, increases the size of the salmon that travel these streams to the ocean. Hence, more salmon survive this trip. Since salmon always return to the same stream where they were spawned, there is then not only more but larger salmon available for the commercial fisheries.
>
> Fish sizes and populations have increased so much that return on fertilizer investment can be anywhere from 3–6 to 1. Trial measurements—fish weights and lengths—will be conducted thoughout the summer, and economic measurements—the number of fish leaving the stream—will be available by early fall. Initial studies have shown fish size doubling with frequent applications of soluble N&P fertilizer.
>
> OSMOCOTE economics seem very favorable assuming fish sizes double with only one fertilizer application. The potential market for Sierra's products could be between 100 to 300 tons per year.
>
> Deciduous fruit and nut trees will also be an area of trial study for Sierra next year. Some are currently under evaluation, while others are scheduled to begin earlier this year. Since the fertilization of mature, bearing trees is currently not economical when compared to standard practice, Sierra is interested in entering the area of establishment fertilization of young deciduous fruit and nut trees. Favorable trial work in Washington has shown that trees which are ex-

pected to mature in five years have begun bearing fruit one year earlier, thus giving the grower an extra year of production. Trials are also being set on citrus trees in Florida, where we believe that the sandy soils, high rainfall, and crop value will be responsive to our product.

Another market where Sierra products can prove their value is in sugar cane fertilization. Trials are currently in place at Maunakae Sugar Plantation in Hawaii, where our custom-blend OSMOCOTE 17-0-23 product is being used on restricted areas.

It is believed that our technology will allow the sugar plantation to provide nutrients for the second half of the crop cycle. Normally, nutrition cannot be applied in these restricted areas as they are underneath power lines. Planes cannot fly over them to supply nutrients, and the thick growth of the sugar cane prohibits ground application.

The near-term market potential is felt to be between 15,000 to 20,000 units if these trials prove successful. We currently believe we have a 50 percent chance of obtaining this business.

Rossi's Challenge

As Jay Rossi and sales manager David Martin saw their problem, it was to:

1. Change the attitude of the sales force from horticultural specialists to aggressive salespeople.
2. Introduce controls that would direct the sales force toward a more productive use of its time.
3. Establish new incentive systems that would redirect the selling effort.
4. Give the organization a sense of mission and direction.
5. Be sure that the sales force was positioned to take advantage of the growth opportunities.

Questions

1. What specific action do you suggest that Rossi take?
2. What specific controls, reports, incentive systems, etc., would you adopt?
3. What would you do with the data?
4. How would you organize for growth?

KRUGER-MONTINI MANUFACTURING COMPANY

The management of Kruger-Montini Manufacturing Company had just entered a new fiscal year and was rethinking its specific policies and general position on transfers of sales representatives. The decision was the responsibility of the sales manager.

Founded many years earlier, this well-established corporation was a medium-sized manufacturer of several related industrial products in rather wide use. The majority of customers were manufacturers. For quite a few years Kruger-Montini did not do its own personal selling. Starting about twenty years ago, it gradually phased out the various intermediaries and manufacturers' agents. After about five years of difficult transition, Kruger-Montini relied strictly on sales representatives who were on the company's payroll and who worked for no one else. Kruger Montini was not truly national in coverage in its early years but became so nine years ago when it added five sales representatives in one year and relocated thirteen.

The size of the sales force had increased as the company grew and prospered and had now reached thirty-eight. The sales manager had found it necessary to divide his organization into four geographical regions because of span of control difficulties as Kruger-Montini grew. Because the product line was fairly narrow, it was decided that geography, not type of products, would be the best basis for the organization structure. Thus each sales representative sold all products. A contributing reason for deciding against product specialization as the basis for organizing selling efforts was that it would have resulted necessarily in a larger geographical territory for each employee to cover. That would have meant his being away from home overnight much more than under the policy adopted. The present sales manager, Henry Rosas, estimated that the average person on his sales force spent six nights a month away from home. This figure was a little lower, he knew, for people in the highly industrialized and densely populated areas of the Northeast, the Michigan, Ohio, Indiana, Illinois, Wisconsin region in the Middle West, and parts of California. The figure was a little higher for his people in all other areas. Rosas estimated that the difference was about five versus eight nights per month. During the past few years the company had noticed a sizable number of its customers relocate to the Sun Belt and many customers open branch factories in those milder climate areas of the nation. The demand for Kruger-Montini's products was slowly becoming more evenly spread across the country, and this trend was expected to continue.

Rosas had been with the organization about three years. He had been a successful salesman with one company and then assistant sales manager with another company before coming with Kruger-Montini. He had a good personality and was well liked by the sales representatives.

Exhibit 1 **Data on Sales Force of Kruger-Montini Manufacturing Company**

	Size of Sales Force	Number Transferred	Mean Distance Transferred (miles)
Last year	38	6	798
Two years ago	37	7	872
Three years ago	37	7	682
Four years ago	36	7	1122
Five years ago	35	7	1254
Six years ago	34	9	1360
Seven years ago	32	9	597
Eight years ago	32	12	1070
Nine years ago	31	13	793
Ten years ago	26	10	1035
Eleven years ago	25	10	640
Twelve years ago	24	11	510

The company had always used a salary plus commission pay plan. For the average representative the commission provided 25 percent of his compensation.

Kruger-Montini manufactured nine products, two of which had been introduced only in the past three years. Prior to that three-year period there had been no new product introductions for a great many years. It appeared highly probable that Kruger-Montini would introduce two more new products, closely related to the existing product line, and delete one during the next two years.

During the most recent fiscal year Kruger-Montini had transferred six sales representatives to different territories. In the four years previous to that, the company had transferred seven each year. Each was moved because of company need and/or the assigning of better territories to deserving sales representatives. See Exhibit 1 for earlier years and additional data on size of the sales force and average distances people were transferred. The mean distance of a relocation at Kruger-Montini had shown a downward trend for several years.

Every person on the sales force had moved at least once. The longest time in one place anyone on the present sales force had experienced with Kruger-Montini was seven years. Rosas was tentatively thinking about moving from five to seven members of the sales force later this year.

The management did not know much about the geographical preferences of its sales representatives or their family life. Rosas could not legally inquire systematically about whether the spouses were also employed and whether that work was professional and managerial, which might make one less willing to move. Dual careers made it difficult for couples to handle relocations well, and some probably would not consider it at all. However, Rosas and his four regional sales managers had been trying recently to make observations and record facts and inferences about these matters for all the sales representatives. Three of the sales representatives were young, unmarried men who seemed to be mobile and flexible. Three middle-aged men were divorced, and one was a widower. The remaining thirty-one were all married. It appeared that twenty of them had working spouses and that fifteen of these women had professional or managerial careers. Rosas also began to understand that most nonworking married women had developed community ties and that moving for them could also be difficult and unsettling.

The unwritten understanding of personnel at Kruger-Montini had been that turning down a transfer would be suicidal. At the minimum such a rejection would classify a person as unaggressive and unambitious. The United States culture for many years had perceived frequent transfers as evidence of fast-track career progress. Staying mobile was a "badge of honor," as business newspapers and magazines usually described it.

No one on the Kruger-Montini sales force had ever declined a transfer until two years ago, as far as Rosas could determine. The sales manager and other headquarters personnel had been surprised and perplexed when Charles Hopkins, a very satisfactory employee, had declined a move from a small, pleasant southeastern city to a much more lucrative territory in another part of the United States. Age thirty-seven and a native of the upper Middle West, Hopkins explained that he liked Kruger-Montini and wanted to continue working for the company but did not want to move. His wife was a business manager in another company, and they had a thirteen-year-old daughter in school.

The costs to relocate a sales representative had been rising quite rapidly. The most recently transferred person was Alex Kendall, a man with a wife and three children. It cost Kruger-Montini $30,880 to move them approximately 2,900 miles from one coast to the other, although the company was not any more generous than the typical American company. Of this amount, $11,475 was to ship household goods, $4,100 was for the pre-move housing search, and $3,680 was for one extra month of this man's average compensation in lieu of incidental expenses. Final travel and temporary living expenses accounted for another $4,550. The remaining costs had to do with company subsidies on the sale of the couple's house and purchase of a replacement house. The management of Kruger-Montini was beginning to note the financial impact of moving costs of the company.

Kruger-Montini also recognized that a transferred sales representative required several months to get his work productivity back to normal. The recovery of productivity was much more difficult for people who worked with the public and who needed to understand the characteristics of a market than for other types of workers. A sales representative also needed time to establish rapport with the regular clients.

One managerial colleague who Rosas respected was outspoken about the issue of moving. Bert Crane, who managed another department at Kruger-Montini and had been with the company about twelve years, believed that if employees were permitted to put down roots in a community they would lose their sense of corporate identity. Loyalties to the geographical community would overcome loyalties to the corporation.

He stated that perhaps this had been an unconscious motivation of Kruger-Montini in past years.

Another colleague, Robert Mason, mentioned that a nice compromise might be to confine transfers to the region in which the sales representative was already living. For example, the ten sales representatives in eleven Northeastern states would be transferred only within that region. Mason noted that each region had some lifestyle characteristics that set it apart from the others. He was an experienced manager and had been with the company for about nine years.

Advise Henry Rosas of the Kruger-Montini Manufacturing Company.

NORTHERN NEW JERSEY MANUFACTURING COMPANY

Northern New Jersey Manufacturing Company was a producer of several kinds of industrial equipment listed in Exhibit 1. It developed from the efforts in the late 1940s of a gifted engineer and inventor, Sidney Hovey, who patented several of his ideas for variations on standard products. He founded and was active in the firm for more than twenty-six years until his death.

Hovey had been very interested in the selling activity of his company and had a strong sense of professionalism that he used in personally selecting people for his sales force. He managed the sales force until it grew to a size of three men, at which time he secured the services of Herbert Staley as sales manager.

Before Staley's arrival and for several years thereafter, Hovey told the salesmen expressly the names of firms he wanted them to call on. The founder was acutely interested in the reputation of his young company. His concern with reputation included product characteristics as promised, delivery on time (critical to customers for these goods), and ethical, highly reserved business conduct by the salesmen. However, this concern for reputation was not restricted to these factors. Hovey also wanted to have as his customers those who enjoyed the finest reputations. For example, he told his salesmen never to solicit the orders of a small firm then known by the name of Reihnan and Loykas, for he considered the owners to be social climbers without proper backgrounds. In addition, he did not like an advertisement of theirs he once saw in a weekly business newspaper. He also instructed his salesmen not to call on Heather Glow, Inc., because it had been turned down for a loan at the bank that Hovey used. This was despite the fact Heather Glow found credit at another bank.

Exhibit 1 **Northern New Jersey Manufacturing Company Sales by Product, Selected Months**

Product	September	July	September Last Year	September Two Years Before
Dryers	$21,000	$34,500	$35,000	$32,200
Sprayers	7,700	7,500	8,000	7,800
Planers	4,100	4,300	4,000	3,900
Power saws	3,200	3,000	3,000	3,100
Drills	4,200	4,100	4,000	3,900
Sanders	9,500	7,300	7,200	7,000
Metal buffers	7,500	4,900	5,000	4,800

Not all the instructions were negative, however. Hovey had the salesmen, all of whom were engineers, visit Camden Mills, Stone & Kruger, and South Coast Metals time after time even though all three were committed to other sellers and other product designs. He wanted Northern New Jersey Manufacturing Company to be a name that such firms knew and respected. He also cultivated several large national companies, such as Combustion Engineering, American Machine and Foundry, Kaiser Industries, Westinghouse, and Melpar.

After Hovey's death, Staley continued these policies for the better part of a year. At that point James Watts, the new president hired from the outside, had a long talk with the sales manager and explained that he thought some changes were desirable. The firm should try to maximize sales and abandon all the "notions and pretentions," as he termed them. The salesmen should be put on a combination salary plus commission. The two other executives in the company, the finance man and the production man, spoke up with thorough endorsements of such changes. The existing policy was straight salary.

With some misgivings, Staley devised a new compensation structure for his four salesmen. Under this plan he estimated that a salesman would earn about 80 percent of his compensation through salary and about 20 percent through commissions. The plan was announced on August 1 and the men were told it would go into effect in thirty days. Sales in August slumped about 17 percent from the same month one year earlier and 14 percent from the same month two years earlier.

After one month of use, the sales manager conducted a preliminary inquiry into the results of the new compensation policy. The results appeared to be that the easier to sell items in the product line were moving well, those of average difficulty to sell were moving adequately, and the one item that was rather difficult to sell (the dryer) was moving very poorly. Exhibit 1 gives the comparisons of September to the last month under the old policy (July) and to September one year before. Staley presented his analysis to Watts but cautioned him about premature inferences from these data. The sales manager said that he would repeat his comparisons after another month. In the meanwhile, the president told the sales manager to urge the salesmen to solicit orders for dryers.

At the beginning of November, Staley anxiously studied the results for October, as presented in Exhibit 2. He had taken a preliminary look at some fragmentary data about October 16 but knew that those data were undependable. In addition, the company had usually experienced a mild upswing in the fall season.

Staley was in his office reflecting on the figures in Exhibits 1 and 2 when Douglas Guglielmi, the production manager, and Richard Acker, the finance and accounting manager, both walked in. After several minutes of friendly conversation about sports and the weather, Guglielmi said that he and Staley jointly had a problem. To be specific, the mix of sales was apparently changing radically, which was upsetting his production schedule, company general plans, and deliveries. Richard Acker then added what Staley already knew, that the dryers had been earning the highest unit

Exhibit 2 **Northern New Jersey Manufacturing Company Sales by Product, Selected Months**

Product	October	October Last Year	October Two Years Before
Dryers	$23,000	$36,000	$35,400
Sprayers	7,900	8,400	8,200
Planers	4,300	4,200	4,000
Power saws	3,300	3,200	3,000
Drills	4,200	4,300	4,100
Sanders	11,500	7,500	7,200
Metal buffers	9,700	5,300	5,100

margin, whereas the sanders and metal buffers had been earning the lowest unit margin. Total profits were beginning to go down.

Advise Herbert Staley, sales manager for the Northern New Jersey Manufacturing Company.

LIBERTY STATESMAN CORPORATION

Liberty Statesman Corporation was a large life insurance company operating throughout the United States and Canada. The manager of the Louisiana-Mississippi district, Cyrus Baker, had just retired after eight years in that post. His replacement was thirty-six-year-old Lyman Danner, who had been with the company six years and with a competitor for about seven years before that. For the past two years Danner, a native of New Jersey, had been manager for his home state for Liberty Statesman. The results in that territory had pleased top management. Danner, his wife, and three young children immediately moved to New Orleans, where district headquarters was located.

The first thing Danner did on arrival was to order the district office refurbished at a cost of about $7,500. He conferred at length during a series of meetings with an interior decorator on how the project was to be done. After about ten days he started a task that he described to many persons as "the most important for any new district manager, learning the sales force." Simultaneously he investigated the paper handling and limited bookkeeping activities the district office engaged in, for his observations indicated that things were not smoothly or efficiently handled and that applicable services of Liberty Statesman's national office were not being fully utilized. Using the national office for any available service might increase the expertise with which it was done and might save the district office some money, he explained.

Danner was accustomed to being in charge of one of the seven leading districts in terms of sales volume. As he discovered when he began to study the records in his new office, the Louisiana-Mississippi district had never finished in this elite group in any year. The best it had ever done was nineteenth among the thirty-eight districts and that was four years ago. The past year it had been twenty-fourth. It had been rumored in the company that Cyrus Baker was winding down toward his retirement the past two years. Therefore, Danner took the view that his new district had much more potential than the actual sales figures of the past implied. He wondered about trying to transfer in some of the highly able and motivated sales representatives he knew from his old district. He discussed the idea briefly with Sam Autier, his assistant district manager and right-hand man. Autier advised him not to waste valuable time and psychic energy even considering it, because insurance sales representatives do not transfer as readily as many other types of sales representatives. They are on their own most of the time and can benefit handsomely from a detailed knowledge of and "feel" for the area in which they work. They need networks of contact and referrals from friends, acquaintances, and customers. Many sales require periodic visits for several years before the sale is consummated. Insurance on one member of the family may lead to insurance on another member.

Exhibit 1 **Selected Results of Sales Contest: The Ten Sales Representatives with the Highest Percentage Increases**

Salesman	Location	Sales During Contest	Sales, Same Period Last Year	Percentage Increase
Leary	Shreveport	$800,000	$705,000	13.4%
Caruthers	New Orleans	720,000	650,000	
Bymel	Baton Rouge	640,000	590,000	
Beatty	Jackson	635,000	590,000	
Verier	Lafayette	620,000	581,000	
Sutkin	Lake Charles	481,000	455,000	
Hemingway	Monroe	422,000	400,000	
Rymanson	Ruston	430,000	409,000	
Breaux	Hammond	430,500	410,000	
Belton	Natchitoches	435,750	415,000	

Danner began to think. He knew all of this as well as Autier did and was embarrassed that he had even brought up such an idea. Perhaps, he reflected to himself, it was symptomatic of his anxiety. But he considered that Sam Autier was a good listener and he had to have someone with whom to "bat ideas around." After all, every manager had some ideas that could be improved on. And everyone in a position of responsibility needs people around him with whom he can talk without entering into commitments and promises.

What he actually said to Autier was: "Of course, you are so right. I was daydreaming. But if I had my druthers, that is about what I would do."

A few days later Danner and Autier set up a contest to furnish additional incentive for the twenty-eight sales representatives in the district. These salesmen did not represent any other company. There had been no contest in this district for about eighteen months. This one would last three months during the slow season and would be based on percentage increases over the same three months and previous year. There were to be three prizes. First prize was an all-expense-paid five-day vacation in Montego Bay, Jamaica. The second prize was a $100 U.S. savings bond, and the third prize was a bond of $50. All three winners would be presented handsome certificates on Danner's next field visit to their vicinity.

As soon as the three-month period was over, Danner eagerly began to examine the results, which are shown in Exhibit 1 for the ten persons with the highest percentage increases. He had never conducted a contest with such an outcome. Aggregate sales had gone up only about 4 per cent. He was suprised and keenly disappointed and said so, but he gave the three awards anyway. Moreover, he immediately announced to the sales force that there would be another contest, the details of which would be given out in a few weeks.

A few days later Danner made a field visit swing through Jackson, Oxford, Starkville, Hattiesburg, and Gulfport. At a party in his honor on this trip there was enough conversation, some of it oblique and some overheard, for him to realize that his remarks about wanting to transfer in some sales representatives from his former territory had gotten out and had apparently been repeated with some enlargement. There were no scenes at the party and Danner deftly avoided saying anything awkward or embarrassing, despite the strong temptation. Nevertheless, he returned to New Orleans perplexed.

Advise Lyman Danner of Liberty Statesman Corporation.

PART SIX

DETERMINING SALESFORCE PERFORMANCE

THE three chapters in Part 6 focus on determining salesforce performance. Chapter 14 presents different forecasting methods used by sales managers and discusses the use of forecasts as a basis for establishing sales quotas and selling budgets. Chapter 15 addresses the evaluation of sales organization effectiveness. Methods for analyzing sales, costs, profitability, and productivity at different sales organization levels are reviewed. Chapter 16 addresses the evaluation of salespeople's individual performance and job satisfaction. Ways of determining the appropriate performance criteria and methods of evaluation, and of using the evaluations to improve salesperson performance and job satisfaction, are discussed.

CHAPTER 14

DEVELOPING FORECASTS AND ESTABLISHING SALES QUOTAS AND SELLING BUDGETS

Learning Objectives:

After completing this chapter, you should be able to

1. Discuss the different types of forecasts used by sales managers.
2. Describe the top-down and bottom-up forecasting approaches used by sales managers.
3. Explain the use of the salesforce composite and market factor forecasting methods.
4. Describe how sales quotas are established, including the use of multiple regression procedures.
5. Discuss the importance of and methods for establishing selling budgets.

INCREASING THE ACCURACY OF SALES FORECASTS: MIRACLE ADHESIVES CORPORATION

Miracle Adhesives Corporation manufactures and sells over 500 items in the field of adhesives, sealants, and coatings. Sales are made to the construction industry and retail trade by 11 company salespeople and 33 manufacturers' representatives. Accurate forecasting of sales and profits is important to firm performance.

Miracle Adhesives employs a multiple-step forecasting procedure:

1. In July of each year, the data processing department prints a three-year sales history and a projection for the coming year. The sales projection is based on historical data and is broken down by division and by department. Monthly figures for total dollar sales, total poundage, and gross profit are assembled.
2. These data are given to each of the divisional sales managers, who review the data and send each salesperson a printout of their sales for the past three years (but *not* the projected sales for next year). The salespeople review their customers and prospects and estimate their monthly sales and gross profits for the next year.
3. The divisional sales managers review the estimates provided by the salespeople. They also consider the forecast from the data processing department, market trends, economic conditions, and new marketing programs planned for the coming year. Based on this analysis, adjustments are made and tentative final forecasts are sent to the vice-president of sales and marketing. After a thorough review and possible adjustments, final forecasts are approved.

This forecasting procedure represents a systematic approach for incorporating the judgments of salespeople, sales managers, and marketing executives. Although management at Miracle Adhesives has generally been pleased with the results of this approach, arriving at accurate forecasts is a difficult task. The major problems that have made forecasting difficult during the past few years are (1) turmoil in

---

Source: Adapted from an example reported in Harry R. White, *Sales Forecasting: Timesaving and Profit-Making Strategies That Work,* (Glenview, Ill.: Scott, Foresman and Company, 1984), 44–50. Used with permission.

the petroleum industry, (2) gauging the condition of the economy, (3) inability of salespeople to judge their customers and prospects accurately, (4) changes in government policies and regulations, (5) influence of the weather, and (6) the actions of competitors.

Since their forecasting approach relies heavily on the estimates provided by salespeople, Miracle Adhesives has taken specific steps to increase the accuracy of these estimates. The company has devised an incentive program whereby a salesperson's bonus is tied to how accurate his or her sales forecasts are. Salespeople achieve the maximum bonus only if their results are within 95 percent and 105 percent of the forecast. Charles R. Van Anden, executive vice-president, said "[I]t's vital for us to estimate sales potential as accurately as possible. The salesperson's bonus for accuracy is an important tool in accomplishing this."

The forecasts are also used to establish quotas for each salesperson. These quotas are baseline sales and profit volumes. Salespeople must reach them before any incentive compensation can be earned; then bonuses of varying percentages are awarded. Thus, forecast accuracy affects when a salesperson will begin to receive incentive compensation and the amount that he or she can earn. Although this type of incentive plan might seem overly complicated, Mr. Van Anden suggests that "it doesn't take long for the salespeople to understand it and to see the logic of it from our point of view and theirs . . . And they really concentrate on getting that extra bonus for forecasting realistically."

THE meteorologist used all of the latest technology to predict a bright and sunny day in the mid 80s. It rained most of the day and never got above 70 degrees. The weather forecast missed the mark on this particular occasion, but the meteorologist will continue to make weather forecasts and to work on improving weather forecasting procedures.

Sales managers face a situation similar to that of the meteorologist. The business environment is complex and dynamic, there are a number of forecasting methods available, and oftentimes forecasts are incorrect. Nevertheless, sales managers must continue to forecast and to work on improving their forecasting procedures. The Miracle Adhesives example discussed in the opening vignette illustrates one firm's approach to the forecasting task.

Why is forecasting so important to sales managers? In one sense, all sales management decisions are based on some type of forecast. The sales manager decides on a certain action because he or she thinks it will produce a certain result. This expected result is a **forecast**, even though the sales manager may not have quantified it or may not have used a mathematical forecasting procedure. More specifically, forecasts provide the basis for the following sales management decisions:[1]

1. Determining salesforce size
2. Designing territories

3. Establishing sales quotas and selling budgets
4. Determining sales compensation levels
5. Evaluating salesperson performance
6. Evaluating prospective accounts.

The purpose of this chapter is to discuss forecasting, first from the perspective of a firm and then from the perspective of sales managers. Finally, we will investigate the use of forecasts in establishing sales quotas and selling budgets.

FORECASTING FROM THE PERSPECTIVE OF THE ORGANIZATION

Forecasts are important to all business functional areas and all management levels. Some of the key questions addressed in determining their use follow:[2]

1. What forecasts are needed (e.g., sales, market share, costs, competitive reactions, etc.)?
2. What are the circumstances surrounding the forecast (e.g., stage of the product life cycle, state of the economy, degree of regulation in the industry, etc.)?
3. What forecast horizon is appropriate (e.g., short-, medium-, long-term, etc.)?
4. What data are relevant and available?
5. With what frequency must the forecast be prepared?
6. Who will prepare the forecast, and how much time and resources will be committed to the task?
7. Who will use the forecast and in what manner?
8. What process and forecasting methods are to be used?
9. How soon is the forecast needed?

Although it is beyond the scope of this chapter to address all of these questions in detail, several comments are in order. The term *forecast* implies some prediction of a future state. Many different types of predictions (forecasts) are typically important (sales, market share, costs, etc.). These forecasts require some assumptions about the future situation that will be facing the firm (economic situation, regulatory environment, etc.). Thus, the forecasts of expected results desired by management are based on assumptions, or forecasts, of the expected environment within which the firm will be operating. The forecasting task is especially difficult for firms operating in international markets, as indicated in "International Sales: Forecasting in Changing Environments."

This complex situation is illustrated in Figure 14.1. Management is typically most interested in forecasts of market share, sales, costs, and profits. Generating these forecasts, however, requires some assumptions, or forecasts, concerning the environment,

INTERNATIONAL SALES

FORECASTING IN CHANGING ENVIRONMENTS

Developing forecasts for different international markets is a challenging task, especially when there are major changes in inflation rates and currency values. For example, inflation ranged from 1,000 percent to close to zero in Argentina during 1984 and 1985. Inflation rates have a direct impact on a firm's costs and on the demand for its products.

Avon Products, the international marketer of cosmetics and accessories, has developed an approach to help its international subsidiaries cope with rapidly changing inflation rates and currency values. Local managers from each functional area meet on a regular basis to assess potential inflation rates and their predicted impact on company costs. Then sales forecasts at different price levels are developed and specific sales campaigns planned for different inflation rate projections. Additional meetings are scheduled to review, revise, and approve the sales campaigns and sales forecasts to reflect the most recent information concerning changes in inflation rates and currency values.

Source: Adapted from examples reported in Michael R. Czinkota and Ilkka A. Ronkainen, *International Marketing* (Hinsdale, Ill.: The Dryden Press, 1988), 448.

market, actions of suppliers, distributors, and government, competitors' actions, and company actions. Firms that have the best information and insight concerning these situational factors are in the best position to forecast expected results.

One study of sales forecasting provides a snapshot of the company forecasting process used by U.S. firms.[3] This study found that 88 percent of responding firms prepared annual forecasts that were typically updated on a monthly or quarterly basis. Only 10 percent of the firms prepared two-year forecasts, while 26 percent forecasted sales on a five-year basis. Managers from different functional areas participated in the forecasting process. Respondent firms indicated major forecasting responsibility for the top marketing executive (41 percent) and for sales managers (19 percent). Many firms distribute the final forecast to field sales managers (34 percent) and to salespeople (19 percent). The sales forecasts are most often used in budget preparation (89 percent) and setting quotas (67 percent). The biggest problems in obtaining accurate sales forecasts were listed as the inability of salespeople or their sales managers to judge their sales prospects accurately (33 percent), difficulty in predicting the actions of competitors (31 percent), and difficulty in predicting the state of the economy (30 percent). Despite these problems, 50 percent of the firms reported that their forecasts have been at least 90 percent accurate. Only 11 percent of the firms indicated forecast accuracy of less than 50 percent.

This overview of forecasting is intended to highlight both the importance and the complexity of the forecasting process. Although sales managers are often involved with company forecasting, sales management activities require a different forecasting perspective.

Figure 14.1 **Forecasting Framework**

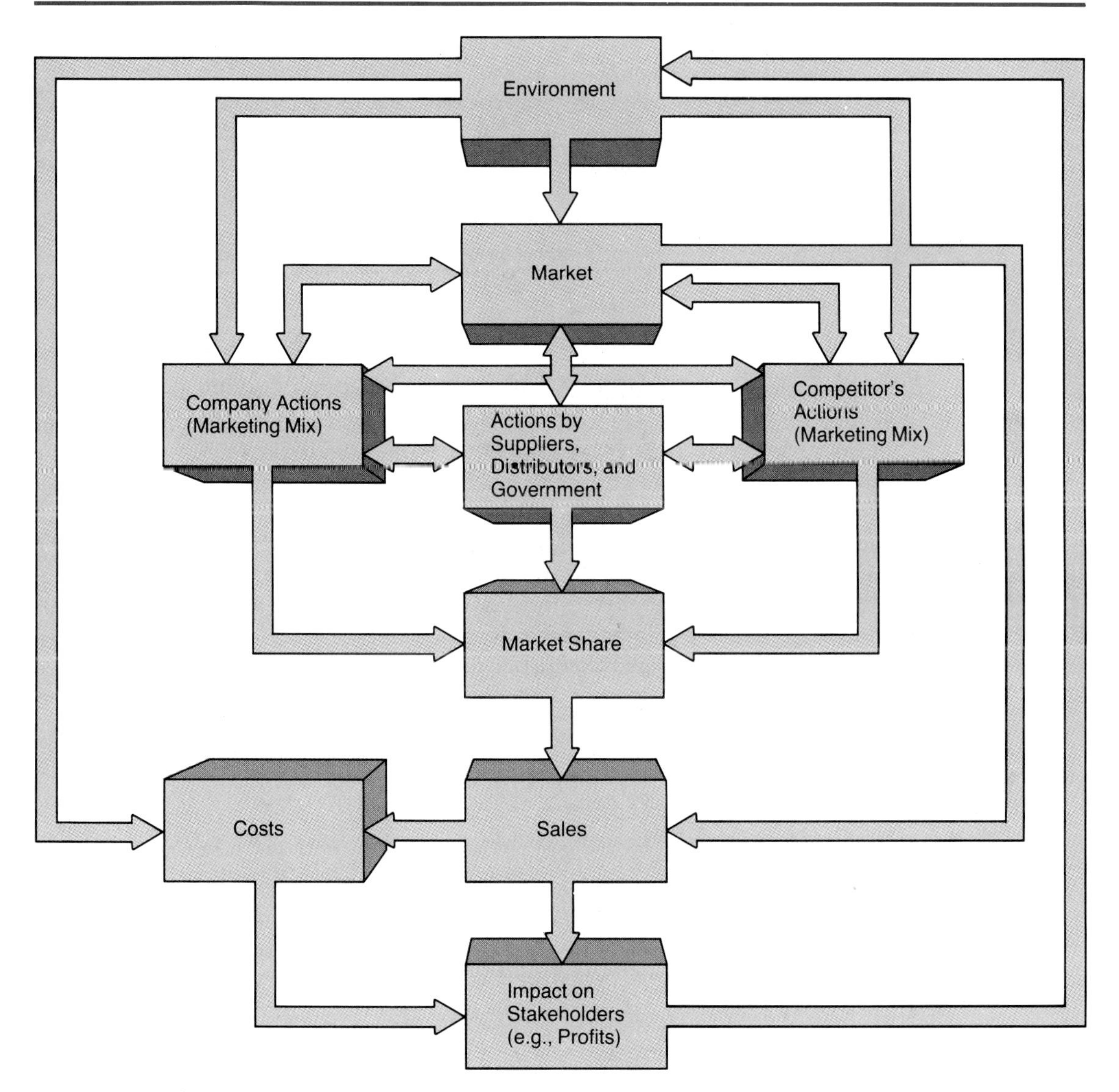

The forecasting process is extremely complex. Forecasts of market share, sales, costs, and/or profits are typically desired. Preparing these forecasts requires information and understanding concerning the environment, market, competitors, channel members, and company actions.

Source: J. Scott Armstrong, Roderick J. Brodie, and Shelby McIntyre, "Forecasting Methods for Marketing: Review of Empirical Research," *Singapore Marketing Review*, March 1987, 9.

FORECASTING FROM THE PERSPECTIVE OF SALES MANAGEMENT

Although top management levels are most concerned with total firm forecasts, sales managers are typically interested in developing and using forecasts for specific areas such as accounts, territories, districts, regions, and/or zones. For example, a district sales manager would be concerned with the district forecast as well as forecasts for individual territories and accounts within the district. There are, however, different types of forecasts that sales managers might use in different ways, and different approaches and methods might be employed to develop these forecasts.

Types of Forecasts

The term *forecast* is ordinarily used to refer to a prediction for a future time period. Although this usage is technically correct, it is too general for managerial value. As illustrated in Figure 14.2, at least three factors must be defined when referring to a forecast: the product level, the geographic area, and the time period. The figure presents 90 different forecasts that might be made, depending upon these factors. Thus, when using the term *forecast,* sales management should be very specific in defining exactly what is being forecast, for what geographic area, and for what time period.

A useful way for viewing what is being forecast is presented in Figure 14.3. This figure suggests that it is important to differentiate between industry and firm product levels and whether the prediction is for the best possible results or for the expected results given a specific strategy. Four different types of forecasts emerge from this classification scheme:

1. **Market potential** — the best possible level of industry sales in a given geographic area for a specific time period.
2. **Market forecast** — the expected level of industry sales given a specific industry strategy in a given geographic area for a specific time period.
3. **Sales potential** — the best possible level of firm sales in a given geographic area for a specific time period.
4. **Sales forecast** — the expected level of company sales given a specific strategy in a given geographic area for a specific time period.

Notice that the geographic area and time period are defined for each of these terms and that a true *sales forecast* must include the consideration of a specific strategy. If a firm changes this strategy, the sales forecast should change also.

As an example, assume that you are the district sales manager for a firm that markets microcomputers to organizational buyers. Your district includes Oklahoma, Texas, Louisiana, and Arkansas. You are preparing forecasts for 1989. You might first try to assess market potential. This market potential forecast would be an estimate of

Figure 14.2 Defining the Forecast

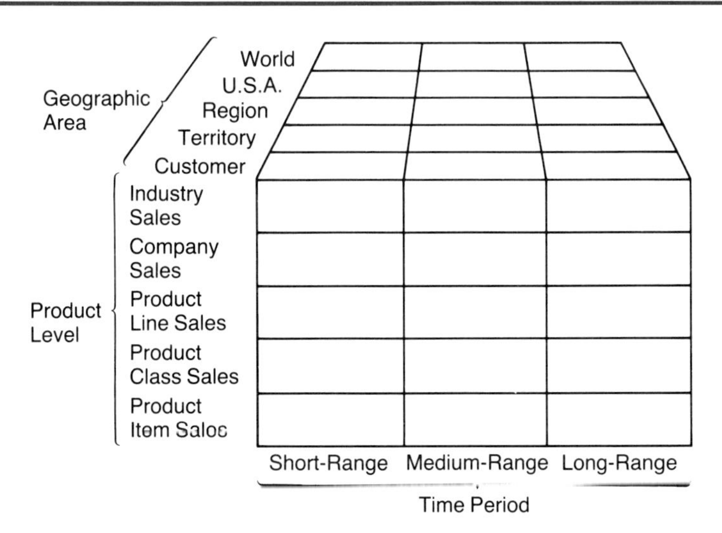

Many different types of forecasts are possible. Every forecast should be defined in terms of geographic area, product level, and time period.

Source: Philip Kotler, *Marketing Management: Analysis, Planning, Implementation, and Control,* 6/e, © 1988, p. 257. Adapted by permission of Prentice Hall, Inc., Englewood Cliffs, New Jersey.

Figure 14.3 Types of Forecasts

	Best Possible Results	Expected Results for Given Strategy
Industry Level	Market Potential	Market Forecast
Firm Level	Sales Potential	Sales Forecast

Four different types of forecasts are typically important to sales managers, depending upon whether a forecast is needed for the industry or the firm, and whether the best possible or expected results are to be forecast.

the highest level of microcomputer sales by all brands in your district for 1989. Then, you might try to develop a market forecast, which would be the expected level of industry microcomputer sales in your district for 1989. This forecast would be based on an assumption of which strategies would be used by all microcomputer firms operating in your district. If you think new firms are going to enter the industry or existing firms leave it, or that existing firms will change their strategies, your industry forecast will change. Another type of forecast might be a determination of the best possible level of 1989 sales for your firm's microcomputers in the district. This would be a sales potential forecast. Finally, you would probably want to predict a specific level of district sales of your firm's microcomputers given your firm's expected strategy. This would result in a sales forecast which would have to be revised whenever strategic changes were made.

Uses of Forecasts

Since different types of forecasts convey different information, sales managers use specific types for specific sales management decisions. Forecasts of market potential and sales potential are most often used to identify opportunities and to guide the allocation of selling efforts. Market potential provides an assessment of overall demand opportunity available to all firms in an industry. Sales potential adjusts market potential to reflect industry competition and thus represents a better assessment of demand opportunity for an individual firm. Both of these forecasts of potential can be used by sales managers to determine where selling effort is needed and how selling effort should be distributed. For example, as discussed in Chapter 8, designing territories requires an assessment of market potential for all planning and control units. Specific territories are then designed by grouping planning and control units together and evaluating the equality of market potential across the territories.

Market forecasts and sales forecasts are used to predict the expected results from various sales management decisions. For example, once territories are designed, sales managers typically want to forecast expected industry and company sales for each specific sales territory. These forecasts are then used to set sales quotas and selling budgets for specific planning periods.

Top-Down and Bottom-Up Forecasting Methods

Forecasting methods can be classified and discussed in a number of ways,[4] but two basic approaches are illustrated in Figure 14.4. **Top-down approaches** generally consist of the development of company forecasts by individuals at the business unit levels. Sales managers break down these company forecasts into zone, region, district, territory, and account forecasts. **Bottom-up approaches** are different in that forecasts are initially made at the account level by salespeople. Sales managers then combine the account forecasts into territory, district, region, zone, and ultimately company forecasts. The top-down and bottom-up approaches represent entirely different perspectives for developing forecasts.

Figure 14.4 Forecasting Approaches

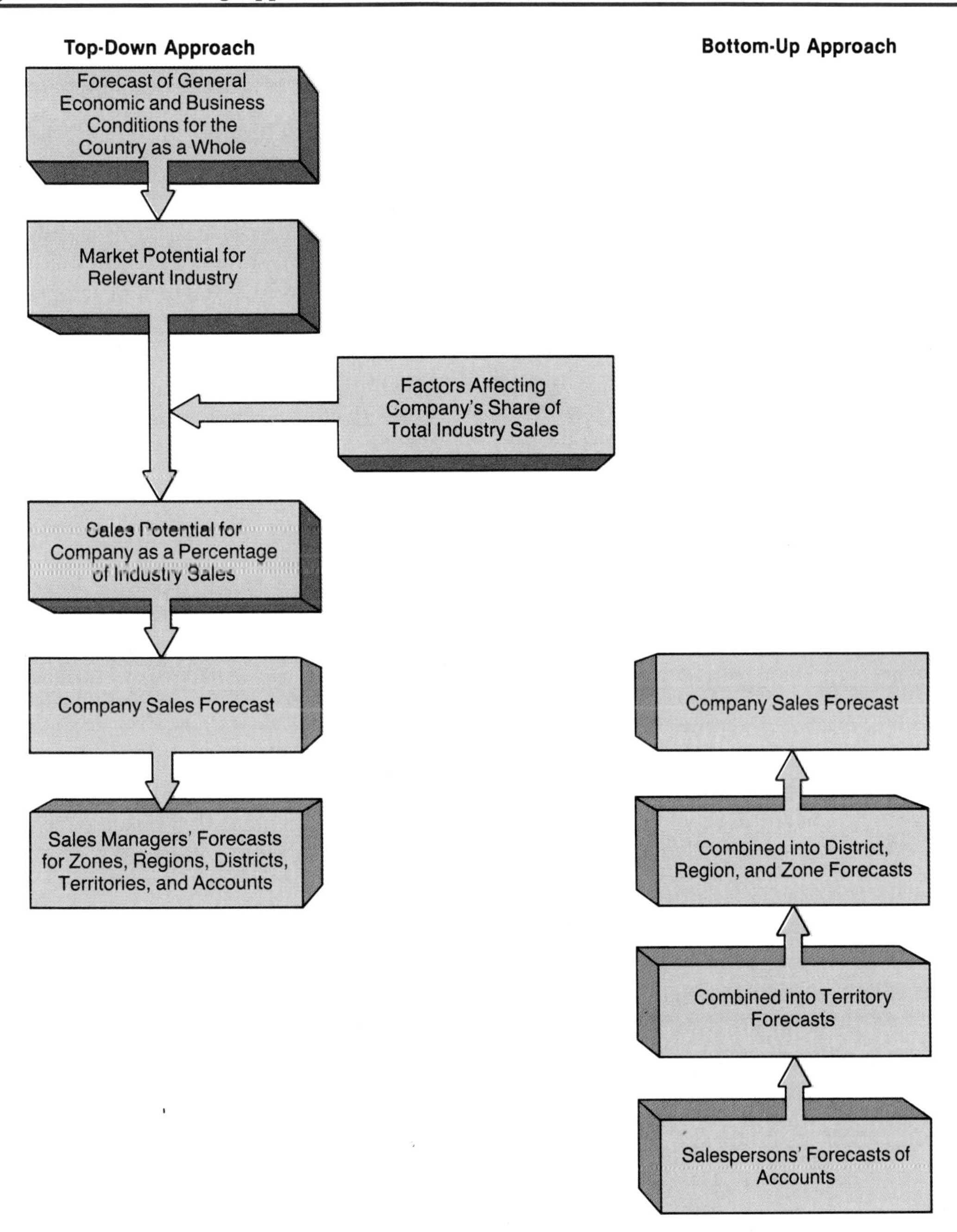

In top-down approaches, company personnel provide aggregate company forecasts that sales managers must break down into zone, region, district, territory, and account forecasts. In bottom-up approaches, salespeople provide account forecasts that are combined into territory, district, region, zone, and company forecasts.

Source: Adapted from C. Robert Patty and Robert Hite, *Managing Salespeople,* Englewood Cliffs, N.J.: Prentice-Hall, Inc., 1988, 71.

Bottom-Up Approach. A bottom-up approach used by many organizations is the **salesforce composite method**. Although variations exist, the basic procedure is to have salespeople provide various types of estimates for their assigned accounts. Estimates of market potentials, market forecasts, sales potentials, and/or sales forecasts for individual accounts might be obtained. An example of one approach is presented in Exhibit 14.1.

Each salesperson completes this form for each assigned account. Notice that the salesperson is asked to supply actual sales to the account for last year, expected sales this year, and forecasted sales for next year, as well as an assessment of account sales potential. Each estimate is made separately for each major product group sold to the account. An account sales potential and account sales forecast are calculated by summing the individual estimates for each product group. Sales managers can then combine these account forecasts to generate forecasts at the territory, district, region, and zone levels. This procedure could also be used to generate company forecasts based on individual forecasts from all accounts served by a firm.

The salesforce composite method takes advantage of the unique account and market information possessed by salespeople. However, salesperson estimates can be biased and lead to inaccurate forecasts, so these potential biases should be addressed when using this method. Many firms appear to be trying to improve the accuracy of salesperson forecasts. The opening vignette to this chapter discusses the approach Miracle Adhesives Corporation uses to tie forecasting accuracy to salesforce compensation. Another example of how firms are emphasizing accuracy in salesperson forecasts is presented in "Sales Trend: Increasing the Accuracy of Salesperson Forecasts."

Top-Down Approach. Although it can take different forms, in a typical top-down approach a firm would use various methods to develop industry or company forecasts and then supply these forecasts to sales managers, who must then divide these aggregate forecasts into forecasts at the account, territory, district, region, or zone levels.

One method sales managers might use is the **market factor method**, in which they identify one or more factors that are related to results at the account, territory, district, region, or zone levels, and use these factors to translate the market or company forecasts into forecasts at the desired levels. A typical approach is to use the **Buying Power Index (BPI)** supplied by *Sales and Marketing Management.*[5] The BPI is a market factor calculated for different areas in the following manner:

$$BPI = 5I + 2P + 3R/10$$

where I = Percentage of U.S. disposable personal income in the area
P = Percentage of U.S. population in the area
R = Percentage of U.S. retail sales in the area

Performing these calculations for any area produces a BPI for the area. This BPI can be translated as the percentage of U.S. buying power residing in the area. The higher the index is, the more buying power in the area. Fortunately, *Sales and Marketing*

Exhibit 14.1 Account Forecasting Form

Account Marketing Plan
Customer Name.*
Current status (continued)

________________ Date

________________ Salesman #

*If split account, indicate % sales credited and only show that portion below

Product (group by division)	19__ Sales $	Estimated 19__ Sales $**	Forecast 19__ Sales		Total Sales Account Potential $
			$	Quantities	

**Estimate based on latest available sales figures.

Source: Harry R. White, *Sales Forecasting,* Glenview, Ill.: Scott, Foresman and Company, 1984), 41. Used with permission.

SALES TREND

INCREASING THE ACCURACY OF SALESPERSON FORECASTS

Ampertif is a manufacturer of data storage systems for mainframe computers. The company operates on a carefully developed five-year plan. The plan details everything from market conditions to projected sales, inventory, production, shipping dates, and cash flow. Management analyzes the plan on a daily basis, reviews it monthly, revises it quarterly, and rewrites it annually. Ampertif had sales of $38 million in 1985 and forecasts sales of $175 million by 1990.

A critical part in the development and implementation of this plan is the forecasting information provided by salespeople. Salespeople file a monthly report that lists prospects, expected closing and shipping dates, and the value and probability of a sale. A salesperson can get into as much trouble for failing to forecast a sale as he or she can for failing to achieve a forecasted sale. The company continually emphasizes the importance of accurate forecasts to their salespeople. For example, if a salesperson indicates a 90 percent chance to close a sale, the company *expects* the sale to be made.

Donald Orr, chief operating officer, suggests, "Some people think we're nuts for being so fine-tuned, but look what it has done for us. If you constantly analyze, you overcome surprises before they happen." The results seem to bear him out, as Ampertif's sales have been within 3 percent of forecasts for the past three years.

Source: "Ampertif Tolerates No Surprises," *Sales and Marketing Management*, February 1987, 18–19.

Management provides these calculations for areas in the United States on an annual basis.

An example of the BPI data provided by *Sales and Marketing Management* is presented in Exhibit 14.2. BPIs and other data are available for all counties in a state and for the major cities and metropolitan areas. The information in the figure suggests that the BPI is 1.2829 for Oklahoma, .2976 for the Tulsa metropolitan area, and .0232 for Payne County. This means that 1.2829 percent, .2976 percent, and .0232 percent of total U.S. buying power resides in Oklahoma, Tulsa metro, and Payne County, respectively. Sales managers can use the BPI to divide total market and company forecasts into more disaggregate forecasts. For example, assume that you are the Oklahoma district sales manager for a marketer of cosmetics. The cosmetic industry forecasts that U.S. sales of cosmetics will be $500 million in 1989. The calculations needed to translate this U. S. market forecast into market and sales forecasts for your district and areas within your district are presented in Exhibit 14.3. Using the appropriate BPIs, you are able to forecast total cosmetic sales in 1989 for Oklahoma, Tulsa metro, and Payne County as $6,414,500, $1,488,000, and $116,000, respectively. Then, by using your firm's market share in each of these areas, you can translate the market forecasts into sales forecasts for your firm.

Exhibit 14.2 **BPI Data**

OKLA. S&MM ESTIMATES — $$ EFFECTIVE BUYING INCOME 1986

METRO AREA / County / City	Total EBI ($000)	Median Hsld. EBI	% of Hslds. by EBI Group: (A) $10,000–$19,999 (B) $20,000–$34,999 (C) $35,000–$49,999 (D) $50,000 & Over — A	B	C	D	Buying Power Index
ENID	**789,542**	**23,126**	**24.0**	**28.8**	**16.6**	**11.8**	**.0275**
Garfield	789,542	23,126	24.0	28.8	16.6	11.8	.0275
• Enid	642,833	22,804	24.4	28.8	16.3	11.5	.0235
SUBURBAN TOTAL	146,709	24,845	22.0	28.9	18.1	13.0	.0040
LAWTON	**1,202,991**	**21,785**	**28.2**	**28.1**	**14.9**	**11.5**	**.0423**
Comanche	1,202,991	21,785	28.2	28.1	14.9	11.5	.0423
• Lawton	913,784	21,650	28.7	27.7	15.2	11.3	.0345
SUBURBAN TOTAL	289,207	22,402	25.8	30.5	13.6	12.3	.0078
OKLAHOMA CITY	**11,916,563**	**23,700**	**23.7**	**28.0**	**16.5**	**13.3**	**.4361**
Canadian	878,749	29,530	18.3	29.5	22.4	16.0	.0286
Cleveland	1,932,107	25,835	22.0	29.2	18.9	13.7	.0701
• Norman	933,784	21,603	25.3	25.3	15.1	13.0	.0406
Logan	329,203	21,855	23.6	26.9	14.9	12.4	.0102
McClain	247,968	22,445	21.9	28.8	15.9	10.3	.0085
Oklahoma	7,881,861	23,127	24.6	27.9	15.6	13.4	.2957
Midwest City	647,662	25,125	25.2	31.2	18.2	13.0	.0245
• Oklahoma City	5,620,413	22,271	24.7	27.2	14.9	12.9	.2157
Pottawatomie	646,675	20,122	24.7	25.8	14.7	9.8	.0230
• Shawnee	300,794	18,327	24.6	24.6	12.9	8.8	.0132
SUBURBAN TOTAL	5,061,572	26,195	22.2	29.8	18.9	14.1	.1666
TULSA	**8,783,228**	**23,388**	**23.4**	**29.6**	**16.1**	**12.6**	**.2976**
Creek	749,766	22,716	22.2	28.8	16.5	10.5	.0244
Osage	422,799	20,308	24.1	29.6	13.2	8.0	.0123
Rogers	613,780	23,408	20.9	28.4	19.3	12.5	.0186
Tulsa	6,440,071	23,409	24.2	28.3	15.8	13.1	.2272
• Tulsa	4,924,022	22,480	25.2	27.3	14.8	13.3	.1773
Wagoner	556,806	25,480	19.3	28.9	17.9	13.5	.0151
SUBURBAN TOTAL	3,859,206	24,510	21.4	30.0	17.7	11.6	.1203
OTHER COUNTIES							
Adair	133,643	13,537	28.2	23.5	7.3	3.3	.0048
Alfalfa	71,947	19,403	25.3	25.8	13.2	9.7	.0025
Atoka	106,344	13,987	29.6	19.6	8.0	6.1	.0041
Beaver	87,838	23,141	23.0	32.4	12.9	11.6	.0024
Beckham	226,305	17,853	24.1	25.2	12.2	8.0	.0105
Blaine	147,868	20,629	22.7	24.8	15.2	11.2	.0049
Bryan	249,353	13,476	30.6	19.3	7.4	4.5	.0095
Caddo	319,494	18,211	25.3	24.7	10.7	10.4	.0118
Carter	482,667	19,541	24.0	26.1	13.1	9.9	.0177
Cherokee	269,236	15,088	30.2	23.0	8.2	6.0	.0097
Choctaw	117,520	12,667	26.4	20.3	7.8	4.1	.0044
Cimarron	36,291	16,833	32.1	25.9	8.9	5.9	.0013
Coal	40,117	12,458	29.6	20.1	4.6	4.3	.0014
Cotton	57,772	14,925	28.8	24.9	8.7	3.2	.0021
Craig	125,449	16,308	30.8	25.6	8.2	5.7	.0054
Custer	396,793	22,852	22.4	24.6	15.2	15.5	.0158
Delaware	216,090	14,242	32.6	22.7	6.8	4.5	.0077
Dewey	73,529	23,415	21.7	21.8	18.2	16.4	.0021
Ellis	61,606	20,208	26.8	25.7	13.5	11.3	.0019
Garvin	304,719	19,359	25.0	25.0	14.0	9.6	.0106
Grady	445,295	19,643	25.6	26.2	13.0	9.9	.0153
Grant	69,995	19,806	26.6	26.5	12.7	10.3	.0023
Greer	57,842	12,686	26.5	21.4	5.8	5.1	.0019
Harmon	27,683	10,029	29.6	12.7	3.3	4.5	.0010
Harper	47,679	21,167	23.9	30.9	12.1	9.3	.0015
Haskell	96,029	13,940	29.3	19.1	8.2	6.3	.0035
Hughes	108,258	12,735	28.8	20.0	6.8	4.3	.0042
Jackson	269,453	17,192	32.2	25.4	9.9	6.5	.0116
Jefferson	58,285	11,926	29.3	19.4	5.3	3.2	.0022
Johnston	69,574	11,377	28.9	15.3	7.1	4.1	.0022
Kay	618,215	22,589	24.3	27.6	15.4	12.4	.0212
Kingfisher	163,638	22,905	22.8	31.0	16.4	9.7	.0061
Kiowa	108,408	13,409	27.9	20.5	8.0	5.1	.0041
Latimer	74,514	13,393	27.1	21.3	7.2	5.0	.0024
Le Flore	357,247	15,494	30.1	24.3	8.7	4.9	.0124
Lincoln	300,106	19,343	24.3	28.5	12.5	7.6	.0097
Love	75,536	17,195	26.0	26.1	9.5	7.5	.0023
McCurtain	242,400	13,123	30.1	19.8	7.9	3.4	.0096
McIntosh	140,650	14,335	29.4	21.9	9.3	3.5	.0056
Major	90,341	20,000	26.9	27.0	12.5	10.5	.0033
Marshall	111,189	14,404	30.8	21.2	8.5	5.8	.0038
Mayes	321,720	18,508	27.5	26.1	13.1	7.3	.0110
Murray	110,544	16,762	28.8	26.0	[illegible]	[illegible]	.0019
Muskogee	655,856	17,287	25.5	25.3	11.0	7.5	.0243
Muskogee	412,025	16,410	26.2	23.7	9.9	8.2	.0172
Noble	134,717	20,776	26.7	27.9	12.6	11.3	.0044
Nowata	119,575	21,031	22.4	29.7	14.0	8.5	.0035
Okfuskee	97,491	14,875	27.7	20.5	10.4	6.5	.0032
Okmulgee	369,374	16,865	26.9	24.2	11.5	7.6	.0126
Ottawa	299,006	16,742	29.8	26.4	9.7	5.5	.0110
Pawnee	190,615	20,622	25.3	27.2	12.6	11.5	.0058
Payne	667,233	17,180	28.2	23.0	11.8	8.7	.0232
Pittsburg	366,266	15,782	29.5	25.3	8.8	4.6	.0132
Pontotoc	322,521	16,846	25.2	25.2	11.1	7.2	.0127
Pushmataha	96,149	12,684	30.7	19.1	5.5	4.3	.0033
Roger Mills	77,417	24,400	21.6	28.7	12.9	18.3	.0024
Seminole	279,438	18,089	24.7	25.0	12.0	9.0	.0092
□ Sequoyah	238,850	14,182	32.3	22.5	6.7	3.5	.0088
Stephens	503,594	21,876	23.5	27.6	15.5	11.1	.0169
Texas	183,614	21,663	26.2	31.3	14.1	9.0	.0069
Tillman	78,895	12,064	31.0	17.4	4.7	4.5	.0030
Washington	713,692	29,353	18.6	25.7	18.3	22.2	.0219
Washita	164,087	22,528	24.2	29.0	13.7	13.1	.0054
Woods	127,092	20,840	26.0	25.8	12.6	13.4	.0045
Woodward	286,383	27,708	20.5	26.7	19.5	17.3	.0111
TOTAL METRO COUNTIES	**22,931,174**	**23,224**	**24.0**	**28.1**	**16.1**	**12.7**	**.8123**
TOTAL STATE	**36,153,371**	**20,814**	**25.1**	**26.8**	**14.1**	**10.9**	**1.2829**

S&MM/1987 SURVEY OF BUYING POWER C-145

Source: "Survey of Buying Power," *Sales and Marketing Management*, July 27, 1987, C-145.

The BPI is an extremely useful tool for forecasting, since it is readily available and updated on an annual basis. It is most appropriate for often purchased consumer goods due to the factors used in calculating the index for each area. Marketers of durable consumer goods or industrial products may not find the BPI sufficiently accurate for their needs. In these situations other market factors must be identified and used. For example, Pitney Bowes's U.S. Business Systems Division uses *growth in business employment* as a market factor for forecasting purposes.[6]

Exhibit 14.3 **Market Factor Calculations**

	Oklahoma	Tulsa Metro	Payne County
1989 U.S. market forecast	$500,000,000	$500,000,000	$500,000,000
BPI	1.2829%	0.2976%	0.0232%
1989 area market forecast	$6,414,500	$1,488,000	$116,000
Area market share	20%	35%	10%
1989 Area sales forecast	$1,282,900	$520,800	$11,600

Another approach is for a firm to develop a buying power index for its specific situation. For example, a general aviation aircraft marketer developed a buying power index for its products in each county in the United States. The basic formula was

$$\text{Index} = 5I + 3AR + 2P/10$$

where I = Percentage of U.S. disposable income in county
AR = Percentage of U.S. aircraft registrations in county
P = Percentage of U.S. registered pilots in county

These calculations produced an index for each county that could be translated and used like the BPI. The firm could take U.S. forecasts provided by the industry trade association and convert them to market and sales forecasts for each county using their calculated indices and market shares.

The use of market factor methods is widespread in the sales management area. Indices such as BPI or those developed by specific firms and other market factor methods can be extremely valuable forecasting tools for sales managers. These indices and market factors should be continually evaluated and improved over time. They can be assessed by comparing actual sales in an area to the market factor value for the area. For example, the general aviation aircraft marketer found high correlations between actual aircraft sales in a county and the county indices. This finding provided support for the use of the calculated index as an indirect forecasting tool.

Combination Approaches and Methods. Since forecasting is such a difficult task, it is generally advisable to use multiple approaches and methods for each forecast. Each forecasting approach and method has certain advantages and disadvantages, and by combining approaches and methods, sales managers can capitalize on the advantages of each. Furthermore, if different approaches and methods produce the same basic forecast, sales management has some support for the validity of the forecast. If not, sales management knows that corrective action is needed.

Thus, the basic task is not to identify one specific forecasting approach or method to be used exclusively, since it is best to use different forecasting methods in combination approaches. The Miracle Adhesives Corporation example illustrates the use of elements of both the bottom-up and top-down approaches to produce accurate forecasts.

ESTABLISHING SALES QUOTAS

Sales managers need valid and timely forecasts for establishing sales quotas and selling budgets. *Quotas* are organizational objectives that are to be achieved by sales managers and salespeople. The use of different types of quotas for evaluating salesperson performance will be discussed in detail in Chapter 16. Our discussion in this section focuses on the development of sales quotas throughout the sales organization.

A **sales quota** represents a reasonable sales objective for a territory, district, region, or zone. Since a sales forecast represents an expected level of firm sales for a defined geographic area, time period, and strategy, there should be a close relationship between the sales forecast and the sales quota. Bottom-up and/or top-down approaches might be used to develop sales forecasts that are translated into sales quotas.

Another recommended approach is to use associative statistical forecasting methods such as multiple regression.[7] A market response framework to guide this type of approach is presented in Figure 14.5. Depending upon the planning and control unit of interest (territory, district, region, or zone), different determinants of market response (sales, market share, etc.) might be important. However, these determinants can be classified as either environmental, organizational, or salesperson factors. Once the determinant and market response factors are identified, their values for each planning and control unit in the previous period must be measured.

Statistical packages can then be used to estimate the parameters of the regression equation. For example, if you are a district sales manager interested in forecasting territory sales, you would identify and measure specific environmental, organizational, and salesperson factors as well as sales for each territory in the previous year. You could then develop a regression model of the following form:

$$\text{Territory sales} = a + (b1)(\text{environmental factor}) + (b2)(\text{organizational factor}) + (b3)(\text{salesperson factor})$$

The a, b1, b2, and b3 values are the model parameters supplied by the regression procedure to define the relationship between the determinant factors and territory sales.

Although this type of model might be useful, it suffers from two basic weaknesses. First, it incorporates only the independent effects of the determinant variables, yet these variables are highly interrelated. Second, this type of equation is linear, yet the determinant variable relationships are probably nonlinear. These weaknesses can

Figure 14.5 **Market Response Framework**

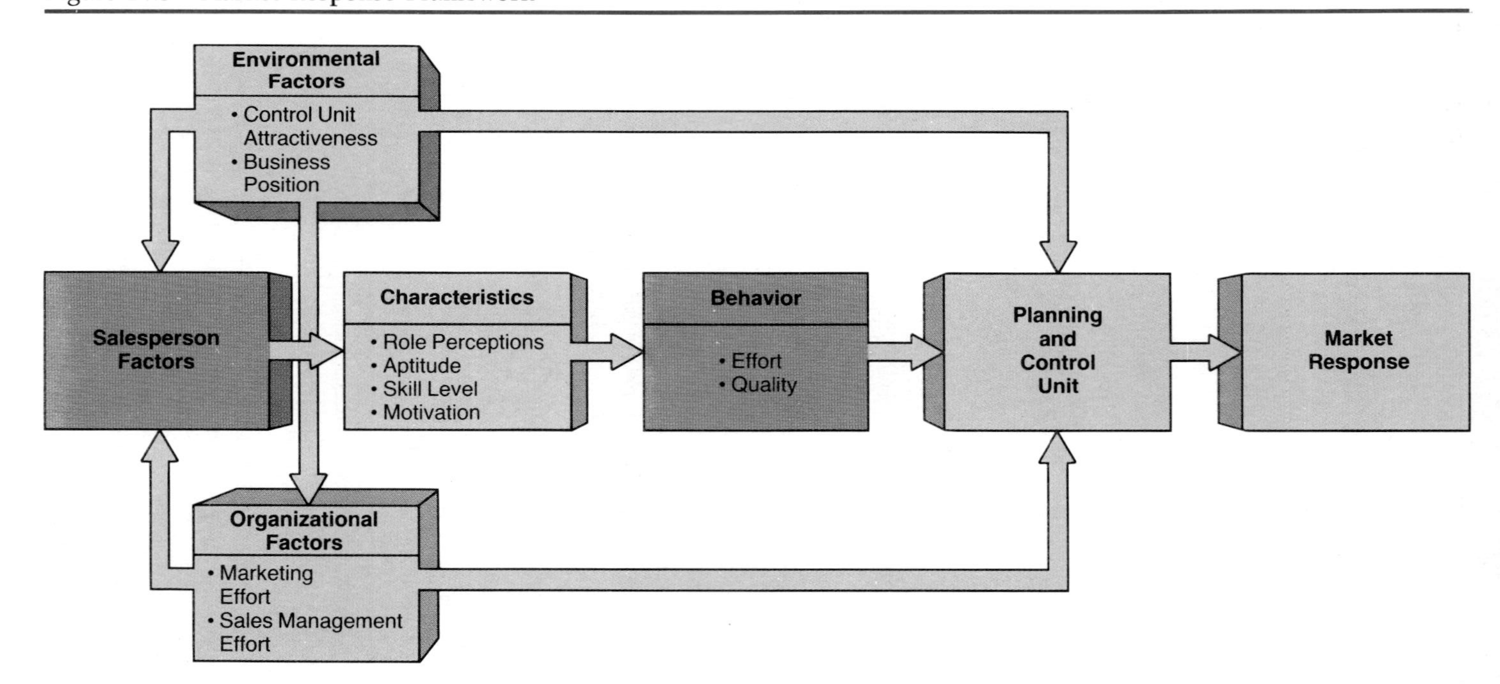

These are the types of factors that affect market response for any planning and control unit, whether it be accounts, territories, districts, regions, or zones. Market response might be profits, market share, or some other response, but sales is usually the market response variable of interest to sales managers.

Source: Raymond W. LaForge and David W. Cravens, "A Market Response Model for Sales Management Decision Making," *Journal of Personal Selling and Sales Management,* Fall/Winter 1981–1982, 14. Used with permission.

Exhibit 14.4 **Regression Model Example**

$$\text{Territory sales} = (800.82)(\text{potential}^{.53})(\text{concentration}^{.03})(\text{experience}^{.08})(\text{span of control}^{-.55})$$

	Territory 1	Territory 2	Territory 3
Potential (no. of persons employed by firms in customer industry located in territory)	114,000	125,000	87,000
Concentration (no. of persons employed by the large plants in customer industry located in territory)	94,000	52,000	12,000
Experience (months salesperson has been with company)	30	10	20
Span of control (no. of salespeople supervised by sales manager)	5	8	10
Territory sales forecast	$586,000	$238,400	$173,200

Source: Adapted from Adrian B. Ryans and Charles B. Weinberg, "Territory Sales Response Models: Stability Over Time," *Journal of Marketing Research,* May 1987, 231, published by the American Marketing Association. Used with permission.

be addressed by performing the linear regression on the logarithms of the actual data, producing a multiplicative power function of the following form:

$$\text{Territory sales} = (a)(\text{environmental factor})^{b1} \times (\text{organizational factor})^{b2} \times (\text{salesperson factor})^{b3}$$

This function is nonlinear and incorporates interactions through the multiplication of determinant variables.

A specific example illustrating this type of function is presented in Exhibit 14.4. The environmental factors are *potential* and *concentration,* the salesperson factor is *experience,* and the organizational factor is *closeness of supervision.* The data are for three territories and are used in the model to generate sales forecasts for each territory individually. This regression model indicates that the higher the territory potential, account concentration, and level of salesperson experience are, the higher the territory sales will be. The larger the span of control is, the lower the territory sales. The exponents in the model suggest that territory sales are most affected by territory potential and span of control. Thus, the regression model generates a specific sales forecast for each territory, and it also provides information concerning relationships between determinant factors and sales.

The regression forecasting approach develops sales forecasts that explicitly consider the characteristics of a territory or other planning and control unit. Thus, these regression forecasts can be translated directly into sales quotas. For example, the sales forecasts for the three territories in Exhibit 14.4 ($586,000, $238,400, and $173,200), represent expected sales levels given the potential, concentration, experience, and span of control evaluations for each territory. Sales management might use these regression sales forecasts as sales quotas for each territory. Alternatively, sales management might adjust the forecasts up or down due to information about the territories not incorporated in the regression model. In any case, the territory sales forecasts provide the basis for establishing the territory sales quotas.

The regression approach can be used to develop sales forecasts and establish sales quotas at all sales organization levels.[8] The determinant variables and measures are typically different depending upon whether the control unit is a territory, district, region, or zone. Nevertheless, accurate sales forecasts are critical for establishing valid sales quotas at all sales organization levels.

ESTABLISHING SELLING BUDGETS

Budgeting takes place throughout a corporate organization. A corporation has limited resources that must be allocated to business units, which in turn must assign resources to the functional departments of each business unit. Within the marketing function the available resources must be allocated across the different elements of the marketing mix. Of special interest to us is the allocation of promotional resources between advertising and personal selling. The resources earmarked for personal selling represent the total **selling budget**. Sales management must then determine the best way to allocate these sales resources throughout the sales organization and across the different selling activities. This is the key sales management budgeting task.

Since we discussed salesforce expenditures at the business unit and marketing strategy levels in Chapter 5, our major concern in this section is the development of specific selling budgets within the sales organization. Our discussion therefore assumes that the total level of selling expenditures has been established and that the sales organization is faced with determining the best way to spend these resources.

This budgeting process takes place after sales forecasts have been generated. The sales forecasts provide sales management with the expected level of sales for the next planning period, usually a year. These forecasts are then translated into sales quotas for each territory, district, region, and zone. The quotas represent a plan for sales results for the next period. Selling budgets represent a plan for selling expenses for the next period. Combining the sales quotas and selling budgets results in a profit plan for the next period. The budgeting process is intended to instill cost consciousness and profit awareness throughout the sales organization.

Exhibit 14.5 **Selling Expense Categories in Budget**

Classification	Actual 1988	Original 1989 budget	April revision	July revision	October revision
Compensation Expenses Salaries Commissions Bonuses Total					
Travel Expenses Lodging Food Transportation Misc. Total					
Administrative Expenses Recruiting Training Meetings Sales offices					

Selling budgets are developed at all levels of the sales organization and for all key expenditure categories. Our discussion will focus on the major selling expense categories and methods for establishing specific expenditure levels within the budget.

Selling Expense Categories

Firms differ considerably in how they define their selling expense categories. Nevertheless, all sales organizations should carefully plan expenditures for the major selling and sales management activities and for the different levels in the sales organization structure. The selling budget addresses controllable expenses, not uncontrollable ones. Typical selling budget expense categories are presented in Exhibit 14.5.

Both the total expenditures for each of these categories and sales management budget responsibility must be determined. Sales management budget responsibility depends upon the degree of centralization or decentralization in the sales organization. In general, more centralized sales organizations will place budget responsibility at higher sales management levels. For example, if salesforce recruitment and selection takes place at the regional level, then the regional sales managers will have responsibility for this budget category. A typical situation is where the sales management activity occurs at all management levels. For example, training activities might be performed at national, zone, regional, and district levels. In this case, the budgeting process must address how much to spend on overall training and how to allocate training expenditures to the different organizational levels.

The basic objective in budgeting for each category is to determine the lowest expenditure level necessary to *achieve the sales quotas*. Notice that we did not say the lowest possible expenditure level. Sales managers might cut costs and improve profitability in the short run, but if expenditures for training, travel, and so forth are too low, long-run sales and profits will be sacrificed. If, however, expenses can be reduced by more effective or more efficient spending, then these productivity improvements can produce increased profitability in the long run. Achieving productivity improvements has been one of the most demanding tasks facing sales managers in recent years, since increases in field selling costs and extremely competitive markets have put tremendous pressure on firm profitability.

Methods for Determining the Selling Budget

Determining expenditure levels for each selling expense category is extremely difficult. Although there is no perfect way to arrive at these expenditure levels, two approaches warrant our attention: the percentage of sales method and the objective and task method.[9]

Probably the most often used, the **percentage of sales method** calculates an expenditure level for each category by multiplying an expenditure percentage times forecasted sales. The effectiveness of the percentage of sales method depends upon the accuracy of sales forecasts and the appropriateness of the expenditure percentages. If the sales forecasts are not accurate, the selling budgets will be incorrect, regardless of the expenditure percentages used. If sales forecasts are accurate, then the key is determining the expenditure percentages. Fortunately, typical expenditure percentages for different industries are readily available from published sources, as illustrated in Exhibit 14.6. These typical percentages should be viewed as guidelines only. Sales

SALES TECHNOLOGY

BUDGETING AND PERSONAL COMPUTERS

Developing the selling budget used to be a dreaded and time-consuming process at Heublin Inc. However, the vodka marketing division has cut the process to under two hours through the use of personal computers. The new process was explained by Neil Kelliher, vice-president of vodka marketing:

> When we developed our 1987 budget last September, three senior managers gathered at six-thirty one evening to evaluate various spending, costing, and volume scenarios for a mix of brands. In a period of about one hour we developed a mini P&L containing all of the necessary variables. Then, we played "what if," inserting the changes on our PCs and seeing the resulting P&L. Forty-five minutes later we had results in hand and a best option to proceed with.

Source: "Creating Budgets is a Snap at Heublin," *Sales and Marketing Management,* January 1987, 76–77.

Exhibit 14.6 **Selling Expense Percentages**

	Compensation		T&E Expenses		Total	
Industry	**1984**	**1983**	**1984**	**1983**	**1984**	**1983**
Consumer goods						
Durable goods	2.1%	4.2%	1.3%	2.2%	3.4%	9.0%
Ethical pharmaceuticals, surgical supplies and equipment	5.2	5.2	1.7	3.1	6.9	16.9
Food	1.9	1.6	0.5	0.4	2.4	3.5
Major household items	3.3	2.1	0.7	0.7	4.0	4.4
Proprietary drugs and toiletries	1.1	1.3	0.8	N.A.	1.9	7.9
Industrial goods						
Automotive parts and accessories	2.6	3.1	1.0	1.6	3.6	5.5
Building materials	1.2	1.5	0.5	0.7	1.7	5.4
Chemicals and petroleum	2.4	1.3	0.4	0.5	2.8	1.4
Computers	4.2	*	1.7	*	5.9	*
Containers, packaging materials, & paper	1.0	0.8	0.2	0.1	1.2	1.6
Electrical materials	1.6	0.6	0.6	0.6	2.2	3.9
Electronics and instruments	3.4	1.9	1.3	1.4	4.7	5.2
Fabricated metals (heavy)	1.0	2.0	0.4	0.8	1.4	3.8
Fabricated metals (light)	2.5	1.9	1.4	0.9	3.9	4.9
Fabrics and apparel	2.2	0.9	0.5	0.4	2.7	5.3
Iron and steel	1.4	0.8	0.6	0.3	2.0	2.4
Machinery (heavy)	2.0	2.3	0.7	0.7	2.7	5.4
Machinery (light)	3.3	3.9	1.3	1.5	4.6	9.2
Office and educational equipment	2.1	*	1.2	*	3.3	*
Printing and publishing	5.2	3.6	1.3	0.9	6.5	9.7
Rubber, plastics, and leather	1.9	1.0	1.0	0.8	2.9	4.4

Source: "Survey of Selling Costs," *Sales and Marketing Management,* February 18, 1985, 56.

management should adjust them up or down to reflect the unique aspects of their sales organization.

The **objective and task method** takes an entirely different approach. In its most basic form, it is a form of zero-based budgeting. In essence, each sales manager prepares a separate budget request that stipulates the objectives to be achieved, the tasks required to achieve these objectives, and the costs associated with performing the necessary tasks. These requests are reviewed, and, through an iterative process, selling budgets are approved. Many variations of the objective and task method are used by different sales organizations.

In reality, the process of establishing a selling budget is an involved one that typically incorporates various types of analysis, many meetings, and much politicizing. The process has, however, been streamlined in many firms through the use of computer technology. An example of using personal computers to improve the budgeting process is presented in "Sales Technology: Budgeting and Personal Computers."

SUMMARY

1. **Discuss the different types of forecasts used by sales managers.** There are four types of forecasts of most interest to sales managers. A market potential forecast predicts the best possible level of total industry sales, while a market forecast predicts the expected level, assuming a specific industry structure and strategy. Similarly, a sales potential forecast predicts the best possible level of firm sales, while a sales forecast predicts the likely firm sales given a specific strategy. All of these forecasts must include a geographic area and time period definition.

2. **Describe the top-down and bottom-up forecasting approaches used by sales managers.** In top-down approaches, company forecasts are made at the business unit level, then are broken down by sales managers into zone, region, district, territory, and account forecasts. In bottom-up approaches, forecasts are initially made at the account level, then sales managers combine them into territory, district, region, zone, and ultimately company forecasts.

3. **Explain the use of the salesforce-composite and market-factor forecasting methods.** The salesforce composite method is a bottom-up approach where salespeople provide forecasts for their accounts. These account forecasts are then combined to produce forecasts at the territory, district, region, and zone levels. The market factor method is a top-down approach where sales managers use some type of market factor to break down aggregate forecasts into territory, district, region, and zone forecasts. The Buying Power Index (BPI) is a popular market factor method for sales managers.

4. **Describe how sales quotas are established, including the use of multiple-regression procedures.** Sales quotas are sales objectives at the territory, district, region, or zone levels. Sales forecasts provide a basis for establishing sales quotas, and they can also be established using bottom-up or top-down approaches. When multiple regression procedures are used, different determinants of market reponse are chosen, depending on the planning and control unit of interest.

5. **Discuss the importance of and methods for establishing selling budgets.** Sales forecasts provide a direct basis for establishing selling budgets. Whereas the sales forecast predicts sales, the selling budget helps to control the selling costs needed to generate these sales. Selling budgets should be established for the major categories of controllable selling expenses and assigned to different sales management levels throughout the sales organization. The percentage of sales and objective and task methods are often used to set the selling budgets. The basic objective of these budgets is to keep selling costs at the lowest level that will still achieve sales quotas. Long-run profitability depends upon sales management's ability to allocate selling expenditures in more productive ways.

Key Terms

- forecast
- market potential
- market forecast
- sales potential
- sales forecast
- top-down approaches
- bottom-up approaches
- salesforce composite method
- market factor method
- buying power index (BPI)
- sales quotas
- selling budget
- percentage of sales method
- objective and task method

Review Questions

1. What is meant by the statement, "All sales management decisions are based on some type of forecast?"
2. Why is it important to differentiate between market potentials, market forecasts, sales potentials, and sales forecasts?
3. What are the sales management implications of the following statement: "The expected amount of sales to an account determines how much selling effort the account should receive, and the amount of selling effort an account receives determines the expected sales from an account."
4. What potential biases might be expected when salespeople are used to provide estimates for forecasts in the salesforce composite method? What can be done to eliminate or reduce these biases and generate more accurate estimates?
5. What is the market factor method for forecasting? How would you develop a market factor method in any selling situation?
6. What is the general approach for using multiple regression analysis to establish sales quotas? What are the advantages and disadvantages of the multiple regression method?
7. What is the Buying Power Index (BPI)? How is it calculated? How is it used?
8. Why should sales managers use multiple forecasting approaches and methods? What should be done when these multiple approaches and methods produce consistent forecasts? Inconsistent forecasts?
9. Why are accurate forecasts necessary for establishing sales quotas and selling budgets? What effect will inaccurate forecasts have on the process of establishing quotas and budgets?
10. Compare and contrast the percentage of sales and the objective and task methods for establishing selling budgets.

Application Exercises

1. You are a sales manager for a manufacturer and marketer of construction equipment. Your firm has reasonably good data concerning its market share in different areas throughout the country. In addition, the trade association for the construction equipment industry

has been able to develop accurate market forecasts. Your firm is, however, having trouble developing sales forecasts for specific sales districts. Describe how you would develop a market factor index that could be used by your firm to translate market forecasts and market share data into sales forecasts for each sales district. Discuss what would be included in the index and how it would be used once developed.

2. Contact three different sales organizations about their selling budget process. Compare and contrast their methods. Evaluate the three approaches.
3. Contact three different sales organizations about their process for establishing sales quotas. Compare and contrast their methods. Evaluate the three approaches.
4. As district sales manager for the XYZ Company, you are interested in establishing sales quotas for the eight salespeople in your district. Sales planners at the XYZ Company have developed the following multiple regression model of territory sales:

$$\text{Territory sales} = 800 \times \text{potential}^{.53} \times \text{concentration}^{.03} \times \text{experience}^{.08} \times \text{span of control}^{-.55}$$

Calculate a sales forecast for each of your salespeople using these data:

Salesperson	Potential	Concentration	Experience	Span of Control
A	75,000	10,000	5	8
B	100,000	50,000	24	8
C	85,000	40,000	12	8
D	110,000	80,000	18	8
E	90,000	20,000	8	8
F	105,000	30,000	36	8
G	120,000	60,000	20	8
H	115,000	85,000	24	8

How would you use your calculations to establish sales quotas for each salesperson?

5. An industrial marketer of bearings and valves has developed the following market factor index for forecasting purposes:

$$\text{Market factor index} = 6\text{ MS} + 4\text{ ME} / 10$$

where MS = Percentage of U.S. manufacturing sales in area
ME = Percentage of U.S. manufacturing employment in area

Industry sales for 1989 are expected to be $300 million. Using the market factor index and data presented here, calculate a market and sales forecast for each state.

State	MS	ME	Company Market Share
South Carolina	1.5%	2.0%	15%
North Carolina	2.5%	2.3%	25%
Virginia	2.2%	2.1%	20%
Georgia	2.0%	2.5%	18%
Alabama	1.2%	1.4%	10%
Florida	3.0%	3.5%	10%
Mississippi	0.8%	1.1%	5%

Notes

[1] Adapted from William E. Cox, Jr., *Industrial Marketing Research* (New York: Wiley, 1979), 146–148.

[2] Taken from J. Scott Armstrong, Roderick J. Brodie, and Shelby McIntyre, "Forecasting Methods for Marketing: Review of Empirical Research," *Singapore Marketing Review,* March 1987, 7–23.

[3] Reported in Harry R. White, *Sales Forecasting: Timesaving and Profit-Making Strategies That Work* (Glenview, Ill.: Scott, Foresman and Company, 1984), 6–19.

[4] For different classification schemes and more detailed discussion of individual forecasting methods, see Harry R. White (1984); David M. Georgoff and Robert G. Murdick, "Manager's Guide to Forecasting," *Harvard Business Review,* January-February 1986, 113–118; and J. Scott Armstrong, Roderick J. Brodie, and Shelby McIntyre (1987).

[5] See "Survey of Buying Power," *Sales and Marketing Management,* August 15, 1988, for a discussion of the Buying Power Index and for the calculated indices throughout the United States.

[6] "And Now, The Home-Brewed Forecast," *Fortune,* January 20, 1986, 54.

[7] For a review and more complete discussion of this approach, see Adrian B. Ryans and Charles B. Weinberg, "Territory Sales Response," *Journal of Marketing Research,* November 1979, 453–465; and Adrian B. Ryans and Charles B. Weinberg, "Territory Sales Response Models: Stability Over Time," *Journal of Marketing Research,* May 1987, 229–233.

[8] For specific examples of using multiple regression analysis to establish territory sales quotas, see David W. Cravens, Robert B. Woodruff, and James C. Stamper, "An Analytical Approach for Evaluating Sales Territory Performance," *Journal of Marketing,* January 1972, 31–37; and David W. Cravens and Robert B. Woodruff, "An Approach for Determining Criteria of Sales Performance," *Journal of Applied Psychology,* June 1973, 240–247.

[9] See Nigel F. Piercy, "The Marketing Budgeting Process: Marketing Management Implications," *Journal of Marketing,* October 1987, 45–59, for results from a study of the overall marketing budgeting process.

CHAPTER 15

EVALUATING SALES ORGANIZATION EFFECTIVENESS: SALES, COST, PROFITABILITY, AND PRODUCTIVITY ANALYSIS

Learning Objectives:

After completing this chapter, you should be able to

1. Differentiate between sales organization effectiveness and salesperson performance.
2. Define a sales organization audit, and discuss how it should be conducted.
3. Describe how to perform different types of sales analysis for different organizational levels and types of sales.
4. Describe how to perform a cost analysis for a sales organization.
5. Describe how to perform income statement, return on assets managed, and residual income analyses to assess sales organization profitability.
6. Describe how to perform a productivity analysis for a sales organization.

EVALUATING SALES ORGANIZATION EFFECTIVENESS: TWO EXAMPLES

Bindicator is a supplier of measuring instruments to various industries. Although a poor economic climate had depressed industry and company sales, management at Bindicator was interested in making strategic changes to improve the recent poor performance. Determining the appropriate strategic changes required a detailed analysis of current sales effectiveness. Management decided to analyze territory sales results for the previous three years. It quickly became obvious that merely viewing territory sales data did not provide useful information, since the territories were of different size and located in different areas. Management therefore decided to compare actual territory sales to sales quotas and to evaluate territory growth rates. Examples of this analysis follow:

	Actual Sales/Sales Quotas × 100 = Sales Rating			Average Annual Sales Growth Rate		
Territory	**1982**	**1983**	**1984**	**1979-1982**	**1979-1983**	**1979-1984**
A	115	145	162	+16.5%	+18.4%	+20.2%
B	246	238	202	−4.3%	−4.9	−3.6%
C	27	31	36	−6.6%	0.0	+2.7%
D	24	26	34	−12.6%	−7.7%	−2.5%

Management found these results gratifyingly informative. Although overall company sales results had been poor, territories differed considerably when actual territory sales were compared to sales quotas and when territory sales growth rates were evaluated. Investigations into the causes of these wide differences in sales results led to strategic changes that improved sales results. For example, advertising expenditure allocations and sales lead development programs were altered, salesforce deployment changes were made, and procedures for establishing sales quotas improved.

Source: Adapted from Karsten Hellebust, "Bindicator Finds a Fair Measure for Sales Territory Performance," *Sales and Marketing Management,* November 11, 1985, 45–47; and Walter Ambrogi and Donald L. Blair, "Quality Management Applications in a Field Marketing Organization," *Survey of Business,* Spring 1986, 30–31.

In contrast to Bindicator, Eastman Chemical Products had been achieving reasonably good sales results. However, the company was engaged in a quality improvement program to increase sales and profits. Sales were determined to be a key result area and sales dollars the appropriate measure of sales results. A weekly analysis of company sales data indicated tremendous sales deviations. The quality improvement team developed a sales management control system to track down the sales deviations. The system evaluated total company sales. If a deviation occurred, it was pinpointed in the eastern or western area. Then, area sales managers could pinpoint the sales deviations at the district level and district sales managers at the product and customer levels. Further analysis of specific products and accounts was performed to determine the exact cause of these deviations and to develop a plan for improving sales results in the future.

The Bindicator and Eastman Chemical examples illustrate several important points. First, analysis of sales and other sales organization results should be performed on a regular basis, regardless of whether overall results have been satisfactory (Eastman Chemical) or poor (Bindicator). Second, as indicated in the Bindicator example, sales and other results can be analyzed in different ways, with each type of analysis providing different diagnostic information. Finally, as the Eastman Chemical example suggests, analysis of sales organization effectiveness often requires a multi-stage approach to identify specific problem areas.

ASSESSING the success of a sales organization is difficult due to the many factors that must be considered. For example, the success of the sales organization must be differentiated from the success of individual salespeople (see Figure 15.1).[1] Whereas sales organization effectiveness is a function of how well the sales organization achieved its goals and objectives overall, salesperson performance is a function of how well each salesperson performed in his or her particular situation. Thus, salesperson performance contributes to, but does not completely determine, sales organization effectiveness.

As indicated by the Bindicator and Eastman Chemical examples in the opening vignette, sales organization effectiveness must be evaluated in order to determine where problems are so that these problems can be solved. The focus is on the overall sales organization as well as the different levels within the sales organization (territories, districts, regions, and zones). The results of such evaluations are normally general strategic or policy changes. For example, Bindicator altered its advertising expenditure allocations, sales lead development program, salesforce deployment, and procedures for establishing sales quotas based on its sales analysis. Eastman Chemical developed programs to improve relationships with all accounts.

Evaluations of salesperson performance are confined to the people themselves, not the sales organization or sales organization levels. The results of these evaluations are typically tactical in nature. In other words, they lead a sales manager to take

Figure 15.1 **Sales Organization Effectiveness versus Salesperson Performance**

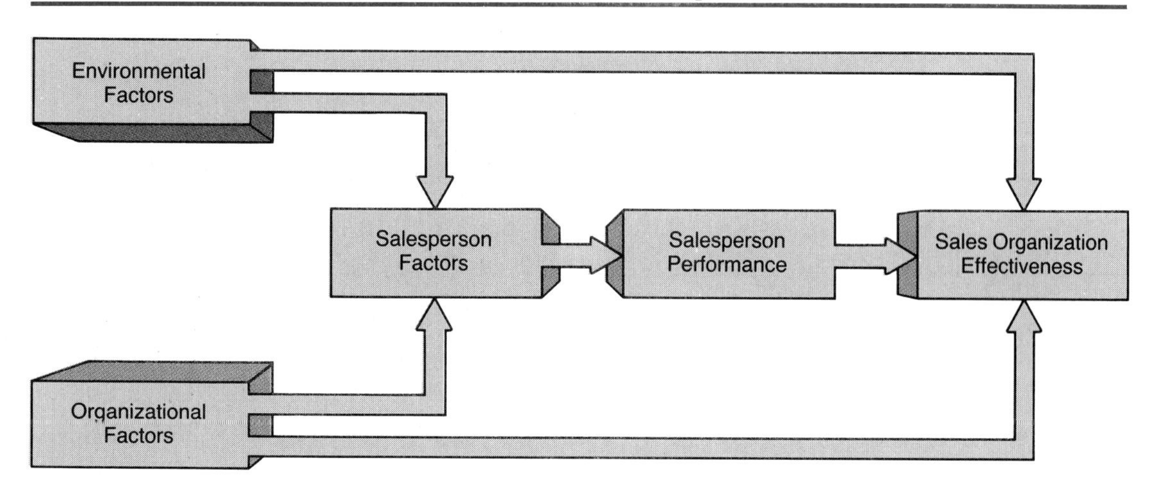

Salesperson performance is an assessment of how well individual salespeople have performed. Sales organization effectiveness is an overall evaluation of the success of the sales organization. Salesperson performance affects, but does not completely determine, sales organization effectiveness.

Source: Adapted from Orville C. Walker, Jr., Gilbert A. Churchill, Jr., and Neil M. Ford, "'Where Do We Go From Here' Selected Conceptual and Empirical Issues Concerning the Motivation and Performance of the Industrial Salesforce," in *Critical Issues in Sales Management: State-of-the-Art and Future Research Needs,* edited by Gerald Albaum and Gilbert A. Churchill, Jr. (Eugene, Ore.: University of Oregon, 1979).

specific actions to improve the performance of an individual salesperson. Generally different actions are warranted for different salespeople, depending upon the areas that need improvement.

This chapter addresses the evaluation of sales organization effectiveness, and Chapter 16 addresses the evaluation of salesperson performance. This chapter begins with a discussion of a sales organization audit, then describes more specific analyses of sales, costs, profits, and productivity to determine sales organization effectiveness.

SALES ORGANIZATION AUDIT

Although the term *audit* is most often used in reference to financial audits performed by accounting firms, the audit concept has been extended to different business functions in recent years. In Chapter 10, a **sales organization audit** was described as a comprehensive, systematic, diagnostic, and prescriptive tool.[2] The purpose of a sales organization audit is:

> . . . to assess the adequacy of a firm's sales management process and to provide direction for improved performance and prescription for needed changes. It is a

tool that should be used by all firms whether or not they are achieving their goals.

This type of audit is the most comprehensive approach for evaluating sales organization effectiveness.

A framework for performing a sales organization audit is presented in Figure 15.2. As indicated in the figure, the audit addresses four major areas: sales organization environment, sales management evaluation, sales organization planning system, and sales management functions. The purpose of the audit is to investigate each of these areas in a systematic and comprehensive way to identify existing or potential problems, determine their causes, and take the necessary corrective action.

The sales organization audit should be performed on a regular basis, not just when problems are evident. One of the major values of an audit is its generation of diagnostic information that can help management correct problems in early stages or eliminate potential problems before they become serious. Since auditing should be of an objective nature, it should be conducted by someone from outside the sales organization. This could be someone from another functional area within the firm or an outside consulting firm.

Although outsiders should conduct the audit, members of the sales organization should be active participants in it. Both sales managers and salespeople often provide much of the information collected. Exhibit 15.1 presents some example questions that should be addressed in a sales organization audit. Answers to these types of questions typically come from members of the sales organization as well as from company records.

Though obviously an expensive and time-consuming process, the sales organization audit generates benefits that usually outweigh the monetary and time costs. This is especially true when they are conducted on a regular basis, since the chances of identifying and correcting potential problems before they become troublesome increases with the regularity of the auditing process.

EVALUATIONS OF SALES ORGANIZATION EFFECTIVENESS

There is no one summary measure of sales organization effectiveness. Sales organizations have multiple goals and objectives and thus multiple factors must be assessed. As illustrated in Figure 15.3, four types of analyses are typically necessary to develop a comprehensive evaluation of any sales organization. Conducting analyses in each of these areas is a complex task for two reasons. First, many different types of analyses can be performed to evaluate sales, cost, profitability, and productivity results. For example, a sales analysis might focus on total sales, sales of specific products, sales to specific customers, or other types of sales and might include sales comparisons to sales quotas, to previous periods, to competitors, or other types of analyses. Second,

Figure 15.2 **Sales Organization Audit Framework**

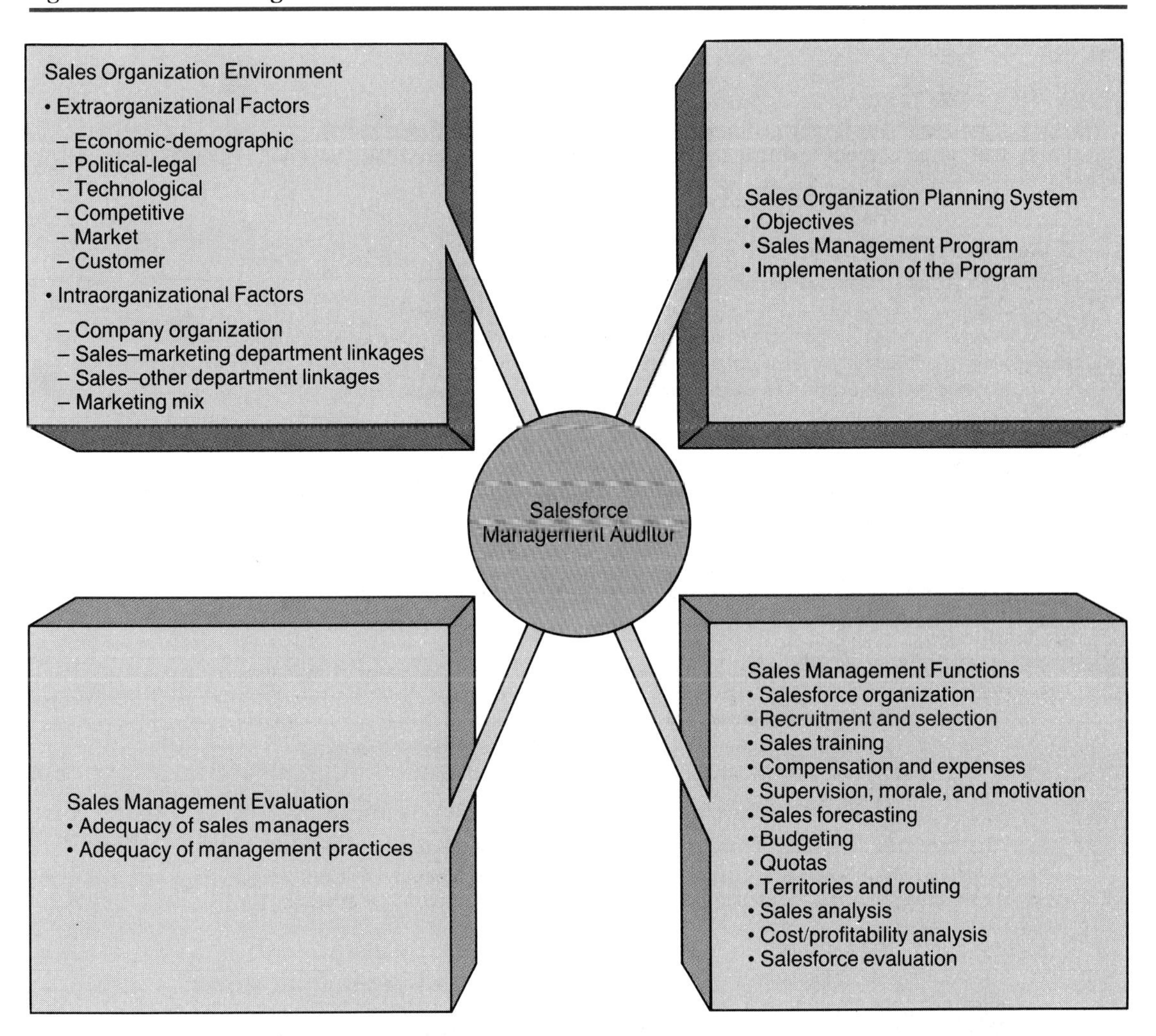

The sales organization audit is the most comprehensive evaluation of sales organization effectiveness. The audit typically provides assessments of the sales organization environment, sales management evaluation, sales organization planning system, and sales management functions.

Source: © 1981 by the Regents of the University of California. Adapted from Alan J. Dubinsky and Richard W. Hansen, "The Sales Force Management Audit," *California Management Review,* Winter 1981, 87, by permission of the Regents.

Exhibit 15.1 Example Questions From A Sales Organization Audit

IV. Sales Management Functions

A. Salesforce Organization

1. How is our salesforce organized (by product, by customer, by territory)?
2. Is this type of organization appropriate, given the current intraorganizational and extraorganizational conditions?
3. Does this type of organization adequately service the needs of our customers?

B. Recruitment and Selection

1. How many salespeople do we have?
2. Is this number adequate in light of our objectives and resources?
3. Are we serving our customers adequately with this number of salespeople?
4. How is our salesforce size determined?
5. What is our turnover rate? What have we done to try to change it?
6. Do we have adequate sources from which to obtain recruits? Have we overlooked some possible sources?
7. Do we have a job description for each of our sales jobs? Is each job description current?
8. Have we enumerated the necessary sales job qualifications? Have they been recently updated? Are they predictive of sales success?
9. Are our selection screening procedures financially feasible and appropriate?
10. Do we use a battery of psychological tests in our selection process? Are the tests valid and reliable?
11. Do our recruitment and selection procedures satisfy the equal employment opportunity guidelines?

C. Sales training

1. How is our sales training program developed? Does it meet the needs of management and sales personnel?
2. Do we establish training objectives before developing and implementing the training program?
3. Is the training program adequate in light of our objectives and resources?
4. What kinds of training do we currently provide our salespeople?
5. Does the training program need revising? What areas of the training program should be improved or deemphasized?
6. What methods do we use to evaluate the effectiveness of our training program?
7. Can we afford to train internally or should we use external sources for training?
8. Do we have an ongoing training program for senior salespeople? Is it adequate?

D. Compensation and Expenses

1. Does our sales compensation plan meet our objectives in light of our financial resources?
2. Is the compensation plan fair, flexible, economical, and easy to understand and to administer?
3. What is the level of compensation, the type of plan, and the frequency of payment?
4. Are the salespeople and management satisfied with the compensation plan?
5. Does the compensation plan ensure that the salespeople perform the necessary sales job activities?
6. Does the compensation plan attract and retain enough quality sales performers?
7. Does the sales expense plan meet our objectives in light of our financial resources?
8. Is the expense plan fair, flexible, and easy to administer? Does it allow for geographical, customer, and/or product differences?
9. Does the expense plan ensure that the necessary sales job activities are performed?
10. Can we easily audit the expenses incurred by our sales personnel?

Source: © 1981 by the Regents of the University of California. Reprinted from Alan J. Dubinsky and Richard W. Hansen, "The Sales Force Management Audit," *California Management Review,* Winter 1981, 90, by permission of the Regents.

Figure 15.3 **Sales Organization Effectiveness Framework**

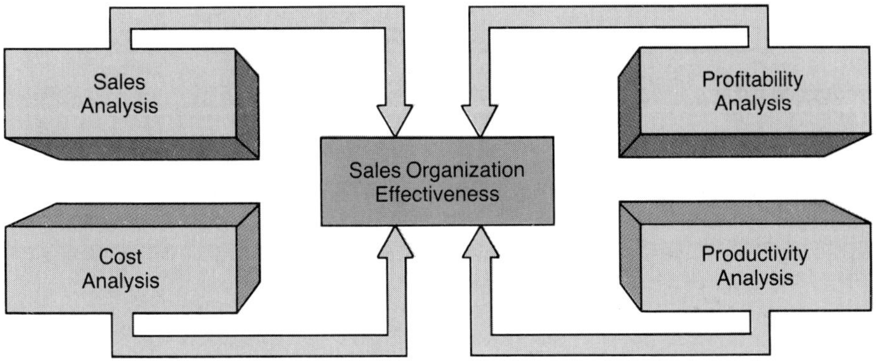

Evaluating sales organization effectiveness requires analyses of sales, costs, profitability, and productivity. Each type of analysis can be performed in different ways, should be performed at different sales organization levels, and produces different evaluative and diagnostic information for sales managers.

separate sales analyses need to be performed for the different levels in the sales organization. Thus, a typical evaluation would include separate sales analyses for sales zones, regions, districts, and territories. This task is even more complex for firms operating in international markets, as suggested in "International Sales: Evaluating Sales Organization Effectiveness."

INTERNATIONAL SALES

EVALUATING SALES ORGANIZATION EFFECTIVENESS

Mastic Corporation is a leading supplier of vinyl construction products. The company developed a computer-based marketing information system to help sales managers monitor market share and product sales by territory and develop market potential forecasts. The information system was limited initially to the U.S. market but has been expanded to cover Canada and other international markets.

Expanding the information system to international markets required that additional data be collected for each included country. For example, information such as prices of foreign siding products, the value of foreign currencies, and differences in tariffs between countries was added to the marketing information system. Mastic Corporation has used this system to evaluate sales organization effectiveness in countries where they currently operate, as well as to help them identify the best international markets for future entry.

Source: Adapted from Tom Eisenhart, "Computer-Aided Marketing," *Business Marketing*, May 1988, 50–52.

Exhibit 15.2 **Use of Sales Organization Effectiveness Analyses**

	Sales Volume	Costs	Profit Contribution	Net Profit	Return on Assets Managed
Product analysis	92%	40%	75%	57%	29%
Customer analysis	91%	18%	41%	24%	10%
Geographic analysis	92%	38%	26%	12%	7%

Source: Adapted from Donald W. Jackson, Jr., Lonnie L. Ostrom, and Kenneth R. Evans, "Measures Used to Evaluate Industrial Marketing Activities," *Industrial Marketing Management,* 11, 1982, 269–274.

Many sales organizations focus their sales organization assessments on sales analysis.[3] The results from one study are presented in Exhibit 15.2. Almost all of the firms in this study employed different types of sales analyses. However, relatively small percentages of firms reported the use of cost, profit contribution, net profit, or return on assets analyses. Each area that should be addressed to evaluate sales organization effectiveness is discussed separately here.

Sales Analysis

Since the basic purpose of a sales organization is to generate sales, **sales analysis** is an obvious and important element of evaluating sales organization effectiveness. The difficulty, however, is in determining exactly what should be analyzed. One key consideration is in defining what is meant by a *sale*. Alternatives include when an order is placed, when an order is shipped, or when payment for an order is received. Defining a sale as when an order is shipped is probably most common. Regardless of the definition used, the sales organization must be consistent and develop an information system to track sales based on whatever sales definition is employed.

Another consideration is whether to focus on *sales dollars* or *sales units*. This can be extremely important in times of price increases or when salespeople have substantial latitude in negotiating selling prices. The sales information in Exhibit 15.3 illustrates how different conclusions may result from analyses of sales dollars or sales units. If just sales dollars are analyzed, all regions in the exhibit would appear to be generating substantial sales growth. However, when sales units are introduced, the dollar sales growth for all regions in 1987 can be attributed almost entirely to price increases, since units sold increased only minimally during this period. The situation is somewhat different in 1988, because all regions increased the number of units sold. However, sales volume for Region 2 is relatively flat, even though units sold increased. This could be caused by either selling more lower-priced products or by using larger price concessions than the other regions. In either case, analysis of sales

Exhibit 15.3 **Sales Dollars versus Sales Units**

	1986		1987		1988	
	Sales Dollars	Sales Units	Sales Dollars	Sales Units	Sales Dollars	Sales Units
Region 1	$40,000,000	400,000	$45,000,000	410,000	$52,000,000	475,000
Region 2	$45,000,000	450,000	$50,000,000	460,000	$52,000,000	500,000
Region 3	$35,000,000	350,000	$40,000,000	360,000	$48,000,000	420,000
Region 4	$50,000,000	500,000	$55,000,000	510,000	$63,000,000	620,000

dollars or sales units provides different types of evaluative information, so it is often useful to include both dollars and units in a sales analysis.

Given a definition of sales and a decision concerning sales dollars versus units, many different sales evaluations can be performed. Several alternative evaluations are presented in Figure 15.4. The critical decision areas are the organizational level of analysis, the type of sales, and the type of analysis.

Organizational Level of Analysis. Sales analysis should be performed for all levels in the sales organization for two basic reasons. First, sales managers at each level need sales analyses at their level and the next level below for evaluation and control purposes. For example, a regional sales manager should have sales analyses for all regions as well as for all districts within his or her region. This makes it possible to assess the sales effectiveness of the region and to determine the sales contribution of each district.

Second, a useful way to identify problem areas in achieving sales effectiveness is to perform a **hierarchical sales analysis**, which consists of evaluating sales results throughout the sales organization from a top-down perspective. Essentially, the analysis begins with total sales for the sales organization and proceeds through each successively lower level in the sales organization. The emphasis is on identifying potential problem areas at each level and then using analysis at lower levels to pinpoint the specific problems. An example of a hierarchical sales analysis is presented in Figure 15.5.

In this example, sales for Region 3 appear to be much lower than those for the other regions, so the analysis proceeds to investigate the sales for all of the districts in Region 3. Low sales are identified for District 4, then District 4 sales are analyzed by territory. The results of this analysis suggest potential sales problems within Territory 5. Additional analyses would be performed to determine why sales are so low for Territory 5 and to take corrective action to increase sales from this territory. The hierarchical approach to sales analysis provides an efficient way to conduct a sales analysis and to identify major areas of sales problems.

Figure 15.4 **Sales Analysis Framework**

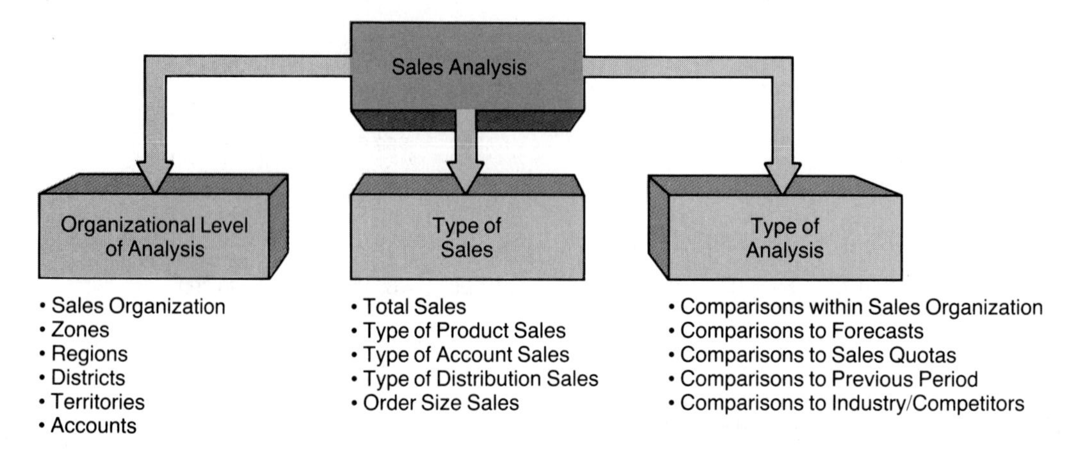

Sales analysis can be performed at different organization levels and for different types of sales, and can employ different types of analysis.

Type of Sales. The analysis in Figure 15.5 addresses only total firm sales at each organizational level. It is usually desirable to evaluate different types of sales such as

- Sales by product type or specific products
- Sales by account type or specific accounts
- Sales by type of distribution method
- Sales by order size

The hierarchical analysis in Figure 15.5 could have included sales by product type, account type, or other type of sales at each level. Or once the potential sales problem in Territory 5 has been isolated, analysis of different types of sales could be performed to define the sales problem more fully. An example analysis is presented in Figure 15.6. This example suggests especially low sales volume for Product Type A and to Account Type B. Additional analyses within these product and account types would be needed to determine why sales are low in these areas and what needs to be done to improve sales effectiveness.

The analysis of different types of sales at different organizational levels increases management's ability to detect and define problem areas in sales performance. However, incorporating different sales types into the analysis complicates the evaluation process and requires an information system capable of providing sales data concerning the desired breakdowns.

Figure 15.5 **Example of Hierarchical Sales Analysis**

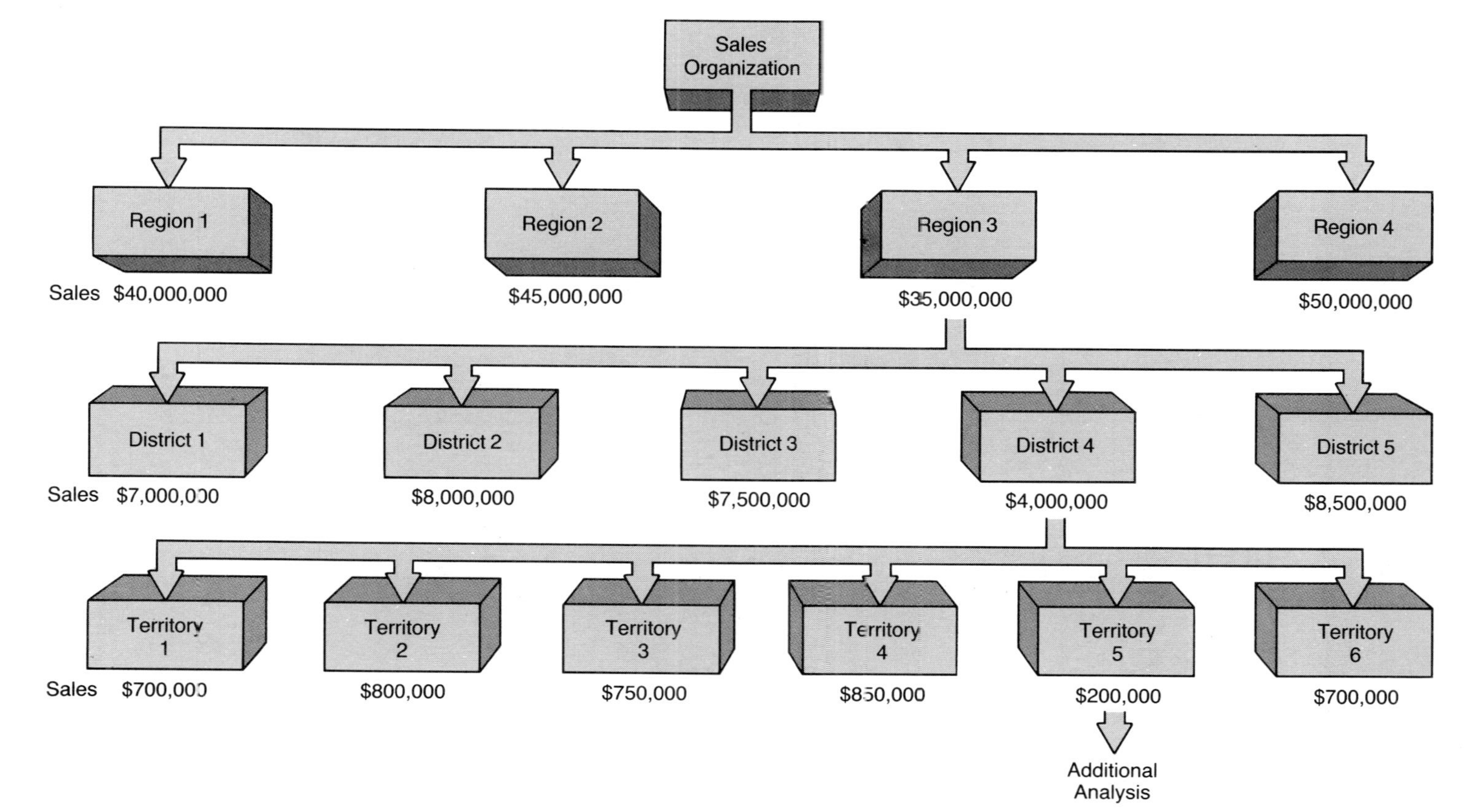

This multi-stage analysis proceeds from one sales organization level to the next by identifying the major deviations and investigating them in more detail at the next lower level. In the present example, Region 3 has the lowest sales, so all districts in Region 3 are examined. District 4 has poor sales results, so all of the territories in District 4 are examined. Additional analysis is indicated for Territory 5.

Figure 15.6 **Example of Type-of-Sales Analysis**

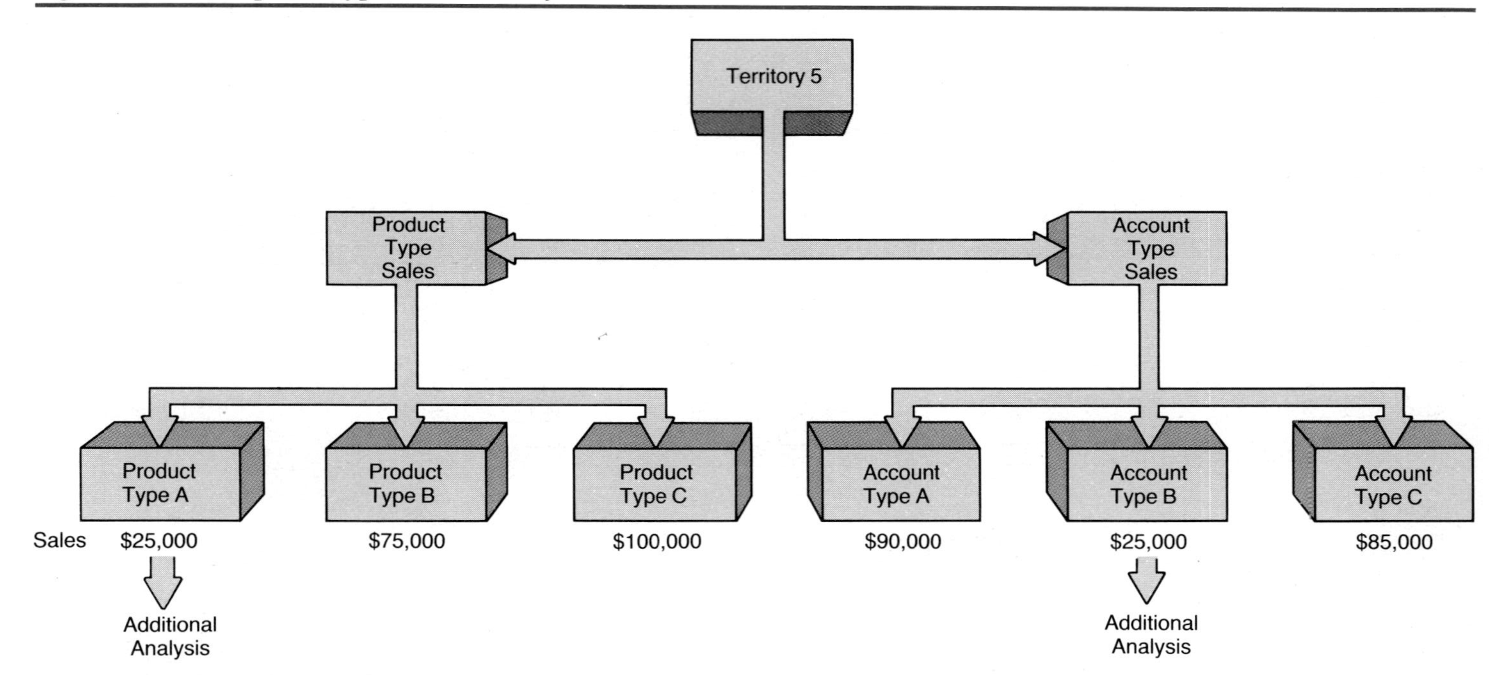

This is a continuation of the hierarchical sales analysis presented in Figure 15.5. Sales in Territory 5 are analyzed by both product type and account type. The analysis suggests poor sales results for Product Type A and Account Type B.

Exhibit 15.4 **Types of Analysis Examples**

	District 1	District 2	District 3	District 4	District 5
Sales	7,000,000	$8,000,000	$7,500,000	$4,000,000	$8,500,000
Sales quota	$7,250,000	$7,500,000	$7,250,000	$7,000,000	$7,500,000
Effectiveness index	97	107	104	57	113
Sales last year	$6,750,000	$7,250,000	$7,000,000	$3,850,000	7,250,000
Sales growth	4%	10%	7%	4%	17%
Industry sales	$22,000,000	$22,000,000	$25,000,000	$20,000,000	$25,000,000
Market share	32%	36%	30%	25%	34%

Type of Analysis. Our discussion to this point has focused on the actual sales results for different organizational levels and for different types of sales. However, the use of actual sales results limits the analysis to comparisons across organizational levels and/or sales types. These within organization comparisons provide some useful information but are insufficient for a comprehensive evaluation of sales effectiveness. Several additional types of analysis are recommended and presented in Exhibit 15.4.

Comparing actual sales results to sales forecasts and quotas is extremely revealing. Remember from Chapter 14 that a *sales forecast* represents an expected level of firm sales for defined products, markets, time periods and for a specified strategy. Based on this definition, a sales forecast provides a basis for establishing specific *sales objectives* and *sales quotas*. An **effectiveness index** can be computed by dividing actual sales results by the sales quota and multiplying by 100. As illustrated in Exhibit 15.4, sales results in excess of quota will have index values greater than 100, while results lower than quota will have index values less than 100. The sales effectiveness index makes it easy to compare directly the sales effectiveness of different organizational levels and different types of sales.

Another type of useful analysis is the comparison of actual results to previous periods. As illustrated in Exhibit 15.4, this type of analysis can be used to determine sales growth rates for different organizational levels and for different sales types. And incorporating sales data for many periods make it possible to assess long-term sales trends.

A final type of analysis to be considered is a comparison of actual sales results to those achieved by competitors. This type of analysis can again be performed at different organizational levels and for different types of sales. If the comparison is extended to overall industry sales, various types of market share can be calculated. Examples of these comparisons are presented in Exhibit 15.4.

Sales analysis is the approach used most often for evaluating sales organization effectiveness. Sales data are typically more readily available than other data types, and

Exhibit 15.5 Cost Analysis Examples

	Compensation Costs			Training Costs		
	Actual Cost	Budgeted Cost	Variance	Actual Cost	Budgeted Cost	Variance
Region 1	$2,650,000	$2,600,000	+ $50,000	$ 975,000	$1,040,000	− $65,000
Region 2	$2,500,000	$2,600,000	−$100,000	$1,100,000	$1,040,000	+ $60,000
Region 3	$2,100,000	$2,400,000	−$300,000	$ 750,000	$ 960,000	−$210,000
Region 4	$3,150,000	$2,900,000	+$250,000	$1,300,000	$1,160,000	+$140,000

	Compensation Costs		Training Costs	
	Actual % Sales	Budgeted % Sales	Actual % Sales	Budgeted % Sales
Region 1	5.1%	5%	1.9%	2%
Region 2	4.8%	5%	2.1%	2%
Region 3	4.4%	5%	1.6%	2%
Region 4	5%	5%	2.1%	2%

sales results are extremely important to sales organizations. However, developing a sales analysis approach that will produce the desired evaluative information is a complex undertaking. Sales data must be available for different organizational levels and for different types of sales. Valid sales forecasts are needed to establish sales quotas for evaluating sales effectiveness in achieving sales objectives. In addition, industry and competitor sales information is also useful. Regardless of the comprehensiveness of the sales analysis, sales organizations need to perform additional analyses to evaluate sales organization effectiveness adequately.

Cost Analysis

A second major element in the evaluation of sales organization effectiveness is **cost analysis.** The emphasis here is on assessing the costs incurred by the sales organization to generate the achieved levels of sales. Just as sales quotas provide benchmarks for evaluating sales results, *selling budgets* set the benchmarks for evaluating selling costs. The general approach is to compare the costs incurred versus planned costs as defined by selling budgets.

Examples of two types of cost analyses are presented in Exhibit 15.5. The first analysis calculates the variance between actual costs and budgeted costs for the regions in a sales organization. Regions with the largest variation, especially where ac-

Exhibit 15.6 **Full Cost Versus Contribution Approaches**

Full Cost Approach		**Contribution Approach**	
	Sales		Sales
Minus:	Cost of Goods Sold	Minus:	Cost of Goods Sold
	Gross Margin		Gross Margin
Minus:	Direct Selling Expenses	Minus:	Direct Selling Expenses
Minus:	Allocated Portion of Shared Expenses		
	Net Profit		Profit Contribution

tual costs far exceed budgeted costs, should be highlighted for further analysis. Large variations are not necessarily bad, but the reasons for the variations should be determined. For example, the ultimate purpose of selling costs is to generate sales. Therefore, the objective is not necessarily to minimize selling costs, but to ensure that a specified relationship between sales and selling costs is maintained.

One way to evaluate this relationship is to calculate the various selling costs as a percentage of sales achieved. As discussed in Chapter 14, the percentage of sales method is often used to establish initial selling budgets. Translating actual selling costs into percentages of sales achieved provides a means for assessing whether the cost-sales relationship has been maintained, even though the actual costs may exceed the absolute level in the selling budget. This situation is illustrated by Region 4 in Exhibit 15.5.

Sales and cost analyses are the two most direct approaches for evaluating sales organization effectiveness. Profitability and productivity analyses extend the evaluation by assessing relationships between sales and costs. These analyses can be quite complex but may provide very useful information.

Profitability Analysis

Sales and cost data can be combined in various ways to produce evaluations of sales organization profitability for different organizational levels or different types of sales. We will cover three types of **profitability analysis**: income statement analysis, return on assets managed analysis, and residual income analysis.

Income Statement Analysis. The different levels in a sales organization and different types of sales can be considered as separate businesses.[4] Consequently, income statements can be developed for profitability analysis. One of the major difficulties in **income statement analysis** is that some costs are shared between organizational levels or sales types.

Two approaches for dealing with the shared costs are illustrated in Exhibit 15.6. The **full cost approach** attempts to allocate the shared costs to individual units based

Exhibit 15.7 **Profitability Analysis Example**

	Full Cost Approach	Contribution Approach		
	Region	District 1	District 2	District 3
Sales	$200,000,000	$100,000,000	$60,000,000	$40,000,000
Cost of goods sold	160,000,000	90,000,000	50,000,000	20,000,000
Gross margin	40,000,000	10,000,000	10,000,000	20,000,000
District selling expenses	10,000,000	5,000,000	3,000,000	2,000,000
Region direct selling expenses	9,000,000	—	—	—
Profit contribution	21,000,000	5,000,000	7,000,000	18,000,000
Allocated portion of shared zone costs	15,000,000			
Net profit	6,000,000			

on some type of cost allocation procedure. This results in a net profit figure for each unit. The **contribution approach** is different in that only direct costs are included in the profitability analysis; the indirect or shared costs are not included. The net contribution calculated from this approach represents the *profit contribution* of the unit being analyzed. This profit contribution must be sufficient to cover indirect costs, other overhead, and provide the net profit for the firm.

An example that incorporates both approaches is presented in Exhibit 15.7. This example employs the direct approach for assessing sales region profitability and the contribution approach for evaluating the districts within this region. Notice that the profitability calculations for each district include only district sales, cost of goods sold, and district direct selling expenses. A *profit contribution* is generated for each district. The profitability calculations for the region include district selling expenses, region direct selling expenses that have not been allocated to the districts, and an allocated portion of shared zone costs. This produces a net profit figure for a profitability evaluation of the region.

Although either approach might be used, there seems to be a trend toward the contribution approach, probably because of the difficulty in arriving at a satisfactory procedure for allocating the shared costs. Different cost allocation methods produce different results. Thus, many firms feel more comfortable with the contribution approach, since it eliminates the need for cost allocation judgments and is viewed as more objective.

Exhibit 15.8 **Return on Assets Managed (ROAM) Example**

	District 1	District 2	District 3	District 4
Sales	$12,000,000	$12,000,000	$12,000,000	$12,000,000
Cost of goods sold	6,000,000	6,000,000	7,000,000	7,000,000
Gross margin	6,000,000	6,000,000	5,000,000	5,000,000
Direct selling expenses	3,600,000	4,800,000	2,600,000	4,400,000
Profit contribution	2,400,000	1,200,000	2,400,000	600,000
Accounts receivable	4,000,000	2,000,000	8,000,000	2,000,000
Inventory	4,000,000	2,000,000	8,000,000	2,000,000
Total assets managed	8,000,000	4,000,000	16,000,000	4,000,000
Profit contribution percentage	20%	10%	20%	5%
Asset turnover	1.5	3.0	.75	3.0
ROAM	30%	30%	15%	15%

Return on Assets Managed Analysis. The income statement approach to profitability assessment produces net profit or profit contribution in dollars or expressed as a percentage of sales. Although necessary and valuable, the income statement approach is incomplete because it does not incorporate any evaluation of the investment in assets required to generate the net profit or profit contribution.

The calculation of **return on assets managed (ROAM)** can extend the income statement analysis to include asset investment considerations. The formula for calculating ROAM is

$$\begin{aligned} \text{ROAM} &= \text{Profit contribution as percentage of sales} \times \text{Asset turnover rate} \\ &= \text{Profit contribution/sales} \times \text{Sales/assets managed} \end{aligned}$$

Profit contribution can be either a net profit figure from a direct approach or profit contribution from a contribution approach. Assets managed typically include inventory, accounts receivable, or other assets at each sales organizational level.

An example of ROAM calculations is presented in Exhibit 15.8. The example illustrates ROAM calculations for sales districts within a region. Notice that District 1 and District 2 produce the same ROAM but achieve their results in different ways.

District 1 generates a relatively high profit contribution percentage, while District 2 operates with a relatively high asset turnover. Both District 3 and District 4 are achieving poor levels of ROAM, but for different reasons. District 3 has an acceptable profit contribution percentage but very low asset turnover ratio. This low asset turnover ratio is due either to both inventory accumulations or problems in payments from accounts. District 4, on the other hand, has an acceptable asset turnover ratio, but low profit contribution percentage. This low profit contribution percentage may be the result of selling low margin products, negotiating low selling prices, or accruing excessive selling expenses.

As illustrated in the preceding example, ROAM calculations provide an assessment of profitability and useful diagnostic information. ROAM is determined by both profit contribution percentage and asset turnover. If ROAM is low in any area, the profit contribution percentage and asset turnover ratio can be examined to determine the reason. Corrective action (reduced selling expenses, stricter credit guidelines, lower inventory levels, etc.) can then be taken to improve future ROAM performance.

Residual Income Analysis. Although ROAM evaluates profitability in relation to asset investment, it does not include any consideration of sales growth. Since most firms have both sales growth and profitability objectives, an approach that incorporates both of these elements is extremely useful to sales managers. **Residual income analysis** has been proposed as such an approach.[5]

The basic concept underlying residual income analysis is that sales organization effectiveness depends upon both sales growth and profitability. Sales growth is desirable as long as the return on sales exceeds the cost of capital for acquiring assets. The formula for residual income analysis is

$$\text{Residual income} = \text{Profit contribution} - \text{Accounts receivable cost} - \text{Inventory carrying cost}$$

Thus, as long as residual income is positive, the return on sales is greater than the cost of assets.

One of the advantages of residual income analysis is that residual income targets can be set for different levels of the sales organization. These targets are based on sales organization goals for both sales growth and profitability. Typically, they would be calculated by top management and supplied to the sales organization as target goals. Therefore, calculating residual income targets is outside the realm of sales managers and beyond the scope of this text. However, sales managers can use the residual income approach and should understand that the target residual income levels are calculated by directly considering a firm's objectives for sales growth and profitability.

An example of residual income analysis is presented in Exhibit 15.9. The firm in this example desired sales growth of 10 percent and profitability expressed by a 10 percent return on assets. Based on the firm's cost of capital, inventory carrying costs of 15 percent and accounts receivable costs of 10 percent were estimated. These figures were used to derive a target residual income of $1,131,167 for the sales re-

Exhibit 15.9 **Residual Income Example**

	District 1	District 2	District 3	District 4
Sales	$5,750,000	$5,750,000	$5,250,000	$5,250,000
Sales growth	15%	15%	5%	5%
ROAM	35%	15%	35%	15%
Profit contribution	$ 520,208	$ 323,437	$ 520,625	$ 295,312
Accounts receivable cost	47,917	71,875	43,750	65,626
Inventory cost	178,500	107,812	157,500	98,438
Residual income	349,791	143,750	319,375	131,248
Target residual income	282,792	282,792	282,792	282,792
Variance	+ 66,999	− 139,042	+ 36,583	− 157,544

Source: Adapted from William L. Cron and Michael Levy, "Sales Management Performance Evaluation: A Residual Income Perspective," *Journal of Personal Selling and Sales Management*, August 1987, 63. Used with permission.

gion. Because the four sales districts were considered to be similar, equal residual income targets were established for each district ($1,131,167/4 = $282,792).

A review of Exhibit 15.9 illustrates the value of residual income analysis. If these districts had been evaluated only on ROAM calculations, District 1 and District 3 would have outperformed the other districts and, accordingly, would have been viewed as equally effective from a profitability perspective. District 2 and District 4 would have also been evaluated as similar in profitability. However, the residual income analysis indicates that when sales growth is included, District 1 was clearly more effective than District 3, and District 2 was more effective than District 4. These evaluations are the same for both total residual income and target residual income, since all districts had the same targets. If different targets had been set for each district, then the comparison of actual residual income to target residual income would be the most meaningful evaluation.

Although the residual income approach has been employed extensively in the retail sector, it is a relatively new approach for the sales management area. The basic advantage of residual income analysis is its integration of sales growth and profitability assessments into one analysis. Even though the computations are somewhat complex, sales managers do not have to perform these computations and merely need to understand what is included in calculating the residual income targets and how to calculate actual residual income and compare it to target residual income.

Exhibit 15.10 **Productivity Analysis Example**

	District 1	District 2	District 3	District 4
Sales	$10,000,000	$12,000,000	$10,000,000	$12,000,000
Selling expenses	1,000,000	1,000,000	1,000,000	1,500,000
Sales calls	5,000	4,500	4,500	6,000
Proposals	100	105	120	120
Number of salespeople	10	15	10	15
Sales/salesperson	1,000,000	800,000	1,000,000	800,000
Expenses/salesperson	100,000	80,000	150,000	100,000
Calls/salesperson	500	300	450	400
Proposals/salesperson	10	7	12	8

Productivity Analysis

Although ROAM and residual income calculations incorporate elements of productivity by comparing profits and asset investments, additional **productivity analysis** is desirable for thorough evaluation of sales organization effectiveness. Productivity is typically measured in terms of ratios between outputs and inputs. For example, as discussed in Chapter 8, one often used measure of salesforce productivity is sales/salesperson. A major advantage of productivity ratios is that they can be compared directly across the entire sales organization and with other sales organizations. This direct comparison is possible because all of the ratios are expressed in terms of the same units.

Since the basic job of sales managers is to manage salespeople, the most useful input unit for productivity analysis is the salesperson. Therefore, various types of productivity ratios are calculated on a per salesperson basis. The specific ratios depend upon the characteristics of a particular selling situation but often include important outputs such as sales, expenses, calls, demonstrations, and proposals. An example of a productivity analysis is presented in Exhibit 15.10; examples of how several firms evaluate *telemarketing* productivity (discussed earlier in this text) are presented in "Sales Trend: Evaluating Telemarketing Productivity."

Exhibit 15.10 illustrates how productivity analysis provides a different and useful perspective for evaluating sales organization effectiveness. As the exhibit reveals, absolute values can be misleading. For example, the highest sales districts are not necessarily the most effective. Although profitability analyses would likely detect this also, productivity analysis presents a vivid and precise evaluation by highlighting

SALES TREND

EVALUATING TELEMARKETING PRODUCTIVITY

The trend toward the use of telemarketing means that sales managers must be prepared to evaluate the effectiveness of their telemarketing sales organizations. Firms such as Rohm and Haas, Capital Preservation Fund, William Wrigley Jr. Company, and CF Air Freight use different measures to evaluate the telemarketing process, the results from telemarketing, and the impact of telemarketing. Examples of these measures are presented below.

Measures	Rohm and Hass	Capital Preservation Fund	Wrigley	CF Air Freight
Process measures	Calls per day Cost per order Calls per telemarketer	Calls per telemarketer Turnover Cost per call		
End-result measures		Number of customer complaints	Dollar revenue per telemarketer New accounts Customer complaints	Dollar revenue per telemarketer New accounts
Impact measures			Leads generated Reduction in field salesforce	Leads generated Decreased field sales training Reduction in field salesforce

Source: Reprinted by persmission from *Business,* "How to Measure Telemarketing Productivity," by Harold E. Glass and Nancy Matthews Kuhn, April–June 1986, p. 28. Copyright 1986 by the College of Business Administration, Georgia State University, Atlanta.

specific areas of both high and low productivity. Take the information concerning District 2. Although sales/salesperson is reasonable and expenses/salesperson is relatively low, both calls/salesperson and proposals/salesperson are much lower than the other districts. This may explain why selling expenses are low, but it also suggests that the salespeople in this district may not be covering the district adequately. The high sales may be due to a few large sales to large customers.

In any case, the productivity analysis provides useful evaluative and diagnostic information that is not directly available from the other types of analyses discussed in this chapter. Sales productivity and profitability are highly interrelated. However, profitability analysis has a financial perspective, while productivity analysis is more managerially oriented. Improvements in sales productivity should translate into increases in profitability.

SALES TECHNOLOGY

USING SPREADSHEETS TO PERFORM ANALYSES

The development of microcomputer spreadsheet software provides sales managers with a useful tool for performing sales, cost, profitability, and productivity analysis. An example of a spreadsheet analysis performed by a district sales manager is presented below.

	Territory 1		Territory 2		Territory 3		District Totals	
	$000	%	$000	%	$000	%	$000	%
Sales	2200	100	2500	100	2000	100	6700	100
Acct-product contribution	479	21.77	613	24.52	457	22.85	1549	23.12
Acct. costs exh. 3								
Freight	63	2.86	65	2.60	60	3.00	188	2.81
Inventory	44	2.00	30	1.20	39	1.95	113	1.69
Accts. receivable	64	2.91	75	3.00	59	2.95	198	2.96
Tech. services	18	0.82	18	0.72	17	0.85	53	0.79
Adv. & prom.	21	0.95	35	1.40	18	0.90	74	1.10
Total customer costs	210	9.55	223	8.92	193	9.65	626	9.34
Personal selling costs								
Compensation	31.50	1.43	33.00	1.32	29.90	1.50	94.40	1.41
Transportation	6.00	0.27	5.00	0.20	7.00	0.35	18.00	0.27
Lodging & meals	3.50	0.16	3.50	0.14	4.00	0.20	11.00	0.16
Telephone	1.35	0.06	1.70	0.07	1.20	0.06	4.25	0.06
Entertainment	3.00	0.14	1.00	0.04	2.50	0.13	6.50	0.10
Samples & literature	2.00	0.09	2.00	0.08	1.50	0.08	5.50	0.08
Misc.	0.50	0.02	0.50	0.02	0.30	0.02	1.30	0.02
Total pers. selling cst	47.85	2.18	46.70	1.87	46.40	2.32	140.95	2.10
Net territory contrib($000)	221.15	10.05	343.30	13.73	217.60	10.88	782.05	11.67
Return on assets managed:								
Territory assets ($000)	800		890		775		2465	
Asset turnover (sales/assts)	2.75		2.81		2.58		2.72	
Add: Interest inv.		2.00		1.20		1.95		1.69
Interest a/r		2.91		3.00		2.95		2.96
Total contribution percent		14.96		17.93		15.78		16.31
Return on assets managed (% contrib. × turnover)		41.14		50.37		40.72		44.34

Source: Reprinted by permission of the *Harvard Business Review*. An exhibit from "Computerized Sales Management" by G. David Hughes (March/April 1983), on p. 109.

Productivity improvements are obtained in one of two basic ways:

1. Increasing output with the same level of input.
2. Maintaining the same level of output but using less input.

Productivity analysis can help determine which of these basic approaches should be pursued.

Concluding Comments

As is obvious from the discussion in this chapter, there is no easy way to evaluate the effectiveness of a sales organization. Our recommendation is to perform separate analyses of sales, costs, profitability, and productivity to assess different aspects of sales organization effectiveness. Each type of analysis offers a piece of the puzzle. Sales managers must put these pieces together for comprehensive evaluations. The objective underlying each of the analyses is to be able to evaluate effectiveness, identify problem areas, and use this information to improve future sales organization effectiveness. The use of microcomputer spreadsheet software can assist sales managers in performing the necessary analysis. An example of an output from a spreadsheet analysis is presented in "Sales Technology: Using Spreadsheets to Perform Analyses."

SUMMARY

1. **Differentiate between sales organization effectiveness and salesperson performance.** Sales organization effectiveness is a summary evaluation of the overall success of a sales organization in meeting its goals and objectives in total and at different organizational levels. In contrast, salesperson performance is a function of individual salesperson performance in individual situations.
2. **Define a sales organization audit, and discuss how it should be conducted.** The most comprehensive type of evaluation is a sales organization audit, which is a systematic assessment of all aspects of a sales organization. The major areas included in the audit are sales organization environment, sales management evaluation, sales organization planning system, and sales management functions. The audit should be conducted on a regular basis by individuals outside the sales organization. It is intended to identify existing or potential problems at an early date so that corrective action can be taken before the problems become serious.
3. **Describe how to perform different types of sales analysis for different organizational levels and types of sales.** Sales analysis is the most common evaluation approach, but it can be extremely complex. Specific definitions of a sale are required, and both sales dollars and units should typically be considered. A hierarchical approach is suggested as a top-down procedure to address sales results at each level of the sales organization with an emphasis on identifying prob-

lem areas. Sales analysis is more useful when sales results are compared to forecasts, quotas, previous time periods, and competitor results.

4. **Describe how to perform a cost analysis for a sales organization.** Cost analysis focuses on the costs incurred to generate sales results. Specific costs can be compared to the planned levels in the selling budget. Areas with large variances require specific attention. Costs can also be evaluated as percentages of sales and compared to comparable industry figures.
5. **Describe how to perform income statement, return on assets managed, and residual income analyses to assess sales organization profitability.** Profitability analysis combines sales and cost data in various ways. The income statement approach focuses on net profit or profit contributions from the different sales organization levels. The return on assets managed approach assesses relationships between profit contributions and the assets used to generate these profit contributions. Residual income analysis combines the return on assets managed concept with sales growth objectives to produce a very useful evaluative tool. The different profitability analyses address different aspects of profitability that are of interest to sales managers.
6. **Describe how to perform a productivity analysis for a sales organization.** Productivity analysis focuses on relationships between outputs and inputs. The most useful input is the number of salespeople, while relevant outputs might be sales, expenses, proposals, and so on. The productivity ratios calculated in this manner are versatile, since they can be used for comparisons within the sales organization and across other sales organizations. Productivity analysis not only provides useful evaluative information, but also produces managerially useful diagnostic information that can suggest ways to improve productivity and increase profitability.

Key Terms

sales organization audit
sales analysis
hierarchical sales analysis
effectiveness index
cost analysis
profitability analysis
income statement analysis
full cost approach
contribution approach
return on assets managed (ROAM)
residual income analysis
productivity analysis

Review Questions

1. Discuss why it is important to differentiate between sales organization effectiveness and salesperson performance.
2. Discuss what is involved in conducting a sales management audit.

3. Describe three different types of sales analysis and indicate the types of evaluative and diagnostic information resulting from each analysis.
4. What is meant by a hierarchical sales analysis? Can a hierarchical approach be used in analyzing costs, profitability, and/or productivity?
5. What is the difference between the full cost and contribution approaches to income statement analysis for a sales organization? Which would you recommend for a sales organization? Why?
6. What are the two basic components of return on assets managed? How is each component calculated, and what does each component tell a sales manager?
7. What is the value of residual income analysis? How should it be used by sales managers?
8. How would you define sales organization productivity? How does sales organization productivity differ from sales organization profitability?
9. Identify five different sales organization productivity ratios that you would recommend. Describe how each would be calculated and what information each would provide.
10. Discuss how you think new computer and information technologies will affect the evaluations of sales organization effectiveness in the future.

Application Exercises

	District 1 ($000)	District 2 ($000)	District 3 ($000)	District 4 ($000)	District 5 ($000)
Sales	8,200	9,500	10,450	13,750	8,400
Cost of goods sold	4,920	5,510	6,479	8,250	4,620
Compensation	615	810	735	1,170	630
Transportation	41	67	42	70	50
Lodging and meals	17	30	16	41	21
Telephone	8	10	12	14	9
Entertainment	10	8	15	12	12
Training	80	95	105	125	110
District inventory	2,000	3,500	3,200	5,250	2,500
District accounts receivable	1,170	1,400	1,450	2,420	1,150
Number of salespeople	8	9	11	12	10
Sales quota	8,100	9,750	10,250	14,125	8,300
Sales last year	7,500	9,250	10,250	13,925	8,200

1. Using this table, develop an income statement for each district by means of the contribution approach. Discuss your results.
2. Using this table, calculate the return on assets managed for each district. Discuss your results.
3. Using this table, perform a sales analysis for each district. Discuss your results.
4. Using this table, perform a productivity analysis for each district. Discuss your results.
5. Based on all of the preceding analyses, prepare an overall evaluation of the effectiveness of each district. Discuss recommendations for improving the effectiveness of each district in the future.

Notes

[1]For a more complete discussion of this issue, see Orville C. Walker, Jr., Gilbert A. Churchill, Jr., and Neil M. Ford, "Where Do We Go From Here? Selected Conceptual and Empirical Issues Concerning the Motivation and Performance of the Industrial Salesforce," in *Critical Issues in Sales Management: State-of-the-Art and Future Research Needs,* edited by Gerald Albaum and Gilbert A. Churchill, Jr. (Eugene, Ore.: University of Oregon, 1979).

[2]Much of the discussion in this section comes from Alan J. Dubinsky and Richard W. Hansen, "The Sales Force Management Audit," *California Management Review,* Winter 1981, 86–95.

[3]For the results of empirical studies that support this point see Alan J. Dubinsky and Thomas E. Barry, "A Survey of Sales Management Practices," *Industrial Marketing Management,* 11, 1982, 133–141; and Donald W. Jackson, Jr., Lonnie L. Ostrom, and Kenneth R. Evans, "Measures Used to Evaluate Industrial Marketing Activities," *Industrial Marketing Management,* 11, 1982, 269–274.

[4]For a more complete presentation of this concept, see J. S. Schiff, "Evaluate the Sales Force as a Business," *Industrial Marketing Management,* 12, 1983, 131–137.

[5]For a comprehensive presentation of this approach, see William L. Cron and Michael Levy, "Sales Management Performance Evaluation: A Residual Income Perspective," *Journal of Personal Selling and Sales Management,* August 1987, 57–66.

CHAPTER 16

EVALUATING AND CONTROLLING SALESPERSON PERFORMANCE AND JOB SATISFACTION

Learning Objectives:

After completing this chapter, you should be able to

1. Discuss the different purposes of salesperson performance evaluations.
2. Differentiate between an outcome-based and behavior-based perspective for evaluating and controlling salesperson performance.
3. Describe the different types of criteria necessary for comprehensive evaluations of salesperson performance.
4. Compare the advantages and disadvantages of different methods of salesperson performance evaluation.
5. Explain how salesperson performance information can be used to identify problems, determine their causes, and suggest sales management actions to solve them.
6. Discuss the measurement and importance of salesperson job satisfaction.

SALESPERSON PERFORMANCE EVALUATIONS: THE PERFORMANCE APPRAISAL PROCESS

A recent study of the performance appraisal process in seven large organizations illustrates some of the complexities involved in evaluating employee performance. Several comments from the executives interviewed in this study portray the performance appraisal process vividly and realistically:

> There is really no getting around the fact that whenever I evaluate one of my people, I stop and think about the impact — the ramifications of my decisions on my relationship with the guy and his future here. I'd be stupid not to. Call it being politically minded, or using managerial discretion, or fine-tuning the guy's ratings, but in the end I've got to live with him, and I'm not going to rate a guy without thinking about the fallout. There are a lot of games played in the rating process and whether we [managers] admit it or not we are all guilty of playing them at our discretion.
>
> As a manager, I will use the review process to do what is best for my people and the division . . . I've got a lot of leeway — call it discretion — to use this process in that manner . . . I've used it to get my people better raises in lean years, to kick a guy in the pants if he really needed it, to pick up a guy when he was down or to tell him that he was no longer welcome here. It is a tool that the manager should use to help him do what it takes to get the job done . . . Accurately describing an employee's performance is really not as important as generating ratings that keep things cooking.
>
> Some organizations are more aggressive and political than others, so it just makes sense that those things carry over into the rating process as well . . . The organization's climate will determine, to a great extent, how successful any rating system will be.

Source: Managerial comments taken from Clinton O. Longenecker, Henry P. Sims, Jr., and Dennis A. Gioia, "Behind the Mask: The Politics of Employee Appraisal," *The Academy of Management Executive,* August 1987, 183–193. Reprinted with permission.

> At the last couple of places I've worked, the formal review process is taken really seriously; they train you how to conduct a good interview, how to handle problems, how to coach and counsel . . . I guess the biggest thing is that people are led to believe that it is a management tool that works.
>
> Most of us try to be fairly accurate in assessing the individual's performance in different categories . . . If you are going to pump up a person's ratings, for whatever reason, it's done on the subordinate's overall evaluation category . . . The problem is these things have to match up, so if you know what the guy's overall rating is in the first place, it will probably color the rest of the appraisal.
>
> Many of us have trouble rating for the entire year. If one of my people has a stellar three months prior to the review . . . you don't want to do anything that impedes that person's momentum and progress.
>
> I've used the appraisal to shock an employee . . . If you've tried to coach a guy to get him back on track and it doesn't work, a low rating will more often than not slap him in the face and tell him you mean business . . . I've dropped a few ratings down to accomplish this because the alternative outcome would be termination down the road, which isn't pretty.

Although these comments were from both sales managers and managers from other functional areas, they are all applicable to situations where sales managers evaluate the performance of salespeople under their supervision. The performance appraisal process is difficult. People evaluating people is always a delicate operation; and added to that is the even more ticklish job of communicating to the salesperson who, of course, realizes that the evaluation can have a major impact on his or her income, promotion possibilities, and tenure with the firm. The way that this is handled will certainly affect the salesperson's motivational level.

As indicated in the comments, the ramifications of performance evaluation are often considered by a sales manager in determining the ratings. Sales managers may therefore strive not for the most accurate evaluation of a salesperson, but rather attempt to use the performance appraisal to accomplish various objectives.

WHEREAS Chapter 15 focused on evaluating sales organization effectiveness, this chapter examines the task of evaluating salesperson performance and job satisfaction. Evaluations of sales organization effectiveness concentrate on the overall results achieved by the different units within the sales organization, with special attention given to determining the effectiveness of territories, districts, regions, and zones, and identifying strategic changes to improve future effectiveness. These effectiveness assessments examine sales organization units and do not directly evaluate people; however, sales managers are responsible for the effectiveness of their assigned units.

Salesperson performance evaluations, on the other hand, consist of people (sales managers) examining the performance of people (salespeople). Although the general purpose of these appraisals is to evaluate salesperson performance accurately, the managerial comments in the opening vignette suggest some of the complexities involved in the appraisal process. Clearly, salesperson performance evaluations in the real world are based on a variety of considerations and are used to accomplish different objectives by sales managers.

The purpose of this chapter is to investigate the key issues involved in evaluating and controlling the performance and job satisfaction of salespeople. The different purposes of salesperson performance evaluations are discussed initially. Then, the performance evaluation procedures currently used by sales organizations are examined. This is followed by a comprehensive assessment of the different areas in salesperson performance evaluation. The assessment addresses the criteria to be used in evaluating salespeople, the methods for evaluating salespeople against these criteria, and the outcomes of salesperson performance evaluations. The chapter concludes by discussing the importance and measurement of salesperson job satisfaction and relationships between salesperson performance and job satisfaction.

PURPOSES OF SALESPERSON PERFORMANCE EVALUATIONS

As the name suggests, the basic objective of salesperson performance evaluations is to determine how well individual salespeople have performed. However, as mentioned in the opening vignette, the results of salesperson performance evaluations can be used for many sales management purposes:[1]

1. To ensure that compensation and other reward disbursements are consistent with actual salesperson performance.
2. To identify salespeople that might be promoted.
3. To identify salespeople whose employment should be terminated and to supply evidence to support the need for termination.
4. To determine the specific training and counseling needs of individual salespeople and the overall salesforce.
5. To provide information for effective human resource planning.
6. To identify criteria that can be used to recruit and select salespeople in the future.

These diverse purposes affect all aspects of the performance evaluation process. For example, performance evaluations for determining compensation and reward disbursements should emphasize activities and results related to the salesperson's current job and situation. Performance evaluations for the purpose of identifying salespeople for promotion into sales management positions should focus on criteria related to potential effectiveness as a sales manager and not just current performance as a salesperson. The best salespeople do not always make the best sales managers. Thus, salesperson performance appraisals must be carefully developed and implemented to provide the types of information necessary to accomplish all of the desired purposes.

CURRENT APPROACHES TO SALESPERSON PERFORMANCE EVALUATIONS

Although it is impossible to determine with precision all the performance evaluation approaches used by sales organizations, several studies have produced sufficiently consistent information to warrant some general conclusions:[2]

1. Most sales organizations evaluate salesperson performance on an annual basis, although many firms conduct evaluations on a semiannual or quarterly basis. Relatively few firms evaluate salesperson performance more often than quarterly.
2. Most sales organizations employ combinations of input and output criteria that are evaluated by quantitative and qualitative measures. However, emphasis seems to be placed on outputs, and as illustrated in Exhibit 16.1, evaluations of sales volume results are the most popular.
3. Sales organizations that set performance standards or quotas tend to enlist the aid of salespeople in establishing these objectives (see Exhibit 16.2). The degree of salesperson input and involvement does, however, appear to vary across firms.
4. As indicated in Exhibit 16.3, most firms use more than one source of information in evaluating salesperson performance. Qualitative information is most often provided by using printed performance evaluation forms, while quantitative information typically comes from the analysis of computer printouts for each territory.

These results offer a glimpse of current practices in evaluating salesperson performance. The remainder of this chapter will address the key decision areas and alternative approaches for developing comprehensive evaluation and control procedures.

KEY ISSUES IN EVALUATING AND CONTROLLING SALESPERSON PERFORMANCE

A useful way to view different perspectives for evaluating and controlling salesperson performance is presented in Figure 16.1. An **outcome-based perspective** focuses on objective measures of results with little monitoring or directing of salesperson

Exhibit 16.1 Salesperson Performance Measures

Evaluation Dimension Items	Percentage of Large Firms Using
Evaluation of sales volume performance	72
Evaluation of personal characteristics	47
Evaluation of post-selling activities	38
Evaluation of profit performance	40
Evaluation of preselling activities	30

Source: Alan J. Dubinsky and Thomas E. Barry, "A Survey of Sales Management Practices," *Industrial Marketing Management,* 11, 1982, 138.

Exhibit 16.2 Salesperson Participation in Setting Objectives

Participation	Percent Using
Salespeople set their own objectives with no inputs from management	0
Salespeople set their own objectives with some inputs from management	3
Salespeople and management jointly set objectives	55
Management sets objectives with some inputs from salespeople	23
Management sets objectives with no inputs from salespeople	8
No response	11

Source: Donald W. Jackson, Jr., Janet E. Keith, and John L. Schlacter, "Evaluation of Selling Performance: A Study of Current Practices," *Journal of Personal Selling and Sales Management,* November 1983, 47. Used with permission.

Exhibit 16.3 Information Sources for Salesperson Performance Evaluations

Source	Percent Using
Printed form for performance evaluation	56
Analysis of computer printouts for each territory	50
Analysis of call reports	48
Other (supervisory calls, feedback from clients)	44

Source: Donald W. Jackson, Jr., Janet E. Keith, and John L. Schlacter, "Evaluation of Selling Performance: A Study of Current Practices," *Journal of Personal Selling and Sales Management,* November 1983, 48. Used with permission.

Figure 16.1 **Perspectives on Salesperson Performance Evaluation**

Outcome-Based Perspective ⟵	⟶ **Behavior-Based Perspective**
•Little monitoring of salespeople	•Considerable monitoring of salespeople
•Little managerial direction of salespeople	•High levels of managerial direction of salespeople
•Straightforward objective measures of results	•Subjective measures of salesperson characteristics, activities, and strategies

The perspectives that a sales organization might take toward salesperson performance evaluation and control lie on a continuum. The two extremes are the outcome-based and behavior-based perspectives.

Source: Adapted from Erin Anderson and Richard L. Oliver, "Perspectives on Behavior-Based Versus Outcome-Based Salesforce Control Systems," *Journal of Marketing,* (October 1987) 86, published by the American Marketing Association. Used with permission.

behavior by sales managers. In contrast, a **behavior-based perspective** incorporates complex and often subjective assessments of salesperson characteristics and behaviors with considerable monitoring and directing of salesperson behavior by sales managers.[3]

The outcome-based and behavior-based perspectives illustrated in Figure 16.1 represent the extreme positions that a sales organization might take concerning salesperson performance evaluation. Although our earlier review of current practice indicates a tendency toward an outcome-based perspective, most sales organizations operate somewhere between the two extreme positions. However, emphasis on either perspective can have far-reaching impacts on the salesforce and important implications for sales managers. Several of these key implications are presented in Exhibit 16.4.

On balance, these implications provide strong support for at least some behavior-based evaluations in most selling situations. In the absence of any behavior-based measures and limited monitoring and direction from sales management, salespeople are likely to focus on the short-term outcomes that are being evaluated. The process of obtaining the desired outcomes may be neglected, causing some activities that produce short-term results (selling pressure, unethical activities, etc.) to be emphasized, and activities related to long-term customer relationships (customer orientation, post-sale service, etc.) to be minimized.

A reasonable conclusion from this discussion is that sales organizations should employ both outcome-based and behavior-based measures when evaluating salesperson performance. However, the relative emphasis on outcome-based and behavior-based measures depends upon environmental, firm, and salesperson considerations. Establishing the desired emphasis should be the initial decision in developing a salesperson performance evaluation and control system. Once this emphasis has been

Exhibit 16.4 **Outcome-Based versus Behavior-Based Implications**

The more behavior-based a salesperson performance evaluation is (versus outcome-based):

- The more product knowledge, company knowledge, and integrated sales expertise the salespeople will have.
- The more professionally competent the salespeople will be.
- The more salespeople will identify with and feel committed to the sales organization.
- The more likely salespeople will be to accept direction and cooperate as part of a sales team, accept the authority of sales management, and welcome management performance reviews.
- The more likely that risk-averse salespeople will be attracted, nurtured, and retained.
- The more likely salespeople will be to have high levels of intrinsic motivation, be motivated by peer recognition, and be motivated to serve the sales organization.
- The more salespeople can be expected to plan for each call, make fewer calls, operate at a lower ratio of selling to nonselling time, spend more time on sales support activities, and use "expertise" and "customer-oriented" selling strategies.
- The closer salespeople will come to achieving sales organization goals and serving customer needs, but the less well they will perform on traditional output measures of individual performance.

Source: Adapted from Erin Anderson and Richard L. Oliver, "Perspectives on Behavior-Based versus Outcome-Based Salesforce Control Systems," *Journal of Marketing*, 51 (October 1987):85–86, published by the American Marketing Association. Used with permission.

established, the sales organization can then address the specific criteria to be evaluated, the methods of evaluation, and how the performance information will be used.

Criteria for Performance Evaluation

The typical salesperson job is multidimensional. Salespeople normally sell multiple products to diverse customers and perform a variety of selling and nonselling activities. Therefore, any comprehensive assessment of salesperson performance must include multiple criteria. As illustrated in "Sales Technology: Computer-Based Performance Evaluations," advances in computer technology are making it easier for sales managers to employ multiple criteria in their evaluations of salespeople.

Although the specific criteria depend upon the characteristics of a given selling situation and the performance evaluation perspective, the four performance dimensions illustrated in Figure 16.2 should be considered: behavioral and professional development (behavior-based perspective) and results and profitability (outcome-based perspective).

Behavioral. The behavioral dimension consists of criteria related to activities performed by individual salespeople. The emphasis is on evaluating exactly what each salesperson does. These **behavioral criteria** should not only address activities related to short-term sales generation, but should also include nonselling activities needed to ensure long-term customer satisfaction and to provide necessary information

SALES TECHNOLOGY

COMPUTER-BASED PERFORMANCE EVALUATION

Computer technology is being used increasingly to help sales managers evaluate the performance of their salespeople against multiple criteria. One interesting approach is the Contingency Management System (CMS).

The CMS approach consists of developing questionnaires to evaluate different salesperson performance dimensions. These questionnaires are completed by the salesperson, the sales manager with direct supervision responsibility for the salesperson, and by a sample of customers served by the salesperson. A congruence ratio is then calculated to determine the level of consistency among these evaluations.

An efficiency index for each performance dimension is also calculated. This efficiency index represents the salesperson's performance for each dimension and can be directly compared to the efficiency indices of other salespeople. CMS also provides color-coded graphs of the performance evaluations of all salespeople. The different colors represent different levels of performance.

Although CMS is used to evaluate salesperson performance, the real focus is toward identifying ways to improve the future performance of each salesperson. Sales managers typically have counseling sessions with each salesperson and use the CMS results to point out areas in which a salesperson needs to improve.

Source: Adapted from Donald F. Harvey, "Managers Use Computer Profile System to Measure and Analyze Sales-Rep Performance," *Marketing News,* March 18, 1983, 12.

to the sales organization. Examples of typical behavioral criteria are presented in Exhibit 16.5.

As might be expected, most sales organizations focus on the number of sales calls made as the key behavioral criterion. However, other activities are also evaluated by at least some sales organizations. Salespeople have the most control over what they do, so evaluations of their performance should include some assessment of their behaviors. As discussed in Exhibit 16.4, the use of behavior-based criteria will also facilitate the development of a professional, customer-oriented, committed, and motivated salesforce.

Professional Development. Another dimension of considerable importance in evaluating the performance of individual salespeople relates to professional development. **Professional development criteria** assess improvements in certain characteristics of salespeople that are related to successful performance in the sales job. For example, if product knowledge is critical in a particular selling situation, then evaluations of the product knowledge of individual salespeople over various time periods should be conducted. Examples of professional development criteria are presented in Exhibit 16.6.

Many sales organizations appear to incorporate multiple professional development criteria into their salesperson performance evaluations. This is appropriate, since salespeople have control over the development of personal characteristics related to

Figure 16.2 **Dimensions of Salesperson Performance Evaluation**

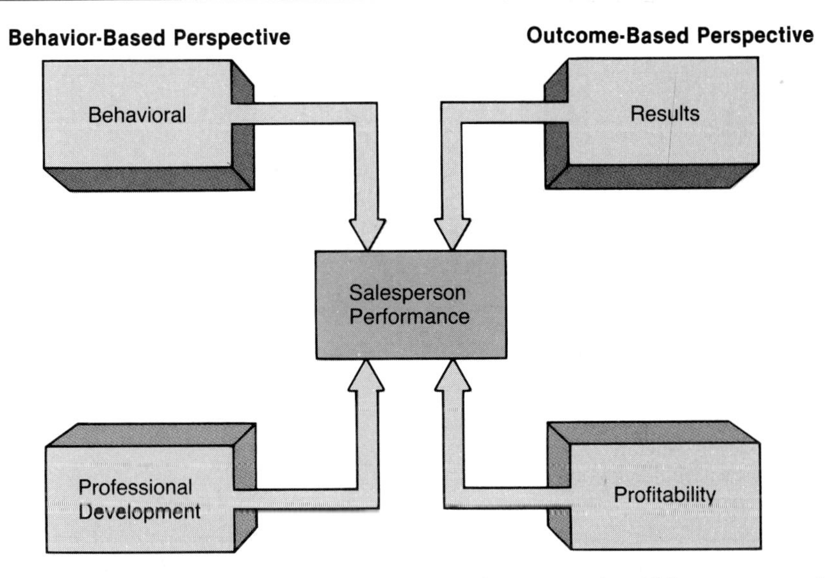

A comprehensive evaluation of salesperson performance should incorporate criteria from these different dimensions. Sales organizations employing a behavior-based perspective would focus on behavioral and professional development criteria, while those following an outcome-based perspective would emphasize results and profitability criteria.

Exhibit 16.5 **Behavioral Criteria**

Base	Percent Using
Calls	
Calls per period	57
Number of calls per number of customers (by product class)	17
Ancillary Activities	
Number of required reports turned in	44
Number of customer complaints	31
Training meetings conducted	28
Number of letters/phone calls to prospects	25
Number of demonstrations conducted	25
Number of service calls made	24
Number of dealer meetings held	15
Advertising displays set up	12

Source: Donald W. Jackson, Jr., Janet E. Keith, and John L. Schlacter, "Evaluation of Selling Performance: A Study of Current Practices," *Journal of Personal Selling and Sales Management,* November 1983, 47. Used with permission.

Exhibit 16.6 **Professional Development Criteria**

Base	Percent Using
Attitude	90
Product knowledge	89
Selling skills	85
Appearance and manner	82
Communication skills	81
Initiative and aggressiveness	80
Planning ability	78
Time management	73
Knowledge of competition	72
Judgment	69
Creativity	61
Knowledge of company policies	59
Report preparation and submission	59
Customer goodwill generated	50
Degree of respect from trade and competition	34
Good citizenship	23

Source: Donald W. Jackson, Jr., Janet E. Keith, and John L. Schlacter, "Evaluation of Selling Performance: A Study of Current Practices," *Journal of Personal Selling and Sales Management,* November 1983, 47. Used with permission.

success in their selling situation. The professional development criteria introduce a long-term perspective into the process of salesperson performance evaluation. Salespeople that are developing professionally are increasing their chances of successful performance over the long run. Although the professional development and behavioral criteria might be combined into one category, we prefer to keep them separate to reflect their different perspectives.

Results. The results achieved by salespeople are extremely important and should be typically evaluated. Examples of **results criteria** used in salesperson performance evaluations are listed in Exhibit 16.7.

A potential problem with the use of results criteria in Exhibit 16.7 is that the overall results measures do not reflect the territory situations faced by individual salespeople. The salesperson with the highest level of sales may have the best territory and may not necessarily be the best performer in generating sales. Aside from the impossible task of developing territories that are exactly equal, the only way to address this potential problem is to compare actual results to standards that reflect the unique territory situation faced by each salesperson. The development of sales quotas was discussed in Chapter 14. Other types of quotas will be discussed later in this chapter. As indicated in Exhibit 16.7, some sales organizations do compare results to quotas for at least some of the results criteria.

Exhibit 16.7 **Results Criteria**

Base	Percent Using
Sales	
Sales volume in dollars	81
Sales volume to previous year's sales	78
Sales volume by product or product line	69
Amount of new account sales	58
Sales volume in units	54
Sales volume to dollar quota	54
Sales volume by customer	49
Sales volume to market potential	34
Sales volume to physical unit quota	24
Sales volume per order	15
Sales volume by outlet type	11
Sales volume per call	10
Percentage of sales made by telephone or mail	8
Market Share	
Market share per quota	18
Accounts	
Number of new accounts	71
Number of accounts lost	43
Number of accounts on which payment is overdue	22
Number of accounts buying the full line	16

Source: Donald W. Jackson, Jr., Janet E. Keith, and John L. Schlacter, "Evaluation of Selling Performance: A Study of Current Practices," *Journal of Personal Selling and Sales Management,* November 1983, 46. Used with permission.

Profitability. A potential problem with focusing on sales results is that the profitability of sales is not assessed. Salespeople can affect profitability in two basic ways. First, salespeople have an impact on gross profits through the specific products they sell and/or through the prices they negotiate for final sale. Thus, two salespeople could generate the same level of sales dollars and achieve the same sales/sales quota evaluation, but one salesperson could produce more gross profits by selling higher margin products and/or maintaining higher prices in sales negotiations.

Second, salespeople affect net profits by the expenses they incur in generating sales. The selling expenses most under the control of salespeople are travel and entertainment expenses. Therefore, two salespeople could generate the same levels of total sales, the same sales/sales quota performance, and even the same levels of gross profits, but one salesperson could contribute more to net profits through lower travel and entertainment costs. Examples of **profitability criteria** are listed in Exhibit 16.8.

Exhibit 16.8 **Profitability Criteria**

Profit	
Net profit dollars	26
Return on investment	16
Net profit contribution	14
Gross margin	14
Gross margin per sales	14
Net profit as a % of sales	13
Orders	
Order/call ratio	26
Net orders per repeat order	17
Number of cancelled orders per orders booked	14
Selling Expense	
Selling expense to sales	41
Selling expense to quota	22
Average cost per call	13

Source: Donald W. Jackson, Jr., Janet E. Keith, and John L. Schlacter, "Evaluation of Selling Performance: A Study of Current Practices," *Journal of Personal Selling and Sales Management,* November 1983, 46. Used with permission.

Surprisingly, relatively few sales organizations seem to incorporate profitability criteria into their salesperson performance evaluations. The most popular profitability criterion is *selling expenses as a percentage of sales.* Very few sales organizations appear to emphasize the gross margins generated by individual salespeople. The need to address profitability criteria is especially important in the current slow growth, competitive environment where sales growth is so difficult and productivity and profitability so important.

Comment on Criteria. Conducting a comprehensive evaluation of salesperson performance typically requires consideration of behavioral, professional development, results, and profitability criteria. Each set of criteria tells a different story as to how well salespeople have performed and provides different diagnostic information for control purposes. We will now discuss different methods for evaluating salespeople against these criteria.

Methods of Performance Evaluation

Sales managers can employ a number of different methods for measuring the behaviors, professional development, results, and profitability of salespeople. Ideally, the method employed should have the following characteristics:[4]

- *Job relatedness.* The performance evaluation method should be designed to meet the needs of each specific sales organization.

Exhibit 16.9 **Comparison of Performance Evaluation Methods**

	Evaluation Criteria							
	Job Relatedness	**Reliability**	**Validity**	**Standard-ization**	**Practicality**	**Compara-bility**	**Discrimin-ability**	**Usefulness**
Performance-Evaluation Method								
Graphic rating/checklist	Very good	Good	Good	Very good	Very good	Very good	Poor	Good
Ranking	Poor	Poor	Poor	Very good	Poor	Good	Excellent	Poor
Objective-setting/MBO	Very good	Good	Good	Poor	Good	Poor	Good	Poor
Behaviorally-Anchored Rating Scale (BARS)	Very good	Good	Good	Poor	Good	Poor	Poor	Good

Source: Adapted from Mark R. Edwards, W. Theodore Cummings, and John L. Schlacter, "The Paris-Peroia Solution: Innovations in Appraising Regional and International Sales Personnel," *Journal of Personal Selling and Sales Management,* November 1984, 29. Used with permission.

- *Reliability*. The measures should be stable over time and exhibit internal consistency.
- *Validity*. The measures should provide accurate assessments of the criteria they are intended to measure.
- *Standardization*. The measurement instruments and evaluation process should be similar throughout the sales organization.
- *Practicality*. Sales managers and salespeople should understand the entire performance appraisal process and should be able to implement it in a reasonable amount of time.
- *Comparability*. The results of the performance evaluation process should make it possible to compare the performance of individual salespeople directly.
- *Discriminability*. The evaluative methods must be capable of detecting differences in the performance of individual salespeople.
- *Usefulness*. The information provided by the performance evaluation must be valuable to sales managers in making various decisions.

Designing methods of salesperson performance evaluation that possess all of these characteristics is a difficult task. As indicated in Exhibit 16.9, each evaluative method has certain strengths and weaknesses. No one method provides a perfect evaluation. Therefore, it is important to understand the strengths and weaknesses of each method so that several can be combined to produce the best evaluative procedure for a given sales organization.

Graphic Rating/Checklist Methods. Graphic rating/checklist methods consist of approaches where salespeople are evaluated using some type of performance evalua-

Exhibit 16.10 **Graphic Rating/Checklist Example**

1. Asks customers for their ideas for promoting business

   Almost Never 1 2 3 4 5 Almost Always NA

2. Offers customers help in solving their problems

   Almost Never 1 2 3 4 5 Almost Always NA

3. Is constantly smiling when interacting with customers

   Almost Never 1 2 3 4 5 Almost Always NA

4. Admits when he doesn't know the answer, but promises to find out

   Almost Never 1 2 3 4 5 Almost Always NA

5. Generates new ways of tackling new or ongoing problems

   Almost Never 1 2 3 4 5 Almost Always NA

6. Returns customers' calls the same day

   Almost Never 1 2 3 4 5 Almost Always NA

7. Retains his composure in front of customers

   Almost Never 1 2 3 4 5 Almost Always NA

8. Delivers what he promises on time

   Almost Never 1 2 3 4 5 Almost Always NA

9. Remains positive about company in front of customers

   Amost Never 1 2 3 4 5 Almost Always NA

Source: Jan P. Muczyk and Myron Gable, "Managing Sales Performance Through a Comprehensive Performance Appraisal System," *Journal of Personal Selling and Sales Management,* May 1987, 46. Used with permission.

tion form. The performance evaluation form contains the criteria to be used in the evaluation as well as some means to provide an assessment of how well each salesperson performed on each criterion. An example of part of such a form is presented in Exhibit 16.10.

This method is very popular in many sales organizations. It is especially useful in evaluating salesperson behavioral and professional development criteria. However, rating methods have been developed to evaluate all of the important salesperson performance dimensions.[5] As evident from Exhibit 16.9, graphic rating/checklist methods possess many desirable characteristics, especially in terms of job relatedness, standardization, practicality, and comparability. The reliability and validity of these methods, however, must be continually assessed and the specific rating scales improved over time.

The major disadvantage of graphic rating/checklist methods is in providing evaluations that discriminate sufficiently among the performances of individual salespeople or among the performances on different criteria for the same salesperson. These

Exhibit 16.11 **Ranking Method Example**

	Performance Criterion: Communication Skills					
	Much Better	**Slightly Better**	**Equal**	**Slightly Better**	**Much Better**	
Jane Haynes	X					***John Evans***
Ron Castaneda		X				***Jane Haynes***
Bill Haroldson			X			***Jane Haynes***

Source: Adapted from Mark R. Edwards, W. Theodore Cummings, and John L. Schlacter, "The Paris-Peoria Solution: Innovations in Appraising Regional and International Sales Personnel," *Journal of Personal Selling and Sales Management,* November 1984, 31. Used with permission.

problems are due to potential biases of sales managers when completing the evaluations (see examples in the opening vignette). For example, some sales managers may be very lenient in their evaluations, may try to play it safe and give all salespeople ratings around the average. Others might evaluate salespeople that they like higher than those they dislike. In addition, when evaluating an individual salesperson, some sales managers are subject to a *halo effect,* meaning that their evaluations on one criteria affect their ratings on other criteria.

The advantages of graphic rating/checklist methods clearly outweigh the disadvantages. However, care must be taken to minimize potential sales management biases when the evaluation forms are completed, and continuous attention to reliability and validity issues is necessary.

Ranking Methods. Otherwise similar to graphic rating/checklist methods, **ranking methods** rank all salespeople according to relative performance on each performance criterion rather than evaluating them against a set of performance criteria. Many different approaches might be used to obtain the rankings. An example of a ranking approach where salespeople are compared in pairs concerning relative communication skills is presented in Exhibit 16.11.

Ranking methods provide a standardized approach to evaluation and thus force discrimination as to the performance of individual salespeople on each criterion. The process of ranking forces this discrimination in performance. Despite these advantages, ranking methods have many shortcomings as indicated in Exhibit 16.9. Of major concern are the constraints on their practicality and usefulness. Ranking all salespeople against each performance criterion can be a complex and cognitively difficult task. The ranking task can be simplified by using paired-comparison approaches like the one presented in Exhibit 16.11. However, the computations required to translate the paired comparisons into overall rankings can be extremely cumbersome.

Even if the evaluative and computative procedures can be simplified, the rankings that are obtained are of limited usefulness. Rank data reveal only relative ordering and omit any assessment of the differences between ranks. For example, the actual differences in the communication skills of salespeople ranked first, second, and third may be very small or very large, but there is no way to tell the degree of these differences from the ranked data. In addition, information obtained from graphic rating/checklist methods can always be transformed into rankings, but rankings cannot be translated into graphic rating/checklist form. Therefore, using ranking methods for salesperson performance evaluations is recommended only as an adjunct to other methods.

Objective Setting Methods. The most common and comprehensive goal setting method is **management by objectives** (MBO). Applied to a salesforce, the typical MBO approach is as follows:[6]

1. Mutual setting of well-defined and measurable goals within a specified time period.
2. Managing activities within the specified time period toward the accomplishment of the stated objectives.
3. Appraisal of performance against objectives.

As with all of the performance evaluation methods, MBO and other goal setting methods have certain strengths and weaknesses (see Exhibit 16.9). Although complete reliance on this or any other goal setting method is inadvisable, the incorporation of some goal setting procedures is normally desirable. This is especially true for performance criteria related to quantitative behavioral, professional development, results, and profitability criteria. Absolute measures of these dimensions are often not very meaningful due to extreme differences in the territory situations of individual salespeople. The setting of objectives or quotas provides a means for controlling for territory differences through the establishment of performance benchmarks that incorporate these territory differences.

The development of sales quotas was discussed in Chapter 14. Quotas can be established for other important results criteria and for specific behavioral, professional development, and profitability criteria. Each type of quota represents a specific objective for a salesperson to achieve during a given time period. Actual performance can be compared to the quota objective and a performance index calculated for each criterion being evaluated. The individual performance indices can then be weighted to reflect their relative importance and combined to produce an overall performance index. An example of this procedure is shown in Exhibit 16.12.

This example illustrates an evaluation of Mary, John, and Nancy on sales, gross profit, and demonstration quotas. The unequal weights reflect that the firm is placing the most importance on gross profits, followed by demonstrations and then sales. Nancy has performed the best overall, but she did not reach her sales quota for this

Exhibit 16.12 **Quota Evaluation Example**

Salesperson	Quota	Weight	Actual Performance	Index	Weighted Performance
Nancy					
Sales	300,000	2	275,000	92	184
Gross Profits	75,000	5	90,000	120	600
Demonstration	100	3	125	125	375
Overall Performance					116
John					
Sales	350,000	2	355,000	101	202
Gross Profits	85,000	5	87,000	102	510
Demonstrations	100	3	100	100	300
Overall Performance					101
Mary					
Sales	275,000	2	325,000	118	236
Gross Profits	70,000	5	50,000	71	355
Demonstrations	90	3	75	83	249
Overall Performance					84

period. John has performed reasonably well on all criteria. Mary's situation is interesting in that she performed the best on the sales quota but poorly overall due to very low performance indices for gross profits and demonstrations. Perhaps she is concentrating too much on short-term sales generation and not concerning herself with the profitability of sales or the number of product demonstrations. In any case, the use of quotas provides an extremely useful method for evaluating salesperson performance and highlighting specific areas where performance is especially good or especially poor.

Behaviorally Anchored Rating Scales. The uniqueness of behaviorally anchored rating scales (BARS) is due to its focus on trying to link salesperson behaviors with specific results. These behavior-results linkages become the basis for salesperson performance evaluation in this method.

The development of a BARS approach is an iterative process that actively incorporates members of the salesforce.[7] Salespeople are used to identify important performance results and the critical behaviors necessary to achieve those results. The critical behaviors are assigned numbers on a rating scale for each performance result. An example of one such BARS rating scale is presented in Figure 16.3.

The performance result in this example is achieving cooperative relations with sales team members. Seven behaviors have been assigned numbers on a 10-point rating scale to reflect the linkage between engaging in the behavior and achieving the result. This scale can then be used to evaluate individual salespeople. For instance,

Figure 16.3 **BARS Scale**

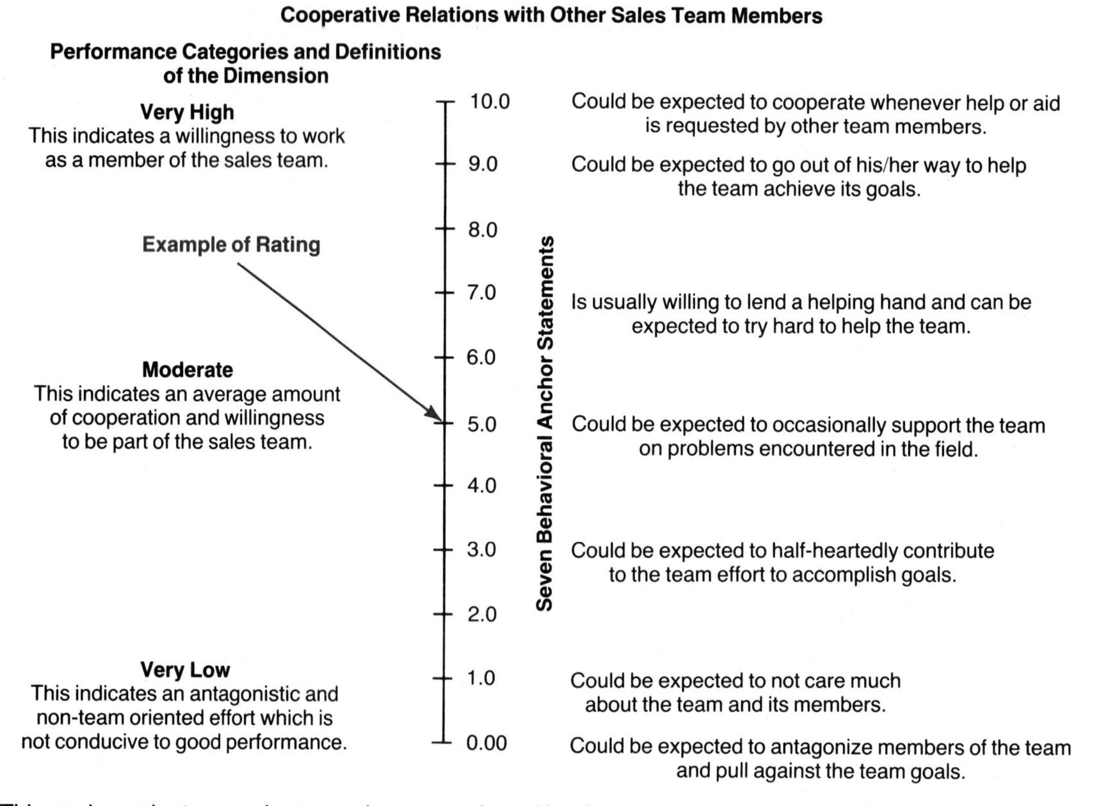

This scale evaluates a salesperson's cooperation with other sales team members. The example rating of 5 suggests a moderate level of cooperation in which the salesperson gives only occasional support to the sales team.

Source: A. Benton Cocanougher and John M. Ivancevich, "'BARS' Performance Rating for Sales Force Personnel." Reprinted from *Journal of Marketing*, 42 (July 1978): 91, published by the American Marketing Association. Used with permission.

the example rating of 5 in the exhibit suggests that the salesperson occasionally supports the sales team on problems encountered in the field and thus achieves only a moderate amount of cooperation with sales team members.

As indicated in Exhibit 16.9, the BARS approach rates high on job relatedness. This is because of the rigorous process used to determine important performance results and critical salesperson behaviors. The results and behaviors identified in this manner are specific to a given selling situation and directly related to the job of the salespeople being evaluated. The really unique aspect of BARS is the focus on linkages between behaviors and results. No other approach incorporates this perspective.

INTERNATIONAL SALES

COMPARING SALESPERSON PERFORMANCE IN DIFFERENT COUNTRIES

Problem: A salesperson from Paris, France, applies for the same International Marketing Information Manager's job as a salesperson from Peoria, Illinois. *Question:* How can these two salespeople from the same company be equitably compared so that the best potential manager is selected and the selection decision is fair to the salespeople, accurate and valid for management, and defensible in court?

Major international corporations such as R. J. Reynolds, Syntex, and Gulf Oil are using various forms of a performance appraisal process termed *team evaluation consensus (TEC)*. The TEC approach consists of direct comparisons of specific salespeople, the use of benchmarks and quotas, the use of multiple raters for each salesperson, and the incorporation of various safeguards to ensure fairness. Over 60 firms have successfully employed the TEC approach to evaluate the performance of their salespeople operating in different countries.

Source: Mark R. Edwards, W. Theodore Cummings, and John L. Schlacter, "The Paris-Peoria Solution: Innovations in Appraising Regional and International Sales Personnel," *Journal of Personal Selling and Sales Management*, November 1984, 27–38.

In sum, the basic methods for evaluating salesperson performance include graphic rating/checklist methods, ranking methods, objective setting methods, and BARS methods. Each approach has specific strengths and weaknesses that should be considered when using a particular approach. Combining different methods into the salesperson performance evaluation process is one way to capitalize on the strengths and minimize the weaknesses inherent in each approach. These combination approaches are especially useful when evaluating international salesperson performance (see "International Sales: Comparing Salesperson Performance in Different Countries"). Our attention will now turn to how the information obtained in the salesperson performance evaluation process might be used by sales managers.

Using Performance Information

Using different methods to evaluate the behavioral, professional development, results, and profitability of salespeople provides extremely important performance information. The critical sales management task is to use this information to improve the performance of individual salespeople and the overall operations of the sales organization. Initially it should be used to determine the absolute and relative performance of each salesperson. These determinations then provide the basis for reward disbursements, special recognition, promotions, and so forth.

The second major use of this performance information is to identify potential problems or areas where salespeople need to improve for better performance in the future. If salespeople are evaluated against multiple criteria, as suggested in this chap-

Figure 16.4 **Framework for Using Performance Information**

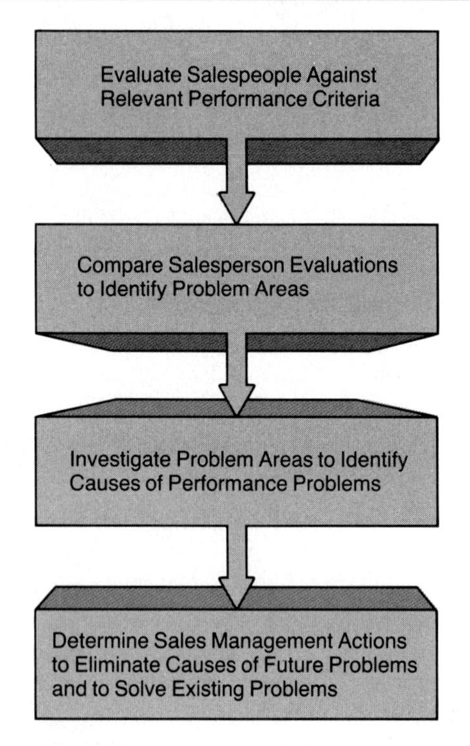

Sales managers need to be able to use the information provided by salesperson performance evaluations in a diagnostic manner. The basic diagnostic approach is to determine problem areas, identify the causes of these problems, and take appropriate action to eliminate the causes and to solve problems that are already present, thus improving future salesperson performance.

ter, useful diagnostic information will be available. The difficulty exists in isolating the specific causes of low performance areas. A framework for performing this analysis is given in Figure 16.4.

The first step in this analysis is to review the performance of each salesperson against each relevant criterion and then to summarize the results across all salespeople being supervised. The purpose of this step is to determine if there are common areas of low performance. For example, the situation is quite different if most salespeople are not meeting their sales quota than if only one or two salespeople do not meet their sales quotas.

Once the poor performance areas have been identified, the sales manager must work backwards to try to identify the cause of the poor performance. Merely deter-

Exhibit 16.13 **Example Problems, Causes, and Management Actions**

Performance Problems	Potential Causes	Sales Management Actions
Not meeting sales or other results quotas	Sales or other results quotas incorrect; poor account coverage; too few sales calls	Revise sales or other results quotas; revise effort allocation; redesign territories; develop motivational programs; provide closer supervision; increase salesforce size
Not meeting behavioral quotas	Behavioral quotas incorrect; too little effort; poor quality of effort	Revise behavioral quotas; develop motivational programs; increase salesforce size; conduct training programs; provide closer supervision
Not meeting profitability quotas	Profitability quotas incorrect; low gross margins; high selling expenses	Revise profitability quotas; change compensation; devise incentive programs; provide closer supervision; conduct training programs
Not meeting professional development quotas	Professional development quotas incorrect	Revise professional development quotas; conduct training programs; provide closer supervision; develop motivational programs; change hiring practices

mining that most salespeople did not meet their sales quotas is not sufficient to improve future performance; the sales manager must try to uncover the reason for this poor performance. The basic approach is to try to answer the question, "What factors affect the achievement of this performance dimension?" For instance, in regard to achieving sales quotas, the key question is, "What factors determine whether salespeople achieve their sales quotas or not?" All of the factors identified should be reviewed to isolate the cause of any poor performance. Several factors that might cause poor performance in different areas are presented in Exhibit 16.13.

After identifying the potential causes of poor performance, the sales manager must determine the appropriate action to reduce or eliminate the cause of the problem so that performance will be improved in the future. Examples of potential management actions for specific problems are also presented in Exhibit 16.13.

Consider again the poor performance on sales quota achievement. Assume that intense review of this problem produces evidence that salespeople not meeting sales quotas also do not make many product demonstrations to prospects. This analysis suggests that if salespeople were to make more product demonstrations, they would be able to generate more sales and thus achieve their sales quotas. The sales management task is to determine what management actions will lead to more product demonstrations by salespeople. Possible actions include more training on product dem-

SALES TREND

SALESFORCE QUALITY IMPROVEMENT

Many firms are beginning to implement quality improvement programs for their salesforces. The basic quality improvement approach is to establish quality improvement teams consisting of salespeople and sales managers, have these teams develop specific programs to improve salesforce quality, and implement the quality improvement program throughout the sales organization.

Eastman Chemical Products provides an interesting example of this approach. One of the company's quality improvement teams identified the need to improve sales call quality. The team spent a great deal of time analyzing sales calls from a customer perspective and decided that there were 17 major elements to a quality sales call. They developed a checklist and grading system for the 17 quality sales call elements. The checklist and grading system is being used as a training vehicle and as a way for salespeople and sales managers to evaluate and improve sales call quality.

Other quality improvement teams at Eastman Chemical Products have used similar approaches to develop programs for improving relationships with customers and for improving the sales organization's market intelligence system.

Source: Adapted from Walter Ambrogi and Donald L. Blair, "Quality Management in a Field Marketing Organization," *Survey of Business*, Spring 1986, 30–31.

onstrations, motivational programs directed toward increasing the number of product demonstrations, direct communication with individual salespeople about the need for more product demonstrations, or some combination of these or other management actions.

This discussion highlights the thought processes that sales managers need to use to identify performance problems, isolate the causes of these problems, and determine the appropriate management actions necessary to solve the problems and improve future salesperson performance. Using this approach successfully requires that sales managers have a detailed understanding of the personal selling and sales management processes and relationships. Such an understanding is essential for them to be able to determine the causes of performance problems and identify the appropriate management actions to solve these problems. In addition to solving problems that have been identified, many firms are focusing on quality improvement programs as suggested in "Sales Trend: Salesforce Quality Improvement."

Our discussion and examples have emphasized problems affecting many salespeople. The same basic approach can be used for performance problems that are unique to one individual salesperson. In fact, many sales organizations use performance reviews as a means for a sales manager to meet with each salesperson, analyze the salesperson's performance on each criterion, and suggest ways to improve future performance. These performance reviews provide one means for communicating the *performance feedback* that is so important to salespeople. Performance feedback is also an important determinant of salesperson job satisfaction, which will be discussed next.

SALESPERSON JOB SATISFACTION

In addition to evaluating salesperson performance, sales managers should be concerned with the **job satisfaction** of salespeople. Research results have consistently found a negative relationship between salesperson job satisfaction and turnover, absenteeism, and motivation.[8] Salespeople who are satisfied with their job tend to stay with the firm and work harder than those who are not satisfied.

Other research has investigated relationships between salesperson performance and salesperson satisfaction. This research has produced conflicting findings concerning the direction of the relationship between performance and satisfaction.[9] In other words, it has not been established whether achieving high performance causes salesperson satisfaction or whether salesperson satisfaction determines salesperson performance. It is clear, however, that sales managers should be concerned with both the performance and satisfaction of their salespeople. Of importance to sales managers is how salesperson satisfaction might be measured and then how this satisfaction information might be used.

Measuring Salesperson Job Satisfaction

Since job satisfaction is based on individual perceptions, measures of salesperson satisfaction must be based on data provided by individual salespeople. In addition, there are many different aspects of a salesperson's job, and these different areas should be incorporated into the satisfaction evaluation. Fortunately, a scale for evaluating the job satisfaction of salespeople, termed INDSALES, has been developed and validated. Portions of this scale are presented in Exhibit 16.14.[10]

On this scale, salespeople indicate their level of agreement with a number of statements concerning their particular sales job. These statements are designed to measure their satisfaction in seven general areas: satisfaction with the job, fellow workers, supervision, company policy and support, pay, promotion and advancement, and customers. Answers to the specific questions for each area are summed to produce a separate satisfaction score for each job dimension. These individual job dimension scores can then be summed to form an overall salesperson satisfaction score. Sales managers can then view the dimensional or overall satisfaction scores for each salesperson or for specified groups of salespeople.

Using Job Satisfaction Information

INDSALES provides extremely useful evaluative and diagnostic information. Since sales managers can evaluate the degree of salesperson satisfaction with specific aspects of the sales job, areas where satisfaction is low can be investigated further by looking at the individual questions for that dimension. For example, if salespeople tended to express dissatisfaction with the supervision they were receiving, management could investigate the answers to the specific questions designed to evaluate the supervision dimension (see Exhibit 16.14). The sales manager in this example might find that

Exhibit 16.14 **Example of INDSALES Scale**

Component	Total number of items	Sample items
The job	12	My work is challenging.
		My job is often dull and monotonous.
		My work gives me a sense of accomplishment.
		My job is exciting.
Fellow workers	12	The people I work with get along well together.
		My fellow workers are selfish.
		My fellow workers are intelligent.
		My fellow workers are responsible.
Supervision	16	My sales manager really tries to get our ideas about things
		My sales manager doesn't seem to try too hard to get our problems across to management.
		My sales manager sees that we have the things we need to do our jobs.
Company policy and support	21	Compared with other companies, employee benefits here are good.
		Sometimes when I learn of management's plans I wonder if they know the territory situation at all.
		The company's sales training is not carried out in a well-planned program.
		The company is highly aggresssive in its sales promotional efforts.
		Management is progressive.
Pay	11	My pay is high in comparison with what others get for similar work in other companies.
		My pay doesn't give me much incentive to increase my sales.
		My selling ability largely determines my earnings in this company.
		My income provides for luxuries.
Promotion and advancement	8	My opportunites for advancement are limited.
		Promotion here is based on ability.
		I have a good chance for promotion.
		Regular promotions are the rule in this company.
Customers	15	My customers are fair.
		My customers blame me for problems that I have no control over.
		My customers respect my judgment.
		I seldom know who really makes the purchase decisions in the companies I call upon.

Source: Gilbert A. Churchill, Jr., Neil M. Ford, and Orville C. Walker, Jr., "Measuring the Job Satisfaction of Industrial Salesmen." Reprinted from *Journal of Marketing Research,* August 1974, 258, published by the American Marketing Association. Used with permission.

most salespeople responded negatively to the statement, "My sales manager really tries to get our ideas about things." The sales manager could then try to increase salesperson satisfaction by using a more participative management style and trying to incorporate salesperson input into the decision making process.

One useful approach is to perform separate analyses of salesperson satisfaction for high-performing and low-performing salespeople. Research results suggest that there may be important differences in job satisfaction between high performers and low performers. Not incorporating these differences could lead sales managers to make changes that would tend to reduce the turnover of low performers but not of high performers.[11]

Research has also found an important relationship between salesperson satisfaction and performance feedback.[12] This finding suggests the need for sales managers to pay attention to the relationships among performance evaluation, performance feedback, and salesperson job satisfaction. Although these exact relationships are not completely understood, they are apparently all important for the effective functioning of a sales organization. Carefully evaluating salesperson performance and satisfaction, identifying problem areas, and solving these problems is really what sales management is all about.

SUMMARY

1. **Discuss the different purposes of salesperson performance evaluations.** Performance evaluations can serve many different purposes and should be designed with specific purposes in mind. They may serve to determine appropriate compensation and other reward disbursements, to identify salespeople who should be promoted or fired, to determine training and counseling needs, to provide information for human resource planning, and to identify criteria for future recruitment and selection of salespeople.
2. **Differentiate between an outcome-based and behavior-based perspective for evaluating and controlling salesperson performance.** An outcome-based perspective focuses on objective measures of results, with little monitoring or direction of salesperson efforts by sales managers. In contrast, a behavior-based perspective focuses on close supervision of salesperson efforts and subjective measures of salesperson characteristics, activities, and strategies. The perspective taken by a sales organization will affect salespeople and has important implications for sales management.
3. **Describe the different types of criteria necessary for comprehensive evaluations of salesperson performance.** The multifaceted nature of sales jobs requires that performance evaluations incorporate multiple criteria. Although the specific criteria depend upon the characteristics of a particular selling situation, comprehensive evaluations of salesperson performance require that four dimensions be

addressed: behavioral, professional development, results, and profitability. Addressing each of these areas is necessary to get a complete picture of salesperson performance and to produce the diagnostic information needed to improve future performance.

4. **Compare the advantages and disadvantages of different methods of salesperson performance evaluation.** Sales managers can use four basic methods to evaluate salesperson behaviors, professional development, results, and profitability: graphic rating/checklist methods, ranking methods, objective setting methods, and behaviorally anchored rating scales (BARS). Each method has certain strengths and weaknesses that must be understood and can be compensated for by using other methods in combination. Special attention should be directed toward developing performance benchmarks or quotas that reflect the unique characteristics of each territory.
5. **Explain how salesperson performance information can be used to identify problems, determine their causes, and suggest actions to solve them.** The suggested approach is to first identify areas of poor performance, then work backwards to try to identify the cause by asking, "What factors affect the achievement of this performance dimension?" Finally, the most effective sales management action to remove the cause of the problem and improve future performance must be decided upon. Examples of possible actions are given in Exhibit 16.13.
6. **Discuss the measurement and importance of salesperson job satisfaction.** Dissatisfied salespeople tend to be absent more, leave the firm more, and work less hard than satisfied salespeople. The INDSALES scale can be used to measure salesperson satisfaction in total and for specific job dimensions. Analysis of the satisfaction with individual job dimensions can be used to determine appropriate action to increase salesperson job satisfaction.

Key Terms

- outcome-based perspective
- behavior-based perspective
- behavioral criteria
- professional development criteria
- results criteria
- profitability criteria
- graphic rating/checklist methods
- ranking methods
- management by objectives (MBO)
- behaviorally anchored rating scales (BARS)
- job satisfaction

Review Questions

1. Discuss the different purposes of an evaluation of salesperson performance and how each purpose affects the performance evaluation process.
2. Characterize the salesforce of a firm that uses an outcome-based perspective for evaluating salespeople.

3. Why should sales managers pay more attention to behavioral criteria when evaluating salespeople?
4. Why should professional development criteria be included in salesperson performance evaluations?
5. Compare and contrast the graphic rating/checklist and ranking methods for evaluating salesperson performance.
6. Discuss the importance of using different types of quotas in evaluating and controlling salesperson performance.
7. What is unique about the BARS method for evaluating salesperson performance?
8. Why should sales managers be concerned with the job satisfaction of salespeople?
9. Do more satisfied salespeople always perform better than less satisfied salespeople? Why or why not?
10. How can evaluations of salesperson performance and satisfaction be used by sales managers?

Application Exercises

1. Contact three sales organizations in the same basic industry. Compare and contrast the procedures they use to evaluate salesperson performance and satisfaction. What are your recommendations for improving their procedures?
2. Contact three sales organizations in different industries. Compare and contrast the procedures they use to evaluate salesperson performance and satisfaction. What are your recommendations for improving their procedures?
3. As the national sales manager for the XYZ Company, you are concerned about the job satisfaction of your salespeople. A random sample of high- and low-performing salespeople have completed the INDSALES instrument, with 1 equaling strong disagreement with the statement and 5 equaling strong agreement with the statement. The results are as follows:

	Average Score		
Item	**High Performers**	**Low Performers**	**All Respondents**
1. My work is challenging.	4.3	4.1	4.2
2. My sales manager sees that we have the things we need to do our jobs.	3.2	2.8	3.0
3. My selling ability largely determines my earnings in this company.	4.5	2.7	3.6
4. Promotion here is based on ability.	3.2	4.2	3.7
5. My fellow workers are responsible.	3.3	3.1	3.2
6. The company's sales training program is not well-planned.	4.2	3.2	3.7
7. My customers blame me for problems that I have no control over.	4.5	4.1	4.3

What actions would you consider to improve salesforce job satisfaction?

4. You are the district sales manager for XYZ Corporation. It is time for the annual performance evaluation for the four salespeople you supervise. The following information has been assembled to help in the evaluation task. Use this information to

   a. Evaluate each individual salesperson.
   b. Compare performance across the salespeople.

	Sales Volume (Weight = 2)		Demonstrations (Weight = 1)		Proposals (Weight = 1)		Net Profit (Weight = 2)	
Salesperson	**Quota**	**Actual**	**Quota**	**Actual**	**Quota**	**Actual**	**Quota**	**Actual**
Bob Smith	$400,000	$425,000	50	40	25	10	$50,000	$60,000
Mary Jones	375,000	350,000	50	35	30	25	40,000	30,000
Sally Little	250,000	225,000	30	45	20	30	30,000	20,000
Sam Johnson	350,000	375,000	40	35	35	35	35,000	40,000

5. Use the SPREE (Salesperson Review and Evaluation) software to evaluate five different salespeople. Then, make the following comparisons:

   a. Compare the information used to evaluate each salesperson. How did the amount and types of information used change as you gained more experience in performing the evaluations?
   b. Compare the performance evaluations of each salesperson, and suggest appropriate sales management actions to improve the future performance of all five salespeople and each individual salesperson.

Notes

[1] Adapted from Jan P. Muczyk and Myron Gable, "Managing Sales Performance Through a Comprehensive Performance Appraisal System," *Journal of Personal Selling and Sales Management,* May 1987, 41.

[2] For more complete results, see Alan J. Dubinsky and Thomas E. Barry, "A Survey of Sales Management Practices," *Industrial Marketing Management,* 11, 1982, 133–141; Donald W. Jackson, Jr., Lonnie L. Ostrom, and Kenneth R. Evans, "Measures Used to Evaluate Industrial Marketing Activities," *Industrial Marketing Management,* 11, 1982, 269–274; and Donald W. Jackson, Janet E. Keith, and John L. Schlacter, "Evaluation of Selling Performance: A Study of Current Practices," *Journal of Personal Selling and Sales Management,* November 1983, 43–51.

[3] For a more complete discussion and theoretical rationale for these perspectives, see Erin Anderson and Richard L. Oliver, "Perspectives on Behavior-Based versus Outcome-Based Salesforce Control Systems," *Journal of Marketing,* October 1987, 76–88.

[4] See Mark R. Edwards, W. Theodore Cummings, and John L. Schlacter, "The Paris-Peoria Solution: Innovations in Appraising Regional and International Sales Personnel," *Journal of Personal Selling and Sales Management,* November 1984, 27–38.

[5] For a comprehensive scale for evaluating salesperson performance, see Douglas N. Behrman and William D. Perreault, Jr., "Measuring the Performance of Industrial Salespersons," *Journal of Business Research,* 10, 1982, 355–370.

[6] Edwards, Cummings, and Schlacter, 1984, 30.

[7] For a more complete discussion of this process, see A. Benton Cocanougher and John M. Ivancevich, "'BARS' Performance Rating for Sales Force Personnel," *Journal of Marketing,* July 1978, 87–95.

[8] For examples of these studies, see A. Parasuraman and Charles M. Futrell, "Demographics, Job Satisfaction, and Propensity to Leave of Industrial Salesmen," *Journal of Business Research,* 11, 1983, 33–48; and Charles M. Futrell and A. Parasuraman, "The Relationship of Satisfaction and Performance to Salesforce Turnover," *Journal of Marketing,* Fall 1984, 33–40.

[9] For examples of this research, see Richard P. Bagozzi, "Performance and Satisfaction in an Industrial Sales Force: An Examination of Their Antecedents and Simultaneity," *Journal of Marketing,* Spring 1980, 65–77; and Douglas N. Behrman and William D. Perreault, Jr., "A Role Stress Model of the Performance and Satisfaction of Industrial Salespersons," *Journal of Marketing,* Fall 1984, 9–21.

[10] For a complete discussion of the scale, see Gilbert A. Churchill, Jr., Neil M. Ford, and Orville C. Walker, Jr., "Measuring the Job Satisfaction of Industrial Salesmen," *Journal of Marketing Research,* August 1974, 254–260. For validation support, see Charles M. Futrell, "Measurement of Salespeople's Job Satisfaction: Convergent and Discriminant Validity of Corresponding INDSALES and Job Descriptive Index Scales," *Journal of Marketing Research,* November 1979, 591–597.

[11] Futrell and Parasuraman, 1984, 33–40.

[12] R. Kenneth Teas and James F. Horrell, "Salespeople Satisfaction and Performance Feedback," *Industrial Marketing Management,* 10, 1981, 49–57.

HANOVER-BATES CHEMICAL CORPORATION

James Sprague, newly appointed northeast district sales manager for the Hanover-Bates Chemical Corporation, leaned back in his chair as the door to his office slammed shut. "Great beginning," he thought. "Three days in my new job and the district's most experienced sales representative is threatening to quit."

On the previous night, James Sprague, Hank Carver (the district's most experienced sales representative), and John Follet, another senior member of the district sales staff, had met for dinner at Jim's suggestion. During dinner Jim had mentioned that one of his top priorities would be to conduct a sales and profit analysis of the district's business in order to identify opportunites to improve the district's profit performance. Jim had stated that he was confident that the analysis would indicate opportunities to reallocate district sales efforts in a manner that would increase profits. As Jim had indicated during the conversation, "My experience in analyzing district sales performance data for the national sales manager has convinced me that any district's allocation of sales effort to products and customer categories can be improved." Both Carver and Follet had nodded as Jim discussed his plans.

Hank Carver was waiting when Jim arrived at the district sales office the next morning. It soon became apparent that Carver was very upset by what he perceived as Jim's criticism of how he and the other district sales representatives were doing their jobs—and, more particularly, how they were allocating their time in terms of customers and products. As he concluded his heated comments, Carver said:

> This company has made it darned clear that thirty-four years of experience don't count for anything . . . and now someone with not much more than two years of selling experience and two years of pushing paper for the national sales manager at corporate headquarters tells me I'm not doing my job. . . . Maybe it's time for me to look for a new job . . . and since Trumbull Chemical [Hanover-Bates's major competitor] is hiring, maybe that's where I should start looking . . . and I'm not the only one who feels this way.

As Jim reflected on the scene that had just occurred, he wondered what he should do. It had been made clear to him when he had been promoted to manager of the

---

Source: This case was prepared by Professor Robert E. Witt, College and Graduate School of Business, the University of Texas, Austin, Texas. The case is intended to serve as a basis for class discussion rather than to illustrate effective or ineffective management.

Exhibit 1 **Hanover-Bates Chemical Corporation: Summary Income Statements, 1981–1985**

	1981	1982	1983	1984	1985
Sales	$19,890,000	$21,710,000	$19,060,000	$21,980,000	$23,890,000
Production expenses	11,934,000	13,497,000	12,198,000	13,612,000	14,563,000
Gross profit	7,956,000	8,213,000	6,862,000	8,368,000	9,327,000
Administrative expenses	2,606,000	2,887,000	2,792,000	2,925,000	3,106,000
Selling expenses	2,024,000	2,241,000	2,134,000	2,274,000	2,399,000
Pretax profit	3,326,000	3,085,000	1,936,000	3,169,000	3,822,000
Taxes	1,512,000	1,388,000	790,000	1,426,000	1,718,000
Net profit	$ 1,814,000	$ 1,697,000	$ 1,146,000	$ 1,743,000	$ 2,104,000

Exhibit 2 **District Sales Quota and Gross Profit Quota Performance, 1985**

District	Number of Sales Reps	Sales Quota	Sales—Actual	Gross Profit Quota[a]	Gross Profit—Actual
1	7	$ 3,880,000	$ 3,906,000	$1,552,000	$1,589,000
2	6	3,750,000	3,740,000	1,500,000	1,529,000
3	6	3,650,000	3,406,000	1,460,000	1,239,000
4	6	3,370,000	3,318,000	1,348,000	1,295,000
5	5	3,300,000	3,210,000	1,320,000	1,186,000
6	5	3,130,000	3,205,000	1,252,000	1,179,000
7	5	2,720,000	3,105,000	1,088,000	1,310,000
		$23,800,000	$23,890,000	$9,520,000	$9,327,000

[a]District gross profit quotas were developed by the national sales manager in consultation with the district managers and took into account price competition in the respective districts.

northeast sales district that one of his top priorities should be improvement of the district's profit performance. As the national sales manager had said, "The northeast sales district may rank third in dollar sales, but it's our worst district in terms of profit performance."

Prior to assuming his new position, Jim had assembled the data presented in Exhibits 1 through 6 to assist him in analyzing district sales and profits. The data had been compiled from records maintained in the national sales manager's office. Although he believed the data would provide a sound base for a preliminary analysis of district sales and profit performance, Jim had recognized that additional data would probably have to be collected when he arrived in the northeast district (District 3).

In response the the national sales manager's comment about the northeast district's poor profit performance, Jim had been particularly interested in how the district had performed on its gross profit quota. He knew that district gross profit quotas were assigned in a manner that took into account variation in price competition. Thus he felt that poor performance in the gross profit quota area reflected misallocated

Exhibit 3 **District Selling Expenses, 1985**

District	Sales Rep Salaries[a]	Sales Commission	Sales Rep Expenses	District Office	District Manager Salary	District Manager Expenses	Sales Support	Total Selling Expenses
1	$177,100	$19,426	$56,280	$21,150	$33,500	$11,460	$69,500	388,416
2	143,220	18,700	50,760	21,312	34,000	12,034	71,320	351,346
3	157,380	17,030	54,436	22,123	35,000[b]	12,382	70,010	368,529
4	150,480	16,590	49,104	22,004	32,500	11,005	66,470	348,153
5	125,950	16,050	42,720	21,115	33,000	11,123	76,600	326,558
6	124,850	16,265	41,520	20,992	33,500	11,428	67,100	315,655
7	114,850	17,530	44,700	22,485	31,500	11,643	58,750	300,258
								$2,398,915

[a]Includes cost of fringe benefit program, which was 10 percent of base salary.

[b]Salary of Jim Sprague's predecessor.

sales efforts either in terms of customers or in the mix of product line items sold. To provide himself with a frame of reference, Jim had also requested data on the north-central sales district (District 7). This district was generally considered to be one of the best, if not the best, in the company. Furthermore, the north-central district sales manager, who was only three years older than Jim, was highly regarded by the national sales manager.

The Company and Industry

The Hanover-Bates Chemical Corporation was a leading producer of processing chemicals for the chemical plating industry. The company's products were produced in four plants located in Los Angeles, Houston, Chicago, and Newark, New Jersey. The company's production process was, in essence, a mixing operation. Chemicals purchased from a broad range of suppliers were mixed acccording to a variety of user-based formulas. Company sales in 1985 had reached a new high of $23.89 million, up from $21.98 million in 1984. Net pretax profit in 1985 had been $3.822 million, up from $3.169 million in 1984. Hanover-Bates had a strong balance sheet, and the company enjoyed a favorable price-earnings ratio on its stock, which traded on the OTC market.

Although Hanover-Bates did not produce commodity-type chemicals (e.g., sulfuric acid and others), industry customers tended to perceive minimal quality differences among the products produced by Hanover-Bates and its competitors. Given the lack of variation in product quality and the industrywide practice of limited advertising expenditures, field sales efforts were of major importance in the marketing programs of all firms in the industry.

Hanover-Bates's market consisted of several thousand job-shop and captive (in-house) plating operations. Chemical platers process a wide variety of materials in-

Exhibit 4 District Contribution to Corporate Administrative Expense and Profit, 1985

District	Sales	Gross Profit	Selling Expenses	Contribution to Administrative Expense and Profit
1	$ 3,906,000	$1,589,000	$ 388,416	$1,200,544
2	3,740,000	1,529,000	351,346	1,177,654
3	3,406,000	1,239,000	368,529	870,471
4	3,318,000	1,295,000	348,153	946,847
5	3,210,000	1,186,000	326,558	859,442
6	3,205,000	1,179,000	315,376	863,624
7	3,105,000	1,310,000	300,258	1,009,724
	$23,890,000	$9,327,000	$2,398,636	$6,928,324

Exhibit 5 Northeast (#3) and North-Central (#7) District Sales and Gross Profit Performance by Account Category, 1985

District	(A)	(B)	(C)	Total
	Sales by Account Category			
Northeast	$915,000	$1,681,000	$810,000	$3,406,000
North-central	751,000	1,702,000	652,000	3,105,000
	Gross Profit by Account Category			
Northeast	$356,000	$623,000	$260,000	$1,239,000
North-central	330,000	725,000	255,000	1,310,000

Exhibit 6 Potential Accounts, Active Accounts, and Account Call Coverage: Northeast and North-Central Districts, 1985

	Potential Accounts			Active Accounts			Account Coverage (Total Calls)		
District	(A)	(B)	(C)	(A)	(B)	(C)	(A)	(B)	(C)
Northeast	90	381	635	53	210	313	1,297	3,051	2,118
North-central	60	386	499	42	182	218	1,030	2,618	1,299

cluding industrial fasteners (e.g., screws, rivets, bolts, washers, and others), industrial components (e.g., clamps, casings, couplings, and others), and miscellaneous items (e.g., umbrella frames, eyelets, decorative items, and others). The chemical plating process involves the electrolytic application of metallic coatings such as zinc, cadmium, nickel, brass, and so forth. The degree of required plating precision varies substantially, with some work being primarily decorative, some involving relatively loose standards (e.g., 0.0002 zinc, which means that anything over two ten-thousandths of an inch of plate is acceptable), and some involving relatively precise standards (e.g., 0.0003–0.0004 zinc).

Regardless of the degree of plating precision involved, quality control is of critical concern to all chemical platers. Extensive variation in the condition of materials received for plating requires a high level of service from the firms supplying chemicals to platers. This service is normally provided by the sales representatives of the firm(s) supplying the plater with processing chemicals.

Hanover-Bates and the majority of the firms in its industry produced the same line of basic processing chemicals for the chemical plating industry. The line consisted of a trisodium phosphate cleaner (SBX), anesic aldahyde brightening agents for zinc plating (ZBX), cadmium plating (CBX) and nickel plating (NBX), a protective post-plating chromate dip (CHX), and a protective burnishing compound (BUX). The company's product line is detailed as follows:

Product	Container Size	List Price	Gross Margin
SPX	400-lb. drum	$ 80	$28
ZBX	50-lb. drum	76	34
CBX	50-lb. drum	76	34
NBX	50-lb. drum	80	35
CHX	100-lb. drum	220	90
BUX	400-lb. drum	120	44

Company Sales Organization

Hanover-Bates's sales organization consisted of forty sales representatives operating in seven sales districts. Sales repesentatives' salaries ranged from $14,000 to $24,000 with fringe-benefit costs amounting to an additional 10 percent of salary. In addition to their salaries, Hanover-Bates's sales representatives received commissions of 0.5 percent of their dollar sales volume on all sales up to their sales quotas. The commission on sales in excess of quota was 1 percent.

In 1983 the national sales manager of Hanover-Bates had developed a sales program based on selling the full line of Hanover-Bates products. He believed that if the sales representatives could successfully carry out his program, benefits would accrue to both Hanover-Bates and its customers:

1. Sales volume per account would be greater and selling costs as a percentage of sales would decrease.

2. A Hanover-Bates's sales representative could justify spending more time with such an account, thus becoming more knowledgeable about the account's business and becoming better able to provide technical assistance and identify selling opportunites.
3. Full-line sales would strengthen Hanover-Bates's competitive position by reducing the likelihood of account loss to other plating chemical suppliers (a problem that existed in multiple-supplier situations).

The national sales manager's 1983 sales program had also included the following account call-frequency guidelines:

A accounts (major accounts generating $12,000 or more in a yearly sales)—two calls per month
B accounts (medium-sized accounts generating $6,000–$11,999 in yearly sales)—one call per month
C accounts (small accounts generating less than $6,000 yearly in sales)—one call every two months

The account call-frequency guidelines were developed by the national sales manager after discussions with the district managers. The national sales manager had been concerned about the optimum allocation of sales effort to accounts and felt that the guidelines would increase the efficiency of the company's sales force, although not all of the district sales managers agreed with this conclusion.

It was common knowledge in Hanover-Bates's corporate sales office that Jim Sprague's predecessor as northeast district sales manager had not been one of the company's better district sales managers. His attitude toward the sales plans and programs of the national sales manager had been one of reluctant compliance rather than acceptance and support. When the national sales manager succeeded in persuading Jim Sprague's predecessor to take early retirement, he had been faced with the lack of an available qualified replacement.

Hank Carver, who most of the sales representatives had assumed would get the district manager job, had been passed over in part because he would be sixty-five in three years. The national sales manager had not wanted to face the same replacement problem again in three years and also had wanted someone in the position who would be more likely to be responsive to the company's sales plans and policies. The appointment of Jim Sprague as district manager had caused considerable talk, not only in the district but also at corporate headquarters. In fact, the national sales manager had warned Jim that "a lot of people are expecting you to fall on your face . . . they don't think you have the experience to handle the job, in particular, and to manage and motivate a group of sales representatives, most of whom are considerably older and more experienced than you." The national sales manager had concluded by saying, "I think you can handle the job, Jim. . . . I think you can manage those sales reps and improve the district's profit performance . . . and I'm depending on you to do both."

THE WEBB OFFICE PRODUCTS COMPANY

The Webb Office Products Company manufactured a wide line of office productions including adhesives, sealers, glue sticks, cleaners and solvents, markers, laundry pens, a variety of inks, stamp pads, and erasers (a relatively new addition). Webb had originally specialized in adhesives and was an old and well-established company. Over the years, it had added office-product lines partly by acquisition and partly by internal development. For the most part, the new products were produced under contract by a number of small manufacturing firms.

Company sales over the past five years (1976–80) had increased substantially despite the business recession. In late 1980, the company's sales manager resigned because of poor health. The new sales manager, Robert Fischer, joined the company early in 1981. He had formerly been employed as a regional sales manager for a large office-products manufacturer specializing in writing instruments. After familiarizing himself with the company's product line and its sales policies, he spent considerable time in the field visiting the trade with the company's sales representatives. While he was generally pleased with what he found, he was concerned that he had no way of evaluating their individual performances. This was made difficult by not only a lack of industry sales data at the national level but by the substantial differences in the individual company sales territories based on number of accounts and geography covered.

The company's regular sales force consisted of 27 manufacturer representatives who, in 1980, generated sales of $14.4 million. Sales were made directly to large retail office-product stores (often called stationers by the trade) and the wholesale office-product companies. Many customers were both wholesalers and retailers. The company did not sell to industrial, institutional, or government agencies since these organizations typically bought from local sources—usually large stationers.

Four company salespeople sold all major chains (regardless of buying office location) and large office supply distributors. The former often required private-label merchandise specially packaged to meet their requirements. The latter were often referred to as brokers, although this was a misnomer, given that they stocked a full line of products which they typically sold over a several-state area to local retailers and wholesalers. More often than not, such distributors served an area which could be reached overnight by truck. For the most part, they were large, highly automated units of a large national organization (e.g., Boise Cascade). Because of their volume and overall efficiency, they were able to operate on low margins; indeed, it was often less expensive for retailers to buy from them than direct from manufacturers—espe-

Source: This case was written by Professor Harper Boyd, College of Business Administration, University of Arkansas. Included in *Stanford Business Cases 1983* with permission. Reprinted with permission of Stanford University Graduate School of Business,

cially when relatively small quantities were involved. Such distributors did not sell to industrial, institutional, and government accounts. Sales reps were not allowed to solicit these accounts.

Company sales reps sold not only the company's products but other noncompetitive lines. It was estimated that on average company products accounted for about 60 percent of their sales, although there was considerable variation between individual reps. An exclusive sales territory was assigned each rep who received credit for all sales from that territory regardless of order mode—i.e., orders could be phoned or mailed in by either the customer or the sales rep. Sales reps received no credit for sales made to chains and the large distributors which, as noted earlier, were sold direct.

Sales reps worked on a commission basis out of which they paid all of their own expenses. Commissions ranged between 5 and 10 percent depending on the product line's margins. Because of their independent middlemen status, it had proved difficult to get them to render call reports. It was also a question of whether it would be wise to do so since the Internal Revenue Service might then classify them as employees and force the company to pay fringe benefits, including contributions to the Social Security system. In any event, call frequency by type and size of account was not known.

The duties of the sales reps included line placement, the introduction of new items, setting up in-store merchandise displays, and handling any complaints. Only a few of the orders placed were written by the reps—over 90 percent of all others were received by phone over the company's toll-free service. The company had 12 incoming WATS lines staffed by 14 experienced order takers. The order processing system was computerized to a point where, within but a few minutes after receipt, the order was delivered to the warehouse for picking, packing, and shipment. The company prided itself on shipping a high percentage of all orders within 48 hours—two working days.

In the past, the company had not used any criteria to evaluate the performance of individual sales reps other than a percentage increase in sales over the prior year. For example, if company rep sales were forecast to grow by 20 percent, then each rep's sales were expected to increase by this amount. Over the past several years, the company's force had remained relatively stable; only four reps had been turned over during the previous three years including one who had been killed in an automobile accident.

One reason why no performance criteria had been set up was, according to the sales manager, a lack of industry sales data. In particular, there were no national sales data by product lines. Thus, the company had no reliable base from which to compute its market share at either the national or individual sales territory levels for each of its product lines.

After considerable discussions with a variety of individuals including the company's senior chain salesman, the sales manager came up with six different evaluation ratios as follows (see Exhibit 1).

Exhibit 1 Sales Territories Evaluation Ratios Based on Sales Credited to Sales Reps

Sales Territory	Sales increase over 1976 (company average = 98.6%)	Average $ sales per outlet (company average = $1,318)	Percent of total sales made by reps	Percent of total population	Average adhesive sales per outlet	Percent erasers to total territory sales (company = 1.1%)	Percent cleaners/ solvents to total territory (company = 19%)
1	34.0%	$ 688	3.74%	8.38%	$239	.50%	10.95%
2	67.2	804	3.30	4.88	326	.83	7.89
3	210.1	728	1.72	4.54	264	.53	5.75
4	202.8	1,365	2.83	2.36	240	1.25	18.21
5	118.5	1,267	4.11	3.55	267	1.14	18.91
6	189.8	2,041	3.85	2.02	381	3.21	8.50
7	103.6	1,276	2.22	3.40	443	1.46	5.19
8*	5.7	916	6.50	5.51	217	.27	29.16
9	72.6	498	1.28	4.88	168	.41	10.38
10	75.5	1,274	2.88	5.33	268	.84	12.72
11	176.3	1,887	4.05	2.30	384	1.75	21.23
12	113.6	1,415	1.56	.94	281	2.01	9.28
13	168.0	1,248	3.48	3.97	298	1.38	14.44
14	155.1	1,701	3.19	1.90	315	2.26	21.15
15	151.0	1,868	5.93	3.41	225	1.07	27.50
16	114.6	1,707	5.85	5.78	321	.89	21.84
17	117.9	1,385	1.62	1.46	398	1.84	1.78
18	81.7	1,456	.85	.74	259	1.16	15.63
19	350.4	1,522	4.93	5.24	317	.84	24.76
20	93.9	1,199	2.10	2.65	288	1.18	5.82
21	134.8	1,465	6.48	5.36	232	.92	24.84
22	94.8	2,216	9.46	4.52	224	.46	35.99
23	78.9	1,526	7.69	6.56	292	1.03	28.66
24	88.3	871	2.91	4.28	270	1.16	7.29
25	121.9	1,604	4.65	4.06	312	.91	14.84
26	149.6	1,622	2.53	1.44	307	2.99	16.35
27	49.8	1,239	.18	.41	305	.48	18.70

*Territory 8 represents a special case. It matched total company percentage increases in 1977 and 1978. In 1979, the sales rep responsible for the territory was killed in an automobile accident, and his successor was let go after some six months. Also in 1979, a super distributor was established in the approximate center of this territory, causing a sharp drop in rep sales.

1. Percent dollar increase 1980 against 1976, company versus territory.
2. Company 1980 average dollar sale per outlet versus territory average dollar.
3. Percent of territory sales 1980 to total sales versus percent territory's population to total U.S. population.
4. Company average sales of adhesives per outlet 1980 versus that of the territory.
5. Percent erasers 1980 to total company sales versus percent to total territory sales. Erasers were a relatively new addition to the company's product line.
6. Percent cleaners and solvent sales 1980 to total company sales versus percent to total territory sales. Cleaners and solvents were long established items.

If the ratios generated in 4 through 6 proved meaningful, it was planned to calculate similar ratios for the company's other product lines.

In commenting on his sales analysis to the company executive vice president, Mr. Fischer noted that the evaluations used were "purely objective with no weights added." He went on to say that "after digesting this information, we should determine if these are the areas we want to use to measure our reps. Perhaps we should be using additional measures, and perhaps we should weight some heavier than others. In any case, what I'm looking for is a way of identifying our weaker reps. Thus, those who exceed the evaluation criteria in four categories are not where we should focus our time and attention. If you agree with what we have done, I plan to use it as a way of taking corrective action with problem reps. I'd appreciate your candid comments as soon as possible."

MODERN PLASTICS (A)

Institutional sales manager Jim Clayton had spent most of Monday morning planning for the rest of the month. It was early July and Jim knew that an extremely busy time was coming with the preparation of the following year's sales plan.

Since starting his current job less than a month ago, Jim had been involved in learning the requirements of the job and making his initial territory visits. Now that he was getting settled, Jim was trying to plan his activities according to priorities. The need for planning had been instilled in him during his college days. As a result of his three years' field sales experience and development of time management skills, he felt prepared for the challenge of the sales manager's job.

While sitting at his desk, Jim recalled a conversation that he had a week ago with Bill Hanson, the former manager, who had been promoted to another division. Bill told him that the sales forecast (annual and monthly) for plastic trash bags in the Southeast region would be due soon as an initial step toward developing the sales plan for the next year. Bill had laughed as he told Jim, "Boy, you ought to have a ball doing the forecast being a rookie sales manager!"

When Jim had asked what Bill meant, he explained by saying that the forecast was often "winged" because the headquarters in New York already knew what they wanted and would change the forecast to meet their figures, particularly if the forecast was for an increase of less than 10 percent. The experienced sales manager could throw numbers together in a short time that would pass as a serious forecast and ultimately be adjusted to fit the plans of headquarters. However, an inexperienced manager would have a difficult time "winging" a credible forecast.

Bill had also told Jim that the other alternative meant gathering mountains of data and putting together a forecast that could be sold to the various levels of Modern Plastics management. This alternative would prove to be time-consuming and could still be changed anywhere along the chain of command before final approval.

Clayton started reviewing pricing and sales volume history (see Exhibit 1). He also looked at the key account performance for the past two and a half years (see Exhibit 2). During the past month Clayton had visited many of the key accounts, and on the average they had indicated that their purchases from Modern would probably increase about 15–20 percent in the coming year.

Schedule for Preparing the Forecast

Jim had received a memo recently from Robert Baxter, the regional marketing manager, detailing the plans for completing the 1986 forecast. The key dates in the memo began in only three weeks:

Source: This case was written by Professor Kenneth L. Bernhardt, Georgia State University, Professor Tom Ingram, Memphis State University, and Professor Danny N. Bellenger, Texas Tech University.

Exhibit 1 Plastic Trash Bags—Sales and Pricing History, 1983–1985

	Pricing dollars per case			Sales volume in cases			Sales volume in dollars		
	1983	**1984**	**1985**	**1983**	**1984**	**1985**	**1983**	**1984**	**1985**
January	$6.88	$ 7.70	$15.40	33,000	46,500	36,500	$ 227,000	$ 358,000	$ 562,000
February	6.82	7.70	14.30	32,500	52,500	23,000	221,500	404,000	329,000
March	6.90	8.39	13.48	32,000	42,000	22,000	221,000	353,000	296,500
April	6.88	10.18	12.24	45,500	42,500	46,500	313,000	432,500	569,000
May	6.85	12.38	11.58	49,000	41,500	45,500	335,500	514,000	527,000
June	6.85	12.65	10.31	47,500	47,000	42,000	325,500	594,500	433,000
July	7.42	13.48	9.90*	40,000	43,500	47,500*	297,000	586,500	470,000*
August	6.90	13.48	10.18	48,500	63,500	43,500	334,500	856,000	443,000
September	7.70	14.30	10.31	43,000	49,000	47,500	331,000	700,500	489,500
October	7.56	15.12	10.31	52,500	50,000	51,000	397,000	756,000	526,000
November	7.15	15.68	10.72	62,000	61,500	47,500	443,500	964,500	509,000
December	7.42	15.43	10.59	49,000	29,000	51,000	363,500	447,500	540,000
Total	$7.13	$12.25	$11.30	534,500	568,500	503,500	$3,810,000	$6,967,000	$5,694,000

*July–December 1985 figures are forecast of sales manager J. A. Clayton and other data comes from historical sales information.

Exhibit 2 1985 Key Account Sales History (in cases)

Customer	1983	1984	First six months 1985	1983 monthly average	1984 monthly average	First half 1985 monthly average	First quarter 1985 monthly average
Transco Paper Company	125,774	134,217	44,970	10,481	11,185	7,495	5,823
Callaway Paper	44,509	46,049	12,114	3,709	3,837	2,019	472
Florida Janitoral Supply	34,746	36,609	20,076	2,896	3,051	3,346	2,359
Jefferson	30,698	34,692	25,004	2,558	2,891	4,174	1,919
Cobb Paper	13,259	23,343	6,414	1,105	1,945	1,069	611
Miami Paper	10,779	22,287	10,938	900	1,857	1,823	745
Milne Surgical Company	23,399	21,930	—	1,950	1,828	—	—
Graham	8,792	15,331	1,691	733	1,278	281	267
Crawford Paper	7,776	14,132	6,102	648	1,178	1,017	1,322
John Steele	8,634	13,277	6,663	720	1,106	1,110	1,517
Henderson Paper	9,185	8,850	2,574	765	738	429	275
Durant Surgical	—	7,766	4,356	—	647	726	953
Master Paper	4,221	5,634	600	352	470	100	—
D.T.A.	—	—	2,895	—	—	482	—
Crane Paper	4,520	5,524	3,400	377	460	566	565
Janitorial Service	3,292	5,361	2,722	274	447	453	117
Georgia Paper	5,466	5,053	2,917	456	421	486	297
Paper Supplies, Inc.	5,117	5,119	1,509	426	427	251	97
Southern Supply	1,649	3,932	531	137	328	88	78
Horizon Hospital Supply	4,181	4,101	618	348	342	103	206
Total cases	346,007	413,217	156,134	28,835	34,436	26,018	17,623

August 1	Presentation of forecast to regional marketing manager.
August 10	Joint presentation with marketing manager to regional general manager.
September 1	Regional general manager presents forecast to division vice president.
September 1–September 30	Review of forecast by staff of division vice president.
October 1	Review forecast with corporate staff.
October 1–October 15	Revision as necessary.
October 15	Final forecast forwarded to division vice president from regional general manager.

Company Background

The plastics division of Modern Chemical Company was founded in 1965 when Modern Chemical purchased Cordco, a small plastics manufacturer with national sales of $15 million. At that time the key products of the plastics division were sandwich bags, plastic tablecloths, trash cans, and plastic-coated clothesline.

Since 1965 the plastics division has grown to a sales level exceeding $200 million with five regional profit centers covering the United States. Each regional center has manufacturing facilities and a regional sales force. There are four product groups in each region:

1. Food packaging: Styrofoam meat and produce trays; plastic bags for various food products.
2. Egg cartons: Styrofoam egg cartons sold to egg packers and supermarket chains.
3. Institutional: Plastic trash bags and disposable tableware (plates, bowls and so on).
4. Industrial: Plastic packaging for the laundry and dry cleaning market; plastic film for use in pallet overwrap systems.

Each product group is supervised jointly by a product manager and a district sales manager, both of whom report to the regional marketing manager. The sales representatives report directly to the district sales manager but also work closely with the product manager on matters concerning pricing and product specifications.

The five regional general managers report to J. R. Hughes, vice president of the plastics division. Hughes is located in New York. Although Modern Chemical is owned by a multinational oil company, the plastics division has been able to operate in a virtually independent manner since its establishment in 1965. The reasons for this include:

1. Limited knowledge of the plastic industry on the part of the oil company management.
2. Excellent growth by the plastics division has been possible without management supervision from the oil company.
3. Profitability of the plastics division has consistently been higher than that of other divisions of the chemical company.

The Institutional Trash Bag Market

The institutional trash bag is a polyethylene bag used to collect and transfer refuse to its final disposition point. There are different sizes and colors available to fit the various uses of the bag. For example, a small bag for desk wastebaskets is available as well as a heavier bag for large containers such as a 55-gallon drum. There are 25 sizes in the Modern line with 13 of those sizes being available in 3 colors—white, buff, and clear. Customers typically buy several different items on an order to cover all their needs.

The institutional trash bag is a separate product from the consumer grade trash bag, which is typically sold to homeowners through retail outlets. The institutional trash bag is sold primarily through paper wholesalers, hospital supply companies, and janitorial supply companies to a variety of end users. Since trash bags are used on such a wide scale, the list of end users could include almost any business or institution. The segments include hospitals, hotels, schools, office buildings, transportation facilities, and restaurants.

Based on historical data and a current survey of key wholesalers and end users in the Southeast, the annual market of institutional trash bags in the region was estimated to be 55 million pounds. Translated into cases, the market potential was close to 2 million cases. During the past five years, the market for trash bags has grown at an average rate of 8.9 percent per year. Now a mature product, future market growth is expected to parallel overall growth in the economy. The 1986 real growth in GNP is forecast to be 4.5 percent.

General Market Conditions

The current market is characterized by a distressing trend. The market is in a position of oversupply with approximately 20 manufacturers competing for the business in the Southeast. Prices have been on the decline for several months but are expected to level out during the last six months of the year.

This problem arose after a record year in 1984 for Modern Plastics. During 1984, supply was very tight due to raw material shortages. Unlike many of its competitors, Modern had only minor problems securing adequate raw material supplies. As a result the competitors were few in 1984, and all who remained in business were prosperous. By early 1985 raw materials were plentiful, and prices began to drop as new competitors tried to buy their way into the market. During the first quarter of 1985 Modern Plastics learned the hard way that a competitive price was a necessity in the current market. Volume fell off drastically in February and March as customers shifted orders to new suppliers when Modern chose to maintain a slightly higher than market price on trash bags.

With the market becoming extremely price competitive and profits declining, the overall quality has dropped to a point of minimum stardard. Most suppliers now make a bag "barely good enough to get the job done." This quality level is acceptable to most buyers who do not demand high quality for this type of product.

Modern Plastics versus Competition

A recent study of Modern versus compeition had been conducted by an outside consultant to see how well Modern measured up in several key areas. Each area was weighted according to its importance in the purchase decision, and Modern was compared to its key competitors in each area and on an overall basis. The key factors and their weights are shown below:

	Weight
1. Pricing	.50
2. Quality	.15
3. Breadth of line	.10
4. Sales coverage	.10
5. Packaging	.05
6. Service	.10
Total	1.00

As shown in Exhibit 3, Modern compared favorably with its key competitors on an overall basis. None of the other suppliers was as strong as Modern in breadth of line nor did any competitor offer as good sales coverage as that provided by Modern. Clayton knew that sales coverage would be even better next year since the Florida and North Carolina territories had grown enough to add two salespeople to the institutional group by January 1, 1986.

Pricing, quality, and packaging seemed to be neither an advantage nor a disadvantage. However, service was a problem area. The main cause for this, Clayton was told, was temporary out-of-stock situations which occurred occasionally primarily due to the wide variety of trash bags offered by Modern.

During the past two years, Modern Plastics had maintained its market share at approximately 27 percent of the market. Some new competitors had entered the market since 1983 while others had left the market (see Exhibit 4). The previous district sales manager, Bill Hanson, had left Clayton some comments regarding the major competitors. These are reproduced in Exhibit 5.

Exhibit 3 Competitive Factors Ratings (by competitor*)

Weight	Factor	Modern	National Film	Bonanza	South-eastern	PBI	BAGCO	South-west Bag	Sun Plastics	East Coast Bag Co.
.50	Price	2	3	2	2	2	2	2	2	3
.15	Quality	3	2	3	4	3	2	3	3	4
.10	Breadth	1	2	2	3	3	3	3	3	3
.10	Sales coverage	1	3	3	3	4	3	3	4	3
.05	Packaging	3	3	2	3	3	1	3	3	3
.10	Service	4	3	3	2	2	2	3	4	3

Overall weighted ranking†

Rank	Score	Rank	Score
1. BAGCO	2.15	6. Southeastern	2.55
2. Modern	2.20	7. Florida Plastics	2.60
3. Bonanza	2.25	8. National Film	2.65
4. Southwest Bag (Tie)	2.50	9. East Coast Bag Co.	3.15
5. PBI (Tie)	2.50		

*Ratings on a 1-to-5 scale with 1 being the best rating and 5 the worst.

†The weighted ranking is the sum of each rank times its weight. The lower the number, the better the overall rating.

Exhibit 4 Market Share by Supplier, 1983 and 1985

Supplier	Percent of market 1983	Percent of market 1985
National Film	11	12
Bertram	16	0*
Bonanza	11	12
Southeastern	5	6
Bay	9	0*
Johnson Graham	8	0*
PBI	2	5
Lewis	2	0*
BAGCO	—	6
Southwest Bag	—	2
Florida Platics	—	4
East Coast Bag Co.	—	4
Miscellaneous and unknown	8	22
Modern	28	27
	100	100

*Out of business in 1985

Source: This information was developed from a field survey conducted by Modern Plastics.

Exhibit 5 Characteristics of Competitors

National Film	Broadest product line in the industry. Quality a definite advantage. Good service. Sales coverage adequate, but not an advantage. Not as aggressive as most suppliers on price. Strong competitor.
Bonanza	Well-established tough competitor. Very aggressive on pricing. Good packaging, quality okay.
Southeastern	Extremely price competitive in southern Florida. Dominates Miami market. Limited product line. Not a threat outside of Florida.
PBI	Extremely aggressive on price. Have made inroads into Transco Paper Company. Good service but poor sales coverage.
BAGCO	New competitor. Very impressive with a high-quality product, excellent service, and strong sales coverage. A real threat, particularly in Florida.
Southwest Bag	A factor in Louisiana and Mississippi. Their strategy is simple—an acceptable product at a rock bottom price.
Sun Plastics	Active when market is at a profitable level with price cutting. When market declines to a low profit range, Sun manufactures other types of plastic packaging and stays out of the trash bag market. Poor reputation as a reliable supplier, but can still "spot-sell" at low prices.
East Coast Bag Co.	Most of their business is from a state bid which began in January 1984 for a two-year period. Not much of a threat to Modern's business in the Southeast as most of their volume is north of Washington, D.C.

Exhibit 6 1986 Real Growth Projections by Segment

Total industry	+5.0%
Commercial	+5.4%
Restaurant	+6.8%
Hotel/motel	+2.0%
Transportation	+1.9%
Office users	+5.0%
Other	+4.2%
Noncommercial	+4.1%
Hospitals	+3.9%
Nursing homes	+4.8%
Colleges/universities	+2.4%
Schools	+7.8%
Employee feeding	+4.3%
Other	+3.9%

Source: Developed from several trade journals.

Developing the Sales Forecast

After a careful study of trade journals, government statistics, and surveys conducted by Modern marketing research personnel, projections for growth potential were formulated by segment and are shown in Exhibit 6. This data was compiled by Bill Hanson just before he had been promoted.

Jim looked back at Baxter's memo giving the time schedule for the forecast and knew he had to get started. As he left the office at 7:15, he wrote himself a large note and pinned it on his wall—"Get Started on the Sales Forecast!"

COMPREHENSIVE CASES

HENDERSON SERVICE CENTER

AURORA LOTION

ANDERSON DISTRIBUTORS INC.

PAUL GORDON REPRESENTATIVES, INCORPORATED

HENDERSON SERVICE CENTER

Tom Henderson, president of Henderson Steel Service Center, felt it necessary to review his company's marketing and sales strategies. Early in 1979, it was apparent that old assumptions and approaches had to be carefully examined and updated due to a number of ongoing changes in the environment. To be specific:

1. Specialist service centers were becoming more important and assuming major positions in such lines as tubing, spring steel, aluminum, and tool steel—products characterized as being of relatively high technical content, diffcult to comprehend technically, consisting of many small volume grades, with considerable risk of obsolescence, and often with limited sources of supply—but, nonetheless, profitable due to their unique characteristics.
2. A decided upsurge in requests for bids, in which major buyers asked for quotes on a six-month supply contract; contracts which unfortunately might not be honored fully and where shipments might not always be in the specified truckload quantities (in short, a price squeeze).
3. The proliferation of brokers and secondary-line houses, who emphasized distress prices, raised havoc with traditional margins, and were in and out of the markets.
4. An ominous industry drift toward commodity selling, in which old trade names (Shelby Tubing, Jalloy) were being superseded by ASTM numbers, with the resulting willingness of customers to accept "or equivalent" products.
5. The merging of small centers into larger, multilocation houses.
6. And the accelerated trend toward sophisticated management, particularly in regard to asset management in general and inventories in particular.

Henderson was a medium-sized general line steel center in California whose growth made it increasingly difficult for management to stay on top of the details and to maintain its earlier entrepreneurial touch. As Tom Henderson said, "This is a business of inches—of exact control and doing the little things right—where success is closely tied to service and employee attitudes. How do I keep a balanced effort among the salesmen when growth results in a one-inch catalog, specialists eat away at our specialty markets, and the individual salesmen tend to gravitate toward their favorite products?"

Thus, it was timely that he review the company's sales and marketing strategies. Did his sales programs enhance the all-important company-customer relationships? Tom wanted to be sure that there weren't new approaches that warranted implementation. Indeed, he had a number of specific concerns about his sales strategies.

The Steel Service Center Industry

As of 1975, there were estimated to be 1,500 steel service centers (SSC) operated by 700 companies and accounting for 20 percent of the country's steel tonnage. The median firm had annual sales of $3 million. The modern steel service center was a vital link in the chain from basic steel producer (the mill) to user. An SSC was both distributor and processor, who not only handled a great range of mill products, but added considerable value to standard mill output. Steel service center processing included, but was not limited to, cutting, sawing, trimming, slitting, blanking, burning, roll forming, and light fabrication.[1] The mills were only too pleased to see most of this small order, specialty business handled by the centers.

Products handled included pipe, spring steel, sheet, tool steel, bar tubing, and structurals, primarily in steel (or aluminum) and involving a great complexity of specifications and basic processing variations—such as cold rolled carbon. Sales were made by the centers to a wide array of primarily industrial customers, including agriculture and commercial establishments. Needless to say, there were many products that were wholesaled primarily (i.e., no processing) by the steel service centers. And as will be shown, there was a wide difference between different types of centers. Separate from the steel service centers were hundreds of brokers—small independents who bought and sold as the opportunity arose, rarely handled the product, and substituted price for service.

A 1974 study by Republic Steel contained some interesting speculations about the future:

Summary[2]

The service center market will be the largest market for steel by 1980, with shipment of 24.8 million tons in a peak year. This will represent a 25 percent increase over 1974's shipments of 19.9 million tons. Shipments of flat rolled products will increase by 29 percent, and shipments of hot rolled bar products will show a gain of 28 percent. Both tubing and cold finished bar shipments will increase by 22 percent, while the volume of stainless and pipe through service centers should register gains of 16 percent and 15 percent, respectively.

Seven products accounted for almost 75 percent of total service center tonnage in 1974. These products included the following: C HR Sheets, C CR Sheets,

[1]Cutting, sawing, and trimming involved reducing mill dimensions to customer requirements. Slitting was represented by the reduction of a wide roll to a narrow one. Blanking was the process of stamping out custom shapes. Burning would involve the "burning out" of a gear design, as an example, from heavy plate. Roll forming would be typified by forming a gutter or down spout. Light fabrication included such activities as punching predetermined holes in structural beams or bending material to a particular shape.

[2]"Steel Service Centers in 1980," Republic Steel, pp. 2, 3.

C Plates, C Structurals, C Standard Pipe, C HD Galvanized, and C HR Bars.[3] The largest single item was C HR Sheets, accounting for 18.6 percent of total service center tonnage.

Service centers will continue to increase their share of total steel shipments. Although they dropped sharply in 1975, we believe they will recover and take 20 percent in a peak year by 1980.

Our survey revealed four distinct types of service centers: super processors, large general line centers, small general line centers, and specialty houses. We forecast the biggest growth to take place among the large general line centers between 1974 and 1980 because trends to larger minimum order quantities by the mills and the continuation of absorption and consolidation of smaller centers will combine to promote strength in this market segment. The super processor, although showing good growth, will be hampered somewhat by its dependence on the automotive market. The specialty houses will just about hold their own in the marketplace. The small general line center will remain a significant part of the market, although many may be absorbed by large general line centers.

The survey findings indicate that two major changes are likely to take place in the service center market by 1980. If the mills increase and maintain higher minimum quantity extras as our survey indicates, there will probably be fewer service center companies but more locations, as some small centers are likely to be absorbed by larger centers. Those small centers remaining in the business will probably turn to larger centers as a source of supply, creating a two-tier service center market. The average service center of 1980 will be larger than the one of 1975 and will be more professionally managed.

Service centers will not be involved in any different types of processing in 1980 than they are in now but will experience growth in virtually everything they are doing currently. Slitting and cut-to-length will continue to be bread-and-butter items, but plate burning, blanking, and roll forming should all show good growth. Pickling and tube manufacturing could show limited growth at the service center level.

We forecast good growth in hot rolled bar products, particularly carbon hot rolled bars, through service centers based largely on the fact that the forecasted level of shipments through the rest of this decade will encourage volume rollings by the mills. Such levels of operations encourage increased minimum order quantity extras at the mill level. This activity in turn would cause the small purchaser to use service centers as a source of supply. Good growth in cold finished bars could result from the same type of circumstances.

[3]C HR Sheets = carbon hot rolled sheets
C CR Sheets = carbon cold rolled sheets
C Plates = carbon plates
C Structurals = carbon structurals (beams, columns, joists)
C Standard Pipe = carbon standard pipe
C HD Galvanized = carbon hand dipped galvanized
C HR Bars = carbon hot rolled bars

> Cold finished bars should continue their excellent growth through service centers, as will tubing products. Stainless and pipe products will not experience the rapid growth of other products, but will still register impressive gains.
>
> We estimate that the four major captive service centers handled approximately 20 percent of all steel shipped through service centers in 1974. Captives should grow faster than the average for all service centers because they fall into the fastest growing category, the large general line center. However, we do not believe their growth will surpass that of the independent large general line centers.
>
> Foreign-owned companies have been increasing their holdings in the domestic service center market. We estimate that 13 percent to 15 percent of the total tonnage handled by domestic service centers goes through foreign-owned outlets.

In addition to these trends, Mr. Henderson foresaw: (1) continued emphasis upon sophisticated computer systems to control operations; (2) increased equipment improvements and costs of investments; (3) the need to ensure solid supplier relationships, due to limited investment funds for capacity increases among U.S. steel companies; and (4) continued downward pressures on price unless growing commodity selling attitudes could be curbed.

The Company

The Henderson company was headquartered in the San Fernando Valley, north of downtown Los Angeles, having been started by Tom Henderson in 1958 after his discharge from the army. Over the years, Tom had developed the company by internal growth and the acquisition of four smaller firms in San Diego, Bakersfield, Modesto, and San Jose (all in California). Bank financing had been used recently, but in his earlier days, Tom relied for financing upon internal funds and the public sales of 60 percent of the ownership.

It is revealing to see how the firm grew with the acquisitions program (see Exhibit 1).

It is reasonably clear that market share was gained fairly early in each market and then maintained or slowly increased over time. Overall growth was primarily a function of acquisition.

As with all steel service centers, profits were sensitive to volume and mix, with different locations having different experiences. Variable costs exceeded 80 percent, which meant that funds available for overhead and profits were narrowly bounded by margins and direct costs. Peak sales for Henderson occurred in 1974, when total volume reached $29 million; 1976 was a poor year for the company and the industry, and by 1978, volume was still below 1974 but recovering.

Tom Henderson was a strong believer in the fact that true profitability was a function of asset turnover and leverage ratio (i.e., relative amount of debt) as opposed to solely conventional profit expressions. To be specific, he had drawn up a simple

Exhibit 1

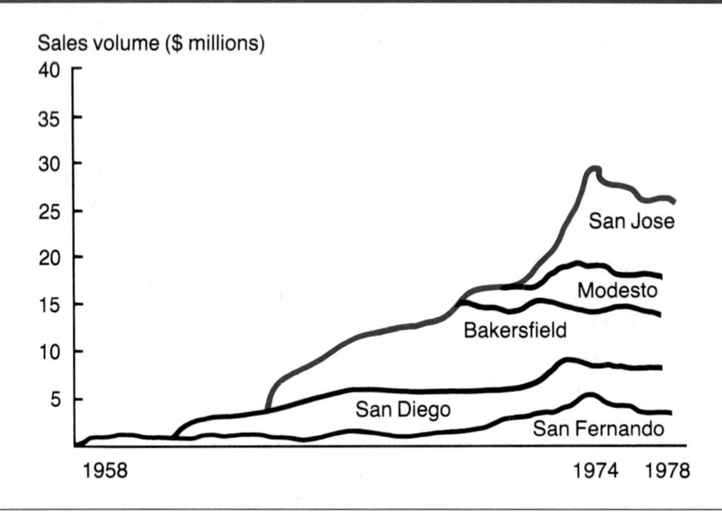

"strategic profit model" which he also used to compare his results to competition (Exhibit 2).

For 1978, to illustrate the model, Tom had drawn the comparisons between his firm and two competitiors shown in Exhibit 3.

It was Tom's conviction that strategy should be stated specifically in terms of the model, such as:

Asset Management. Improve asset turnovers to 2.5:

1. Improve inventory turnover to minimum of three times.
2. Eliminate delete when out of items.
3. Maximum use of mother warehouse concept.
4. Maintain accounts receivables at 41 days.
5. Review all fixed assets and remove all nonproductive assets.
6. Study balance of fixed assets to improve their earning power.

Profit Management.

1. Tight cost control.
2. Improve plant operating procedure to reduce cost.
3. Better systems to cut out unnecessary work.
4. Improve pricing where possible.
5. Study product lines to emphasize profit opportunities.

Exhibit 2 The Strategic Profit Model*

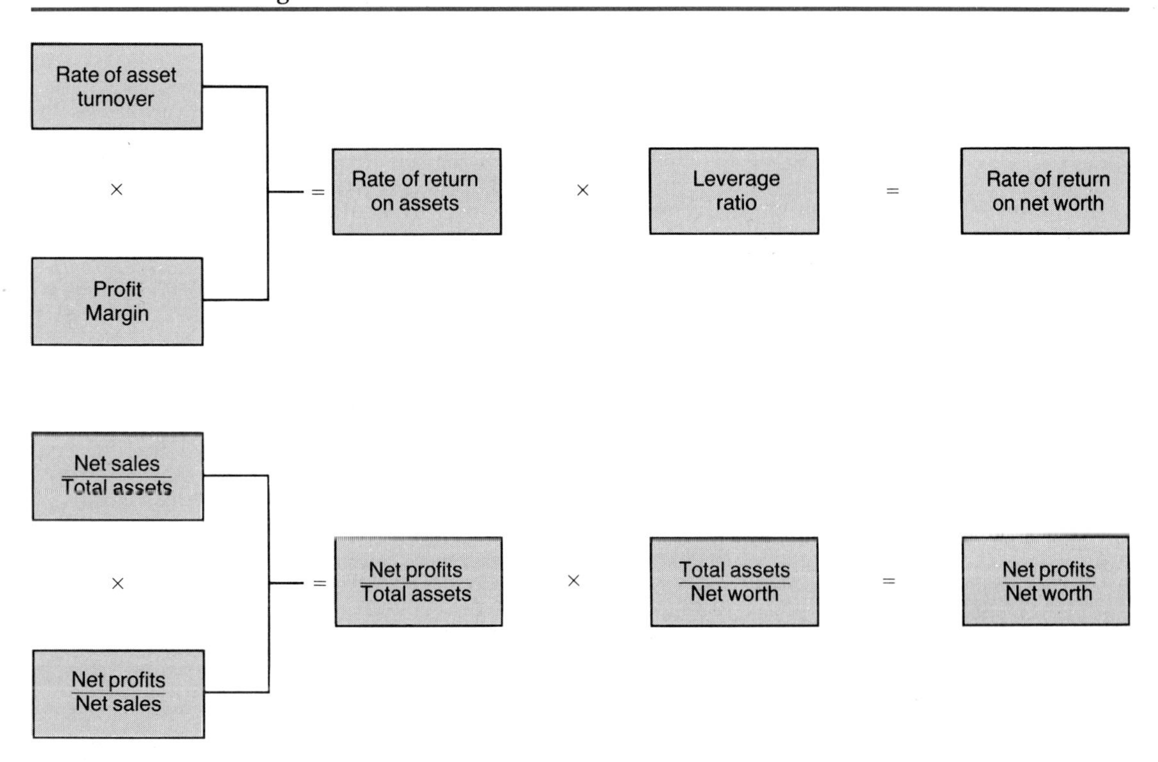

*The strategic profit model excludes leased equipment, fixtures, and facilities. The model also excludes the capital structure of nonconsolidated subsidiaries.

Exhibit 3

Competitor	Asset turnover ×	Percent profit margin =	Percent return on assets ×	Tax return rate =	Net return on assets ×	Financial LVRG =	Net return on equity ×	Earn return rate =	Reinvest rate	Working capital percent sales
No. 1	2.7	1.7	4.4	53.2	2.4	2.2	5.2	32.6	1.7	17.0
No. 2	2.7	4.7	12.6	54.8	6.9	1.7	12.0	76.5	9.2	13.1
Henderson . . .	1.6	4.1	6.6	53.9	3.6	1.7	6.1	100.0	6.1	22.1

Financial Management.

1. Find expansion opportunities that meet or equal our asset and profit objectives.
2. Expand debt to 38 percent of total assets.

Competition and Markets

Competition for Henderson was strong—from five majors and 20 times that number of specialists and brokers. It was Henderson's experience that the large, full-line houses were strong but reasonable competitors. Market disruption and cost cutting came from the brokers and a fringe handful of smaller firms whose approach to selling centered around "a good deal." Such tactics were particularly effective with those buyers, who seemed to be increasing in numbers, who preferred to shop around for the lowest offer and who thought that loyalty was for boy scouts.

Henderson's marketing/sales strategy was straightforward. The policy was to carry a good inventory of prime (as opposed to secondary) merchandise, to offer fast response time, and to concentrate on stock parts and cutting at the expense (relatively) of first-stage processing, though 20 percent of sales did come from processing. Whenever the company had to buy out, it examined carefully whether demand for that item would warrant future stocking.

Henderson's markets were diverse, reflecting basic differences among the California territories; 90 percent of the sales, to be specific, were into the farming and farm equipment, railroad, mechanical contractors, industrial equipment, mining, appliance, and furniture segments. Although there were several automobile assembly plants in the state, Henderson had chosen to not go after that very specialized and competitive business. Each market segment represented, obviously, a unique selling problem.

Farm equipment. There were six short-line producers in the Henderson territories, firms which manufactured and sold for their own account or acted as suppliers to full-line houses (such as Deere). By and large, these manufacturers wanted reliability, on-time service, and product quality, as opposed to minimum cost. The service center salesperson was a critical variable in the selling process, though much of his influence was due to the entertainment between supplier and buyer that was common practice. Apparently, the buyers preferred to purchase "from a friend," all other things being equal, and equated supplier reliability with the salesperson's interpersonal skills. This was not meant to imply that product knowledge and service were unimportant; it was rather that the essential catalyst was the salesperson's personal input. Multiple sourcing and bidding, nonetheless, were common, although trusted salespeople typically got "the last look." Buying decisions were made by the purchasing vice president or his buyer (if the firm were big enough).

Railroads were a good market on the West Coast, but in these firms it was difficult to find who buys. The successful salesperson did lots of legwork in engineering, purchasing, and even top management in order to get drawings. As in the case of the farm equipment segment, the role of the salesperson was critical. Cronyism was common, and most sales relationships had been established slowly over the years.

In the case of both segments, Henderson tried to sell the idea of "cost of position," that is, why invest as a buyer in expensive processing equipment when you can share the capital costs with the buyers by dealing with a Service Center?

Mechanical contractors (plumbing and heating, sheet and metal working), on the other hand, were easy to sell in that they bought "off the shelf," but they were price buyers of mixed credit reliability who shopped around. The nature of contractors' businesses caused them to be single job oriented. The salesperson's role was minimal in these instances, and entertainment was of little importance.

Appliance manufacturers (mostly in Los Angeles) were somewhat the same. They were tough buyers who appeared to have little loyalty. They were auction oriented and usually purchased flat rolled products with few components. Salespeople were significant only in respect to maintenance and repair.

Furniture accounts had little need for maintenance and repair. Price, not selling, was the name of the game. Theirs also was a fragmented industry of small, unstable producers.

The **industrial equipment** and **mining** segments were more solid and resembled the farm equipment market—sophisticated, insistent upon reliability and service, and sympathetic to constructive salesperson relationships.

Pricing, Advertising, and Distribution

Henderson was not a price house, although its prices were competitive. In periods of short supply, in fact, the firm had deliberately refrained from gouging its accounts in the hopes that the ensuring goodwill would carry over into buyer markets. Whether this policy was paying off was not at all clear: in 1977 and 1978, there had been a tendency for Henderson margins to slip and for the field salespeople to sacrifice service for discounted prices. Price pressures were growing. In fact, Tom Henderson figured that one of his most pressing needs was to give his salespeople more backbone to withstand such pressures and to sell service instead.

Advertising was a small but useful adjunct to the firm's strategy. Because there were no obvious regional media that matched Henderson's customer base, emphasis was put upon a modest direct mail campaign (which stressed the service dedication of the company, i.e., "Henderson Means Service"), a biannual house publication which went to employees and customers alike, appearance at all relevant conventions, some public relations, and hopefully, positive word of mouth.

The distribution strategy was simple. There were five warehouses in five cities, each stocked to its own market needs. Particular items could be shipped from branch to branch in a matter of hours and were in order to meet special requests. Buyouts were made whenever necesssary.

Exhibit 4

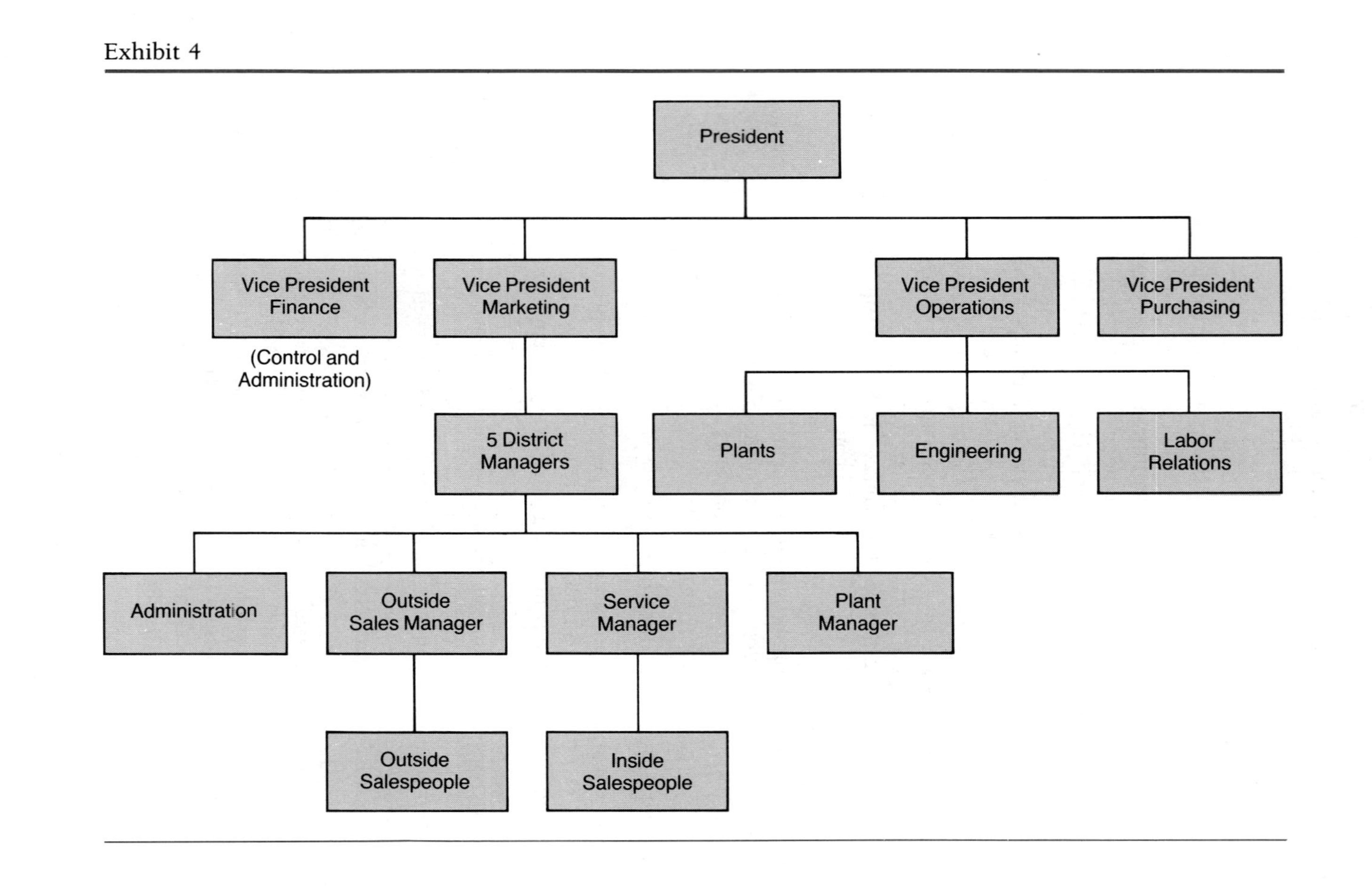
President
Vice President Finance
(Control and Administration)
Vice President Marketing
Vice President Operations
Vice President Purchasing
5 District Managers
Plants
Engineering
Labor Relations
Administration
Outside Sales Manager
Service Manager
Plant Manager
Outside Salespeople
Inside Salespeople

Organization

Henderson's organization was probably representative of the industry (see Exhibit 4).

Even though the local plant managers reported to the district managers (for daily administration), they had a dotted-line relationship to the vice president of operations for functional matters. The reporting duality seemed to work.

The sales and service end of the business, because it was of particular concern to Mr. Henderson, deserves more elaboration. Including the San Fernando headquarters, there were five district managers who reported to a marketing vice president. Each manager operated out of a plant and supervised the sales manager, the plant manager, and inside service (sales) manager, and an adminstrative staff.

Reporting to the outside sales managers were 16 salespeople, for each of whom (with a few exceptions) there was a corresponding inside person. The two worked as a team, although they reported to separate bosses. The team idea was important because most ongoing sales were placed by customers calling in. The role of the outside salespeople was, therefore, to prospect for new accounts, to build established accounts, and to ensure post purchase service. The inside person's responsibility was to maintain the business.

The district manager was the local authority. He had considerable decision-making leeway, although credit, purchasing, inventory policy, compensation, finance, and labor relations were controlled out of headquarters. The district manager could fire or add to the sales forces (with the concurrence of the marketing vice president), deploy his labor force as he saw fit, and train, supervise, and generally decide sales strategy. He was further responsible for making sure that the plant could meet customer requirements on time.

In a real sense, the district manager was "the leader" and was expected to know intimately the needs of the market. Suffice it to say he reinforced his own observations with data from the field concerning quantity changes, customer new product plans, customer switches in mill purchases, self-fabrication plans, and competitive activity.

The typical district manager earned between $30,000 to $35,000, including a maximum 20 percent of salary bonus based on district profitability. He received a percentage of the profit beyond the plan up to 20 percent of his base pay. Profit was calculated before headquarter's allocations for overhead and support.

The People

The five district managers came from different backgrounds. To single out three as representative:

> **San Fernando**. Started in accounting and then to inside selling. After two years, became an outside salesman and after three years, fabrications manager. Next, sales manager in a district and finally, at age 40, to district manager. One

year of college but . . . "a very strong manager. Pushes hard, sets high standards, lets everyone know where they stand, good on strategy and market penetration."

San Jose. College graduate, age 45, formerly manager of an advertising agency. Joined Henderson at 34 as outside salesman, then sales manager, manager of corporate development (a staff assignment reporting to the president), and finally district manager. "Sales oriented, well liked, polished, comfortable anywhere, runs tight team, well informed."

Bakersfield. "Too long in his market. 37 years in the industry, close to retirement, resistant to new techniques but thoroughly conversant with his territory and key accounts. The customers love him, but he is a poor trainer."

The local sales managers had three responsibilities: to supervise and train their salespeople; to handle the key accounts directly; and to establish "executive level" contacts at all accounts. This was a heavy work load, needless to say, and different managers excelled in one or two of the three areas depending upon their strengths and territorial idiosyncracies.

One of them, for example, said that he saw his major job as exciting the salespeople because "attitude is everything in this business." Another felt that sorting out his 900 accounts was a crucial responsibility because "without organization you can't make any territorial headway." A third defined his role as "keeping the men on plan because it's too easy to deviate and do things your own way."

The salespeople were, of course, the prime contact between account and company. They were scheduled to average eight calls each day and to cover their accounts in a three- to four-week cycle. They determined their own callback patterns and varied them by account. Although it is unfair to single out one, the remarks of Harold Murphy (Modesto) are interesting:

> I used to sell insurance. Didn't do well in that environment. All they cared about was the one-time sale. They weren't concerned with building a lasting sales relationship.
>
> I like to think I'm a personal friend of my customers. The two most important things as a salesman are *credibility* and *sincerity*. Customers have got to believe me, or I'm wasting my time. I try to get my inside person out to the customers as much as possible too, so she is more than just a voice on the phone. If they're going to call in an order, then they're more likely to call someone pleasant whom they know.
>
> I've got to have good office support. My job is to introduce customers to Henderson Steel. Then after that, I have to depend on shipping, on production, and especially on my inside person. They make me look good. The first order from a potential new customer is often a token for having visited him three or four times, to "see how the salesman will do." Then I have got to have good support to impress him with my service.
>
> The importance of the inside salespeople isn't recognized adequately at Henderson. Bad inside people slow down a salesman, waste his time and effort doing

their jobs for them. The customer may not see any difference and sales may not fall, but the salesman has to cover for his inside person. Inside people were strictly a training grounds for outside salesmen in the past. Now people are beginning to see that some people are best suited there. Some want to stay in the inside.

We're number one in Modesto (the inside person and me), and half the credit goes to her. The inside people don't get an incentive bonus, though they should, since they really generate sales. I'm going to share part of my bonus with my inside person. She deserves it.

I run my territory on the basis of customer demand. I go where I can do the most good, be most influential, not based on the size of the account or a certain call frequency. I go to customers with a reason in mind, for a specific purpose. Some of my best customers told me when I first visited them three years ago, "Look, we've been buying from Henderson for years. You can't tell us anything new about Henderson and its service. Don't keep just coming around. We'll call you when we need you!" So I visit them maybe once a month and let my inside person deal with them. If they have a problem, then I am right there. They know whatever the problem is, I take care of it.

At one of my most sophisticated accounts, one of my competitors insists on going out every Tuesday morning to their plant. I don't think it's ever influenced a purchase decision. They joked about his coming every Tuesday.

Henderson Steel gives its sales force too much leeway on how to sell, especially the young ones. But I like it loose. I call my manager daily, and I feel good about calling him in to help if needed.

A rundown of the five districts indicated the situation at the start of 1979 as shown in Exhibit 5.

The salespeople specifics are depicted in Exhibit 6.

Tom Henderson provided a thumbnail sketch on each of the individual salesmen and sales managers:

San Fernando

Smith. An old pro; knows the territory; needs incentives to get full attention; overlooks possibilities in established accounts; about 46 years old; has a "good way" about him; the sales manager, but spends most of his time in his territory; has team which needs little supervision.

Smiley. With us three years; young, comer, eager, wants to advance; liked by customers; only 28; tends to high spot the accounts; somewhat weak on product knowledge; sells service aggressively.

South. Foremerly plant superintendent; has done exceptionally well; best suited to country area and will probably have to be transferred; likes farm and mining contacts; thorough but unimaginative; has several key accounts who think the world of him.

Exhibit 5

District and plant	1978 Sales ($000)	1978 Quota	Number of salespeople (including management)	Sales per salesperson ($000)	Gross margin ($000)	Average gross margin per salesperson	Approximate number of accounts	Estimated share of market
San Fernando	$ 7,188	$ 7,000	3	$2,396	$1,798	599	2,500	12%
San Diego	3,456	3,850	3	1,155	917	306	2,500	7.5
Bakersfield	4,727	4,650	2 + district manager/ sales manager combined	1,576	1,128	376	1,100	11
Modesto	2,423	2,600	2 + district manager/ sales manager combined	808	591	197	1,500	10
San Jose/Salinas	5,531	5,100	5	1,106	1,330	265	2,400	8
Total	$23,325*	$23,200						

*In addition there were home office house accounts of $2,550,000 handled by the senior management (but serviced locally).

Exhibit 6

District and territory	Salesperson	1978 Percent of quota	1978 Gross margin	Compensation	As percent of gross margin
San Fernando					
No. 1	Smith	87%	$552,630	$21,166	3.8%
No. 2	Smiley	104	470,912	14,811	3.1
No. 3	South	112	763,215	21,608	2.8
No. 4	Open	—	—	—	—
San Diego					
No. 11	Drudge	61	187,184	—	—
No. 12	Dodge	82	380,747	17,268	4.5
No. 13	Davis	118	320,098	17,963	5.6
Bakersfield					
No. 21	Brown	92	162,165	19,667	12.1
No. 22	Benton	137	468,371	24,005	5.1
No. 23	Bowles*	93	494,120	18,600	—
San Jose					
No. 41	Johnson	86	254,819	22,733	8.9
No. 42	Judas*	65	196,014	16,768	8.6
No. 44	Judd	98	316,592	19,816	6.3
No. 45	James	118	418,211	21,185	5.1
No. 46	Jaedeke	115	143,640	—	—
No. 48	Open	—	—	—	—
Modesto					
No. 51	Murphy	102	301,951	18,355	6.1
No. 52	Minnow*	65	57,853	16,500	28.0
No. 53	Morris*	80	243,582	15,410	6.3

*In territory less than full year. Compensation annualized for comparison.

San Diego

Drudge. The sales manager; well trained but emotional; orthodox in his approach; tends to concentrate on his favorite accounts; 38 years old; has potential; has trouble organizing but does reasonably well as SM.

Dodge. A problem—seems to be drinking too much; recently went through a nasty divorce; was once our best man, now I'm not so sure.

Davis. Shop background; formerly inside salesman; 15 years on the job; seems to be getting bored; OK if closely supervised; no apparent potential; has some well established accounts which he's comfortable with.

Bakersfield

Brown. Combination DM and SM; knows everyone in town; sells entirely on basis of friendship; not running too hard; needs lots of management time; in a tough market, inflexible, close to retirement, good with the petroleum accounts.

Benton. The old pro; a jewel; can always get business; positive; not good on systems or administration; knows markets and products; doesn't want a promotion.

Bowles. Very new in the territory (six month); comes from a competitor where he left under some kind of a cloud; I'm still not comfortable with him—seems slippery, not quite open and honest—though these may be unfair generalizations; I let my DM hire him against my better judgment; has some of our most loyal accounts; shows signs of selling price.

San Jose

Johnson. Lots of experience; was a sales manager but demoted because he couldn't motivate others; needs supervision; knows his product but is easily discouraged; great at knowing the people; spends lots of time on his real estate investments where he has done well; is well-off financially.

Judas. Came from another company where he was a purchasing agent; inside selling for us and has been outside for less than one year; highly religious individual, who occasionally offends others by his inflexible beliefs; not at ease in his territory but seems to be catching on; still a question mark; not fully able to sell on basis of service.

Judd. With us 1½ years from an outside company; good product knowledge but in a tough market; inclined to sell on price; not a strong competitor—wants everyone to like him.

James. An old pro; age 49; lots of experience but needs occasional pumping up; not promotable; the mayor of his town; likes new products and new accounts.

Jaedeke. Recently made SM; too new to judge; has an MBA, which he earned at night; very control oriented; sees the need to concentrate on key accounts and senior managers; well balanced; says he wants to get into marketing management soon; very sharp; should go a long way if handled well.

Modesto

Murphy. 24 years in the industry after a short career in insurance; once a DM but had a nervous breakdown; excellent salesman but very excitable; sees himself as a lady's man; separated from his wife; not fully reliable—some indication that he is slacking off.

Nimow. A new DM; doubles as SM; only three months on the job; has a strong sales background and leads by doing; seems to be a good planner; thorough; tends to be impatient if things don't go his way.

Morris. A new man; just finished his training; college degree; age 24; his father owned and operated a small center but sold out five years ago; seems to be floundering.

Sales Management. The Henderson company's hiring procedures were somewhat a function of local management. Although headquarters set some broad parameters, the district managers were pretty much left to their own. Consider, for example, the remarks of one district manager;

> We hire salesmen primarily through employment agencies. They often have no prior steel experience, though some do. Few even have sales experience; usually they know nothing about sales. We don't require a college degree or screen them with a sales test. What we look for is ambition and good recommendations. Does he want to succeed? The outside salesperson alone is reponsible for the territory. Most sales managers, on the other hand, have been with the company many years, since we promote from within.

The training of a new salesperson was supposed to consist of six weeks in the shop learning terminology and the production processes used at Henderson. The content and duration of training varied greatly with the individual managers. Some managers gave trainees two weeks in the plant, some outside selling time, and then four weeks again in the plant. Other managers used six weeks in the plant. One salesman reported that he spent 12 weeks training in the plant, followed by one week each in the credit, billing, and inventory departments. Upon completing the training, the new salesman moved into inside sales. It was not unusual for competition to hire the new employee after his training was completed—at least this was an ongoing threat because a good labor force was at a premium in the industry.

Territorial assignments were largely a function of local needs. A new person might move into an unexpected assignment because of some sudden emergency (i.e., salesperson turnover was 25 percent a year), or territory boundaries might be changed to accommodate a new multilocation account. By and large, however, a salesperson was assigned to a geographic area containing between 500 and 2,500 potential customers and with an industry mix that reflected the local economy.

Sales quotas were established early and were arrived at by adding 10 percent to the person's last year's sales. The marketing vice president recognized that this was a simplistic approach (in fact, the 10 percent figure was only an average; the vice president would vary it by territory depending upon local requirements), but he took comfort in the fact that the resulting target closely reflected what the organization *could* do. Actual results over the years had been remarkably close to the 10 percent average increase, and the firm seemed to be gaining market share (though there were no real data to measure this relative gain).

Sales compensation was tied to the quota. Each person received a salary and a quarterly commission based upon quota. Between 80 and 90 percent of quota, the commission was $10 times the percentage over 80 percent but under 90 percent; $30 between 90 and 100 percent; $35 between 100 percent and 120 percent, and $10 over 120 percent. If a person hit 129 percent of quota during a three-month period, therefore he would receive:

$$
\begin{aligned}
\$10 \times 10 &= \$\ \ 100 \\
\$30 \times 10 &= \quad 300 \\
\$35 \times 20 &= \quad 700 \\
\$10 \times \ \ 9 &= \quad\ \ 90 \\
\text{Total} &= \$1{,}190
\end{aligned}
$$

At 98 percent of quota his commission was:

$$
\begin{aligned}
\$10 \times 10 &= \$100 \\
\$30 \times \ \ 8 &= \ \ 240 \\
\text{Total} &= \$340
\end{aligned}
$$

One hundred percent of quota was the expected sales target and represented the "10 percent average over last year" previously described. It was hoped that the typical salesperson would earn about 10 percent of salary in bonus.

Sales supervision, as explained, was centerd in the local sales manager, who was both salesperson and supervisor. Normally, however, the sales manager carried a lighter customer load than the full-time salespeople. One manager had this to say about his position:

> I don't think a sales manager can also be his own salesman. Our outside salespeople deserve more attention than I can give them. For example, I don't get out often enough to see other customers. I want to travel more with the sales force, and I plan to. I try to have fewer short sessions with them in favor of longer talks.
>
> Now, Tom Henderson thinks the sales manager can also act as salesman. I'm one reason he thinks so. Sales here have gone up since I took over as sales manager. But I'm the only one who knows I am not doing justice to either job. Our sales are good, but they could be even better. Somewhere between supervising three and seven salespeople, a sales manager becomes necessary. I work hard to do both jobs.

Some Alternatives

As he reviewed his sales strategy, Mr. Henderson singled out a number of issues.

1. **Deployment.** Was the company's policy of assigning salespeople contiguous geographic areas the best one? After all, the buying habits of the various segments were different and some salespeople seemed better equipped to sell to sophisticated buyers, while others were at home with more mundane accounts, such as contractors or farmers. Some people were more comfortable in small-town, small-company environments, while others thrived on the big, complex situations. Finally, it was appar-

ent that different salespeople preferred different tasks. For some, prospecting was the challenge. For others, it was developing more business from existing accounts. A few liked to work with development engineers and others with the more commercial side of the customer's operation.

Without even considering the economics of various territory assignment alternatives, Mr. Henderson pondered what were the best overall ways to organize in today's markets. What were the fundamental advantages and disadvantages of each variation?

A part of the development problem was the additional fact that company sales were concentrated. To be exact, volume was distributed as follows:

Percent of customers	Percent of sales
Largest 20 percent	78.5%
Next 30 percent	12.5
Remaining 50 percent	9.0

This concentration was typical of all of the district offices. In fact, out of ±10,000 customers throughout the company, 250 represented 60 percent of the sales, while the smallest 2,000 averaged only $500 per year. They represented, on the other hand, 18 percent of the calls.

2. Training and Career Development. A 25 percent turnover of salespeople struck Mr. Henderson as expensively high. He could figure the initial costs of hiring and training a new employee at $18,000. Nor did it make sense that his company should invest heavily in the selection and training of a new salesperson only to have competition raid his ranks with alarming degrees of success. Somehow the company had to convince the new hires that a few more dollars from a competitive firm were a poor trade-off for Henerson's generous retirement and benefit plans. Henderson wondered if more detailed individual career development programs would alleviate the problem and whether ongoing training couldn't be more specifically tied into additional job responsibilities and salary increases. In short, how could Mr. Henderson structure the job, compensation, and career development steps in order to attract and hold superior sales candidates?

One of his friends in the industry sent Tom a summary of a personnel development program that he was using. Excerpts are included below, and Tom wondered whether he should adopt a similar program, one which his friend estimated would add 50 percent to the costs of the normal training program:

Personnel Development Program

The objective of this memorandum is to establish a minimum program to be used in developing new salespeople. The requirements should be expanded to meet the needs of the individual district. For example, those districts with light fab, slitting, etc., should include training in those areas.

The requirements shown should be completed within the time frame of the program, and all portions of one step, including the time involved, must be completed before the change in title is certified.

The district manager will be responsible for arranging outside training, which will have to be adapted to what is available in each area.

Special attention should be directed throughout the program to developing selling skills. Reading material pertaining to products and the industry should be available.

A conference with the district manager is required at the completion of each step of the personnel development program.

Sales trainee—I	0 to 4 months
Sales trainee—II.................	5 to 8 months
Sales trainee—III	9 to 12 months
Salesperson......................	Completion

The summary went on to detail each step, listing the specific activities, tasks, and assignments required of the trainees before they could be certified for the next step. Salary adjustments were dependent upon the separate steps. To illustrate, the details under "Sales Trainee I" follow:

STEP 1 + 0 to 4 Months

A. Company Orientation
1. Salary and review date.
2. Insurance programs.
3. Savings plan.
4. Retirement program.
5. Vacations and holidays.
6. Safety program.
7. Personnel development program written test.

The manager of employee relations will furnish a written test concerning these programs. Completion of this phase will be upon recommendation of the department head and certification by the district manager.

B. Plant Experience
1. People identification.
2. Equipment indentification.
3. Equipment capacities.
4. Material identification.
5. Receiving systems.
6. Storage systems.
7. Delivery experience.
8. Order paper flow procedures.

Completion of these requirements will be upon recommendation of the plant superintendent and department head. Certification will be required by the district manager.

3. **Future Managers.** Closely related to the problem of salesperson retention was that of preparing a cadre of managers suited to the environment of the 1980s. It was Tom Henderson's conviction that the manager of tomorrow would have to be a true professional—able to think for herself or himself, to strategize, to work with profit models, to analyze, and to lead a group of better trained subordinates.

Would such requirements permit the traditional policy of promotion from within, or should the company begin to go outside for highly talented individuals? It was possible to spot attractive candidates from outside the industry, but whether the risk of force-feeding them upon the existing culture was worthwhile was unclear. To avoid this risk, why wouldn't it be possible for Tom to retrain current managers to fit the new pattern? Such a move would, if course, require a special training effort—one which would be costly and which might or might not work.

4. **Quotas and Compensation.** The quota system, as described, concentrated upon experience (10 percent over last year). Why not, wondered Tom, include some measures of potential? After all, the quality of a particular level of performance was a function of both experience *and* potential. It should be possible, he thought, to qualify quotas by such potential measures as industrial activity, level of employment per district, freight car loadings, and changes in employment. If the company were to include such variables, how should they be worked into the present system? How much weight should be placed upon experience? Upon potential?

And even more critical, if there were changes made in the quotas, how should the salespeople be paid? Was straight salary to be preferred, or did there need to be an incentive payment? Similar or different from what now existed?

Another friend of Tom's had suggested a simple diagram for thinking out the problem of compensation (Exhibit 7).

First, you must decide how much the "average salesperson doing an average job" should earn. In this illustration, it was $20,000 as seen at the bottom left. Across the top, the key salesperson jobs and their relative values were listed. Hence, the $20,000 pie was allocated across the tasks. Finally, all of the possible payment techniques were enumerated vertically. The dollars and payment methods were then matched by asking "How do I best pay for this task, and how much?" Obviously a particular task might warrant more than one payment technique.

The resulting matrix would form the base for telescoping the various payment alternatives into a simpler, less complicated compensation plan. But at least the implications of each sales task and the ideal way of paying for it would have been considered.

Exhibit 7

Payment alternatives \ Tasks and relative importance	1 To maintain sales* 40%	2 To open new accounts* 30%	3 To sell full line* 20%	4 To supply intelligence* 10%
Salary	$?		$?	
Commission		$?		
Contests				
Bonus		$?		
Expense Accounts				$?
Profit Share				
Other				
			$?	
Dollars for Each Task	$8,000	$6,000	$4,000	$2,000

Note: Total Expected Pay = $20,000

*Assumed for this example only.

5. **Organization.** It was clear, as pointed out earlier, that company growth had come principally from acquisition. Was it possible, considered Tom, to reorganize so as to develop more market share in the existing districts?

For example, would it help to have product managers or even key account managers? After all, business was concentrated both in selected products and customers. Wouldn't specialization in one or both of those dimensions result in better account penetration? But if such a move were to be made, Tom was concerned about how such a modification could be built into the existing structure. Moreover, he estimated that the incremental costs of new managers would be about $60,000 each.

From a field management vantage point, there was the ongoing question of whether the sales managers should supervise and sell, or supervise alone. It was easy to say that supervision was the critical function, but the economics of small districts made it tough to support sales managers who only managed. As the senior salespeople in their territories, their customer know-how was so great that Tom hesitated to set it aside. Could a full-time manager, in other words, pay his own way when he had only two or three salespeople to lead? How best could his job be structured?

6. **Product Lines.** Finally, Tom thought it important to reconsider his product policies. Specialists were growing as were price-oriented brokers and purveyors of secondary lines. Could Henerson hope to survive unless his firm somehow insulated the impact of these competitors from its major markets? Should the company work with one or more of these specialists, become one, or fight them?

Tom knew that he had raised a number of hard questions. It wasn't easy to answer them but he thought that a good starting point would be to evaluate the effectiveness of his present strategy and to match that strategy against the needs of the marketplace.

AURORA LOTION

John Fairchild frowned as he hung up the telephone. He had just finished another conversation with Urs Brunner, the general manager of Produits Pour Femmes, SA (PPF), on a subject that had become increasingly troublesome over the last three years: how to respond to the problem of parallel importing of Aurora Lotion into Switzerland. Fairchild was the general manager of the Overseas Division of Smythe-Dabney International, Ltd., a British company which marketed Aurora and other women's cosmetics. A large portion of his job was devoted to offering information and recommendations to the managers of the subsidiary companies which made up the division.

The management of PPF, the Swiss subsidiary, had reported a growing rash of price cutting on Aurora Lotion, one of its most important products, by a group of independent distributors who were buying Aurora in England and bringing it to Switzerland themselves. This practice, which had been dubbed "parallel importing" or "black importing" in the trade, had put PPF's gross margins under pressure and squeezed the company's return on sales. The situation had reached the point that Urs Brunner had asked John Fairchild to intervene and recommend a strategy to counter the threat, including a substantial reduction of PPF's selling price for Aurora if necessary.

Smythe-Dabney International, Ltd.

The parent company for PPF was Smythe-Dabney International, Ltd. (SDI), with headquarters outside London. In 1977 SDI's sales were £25.8 million and its trading profits were £2.6 million. In the last 10 years earnings per share had increased at the compound rate of 20 percent a year. Sir Anthony Carburton, the chairman of SDI, felt that the impressive record was the result of several factors, including the quality of the company's product, the energies and talents of a closeknit management team, and the ability to stay a step ahead of competitors in the marketplace.

From the earliest days with the introduction of Aurora Lotion, SDI had marketed only products of high quality and had stressed that theme in advertising and promotion campaigns. As a result the various SDI cosmetics, under the Aurora name and in several other well-known brand families, enjoyed widespread brand recognition and consumer loyalty.

A keen sensitivity to the needs of both the channels of distribution and consumers caused the company's directors to search continually for ways to make their products and services more competitive. They had defined the market they served as the

---

Source: The case was prepared by Research Associate Thomas Kosnik under the direction of Professor Christopher Gale as a basis for class discussion rather than to illustrate either effective or ineffective handling of an administrative situation.

women's beauty care market and had acquired a wide line of products that complemented each other and ensured efficient utilization of the sales force and marketing staff. They quickly learned that the ability to supply the trade was critical and earned a reputation for having the company's products in stock in a timely fashion, providing a valuable service for their distributors. They used extensive television advertising to stimulate demand, and point-of-purchase displays in retail outlets to make it easier for consumers to select the products they needed.

The objectives of the company for the next three years were to increase sales and earnings per share 20 percent a year and to maintain a pretax income/sales ratio of 10 percent. The basic guidelines the corporate management had drafted to reach those objectives were to:

1. Increase unit volume of sales in all product lines.
2. Maintain historic direct (gross) margins.
3. Keep corporate overhead expenses low by maintaining a lean home office staff.
4. Give management of subsidiary companies decision-making authority on all tactical matters, with consultation with corporate management on strategic issues.

The Overseas Division

SDI was composed of the UK Division and the Overseas Division. In 1977 the Overseas Division sold £10.8 million worth of women's beauty products in continental Europe, North America, and the Far East. In Europe, SDI had company-owned subsidiaries in France, Germany, and Switzerland and marketed its products in other countries through independent wholesale distributors.

Both Fairchild and Carburton shared the view that the most promising markets for future growth were in Europe and North America. In 1977 much of the 20 percent growth in sales and profits projected for the company as a whole was expected to come from the Overseas Division.

Produits Pour Femmes, SA

PPF was responsible for the marketing of Aurora and other SDI products in Switzerland. Its reporting relationship in the Overseas Division is shown in Exhibit 1. The organization was small, with 14 people in all comprising a sales force, marketing department, accounting department, and warehouse crew.

Sales of the company in 1977 were SFr. 4.3 million, up 22 percent from the year before. Exhibit 2 shows PPF's income statement for 1976 and 1977.

Urs Brunner had recently taken over as general manager. He and his marketing manager were the key decision makers in day-to-day activities; John Fairchild and Dustin Cushman, the general manager for Europe, involved themselves with PPF only on matters of strategic importance.

Exhibit 1 **Smythe-Dabney International Ltd. Overseas Division Organization Chart**

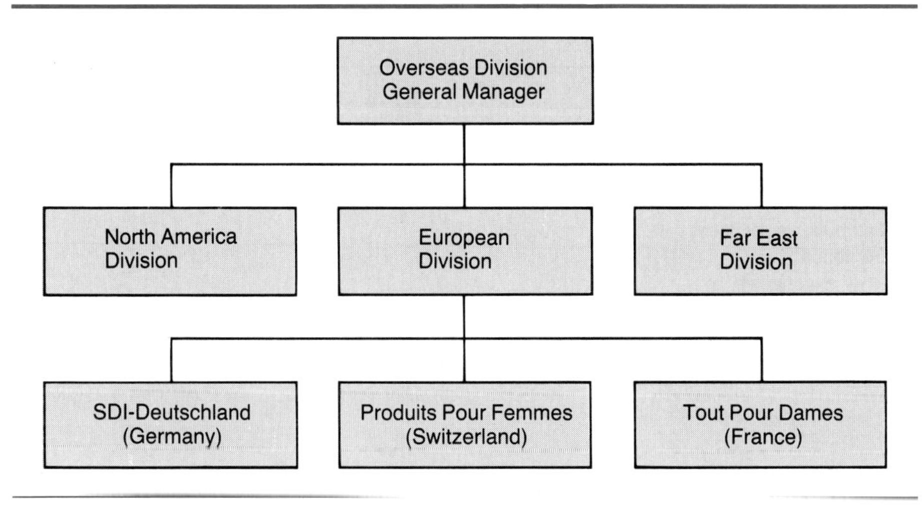

Source: SDI company records.

Exhibit 2 **Produits Pour Femmes, SA Division Income Statement 1976 and 1977 (SFr.000)**

	1976	1977
Sales	3,525	4,300
Less: Cost of goods sold	1,160	1,720
Direct margin	2,365	2,580
Less:		
Advertising	405	403
Distribution	204	330
Promotion*	175	230
Other expenses†	55	70
Brand contribution	1,490	1,520
Less:		
Sales force expenses	410	430
General and administration	670	610
Trading profit (before tax)	410	480

*Does not include trade discounts on Aurora Lotion.

†Other expenses included marketing research, product research, public relations, depreciation, and inventory losses through obsolescence, damage etc.

Source: SDI company records (disguised).

Exhibit 3 **Aurora Product Group PPF**
Brand Contribution Statement, 1976 and 1977 (SFr.000)

	1976	1977
Sales	850	1,140
Less: Cost of goods sold	290	526
Direct margin	560	614
Less:		
Advertising	94	106
Distribution expenses	50	55
Promotion*	74	150
Other expenses†	15	12
Brand contribution	327	291

*Does not include trade discounts on Aurora Lotion.
†Other expenses included marketing research, product research, public relations, depreciation, and inventory losses.
Source: SDI company records (disguised).

The Product

Aurora Lotion was a high-quality, all-purpose lotion for women. It was applied by being spread lightly over the skin of the face, arms, legs, and other parts of the body and then rubbing gently until the lotion was completely absorbed into the skin. The company stressed in its advertising that Aurora relieved dryness due to sun, wind, water, or detergents and made skin feel soft, clean, and gentle to the touch. It also stated that the effects of the lotion were longer lasting than those of many similar products. A single application of Aurora before bedtime each evening kept the skin "soft and beautiful," while it was necessary to apply other lotions as often as three or four times a day to get the same protection. The secret of Aurora's long-lasting effectiveness was a unique formula which allowed the lotion to penetrate the skin more completely than competing brands.

Aurora Lotion was the brand leader in a growing line of beauty products which included hand lotion, moisturizers, and bath preparations. Exhibit 3 contains the Aurora product line's brand contribution statement to PPF. The company also marketed the full line of SDI products under other brands, including facial cosmetics, eye cosmetics, hair preparations, nail polish, and deodorants. In 1977 Aurora Lotion sales accounted for 20 percent of the total sales of PPF.

Over the years, Aurora Lotion had become increasingly familiar to women in many European countries. In fact, parallel importers capitalized on this brand recognition and easily sold Aurora Lotion in Switzerland that had been shipped directly from Britain, even though the directions for use of the lotion were in English. Fairchild and Brunner estimated that 120,000 bottles of Aurora were parallel-imported into Switzerland in 1977, compared with PPF sales of 200,000 bottles in the same period.

Exhibit 4 **Sample of All-Purpose Lotions Available in Switzerland**

Product	Size of selling unit	Retail selling price per selling unit
High-price		
Caron	120 cl	SFr. 28.00
Chanel	80 g	24.50
Je Reviens	100 cl	22.50
Amnioderm	200 cl	30.00
Medium-price		
Aurora Lotion	200 cl	SFr. 15.00
Bea Kasser	150 cl	14.50
Janine D	200 cl	13.50
4711	200 cl	9.50
Ma Garde	125 cl	7.50
Oil of Olay	200 cl	7.50
Fenjal	250 cl	7.50
Winston's	300 cl	8.40
Low-price		
Rose Milk	240 cl	SFr. 5.90
Nivea	250 cl	4.95
Kaloderma	300 cl	4.50
Jana Lait de Toilette (Migros)	430 cl	3.50

Source: Field research at retail outlets, Lausanne, Switzerland.

Competitive Products

All-purpose lotions for women were available in great variety and a wide range of price and quality. However, they tended to cluster in three main groups.

1. *High-priced products.* These lotions were most often produced by companies making fashionable women's perfumes. They had the same scents as popular women's fragrances, so the consumer could use the lotion along with her favorite cologne or perfume. These lotions were sold for SFr. 20 to SFr. 50 in retail outlets, for bottles of 100 to 200 centiliters (cl). Some packages were annotated in grams rather than centiliters.
2. *Medium-price lotions.* Many of these lotions were imported to Switzerland from France and England. They were attractively packaged and often made claims to characteristics that differentiated them from other lotions. Some were made by perfume houses to match less expensive fragrances. They sold for between SFr. 7.50 and SFr. 15, and the most common bottle size was 200 cl.
3. *Low-price lotions.* These products were the simple, functional answer to the everyday problems of dry, rough skin due to water, weather, and housework. Prices ranged from SFr. 3 to SFr. 6 for a plastic container of 240 cl to 450 cl.

Exhibit 4 provides examples of all-purpose lotions in the three price ranges. Aurora Lotion, with a suggested retail price of SFr. 15 for 200 cl, was positioned near the top of the middle range of lotions.

Consumers cited several problems that sometimes arose when using an all-purpose lotion. These related to the fragrance of the lotion and its ability to penetrate the skin. Some products had a heavy, sweet, or powerful scent that could potentially clash with or mask the fragrance of perfume. Some lotions left the skin feeling slippery, greasy, or wet after application, while others were not absorbed into the skin and washed off immediately upon contact with water. In the former case the lotion might stain clothing or furniture. In the latter case it was necessary to apply the lotion several times a day, after bathing, doing dishes, or returning from out of doors. The popularity of Aurora Lotion was due in large part to the fact that it had a light, clean scent that did not clash with perfumes and also that it penetrated deeply without leaving the skin slick or greasy.

The Beauty Care Market in Switzerland

Switzerland was a small, topographically rugged country in the center of Western Europe. The Swiss enjoyed a relatively high standard of living; the per capita GNP in 1975 was SFr. 22,500, the highest in Europe. The population was 6.4 million people, and the diversity of the Swiss was reflected in the fact that there were four official languages, as follows:

First language	Percentage of population
German	65%
French	18
Italian	12
Romansh	1
Other	4
Total	100%

Source: Market research report, Swiss Federal Railway.

There were 3.28 million women in Switzerland who were distributed among the following age groups:

Age group	Number of women (000)
0–14	700
15–19	240
20–29	510
30–39	450
40–49	400
50–59	340
Over 60	640
Total	3,280

Source: Consumer Europe 1977.

Retail sales of all beauty products in Switzerland were SFr. 535.3 million in 1975. The per capita expenditure for the Swiss adult woman was nearly SFr. 210. The women's cosmetic market comprised several segments, which in 1975 accounted for the following percentages of the total retail sales:

Product category	Percentage of beauty product sales
Face cosmetics	12%
Eye cosmetics	4
Hair preparations	22
Skin preparations	18
Fragrances	18
Deodorants	8
Bath preparations	4
Other	14
Total	100%

Source: Consumer Europe 1977.

Total sales of beauty products increased 12.6 percent from 1974 to 1975 in Switzerland. There were also changes in the structure of the market. Sales of fragrances and skin preparations, which included all-purpose lotions, rose sharply, while there was a decline in the volume of face and eye cosmetics and bath preparations.

According to some experts, the potential for the skin preparations market varied significantly among European countries. Sales levels depended not only upon the predominant skin types in a country but also upon the affluence of the women. Partly because of the standard of living in Switzerland and the fact that a relatively large proportion of the women were fair skinned, the expenditure per adult woman on skin preparations was higher than in every other Western European country but Germany. In 1973 the "average" Swiss woman spent about SFr. 37 on skin lotions of various types. Exhibit 5 gives a breakdown of sales and usership of various categories of skin preparations, including all-purpose lotions.

Exhibit 5 **Swiss Market for Skin Preparations, 1975**

	Retail sales (SFr. million)	Unit sales (packs)	Usership (million women)	Percent of usership
Hand cream/lotion	22.8	7.8	1.85	72
Body cream/lotion	12.2	2.5	0.98	38
Moisturizers	7.5	1.2	0.73	29
All-purpose lotions	34.0	6.4	1.74	67
Others	18.8	+	+	+
	95.3			

Source: Consumer Europe 1977.

Channels and Pricing

Smythe-Dabney products reached the buying public through a variety of channels of distribution, each with its own pricing arrangement. Aurora Lotion was manufactured in England and then sold in the United Kingdom to independent wholesalers or large retail chains. In countries with an SDI subsidiary, such as Switzerland, Aurora was sold to the affiliated company, which then resold it to wholesalers and retail stores. SDI billed all customers in pounds sterling. Company-owned subsidiaries were charged a transfer price, which was the standard manufacturing cost of the product, including:

- Raw materials.
- Direct labor.
- Factory overhead.
- Handling and warehousing.

The senior management of SDI adopted this transfer pricing arrangement in order to give the managers of each subsidiary maximum discretion over margins and profits. The reasons for this strategy were:

1. The majority of marketing costs were, in fact, incurred in the country where the product was sold.
2. Advertising, price promotions, and sales force management decisions were under the control of the subsidiary's management.
3. The practice reinforced the SDI concept of division autonomy on day-to-day decisions and fostered good relationships between subsidiary managers and corporate officers.

SDI's price to independent customers in Britain was standard manufacturing cost plus a percentage of the cost for contribution to overhead and profit. All customers paid freight charges from factory to their warehouses.

SDI gave independent distributors in the United Kingdom a 3.75 percent discount for cash purchases and up to 6 percent volume rebate for purchases of large amounts of any product. In addition, each month, the company ran price promotions for groups of products in order to encourage British distributors to increase the volume of products they carried.

In England, wholesalers' markups on cosmetics were usually between 15 percent and 25 percent; retail margins were 35 percent to 45 percent of the selling price to the consumer. On the the other hand, wholesale margins for beauty products in Switzerland were between 40 percent and 55 percent of the selling price to retail outlets, and retail margins were 42 percent to 50 percent. In Switzerland, Aurora Lotion and other PPF products were sold at the retail level in a wide variety of outlets. Exhibit 6 shows the percentage of total sales of beauty care products that were sold through various outlets in 1975. While the data were incomplete, there was evidence of a rapid increase in the portion of total sales that were accounted for by hypermarkets in the last few years.

Exhibit 6 **Percentage of Retail Sales of Women's Beauty Care Products Sold through Various Outlets in Switzerland**

Outlet	Description	Percent of total sales
Department and cosmetics stores	Cosmetic departments of large department stores and small shops and "parfumeries" specializing in cosmetics.	20%
Drugstores and pharmacies	Drugstores sold cleaning compounds, preparations, and parapharmaceuticals; pharmacies sold prescription drugs and other products.	40
Multiple stores/hypermarkets	Large chains selling food items as well as many nonfood products, from clothing to hardware to beauty products, often at discount prices (e.g., Migros and Carrefour).	25
Direct sales	Door-to-door salespersons.	3
Supermarkets/food outlets	Small and medium-size retail stores selling mainly food, with some nonfood lines.	9
Other		3
Total		100%

Source: *Consumer Europe 1977.*

Parallel Imports

Perhaps the biggest single problem that confronted the management of PPF was the parallel importing of Aurora Lotion. The difference in the wholesale price in Britain and Switzerland made it profitable for a distributor to send a buyer to England, purchase the product at the British wholesale price, and ship it to Switzerland for eventual resale to retail outlets. The process had become increasingly common in the last several years, and the management of PPF counted several large distributors who parallel imported Aurora Lotion among their main competitors in the marketplace. Although parallel importing was irritating to the sales force and management of PPF, it was not illegal and it was impossible to monitor.

There were three main reasons that the wholesale price of Aurora Lotion was lower in England than in Switzerland. First, retail prices were higher on the Continent than in Britain, reflecting a higher cost of living. Second, SDI conducted aggressive promotions in the United Kingdom each month, and the resulting average level of wholesale prices was lower than in Europe, where such promotions occurred less frequently. Finally, from 1972 through 1978 there had been a substantial decline in the value of the British pound against other currencies, including the Swiss franc. As a result of this trend, Swiss distributors had not had to increase the price of Aurora Lotion to the retail trade in five years, although SDI had hiked prices in Britain by as much as 25 percent a year in the same period. Since SDI billed its customers in pounds sterling, the fall of the pound against the Swiss franc had offset the British price increase.

Table 1 **Hypothetical Example of Parallel Importer's Cost per Bottle of Aurora Lotion***

SDI price/case	£10.55
SDI price/bottle	0.88
Less: 3.75 percent cash discount	0.04
Net purchase	0.84
Less: 6 percent volume rebate	0.05
British distributor's cost	0.79
Add: 15 percent markup	0.14
Wholesale price	0.93
Add: transport cost at 6 percent	0.06
Landed cost/bottle	£ 0.99
Landed cost/bottle†	SFr.3.70

*Figures have been rounded.

†Assumes 3.75 SFr./pound.

Source: Discussions with SDI directors.

Table 1 contains a hypothetical example of the landed cost per bottle of parallel-imported Aurora Lotion.

A large British wholesaler purchased Aurora Lotion at £10.55 per case of 12 bottles. Normally the distributor was expected to take a 3.75 percent cash discount and to be eligible for a volume rebate of 6 percent of his net purchases. When reselling these goods in large volume, he was content to receive a 15 percent markup.

A wholesale distributor or large retailer doing business in Switzerland sent a representative across the English Channel to buy from the British supplier. He paid £0.93 for each bottle and incurred additional freight charges at 4 percent to 8 percent of the cost of goods, depending upon the volume shipped to Switzerland. Assuming at the time of the transaction an exchange rate of 3.75 Swiss francs per pound, his cost for a 200 cl bottle of Aurora Lotion landed in Switzerland was SFr. 3.70. The price list for PPF recommended the following price structure for the 200 cl bottle of Aurora (including freight):

PPF suggested list price to distributors	SFr. 5.00
Distributor's suggested list price to retail outlets	8.70
Retailer's suggested list price to consumers	15.00

According to Urs Brunner, the retail price of Aurora Lotion had not declined in the last few years despite the parallel imports. Since the consumer was paying the same price, the channels were apparently enjoying higher margins.

It was difficult to assess the impact of parallel importing on PPF or SDI as a whole. On the one hand the average price of Aurora Lotion sold by PPF to the trade had declined over 20 percent in the past three years. Although PPF's list price for the product had not been reduced, the company had run a series of trade promotions

Exhibit 7 **Trends in Average Selling Price and Landed Cost of Aurora Lotion (200 cl) by Produits Pour Femmes, SA 1975–1978**

	1975	1976	1977	1978*
Average selling price per bottle (SFr.)†	5.00	4.70	4.30	4.00
Average landed cost per bottle (pounds)	0.35	0.40	0.45	0.50
Average exchange rate (SFr./£)‡	5.40	4.05	3.95	3.75

*1978 is average for the first quarter of the year.

†"Average price" is list price less discounts given in trade promotions.

‡Average rate during fourth quarter 1975–77; during first quarter 1978.

Source: SDI company records (disguised).

which gave discounts to distributors, aimed at countering the competition from parallel imports. Exhibit 7 provides details in the trend of PPF's selling price for Aurora.

Sales of Aurora Lotion had increased in units and in Swiss francs, and Fairchild was not sure whether the increases were in spite of the parallel imports or because of them. Probable effects of the activity had been higher market penetration of the product and increased brand recognition, both of which were beneficial to PPF. Besides, from SDI's point of view, the sales of Aurora parallel imported from England benefited the parent company by the contribution from the SDI sales to the British wholesalers.

Even if the practice had mixed results Fairchild knew that he could not shrug off the situation. It was clear from his conversation with Brunner that it had resulted in low morale in the Swiss subsidiary's sales force. Salespersons were rewarded for units sold and wanted to cut the price of Aurora to make them more competitive with the parallel importers.

Alternatives

John Fairchild reviewed the possible responses he had considered to the problem at hand. One alternative was to lower PPF's recommended selling price for Aurora Lotion to distributors. He was concerned about the possible financial consequences of such a price cut, both for PPF and for SDI. Moreover he wondered what steps he should take to ensure that trading profits would not be sacrificed. He believed that related options included cutting the subsidiary's advertising budget, trimming the sales force, and raising the prices of other products.

On the other hand, he wondered whether PPF could simply adhere to the policy that had been followed in the past. Such a strategy would continue to consist of three elements:

1. Avoid direct competition in published list prices.
2. Use trade promotions such as price-off discounts or "buy two, get one free" to respond to competitive pricing.

3. Stress the advantages provided by PPF to the trade, such as continuity of supply, advertising to stimulate demand, and a full line of related products.

Although the problem of what to do about the price of Aurora Lotion demanded action in the short run, it also had implications for the future of the subsidiary over the long term. Fairchild wondered whether the independent Swiss wholesalers would begin to parallel import more SDI products across the channel. Aurora Lotion, which accounted for 20 percent of PPF sales, might only be the first of a growing number of products on which the subsidiary would face increasing price competition.

Perhaps the existence of parallel importers was a signal that PPF was not an efficient channel of distribution. SDI might be better off to conduct its business directly with the independent distributors in Switzerland. This issue took on added significance because of SDI's plans to expand abroad in the future. The corporate directors would be faced with the decision of whether to set up a company subsidiary or to sell SDI products through existing independent wholesalers each time they entered a market in a new country or region.

A meeting with Sir Anthony Carburton and the other SDI directors was scheduled soon. Fairchild decided that this would be the best time to present his views on the situation at PPF and make his recommendations to the group.

ANDERSON DISTRIBUTORS INC.

Anderson Distributors Inc. was a Phoenix Corporation which wholesaled a full line of dry groceries. The line included 12,000 items and was sold primarily to independent food retailers in Arizona and parts of Southern California. Stocks were held in three warehouses scattered throughout the territory. The company had prospered since it was formed thirty years earlier by three brothers who had earlier managed a successful small chain of three retail stores. Sales were made by forty-five salespeople who operated out of eight district offices. In brief, the sales organization consisted of the following:

45 Salespeople
8 District Managers
2 Regional Managers
Sales Vice President

Salesperson compensation ranged from $280 to $370 a week, district managers from $380 to $450. Anderson operated as a voluntary cooperative. That is, the member retailers agreed to concentrate the bulk of their purchases with Anderson in return for quantity discounts, a standard, simplified ordering system, special merchandising and promotional programs, and a convenient delivery system by Anderson trucks. All retailers in the system were allowed to use the co-op logo "Best Stores." In 1980, Anderson had over 3000 affiliated retailers, most of whom did concentrate their dry grocery purchases.

As was true with any extensive field sales organization, Anderson experienced most of the routine field management problems concerning salesperson evaluation, compensation, and supervision. A handful of these problems has been summarized in the following pages.

Evaluating Salesmen

District managers were required to make quarterly and annual evaluations of their salespeople. Clark Philbin had been a district manager for one month when he received a memo from Dan Pace, his regional manager, stating that all current quarterly evaluations were due in three weeks. The memo concerned Clark because he felt that he could not honestly evaluate his sales force after such a short time in his new position. He had had no management training or experience in evaluating people except for the infrequent occasions when his previous boss had asked him to take over a sales meeting.

Clark knew that he could accept the recommendations of the former district manager in writing his first quarterly evaluations, but there were several which he considered questionable. He could not easily identify specific reasons for his disagreement, but felt strongly nonetheless. Not wanting to make any serious mistakes, he decided to talk with his regional manager about evaluation techniques and standards before making any recommendations:

Pace: Well, Clark, what's on your mind?

Philbin: Dan, I'm worried about this rating business. I've never evaluated anyone for anything before, and rather than make some real blunder, I wanted to ask you if you could offer me any guides or ground rules to follow.

Pace: Well, you've really picked a good question. What's bothering you now has been, and still is, a problem for most managers. As far as I know, there is no effective form or rating chart for evaluating people. This is something you just have to pick up from experience.

Philbin: Yes, Dan, but this is quite a responsibility and I'm afraid of making some big mistakes during the learning process.

Pace: True, Clark, but it's hard for me to be specific. It's something all managers go through. You learn by doing, and basically have to develop your own standards. What I find acceptable performance, you might question. There's a lot of "feel" to it.

Philbin: O.K., Dan. I'll do the best I can. I have one question, though—this business of looking for people with management potential rather than sales potential. I don't understand why there should be so much emphasis on management. Aren't good salespersons just as important to the company as potential managers? After all, the business is becoming so competitive that we have to have top caliber salespeople. Today most of the buyers are pretty sophisticated and the old-fashioned drummer has no place anymore. We need people who can read income statements and talk in terms of profits and other customer benefits.

Pace: I agree with you on the last part, Clark, and I guess the argument can be made that the best salespeople under these new conditions have to be more like managers. And if we continue to grow there will always be room for the best young managers. Good luck with your evaluations!

After returning to his office, Clark began to think over the interview. He realized that experience was undoubtedly a good, if not the best, teacher but he still felt that some effective evaluation technique would be helpful. He decided to try one other approach. He called an old boss, Kelly O'Brien, and asked him for his opinion on the problem. Kelly indicated that he would be glad to help. He said that the same problem had bothered him when he first became a district manager. Consequently, he had attempted to quantify some of the criteria commonly used in determining a person's management and sales potential. He had drawn up a rough chart which was divided into two separate areas of recognition: one for people with management potential and one for those with sales potential. The chart had proven useful to him

Exhibit 1 **Evaluation of Sales and Management Potential**

Management	Points	Sales	Points
1. Judgment	25–35	1. Aggressiveness	20–25
2. Maturity	15–25	2. Enthusiasm	25–30
3. Aggressiveness	15–20	3. Adaptability	25–35
4. Enthusiasm	20–30	4. Planning (sales calls)	30–40
5. Adaptability	20–30	5. Initiative	20–25
6. Planning (organizing ability)	20–25	6. Dependability	25–30
7. Creativity	15–25	7. Promptness	15–18
8. Dependability	10–15		160–203
9. Report Writing	1–15	1. Making quota	48–62
10. Motivating	10–15	2. Reports (clean, concise and factual)	8–12
11. Controlling	10–15	3. Servicing accounts	14–18
	170–250	4. New account generation	15–25
		5. Calls/day (quarter beds)	6–10
		6. Appearance	12–14
		7. Care of company property	10–12
			113–153

Rating Scale:	70	80	90	100
	poor	fair	good	excellent

and he offered it to Clark to use in making his evaluations (see Exhibit 1). Clark, of course, wasn't sure if he could separate the requirements for selling and management, nor was he even sure if an "attribute" approach was reasonable.

Recommending Salary Increases

After Clark had finished making his evaluations, he reviewed the salary levels of the salespeople in his territory. He noticed that one man, Larry Gilbert, had been recommended for an increase six weeks earlier by the former manager. Since Clark had just completed his own evaluation of this man, he was interested in seeing how Gilbert had been rated over the years. Gilbert's file showed that he had been with Anderson as a salesman for 12 years but had only progressed to the middle of the current salary range. He had not been granted a salary increase for 22 months, although most salesmen received increases every ten to twelve months. The recommendation written by the former district manager stated, "Larry is continually trying to improve, and some progress is noted every so often. He hasn't had an increase for over a year and a half and should be considered for one soon."

In his own evaluation Clark had ranked Gilbert as one of his poorest salespersons—one who had little or no probability of improving and who should possibly be terminated. Clark realized that he had only worked with Larry for a short time, and felt he should take a second look at Gilbert. However, he felt strongly about his own evaluation in this case and was absolutely against recommending a raise. Although the increase had already been submitted by the former district manager, Clark did not know whether it had been reviewed by the regional manager yet. Clark thought to himself how difficult it would be to give someone an increase and then fire him/her a month later.

Awarding Salary Increases

The regional manager approved the salary increases that Clark had recommended for his sales staff. Awarding an increase was generally considered fairly routine, but Clark could remember well how, as a young salesman, he had reacted to the way his supervisors had awarded increases to him. Once his local manager called him long distance and said, "Next week your paycheck will be $10 larger. . . ." Before Clark had a chance to say a word his manager had hung up. On another occasion with a different manager, both he and his wife were taken out to dinner by the district manager on the day he had received his raise.

Clark felt that the way in which increases were awarded could make a significant difference in a person's future performance. Moreover, he believed that one should be told why he/she was receiving the raise. However, he was undecided about two things: whether it was a good idea to involve the family in company business by including the spouse; and whether one would be motivated to a greater degree if salary increases were constantly promised.

Compensation Policy

Anderson's policy was to give fairly quick salary increases (perhaps six to nine months apart) up to the median of the salary range. It was more difficult to earn a salary increase over the median; generally, a person did not receive a raise for ten months or more, depending on his/her efficiency and potential for promotion.

In April, Clark Philbin recommended a salary increase for one of his salesmen, Al Peters. Peters was making $325 per week and had not had a raise in three years. He had been a salesman with the company for about fourteen years. Clark wrote the following as a basis for the salary increase: "Peters has demonstrated consistent upgrading of accounts and increased sales to key accounts and has shown marked improvement in establishing better relations with his customers." Philbin indicated that, after working closely with Peters, he was convinced an increase was warranted. He believed that salary administration was a serious responsibility and that increases should be recommended only when merited by performance.

The regional manager, Dan Pace, thought that Peters was about average. Due to the lapse of time since the last salary increase, however, he approved recommendation and passed it along to the sales vice president for final approval.

The vice president knew that Al Peters had not had an increase for over 18 months, but from past experience he had also considered Peters an average performer. He believed, however, that Clark Philbin was very conscientious about awarding salary increases solely on a merit basis rather than time elapsed since the last raise.

The incident brought a matter to the vice president's mind which he had been pondering for some time. He wondered whether senior salespeople should be given automatic salary increases (other than cost of living increases) or whether (in line with company policy) increases should be awarded strictly on a merit basis. In the case of Philbin's recommendation on behalf of Al Peters, the vice president was not convinced that Peters deserved a merit increase. Possibly this was a case in which a salesperson should be considered for an automatic annual increase. In either event Ken was reluctant to turn down the application since it had been passed by the regional manager and district manager, both of whom he considered very capable. Moreover, these people knew Peters and his capabilities far better than he did because of their closer association with him.

Bonus Incentive Plan

Clark Philbin was concerned about unrest exhibited by his sales force. He attributed it to the company's newly instituted bonus incentive plan.

Formerly, Anderson had an individual incentive plan based on each man or woman's sales volume over and above his or her quota. Each person was directly responsible for attaining the individual quota assigned. The percentage by which a salesperson surpassed that quota was applied to his or her base salary for that period, as a bonus.

The new bonus incentive plan was based on the performance of the group rather than the individual. Each district was a team which consisted of the district manager and the salespeople. At the end of a quarter the district bonus was computed on the basis of combined sales over quotas, and the quota was set so that it would be almost impossible to meet the total requirements unless each team member contributed his/her share. Consequently, if one territory fell short due to a weak salesperson, the whole district could lose its chance for a bonus. It was expected that any staff member would be willing to help out those who were falling behind.

Each individual's share under the new system was based on a "stated percentage" of his/her salary for the preceding quarter (see Exhibit 2). This percentage was determined by the amount by which the district exceeded its budget.

Philbin questioned whether the new plan was better or worse than the old one, and in order to evaluate the two plans he wondered how he could get honest opinions from the sales force. Clark decided that a good way to find out what was troubling everyone was to have a post-sales meeting "gripe" session. He had tried this once before and it had yielded favorable results. The salespeople were asked to participate by writing down any complaints they might have and by bringing them to

Exhibit 2 **Computation Table—Quarterly Incentive**

Quarterly Invoiced Sales vs. Total Budget	% Gross Salary* at End of Quarter
I. 100.0 to 105	7%
II. 106 to 110	8%
III. 110 to 115	9%
IV. 115 to beyond	10%

*Weekly Salary Rate × 13.

the "gripe" session. At a previous session Clark had assured them that anything they said would be confidential, and that the point of the meeting was to improve understanding between management and the sales force. Because confidences had been maintained in the past, Clark hoped that the meeting might be beneficial.

At the meeting the following opinions were expressed:

Salesperson 1: Clark, this new incentive plan has killed individual effort. Not only is the weakest person boosted up in each territory, but also one weak territory is helped by stronger or harder working ones. . . .

Salesperson 2: Yes, and that brings up something else. I don't mean to offend you (turning to a new man), but under this system you guys get the same share of the bonus as we old timers do. I know that we all had to start from scratch and I'm not objecting to that. But, and I think everyone will agree, a new man just isn't worth as much to the company as an older man in terms of actual sales volume. Under the old system a guy really got paid for what he was worth. Any extra effort was rewarded by extra pay.

Salesperson 3: You bet. This place is becoming a loafer's paradise!

Salesperson 4: You guys have a point on this "individual effort business," but I still think the team effort idea is good. Everyone works together for the benefit of all. We're all interested in how we do as a district.

Salesperson 2: Sure, that's fine if everyone works together but how do we know that some guy can't improve his performance?

Salesperson 4: Well, I'm sure we all want the extra cash flow, as much as we did before under the old system, so I think everyone will work just as hard if not harder.

Clark Philbin began to wonder if the new system really was better than the old one. Just as the meeting was breaking up one of the men approached Clark.

Salesperson 5: Clark, one of our men puts in about a four day week but still makes quota. There's something strange about this system if things like that can go on.

Philbin: Well, I think we all know that these things can happen in any territory—even in this one—but they happened under the old incentive plan, too.

Suppose we have two salesmen. One is a plugger, putting in a ten- to twelve-hour day and barely making quota each time. The other is a whiz-kid. Works six to seven hours a day, four days a week, but is way over quota each time. Now under these conditions is the second person getting away with anything if the quotas are fairly set? Under the new system that person is really helping the other.

Salesperson 5: Well, I just can't see a guy or gal working only four days a week when everyone else is working five. Somehow it's different when someone overworks—sort of makes a healthy competitive environment.

Philbin: Yes, but don't you resent someone who is *always* putting in extra time trying to get ahead, especially if he or she is barely making quota?

Salesperson 5: No, as I said, I think it makes a healthier working environment.

Clark Philbin was very interested in this discussion because he felt that the issues were causing the unrest in the sales force. There was not much he could do about the new incentive plan, but he felt he should do something to correct the situation concerning the short work week.

Compensating Managers

The Sales Training department of Anderson was reviewing its current hiring policy for college graduates and MBA's. In the past few years the company had been hiring more and more well-educated people. There was, however, a problem which involved paying these people the salary required to attract them to Anderson. For example, those hired for the product management group were first sent to the field as sales trainees, and in order to get top caliber people, it was necessary to pay them more than the salesperson scale.

One MBA, for example, was hired recently by the Product and Research department and was assigned to the field as a salesman for five months as the first phase of his training. His initial salary was well above the maximum that could be earned by a salesperson. Thus, he had been told by the head office not to discuss his salary with anyone, not even his district manager. All went well for about three weeks until, through the grapevine, the others found out that the new hire was earning more than any of them.

The Sales Training department was stumped as far as future hiring and salary ranges were concerned. They realized that they had to continue to pay high salaries in order to get top caliber people, but on the other hand, it was risky to continue to antagonize the sales force.

Internal Corporate Politics

The sales vice president was due to visit Clark Philbin after spending a few days with Dan Pace at the regional office. Clark was uneasy about the forthcoming visit because he had heard a number of unpleasant rumors about the vice president from his regional manager. Clark thought highly of Dan, but he felt that it had been poor practice on Dan's part to have passed the rumors down. Clark believed that no matter how well deserved, remarks such as these should not be transmitted to lower levels in the organization.

The vice president's visit went smoothly except for two incidents. The first concerned Andy Smith, a salesman, whom Clark considered an "average to good" performer. The salesman had recently grown a long handlebar mustache and the vice president commented to Philbin, "Clark, why don't you tell Andy to shave off that damn thing, or at least bring it back to normal size. It's so out of keeping with what our customers are used to."

The second incident concerned a saleswoman, Lee Beckwith. The vice president had previously met Lee at a sales meeting shortly after Lee was hired and had been very impressed with her after this brief contact. Now, after spending a few more hours with Lee, he commented to Clark, "That certainly is an outstanding girl; if she receives the proper training she'll make a good manager."

After the vice president had left, Clark pondered what had been said. In recalling the mustache situation he remembered that his regional manager once had expressed a concern about the vice president interfering in the evaluation of his staff. The promotion record showed that, over the years, many of the vice president's favorites had followed him up the corporate ladder.

With these points in mind, Clark wondered what he should do about Andy and Lee. In the recent evaluations he had recommended Andy both for a salary increase and for a possible promotion. On the other hand, he had characterized Lee as an opportunist with not too much potential for sales or management. Clark felt that Pace was a "fair-shooter" and would back him up, but the fact that the vice president had the final say in approving all recommendations could negate Dan's influence.

Characteristics of A Good Sales Manager

After attending a management training seminar at a nearby university, Dan Pace returned to his office with several ideas in mind for improving the performance of his districts. First, he decided to examine the characteristics of his managers in order to determine what qualities were important.

He summarized his conclusions as follows:

Clark Philbin: Clark is very systematic in his approach to evaluating his staff. He carefully weighs all the important factors which contribute to a person's potential and actual sales ability. So far Clark's recommendations for promotions and increases have been granted exactly as requested. He is neither consistently high nor low in his raise pattern: rather he awards increases as he feels they are due. If someone is worth $40/week raise, then it is requested. Similarly for a $10/week raise. Clark keeps running files on all of his people, so there are few, if any, last minute or "impulse" decisions on a man or woman's value. Clark once commented, "After a framework is outlined, a manager should be permitted to operate autonomously within it." He motivates his staff largely through recognition of jobs well done. On a person's anniversary with the company or on a birthday, he always sends out a card. Also, if someone makes a single outstanding contribution, such as getting a large new account, then in addition to counting it toward a raise or promotion, Clark may take that person out to dinner, give a "pat on the back," or send a letter of commendation.

Jack Steelman: It seems that Jack is always sending in a raise request for one of his staff. He seldom changes the amount; it is always a minimum amount. A number of Jack's raise requests have been turned down because they seem like automatic increases. In many cases the people haven't actually earned them. Jack, however, is a very aggressive guy and an excellent salesman, as well as a good manager. He was once asked whether there was much variance in the quality of his sales force and he commented: "No, they are all great guys and gals, who work hard and deserve to be paid well." Jack is sometimes referred to as the "Little King." He tries to maintain self respect and to motivate salespeople by always doing things for them such as recommending raises. On the other hand, he usually keeps all but the most general information quite private. This makes his position appear to have a little more prestige.

Ozzie Davidson: Ozzie is sort of impulsive in the way he awards increases and promotions. On several occasions good salespeople have gone without raises for over a year even though their quality evaluation forms showed excellent progress. In each case, however, when Ozzie worked with someone just before an evaluation, something happened which, in Ozzie's eyes, ruined the person's chances for an increase. He apparently is fairly well liked by his staff and is always promising one of them a raise or promotion. This was often done before the increase was sent in for approval. In several instances this method of motivation caused difficulty when raises were not sanctioned by senior supervisors.

Jerry Hatch: Jerry does not believe in using pats on the back for jobs well done or any other type of non-financial recognition. He thinks that the dollar reward is sufficient, and if his people produce, they get paid for it; if they don't, they get fired. Jerry has always worked hard himself and is very fond of a dollar. He also feels that actual performance is the best measure of whether or not a person deserves an increase or promotion.

In reviewing his findings, Dan Pace found it difficult to decide which techniques or characteristics peculiar to each manager contributed the most to success in the job. He was not thinking solely in terms of an Anderson manager but more of a sales manager in general.

PAUL GORDON REPRESENTATIVES, INCORPORATED

Background

Paul Gordon Representatives, Inc. was founded in 1955 by Paul Gordon. He had worked for a medium-size component manufacturing company prior to setting up his own manufacturers' representatives firm. He left because he felt there was a great deal of opportunity in the rep industry and he desired to be his own boss. His firm was located in the Delaware Valley, PA., near Philadelphia. Over the years, as the firm grew, he moved to a large facility in Cherry Hill, NJ. His territory covers Eastern Pennsylvania, Southern New Jersey, and parts of Virginia, Maryland, and Delaware. Currently his firm has four employees and five principals. Their sales have been steadily increasing over the last five years, with last year's revenues at $9.25 million. Mr. Gordon is married and has a 22-year-old daughter, Jeanne, and a 19-year-old son, Sam. Sam is a sophomore at Cornell and is studying the theatre arts. His daughter has expressed interest in the business and has spent several summers doing clerical work in the office. His wife did some bookkeeping in the early days of the company but had stopped to raise their children and was no longer active in the business. (Background information on manufacturers' representatives and on PGR, Inc. is contained in appendices A and B.)

As 1984 was drawing to an end, Mr. Gordon sat in his living room, reflecting how his company has grown. He was very pleased with the success of his firm, yet thoughts of retiring flitted in and out of his mind. The company had had its share of ups and downs, but during the last few years business had been very good. Unfortunately, he was not totally content with his present state of affairs. Although profits were not down, the makeup of revenues was taking what Gordon considered an undesirable change. (Exhibits 1 through 6)

North American Semiconductor has been with PGR Inc. for six years. NAS accounted for approximately 65% of sales for PGR. While revenue from NAS has consistently increased over each of the past six years, and total revenue for PGR has been increasing at a 20 to 40% rate (about twice the industry average), sales have not been increasing proportionally for Mr. Gordon's other principals. At one point, four of the five principals accounted for about 25% of sales each, but NAS had experienced tremendous growth over the past five years. Mr. Gordon was trying to figure out why sales for his other principals had slowed down recently.

Source: This case was prepared by Marc Haberman and Amy Hoberman under the supervision of Assistant Professor Erin Anderson of the Wharton School of the University of Pennsylvania. Funding from the Manufacturer's Representatives Educational Research Foundation is gratefully acknowledged. The authors thank several anonymous companies from the Mid-Atlantic Chapter of The Electronic Representatives Association for sharing their ideas and experiences.

Exhibit 1 **Sales in Millions per Year, per Principal**

		1979	1980	1981	1982	1983	1984
NAS	%	23	27	34.4	42.5	52.3	64.9
	$	.53	.795	1.275	1.96	3.37	5.995
Technologics	%	26	24.5	21.2	19.5	15.1	11.4
	$	.60	.72	.79	.91	.98	1.045
Gerber	%	25	24	22.8	20	15.8	11.75
	$	.575	.705	.845	.935	1.015	1.085
Lapat	%	—	—	—	—	3	2.1
	$	—	—	—	—	.195	.2
Glasco	%	26	24.5	21.6	18	13.8	9.85
	$	.6	.71	.8	.855	.885	.91
Total	%	100	100	100	100	100	100
	$	2.305	2.93	3.71	4.66	6.45	9.25

% Increase in Sales from Previous Year

		1980	1981	1982	1983	1984
NAS	%	50	60	53	71	77
Technologics	%	20	9.7	15	7.6	6.6
Gerber	%	22.6	19.8	10.6	8.5	6.9
Lapat	%	—	—	—	—	2.5
Glasco	%	18.3	12.6	6.8	3.5	2.8
Total	%	27	26.6	25.6	38	43

His daughter, Jeanne, walked into the room. Jeanne was a recent graduate of the Wharton School, University of Pennsylvania, and was well aquainted with the manufacturers' representative industry.

"What's the matter, Dad? You look so serious. Is there something wrong at work?"

"I'm just thinking about some of my smaller lines. I'm afraid my relations with NAS might be affecting the overall performance of the company."

"Well, what do you expect, Dad? They have to okay every step you take. Every time you think about adding another principal, you have to clear it with NAS first. They demand extra paperwork from your salespeople, too. And you told me that last month they insisted you fly the whole crew out to the Chicago semiconductor trade show for two days. Your other accounts wouldn't ask that from you."

"Of course they make demands like that. They're 65% of our sales, so they deserve a proportional amount of my time. It's still my company and I make the decisions. Listen, NAS has put you through college! They are an excellent source of sales for the company, and we've had a pretty stable relationship for six years, and they haven't given me any indication of going direct. They have a strong R & D depart-

Exhibit 2 **NAS 1979–1984**

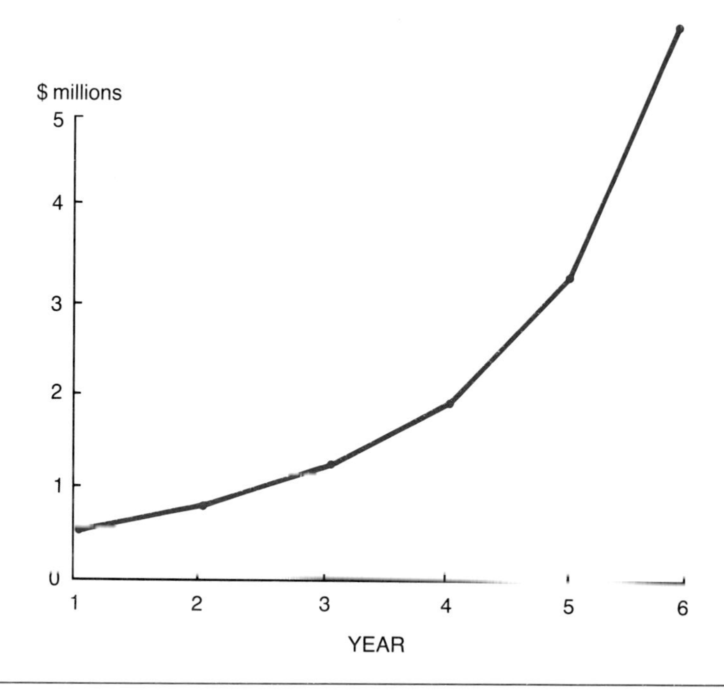

Exhibit 3 **Technologics 1979–1984**

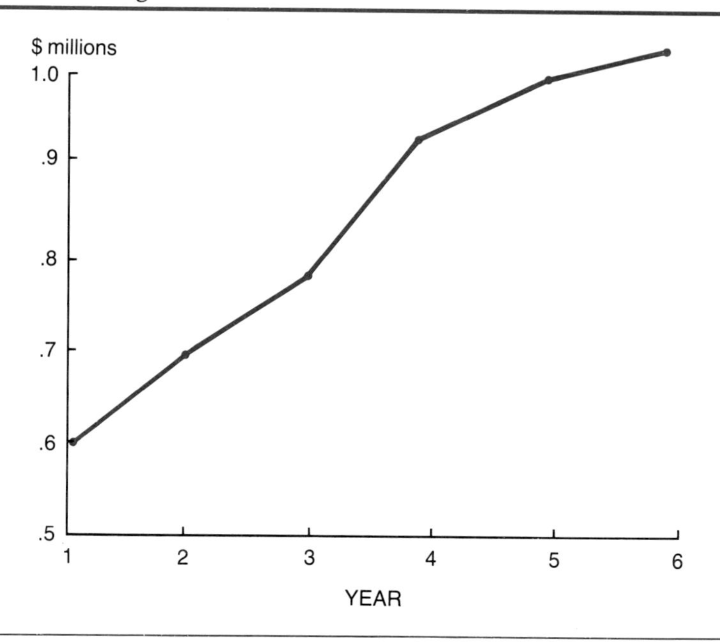

Exhibit 4 **Gerber 1979–1984**

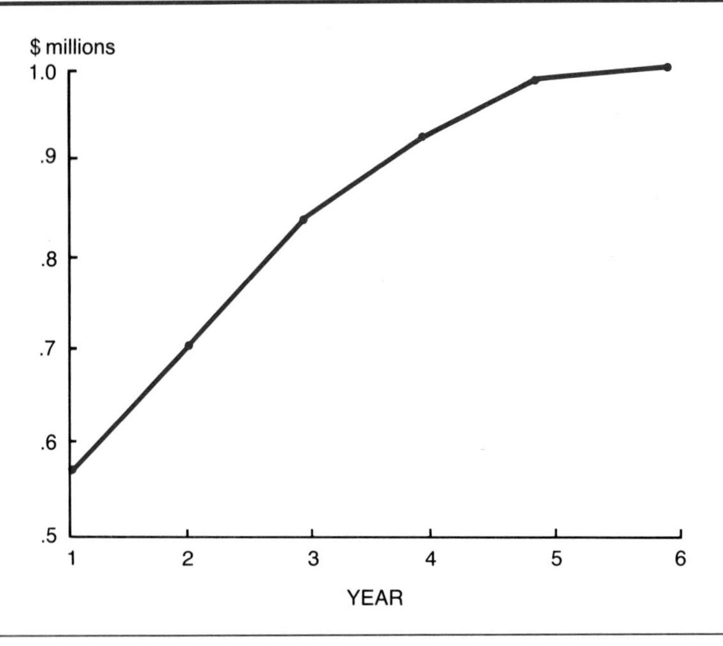

Exhibit 5 **Lapat 1979–1984**

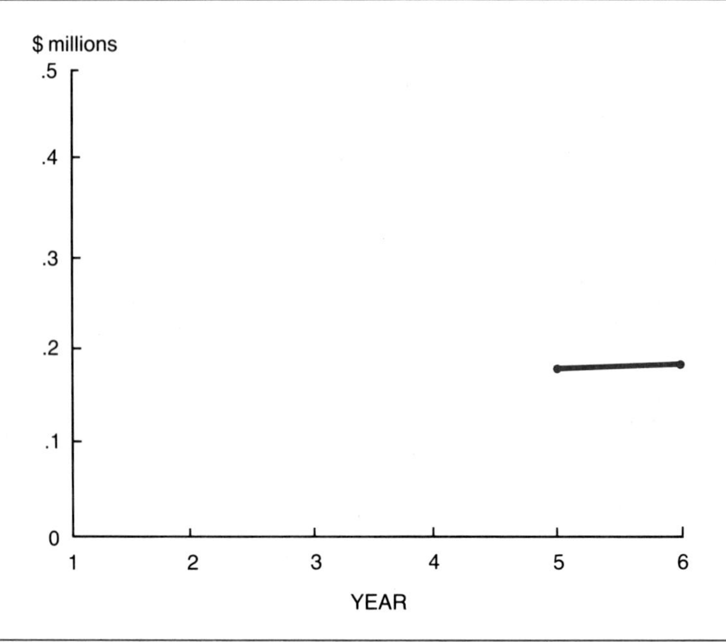

Exhibit 6 **Glasco 1979–1984**

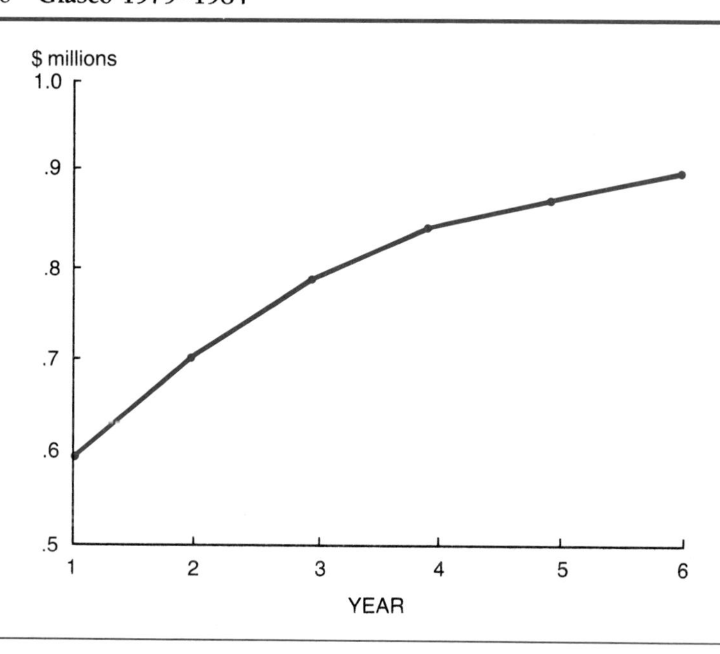

ment and are always working to bring out new products. I wouldn't trade them for any other line."

"But they could just dump you in a second, Dad. You know if they want out of a contract they could find a way to break it. Aren't you putting all your eggs in one basket?"

"Listen, Jeanne, NAS is lucky to have PGR representing them. I've worked this territory for 35 years and I've gotten one of the best reputations in this area. I know they couldn't do a better job on their own. Sure, they do have a few direct people on some larger accounts, but they've shown a great deal of commitment to maintaining the representative firms they use. There are plenty of semiconductor firms out there, and if NAS went direct I could just as easily replace them. They'd have to take some pretty big losses if they went direct. Remember, they may be 65% of our sales, but we are 12% of theirs."

"But, still, Dad, profits are down for your other accounts, and if it's because of NAS's overbearing attitude, you can't let it get out of hand."

"Listen, if you think you can prove that NAS is responsible for our dwindling sales, be my guest. How about if, next week, you go out with the guys to all the principals and see if you can find out what's really happening. I want to be absolutely sure the problem is NAS before I decide how to handle the situation. If you do well, we'll talk about getting you started in the business."

Calls with Ben Taylor

On Monday morning, Jeanne met Ben Taylor. Ben had been with the firm for 23 years. His Ivy League background and extensive knowledge of the manufacturers' rep industry helped earn him his reputation as one of the finest in the area. Ben had an outstanding record of sales. He was an ambitious and hard worker, who had only recently taken off for his first trip abroad, a two-week luxurious family vaction in Greece. Jeanne commented about his healthy tan and European-styled business suit.

Their first stop was at Glasco Industries, a small, passive components firm that had seen better days before active components took over the market. As they drove along in Ben's new BMW, he briefed her about Glasco.

"The sales manager with Glasco is Gerry Gifford. He's fairly new to the position, been there about a year, but has worked his way up the ladder. I give him about another year; they never seem to last long at this job. Besides, he just doesn't seem as skilled as the last guy. Orders have been late; I can't get all the production I need. It's difficult meeting with him. I'm thinking of maybe going over his head."

They arrived at the plant and had a brief meeting with Gerry. Gerry was in his mid-twenties and was not college educated. As the three of them sat down, Gerry joked, "Well, it looks like you have yourself an assistant now. You'll have even more time to spend out at the club."

The three laughed and the ensuing discussion was tense, but not hostile.

"We're having problems getting your orders delivered on time, Ger. Do you want me to see if I can get you some more help down here?"

"Give me a break, Ben. I don't know what you could do that I couldn't. We've been busting our butts trying to get these shipments out on time. You have it easy, just write a few orders and take the rest of the day off. It's really tough down here, you know."

Jeanne noticed Gerry's face getting red as he listened to Ben. She was a little surprised that Ben was telling him how to run his job. She suspected that, although he had the power to fire and hire Ben, Gerry wouldn't want to make waves because he had recently been promoted to this position. She noticed that he regained his composure.

"OK, Ben, you can try, but I don't think it'll help . . . "

As they left, Jeanne thought there must be a communciation problem. Gerry didn't think Ben was spending much time on Glasco. Perhaps Ben was spending too much time on NAS and Gerry was upset about being ignored. . . .

After Glasco, Ben and Jeanne headed to a nearby principal, Technologics, so he could introduce her to the sales manager there. Technologics was a manufacturer of active components and held a small but profitable niche in the market. Their name was known in the industry, and they were well respected.

As they walked into the office, Ben was warmly greeted by Bob Wilkes. "What a nice surprise! It's always nice to see the fella who does such a good job selling our products."

Ben explained that he wasn't there on business; he just wanted to introduce Jeanne to Technologics. The two men proceeded to talk mostly about business, but in a very informal way. Although sales had slowed down for Technologics recently, Bob appeared confident in Ben's ability.

Ben dropped Jeanne off at PGR headquarters and went off to make two sales calls.

Calls with Greg Watson

Later that day, Jeanne met with Greg Watson. He was fairly new to the firm, having been hired about nine months ago. Previously, he had been a direct salesperson for another semiconductor firm and been one of the top salespersons there. He explained the reason he left his old position was that the idea of being an independent rep and having greater control had appealed to him. He also relished the idea of making a commission versus a salary for his efforts. Jeanne wondered about this, though. She had heard her father mention that Greg's former company had a habit of transferring its salespeople more often than most firms, and as a consequence, they were experiencing a lot of turnover.

Most of the morning was spent making cold calls, and Greg seemed to present himself well. He made a few sales of semiconductors and had some good leads. Later in the afternoon they stopped at a fairly steady account. He picked up a new order from an engineer at the plant. As expected, they were in and out in five minutes.

"Business as usual." said Greg, "It's easy with NAS."

"What about your other lines," asked Jeanne. "Why don't you push those? That account uses at least two of our other principals' products."

"I don't have much experience in pushing those other lines. I'm waiting until I feel really comfortable with semiconductors before I put a lot of emphasis on other lines. Besides, NAS is your father's bread and butter. I'd prefer using my time to sell something I know a lot of customers are going to buy, rather than waste my time selling something they're not interested in and I'm not familiar with. When I have more time, I'll start pushing the other lines. If sales of semiconductors go down, we're gonna hear it from NAS. We don't have to worry if sales of the other principals go down a little. Jeanne, this isn't easy, you know. I'm already 20% above my sales quota (Exhibit 7). The bottom line says it all."

Jeanne thought about this as she looked at Greg's sales levels. He had done an impressive job so far. She wondered how much more his sales would go up once he started pushing all the accounts.

The next day, Jeanne and Greg set off for the next principal, Gerber Industries, a medium-size connectors manufacturer. A half an hour after arriving, Greg and Jean were still waiting to see the sales manager, Harry Fuchs, a young and ambitious man. When they were finally called into his office, within minutes of sitting down, Harry started in on his "suggestions" for Greg.

"I haven't been real impressed with your sales recently. I've noticed you've been dropping over the last 6 months. Try making more cold calls, and I'd like to see some forecasting charts and itineraries on Monday. Otherwise, I'm satisfied with your sales reports and bimonthly newsletters. In the future, I want you to have more to write about."

Harry dominated the rest of the conversation, talking at Greg, rather than to him. The meeting ended with Greg assuring Harry that his sales would increase.

Outside the office, Greg whispered to Jeanne, "He reminds me of my old boss—do this, do that. I'm glad I don't work for him anymore."

Calls with Nick Gerzog

Nick Gerzog, 42, had been with the firm for 8 years. He was very good in both active and passive component selling, although he was less motivated by money than personal satisfaction. Jeanne knew Nick was financially secure, and with no children to put through school, he could afford to slow down a bit or, alternatively, take a new direction in work. He could afford to chance a risky venture. Jeanne wondered if he had ever considered leaving PGR to start is own firm.

Lapat Industries was a young, innovative company that manufactured controllers. It hadn't established a name yet, but was known by a few insiders as a firm with a lot of potential. Lapat was very short on capital and had scuttled most of its ambitious marketing plans. Consequently, it rarely advertised in trade journals and its brochures were unattractive and uninformative. After four years of trying to sell the product itself, Lapat approached PGR. PGR took it on as a principal and had had some measured success with Lapat's first product (Exhibit 5). The salespeople made mostly cold calls for this line and received virtually no support from Lapat.

On her calls, Jeanne saw that PGR was having difficulties selling Lapat, although new principals are always hard to establish. Jeanne was impressed by the organization of the company and wondered if NAS was preventing the salespeople from spending enough time on a principal with such good prospects. She asked Nick how he felt.

"You know, Lapat has a lot of untapped potential. Unfortunately, they are not the easiest lines to push because virtually no one has ever heard of them. I have discussed advertising to the trade or designing a new brochure, but they just don't have the funds right now. They keep saying that next year they'll be able to afford some promotions. Yet, no matter how many times I tell them, they say they don't think they need to spend the extra capital on advertising. They think that it's our job to do all their promoting."

"Have you mentioned this to my father?"

"On several occasions, yes. The poor guy's been rather preoccupied with NAS lately. I have a feeling he just hasn't gotten around to it yet."

Nick dropped Jeanne off at the office because he had a dinner appointment with a new customer. The first thing she did was skim sales data (Exhibit 7) and read through her father's monthly reports containing the sales evaluations of the three men for the last year. Each month was pretty much the same. (Exhibits 1 through 10 show typical evaluation forms.) Jeanne mulled over her notes and began to list her recommendations. She and her father would meet first thing Monday morning to discuss her findings.

Exhibit 7 % of Sales for Last Fiscal Year

	Nas	Technologics	Glasco	Lapat	Gerber	
Ben Taylor	70	15	4	3	8	100
Greg Watson	93	2	5	0	0	100
Nick Gerzog	60	15	10	5	5	100
Paul Gordon	55	12	7	8	10	100

Exhibit 8 Salesman Evaluation Report

Name Ben Taylor Date 6/84

Sales Performance	*Rating circle one	Comments
1. Key Account Penetration	0 1 2 3④	Ben's been having excellent results with PGR.
2. Forecasting Accuracy — on all lines and customers	1 2 3④	Ben is fairly consistent here.
3. Forecasting Timeliness and Awareness of Revisions	1 2③	As usual, Ben is very adept at this.
4. Multi-Line Sales Effectiveness	0 1 2③4	Ben has been doing well, although some complaints have come in about orders for Glasco recently.
5. New Account Penetration	0 1②3 4	
6. Maintenance of Old Accounts	0 1 2 3④	Ben has built many strong relationships with his accounts.
7. Overall sales	0 1 2 3④	
8. Sells PGR and Its Principals	0 1 2 3④	Ben is a great salesman and a super guy.

Exhibit 9 Salesman Evaluation Report

Name Nick Gerzog Date 6/84

Sales Performance	*Rating circle one	Comments
1. Key Account Penetration	0 1 2 3 ④	Can really push NAS when I need him to.
2. Forecasting Accuracy — on all lines and customers	1 2 3 ④	He always attains his forecast, although I wonder whether they are as high as they could be.
3. Forecasting Timeliness and Awareness of Revisions	1 2 ③	
4. Multi-Line Sales Effectiveness	0 1 2 3 ④	Has good understanding of interdependence of products. Sells more than one line almost every sale.
5. New Account Penetration	0 1 ② 3 4	Doesn't seem to put as much effort here as I'd like to see.
6. Maintenance of Old Accounts	0 1 2 3 ④	Has excellent rapport with most of our steady customers.
7. Overall sales	0 1 2 3 ④	
8. Sells PGR and Its Principals	0 1 2 ③ 4	

Exhibit 10 Salesman Evaluation Report

Name Greg Watson Date 6/84

Sales Performance	*Rating circle one	Comments
1. Key Account Penetration	0 1 2 3 (4)	He seems to have capitalized on his previous experience here.
2. Forecasting Accuracy — on all lines and customers	1 2 (3) 4	Has predicted fairly well, although has had some problems with Lapat and Gerber.
3. Forecasting Timeliness and Awareness of Revisions	1 (2) 3	
4. Multi-Line Sales Effectiveness	0 (1) 2 3 4	Greg is still fairly wet behind the ears at MLS but his sales levels are very impressive in the lines he has had success with.
5. New Account Penetration	0 1 2 (3) 4	Has had most of his success with NAS; seems to be making some headway with Lapat.
6. Maintenance of Old Accounts	0 1 (2) 3 4	
7. Overall sales	0 1 2 3 (4)	Greg shows good potential. With continued efforts he'll become a top rep.
8. Sells PGR and Its Principals	0 1 2 (3) 4	

Appendix A: Definitions

Manufacturers' Representatives—Manufacturers' representatives are independent sales companies who contract with manufacturers to sell their product lines. They are not employees of the manufacturer. The rep firm pays for its own transportation, entertainment, promotion, and product training. In addition, the firm may carry considerable overhead; this may include a complete office staff, data processing equipment, salaries and benefits for firm employees, and so forth. The rep firm is compensated by commission on sales of the manufacturers' product. A rep's accounts [retailers, Original Equipment Manufacturers (OEMs)], are generally within a specific geographic area. The rep carries the products of several different manufacturers, although many contracts specify that the rep cannot sell competing lines. Rep firms (agencies) usually deal with a principal's sales manager but, being independent, do not "report" to the manager as does a sales force.

Direct Sales Force—Direct salespeople are employees of the manufacturer. The manufacturer pays the salesperson's salary, bonus, expenses, and benefits and/or commission. The employer generally trains the salesperson. Direct salespeople are generally given a geographic territory or selected accounts. They sell only their employer's products to their customers. Organizationally, the salesperson usually reports to a district or regional sales manager.

Principals—A principal is another name for a manufacturer. Principals may use a direct sales force, manufacturers' representatives, or distributors to sell their products. "Principal" is a legal term used here because of the contractual arrangement set up between the manufacturer and its "agents" (employee salespeople, manufacturers' representatives, distributors.)

Captivity—Occurs when a principal can exert more than typical control over a representative firm because the principal provides such a large proportion of commission income that the rep firm cannot maintain independence. The principal can make unusual requests and detract resources from other lines. "Captors" are usually larger, national firms and tend to experience faster growth. When a line grows very large, the principal can dominate the rep firm, i.e., hold it captive. Hence, the rep can become a psuedo employee.

Appendix B

Manufacturers' Representative firms usually pay on a salary plus commission basis or, less frequently, on a straight commission rate of approximately 2.5% for each line, with little variation across lines. In addition, PGR salespeople cover their own expenses and fringe benefits. Gordon fills out monthly sales reports on each employee but supervises them very loosely. Gordon himself also does a considerable amount of selling.

INDEX

NAME INDEX

SUBJECT INDEX